# Apps and Services w
## First Edition

Build practical projects with Blazor, .NET MAUI, gRPC, GraphQL, and other enterprise technologies

**Mark J. Price**

BIRMINGHAM—MUMBAI

# Apps and Services with .NET 7

First Edition

**Senior Publishing Product Manager:** Suman Sen

**Acquisition Editor – Peer Reviews:** Saby Dsilva

**Project Editor:** Janice Gonsalves

**Content Development Editor:** Lucy Wan

**Copy Editor:** Safis Editing

**Technical Editor:** Aniket Shetty

**Proofreader:** Safis Editing

**Indexer:** Subalakshmi Govindhan

**Presentation Designer:** Rajesh Shirsath

First published: November 2022

Production reference: 2060423

Published by Packt Publishing Ltd.
Livery Place
35 Livery Street
Birmingham
B3 2PB, UK.

ISBN 978-1-80181-343-3

www.packt.com

# Contributors

## About the author

**Mark J. Price** is a Microsoft Specialist: Programming in C# and Architecting Microsoft Azure Solutions, with over 20 years of experience. Since 1993, he has passed more than 80 Microsoft programming exams and specializes in preparing others to pass them. Between 2001 and 2003, Mark was employed to write official courseware for Microsoft in Redmond, USA. His team wrote the first training courses for C# while it was still an early alpha version. While with Microsoft, he taught "train-the-trainer" classes to get Microsoft Certified Trainers up to speed on C# and .NET. Mark has spent most of his career training a wide variety of students, from 16-year-old apprentices to 70-year-old retirees, with the majority being professional developers. Mark holds a Computer Science BSc. Hons. degree.

# About the reviewers

**Damir Arh** has many years of experience with software development and maintenance, from complex enterprise software projects to modern consumer-oriented mobile applications. Although he has worked with a wide spectrum of different languages, his favorite language remains C#. In his drive towards better development processes, he is a proponent of test-driven development, continuous integration, and continuous deployment. He shares his knowledge by speaking at local user groups and conferences, blogging, and writing articles. He has received the prestigious Microsoft MVP award for developer technologies 12 times in a row. In his spare time, he's always on the move: hiking, geocaching, running, and rock climbing.

**Tomasz Pęczek** is a passionate developer, architect, blogger, speaker, and OSS contributor/maintainer in the .NET and Azure space. His commitment to sharing his knowledge and experiences has earned him a Microsoft MVP title in the Developer Technologies category.

Throughout his 18+ years of professional career, he has been designing and developing software that powers companies across the healthcare, banking, e-learning, and e-discovery industries. Currently, he is a Technical Fellow at Predica, where he focuses on ensuring that projects deliver true business value for clients and adhere to the highest industry standards.

His blog is at `https://www.tpeczek.com/`, and he can be found on Twitter as @tpeczek.

**Target audience:**
Beginner-to-intermediate in the C# language, .NET libraries, and ASP.NET Core web development

**Topics include:**
C# language, .NET libraries, ASP.NET Core, object-oriented programming, testing, EF Core, and more

# Learn the fundamentals

# Take your apps to the next level

**Target audience:**
Beginner-to-intermediate in building apps and services

**Topics include:**
Common .NET-adjacent technologies like Cosmos DB, GraphQL, .NET MAUI, Blazor, gRPC, and more

# Join our book's Discord space

Join the book's Discord workspace for *Ask me Anything* sessions with the author.

https://packt.link/apps_and_services_dotnet7

# Quick Chapter Reference

# Table of Contents

## Chapter 2: Managing Relational Data Using SQL Server                43

## Chapter 14: Building Serverless Nanoservices Using Azure Functions 483

## Chapter 15: Building Web User Interfaces Using ASP.NET Core      525

# Preface

There are programming books that are thousands of pages long that aim to be comprehensive references to the C# language, the .NET libraries, and app models like websites, services, and desktop and mobile apps.

This book is different. It is a step-by-step guide to learning various technologies for building apps and services with .NET. It is concise and aims to be a brisk, fun read packed with practical hands-on walkthroughs of each topic. The breadth of the overarching narrative comes at the cost of some depth, but you will find many signposts to explore further if you wish.

In my experience, the hardest part of learning a new technology is getting started. Once I have had the most important concepts explained and seen some practical code in action, I feel comfortable going deeper by exploring the official documentation on my own. You can feel confident experimenting on your own once you have seen how the basics work correctly.

This book is best for those who already know the fundamentals of C# and .NET and programmers who have worked with C# in the past but feel left behind by the changes in the past few years.

If you already have experience with older versions of the C# language and .NET libraries, then I cover what is new in C# 8 and .NET Core 3 and later in *Chapter 1, Introducing Apps and Services with .NET*.

I will call out the most important aspects of app models and frameworks for building modern user interfaces and implementing services, so you can participate in conversations with colleagues about technology and architectural choices and get productive with their implementation fast.

## Where to find the code solutions

You can download or clone solutions for the step-by-step guided tasks and exercises from the GitHub repository at the following link: `https://github.com/markjprice/apps-services-net7`.

If you don't know how, then I provide instructions on how to do this at the end of *Chapter 1, Introducing Apps and Services with .NET*.

## What this book covers

*Chapter 1, Introducing Apps and Services with .NET*, is about setting up your development environment and using Visual Studio 2022 and/or Visual Studio Code. I review the new features added to the language and libraries in modern C# and .NET.

You will also learn about some good places to look for help and ways to contact the author to get help with an issue or give me feedback to improve the book.

*Chapter 2, Managing Relational Data Using SQL Server*, is about setting up SQL Server on Windows, in a Docker container on macOS or Linux, or the Azure cloud using SQL Database. You will learn how to read and write at a low level using ADO.NET libraries (`Microsoft.Data.SqlClient`) and by using the higher-level object-to-data store mapping technology named **Entity Framework Core** (**EF Core**). You will set up an example database named Northwind and create class libraries to define an EF Core model to work with it. These class libraries are then used in many of the subsequent chapters.

*Chapter 3, Managing NoSQL Data Using Azure Cosmos DB*, is about the cloud-native non-SQL data store Azure Cosmos DB. You will learn how to read and write using its native API as well as the more specialized graph-based Gremlin API in an online section.

*Chapter 4, Benchmarking Performance, Multitasking, and Concurrency*, shows how to allow multiple actions to occur at the same time to improve performance, scalability, and user productivity by using threads and tasks. You will learn how to use types in the `System.Diagnostics` namespace and the Benchmark.NET library to monitor your code to measure performance and efficiency.

*Chapter 5, Implementing Popular Third-Party Libraries*, discusses the types that allow your code to perform common practical tasks, such as manipulating images with ImageSharp, logging with Serilog, mapping objects to other objects with AutoMapper, making unit test assertions with FluentAssertions, validating data with FluentValidation, and generating PDFs with QuestPDF.

*Chapter 6, Observing and Modifying Code Execution Dynamically*, covers working with types for reflection and attributes, expression trees, and dynamically generating source code during the compilation process.

*Chapter 7, Handling Dates, Times, and Internationalization*, covers the types that allow your code to perform common tasks like handling dates and times, time zones, and globalizing and localizing data and the user interface of an app for internationalization.

*Chapter 8, Protecting Your Data and Applications*, is about protecting your data from being viewed by malicious users using encryption and from being manipulated or corrupted using hashing and signing. You will also learn about authentication and authorization to protect applications from unauthorized users.

*Chapter 9, Building and Securing Web Services Using Minimal APIs*, introduces a simpler way to build web services using ASP.NET Core Minimal APIs that avoids the need for controller classes. You then learn how to protect and secure a web service using rate limiting, CORS, and authentication and authorization.

*Chapter 10, Exposing Data via the Web Using OData*, introduces building services that quickly expose data models using the Open Data protocol with multiple HTTP endpoints. You will see why one of the best ways to test a web service is using the REST Client extension for Visual Studio Code.

*Chapter 11, Combining Data Sources Using GraphQL*, introduces building services that provide a simple single endpoint for exposing data from multiple sources to appear as a single combined source of data. You will use the ChilliCream GraphQL platform to implement the service, including Hot Chocolate.

*Chapter 12, Building Efficient Microservices Using gRPC*, introduces building microservices using the efficient gRPC standard. You will learn about the `.proto` file format for defining services contracts and the Protobuf binary format for message serialization. You will also learn how to enable web browsers to call gRPC services using gRPC JSON transcoding.

*Chapter 13, Broadcasting Real-Time Communication Using SignalR*, introduces you to SignalR, a technology that enables a developer to create a service that can have multiple clients and broadcast messages to all of them or a subset of them live in real time. For example, notification systems and dashboards that need instantly up-to-date information like stock prices.

*Chapter 14, Building Serverless Nanoservices Using Azure Functions*, introduces you to Azure functions that can be configured to only require server-side resources while they execute. They execute when they are triggered by an activity like a message sent to a queue, a file uploaded to storage, or at a regularly scheduled interval.

*Chapter 15, Building Web User Interfaces Using ASP.NET Core*, is about building web user interfaces with ASP.NET Core MVC. You will learn Razor syntax, tag helpers, and Bootstrap for quick user interface prototyping.

*Chapter 16, Building Web Components Using Blazor WebAssembly*, is about how to build user interface components using Blazor WebAssembly on the client side for cross-platform uses.

*Chapter 17, Leveraging Open-Source Blazor Component Libraries*, introduces some popular open-source libraries of Blazor components.

*Chapter 18, Building Mobile and Desktop Apps Using .NET MAUI*, introduces you to building cross-platform mobile and desktop apps for Android, iOS, macOS, and Windows. You will learn the basics of XAML, which can be used to define the user interface for a graphical app.

*Chapter 19, Integrating .NET MAUI Apps with Blazor and Native Platforms*, covers building hybrid native and web apps that make the most of the operating system they run on. You will integrate native platform features like the system clipboard, filesystem, retrieving device and display information, and popup notifications. For desktop apps, you will add menus and manage windows.

*Chapter 20, Introducing the Survey Project Challenge*, documents the product requirements for a survey/polling software solution that the reader can optionally attempt to implement and publish to a public GitHub repository to get feedback from the author and other readers.

*Epilogue* describes your options for further study about building apps and services with C# and .NET, and the tools and skills you should learn to become a well-rounded professional .NET developer.

*Appendix, Answers to the Test Your Knowledge Questions*, has the answers to the test questions at the end of each chapter.

You can read the appendix at the following link: `https://static.packt-cdn.com/downloads/9781801813433_Appendix.pdf`.

# What you need for this book

You can develop and deploy C# and .NET apps using Visual Studio 2022 for Windows or Mac, or Visual Studio Code and the command-line tools on most operating systems, including Windows, macOS, and many varieties of Linux. An operating system that supports Visual Studio Code and an internet connection are all you need to complete this book. If you prefer to use a third-party tool like JetBrains Rider, then you can.

# Downloading the color images of this book

We also provide you with a PDF file that has color images of the screenshots and diagrams used in this book. The color images will help you better understand the changes in the output.

You can download this file from `https://packt.link/5Y6E2`.

# Conventions

In this book, you will find several text styles that distinguish between different kinds of information. Here are some examples of these styles and an explanation of their meaning.

`CodeInText`: Indicates code words in text, database table names, folder names, filenames, file extensions, pathnames, dummy URLs, user input, and Twitter handles. For example: "The `Controllers`, `Models`, and `Views` folders contain ASP.NET Core classes and the `.cshtml` files for execution on the server."

A block of code is set as follows:

```
// storing items at index positions
names[0] = "Kate";
names[1] = "Jack";
names[2] = "Rebecca";
names[3] = "Tom";
```

When we wish to draw your attention to a particular part of a code block, the relevant lines or items are highlighted:

```
// storing items at index positions
names[0] = "Kate";
names[1] = "Jack";
names[2] = "Rebecca";
names[3] = "Tom";
```

Any command-line input or output is written as follows:

```
dotnet new console
```

**Bold**: Indicates a new **term**, an important **word**, or words that you see on the screen, for example, in menus or dialog boxes. For example: "Clicking on the **Next** button moves you to the next screen."

Important notes and links to external sources of further reading appear in a box like this.

 **Good Practice:** Recommendations for how to program like an expert appear like this.

# Get in touch

Feedback from our readers is always welcome.

**General feedback:** Email `feedback@packtpub.com` and mention the book's title in the subject of your message. If you have questions about any aspect of this book, please email us at `questions@packtpub.com`.

**Errata:** Although we have taken every care to ensure the accuracy of our content, mistakes do happen. If you have found a mistake in this book, we would be grateful if you reported this to us. Please visit `https://subscription.packtpub.com/help`, click **Submit Errata**, search for your book, and fill in the form.

**Piracy:** If you come across any illegal copies of our works in any form on the internet, we would be grateful if you would provide us with the location address or website name. Please contact us at `copyright@packtpub.com` with a link to the material.

**If you are interested in becoming an author:** If there is a topic that you have expertise in and you are interested in either writing or contributing to a book, please visit `http://authors.packtpub.com`.

# Share your thoughts

Once you've read *Apps and Services with .NET 7*, we'd love to hear your thoughts! Scan the QR code below to go straight to the Amazon review page for this book and share your feedback.

*https://packt.link/r/1801813434*

Your review is important to us and the tech community and will help us make sure we're delivering excellent quality content.

# Download a free PDF copy of this book

Thanks for purchasing this book!

Do you like to read on the go but are unable to carry your print books everywhere?

Is your eBook purchase not compatible with the device of your choice?

Don't worry, now with every Packt book you get a DRM-free PDF version of that book at no cost.

Read anywhere, any place, on any device. Search, copy, and paste code from your favorite technical books directly into your application.

The perks don't stop there. You can get exclusive access to discounts, newsletters, and great free content in your inbox daily.

Follow these simple steps to get the benefits:

1. Scan the QR code or visit the link below:

https://packt.link/free-ebook/9781801813433

2. Submit your proof of purchase.
3. That's it! We'll send your free PDF and other benefits to your email directly

# 1

# Introducing Apps and Services with .NET

In this first chapter, the goals are setting up your development environment to use Visual Studio 2022 and Visual Studio Code, reviewing what is new with C# 8 up to C# 11 and what is new with .NET Core 3.1 up to .NET 7, and understanding your choices for building apps and services. Finally, we will review good places to look for help.

The GitHub repository for this book has solutions using full application projects for all code tasks:

```
https://github.com/markjprice/apps-services-net7/
```

After going to the GitHub repository, simply press the . (dot) key or change .com to .dev to change the repository into a live code editor based on Visual Studio Code using GitHub Codespaces.

Visual Studio Code in a web browser is great to run alongside your chosen code editor as you work through the book's coding tasks. You can compare your code to the solution code and easily copy and paste parts if needed.

Throughout this book, I use the term **modern .NET** to refer to .NET 7 and its predecessors like .NET 5 and .NET 6, which come from .NET Core. I use the term **legacy .NET** to refer to .NET Framework, Mono, Xamarin, and .NET Standard. Modern .NET is a unification of those legacy platforms and standards.

This chapter covers the following topics:

- Introducing this book and its contents
- Setting up your development environment
- Using an analyzer to write better code
- What's new in C# and .NET?
- Making good use of the GitHub repository for this book
- Where to go for help

# Introducing this book and its contents

This book attempts to cater to two related audiences:

- Readers who have completed my book for beginners, *C# 11 and .NET 7 – Modern Cross-Platform Development Fundamentals*, and now want to take their learning further.
- Readers who already have basic skills and knowledge about C# and .NET and want to learn practical skills and knowledge to build real-world applications and services.

## A companion book to continue your learning journey

This book is the second of two books that continues your learning journey through .NET 7.

The first book covers the C# language, the .NET libraries, and the fundamentals of ASP.NET Core for web development. It is designed to be read linearly because skills and knowledge from earlier chapters build up and are needed to understand later chapters.

This second book covers more specialized topics like internationalization, protecting your data and apps, benchmarking and improving performance, and building services with OData, GraphQL, gRPC, SignalR, and Azure Functions. Finally, you will learn how to build graphical user interfaces for websites, desktop, and mobile apps with Blazor and .NET MAUI.

A summary of the two books and their important topics is shown in *Figure 1.1*:

1. **C# language,** including new C# 11 features, object-oriented programming, and debugging and unit testing.
2. **.NET libraries,** including numbers, text, and collections, file I/O, and data with EF Core 7.
3. **Websites and web services** with ASP.NET Core 7 and Blazor.

1. **More .NET libraries** like internationalization, multitasking, and security.
2. **More data** with SQL Server and Azure Cosmos DB.
3. **More services** with Minimal Web API, OData, GraphQL, gRPC, SignalR, and Azure Functions.
4. **More graphical user interfaces** with ASP.NET Core MVC, Razor, Blazor, and .NET MAUI.

*Fundamentals*                                                             *Practical Applications*

Figure 1.1: Companion books for learning C# 11 and .NET 7 and the apps and services that can be built with them

 We provide you with a PDF file that has color images of the screenshots and diagrams used in this book. You can download this file from `https://packt.link/5Y6E2`.

# What you will learn in this book

After this first chapter, this book can be divided into four parts:

1. **Storing and managing data:** How to store and manage data locally and in the cloud with SQL Server and Azure Cosmos DB. Later chapters use the SQL Server database and entity models that you create at the end of *Chapter 2, Managing Relational Data Using SQL Server*.

2. **Specialized libraries:** Dates, times, and internationalization; protecting data with encryption, hashing, and signing; protecting apps with authentication and authorization; monitoring and improving performance with threads and tasks; third-party libraries for image handling, data validation rules, and so on. These chapters can be treated like a cookbook of recipes. If you are not interested in any topic, you can skip it, and you can read them in any order.

3. **Service technologies:** How to build and secure services with ASP.NET Core Web API Minimal APIs, OData, GraphQL, gRPC, SignalR, and Azure Functions.

4. **User interface technologies:** How to build user interfaces with ASP.NET Core, Blazor WebAssembly, and .NET MAUI.

# My learning philosophy

Most people learn complex topics best by imitation and repetition rather than reading a detailed explanation of the theory; therefore, I will not overload you with detailed explanations of every step throughout this book. The idea is to get you to write some code and see it run.

You don't need to know all the nitty-gritty details immediately. That will be something that comes with time as you build your own apps and go beyond what any book can teach you.

# Fixing my mistakes

In the words of Samuel Johnson, author of the English dictionary in 1755, I have committed "a few wild blunders, and risible absurdities, from which no work of such multiplicity is free." I take sole responsibility for these and hope you appreciate the challenge of my attempt to lash the wind by writing this book about rapidly evolving technologies like C# and .NET, and the apps and services that you can build with them.

If you have an issue with something in this book, then please contact me before resorting to a negative review on Amazon. Authors cannot respond to Amazon reviews so I cannot contact you to resolve the problem. I want to help you to get the best from my book, and I want to listen to your feedback and do better in the next edition. Please email me (my address is on the GitHub repository for the book), chat to me in the Discord channel for the book (`https://packt.link/apps_and_services_dotnet7`), or raise an issue at the following link: `https://github.com/markjprice/apps-services-net7/issues`.

# Project naming and port numbering conventions

If you complete all the coding tasks in this book, then you will end up with dozens of projects. Many of those will be websites and services that require port numbers for hosting on the `localhost` domain.

With large, complex solutions, it can be difficult to navigate amongst all the code. So, a good reason to structure your projects well is to make it easier to find components. It is good to have an overall name for your solution or workspace that reflects the application or solution.

In the 1990s, Microsoft registered **Northwind** as a fictional company name for use in database and code samples. It was first used as the sample database for their Access product and then also used in SQL Server. We will build multiple projects for this fictional company, so we will use the name `Northwind` as a prefix for all the project names.

There are many ways to structure and name projects and solutions, for example, using a folder hierarchy as well as a naming convention. If you work in a team, make sure you know how your team does it.

It is good to have a naming convention for your projects in a solution or workspace so that any developer can tell what each one does instantly. A common choice is to use the type of project, for example, class library, console app, website, and so on, as shown in the following table:

| Name | Description |
|---|---|
| `Northwind.Common` | A class library project for common types like interfaces, enums, classes, records, and structs, used across multiple projects. |
| `Northwind.Common.EntityModels` | A class library project for common EF Core entity models. Entity models are often used on both the server and client side, so it is best to separate dependencies on specific database providers. |
| `Northwind.Common.DataContext` | A class library project for the EF Core database context with dependencies on specific database providers. |
| `Northwind.Mvc` | An ASP.NET Core project for a complex website that uses the MVC pattern and can be more easily unit tested. |
| `Northwind.WebApi.Service` | An ASP.NET Core project for an HTTP API service. A good choice for integrating with websites because it can use any JavaScript library or Blazor to interact with the service. |
| `Northwind.WebApi.Client.Console` | A client to a web service. The last part of the name indicates that it is a console app. |
| `Northwind.gRPC.Service` | An ASP.NET Core project for a gRPC service. |

| | |
|---|---|
| `Northwind.gRPC.Client.Mvc` | A client to a gRPC service. The last part of the name indicates that it is an ASP.NET Core MVC website project. |
| `Northwind.BlazorWasm.Client` | An ASP.NET Core Blazor WebAssembly client-side project. |
| `Northwind.BlazorWasm.Server` | An ASP.NET Core Blazor WebAssembly server-side project. |
| `Northwind.BlazorWasm.Shared` | A class library shared between client- and server-side Blazor projects. |

To enable you to run any of these projects simultaneously, we must make sure that we do not configure duplicated port numbers. I have used the following convention:

```
https://localhost:5[chapternumber]1/
```

```
http://localhost:5[chapternumber]2/
```

For example, for the encrypted connection to the website built in *Chapter 15*, *Building Web User Interfaces Using ASP.NET Core*, I used port 5151, as shown in the following link:

```
https://localhost:5151/
```

## Treating warnings as errors

By default, compiler warnings may appear if there are potential problems with your code when you first build a project, but they do not prevent compilation and they hide if you rebuild. Warnings are given for a reason, so ignoring warnings encourages poor development practice.

Some developers would prefer to be forced to fix warnings, so .NET provides a project setting to do this, as shown highlighted in the following markup:

```xml
<Project Sdk="Microsoft.NET.Sdk">

  <PropertyGroup>
    <OutputType>Exe</OutputType>
    <TargetFramework>net7.0</TargetFramework>
    <ImplicitUsings>enable</ImplicitUsings>
    <Nullable>enable</Nullable>
    <TreatWarningsAsErrors>true</TreatWarningsAsErrors>
  </PropertyGroup>
```

I have enabled the option to treat warnings as errors in (almost) all the solutions in the GitHub repository.

The exceptions are the gRPC projects. This is due to a combination of factors. In .NET 7, the compiler will warn if you compile source files that contain only lowercase letters in the name of a type.

For example, if you defined a person class, as shown in the following code:

```
public class person
{
}
```

This compiler warning has been introduced so that a future version of C# can safely add a new keyword knowing it will not conflict with the name of a type that you have used, because only C# keywords should contain only lowercase letters.

Unfortunately, the Google tools for generating C# source files from .proto files generate aliases for class names that only contain lowercase letters, as shown in the following code:

```
#region Designer generated code

using pb = global::Google.Protobuf;
```

If you treat warnings as errors, then the compiler complains and refuses to compile the source code, as shown in the following output:

```
Error      CS8981    The type name 'pb' only contains lower-cased ascii
characters. Such names may become reserved for the language.    Northwind.Grpc.
Service     C:\apps-services-net7\Chapter12\Northwind.Grpc.Service\obj\Debug\
net7.0\Protos\Greet.cs
```

 **Good Practice:** Always treat warnings as errors in your .NET projects (except for gRPC projects until Google updates their code generation tools).

# App and service technologies

Microsoft calls platforms for building applications and services **app models** or **workloads**.

## Building websites and apps using ASP.NET Core

Websites are made up of multiple web pages loaded statically from the filesystem or generated dynamically by a server-side technology such as ASP.NET Core. A web browser makes GET requests using **Uniform Resource Locators** (**URLs**) that identify each page and can manipulate data stored on the server using POST, PUT, and DELETE requests.

With many websites, the web browser is treated as a presentation layer, with almost all the processing performed on the server side. Some JavaScript might be used on the client side to implement some presentation features, such as carousels or to perform data validation.

ASP.NET Core provides multiple technologies for building websites:

- **ASP.NET Core Razor Pages** can dynamically generate HTML for simple websites.

- **ASP.NET Core MVC** is an implementation of the **Model-View-Controller** (**MVC**) design pattern that is popular for developing complex websites. You will learn about using it to build user interfaces in *Chapter 15, Building Web User Interfaces Using ASP.NET Core*.

- **Razor class libraries** provide a way to package reusable functionality for ASP.NET Core projects including user interface components.

- **Blazor** lets you build user interface components using C# and .NET and then run them in a web browser or embedded web component instead of a JavaScript-based UI framework like Angular, React, or Vue. **Blazor WebAssembly** runs your code in the browser like a JavaScript-based framework would. **Blazor Server** runs your code on the server and updates the web page dynamically. You will learn about Blazor in detail in *Chapter 16, Building Web Components Using Blazor WebAssembly*, and *Chapter 17, Leveraging Open-Source Blazor Component Libraries*.

 Blazor is not just for building websites; it can also be used to create hybrid mobile and desktop apps when combined with .NET MAUI.

## Building web and other services

There are no formal definitions, but services are sometimes described based on their complexity:

- **Service:** All functionality needed by a client app in one monolithic service.

- **Microservice:** Multiple services that each focus on a smaller set of functionalities.

- **Nanoservice:** A single function provided as a service. Unlike services and microservices that are hosted 24/7/365, nanoservices are often inactive until called upon to reduce resources and costs.

As well as ASP.NET Core Web API and Minimal APIs web services that use HTTP as the underlying communication technology and follow the design principles of Roy Fielding's REST architecture, we will learn how to build services using web and other technologies that extend basic web APIs, including:

- **gRPC:** For building highly efficient and performant microservices with support for almost any platform.

- **SignalR:** For implementing real-time communications between components.

- **OData:** For easily wrapping Entity Framework Core and other data models as a web service.

- **GraphQL:** For letting the client control what data is retrieved across multiple data sources. Although GraphQL can use HTTP, it does not have to, and it does not follow web design principles defined by Roy Fielding in his dissertation about REST APIs.

- **Azure Functions:** For hosting serverless nanoservices in the cloud.

## Windows Communication Foundation (WCF)

In 2006, Microsoft released .NET Framework 3.0 with some major new frameworks, one of which was **Windows Communication Foundation** (**WCF**). It abstracted the business logic implementation of a service from the communication technology infrastructure so that you could easily switch to an alternative in the future or even have multiple mechanisms to communicate with the service.

WCF heavily uses XML configuration to declaratively define endpoints, including their address, binding, and contract. This is known as the ABCs of WCF endpoints. Once you understand how to do this, WCF is a powerful yet flexible technology.

Microsoft decided not to officially port WCF to modern .NET, but there is a community-owned OSS project named **Core WCF** managed by the .NET Foundation. If you need to migrate an existing service from .NET Framework to modern .NET, or build a client to a WCF service, then you could use Core WCF. Be aware that it can never be a full port since parts of WCF are Windows-specific.

Technologies like WCF allow for the building of distributed applications. A client application can make **remote procedure calls** (**RPCs**) to a server application. Instead of using a port of WCF to do this, we should use an alternative RPC technology like gRPC, which is covered in this book.

## Summary of choices for services

Each service technology has its pros and cons based on its feature support, as shown in the following table:

| Feature | Web API | OData | GraphQL | gRPC | SignalR |
|---|---|---|---|---|---|
| Client can request just the data they need | No | Yes | Yes | No | No |
| Minimum HTTP version | 1.1 | 1.1 | 1.1 | 2.0 | 1.1 |
| Browser support | Yes | Yes | Yes | No | Yes |
| Data format | XML, JSON | XML, JSON | GraphQL (JSONish) | Binary | Varies |
| Service documentation | Swagger | Swagger | No | No | No |
| Code generation | Third-party | Third-party | Third-party | Google | Microsoft |
| Caching | Easy | Easy | Hard | Hard | Hard |

Use these recommendations for various scenarios as guidance, as shown in the following table:

| Scenario | Recommendation |
|---|---|
| Public services | HTTP/1.1-based services are best for services that need to be publicly accessible, especially if they need to be called from a browser or mobile device. |
| Public data services | OData and GraphQL are both good choices for exposing complex hierarchical datasets that could come from different data stores. OData is designed and supported by Microsoft via official .NET packages. GraphQL is designed by Facebook and supported by third-party packages. |

| Service-to-services | gRPC is designed for low latency and high throughput communication. gRPC is great for lightweight internal microservices where efficiency is critical. |
|---|---|
| Point-to-point real-time communication | gRPC has excellent support for bidirectional streaming. gRPC services can push messages in real time without polling. SignalR is designed for real-time communication of many kinds, so it tends to be easier to implement than gRPC although it is less efficient. |
| Broadcast real-time communication | SignalR has great support for broadcasting real-time communication to many clients. |
| Polyglot environments | gRPC tooling supports all popular development languages, making gRPC a good choice for multi-language and platform environments. |
| Network bandwidth constrained environments | gRPC messages are serialized with Protobuf, a lightweight message format. A gRPC message is always smaller than an equivalent JSON message. |
| Nanoservices | Azure Functions do not need to be hosted 24/7 so they are a good choice for nanoservices that usually do not need to be running constantly. Amazon Web Services (AWS) Lambdas are an alternative. |

## Building Windows-only apps

Technologies for building Windows-only apps, primarily for the desktop, include:

- **Windows Forms**, 2002.
- **Windows Presentation Foundation** (**WPF**), 2006.
- **Windows Store** apps, 2012.
- **Universal Windows Platform** (**UWP**) apps, 2015.
- **Windows App SDK** (formerly **WinUI 3** and **Project Reunion**) apps, 2021.

## Understanding legacy Windows application platforms

With the Microsoft Windows 1.0 release in 1985, the only way to create Windows applications was to use the C language and call functions in three core DLLs named kernel, user, and GDI. Once Windows became 32-bit with Windows 95, the DLLs were suffixed with 32 and became known as **Win32 API**.

In 1991, Microsoft introduced Visual Basic, which provided developers a visual, drag-and-drop-from-a-toolbox-of-controls way to build the user interface for Windows applications. It was immensely popular, and the Visual Basic runtime is still distributed as part of Windows 11 today.

With the first version of C# and .NET Framework released in 2002, Microsoft provided technology for building Windows desktop applications named **Windows Forms**. The equivalent at the time for web development was named **Web Forms**, hence the complementary names. The code could be written in either Visual Basic or C# languages. Windows Forms had a similar drag-and-drop visual designer, although it generated C# or Visual Basic code to define the user interface, which can be difficult for humans to understand and edit directly.

In 2006, Microsoft released a more powerful technology for building Windows desktop applications, named **Windows Presentation Foundation** (**WPF**), as a key component of .NET Framework 3.0 alongside **Windows Communication Foundation** (**WCF**) and **Windows Workflow** (**WF**).

Although a WPF app can be created by writing only C# statements, it can also use **eXtensible Application Markup Language** (**XAML**) to specify its user interface, which is easy for both humans and code to understand. Visual Studio for Windows is partially built with WPF.

In 2012, Microsoft released Windows 8 with its Windows Store apps that run in a protected sandbox.

In 2015, Microsoft released Windows 10 with an updated Windows Store app concept named **Universal Windows Platform** (**UWP**). UWP apps can be built using C++ and DirectX UI, or JavaScript and HTML, or C# using a custom fork of modern .NET that is not cross-platform but provides full access to the underlying WinRT APIs.

UWP apps can only execute on the Windows 10 or Windows 11 platforms, not earlier versions of Windows, but UWP apps can run on Xbox and Windows Mixed Reality headsets with motion controllers.

Many Windows developers rejected Windows Store and UWP apps because they have limited access to the underlying system. Microsoft recently created **Project Reunion** and **WinUI 3**, which work together to allow Windows developers to bring some of the benefits of modern Windows development to their existing WPF apps and allow them to have the same benefits and system integrations that UWP apps have. This initiative is now known as **Windows App SDK**.

## Understanding modern .NET support for legacy Windows platforms

The on-disk size of the .NET SDKs for Linux and macOS are about 330 MB. The on-disk size of the .NET SDK for Windows is about 440 MB. This is because it includes the Windows Desktop Runtime, which allows the legacy Windows application platforms Windows Forms and WPF to be run on modern .NET.

There are many enterprise applications built using Windows Forms and WPF that need to be maintained or enhanced with new features, but until recently they were stuck on .NET Framework, which is now a legacy platform. With modern .NET and its Windows Desktop Pack, these apps can now use the full modern capabilities of .NET.

## Building cross-platform mobile and desktop apps

There are two major mobile platforms: Apple's iOS and Google's Android, each with their own programming languages and platform APIs. There are also two major desktop platforms: Apple's macOS and Microsoft's Windows, each with their own programming languages and platform APIs, as shown in the following list:

- **iOS**: Objective C or Swift and UIKit.
- **Android**: Java or Kotlin and Android API.
- **macOS**: Objective C or Swift and AppKit or Catalyst.
- **Windows**: C, C++, or many other languages and Win32 API or Windows App SDK.

Cross-platform mobile and desktop apps can be built once for the **.NET Multi-platform App UI** (**MAUI**) platform, and then can run on many mobile and desktop platforms.

.NET MAUI makes it easy to develop those apps by sharing user interface components as well as business logic; they can target the same .NET APIs as used by console apps, websites, and web services.

The apps can exist standalone, but they usually call services to provide an experience that spans across all your computing devices, from servers and laptops to phones and gaming systems.

.NET MAUI supports existing MVVM and XAML patterns. The team also plans to add support in the future for **Model-View-Update** (**MVU**) with C#, which is like Apple's Swift UI.

# .NET MAUI alternatives

Before Microsoft created .NET MAUI, third parties created open-source initiatives to enable .NET developers to build cross-platform apps using XAML, named **Uno** and **Avalonia**.

## Understanding Uno platform

Uno is "the first C# & XAML, free and open-source platform for creating true single-source, multi-platform applications", stated on their own website at the following link: `https://platform.uno/`.

Developers can reuse 99% of the business logic and UI layer across native mobile, web, and desktop.

Uno platform uses the Xamarin native platform but not Xamarin.Forms. For WebAssembly, Uno uses the Mono-WASM runtime just like Blazor WebAssembly. For Linux, Uno uses Skia to draw the user interface on canvas.

> A book to learn Uno platform can be found at the following link: `https://www.packtpub.com/product/creating-cross-platform-c-applications-with-uno-platform/9781801078498`.

## Understanding Avalonia

Avalonia "is a cross-platform UI framework for .NET." It "creates pixel-perfect, native apps," It "is supported on all major platforms." Avalonia "is the trusted UI framework for complex apps", as stated on their official website home page at the following link: `https://avaloniaui.net/`.

You can think of Avalonia as a spiritual successor to WPF. WPF, Silverlight, and UWP developers can continue to benefit from their years of pre-existing knowledge and skills.

It was used by JetBrains to modernize their WPF-based tools and take them cross-platform.

The Avalonia extension for Visual Studio and deep integration with JetBrains Rider makes development easier and more productive.

# Setting up your development environment

Before you start programming, you'll need a code editor for C#. Microsoft has a family of code editors and **Integrated Development Environments (IDEs)**, which include:

- Visual Studio 2022 for Windows
- Visual Studio 2022 for Mac
- Visual Studio Code for Windows, Mac, or Linux
- Visual Studio Code for Web
- GitHub Codespaces

Third parties have created their own C# code editors, for example, JetBrains Rider.

In *Chapters 1* to *17*, you can use OS-specific Visual Studio 2022 or cross-platform Visual Studio Code and JetBrains Rider to build all the apps and services. In *Chapter 18*, *Building Mobile and Desktop Apps Using .NET MAUI*, and *Chapter 19*, *Integrating .NET MAUI Apps with Blazor and Native Platforms*, although you could use Visual Studio Code to build the mobile and desktop app, it is not easy. Visual Studio 2022 for Windows or Mac has better support for .NET MAUI than Visual Studio Code does (for now).

# Choosing the appropriate tool and application type for learning

What is the best tool and application type for building apps and services with C# and .NET?

I want you to be free to choose any C# code editor or IDE to complete the coding tasks in this book, including Visual Studio Code, Visual Studio for Windows, Visual Studio for Mac, or even JetBrains Rider.

For building user interfaces, Visual Studio 2022 for either Windows or Mac is best because it provides a GUI editor. Visual Studio Code does not yet have a GUI editor for XAML-based platforms like WPF or .NET MAUI.

In this book, I give general instructions that work with all tools so you can use whichever tool you prefer.

# Using Visual Studio Code for cross-platform development

The most modern and lightweight code editor to choose from, and the only one from Microsoft that is cross-platform, is Visual Studio Code. It can run on all common operating systems, including Windows, macOS, and many varieties of Linux, including **Red Hat Enterprise Linux** (**RHEL**) and Ubuntu.

Visual Studio Code is a good choice for modern cross-platform development because it has an extensive and growing set of extensions to support many languages beyond C#.

Being cross-platform and lightweight, it can be installed on all platforms that your apps will be deployed to for quick bug fixes and so on. Choosing Visual Studio Code means a developer can use a cross-platform code editor to develop cross-platform apps.

Visual Studio Code has strong support for web development, although it currently has weak support for mobile and desktop development.

Visual Studio Code is supported on ARM processors, so you can develop on Apple Silicon computers and Raspberry Pi.

Visual Studio Code is by far the most popular integrated development environment, with over 70% of professional developers selecting it in the Stack Overflow 2021 survey.

## Using GitHub Codespaces for development in the cloud

GitHub Codespaces is a fully configured development environment based on Visual Studio Code that can be spun up in an environment hosted in the cloud and accessed through any web browser. It supports Git repos, extensions, and a built-in command-line interface so you can edit, run, and test from any device.

## Using Visual Studio for Mac for general development

Visual Studio 2022 for Mac can create most types of applications, including console apps, websites, web services, desktop, and mobile apps.

To compile apps for Apple operating systems like iOS to run on devices like the iPhone and iPad, you must have Xcode, which only runs on macOS.

## Using Visual Studio for Windows for general development

Visual Studio 2022 for Windows can create most types of applications, including console apps, websites, web services, desktop, and mobile apps.

Although you can use Visual Studio 2022 for Windows with a .NET MAUI project to write a cross-platform mobile app, you still need macOS and Xcode to compile it.

Visual Studio 2022 for Windows only runs on Windows 10 version 1909 or later, or Windows Server 2016 or later, and only on 64-bit versions. Version 17.4 is the first version to support native Arm64.

## What I used

To write and test the code for this book, I used the following hardware:

- HP Spectre (Intel) laptop
- Apple Silicon Mac mini (M1) desktop
- Raspberry Pi 400 (ARM v8) desktop

I used the following software:

- Visual Studio Code on:

    - macOS on the Apple Silicon Mac mini (M1) desktop
    - Windows 11 on the HP Spectre (Intel) laptop
    - Ubuntu 64 on the Raspberry Pi 400

- Visual Studio 2022 for Windows on:

    - Windows 11 on the HP Spectre (Intel) laptop

- Visual Studio 2022 for Mac on:

    - macOS on the Apple Silicon Mac mini (M1) desktop

I hope that you have access to a variety of hardware and software too, because seeing the differences on various platforms deepens your understanding of development challenges, although any one of the above combinations is enough to learn how to build practical apps and websites.

 You can learn how to write code with C# and .NET using a Raspberry Pi 400 with Ubuntu Desktop 64-bit by reading an extra article that I wrote at the following link: `https://github.com/markjprice/apps-services-net7/tree/main/docs/raspberry-pi-ubuntu64`.

## Deploying cross-platform

Your choice of code editor and operating system for development does not limit where your code gets deployed.

.NET 7 supports the following platforms for deployment:

- **Windows**: Windows 10 version 1607, or later, including Windows 11, on x86, x64 or Arm64. Windows Server 2012 R2 SP1, or later. Nano Server version 1809, or later.
- **Mac**: macOS Catalina (version 10.15), or later.
- **Linux**: Alpine Linux 3.15, or later. CentOS 7, or later. Debian 10, or later. Fedora 33, or later. openSUSE 15, or later. RHEL 7, or later. SUSE Enterprise Linux 12 SP2, or later. Ubuntu 18.04, or later.
- **Android**: API 21, or later.
- **iOS**: 10, or later.

Windows ARM64 support in .NET 5 and later means you can develop on, and deploy to, Windows ARM devices like Microsoft Surface Pro X. Developing on an Apple M1 Mac using Parallels and a Windows 11 ARM virtual machine is twice as fast.

 Windows 7 and Windows 8.1 are only supported with .NET 6 until January 2023. They are not supported with .NET 7 or later. You can read more at the following link: `https://github.com/dotnet/core/issues/7556`.

## Downloading and installing Visual Studio 2022 for Windows

Many professional Microsoft developers use Visual Studio 2022 for Windows in their day-to-day development work. Even if you choose to use Visual Studio Code to complete the coding tasks in this book, you might want to familiarize yourself with Visual Studio 2022 for Windows too.

If you do not have a Windows computer, then you can skip this section and continue to the next section where you will download and install Visual Studio Code on macOS or Linux.

Since October 2014, Microsoft has made a professional quality edition of Visual Studio for Windows available to students, open-source contributors, and individuals for free. It is called Community Edition. Any of the editions are suitable for this book. If you have not already installed it, let's do so now:

1.  Download Visual Studio 2022 version 17.4 or later for Windows from the following link: `https://visualstudio.microsoft.com/downloads/`.

2.  Start the installer.

3.  On the **Workloads** tab, select the following:

    *   ASP.NET and web development
    *   Azure development
    *   .NET Multi-platform App UI development
    *   .NET desktop development (because this includes console apps)

4.  On the **Individual components** tab, in the **Code tools** section, select the following:

    *   Git for Windows

5.  Click **Install** and wait for the installer to acquire the selected software and install it.

6.  When the installation is complete, click **Launch**.

7.  The first time that you run Visual Studio, you will be prompted to sign in. If you have a Microsoft account, you can use that account. If you don't, then register for a new one at the following link: `https://signup.live.com/`.

8.  The first time that you run Visual Studio, you will be prompted to configure your environment. For **Development Settings**, choose **Visual C#**. For the color theme, I chose **Blue**, but you can choose whatever tickles your fancy.

9.  If you want to customize your keyboard shortcuts, navigate to **Tools | Options...**, and then select the **Environment | Keyboard** option.

## Visual Studio 2022 for Windows keyboard shortcuts

In this book, I will avoid showing keyboard shortcuts since they are often customized. Where they are consistent across code editors and commonly used, I will try to show them.

If you want to identify and customize your keyboard shortcuts, then you can, as shown at the following link: `https://docs.microsoft.com/en-us/visualstudio/ide/identifying-and-customizing-keyboard-shortcuts-in-visual-studio`.

## Downloading and installing Visual Studio Code

Visual Studio Code has rapidly improved over the past couple of years and has pleasantly surprised Microsoft with its popularity. If you are brave and like to live on the bleeding edge, then there is an **Insiders** edition, which is a daily build of the next version.

 **Good Practice:** Even if you plan to only use Visual Studio 2022 for Windows for development, you must install Visual Studio Code so that you can use some of its extensions, like the REST Client, that we will use in this book for testing of web and data services.

Let's now download and install Visual Studio Code, the .NET SDK, and the C# extension:

1.  Download and install either the Stable build or the Insiders edition of Visual Studio Code from the following link: `https://code.visualstudio.com/`.

 **More Information:** If you need more help installing Visual Studio Code, you can read the official setup guide at the following link: `https://code.visualstudio.com/docs/setup/setup-overview`.

2.  Download and install the .NET SDKs for versions 6.0 and 7.0 from the following link: `https://www.microsoft.com/net/download`.

 To fully learn how to control .NET SDKs, we need multiple versions installed. .NET 6.0 and .NET 7.0 are two currently supported versions. You can safely install multiple SDKs side by side. Although .NET 6.0 is not the most recent, it is the most recent **Long Term Support** (**LTS**) version so it has an end of life six months after .NET 7.0; that is another good reason to install it.

3.  To install the C# extension, you must first launch the Visual Studio Code application.
4.  In Visual Studio Code, click the **Extensions** icon or navigate to **View | Extensions**.
5.  C# is one of the most popular extensions available, so you should see it at the top of the list, or you can enter C# in the search box.
6.  Click **Install** and wait for supporting packages to download and install.

## Installing other extensions

In later chapters of this book, you will use more Visual Studio Code extensions. If you want to install them now, all the extensions that we will use are shown in the following table:

| Extension name and identifier | Description |
| --- | --- |
| C# for Visual Studio Code (powered by OmniSharp) `ms-dotnettools.csharp` | C# editing support, including syntax highlighting, IntelliSense, Go To Definition, Find All References, debugging support for .NET, and support for `csproj` projects on Windows, macOS, and Linux. |
| MSBuild project tools `tintoy.msbuild-project-tools` | Provides IntelliSense for MSBuild project files, including autocomplete for `<PackageReference>` elements. |
| REST Client `humao.rest-client` | Send an HTTP request and view the response directly in Visual Studio Code. |
| ilspy-vscode `icsharpcode.ilspy-vscode` | Decompile MSIL assemblies – support for modern .NET, .NET Framework, .NET Core, and .NET Standard. |

| Azure Functions for Visual Studio Code<br>`ms-azuretools.vscode-azurefunctions` | Create, debug, manage, and deploy serverless apps directly from VS Code. It has dependencies on Azure Account (`ms-vscode.azure-account`) and Azure Resources (`ms-azuretools.vscode-azureresourcegroups`) extensions. |
|---|---|
| GitHub repositories<br>`github.remotehub` | Browse, search, edit, and commit to any remote GitHub repository directly from within Visual Studio Code. |
| SQL Server (mssql) for Visual Studio Code<br>`ms-mssql.mssql` | For developing SQL Server, Azure SQL Database, and SQL Data Warehouse everywhere with a rich set of functionalities. |
| vscode-proto3<br>`zxh404.vscode-proto3` | Syntax highlighting, syntax validation, code snippets, code completion, code formatting, brace matching, and line and block commenting. |

## Understanding Visual Studio Code versions

Microsoft releases a new feature version of Visual Studio Code (almost) every month and bug fix versions more frequently. For example:

- Version 1.66, March 2022 feature release
- Version 1.66.1, March 2022 bug fix release

The version used in this book is 1.71, but the version of Visual Studio Code is less important than the version of the C# for Visual Studio Code extension that you installed. For example, to support C# 11 features, you should install C# extension 1.25 or later.

While the C# extension is not required, it provides IntelliSense as you type, code navigation, and debugging features, so it's something that's very handy to install and keep updated to support the latest C# language features.

## Visual Studio Code keyboard shortcuts

In this book, I will avoid showing keyboard shortcuts used for tasks like creating a new file since they are often different on different operating systems. The situations where I will show keyboard shortcuts are when you need to repeatedly press the key, for example, while debugging. These are also more likely to be consistent across operating systems.

If you want to customize your keyboard shortcuts for Visual Studio Code, then you can, as shown at the following link: `https://code.visualstudio.com/docs/getstarted/keybindings`.

I recommend that you download a PDF of keyboard shortcuts for your operating system from the following list:

- Windows: `https://code.visualstudio.com/shortcuts/keyboard-shortcuts-windows.pdf`

- macOS: `https://code.visualstudio.com/shortcuts/keyboard-shortcuts-macos.pdf`
- Linux: `https://code.visualstudio.com/shortcuts/keyboard-shortcuts-linux.pdf`

## Finding the solution code on GitHub

The solution code in the GitHub repository for this book includes separate folders for Visual Studio 2022 for Windows and Visual Studio Code, as shown in the following list:

- Visual Studio 2022 solutions: `https://github.com/markjprice/apps-services-net7/tree/main/vs4win`
- Visual Studio Code solutions: `https://github.com/markjprice/apps-services-net7/tree/main/vscode`

## Consuming Azure resources

Some of the chapters in this book will require you to sign up for an Azure account and create Azure resources. Frequently, there are free tiers or local development versions of these services, but sometimes you will have to create a resource that has a cost while it exists.

Microsoft currently says, "Eligible new users get $200 Azure credit in your billing currency for the first 30 days and a limited quantity of free services for 12 months with your Azure free account." You can learn more at the following link:

`https://docs.microsoft.com/en-us/azure/cost-management-billing/manage/avoid-charges-free-account`

 **Good Practice:** Delete Azure resources as soon as you do not need them to keep your costs low.

A summary of which chapters need Azure resources and if a local development alternative is available is shown in the following table:

| Chapter | Azure resource | Free tier | Local development alternative |
|---|---|---|---|
| 2 | SQL Database | As part of free first year. | SQL Server Developer Edition on Windows, or SQL Edge in a Docker container on Windows, Linux, and macOS. |
| 3 | Cosmos DB database | 1,000 RU/s and 25 GB of storage. | Azure Cosmos DB Emulator on Windows or the preview version on Linux. |
| 13 | Azure SignalR Service | 20 concurrent connections and 20,000 messages per day with 99.9% SLA. | Add SignalR to any ASP.NET Core project for local development. |

| 14 | Azure Functions | 1 million requests and 400,000 GB-s of resource consumption per month. | Azurite open-source emulator for testing Azure blob, queue storage, and table storage applications like Azure Functions. |
|---|---|---|---|

 You can find out how to check your usage of free Azure resources at the following link: https://docs.microsoft.com/en-us/azure/cost-management-billing/manage/ check-free-service-usage.

# Using an analyzer to write better code

.NET analyzers find potential issues and suggest fixes for them. **StyleCop** is a commonly used analyzer for helping you write better C# code.

Let's see it in action:

1. Use your preferred code editor to create a **Console App**/console project named CodeAnalyzing in a Chapter01 solution/workspace.
2. In the CodeAnalyzing project, add a package reference for StyleCop.Analyzers.
3. Add a JSON file to your project named stylecop.json for controlling StyleCop settings.
4. Modify its contents, as shown in the following markup:

```
{
  "$schema": "https://raw.githubusercontent.com/DotNetAnalyzers/
StyleCopAnalyzers/master/StyleCop.Analyzers/StyleCop.Analyzers/Settings/
stylecop.schema.json",
  "settings": {

  }
}
```

The $schema entry enables IntelliSense while editing the stylecop.json file in your code editor.

5. Move the insertion point inside the settings section and press *Ctrl + Space*, and note the IntelliSense showing valid subsections of settings, as shown in *Figure 1.2*:

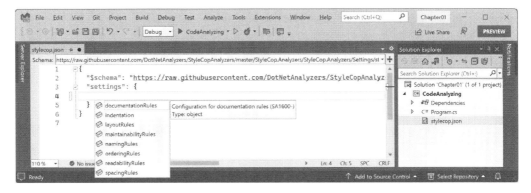

*Figure 1.2: stylecop.json IntelliSense showing valid subsections of settings*

6.  In the CodeAnalyzing project file, add entries to configure the file named stylecop.json to not be included in published deployments, and to enable it as an additional file for processing during development, as shown highlighted in the following markup:

```xml
<Project Sdk="Microsoft.NET.Sdk">

  <PropertyGroup>
    <OutputType>Exe</OutputType>
    <TargetFramework>net7.0</TargetFramework>
    <ImplicitUsings>enable</ImplicitUsings>
    <Nullable>enable</Nullable>
  </PropertyGroup>
  <ItemGroup>
    <PackageReference Include="StyleCop.Analyzers" Version="1.2.0-*">
      <PrivateAssets>all</PrivateAssets>
      <IncludeAssets>runtime; build; native; contentfiles; analyzers</IncludeAssets>
    </PackageReference>
  </ItemGroup>

  <ItemGroup>
    <None Remove="stylecop.json" />
  </ItemGroup>

  <ItemGroup>
    <AdditionalFiles Include="stylecop.json" />
  </ItemGroup>

</Project>
```

 At the time of writing, the StyleCop.Analyzers package is in preview. I have set the version to 1.2.0-* to make sure that as soon as a newer preview version is released, it will upgrade automatically. Once a stable version is available, I recommend fixing the version.

7.  In Program.cs, delete the existing statements and then add some statements to explicitly define the Program class with its Main method, as shown in the following code:

```csharp
using System.Diagnostics;

namespace CodeAnalyzing;

class Program
{
  static void Main(string[] args)
```

```
    {
        Debug.WriteLine("Hello, Debugger!");
    }
}
```

8.  Build the `CodeAnalyzing` project.

9.  You will see warnings for everything it thinks is wrong, as shown in *Figure 1.3*:

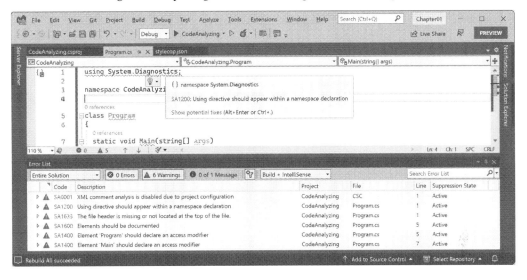

*Figure 1.3: StyleCop code analyzer warnings*

10. For example, it wants `using` directives to be put within the namespace declaration, as shown in the following output:

```
C:\apps-services-net7\Chapter01\CodeAnalyzing\Program.cs(1,1): warning
SA1200: Using directive should appear within a namespace declaration [C:\
apps-services-net7\Chapter01\CodeAnalyzing\CodeAnalyzing.csproj]
```

## Suppressing warnings

To suppress a warning, you have several options, including adding code and setting configuration.

To suppress a warning using an attribute, add an assembly-level attribute, as shown in the following code:

```
[assembly:SuppressMessage("StyleCop.CSharp.OrderingRules",
"SA1200:UsingDirectivesMustBePlacedWithinNamespace", Justification =
"Reviewed.")]
```

To suppress a warning using a directive, add `#pragma` statements around the statement that is causing the warning, as shown in the following code:

```
#pragma warning disable SA1200 // UsingDirectivesMustBePlacedWithinNamespace
using System.Diagnostics;
#pragma warning restore SA1200 // UsingDirectivesMustBePlacedWithinNamespace
```

Let's suppress the warning by modifying the `stylecop.json` file:

1.  In `stylecop.json`, add a configuration option to set `using` statements to be allowable outside a namespace, as shown highlighted in the following markup:

```
{
  "$schema": "https://raw.githubusercontent.com/DotNetAnalyzers/
StyleCopAnalyzers/master/StyleCop.Analyzers/StyleCop.Analyzers/Settings/
stylecop.schema.json",
  "settings": {
    "orderingRules": {
      "usingDirectivesPlacement": "outsideNamespace"
    }
  }
}
```

2.  Build the project and note that warning SA1200 has disappeared.

3.  In `stylecop.json`, set the using directives placement to `preserve`, which allows `using` statements both inside and outside a namespace, as shown highlighted in the following markup:

```
"orderingRules": {
  "usingDirectivesPlacement": "preserve"
}
```

# Fixing the code

Now, let's fix all the other warnings:

1.  In `CodeAnalyzing.csproj`, add an element to automatically generate an XML file for documentation and add an element to treat warnings as errors, as shown highlighted in the following markup:

```
<Project Sdk="Microsoft.NET.Sdk">

  <PropertyGroup>
    <OutputType>Exe</OutputType>
    <TargetFramework>net7.0</TargetFramework>
    <ImplicitUsings>enable</ImplicitUsings>
    <Nullable>enable</Nullable>
    <GenerateDocumentationFile>true</GenerateDocumentationFile>
    <TreatWarningsAsErrors>true</TreatWarningsAsErrors>
  </PropertyGroup>
```

2.  In `stylecop.json`, add a configuration option to provide values for documentation for the company name and copyright text, as shown highlighted in the following markup:

```
{
  "$schema": "https://raw.githubusercontent.com/DotNetAnalyzers/
StyleCopAnalyzers/master/StyleCop.Analyzers/StyleCop.Analyzers/Settings/
stylecop.schema.json",
```

```
    "settings": {
      "orderingRules": {
        "usingDirectivesPlacement": "preserve"
      },
      "documentationRules": {
        "companyName": "Packt",
        "copyrightText": "Copyright (c) Packt. All rights reserved."
      }
    }
}
```

3.  In `Program.cs`, add comments for a file header with company and copyright text, move the `using System;` declaration inside the namespace, and set explicit access modifiers and XML comments for the class and method, as shown in the following code:

```csharp
// <copyright file="Program.cs" company="Packt">
// Copyright (c) Packt. All rights reserved.
// </copyright>
namespace CodeAnalyzing;

using System.Diagnostics;

/// <summary>
/// The main class for this console app.
/// </summary>
public class Program
{
    /// <summary>
    /// The main entry point for this console app.
    /// </summary>
    /// <param name="args">
    /// A string array of arguments passed to the console app.
    /// </param>
    public static void Main(string[] args)
    {
        Debug.WriteLine("Hello, Debugger!");
    }
}
```

4.  Build the project.

5.  Expand the `bin/Debug/net7.0` folder (remember to **Show All Files** if you are using Visual Studio 2022) and note the autogenerated file named `CodeAnalyzing.xml`, as shown in the following markup:

```xml
<?xml version="1.0"?>
<doc>
    <assembly>
```

```
        <name>CodeAnalyzing</name>
    </assembly>
    <members>
        <member name="T:CodeAnalyzing.Program">
            <summary>
            The main class for this console app.
            </summary>
        </member>
        <member name="M:CodeAnalyzing.Program.Main(System.String[])">
            <summary>
            The main entry point for this console app.
            </summary>
            <param name="args">
            A string array of arguments passed to the console app.
            </param>
        </member>
    </members>
</doc>
```

The `CodeAnalyzing.xml` file can then be processed by a tool like DocFX to convert it into documentation files, as shown at the following link: `https://www.jamescroft.co.uk/building-net-project-docs-with-docfx-on-github-pages/`.

# What's new in C# and .NET?

In 2020, .NET Core was rebranded .NET and the major version number skipped 4 to avoid confusion with .NET Framework 4.x. Microsoft plans on annual major version releases every November, rather like Apple does major version number releases of iOS every September.

The following table shows when the key versions of modern .NET were released, when future releases are planned, and when they reach end of life and are therefore unsupported and receive no more bug fixes and security updates:

| Version | Released | End of life |
| --- | --- | --- |
| .NET Core 3.1 (LTS) | December 3, 2019 | December 3, 2022 |
| .NET 5.0 (Current) | November 8, 2020 | May 8, 2022 |
| .NET 6.0 (LTS) | November 8, 2021 | November 8, 2024 |
| .NET 7.0 (STS) | November 8, 2022 | May 2024 |
| .NET 8.0 (LTS) | November 2023 | November 2026 |
| .NET 9.0 (STS) | November 2024 | May 2026 |
| .NET 10.0 (LTS) | November 2025 | November 2028 |

# Understanding .NET support

.NET versions are either **LTS**, **STS** (formerly known as **Current**), or **Preview**, as described in the following list:

- **Long Term Support** (**LTS**) releases are stable and require fewer updates over their lifetime. These are a good choice for applications that you do not intend to update frequently. LTS releases are supported by Microsoft for 3 years after general availability, or 1 year after the next LTS release ships, whichever is longer.

- **Standard Term Support** (**STS**) releases include features that may change based on feedback. These are a good choice for applications that you are actively developing because they provide access to the latest improvements. STS releases are supported by Microsoft for 18 months after general availability, or 6 months after the next release ships, whichever is longer.

- **Preview** releases are for public testing. These are a good choice for adventurous programmers who want to live on the bleeding edge, or programming book writers who need to have early access to new language features, libraries, and app platforms. Preview releases are not supported by Microsoft but Preview or **Release Candidate** (**RC**) releases may be declared **Go Live**, meaning they are supported by Microsoft in production.

STS and LTS releases receive critical fixes throughout their lifetime for security and reliability. You must stay up to date with the latest patches to get support. For example, if a system is running 1.0 and 1.0.1 has been released, 1.0.1 must be installed to get support.

 **End of support** or **end of life** means the date after which bug fixes, security updates, or technical assistance are no longer available from Microsoft.

# Understanding .NET Runtime and .NET SDK versions

.NET Runtime versioning follows semantic versioning; that is, a major increment indicates breaking changes, minor increments indicate new features, and patch increments indicate bug fixes.

.NET SDK versioning does not follow semantic versioning. The major and minor version numbers are tied to the runtime version it is matched with. The patch number follows a convention that indicates the major and minor versions of the SDK. For example, patch number 100 means SDK version 1.0, patch number 101 means SDK version 1.1, and patch number 200 means SDK version 2.0. To summarize, version 7.0.213 would mean .NET 7 SDK version 2.13.

You can see an example of this in the following table:

| Change | Runtime | SDK |
|---|---|---|
| Initial release | 7.0.0 | 7.0.100 |
| SDK bug fix | 7.0.0 | 7.0.101 |
| Runtime and SDK bug fix | 7.0.1 | 7.0.102 |
| SDK new feature | 7.0.1 | 7.0.200 |

# What's new in C# 8 and .NET Core 3?

There were many language and library features introduced with C# 8 and .NET Core 3:

- You can apply `readonly` to members of a `struct`.
- You can use `??=` to assign the value only if the left-hand operand evaluates to `null`.
- You can use both `$@"..."` and `@$"..."` as valid interpolated verbatim strings.
- There are more ways to perform pattern matching.
- You can make local functions static.
- You can create and consume async streams, meaning iterators that implement `IAsyncEnumerable<T>`, not streams that derive from the abstract `Stream` class. You will see an example in *Chapter 4, Benchmarking Performance, Multitasking, and Concurrency*.
- You can use `await using` to work with an asynchronously disposable object that implements the `System.IAsyncDisposable` interface.

Let's see some others in more detail.

## Default interface methods

You can provide implementations of members in an interface. This is most useful when you have defined an interface, and in a later version you want to extend it. Normally you would not be able to without breaking any clients that consume your interface, because any types that implement the interface will not provide implementations for the new members. Now you can add new members with implementations in the interface and the types will inherit the default implementations in the interface. This is also useful for interactions with APIs for Android or Swift that also support this functionality.

## Switch expressions

Switch expressions are a more compact switch syntax. For example, a `switch` *statement*, as shown in the following code:

```
Stream? s;
...
string message;
switch (s)
{
  case FileStream writeableFile when s.CanWrite:
```

```
      message = "The stream is a file that I can write to.";
      break;
   case FileStream readOnlyFile:
      message = "The stream is a read-only file.";
      break;
   case MemoryStream ms:
      message = "The stream is a memory address.";
      break;
   default: // always evaluated last despite its current position
      message = "The stream is some other type.";
      break;
   case null:
      message = "The stream is null.";
      break;
}
```

Could be more succinctly expressed as a `switch` *expression*, as shown in the following code:

```
Stream? s;
...
string message = s switch
{
   FileStream writeableFile when s.CanWrite
      => "The stream is a file that I can write to.",
   FileStream readOnlyFile
      => "The stream is a read-only file.",
   MemoryStream ms
      => "The stream is a memory address.",
   null
      => "The stream is null.",

   _
      => "The stream is some other type."
};
```

## Using declarations

You can simplify `using` blocks by removing the curly braces. For example, when working with a disposable resource like a file, as shown in the following code:

```
using (FileStream file = File.OpenWrite(Path.Combine(path, "file.txt")))
{
   ...
} // automatically calls Dispose if the file is not null
```

This could be simplified, as shown in the following code:

```
using (FileStream file = File.OpenWrite(Path.Combine(path, "file.txt")));
   ...
```

```
// automatically calls Dispose at the end of current scope if the file is not
null
```

# Nullable reference types

The use of the `null` value is so common, in so many languages, that many experienced programmers never question the need for its existence. But there are many scenarios where we could write better, simpler code if a variable is not allowed to have a `null` value.

The most significant change to the C# 8 language compiler was the introduction of checks and warnings for nullable and non-nullable reference types. "But wait!", you are probably thinking, "Reference types are already nullable!"

And you would be right, but in C# 8 and later, reference types can be configured to no longer allow the `null` value by setting a file- or project-level option to enable this useful new feature. Since this is a big change for C#, Microsoft decided to make the feature opt-in.

It will take multiple years for this new C# language compiler feature to make an impact since thousands of existing library packages and apps will expect the old behavior. Even Microsoft did not have time to fully implement this new feature in all the main .NET packages until .NET 6. Important libraries like `Microsoft.Extensions` for logging, dependency injections, and configuration were not annotated until .NET 7.

For example, in Microsoft's implementation of the `System.String` class, the `IsNullOrEmpty` method is annotated to indicate expected nullability. Since the purpose of the method is to return `true` only when the `value` parameter is either `null` or empty, if the method returns `false`, the `value` must not be `null`, so the static compiler analysis can be informed that the parameter will not be `null` when the method returns `false`, as shown in the following code:

```
bool IsNullOrEmpty([NotNullWhen(false)] string? value)
```

 I am considering adding a chapter about the details of nullability to the second edition of this book in 2023. Please let me know if that should be a priority for me over other potential topics.

During the transition, you can choose between several approaches for your own projects:

*   **Default:** For projects created using .NET 5 or earlier, no changes are needed. Non-nullable reference types are not checked. For projects created using .NET 6 or later, nullability checks are enabled by default, but this can be disabled by either deleting the `<Nullable>` entry in the project file or setting it to `disable`.
*   **Opt-in project, opt-out files:** Enable the feature at the project level and, for any files that need to remain compatible with old behavior, opt out. This was the approach Microsoft was using internally while it updated its own packages to use this new feature.
*   **Opt-in files:** Only enable the feature for individual files.

To enable the nullability warning check feature at the project level, add the following to your project file:

```
<PropertyGroup>
  ...
  <Nullable>enable</Nullable>
</PropertyGroup>
```

To disable the nullability warning check feature at the project level, add the following to your project file:

```
<PropertyGroup>
  ...
  <Nullable>disable</Nullable>
</PropertyGroup>
```

To disable the feature at the file level, add the following to the top of a code file:

```
#nullable disable
```

To enable the feature at the file level, add the following to the top of a code file:

```
#nullable enable
```

If you enable nullable reference types and you want a reference type to be assigned the null value, then you will have to use the same syntax as making a value type nullable, that is, adding a ? symbol after the type declaration.

## Indices and ranges

Indices and ranges enable efficient access to elements and slices of elements with an array:

- Define a position using System.Index
- Define a slice using System.Range

Items in an array can be accessed by passing an integer into their indexer, as shown in the following code:

```
int index = 3;
Person p = people[index]; // fourth person in array
char letter = name[index]; // fourth letter in name
```

The Index value type is a more formal way of identifying a position, and supports counting from the end, as shown in the following code:

```
// two ways to define the same index, 3 in from the start
Index i1 = new Index(value: 3); // counts from the start
Index i2 = 3; // using implicit int conversion operator

// two ways to define the same index, 5 in from the end
Index i3 = new Index(value: 5, fromEnd: true);
Index i4 = ^5; // using the caret operator
```

The Range value type uses Index values to indicate the start and end of its range, using its constructor, C# syntax, or its static methods, as shown in the following code:

```
Range r1 = new Range(start: new Index(3), end: new Index(7));
Range r2 = new Range(start: 3, end: 7); // using implicit int conversion
Range r3 = 3..7; // using C# 8.0 or later syntax
Range r4 = Range.StartAt(3); // from index 3 to last index
Range r5 = 3..; // from index 3 to last index
Range r6 = Range.EndAt(3); // from index 0 to index 3
Range r7 = ..3; // from index 0 to index 3
```

# What's new in C# 9 and .NET 5?

There were some important language and library features introduced with C# 9 and .NET 5:

- More pattern matching enhancements like type patterns, parenthesized patterns, use of and, or, and not in patterns, relational patterns with <, >, and so on.
- Support for source code generators. They can only add code, not modify existing code.

Let's see some others in more detail.

## Record types and init-only setters

The biggest new language feature in C# 9 was **records**. Sometimes you want to treat properties like readonly fields so they can be set during instantiation but not after. The new init keyword enables this. It can be used in place of the set keyword, as shown in the following code:

```
namespace Packt.Shared;

public class ImmutablePerson
{
  public string? FirstName { get; init; }
  public string? LastName { get; init; }
}

ImmutablePerson jeff = new()
{
  FirstName = "Jeff", // allowed
  LastName = "Winger"
};

jeff.FirstName = "Geoff"; // compile error!
```

The syntax for defining a record can be greatly simplified using positional data members, as shown in the following code:

```
// simpler way to define a record
// auto-generates the properties, constructor, and deconstructor
public record ImmutableAnimal(string Name, string Species);
```

## Top-level statements

Before the C# 9 compiler, a console app and its `Program.cs` file needed to define a class with a `Main` method as its entry point, as shown in the following code:

```
using System;

namespace HelloCS
{
  class Program
  {
    static void Main(string[] args)
    {
      Console.WriteLine("Hello World!");
    }
  }
}
```

With C# 9, the top-level statements feature allows the `Program` class to be created by the compiler, as shown in the following code:

```
using System;

Console.WriteLine("Hello World!");
```

All the boilerplate code to define a namespace, the `Program` class, and its `Main` method is generated and wrapped around the statements you write.

Key points to remember about top-level programs include the following:

- There can be only one file like this in a project.
- Any `using` statements must go at the top of the file.
- You must have at least one executable statement, like `Console.WriteLine`, or you will get a compile error because the compiler cannot identify where the statements that need to go inside the `Main` method are. This is one reason why the Microsoft project template writes `Hello World!` to the console instead of just having a comment!
- If you declare any classes or other types, they must go at the bottom of the file.
- Although you should name the method `Main` if you explicitly define it, the method is named `<Main>$` when created by the compiler.

## Target-typed new

With C# 9, Microsoft introduced another syntax for instantiating objects known as **target-typed new**. When instantiating an object, you can specify the type first and then use `new` without repeating the type, as shown in the following code:

```
XmlDocument xmlDoc = new(); // target-typed new in C# 9 or later
```

If you have a type with a field or property that needs to be set, then the type can be inferred, as shown in the following code:

```
// In Program.cs
Person kim = new();
kim.BirthDate = new(1967, 12, 26); // instead of: new DateTime(1967, 12, 26)

// In a separate Person.cs file or at the bottom of Program.cs
class Person
{
  public DateTime BirthDate;
}
```

# What's new in C# 10 and .NET 6?

There were many language and library features introduced with C# 10 and .NET 6:

- Project templates enable nullability checks by default.
- Project templates enable implicitly globally imported namespaces by default.
- You can define value type records using `record struct`.
- Constant interpolated strings.
- File-scoped namespace declarations.
- Lambda expressions are easier to write because the compiler can infer a delegate type from the expression.

Let's see some others in more detail.

## Top-level statements and implicitly imported namespaces by default

With .NET 6 and later, Microsoft updated the project template for console apps to use top-level statements by default. It also implicitly imports common namespaces globally by default.

Traditionally, every `.cs` file that needs to import namespaces would have to start with `using` statements to import those namespaces. Namespaces like `System` and `System.Linq` are needed in almost all `.cs` files, so the first few lines of every `.cs` file often had at least a few `using` statements, as shown in the following code:

```
using System;
using System.Linq;
using System.Collections.Generic;
```

When creating websites and services using ASP.NET Core, there are often dozens of namespaces that each file would have to import.

C# 10 introduced a new keyword combination and .NET SDK 6 introduced a new project setting that work together to simplify importing common namespaces.

The global using keyword combination means you only need to import a namespace in one .cs file and it will be available throughout all .cs files. You could put global using statements in the Program.cs file, but I recommend creating a separate file for those statements named something like GlobalUsings.cs with the contents being all your global using statements, as shown in the following code:

```
global using System;
global using System.Linq;
global using System.Collections.Generic;
```

Any projects that target .NET 6.0 or later, and that therefore use the C# 10 or later compiler, can generate a <ProjectName>.GlobalUsings.g.cs file in the obj folder to implicitly globally import some common namespaces like System, as shown in the following code:

```
// <autogenerated />
global using global::System;
global using global::System.Collections.Generic;
global using global::System.IO;
global using global::System.Linq;
global using global::System.Net.Http;
global using global::System.Threading;
global using global::System.Threading.Tasks;
```

The specific list of implicitly imported namespaces depends on which SDK you target, as shown in the following table:

| SDK | Implicitly imported namespaces |
|---|---|
| Microsoft.NET.Sdk | System<br>System.Collections.Generic<br>System.IO<br>System.Linq<br>System.Net.Http<br>System.Threading<br>System.Threading.Tasks |
| Microsoft.NET.Sdk.Web | Same as Microsoft.NET.Sdk and:<br>System.Net.Http.Json<br>Microsoft.AspNetCore.Builder<br>Microsoft.AspNetCore.Hosting<br>Microsoft.AspNetCore.Http<br>Microsoft.AspNetCore.Routing<br>Microsoft.Extensions.Configuration<br>Microsoft.Extensions.DependencyInjection<br>Microsoft.Extensions.Hosting<br>Microsoft.Extensions.Logging |

| | Same as `Microsoft.NET.Sdk` and: |
|---|---|
| `Microsoft.NET.Sdk.Worker` | `Microsoft.Extensions.Configuration` |
| | `Microsoft.Extensions.DependencyInjection` |
| | `Microsoft.Extensions.Hosting` |
| | `Microsoft.Extensions.Logging` |

To control the implicit generation of this file and to control which namespaces are implicitly imported, you can create an item group in the project file, as highlighted in the following markup:

```xml
<Project Sdk="Microsoft.NET.Sdk">

  <PropertyGroup>
    <OutputType>Exe</OutputType>
    <TargetFramework>net7.0</TargetFramework>
    <Nullable>enable</Nullable>
    <ImplicitUsings>enable</ImplicitUsings>
  </PropertyGroup>

  <ItemGroup>
    <Using Remove="System.Threading" />
    <Using Include="System.Numerics" />
    <Using Include="System.Console" Static="true" />
  </ItemGroup>

</Project>
```

## Checking for null in method parameters

When defining methods with parameters, it is good practice to check for `null` values.

In earlier versions of C#, you would have to write `if` statements to check for `null` parameter values and then throw an `ArgumentNullException` for any parameter that is `null`, as shown in the following code:

```csharp
public void Hire(Person manager, Person employee)
{
  if (manager == null)
  {
    throw new ArgumentNullException(nameof(manager));
  }

  if (employee == null)
  {
    throw new ArgumentNullException(nameof(employee));
  }
  ...
}
```

.NET 6 introduced a convenient method to throw an exception if an argument is `null`, as shown in the following code:

```
public void Hire(Person manager, Person employee)
{
  ArgumentNullException.ThrowIfNull(manager);
  ArgumentNullException.ThrowIfNull(employee);

  ...
}
```

C# 11 previews in early 2022 introduced a new `!!` operator that did this for you when you applied the operator as a suffix to parameter names, as shown in the following code:

```
public void Hire(Person manager!!, Person employee!!)
{
  ...
}
```

The `if` statement and throwing of the exception are done for you. The code is injected and executes before any statements that you write.

The .NET product team claims to have saved more than 10,000 lines of code throughout the .NET libraries by using this feature. But this syntax is controversial within the C# developer community and unfortunately there were enough complaints during the previews that Microsoft reversed their decision and removed the feature from previews. It is unlikely to return.

# What's new in C# 11 and .NET 7?

There were many language and library features introduced with C# 11 and .NET 7:

- C# 11 is available in preview with .NET 6 SDK 6.0.200 or later.
- You can use newlines in `string` interpolations.
- You can use static abstract members in interfaces.
- You can define generic attributes.

Let's see some others in more detail.

## Raw string literals

Raw string literals are convenient for entering any arbitrary text without needing to escape the contents. They make it easy to define literals containing other languages like XML, HTML, or JSON.

Raw string literals start and end with three or more double-quote characters, as shown in the following code:

```
string xml = """
              <person age="50">
                <first_name>Mark</first_name>
              </person>
              """;
```

In the previous code, the XML is indented by 13 spaces. The compiler looks at the indentation of the last three double-quote characters, and then automatically removes that level of indentation from all the content inside the raw string literal, as shown in the following markup:

```
<person age="50">
  <first_name>Mark</first_name>
</person>
```

You can mix interpolated with raw string literals. You specify the number of braces that indicate a replaced expression by adding that number of dollar signs to the start of the literal. Any fewer braces than that are treated as raw content.

For example, if we want to define some JSON, single braces will be treated as normal braces, but the two dollar symbols tell the compiler that any two curly braces indicate a replaced expression value, as shown in the following code:

```
string json = $$"""
              {
                "first_name": "{{person.FirstName}}",
                "age": {{person.Age}},
              };
              """
```

## Requiring properties to be set during instantiation

The `required` modifier can be applied to a field or property. The compiler will ensure that you set the field or property to a value when you instantiate it.

For example, you might have two properties, one of which should be required, as shown in the following code:

```
namespace Packt.Shared;

public class Book
{
  public required string Isbn { get; set; }
  public string? Title { get; set; }
}
```

If you attempt to instantiate a `Book` without setting the `Isbn` property, as shown in the following code:

```
Book book = new();
book.Title = "C# 11 and .NET 7 - Modern Cross-Platform Development";
```

Then you will see a compiler error, as shown in the following output:

```
Error    CS9035    Required member 'Book.Isbn' must be set in the object
initializer or attribute constructor.
```

You would therefore have to set the property during initialization, as shown in the following code:

```
Book book = new() { Isbn = "1234-5678"};
```

## Generic math support

C# has supported math operations like addition and division using operators like + and / since its first version. But that support was implemented only for the numeric data types that were built into the language like `int` and `double`.

What if a developer needs to define a new type of number? They could override the standard operators, but that is a lot of work.

Microsoft has added features like static virtual members in interfaces, checked user defined operators, relaxed shift operators, and an unsigned right-shift operator, which are needed to enable anyone to define new types of number that can implement some new interfaces and then work just like all the built-in number types.

For example, you would implement the `System.IAdditionOperators<TSelf, TOther, TResult>` interface in a new number type that implements the + operator.

As you can imagine, defining your own numeric types is a rare and advanced capability, so I do not cover it in this book. If you are interested in learning more, then I recommend reading the blog article at the following link: `https://devblogs.microsoft.com/dotnet/preview-features-in-net-6-generic-math/`.

# Making good use of the GitHub repository for this book

Git is a commonly used source code management system. GitHub is a company, website, and desktop application that makes it easier to manage Git. Microsoft purchased GitHub in 2018, so it will continue to be closely integrated with Microsoft tools.

I created a GitHub repository for this book, and I use it for the following:

- To store the solution code for the book, which will be maintained after the print publication date.
- To provide extra materials that extend the book, like errata fixes, small improvements, lists of useful links, and longer articles that cannot fit in the printed book.
- To provide a place for readers to get in touch with me if they have issues with the book.

## Raising issues with the book

If you get stuck following any of the instructions in this book, or if you spot a mistake in the text or the code in the solutions, please raise an issue in the GitHub repository:

1. Use your favorite browser to navigate to the following link: `https://github.com/markjprice/apps-services-net7/issues`.
2. Click **New Issue**.

3.  Enter as much detail as possible that will help me to diagnose the issue. For example:

    •   For a mistake in the book, the page number and section title.

    •   Your operating system, for example, Windows 11 64-bit, or macOS Big Sur version 11.2.3.

    •   Your hardware, for example, Intel, Apple Silicon, or ARM CPU.

    •   Your code editor, for example, Visual Studio 2022, Visual Studio Code, or something else, including the version number.

    •   As much of your code and configuration that you feel is relevant and necessary.

    •   A description of the expected behavior and the behavior experienced.

    •   Screenshots (you can drag and drop image files into the issue box).

I want all my readers to be successful with my book, so if I can help you (and others) without too much trouble, then I will gladly do so.

## Giving me feedback

If you'd like to give me more general feedback about the book, then you can email me or navigate to the GitHub repository `README.md` page, which has links to some surveys. You can provide the feedback anonymously, or if you would like a response from me, then you can supply an email address. I will only use this email address to respond to your feedback.

My publisher, Packt, has set up Discord channels for readers to interact with authors and other readers. You are welcome to join us at the following link: `https://packt.link/apps_and_services_dotnet7`.

I love to hear from my readers about what they like about my books, as well as suggestions for improvements and how they are working with C# and .NET, so don't be shy. Please get in touch!

Thank you in advance for your thoughtful and constructive feedback.

## Downloading solution code from the GitHub repository

I use GitHub to store solutions to all the hands-on, step-by-step coding examples throughout chapters and the practical exercises that are featured at the end of each chapter. You will find the repository at the following link: `https://github.com/markjprice/apps-services-net7`.

If you just want to download all the solution files without using Git, click the green **Code** button and then select **Download ZIP**.

I recommend that you add the preceding link to your favorites or bookmarks.

 **Good Practice:** It is best to clone or download the code solutions to a short folder path like `C:\dev\` to avoid build-generated files exceeding the maximum path length.

## Where to go for help

This section is all about how to find quality information about programming on the web.

# Reading Microsoft documentation

The definitive resource for getting help with Microsoft developer tools and platforms is Microsoft Docs, and you can find it at the following link: https://docs.microsoft.com/.

# Getting help for the dotnet tool

At the command line, you can ask the dotnet tool for help with its commands:

1. To open the official documentation in a browser window for the dotnet build command, enter the following at the command line or in the Visual Studio Code terminal:

```
dotnet help build
```

2. To get help output at the command line, use the -h or --help flag, as shown in the following command:

```
dotnet new console -h
```

3. You will see the following partial output:

```
Console App (C#)
Author: Microsoft
Description: A project for creating a command-line application that can
run on .NET on Windows, Linux and macOS

Usage:
  dotnet new console [options] [template options]
Options:
  -n, --name <name>       The name for the output being created. If no
name is specified, the name of the output directory is used.
  -o, --output <output>   Location to place the generated output.
  --dry-run               Displays a summary of what would happen if the
given command line were run if it would result in a template creation.
  --force                 Forces content to be generated even if it would
change existing files.
  --no-update-check       Disables checking for the template package
updates when instantiating a template.
  -lang, --language <C#>  Specifies the template language to instantiate.
  --type <project>        Specifies the template type to instantiate.

Template options:
  -f|--framework <net7.0|net6.0|...> The target framework for the
project.
                    Type: choice
                        net7.0            - Target net7.0
                        net6.0            - Target net6.0
                        net5.0            - Target net5.0
                        netcoreapp3.1.    - Target netcoreapp3.1
                    Default: net7.0
```

```
    --langVersion <langVersion>    Sets the LangVersion property in the
created project file
                        Type: text


    --no-restore    If specified, skips the automatic restore of the
project on create.
                        Type: bool
                        Default: false


    --use-program-main  Whether to generate an explicit Program class and
Main method instead of top-level statements.
                        Type: bool
                        Default: false


To see help for other template languages (F#, VB), use --language option:
    dotnet new console -h --language F#
```

# Searching for answers using Google

You can search Google with advanced search options to increase the likelihood of finding what you need:

1. Navigate to Google.
2. Search for information about garbage collection using a simple Google query and note that you will probably see a lot of ads for garbage collection services in your local area before you see the Wikipedia definition of garbage collection in computer science.
3. Improve the search by restricting it to a useful site such as Stack Overflow, and by removing languages that we might not care about, such as C++, Rust, and Python, or by adding C# and .NET explicitly, as shown in the following search query:

```
garbage collection site:stackoverflow.com +C# -Java
```

# Subscribing to the official .NET blog

To keep up to date with .NET, an excellent blog to subscribe to is the official .NET Blog, written by the .NET engineering teams, and you can find it at the following link: https://devblogs.microsoft.com/dotnet/.

# Watching Scott Hanselman's videos

Scott Hanselman from Microsoft has an excellent YouTube channel about *computer stuff they didn't teach you*: http://computerstufftheydidntteachyou.com/.

I recommend it to everyone working with computers.

# Practicing and exploring

Test your knowledge and understanding by answering some questions, getting some hands-on practice, and exploring with deeper research the topics in this chapter.

## Exercise 1.1 – Test your knowledge

Use the web to answer the following questions:

1. Why is it good practice to add the following setting to your project files? And when should you not set it?

   ```
   <TreatWarningsAsErrors>true</TreatWarningsAsErrors>
   ```

2. Which service technology requires a minimum HTTP version of 2?

3. In 2010, your organization created a service using .NET Framework and Windows Communication Foundation. What is the best technology to migrate it to and why?

4. Which code editor or IDE should you install for .NET development?

5. What should you be aware of when creating Azure resources?

6. Which type of .NET release is higher quality, STS or LTS?

7. In new .NET projects, nullable checks are enabled. What are two ways to disable them?

8. If you define any types in a top-level program, where must they go in the `Program.cs` file?

9. How do you import a class like `Console` so that its static members like `WriteLine` are available in all code files throughout a project?

10. What is the best new C# 11 language feature?

## Exercise 1.2 – Explore topics

Use the links on the following GitHub page to learn more about the topics covered in this chapter:

https://github.com/markjprice/apps-services-net7/blob/main/book-links.md#chapter-1---introducing-apps-and-services-with-net

# Summary

In this chapter, you:

- Were introduced to the app and service technologies that you will learn about in this book.
- Set up your development environment.
- Used an analyzer to write better code.
- Reviewed some of the new features in the C# compiler and the .NET libraries in modern versions.
- Learned where to look for help.

In the next chapter, you will learn how to use SQL Server to store and manage relational data.

# Join our book's Discord space

Join the book's Discord workspace for *Ask me Anything* sessions with the author.

https://packt.link/apps_and_services_dotnet7

# 2

# Managing Relational Data Using SQL Server

This chapter is about managing relational data stored in SQL Server, Azure SQL Database, or Azure SQL Edge. First, you will learn how to manage the data using native Transact-SQL statements. Next, you will learn how to manage data at a low level using ADO.NET libraries (`Microsoft.Data.SqlClient`). You will also learn how to manage the data by using the higher-level object-to-data store mapping technology named **Entity Framework Core** (**EF Core**). Then, you will learn how to store entity models that use inheritance hierarchies using three different mapping strategies. Finally, you will build class libraries for a SQL Server database that will be used in code examples throughout the rest of this book.

This chapter will cover the following topics:

- Understanding modern databases
- Managing data with Transact-SQL
- Managing SQL Server data with low-level APIs
- Managing SQL Server data with EF Core
- Mapping inheritance hierarchies with EF Core
- Building a reusable entity data model
- Cleaning up data resources

## Understanding modern databases

Two of the most common places to store data are in a **Relational Database Management System** (**RDBMS**) such as **SQL Server**, PostgreSQL, MySQL, and SQLite, or in a **NoSQL** database such as **Azure Cosmos DB**, MongoDB, Redis, and Apache Cassandra.

In this chapter, we will focus on the most popular RDBMS for Windows, which is SQL Server. This product is also available in a version for Linux. For cross-platform development, you can use either Azure SQL Database, which stores the data in the cloud, or Azure SQL Edge, which can run in a Docker container on Windows, macOS, or Linux.

# Using a sample relational database

To learn how to manage an RDBMS using .NET, it would be useful to have a sample one so that you can practice on a database that has a medium complexity and a decent number of sample records. Microsoft offers several sample databases, most of which are too complex for our needs, so instead, we will use a database that was first created in the early 1990s known as **Northwind**.

Let's take a minute to look at a diagram of the Northwind database and its eight most important tables. You can use the diagram in *Figure 2.1* to refer to as we write code and queries throughout this book:

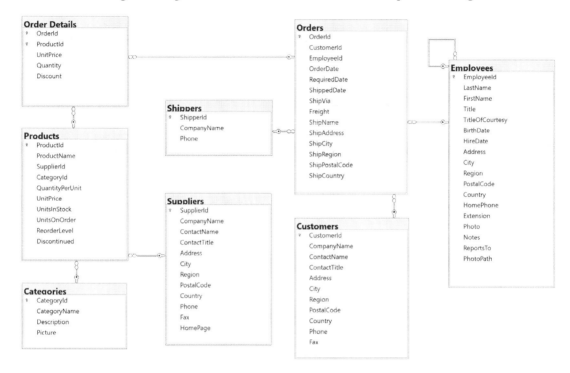

*Figure 2.1: The Northwind database tables and relationships*

Note that:

- Each category has a unique identifier, name, description, and picture. The picture is stored as a byte array in JPEG format.

- Each product has a unique identifier, name, unit price, number of units in stock, and other columns.

- Each product is associated with a category by storing the category's unique identifier.

- The relationship between `Categories` and `Products` is one-to-many, meaning each category can have zero, one, or more products.

- Each product is supplied by a supplier company, indicated by storing the supplier's unique identifier.

- A quantity and unit price of a product is stored for each detail of an order.

- Each order is made by a customer, taken by an employee, and shipped by a shipping company.
- Each employee has a name, address, contact details, birth and hire dates, a reference to their manager (except for the boss whose ReportsTo field is null), and a photo stored as a byte array in JPEG format. The table has a one-to-many relationship to itself because one employee can manage many other employees.

## Connecting to a SQL Server database

To connect to a SQL Server database, we need to know multiple pieces of information, as shown in the following list:

- The name of the server (and the instance if it has one). This can include the protocol, IP address, and port number if connecting over a network.
- The name of the database.
- Security information, such as the username and password, or if we should pass the currently logged-on user's credentials automatically using Windows Authentication.

We specify this information in a **connection string**.

For backward compatibility, there are multiple possible keywords we can use in a SQL Server connection string for the various parameters, as shown in the following list:

- `Data Source`, `server`, or `addr`: These keywords are the name of the server (and an optional instance). You can use a dot . to mean the local server.
- `Initial Catalog` or `database`: These keywords are the name of the database.
- `Integrated Security` or `trusted_connection`: These keywords are set to `true` or `SSPI` to pass the thread's current user credentials using Windows Authentication.
- `User Id` and `Password`: These keywords are used to authenticate with any edition of SQL Server. This is important for Azure SQL Database or Azure SQL Edge because they do not support Windows Authentication. The full edition of SQL Server on Windows supports both username with password, and Windows Authentication.
- `Authentication`: This keyword is used to authenticate by using Azure AD identities that can enable password-less authentication. Values can be `Active Directory Integrated`, `Active Directory Password`, and `Sql Password`.
- `Persist Security Info`: If set to `false`, this keyword tells the connection to remove the `Password` from the connection string after authenticating.
- `Encrypt`: If set to `true`, this keyword tells the connections to use SSL to encrypt transmissions between client and server.
- `TrustServerCertificate`: Set to `true` if hosting locally and you get the error "A connection was successfully established with the server, but then an error occurred during the login process. (provider: SSL Provider, error: 0 - The certificate chain was issued by an authority that is not trusted.)"
- `Connection Timeout`: This keyword defaults to 30 seconds.

- `MultipleActiveResultSets`: This keyword is set to `true` to enable a single connection to be used to work with multiple tables simultaneously to improve efficiency. It is used for lazy loading rows from related tables.

As described in the list above, when you write code to connect to a SQL Server database, you need to know its server name. The server name depends on the edition and version of SQL Server that you will connect to, as shown in the following table:

| SQL Server edition | Server name \ Instance name |
|---|---|
| LocalDB 2012 | `(localdb)\v11.0` |
| LocalDB 2016 or later | `(localdb)\mssqllocaldb` |
| Express | `.\sqlexpress` |
| Full/Developer (default instance) | `.` |
| Full/Developer (named instance) | `.\apps-services-net7` |
| Azure SQL Edge (local Docker) | `tcp:127.0.0.1,1433` |
| Azure SQL Database | `tcp:[custom server name].database.windows.net,1433` |

**Good Practice:** Use a dot `.` as shorthand for the local computer name. Remember that server names for SQL Server can be made up of two parts: the name of the computer and the name of a SQL Server instance. You provide instance names during custom installation.

## Installing and setting up SQL Server

Microsoft offers various editions of its popular and capable SQL Server product for Windows, Linux, and Docker containers. If you have Windows, then you can use a free version that runs standalone, known as SQL Server Developer Edition. You can also use the Express edition or the free SQL Server LocalDB edition that can be installed with Visual Studio 2022 for Windows.

If you do not have a Windows computer or if you want to use a cross-platform database system, then you can skip ahead to *Setting up Azure SQL Database* or *Installing Azure SQL Edge in Docker*. Be sure to read the *Creating the Northwind sample database* section to learn where to find the SQL scripts that create the sample database.

### Installing SQL Server Developer Edition for Windows

On Windows, if you want to use the full edition of SQL Server instead of the simplified LocalDB or Express editions, then you can find all SQL Server editions at the following link: `https://www.microsoft.com/en-us/sql-server/sql-server-downloads`.

To download and configure SQL Server Developer Edition, use the following steps:

1. Download the **Developer** edition.
2. Run the installer.

3.  Select the **Custom** installation type.

4.  Select a folder for the installation files and then click **Install**.

5.  Wait for the 1.5 GB of installer files to download.

6.  In **SQL Server Installation Center**, click **Installation**, and then click **New SQL Server stand-alone installation or add features to an existing installation**.

7.  Select **Developer** as the free edition and then click **Next**.

8.  Accept the license terms and then click **Next**.

9.  Review the **Microsoft Update** options, and then click **Next**.

10. Review the install rules, fix any issues, and then click **Next**.

11. In **Feature Selection**, select **Database Engine Services**, and then click **Next**.

12. In **Instance Configuration**, select **Default instance**, and then click **Next**. If you already have a default instance configured, then you could create a named instance, perhaps called net7book.

13. In **Server Configuration**, note the **SQL Server Database Engine** is configured to start automatically. Set the **SQL Server Browser** to start automatically, and then click **Next**.

14. In **Database Engine Configuration**, on the **Server Configuration** tab, set **Authentication Mode** to **Mixed**, set the **sa** account password to a strong password, click **Add Current User**, and then click **Next**.

15. In **Ready to Install**, review the actions that will be taken, and then click **Install**.

16. In **Complete**, note the successful actions taken, and then click **Close**.

17. In **SQL Server Installation Center**, in **Installation**, click **Install SQL Server Management Tools**.

18. In the browser window, click to download the latest version of SSMS.

The direct link to download SSMS is as follows: https://docs.microsoft.com/en-us/sql/ssms/download-sql-server-management-studio-ssms.

19. Run the SSMS installer and click **Install**.

20. When the installer has finished, click **Restart** if needed or **Close**.

**Azure Data Studio** (**ADS**) is automatically installed alongside SSMS. ADS is cross-platform and open-source, so you can use it to work with SQL Server databases on any desktop operating system.

## Visual Studio Code extension for working with SQL Server

There are many tools that make it easy to work with SQL Server. If you are using Visual Studio Code, then you can install the **SQL Server (mssql)** ms-mssql.mssql extension.

If you install the extension, it adds a new view to the **Primary Side Bar** titled **SQL Server**, as shown in *Figure 2.2*:

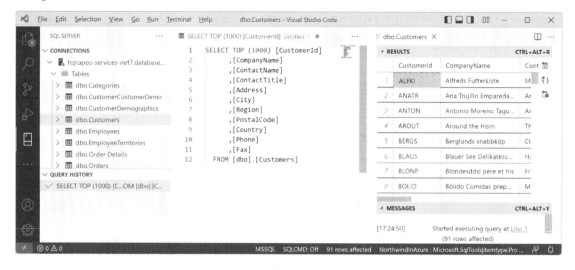

Figure 2.2: SQL Server (mssql) extension for Visual Studio Code

# Creating the Northwind sample database on Windows

Now we can run a database script to create the Northwind sample database on Windows using **SQL Server Management Studio (SSMS)**:

1.  If you have not previously downloaded or cloned the GitHub repository for this book, then do so now using the following link: https://github.com/markjprice/apps-services-net7/.

2.  In your apps-services-net7 folder, create a folder named Chapter02.

3.  Copy the script to create the Northwind database for SQL Server from the following path in your local Git repository: /sql-scripts/Northwind4SQLServer.sql into the Chapter02 folder.

4.  Start **SQL Server Management Studio**.

5.  In the **Connect to Server** dialog, for **Server name**, enter . (a dot), meaning the local computer name, and then click **Connect**.

> If you had to create a named instance, like net7book, then enter .\net7book.

6.  Navigate to **File** | **Open** | **File...**.

7.  Browse to select the Northwind4SQLServer.sql file and then click **Open**.

8.  In the toolbar, click **Execute**, and note the **Command(s) completed successfully** message.

9.  In **Object Explorer**, expand the **Northwind** database, and then expand **Tables**.

10. Right-click **Products**, click **Select Top 1000 Rows**, and note the returned results, as shown in *Figure 2.3*:

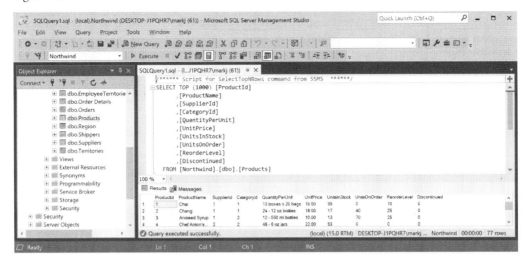

*Figure 2.3: The Products table in SQL Server Management Studio*

11. In the **Object Explorer** toolbar, click the **Disconnect** button.

12. Exit **SQL Server Management Studio**.

> We did not have to use **SQL Server Management Studio** to execute the database script. We can also use tools in Visual Studio 2022, including the **SQL Server Object Explorer** and **Server Explorer,** or cross-platform tools like the Visual Studio Code extension for SQL Server, or **Azure Data Studio,** which you can download and install from the following link: https://aka.ms/getazuredatastudio.

# Setting up Azure SQL Database

If you do not have a Windows computer, then you can create a cloud-hosted instance of SQL Server. You will need an Azure account. You can sign up at the following link: https://signup.azure.com.

1. Log in to your Azure account: https://portal.azure.com/.

2. Navigate to https://portal.azure.com/#create/hub.

3. Search for **Resource group** and then click the **Create** button.

4. Enter a resource group name of apps-services-net7 and select a suitable region close to you, and then click the **Review + create** button.

5. Review your choices and then click the **Create** button.

6. Create another resource, search for **SQL Database**, and click **Create**.

7. In the **Create SQL Database** page, in the **Basics** tab, for the **Database name** enter Northwind, and select the resource group that you created before.

8. In the **Server** section, click **Create New**.

9.   Enter the following details for the SQL Database server, as shown in *Figure 2.4*:

   • **Server name:** `apps-services-net7-[your initials]` or something else entirely. The server name must be globally unique because it becomes part of a public URL.

   • **Location:** A region close to you. I chose **(Europe) UK South**. Not all regions support all types of resource. You will see an error if the region you select does not support SQL Database server resources.

   • **Authentication method:** Use SQL authentication.

   • **Server admin login:** [Your email or another username], for example, I entered `markjprice`.

   • **Password/Confirm password:** [Enter a strong password].

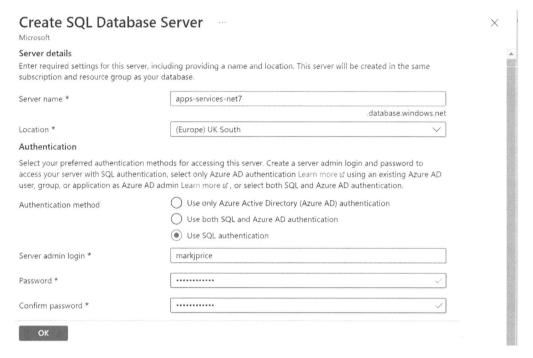

*Figure 2.4: Entering the server details for a SQL Database instance*

10.  Click **OK**.

11.  In the **Create SQL Database** page, in the **Compute + storage** section, click **Configure database**.

12.  For **Service tier**, select **Basic (For less demanding workloads)**. Note the maximum database size is 2 GB and the estimated cost is about $6.23 per month. You can delete the resources as soon as you have completed this chapter to reduce the cost further.

13.  Click **Apply**.

14.  In the **Create SQL Database** page, set **Backup storage redundancy** to **Locally-redundant backup storage**.

15.  Click the **Next : Networking** button.

16.  In the **Network connectivity** section, select **Public endpoint**.

17. In the **Firewall rules** section, set **Add current client IP address** to **Yes**.

18. Click the **Next : Security** button.

19. Review the options but leave them as the defaults.

20. Click the **Next : Additional settings** button.

21. Review the options but leave them as the defaults.

22. Click the **Review + create** button.

23. Click the **Create** button.

24. Wait for the deployment, as shown in *Figure 2.5*:

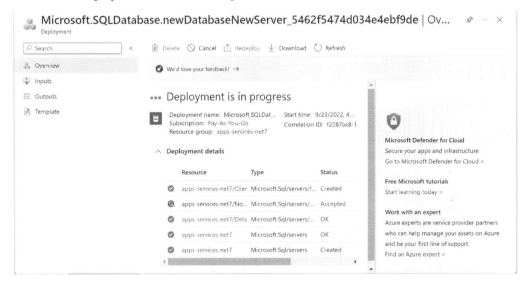

*Figure 2.5: Deployment progress for SQL Database*

25. Click **Go to resource**.

26. Click **Overview** and note the database details, as shown in *Figure 2.6*:

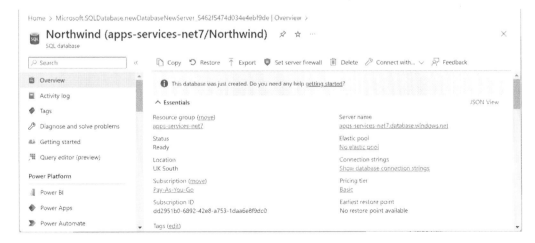

*Figure 2.6: SQL Database details*

27. Click **Show database connection strings**.

28. Copy the **ADO.NET** connection string to your clipboard.

29. Start **Notepad** or your preferred plain text editor, paste the connection string, and add carriage returns after each semicolon to separate each part to make them easier to work with, as shown in the following text:

```
Server=tcp:apps-services-net7.database.windows.net,1433;
Initial Catalog=Northwind;
Persist Security Info=False;
User ID=markjprice;
Password={your_password};
MultipleActiveResultSets=False;
Encrypt=True;
TrustServerCertificate=False;
Connection Timeout=30;
```

 Your `Server` value will be different because the custom server name part, for example, `apps-services-net7`, is public and must be globally unique.

30. Use your preferred database tool to connect to the SQL server:

   •   In Visual Studio 2022, view **Server Explorer**.

   •   On Windows, start **SQL Server Management Studio**.

   •   In Visual Studio Code, view the **SQL Server** tool. You can install the **SQL Server (mssql)** extension if you have not done so already: `https://marketplace.visualstudio.com/items?itemName=ms-mssql.mssql`.

   •   Alternatively, you can use the cross-platform **Azure Data Studio**. You can install it from the following link: `https://aka.ms/getazuredatastudio`.

31. Add a data connection, and fill in the dialog box, as shown in *Figure 2.7*:

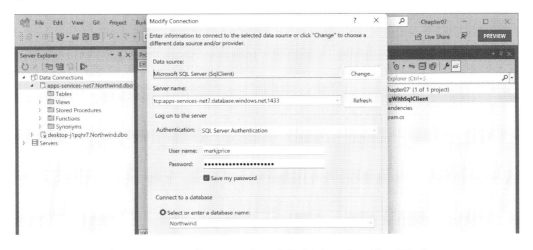

*Figure 2.7: Connecting to your Azure SQL database from Visual Studio*

In Visual Studio Server Explorer, you might also be prompted to **Choose Data Source**. Choose **Microsoft SQL Server**. You can select a checkbox to always use this selection.

32. Right-click the data connection and choose **New Query**.

33. Copy and paste the contents of the `Northwind4AzureSQLdatabase.sql` file into the query window and execute it.

The main difference between the `Northwind4SQLServer.sql` and `Northwind4AzureSQLdatabase.sql` scripts is that the local SQL Server script will delete and recreate the Northwind database. The Azure SQL database script will not, because the database needs to be created as an Azure resource. You can download SQL script files from the following link: `https://github.com/markjprice/apps-services-net7/tree/main/sql-scripts`.

34. Wait to see the **Command completed successfully** message.

35. In **Server Explorer**, right-click **Tables** and select **Refresh**, and note that 13 tables have been created, for example, **Categories**, **Customers**, and **Products**. Also note that dozens of views and stored procedures have also been created.

You now have a running Azure SQL database that you can connect to from a .NET project.

# Installing Azure SQL Edge in Docker

If you do not have a Windows computer, and you do not want to pay for Azure resources, then you can install Docker and use a container that has Azure SQL Edge, a cross-platform minimal featured version of SQL Server that only includes the database engine.

The Docker image we will use has Azure SQL Edge based on Ubuntu 18.4. It is supported with the Docker Engine 1.8 or later on Linux, or on Docker for Mac or Windows. Azure SQL Edge requires a 64-bit processor (either x64 or ARM64), with a minimum of one processor and 1 GB RAM on the host.

1. Install **Docker** from the following link: `https://docs.docker.com/engine/install/`.

2. Start **Docker**.

3. At the command prompt or terminal, pull down the latest container image for Azure SQL Edge, as shown in the following command:

```
docker pull mcr.microsoft.com/azure-sql-edge:latest
```

4. Note the results, as shown in the following output:

```
latest: Pulling from azure-sql-edge
2f94e549220a: Pull complete
830b1adc1e72: Pull complete
f6caea6b4bd2: Pull complete
ef3b33eb5a27: Pull complete
8a42011e5477: Pull complete
f173534aa1e4: Pull complete
6c1894e17f11: Pull complete
a81c43e790ea: Pull complete
c3982946560a: Pull complete
25f31208d245: Pull complete
Digest:
sha256:7c203ad8b240ef3bff81ca9794f31936c9b864cc165dd187c23c5bfe06cf0340
Status: Downloaded newer image for mcr.microsoft.com/azure-sql-
edge:latest
mcr.microsoft.com/azure-sql-edge:latest
```

5. At the command prompt or terminal, run the container image for Azure SQL Edge with a strong password and name the container `azuresqledge`, as shown in the following command:

```
docker run --cap-add SYS_PTRACE -e 'ACCEPT_EULA=1' -e 'MSSQL_SA_
PASSWORD=s3cret-Ninja' -p 1433:1433 --name azuresqledge -d mcr.microsoft.
com/azure-sql-edge
```

**Good Practice:** The password must be at least 8 characters long and contain characters from three of the following four sets: uppercase letters, lowercase letters, digits, and symbols; otherwise, the container cannot set up the SQL Edge engine and will stop working.

6.  If your operating system firewall blocks access, then allow access.

7.  In Docker, confirm that the image is running, as shown in *Figure 2.8*:

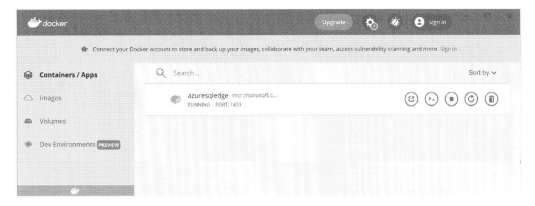

*Figure 2.8: SQL Edge running in Docker Desktop on Windows*

8.  At the command prompt or terminal, ask Docker to list all containers, both running and stopped, as shown in the following command:

```
docker ps -a
```

9.  Note the container is "Up" and listening externally on port 1433, which is mapped to its internal port 1433, as shown highlighted in the following output:

```
CONTAINER ID    IMAGE                                COMMAND
CREATED          STATUS          PORTS                         NAMES
183f02e84b2a    mcr.microsoft.com/azure-sql-edge    "/opt/mssql/bin/
perm…"    8 minutes ago    Up 8 minutes    1401/tcp, 0.0.0.0:1433->1433/tcp
azuresqledge
```

 You can learn more about the docker ps command at the following link: https://docs.docker.com/engine/reference/commandline/ps/.

10. Use your preferred database tool to connect to the SQL server:

   •  In Visual Studio 2022, view **Server Explorer**.

   •  On Windows, start **SQL Server Management Studio**.

   •  In Visual Studio Code, view the **SQL Server** tool.

   •  Alternatively, you can use the cross-platform **Azure Data Studio**.

11. Add a data connection, and fill in the dialog box, as shown in *Figure 2.9*:

*Figure 2.9: Connecting to your Azure SQL Edge server from Visual Studio*

12. Right-click the data connection and choose **New Query**.

13. Copy and paste the contents of the `Northwind4AzureSQLedge.sql` file into the query window and execute it.

14. Wait to see the **Command completed successfully** message.

15. In **Server Explorer**, refresh the data connection if needed, right-click **Tables** and select **Refresh**, and note that 13 tables have been created, for example, **Categories**, **Customers**, and **Products**. Also note that dozens of views and stored procedures have also been created.

You now have a running instance of Azure SQL Edge containing the Northwind database that you can connect to from a console app.

# Managing data with Transact-SQL

Transact-SQL (T-SQL) is SQL Server's dialect of **Structured Query Language** (SQL). Some pronounce it *tee-sequel*, others *tee-es-queue-el*.

Unlike C#, T-SQL is not case-sensitive; for example, you can use int or INT to specify the 32-bit integer data type, and you can use SELECT or select to start a query expression. Text stored in SQL Server can be treated as case-sensitive or not depending on configuration.

> The complete reference for T-SQL is found at the following link: `https://learn.microsoft.com/en-us/sql/t-sql/language-reference`.

# T-SQL data types

T-SQL has data types that are used for columns, variables, parameters, and so on.

| Category | Examples |
| --- | --- |
| Numbers | `bigint`, `bit`, `decimal`, `float`, `int`, `money`, `numeric`, `real`, `smallint`, `smallmoney`, `tinyint` |
| Date and time | `date`, `datetime2`, `datetime`, `datetimeoffset`, `smalldatetime`, `time` |
| Text | `char`, `nchar`, `ntext`, `nvarchar`, `text`, `varchar` |
| Binary | `binary`, `image`, `varbinary` |
| Other | `cursor`, `hierarchyid`, `sql_variant`, `table`, `rowversion`, `uniqueidentifier`, `xml` |

 T-SQL also has support for spatial **geometry** and **geography** types.

## Documenting with comments

To comment out the rest of a line, use `--` which is the equivalent of `//`.

To comment out a block, use `/*` and the start and `*/` at the end, just like in C#.

## Declaring variables

Local variable names are prefixed with @ and they are defined using SET, SELECT, or DECLARE, as shown in the following code:

```
DECLARE @WholeNumber INT; -- Declare a variable and specify its type.
SET @WholeNumber = 3; -- Set the variable to a literal value.
SET @WholeNumber = @WholeNumber + 1; -- Increment the variable.
SELECT @WholeNumber = COUNT(*) FROM Employees; -- Set to the number of
employees.
SELECT @WholeNumber = EmployeeId FROM Employees WHERE FirstName = 'Janet';
```

Global variables are prefixed with @@. For example, @@ROWCOUNT is a context-dependent value that returns the number of rows affected by a statement executed within the current scope, for example, the number of rows updated or deleted.

## Specifying data types

Most types have a fixed size. For example, an int uses four bytes, a smallint uses two bytes, and a tinyint uses one byte.

For text and binary types, you can either specify a type prefixed with var or nvar (meaning variable size) that will automatically change its size based on its current value up to a maximum, as shown in the following example: varchar(40); or you can specify a fixed number of characters that will always be allocated, as shown in the following example: char(40).

For text types, the n prefix indicates Unicode, meaning it will use two bytes per character. Text types not prefixed with n use one byte per character.

## Controlling flow

T-SQL has similar flow control keywords as C#, for example, BREAK, CONTINUE, GOTO, IF...ELSE, CASE, THROW, TRY...CATCH, WHILE, and RETURN. The main difference is the use of BEGIN and END to indicate the start and end of a block, the equivalent of curly braces in C#.

## Operators

T-SQL has similar operators as C#, for example, = (assignment), +, -, *, /, %, <, >, <=, ==, !=, &, |, ^, and so on. It has logical operators like AND, OR, NOT, and LINQ-like operators like ANY, ALL, SOME, EXISTS, BETWEEN, and IN.

LIKE is used for text pattern matching. The pattern can use % for any number of characters. The pattern can use _ for a single character. The pattern can use [ ] to specify a range and set of allowed characters, for example, [0-9A-Z.-,].

 If a table or column name contains spaces, then you must surround the name in square brackets like [Order Details]. The SQL scripts to create the Northwind database include the command set quoted_identifier on, so you can also use double-quotes like "Order Details". Single quotes are used for literal text like 'USA'.

## Data Manipulation Language (DML)

DML is used to query and change data.

The most common statement in DML is SELECT, which is used to retrieve data from one or more tables. SELECT is extremely complicated because it is so powerful. This book is not about learning T-SQL, so the quickest way to get a feel for SELECT is to see some examples, as shown in the following table:

| Example | Description |
|---|---|
| SELECT * <br> FROM Employees | Get all columns of all the employees. |
| SELECT FirstName, LastName <br> FROM Employees | Get the first and last name columns of all employees. |
| SELECT emp.FirstName, emp.LastName <br> FROM Employees AS emp | Give an alias for the table name. |
| SELECT emp.FirstName, emp.LastName <br> FROM Employees emp | Give an alias for the table name. |
| SELECT FirstName, LastName AS Surname <br> FROM Employees | Give an alias for the column name. |

| | |
|---|---|
| `SELECT FirstName, LastName`<br>`FROM Employees`<br>`WHERE Country = 'USA'` | Filter the results to only include employees in the USA. |
| `SELECT DISTINCT Country`<br>`FROM Employees` | Get a list of countries without duplicates. |
| `SELECT UnitPrice * Quantity AS`<br>`Subtotal`<br>`FROM [Order Details]` | Calculate a subtotal for each order detail row. |
| `SELECT OrderId,`<br>`   SUM(UnitPrice * Quantity) AS Total`<br>`FROM [Order Details]`<br>`GROUP BY OrderId`<br>`ORDER BY Total DESC` | Calculate a total for each order and sort with the largest order value at the top. |
| `SELECT CompanyName`<br>`FROM Customers`<br>`UNION`<br>`SELECT CompanyName`<br>`FROM Suppliers` | Return all the company names of all customers and suppliers. |
| `SELECT CategoryName, ProductName`<br>`FROM Categories, Products` | Match *every* category with *every* product using a Cartesian join and output their names (not what you normally want!)<br><br>616 rows (8 categories x 77 products). |
| `SELECT CategoryName, ProductName`<br>`FROM Categories c, Products p`<br>`WHERE c.CategoryId = p.CategoryId` | Match each product with its category using a WHERE clause for the `CategoryId` column in each table, and output the category name and product name.<br><br>77 rows. |
| `SELECT CategoryName, ProductName`<br>`FROM Categories c`<br>`INNER JOIN Products p`<br>`ON c.CategoryId = p.CategoryId` | Match each product with its category using an INNER JOIN...ON clause for the `CategoryId` column in each table, and output the category name and product name.<br><br>77 rows. |

 You can read the full documentation for SELECT at the following link: `https://docs.microsoft.com/en-us/sql/t-sql/queries/select-transact-sql`.

Use your favorite database querying tool, like Visual Studio Server Explorer or Visual Studio Code's mssql extension, to connect to your Northwind database and try out some of the queries above, as shown in *Figure 2.10* and *Figure 2.11*:

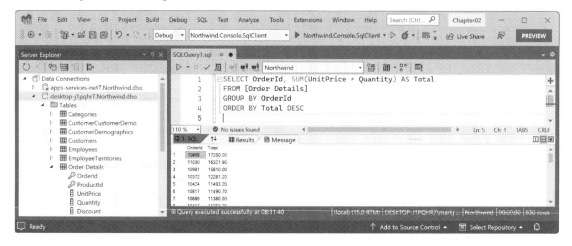

*Figure 2.10: Executing T-SQL queries using Visual Studio's Server Explorer*

*Figure 2.11: Executing T-SQL queries using Visual Studio Code's mssql extension*

# DML for adding, updating, and deleting data

DML statements for adding, updating, and deleting data include:

| Example | Description |
|---|---|
| `INSERT Employees(FirstName, LastName) VALUES('Mark', 'Price')` | Add a new row into the Employees table. The EmployeeId primary key value is automatically assigned. Use @@IDENTITY to get this value. |

| | |
|---|---|
| UPDATE Employees<br>SET Country = 'UK'<br>WHERE FirstName = 'Mark'<br>  AND LastName = 'Price' | Update my employee row to set my Country to UK. |
| DELETE Employees<br>WHERE FirstName = 'Mark'<br>  AND LastName = 'Price' | Delete my employee row. |
| DELETE Employees | Delete all rows in the Employees table. |
| TRUNCATE TABLE Employees | Delete all rows in the Employees table more efficiently because it does not log the individual row deletions. |

 The above examples use the Employees table in the Northwind database. That table has referential integrity constraints that mean that, for example, deleting all rows in the table cannot happen, because every employee has related data in other tables like Orders.

## Data Definition Language (DDL)

DDL statements change the structure of the database, including creating new objects like tables, functions, and stored procedures. The following table shows some examples of DDL statements to give you an idea, but the examples are simple and cannot be executed within the Northwind database.

| Example | Description |
|---|---|
| CREATE TABLE dbo.Shippers (<br>  ShipperId INT PRIMARY KEY<br>CLUSTERED,<br>  CompanyName NVARCHAR(40)<br>); | Create a table to store shippers. |
| ALTER TABLE Shippers<br>ADD Country NVARCHAR(40) | Add a column to a table. |
| CREATE NONCLUSTERED INDEX IX_Country<br>ON Shippers(Country) | Add a non-clustered index for a column in a table. |
| CREATE INDEX IX_FullName<br>ON Employees(LastName, FirstName DESC)<br>WITH (DROP_EXISTING = ON) | Change an aggregate index with multiple columns and control the sort order. |
| DROP TABLE Employees | Delete the Employees table. |
| DROP TABLE IF EXISTS Employees | Delete the Employees table if it already exists. |

| | |
|---|---|
| `IF OBJECT_ID(N'Employees', N'U')`<br>`    IS NOT NULL` | Check if a table exists. The `N` prefix before a text literal means Unicode. `'U'` means a user table as opposed to a system table. |

# Managing data with low-level APIs

`Microsoft.Data.SqlClient` provides database connectivity to SQL Server for .NET applications. It is known as the Microsoft ADO.NET driver for SQL Server and Azure SQL Database.

 You can find the GitHub repository for ADO.NET at the following link: `https://github.com/dotnet/SqlClient`.

The `Microsoft.Data.SqlClient` package supports the following .NET platforms:

- .NET Framework 4.6.2 and later.
- .NET Core 3.1 and later.
- .NET Standard 2.0 and later.

# Understanding the types in ADO.NET

ADO.NET defines abstract types that represent minimal objects for working with data, like `DbConnection`, `DbCommand`, and `DbDataReader`. Database software manufacturers can inherit from and provide specific implementations that are optimized for and expose additional features for their database. Microsoft has done this for SQL Server. The most important types with their most used members are shown in the following table:

| Type | Properties | Methods | Description |
|---|---|---|---|
| `SqlConnection` | `ConnectionString`, `State`, `ServerVersion` | `Open`, `Close`, `CreateCommand`, `Retrieve Statistics` | Manage the connection to the database. |
| `SqlConnection StringBuilder` | `InitialCatalog`, `DataSource`, `Encrypt`, `UserID`, `Password`, `ConnectTimeout`, and so on | `Clear`, `ContainsKey`, `Remove` | Build a valid connection string for a SQL Server database.<br>After setting all the relevant individual properties, get the `ConnectionString` property. |

| SqlCommand | Connection, CommandType, CommandText, Parameters, Transaction | ExecuteReader, ExecuteNonQuery, ExecuteXmlReader, CreateParameter | Configure the command to execute. |
| --- | --- | --- | --- |
| SqlParameter | ParameterName, Value, DbType, SqlValue, SqlDbType, Direction, IsNullable | | Configure a parameter for a command. |
| SqlDataReader | FieldCount, HasRows, IsClosed, RecordsAffected | Read, Close, GetOrdinal, GetInt32, GetString, GetDecimal, GetFieldValue<T> | Process the result set from executing a query. |

SqlConnection has two useful events: StateChange and InfoMessage.

All the ExecuteXxx methods will execute any command. The one you use depends on what you expect to get back:

- If the command includes at least one SELECT statement that returns a result set, then call ExecuteReader to execute the command. This method returns a DbDataReader-derived object for reading row-by-row through the result set.
- If the command does not include at least one SELECT statement, then it is more efficient to call ExecuteNonQuery. This method returns an integer for the number of rows affected.
- If the command includes at least one SELECT statement that returns XML because it uses the AS XML command, then call ExecuteXmlReader to execute the command.

## Creating a console app for working with ADO.NET

First, we will create a console app project for working with ADO.NET:

1. Use your preferred code editor to create a new solution/workspace named Chapter02.
2. Add a console app project, as defined in the following list:

    - Project template: **Console App**/console
    - Workspace/solution file and folder: Chapter02
    - Project file and folder: Northwind.Console.SqlClient

**Good Practice:** For all the projects that you create for this book, keep your root path short and avoid using # in your folder and file names, or you might see compiler errors like RSG002: TargetPath not specified for additional file. For example, do *not* use C:\My C# projects\ as your root path!

3.  In the project file, treat warnings as errors, add a package reference for the latest version of Microsoft.Data.SqlClient, and statically and globally import System.Console, as shown highlighted in the following markup:

```xml
<Project Sdk="Microsoft.NET.Sdk">

  <PropertyGroup>
    <OutputType>Exe</OutputType>
    <TargetFramework>net7.0</TargetFramework>
    <ImplicitUsings>enable</ImplicitUsings>
    <Nullable>enable</Nullable>
    <TreatWarningsAsErrors>true</TreatWarningsAsErrors>
  </PropertyGroup>

  <ItemGroup>
    <PackageReference Include="Microsoft.Data.SqlClient" Version="5.0.0" />
  </ItemGroup>

  <ItemGroup>
    <Using Include="System.Console" Static="true" />
  </ItemGroup>

</Project>
```

4.  Build the project to restore the referenced package.
5.  Add a new class file named Program.EventHandlers.cs, and modify its contents to define methods that will act as event handlers for a database connection state change by showing the original and current states, and for when the database sends an InfoMessage, as shown in the following code:

```csharp
using Microsoft.Data.SqlClient; // SqlInfoMessageEventArgs
using System.Data; // StateChangeEventArgs

partial class Program
{
  static void Connection_StateChange(object sender, StateChangeEventArgs e)
  {
    ConsoleColor previousColor = ForegroundColor;
    ForegroundColor = ConsoleColor.DarkYellow;
```

```
      WriteLine($"State change from {e.OriginalState} to
  {e.CurrentState}.");
      ForegroundColor = previousColor;
    }

    static void Connection_InfoMessage(object sender,
  SqlInfoMessageEventArgs e)
    {
      ConsoleColor previousColor = ForegroundColor;
      ForegroundColor = ConsoleColor.DarkBlue;
      WriteLine($"Info: {e.Message}.");
      foreach(SqlError error in e.Errors)
      {
        WriteLine($"  Error: {error.Message}.");
      }
      ForegroundColor = previousColor;
    }
  }
```

6. In `Program.cs`, delete the existing statements. Add statements to connect to SQL Server locally, to Azure SQL Database, or to SQL Edge, using either SQL authentication with a user ID and password or Windows Authentication without a user ID and password, as shown in the following code:

```
using Microsoft.Data.SqlClient; // SqlConnection and so on

SqlConnectionStringBuilder builder = new();

builder.InitialCatalog = "Northwind";
builder.MultipleActiveResultSets = true;
builder.Encrypt = true;
builder.TrustServerCertificate = true;
builder.ConnectTimeout = 10;

WriteLine("Connect to:");
WriteLine("  1 - SQL Server on local machine");
WriteLine("  2 - Azure SQL Database");
WriteLine("  3 - Azure SQL Edge");
WriteLine();
Write("Press a key: ");

ConsoleKey key = ReadKey().Key;
WriteLine(); WriteLine();

if (key is ConsoleKey.D1 or ConsoleKey.NumPad1)
{
  builder.DataSource = "."; // Local SQL Server
```

```csharp
    // @".\net7book"; // Local SQL Server with an instance name
}
else if (key is ConsoleKey.D2 or ConsoleKey.NumPad2)
{
  builder.DataSource = // Azure SQL Database
    "tcp:apps-services-net7.database.windows.net,1433";
}
else if (key is ConsoleKey.D3 or ConsoleKey.NumPad3)
{
  builder.DataSource = "tcp:127.0.0.1,1433"; // Azure SQL Edge
}
else
{
  WriteLine("No data source selected.");
  return;
}

WriteLine("Authenticate using:");
WriteLine("  1 - Windows Integrated Security");
WriteLine("  2 - SQL Login, for example, sa");
WriteLine();
Write("Press a key: ");

key = ReadKey().Key;
WriteLine(); WriteLine();

if (key is ConsoleKey.D1 or ConsoleKey.NumPad1)
{
  builder.IntegratedSecurity = true;
}
else if (key is ConsoleKey.D2 or ConsoleKey.NumPad2)
{
  builder.UserID = "sa"; // Azure SQL Edge
    // "markjprice"; // change to your username

  Write("Enter your SQL Server password: ");
  string? password = ReadLine();
  if (string.IsNullOrWhiteSpace(password))
  {
    WriteLine("Password cannot be empty or null.");
    return;
  }

  builder.Password = password;
  builder.PersistSecurityInfo = false;
}
```

```
else
{
  WriteLine("No authentication selected.");
  return;
}

SqlConnection connection = new(builder.ConnectionString);

WriteLine(connection.ConnectionString);
WriteLine();

connection.StateChange += Connection_StateChange;
connection.InfoMessage += Connection_InfoMessage;

try
{
  WriteLine("Opening connection. Please wait up to {0} seconds...",
    builder.ConnectTimeout);
  WriteLine();
  connection.Open();

  WriteLine($"SQL Server version: {connection.ServerVersion}");

  connection.StatisticsEnabled = true;
}
catch (SqlException ex)
{
  WriteLine($"SQL exception: {ex.Message}");
  return;
}

connection.Close();
```

7.  Run the console app, select options that work with your SQL Server set up, and note the results, as shown in the following output:

```
Connect to:
   1 - SQL Server on local machine
   2 - Azure SQL Database
   3 - Azure SQL Edge

Press a key: 1

Authenticate using:
   1 - Windows Integrated Security
   2 - SQL Login, for example, sa
```

```
Press a key: 1

Data Source=.;Initial Catalog=Northwind;Integrated Security=True;Multiple
Active Result Sets=True;Connect Timeout=10;Encrypt=True;Trust Server
Certificate=True

Opening connection. Please wait up to 10 seconds...

State change from Closed to Open.
SQL Server version: 15.00.2095
State change from Open to Closed.
```

The following steps show the experience when connecting to Azure SQL Database or Azure SQL Edge, which require a username and password. If you are connecting to a local SQL Server using Windows Integrated Security, then you will not need to enter a password.

8.  Run the console app, select either **Azure SQL Database** or **Azure SQL Edge**, enter your password, and note the result, as shown in the following output:

```
Connect to:
  1 - SQL Server on local machine
  2 - Azure SQL Database
  3 - Azure SQL Edge

Press a key: 3

Authenticate using:
  1 - Windows Integrated Security
  2 - SQL Login, for example, sa

Press a key: 2

Enter your SQL Server password: s3cret-Ninja

State change from Closed to Open.
SQL Server version: 15.00.0041
State change from Open to Closed.
```

9.  Run the console app, enter a wrong password, and note the result, as shown in the following output:

```
Enter your SQL Server password: silly-ninja
SQL exception: Login failed for user 'sa'.
```

10. In `Program.cs`, change the server name to something wrong.

11. Run the console app and note the result, as shown in the following output:

```
SQL exception: A network-related or instance-specific error occurred
while establishing a connection to SQL Server. The server was not found
or was not accessible. Verify that the instance name is correct and that
SQL Server is configured to allow remote connections. (provider: TCP
Provider, error: 0 - No such host is known.)
```

 When opening a SQL Server connection, the default timeout is 30 seconds for server connection problems, so be patient! We changed the timeout to 10 seconds to avoid having to wait so long.

## Executing queries and working with data readers using ADO.NET

Now that we have a successful connection to the SQL Server database, we can run commands and process the results using a data reader.

1. In `Program.cs`, import the namespace for working with ADO.NET command types, as shown in the following code:

   ```
   using System.Data; // CommandType
   ```

2. Before the statement that closes the connection, add statements to define a command that selects the ID, name, and price from the `Products` table, executes it, and outputs the product IDs, names, and prices using a data reader, as shown in the following code:

   ```
   SqlCommand cmd = connection.CreateCommand();

   cmd.CommandType = CommandType.Text;
   cmd.CommandText = "SELECT ProductId, ProductName, UnitPrice FROM
   Products";

   SqlDataReader r = cmd.ExecuteReader();

   WriteLine("---------------------------------------------------------------");
   WriteLine("| {0,5} | {1,-35} | {2,8} |", "Id", "Name", "Price");
   WriteLine("---------------------------------------------------------------");

   while (r.Read())
   {
     WriteLine("| {0,5} | {1,-35} | {2,8:C} |",
       r.GetInt32("ProductId"),
       r.GetString("ProductName"),
       r.GetDecimal("UnitPrice"));
   }

   WriteLine("---------------------------------------------------------------");
   ```

```
r.Close();
```

 We format the unit price using the C format which uses your OS current culture to format currency values. My output uses £ because I am in the UK. You will learn how to control the current culture in *Chapter 7, Handling Dates, Times, and Internationalization*.

3.  Run the console app and note the results, as shown in the following partial output:

```
------------------------------------------------------------------
|   Id | Name                                  |        Price |
------------------------------------------------------------------
|    1 | Chai                                  |      £18.00 |
|    2 | Chang                                 |      £19.00 |
...
|   76 | Lakkalikööri                          |      £18.00 |
|   77 | Original Frankfurter grüne Soße       |      £13.00 |
------------------------------------------------------------------
```

4.  In `Program.cs`, modify the SQL statement to define a parameter for the unit price and use it to filter the results to products that cost more than that unit price, as shown highlighted in the following code:

```
Write("Enter a unit price: ");
string? priceText = ReadLine();

if(!decimal.TryParse(priceText, out decimal price))
{
  WriteLine("You must enter a valid unit price.");
  return;
}

SqlCommand cmd = connection.CreateCommand();

cmd.CommandType = CommandType.Text;

cmd.CommandText = "SELECT ProductId, ProductName, UnitPrice FROM
Products"
  + " WHERE UnitPrice > @price";

cmd.Parameters.AddWithValue("price", price);
```

5.  Run the console app, enter a unit price like 50, and note the results, as shown in the following partial output:

```
Enter a unit price: 50
------------------------------------------------------------------
|   Id | Name                                  |        Price |
```

```
|       9 | Mishi Kobe Niku                      |    £97.00 |
|      18 | Carnarvon Tigers                     |    £62.50 |
|      20 | Sir Rodney's Marmalade               |    £81.00 |
|      29 | Thüringer Rostbratwurst              |   £123.79 |
|      38 | Côte de Blaye                        |   £263.50 |
|      51 | Manjimup Dried Apples                |    £53.00 |
|      59 | Raclette Courdavault                 |    £55.00 |
```

## Working with ADO.NET asynchronously

You can improve the responsiveness of data access code by making it asynchronous. You will see more details of how asynchronous operations work in *Chapter 4, Benchmarking Performance, Multitasking, and Concurrency*. For now, just enter the code as instructed.

Let's see how to change the statements to work asynchronously:

1.  In `Program.cs`, change the statement to open the connection to make it asynchronous, as shown in the following code:

    ```
    await connection.OpenAsync();
    ```

2.  In `Program.cs`, change the statement to execute the command to make it asynchronous, as shown in the following code:

    ```
    SqlDataReader r = await cmd.ExecuteReaderAsync();
    ```

3.  In `Program.cs`, change the statements to read the next row and get the field values to make them asynchronous, as shown in the following code:

    ```
    while (await r.ReadAsync())
    {
      WriteLine("| {0,5} | {1,-35} | {2,8:C} |",
        await r.GetFieldValueAsync<int>("ProductId"),
        await r.GetFieldValueAsync<string>("ProductName"),
        await r.GetFieldValueAsync<decimal>("UnitPrice"));
    }
    ```

4.  In `Program.cs`, change the statements to close the data reader and connection to make them asynchronous, as shown in the following code:

    ```
    await r.CloseAsync();
    await connection.CloseAsync();
    ```

5.  Run the console app and confirm that it has the same results as before, but it would run better in a multithreaded system, for example, not blocking the user interface in a GUI app, and not blocking IO threads in a website.

# Executing stored procedures using ADO.NET

If you need to execute the same query or another SQL statement multiple times, it is best to create a **stored procedure**, often with parameters, so that it can be precompiled and optimized. Parameters have a direction to indicate if they are inputs, outputs, or return values.

Let's see an example that uses all three types of direction:

1. In your preferred database tool, connect to the Northwind database.

2. In your preferred database tool, add a new stored procedure. For example, if you are using SQL Server Management Studio, then right-click **Stored Procedures** and select **Add New Stored Procedure**.

3. Modify the SQL statements to define a stored procedure named GetExpensiveProducts with two parameters, an input parameter for the minimum unit price and an output parameter for the row count of matching products, as shown in the following code:

```
CREATE PROCEDURE [dbo].[GetExpensiveProducts]
    @price money,
    @count int OUT
AS
    SELECT @count = COUNT(*)
    FROM Products
    WHERE UnitPrice > @price

    SELECT *
    FROM Products
    WHERE UnitPrice > @price

RETURN 0
```

 The stored procedure uses two SELECT statements. The first sets the @count output parameter to a count of the matching product rows. The second returns the matching product rows.

4. Right-click in the SQL statements and select **Execute**.

5. Right-click **Stored Procedures** and select **Refresh**.

6. Expand **GetExpensiveProducts** and note the input and output parameters, as shown in Visual Studio's **Server Explorer** in *Figure 2.12*:

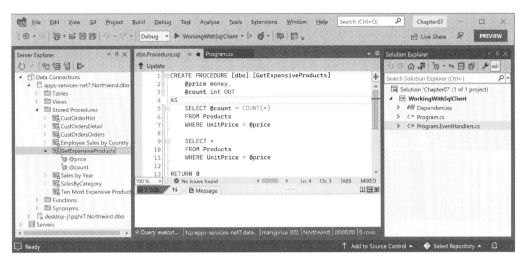

*Figure 2.12: Parameters of the GetExpensiveProducts stored procedure*

7. Close the SQL query without saving changes.

8. In `Program.cs`, add statements to allow the user to choose between running the text command and the stored procedure. Add statements defining the stored procedure and its parameters, and then execute the command, as shown highlighted in the following code:

```csharp
SqlCommand cmd = connection.CreateCommand();

WriteLine("Execute command using:");
WriteLine("  1 - Text");
WriteLine("  2 - Stored Procedure");
WriteLine();
Write("Press a key: ");

key = ReadKey().Key;
WriteLine(); WriteLine();

SqlParameter p1, p2 = new(), p3 = new();

if (key is ConsoleKey.D1 or ConsoleKey.NumPad1)
{
  cmd.CommandType = CommandType.Text;

  cmd.CommandText = "SELECT ProductId, ProductName, UnitPrice FROM Products"
    + " WHERE UnitPrice > @price";

  cmd.Parameters.AddWithValue("price", price);
}
else if (key is ConsoleKey.D2 or ConsoleKey.NumPad2)
```

```
{
  cmd.CommandType = CommandType.StoredProcedure;
  cmd.CommandText = "GetExpensiveProducts";

  p1 = new()
  {
    ParameterName = "price",
    SqlDbType = SqlDbType.Money,
    SqlValue = price
  };

  p2 = new()
  {
    Direction = ParameterDirection.Output,
    ParameterName = "count",
    SqlDbType = SqlDbType.Int
  };

  p3 = new()
  {
    Direction= ParameterDirection.ReturnValue,
    ParameterName = "rv",
    SqlDbType = SqlDbType.Int
  };

  cmd.Parameters.Add(p1);
  cmd.Parameters.Add(p2);
  cmd.Parameters.Add(p3);
}

SqlDataReader r = await cmd.ExecuteReaderAsync();
```

9.  After the statement that closes the data reader, add statements to output the output parameter and the return value, as shown highlighted in the following code:

```
await r.CloseAsync();

WriteLine($"Output count: {p2.Value}");
WriteLine($"Return value: {p3.Value}");

await connection.CloseAsync();
```

 If a stored procedure returns result sets as well as parameters, then the data reader for the result sets must be closed before the parameters can be read.

10. Run the console app and note the results if the price entered is 60, as shown in the following output:

```
Enter a unit price: 60
Execute command using:
  1 - Text
  2 - Stored Procedure

Press a key: 2
-------------------------------------------------------------
|    Id | Name                           |          Price |
-------------------------------------------------------------
|     9 | Mishi Kobe Niku                |         £97.00 |
|    18 | Carnarvon Tigers               |         £62.50 |
|    20 | Sir Rodney's Marmalade         |         £81.00 |
|    29 | Thüringer Rostbratwurst        |        £123.79 |
|    38 | Côte de Blaye                  |        £263.50 |
-------------------------------------------------------------
Output count: 5
Return value: 0
State change from Open to Closed.
```

# Managing data with EF Core

EF Core is an **object-relational mapper** (**ORM**) that uses ADO.NET underneath when working with SQL Server. Because it is a higher-level technology, it is not as efficient as using ADO.NET directly but it can be easier.

EF Core 7 targets .NET 6 so it can be used with both the **Long Term Support** (**LTS**) release of .NET 6 and the **Standard Term Support** (**STS**) release of .NET 7.

## Understanding Entity Framework Core

As well as traditional RDBMSes like SQL Server, EF Core supports modern cloud-based, nonrelational, schema-less data stores, such as Azure Cosmos DB and MongoDB, sometimes with third-party providers.

There are two approaches to working with EF Core:

- **Database First:** A database already exists, so you build a model that matches its structure and features.
- **Code First:** No database exists, so you build a model and then use EF Core to create a database that matches its structure and features.

We will use EF Core with an existing database.

# Scaffolding models using an existing database

Scaffolding is the process of using a tool to create classes that represent the model of an existing database using reverse engineering. A good scaffolding tool allows you to extend the automatically generated classes and then regenerate those classes without losing your extended classes.

If you know that you will never regenerate the classes using the tool, then feel free to change the code for the automatically generated classes as much as you want. The code generated by the tool is just the best approximation.

 **Good Practice:** Do not be afraid to overrule a tool when you know better.

# Setting up the dotnet-ef tool

.NET has a command-line tool named dotnet. It can be extended with capabilities useful for working with EF Core. It can perform design-time tasks like creating and applying migrations from an older model to a newer model and generating code for a model from an existing database.

The dotnet-ef command-line tool is not automatically installed. You must install this package as either a **global** or **local tool**. If you have already installed an older version of the tool, then you should uninstall any existing version:

1.  At a command prompt or terminal, check if you have already installed dotnet-ef as a global tool, as shown in the following command:

    ```
    dotnet tool list --global
    ```

2.  Check in the list if an older version of the tool has been installed, like the one for .NET 5.0, as shown in the following output:

    ```
    Package Id       Version      Commands
    ------------------------------------------
    dotnet-ef        5.0.0        dotnet-ef
    ```

3.  If an old version is already installed, then uninstall the tool, as shown in the following command:

    ```
    dotnet tool uninstall --global dotnet-ef
    ```

4.  Install the latest version, as shown in the following command:

    ```
    dotnet tool install --global dotnet-ef --version 7.0.0
    ```

5.  If necessary, follow any OS-specific instructions to add the dotnet tools directory to your PATH environment variable, as described in the output of installing the dotnet-ef tool.

# Defining EF Core models

EF Core uses a combination of **conventions, annotation attributes,** and **Fluent API** statements to build an **entity model** at runtime so that any actions performed on the classes can later be automatically translated into actions performed on the actual database. An **entity class** represents the structure of a table, and an instance of the class represents a row in that table.

First, we will review the three ways to define a model, with code examples, and then we will create some classes that implement those techniques.

## Using EF Core conventions to define the model

The code we will write will use the following conventions:

- The name of a table is assumed to match the name of a DbSet<T> property in the DbContext class, for example, Products.
- The names of the columns are assumed to match the names of properties in the entity model class, for example, ProductId.
- The string .NET type is assumed to be a nvarchar type in the database.
- The int .NET type is assumed to be an int type in the database.
- The primary key is assumed to be a property that is named Id or ID, or when the entity model class is named Product, then the property can be named ProductId or ProductID. If this property is of an integer type or the Guid type, then it is also assumed to be an IDENTITY column (a column type that automatically assigns a value when inserting).

 **Good Practice:** There are many other conventions that you should know, and you can even define your own, but that is beyond the scope of this book. You can read about them at the following link: https://docs.microsoft.com/en-us/ef/core/modeling/.

## Using EF Core annotation attributes to define the model

Conventions often aren't enough to completely map the classes to the database objects. A simple way of adding more smarts to your model is to apply annotation attributes.

Some common attributes are shown in the following table:

| Attribute | Description |
|---|---|
| [Required] | Ensures the value is not null. |
| [StringLength(50)] | Ensures the value is up to 50 characters in length. |
| [RegularExpression(expression)] | Ensures the value matches the specified regular expression. |
| [Column(TypeName = "money", Name = "UnitPrice")] | Specifies the column type and column name used in the table. |

For example, in the database, the maximum length of a product name is 40, and the value cannot be null, as shown highlighted in the following DDL code that defines how to create a table named Products along with its columns, data types, keys, and other constraints:

```
CREATE TABLE Products (
    ProductId         INTEGER         PRIMARY KEY,
    ProductName       NVARCHAR (40) NOT NULL,
    SupplierId        "INT",
    CategoryId        "INT",
    QuantityPerUnit   NVARCHAR (20),
    UnitPrice         "MONEY"         CONSTRAINT DF_Products_UnitPrice DEFAULT (0),
    UnitsInStock      "SMALLINT"      CONSTRAINT DF_Products_UnitsInStock DEFAULT
(0),
    UnitsOnOrder      "SMALLINT"      CONSTRAINT DF_Products_UnitsOnOrder DEFAULT
(0),
    ReorderLevel      "SMALLINT"      CONSTRAINT DF_Products_ReorderLevel DEFAULT
(0),
    Discontinued      "BIT"           NOT NULL
                                      CONSTRAINT DF_Products_Discontinued DEFAULT
(0),
    CONSTRAINT FK_Products_Categories FOREIGN KEY (
        CategoryId
    )
    REFERENCES Categories (CategoryId),
    CONSTRAINT FK_Products_Suppliers FOREIGN KEY (
        SupplierId
    )
    REFERENCES Suppliers (SupplierId),
    CONSTRAINT CK_Products_UnitPrice CHECK (UnitPrice >= 0),
    CONSTRAINT CK_ReorderLevel CHECK (ReorderLevel >= 0),
    CONSTRAINT CK_UnitsInStock CHECK (UnitsInStock >= 0),
    CONSTRAINT CK_UnitsOnOrder CHECK (UnitsOnOrder >= 0)
);
```

In a Product class, we could apply attributes to specify this, as shown in the following code:

```
[Required]
[StringLength(40)]
public string ProductName { get; set; }
```

 **Good Practice:** If you have nullability checks enabled, then you do not need to decorate a non-nullable reference type with the [Required] attribute as shown above. This is because the C# nullability will flow to the EF Core model. A string property will be required; a string? property will be optional, in other words, nullable. You can read more about this at the following link: https://docs.microsoft.com/en-us/ef/core/modeling/entity-properties?tabs=data-annotations%2Cwith-nrt#required-and-optional-properties.

When there isn't an obvious map between .NET types and database types, an attribute can be used.

For example, in the database, the column type of UnitPrice for the Products table is money. .NET does not have a money type, so it should use decimal instead, as shown in the following code:

```
[Column(TypeName = "money")]
public decimal? UnitPrice { get; set; }
```

Another example is for the Categories table, as shown in the following DDL code:

```
CREATE TABLE Categories (
    CategoryId    INTEGER        PRIMARY KEY,
    CategoryName NVARCHAR (15) NOT NULL,
    Description   "NTEXT",
    Picture       "IMAGE"
);
```

The Description column can be longer than the maximum 8,000 characters that can be stored in a nvarchar variable, so it needs to map to ntext instead, as shown in the following code:

```
[Column(TypeName = "ntext")]
public string? Description { get; set; }
```

## Using the EF Core Fluent API to define the model

The last way that the model can be defined is by using the Fluent API. This API can be used instead of attributes, as well as being used in addition to them. For example, to define the ProductName property, instead of decorating the property with two attributes, an equivalent Fluent API statement could be written in the OnModelCreating method of the database context class, as shown in the following code:

```
modelBuilder.Entity<Product>()
  .Property(product => product.ProductName)
  .IsRequired() // only needed if you have disabled nullability checks
  .HasMaxLength(40);
```

This keeps the entity model class simpler. You will see an example of this in the coding task below.

## Understanding data seeding with the Fluent API

Another benefit of the Fluent API is to provide initial data to populate a database. EF Core automatically works out what insert, update, or delete operations must be executed.

For example, if we wanted to make sure that a new database has at least one row in the Product table, then we would call the HasData method, as shown in the following code:

```
modelBuilder.Entity<Product>()
  .HasData(new Product
  {
    ProductId = 1,
    ProductName = "Chai",
    UnitPrice = 8.99M
  });
```

Our model will map to an existing database that is already populated with data, so we will not need to use this technique in our code.

## Defining the Northwind database model

A Northwind class will be used to represent the database. To use EF Core, the class must inherit from DbContext. This class understands how to communicate with databases and dynamically generate SQL statements to query and manipulate data.

Your DbContext-derived class should have an overridden method named OnConfiguring, which will set the database connection string.

Inside your DbContext-derived class, you must define at least one property of the DbSet<T> type. These properties represent the tables. To tell EF Core what columns each table has, the DbSet<T> properties use generics to specify a class that represents a row in the table. That entity model class has properties that represent its columns.

The DbContext-derived class can optionally have an overridden method named OnModelCreating. This is where you can write Fluent API statements as an alternative to decorating your entity classes with attributes.

1.  Use your preferred code editor to add a console app project, as defined in the following list:

    *   Project template: **Console App**/console
    *   Workspace/solution file and folder: Chapter02
    *   Project file and folder: Northwind.Console.EFCore

2.  In the Northwind.Console.EFCore project, treat warnings as errors, add package references to the EF Core data provider for SQL Server, and globally and statically import the System. Console class, as shown highlighted in the following markup:

```xml
<Project Sdk="Microsoft.NET.Sdk">

  <PropertyGroup>
    <OutputType>Exe</OutputType>
    <TargetFramework>net7.0</TargetFramework>
    <ImplicitUsings>enable</ImplicitUsings>
    <Nullable>enable</Nullable>
    <TreatWarningsAsErrors>true</TreatWarningsAsErrors>
  </PropertyGroup>

  <ItemGroup>
    <PackageReference
      Include="Microsoft.EntityFrameworkCore.Design"
      Version="7.0.0" />
    <PackageReference
      Include="Microsoft.EntityFrameworkCore.SqlServer"
      Version="7.0.0" />
```

```
    </ItemGroup>

    <ItemGroup>
      <Using Include="System.Console" Static="true" />
    </ItemGroup>

  </Project>
```

3. Build the project to restore packages.

4. At a command prompt or terminal in the `Northwind.Console.EFCore` folder, generate a model for all the tables in a new folder named `Models`, as shown in the following command:

```
dotnet ef dbcontext scaffold "Data Source=.;Initial
Catalog=Northwind;Integrated Security=true;TrustServerCertificate=true;"
Microsoft.EntityFrameworkCore.SqlServer --output-dir Models --namespace
Northwind.Console.EFCore.Models --data-annotations --context NorthwindDb
```

Note the following:

- The command action: `dbcontext scaffold`
- The connection string: This will be different depending on if you are connecting to a local SQL Server (with or without an instance name) or Azure SQL Database.
- The database provider: `Microsoft.EntityFrameworkCore.SqlServer`
- The output folder: `--output-dir Models`
- The namespace: `--namespace Northwind.Console.EFCore.Models`
- The use of data annotations as well as the Fluent API: `--data-annotations`
- Renaming the context from `[database_name]Context`: `--context NorthwindDb`

 If you are using Azure SQL Database or Azure SQL Edge, you will need to change the connection string appropriately.

5. Note the build messages and warnings, as shown in the following output:

```
Build started...
Build succeeded.
To protect potentially sensitive information in your connection string,
you should move it out of source code. You can avoid scaffolding the
connection string by using the Name= syntax to read it from configuration
- see https://go.microsoft.com/fwlink/?linkid=2131148. For more
guidance on storing connection strings, see http://go.microsoft.com/
fwlink/?LinkId=723263.
```

6. Open the `Models` folder and note the 25+ class files that were automatically generated.

7.  Open `Category.cs` and note that it represents a row in the `Categories` table, as shown in the following code:

```
using System;
using System.Collections.Generic;
using System.ComponentModel.DataAnnotations;
using System.ComponentModel.DataAnnotations.Schema;
using Microsoft.EntityFrameworkCore;

namespace Northwind.Console.EFCore.Models
{
  [Index("CategoryName", Name = "CategoryName")]
  public partial class Category
  {
    public Category()
    {
      Products = new HashSet<Product>();
    }

    [Key]
    public int CategoryId { get; set; }
    [StringLength(15)]
    public string CategoryName { get; set; } = null!;
    [Column(TypeName = "ntext")]
    public string? Description { get; set; }
    [Column(TypeName = "image")]
    public byte[]? Picture { get; set; }

    [InverseProperty("Category")]
    public virtual ICollection<Product> Products { get; set; }
  }
}
```

Note the following:

*   It decorates the entity class with the [`Index`] attribute that was introduced in EF Core 5.0. This indicates properties that should have an index. In earlier versions, only the Fluent API was supported for defining indexes. Since we are working with an existing database, this is not needed. But if we want to recreate a new empty database from our code, then this information will be used to create indexes.

*   The table name in the database is `Categories` but the `dotnet-ef` tool uses the **Humanizer** third-party library to automatically singularize the class name to `Category`, which is a more natural name when creating a single entity.

*   The entity class is declared using the `partial` keyword so that you can create a matching `partial` class for adding additional code. This allows you to rerun the tool and regenerate the entity class without losing that extra code.

- The CategoryId property is decorated with the [Key] attribute to indicate that it is the primary key for this entity.

- The Products property uses the [InverseProperty] attribute to define the foreign key relationship to the Category property on the Product entity class.

8. Open ProductsAboveAveragePrice.cs and note it represents a row returned by a database view rather than a table, so it is decorated with the [Keyless] attribute.

9. Open NorthwindDb.cs and review the class, as shown in the following edited-for-space code:

```
using System;
using System.Collections.Generic;
using Microsoft.EntityFrameworkCore;
using Microsoft.EntityFrameworkCore.Metadata;

namespace Northwind.Console.EFCore.Models
{
  public partial class NorthwindDb : DbContext
  {
    public NorthwindDb()
    {
    }

    public NorthwindDb(DbContextOptions<Northwind> options)
        : base(options)
    {
    }

    public virtual DbSet<AlphabeticalListOfProduct>
      AlphabeticalListOfProducts { get; set; } = null!;
    public virtual DbSet<Category> Categories { get; set; } = null!;
    ...
    public virtual DbSet<Supplier> Suppliers { get; set; } = null!;
    public virtual DbSet<Territory> Territories { get; set; } = null!;

    protected override void OnConfiguring(
      DbContextOptionsBuilder optionsBuilder)
    {
      if (!optionsBuilder.IsConfigured)
      {
#warning To protect potentially sensitive ...
        optionsBuilder.UseSqlServer("Data
Source=.;Initial Catalog=Northwind;Integrated
Security=true;TrustServerCertificate=true;");
      }
    }

    protected override void OnModelCreating(ModelBuilder modelBuilder)
```

```
    {
      modelBuilder.Entity<AlphabeticalListOfProduct>(entity =>
      {
        entity.ToView("Alphabetical list of products");
      });

      ...

      modelBuilder.Entity<Product>(entity =>
      {
        entity.Property(e => e.ReorderLevel).HasDefaultValueSql("((0))");

        entity.Property(e => e.UnitPrice).HasDefaultValueSql("((0))");

        entity.Property(e => e.UnitsInStock).HasDefaultValueSql("((0))");

        entity.Property(e => e.UnitsOnOrder).HasDefaultValueSql("((0))");

        entity.HasOne(d => d.Category)
                  .WithMany(p => p.Products)
                  .HasForeignKey(d => d.CategoryId)
                  .HasConstraintName("FK_Products_Categories");

        entity.HasOne(d => d.Supplier)
                  .WithMany(p => p.Products)
                  .HasForeignKey(d => d.SupplierId)
                  .HasConstraintName("FK_Products_Suppliers");
      });

      ...

      OnModelCreatingPartial(modelBuilder);
    }

    partial void OnModelCreatingPartial(ModelBuilder modelBuilder);
  }
}
```

Note the following:

- The NorthwindDb data context class is partial to allow you to extend it and regenerate it in the future. We used the name NorthwindDb because Northwind is used for a namespace.

- NorthwindDb has two constructors: a default parameter-less one and one that allows options to be passed in. This is useful in apps where you want to specify the connection string at runtime.

- The `DbSet<T>` properties that represent tables are set to the `null`-forgiving value to prevent static compiler analysis warnings at compile time. It has no effect at runtime.

- In the `OnConfiguring` method, if options have not been specified in the constructor, then it defaults to using the connection string used during scaffolding. It has a compiler warning to remind you that you should not hardcode security information in this connection string.

- In the `OnModelCreating` method, the Fluent API is used to configure the entity classes, and then a partial method named `OnModelCreatingPartial` is invoked. This allows you to implement that partial method in your own partial `Northwind` class to add your own Fluent API configuration, which will not be lost if you regenerate the model classes.

10. Delete the `#warning` statement. We are treating warnings as errors so we cannot leave this in.

11. Close the automatically generated class files.

## Querying the Northwind model

Now we can query the model:

1. In `Program.cs`, delete the existing statements. Add statements to create an instance of the `NorthwindDb` data context class and use it to query the products table for those that cost more than a given price, as shown in the following code:

```
using Microsoft.Data.SqlClient; // SqlConnectionStringBuilder
using Microsoft.EntityFrameworkCore; // ToQueryString,
GetConnectionString
using Northwind.Console.EFCore.Models; // NorthwindDb

SqlConnectionStringBuilder builder = new();

builder.InitialCatalog = "Northwind";
builder.MultipleActiveResultSets = true;
builder.Encrypt = true;
builder.TrustServerCertificate = true;
builder.ConnectTimeout = 10;

WriteLine("Connect to:");
WriteLine("   1 - SQL Server on local machine");
WriteLine("   2 - Azure SQL Database");
WriteLine("   3 - Azure SQL Edge");
WriteLine();
Write("Press a key: ");

ConsoleKey key = ReadKey().Key;
WriteLine(); WriteLine();

if (key is ConsoleKey.D1 or ConsoleKey.NumPad1)
{
```

```
  builder.DataSource = "."; // Local SQL Server
  // @".\net7book"; // Local SQL Server with an instance name
}
else if (key is ConsoleKey.D2 or ConsoleKey.NumPad2)
{
  builder.DataSource = // Azure SQL Database
    "tcp:apps-services-net7.database.windows.net,1433";
}
else if (key is ConsoleKey.D3 or ConsoleKey.NumPad3)
{
  builder.DataSource = "tcp:127.0.0.1,1433"; // Azure SQL Edge
}
else
{
  WriteLine("No data source selected.");
  return;
}

WriteLine("Authenticate using:");
WriteLine("  1 - Windows Integrated Security");
WriteLine("  2 - SQL Login, for example, sa");
WriteLine();
Write("Press a key: ");

key = ReadKey().Key;
WriteLine(); WriteLine();

if (key is ConsoleKey.D1 or ConsoleKey.NumPad1)
{
  builder.IntegratedSecurity = true;
}
else if (key is ConsoleKey.D2 or ConsoleKey.NumPad2)
{
  builder.UserID = "sa"; // Azure SQL Edge
                         // "markjprice"; // change to your username

  Write("Enter your SQL Server password: ");
  string? password = ReadLine();
  if (string.IsNullOrWhiteSpace(password))
  {
    WriteLine("Password cannot be empty or null.");
    return;
  }

  builder.Password = password;
  builder.PersistSecurityInfo = false;
```

```
  }
  else
  {
    WriteLine("No authentication selected.");
    return;
  }

  DbContextOptionsBuilder<NorthwindDb> options = new();
  options.UseSqlServer(builder.ConnectionString);

  using (NorthwindDb db = new(options.Options))
  {
    Write("Enter a unit price: ");
    string? priceText = ReadLine();

    if (!decimal.TryParse(priceText, out decimal price))
    {
      WriteLine("You must enter a valid unit price.");
      return;
    }

    // We have to use var because we are projecting into an anonymous type.
    var products = db.Products
      .Where(p => p.UnitPrice > price)
      .Select(p => new { p.ProductId, p.ProductName, p.UnitPrice });

    WriteLine("------------------------------------------------------------");
    WriteLine("| {0,5} | {1,-35} | {2,8} |", "Id", "Name", "Price");
    WriteLine("------------------------------------------------------------");

    foreach (var p in products)
    {
      WriteLine("| {0,5} | {1,-35} | {2,8:C} |",
        p.ProductId, p.ProductName, p.UnitPrice);
    }

    WriteLine("------------------------------------------------------------");

    WriteLine(products.ToQueryString());
    WriteLine();
    WriteLine($"Provider:   {db.Database.ProviderName}");
    WriteLine($"Connection: {db.Database.GetConnectionString()}");
  }
```

2.  Run the console app and note the results, as shown in the following partial output:

```
Enter a unit price: 60
```

```
--------------------------------------------------------
|    Id | Name                              |     Price |
--------------------------------------------------------
|     9 | Mishi Kobe Niku                   |    £97.00 |
|    18 | Carnarvon Tigers                  |    £62.50 |
|    20 | Sir Rodney's Marmalade            |    £81.00 |
|    29 | Thüringer Rostbratwurst           |   £123.79 |
|    38 | Côte de Blaye                     |   £263.50 |
--------------------------------------------------------

DECLARE @__price_0 decimal(2) = 60.0;


SELECT [p].[ProductId], [p].[ProductName], [p].[UnitPrice]
FROM [Products] AS [p]
WHERE [p].[UnitPrice] > @__price_0


Provider:   Microsoft.EntityFrameworkCore.SqlServer
Connection: Data Source=tcp:apps-services-net7.database.windows.
net,1433;Initial Catalog=Northwind;Persist Security Info=False;User
ID=markjprice;Password=s3cret-Ninja;Multiple Active Result
Sets=False;Encrypt=True;Trust Server Certificate=False;Connection
Timeout=10;
```

Your connection string will be different. For example, your user ID and password, and if you are using a local SQL Server with Windows integrated security authentication, then it would be `Data Source=.;Initial Catalog=Northwind;Integrated Security=True;Multiple Active Result Sets=True;Connect Timeout=10;Encrypt=True;Trust Server Certificate=True.`

# Mapping inheritance hierarchies with EF Core

Imagine that you have an inheritance hierarchy for some C# classes to store information about students and employees, both of which are types of people. All people have a name and an ID to uniquely identify them, students have a subject they are studying, and employees have a hire date, as shown in the following code:

```
public abstract class Person
{
  public int Id { get; set; }
  public string? Name { get; set; }
}

public class Student : Person
{
  public string? Subject { get; set; }
}
```

```
public class Employee : Person
{
    public DateTime HireDate { get; set; }
}
```

By default, EF Core will map these to a single table using the **table-per-hierarchy** (TPH) mapping strategy. EF Core 5 introduced support for the **table-per-type** (TPT) mapping strategy. EF Core 7 introduces support for the **table-per-concrete-type** (TPC) mapping strategy. Let's explore the differences between these mapping strategies.

## Table-per-hierarchy (TPH) mapping strategy

For the `Person-Student-Employee` hierarchy, TPH will use a single table structure with a discriminator column to indicate which type of person, a student or employee, the row is, as shown in the following code:

```
CREATE TABLE [People] (
    [Id] int NOT NULL IDENTITY,
    [Name] nvarchar(max) NOT NULL,
    [Discriminator] nvarchar(max) NOT NULL,
    [Subject] nvarchar(max) NULL,
    [HireDate] nvarchar(max) NULL,
    CONSTRAINT [PK_People] PRIMARY KEY ([Id])
);
```

Some data in the table might look like the following:

| Id | Name | Discriminator | Subject | HireDate |
|----|------|---------------|---------|----------|
| 1 | Roman Roy | Student | History | NULL |
| 2 | Kendall Roy | Employee | NULL | 02/04/2014 |
| 3 | Siobhan Roy | Employee | NULL | 12/09/2020 |

TPH requires the `Discriminator` column to store the class name of the type for each row. TPH requires the columns for properties of derived types to be nullable, like `Subject` and `HireDate`. This can cause an issue if those properties are required (non-null) at the class level. EF Core does not handle this by default.

The main benefits of the TPH mapping strategy are simplicity and performance, which is why it is used by default.

 **Good Practice:** If the discriminator column has many different values, then you can improve performance even more by defining an index on the discriminator. But if there are only a few different values, an index may make overall performance worse because it affects updating time.

# Table-per-type (TPT) mapping strategy

For the `Person-Student-Employee` hierarchy, TPT will use a table for every type, as shown in the following code:

```
CREATE TABLE [People] (
  [Id] int NOT NULL IDENTITY,
  [Name] nvarchar(max) NOT NULL,
  CONSTRAINT [PK_People] PRIMARY KEY ([Id])
);

CREATE TABLE [Students] (
  [Id] int NOT NULL,
  [Subject] nvarchar(max) NULL,
  CONSTRAINT [PK_Students] PRIMARY KEY ([Id])
  CONSTRAINT [FK_Students_People] FOREIGN KEY ([Id]) REFERENCES [People] ([Id])
);

CREATE TABLE [Employees] (
  [Id] int NOT NULL,
  [HireDate] nvarchar(max) NULL,
  CONSTRAINT [PK_Employees] PRIMARY KEY ([Id])
  CONSTRAINT [FK_Employees_People] FOREIGN KEY ([Id]) REFERENCES [People]
([Id])
);
```

Some data in the tables might look like the following.

People table:

| Id | Name |
|----|------|
| 1 | Roman Roy |
| 2 | Kendall Roy |
| 3 | Siobhan Roy |

Students table:

| Id | Subject |
|----|---------|
| 1 | History |

Employees table:

| Id | HireDate |
|----|----------|
| 2 | 02/04/2014 |
| 3 | 12/09/2020 |

The main benefit of the TPT mapping strategy is reduced storage due to the full normalization of the data. The main disadvantage is that a single entity is spread over multiple tables and reconstructing it takes more effort and therefore reduces overall performance. TPT is usually a poor choice, so only use it if the table structure is already normalized and cannot be restructured.

## Table-per-concrete-type (TPC) mapping strategy

For the `Person-Student-Employee` hierarchy, TPC will use a table for each non-abstract type, as shown in the following code:

```
CREATE TABLE [Students] (
  [Id] int NOT NULL DEFAULT (NEXT VALUE FOR [PersonIds]),
  [Name] nvarchar(max) NOT NULL,
  [Subject] nvarchar(max) NULL,
  CONSTRAINT [PK_Students] PRIMARY KEY ([Id])
  CONSTRAINT [FK_Students_People] FOREIGN KEY ([Id]) REFERENCES [People] ([Id])
);

CREATE TABLE [Employees] (
  [Id] int NOT NULL DEFAULT (NEXT VALUE FOR [PersonIds]),
  [Name] nvarchar(max) NOT NULL,
  [HireDate] nvarchar(max) NULL,
  CONSTRAINT [PK_Employees] PRIMARY KEY ([Id])
  CONSTRAINT [FK_Employees_People] FOREIGN KEY ([Id]) REFERENCES [People]
([Id])
);
```

 Since there is not a single table with an **IDENTITY** column to assign Id values, we can use the (**NEXT VALUE FOR [PersonIds]**) command to define a sequence shared between the two tables so they do not assign the same **Id** values.

Some data in the tables might look like the following.

`Students` table:

| Id | Name | Subject |
|----|------|---------|
| 1 | Roman Roy | History |

`Employees` table:

| Id | Name | HireDate |
|----|------|----------|
| 2 | Kendall Roy | 02/04/2014 |
| 3 | Siobhan Roy | 12/09/2020 |

The main benefit of the TPC mapping strategy is performance, because when querying a single concrete type only one table is needed so we avoid expensive joins. It works best for large inheritance hierarchies of many concrete types, each with many type-specific properties.

## Configuring inheritance hierarchy mapping strategies

First, all types must be included in the model, as shown in the following code:

```
public DbSet<Person> People { get; set; }
public DbSet<Student> Students { get; set; }
public DbSet<Employee> Employees { get; set; }
```

For TPH, you are now finished, because it is the default! If you want to make this explicit, then in the data context class OnModelCreating method call the appropriate use mapping strategy method on the base class of the hierarchy, as shown in the following code:

```
modelBuilder.Entity<Person>().UseTphMappingStrategy();
```

To use either of the other two mapping strategies, call the appropriate method, as shown in the following code:

```
modelBuilder.Entity<Person>().UseTptMappingStrategy();
modelBuilder.Entity<Person>().UseTpcMappingStrategy();
```

Next, you can optionally specify the table name to use for each entity class, as shown in the following code:

```
modelBuilder.Entity<Student>().ToTable("Students");
modelBuilder.Entity<Employee>().ToTable("Employees");
```

The TPC strategy should have a shared sequence, so we should configure that too, as shown in the following code:

```
modelBuilder.HasSequence<int>("PersonIds");

modelBuilder.Entity<Person>().UseTpcMappingStrategy()
  .Property(e => e.Id).HasDefaultValueSql("NEXT VALUE FOR [PersonIds]");
```

## Example of hierarchy mapping strategies

Now let's see this in action:

1.  Use your preferred code editor to add a console app project, as defined in the following list:

    *   Project template: **Console App**/console
    *   Workspace/solution file and folder: Chapter02
    *   Project file and folder: Northwind.Console.HierarchyMapping

2.  In the Northwind.Console.HierarchyMapping project, treat warnings as errors, add package references to the EF Core data provider for SQL Server, and globally and statically import the System.Console class, as shown highlighted in the following markup:

```xml
<Project Sdk="Microsoft.NET.Sdk">

  <PropertyGroup>
    <OutputType>Exe</OutputType>
    <TargetFramework>net7.0</TargetFramework>
    <ImplicitUsings>enable</ImplicitUsings>
    <Nullable>enable</Nullable>
    <TreatWarningsAsErrors>true</TreatWarningsAsErrors>
  </PropertyGroup>

  <ItemGroup>
    <PackageReference
      Include="Microsoft.EntityFrameworkCore.Design"
      Version="7.0.0" />
    <PackageReference
      Include="Microsoft.EntityFrameworkCore.SqlServer"
      Version="7.0.0" />
  </ItemGroup>

  <ItemGroup>
    <Using Include="System.Console" Static="true" />
  </ItemGroup>

</Project>
```

3. Build the project to restore packages.

4. Add a new class file named `Person.cs`, and modify its contents, as shown in the following code:

```csharp
using System.ComponentModel.DataAnnotations;

namespace Northwind.Console.HierarchyMapping;

public abstract class Person
{
  public int Id { get; set; }

  [Required]
  [StringLength(40)]
  public string? Name { get; set; }
}
```

5. Add a new class file named `Student.cs`, and modify its contents, as shown in the following code:

```csharp
namespace Northwind.Console.HierarchyMapping;

public class Student : Person
{
  public string? Subject { get; set; }
```

```
    }
```

6. Add a new class file named `Employee.cs`, and modify its contents, as shown in the following code:

```
namespace Northwind.Console.HierarchyMapping;

public class Employee : Person
{
  public DateTime HireDate { get; set; }
}
```

7. Add a new class file named `HierarchyDb.cs`, and modify its contents, as shown in the following code:

```
using Microsoft.EntityFrameworkCore; // DbSet<T>

namespace Northwind.Console.HierarchyMapping;

public class HierarchyDb : DbContext
{
  public DbSet<Person>? People { get; set; }
  public DbSet<Student>? Students { get; set; }
  public DbSet<Employee>? Employees { get; set; }

  public HierarchyDb(DbContextOptions<HierarchyDb> options)
      : base(options)
  {
  }

  protected override void OnModelCreating(ModelBuilder modelBuilder)
  {
    modelBuilder.Entity<Person>()
      .UseTphMappingStrategy();

    // Populate database with sample data.

    Student p1 = new() { Id = 1, Name = "Roman Roy", Subject = "History"
};

    Employee p2 = new() { Id = 2, Name = "Kendall Roy",
      HireDate = new(year: 2014, month: 4, day: 2) };

    Employee p3 = new() { Id = 3, Name = "Siobhan Roy",
      HireDate = new(year: 2020, month: 9, day: 12) };

    modelBuilder.Entity<Student>().HasData(p1);
```

```
    modelBuilder.Entity<Employee>().HasData(p2, p3);
  }
}
```

8. In `Program.cs`, delete the existing statements. Add statements to configure the connection string for the `HierarchyDb` data context and then use it to delete and then create the database, show the automatically generated SQL script, and then output the students, employees, and people, as shown in the following code:

```
using Microsoft.EntityFrameworkCore; // GenerateCreateScript()
using Northwind.Console.HierarchyMapping; // HierarchyDb, Student,
Employee

DbContextOptionsBuilder<HierarchyDb> options = new();

// Modify the connection string manually to use Azure SQL Database or
Edge.
options.UseSqlServer("Data Source=.;Initial
Catalog=HierarchyMapping;Integrated
Security=true;TrustServerCertificate=true;");

using (HierarchyDb db = new(options.Options))
{
  bool deleted = await db.Database.EnsureDeletedAsync();
  WriteLine($"Database deleted: {deleted}");

  bool created = await db.Database.EnsureCreatedAsync();
  WriteLine($"Database created: {created}");

  WriteLine("SQL script used to create the database:");
  WriteLine(db.Database.GenerateCreateScript());

  if (db.Students is null || db.Students.Count() == 0)
  {
    WriteLine("There are no students.");
  }
  else
  {
    foreach (Student student in db.Students)
    {
      WriteLine("{0} studies {1}",
        student.Name, student.Subject);
    }
  }

  if (db.Employees is null || db.Employees.Count() == 0)
```

```
  {
    WriteLine("There are no employees.");
  }
  else
  {
    foreach (Employee employee in db.Employees)
    {
      WriteLine("{0} was hired on {1}",
        employee.Name, employee.HireDate);
    }
  }

  if (db.People is null || db.People.Count() == 0)
  {
    WriteLine("There are no people.");
  }
  else
  {
    foreach (Person person in db.People)
    {
      WriteLine("{0} has ID of {1}",
        person.Name, person.Id);
    }
  }
}
```

9. Start the console app, and note the results including the single table named `People` that is created, as shown in the following output:

```
Database deleted: False
Database created: True
SQL script used to create the database:
CREATE TABLE [People] (
    [Id] int NOT NULL IDENTITY,
    [Name] nvarchar(40) NOT NULL,
    [Discriminator] nvarchar(max) NOT NULL,
    [HireDate] datetime2 NULL,
    [Subject] nvarchar(max) NULL,
    CONSTRAINT [PK_People] PRIMARY KEY ([Id])
);
GO

IF EXISTS (SELECT * FROM [sys].[identity_columns] WHERE [name] IN
(N'Id', N'Discriminator', N'Name', N'Subject') AND [object_id] = OBJECT_
ID(N'[People]'))
    SET IDENTITY_INSERT [People] ON;
INSERT INTO [People] ([Id], [Discriminator], [Name], [Subject])
```

```
    VALUES (1, N'Student', N'Roman Roy', N'History');
    IF EXISTS (SELECT * FROM [sys].[identity_columns] WHERE [name] IN
    (N'Id', N'Discriminator', N'Name', N'Subject') AND [object_id] = OBJECT_
    ID(N'[People]'))
        SET IDENTITY_INSERT [People] OFF;
    GO


    IF EXISTS (SELECT * FROM [sys].[identity_columns] WHERE [name] IN
    (N'Id', N'Discriminator', N'HireDate', N'Name') AND [object_id] = OBJECT_
    ID(N'[People]'))
        SET IDENTITY_INSERT [People] ON;
    INSERT INTO [People] ([Id], [Discriminator], [HireDate], [Name])
    VALUES (2, N'Employee', '2014-04-02T00:00:00.0000000', N'Kendall Roy'),
    (3, N'Employee', '2020-09-12T00:00:00.0000000', N'Siobhan Roy');
    IF EXISTS (SELECT * FROM [sys].[identity_columns] WHERE [name] IN
    (N'Id', N'Discriminator', N'HireDate', N'Name') AND [object_id] = OBJECT_
    ID(N'[People]'))
        SET IDENTITY_INSERT [People] OFF;
    GO


    Roman Roy studies History
    Kendall Roy was hired on 02/04/2014 00:00:00
    Siobhan Roy was hired on 12/09/2020 00:00:00
    Roman Roy has ID of 1
    Kendall Roy has ID of 2
    Siobhan Roy has ID of 3
```

10. In your preferred database tool, view the contents of the People table, as shown in *Figure 2.13*:

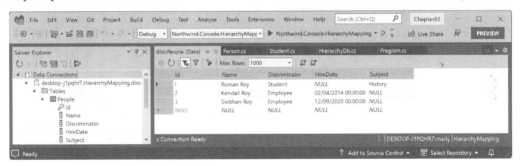

*Figure 2.13: The People table when using the TPH mapping strategy*

11. Close the connection to the HierarchyMapping database.

12. In HierarchyDb.cs, comment out the method call that configures TPH and add a call to the method that configures TPT, as shown highlighted in the following code:

```
protected override void OnModelCreating(ModelBuilder modelBuilder)
{
  modelBuilder.Entity<Person>()
    // .UseTphMappingStrategy();
```

```
.UseTptMappingStrategy();
```

13. Start the console app, and note the results including the three tables named People, Students, and Employees that are created, as shown in the following partial output:

```
Database deleted: True
Database created: True
SQL script used to create the database:
CREATE TABLE [People] (
    [Id] int NOT NULL IDENTITY,
    [Name] nvarchar(40) NOT NULL,
    CONSTRAINT [PK_People] PRIMARY KEY ([Id])
);
GO


CREATE TABLE [Employees] (
    [Id] int NOT NULL,
    [HireDate] datetime2 NOT NULL,
    CONSTRAINT [PK_Employees] PRIMARY KEY ([Id]),
    CONSTRAINT [FK_Employees_People_Id] FOREIGN KEY ([Id]) REFERENCES
[People] ([Id])
);
GO


CREATE TABLE [Students] (
    [Id] int NOT NULL,
    [Subject] nvarchar(max) NULL,
    CONSTRAINT [PK_Students] PRIMARY KEY ([Id]),
    CONSTRAINT [FK_Students_People_Id] FOREIGN KEY ([Id]) REFERENCES
[People] ([Id])
);
GO
```

14. In your preferred database tool, view the contents of the tables, as shown in *Figure 2.14*:

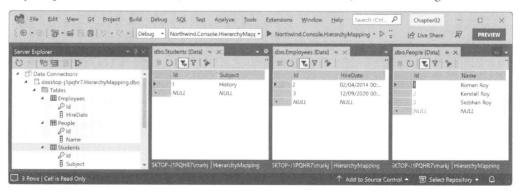

*Figure 2.14: The tables when using the TPT mapping strategy*

15. Close the connection to the `HierarchyMapping` database.

16. In `HierarchyDb.cs`, comment out the method call that configures TPT. Add a call to the method that configures TPC and configure a sequence to track assigned ID values starting at four because we always add three sample rows, as shown highlighted in the following code:

```
protected override void OnModelCreating(ModelBuilder modelBuilder)
{
    modelBuilder.Entity<Person>()
        // .UseTphMappingStrategy();
        // .UseTptMappingStrategy();
        .UseTpcMappingStrategy()
        .Property(person => person.Id)
        .HasDefaultValueSql("NEXT VALUE FOR [PersonIds]");

    modelBuilder.HasSequence<int>("PersonIds", builder =>
    {
        builder.StartsAt(4);
    });
```

17. Start the console app, and note the results including the two tables named `Students` and `Employees` that are created as well as the shared sequence that starts at 4, as shown in the following partial output:

```
CREATE SEQUENCE [PersonIds] AS int START WITH 4 INCREMENT BY 1 NO
MINVALUE NO MAXVALUE NO CYCLE;
GO

CREATE TABLE [Employees] (
    [Id] int NOT NULL DEFAULT (NEXT VALUE FOR [PersonIds]),
    [Name] nvarchar(40) NOT NULL,
    [HireDate] datetime2 NOT NULL,
    CONSTRAINT [PK_Employees] PRIMARY KEY ([Id])
);
GO

CREATE TABLE [Students] (
    [Id] int NOT NULL DEFAULT (NEXT VALUE FOR [PersonIds]),
    [Name] nvarchar(40) NOT NULL,
    [Subject] nvarchar(max) NULL,
    CONSTRAINT [PK_Students] PRIMARY KEY ([Id])
);
GO
```

18. In your preferred database tool, view the contents of the tables, as shown in *Figure 2.15*:

*Figure 2.15: The tables when using the TPC mapping strategy*

19. Close the connection to the `HierarchyMapping` database.

# Building a reusable entity data model

Practical applications usually need to work with data in a relational database or another data store. Earlier in this chapter, we defined EF Core models in the same console app project that we used them in. Now, we will define an entity data model for the Northwind database as a pair of reusable class libraries. One part of the pair will define the entities like `Product` and `Customer`. The second part of the pair will define the tables in the database, default configuration for how to connect to the database, and use fluent API to configure additional options for the model. This pair of class libraries will be used in many of the apps and services that you create in subsequent chapters.

> **Good Practice:** You should create a separate class library project for your entity data models. This allows easier sharing between backend web servers and frontend desktop, mobile, and Blazor WebAssembly clients.

## Creating a class library for entity models using SQL Server

You will now create the entity models using the `dotnet-ef` tool:

1. Add a new project, as defined in the following list:

    • Project template: **Class Library**/`classlib`

    • Project file and folder: `Northwind.Common.EntityModels.SqlServer`

    • Workspace/solution file and folder: `Chapter02`

2. In the `Northwind.Common.EntityModels.SqlServer` project, treat warnings as errors, and add package references for the SQL Server database provider and EF Core design-time support, as shown highlighted in the following markup:

```
<Project Sdk="Microsoft.NET.Sdk">
```

```
  <PropertyGroup>
    <TargetFramework>net7.0</TargetFramework>
    <ImplicitUsings>enable</ImplicitUsings>
    <Nullable>enable</Nullable>
    <TreatWarningsAsErrors>true</TreatWarningsAsErrors>
  </PropertyGroup>

  <ItemGroup>
    <PackageReference
      Include="Microsoft.EntityFrameworkCore.SqlServer" Version="7.0.0"
/>
    <PackageReference
      Include="Microsoft.EntityFrameworkCore.Design" Version="7.0.0">
      <PrivateAssets>all</PrivateAssets>
    <IncludeAssets>runtime; build; native; contentfiles; analyzers;
buildtransitive</IncludeAssets>
    </PackageReference>
  </ItemGroup>

</Project>
```

3. Delete the `Class1.cs` file.

4. Build the `Northwind.Common.EntityModels.SqlServer` project.

5. Open a command prompt or terminal for the `Northwind.Common.EntityModels.SqlServer` folder.

 The next step assumes a database connection string for a local SQL Server authenticated with Windows Integrated security. Modify it for Azure SQL Database or Azure SQL Edge with a user ID and password if necessary.

6. At the command line, generate entity class models for all tables, as shown in the following commands:

```
dotnet ef dbcontext scaffold "Data Source=.;Initial
Catalog=Northwind;Integrated Security=true;TrustServerCertificate=True;"
Microsoft.EntityFrameworkCore.SqlServer --namespace Packt.Shared --data-
annotations
```

Note the following:

- The command to perform: `dbcontext scaffold`
- The connection string: `"Data Source=.;Initial Catalog=Northwind;Integrated Security=true;TrustServerCertificate=True;"`
- The database provider: `Microsoft.EntityFrameworkCore.SqlServer`
- The namespace for the generated classes: `--namespace Packt.Shared`

- To use data annotations as well as the Fluent API: `--data-annotations`

7.  Note that 28 classes were generated, from `AlphabeticalListOfProduct.cs` to `Territory.cs`.

8.  In `Customer.cs`, the `dotnet-ef` tool correctly identified that the `CustomerId` column is the primary key and it is limited to a maximum of five characters, but we also want the values to always be uppercase. So, add a regular expression to validate its primary key value to only allow uppercase Western characters, as shown highlighted in the following code:

```
[Key]
[StringLength(5)]
[RegularExpression("[A-Z]{5}")]
public string CustomerId { get; set; } = null!;
```

# Creating a class library for the data context using SQL Server

Next, you will move the context model that represents the database to a separate class library:

1.  Add a new project, as defined in the following list:

    - Project template: **Class Library**/`classlib`
    - Project file and folder: `Northwind.Common.DataContext.SqlServer`
    - Workspace/solution file and folder: `Chapter02`
    - In Visual Studio Code, select `Northwind.Common.DataContext.SqlServer` as the active OmniSharp project.

2.  In the `DataContext` project, treat warnings as errors, add a project reference to the `EntityModels` project, and add a package reference to the EF Core data provider for SQL Server, as shown highlighted in the following markup:

```
<Project Sdk="Microsoft.NET.Sdk">

  <PropertyGroup>
    <TargetFramework>net7.0</TargetFramework>
    <ImplicitUsings>enable</ImplicitUsings>
    <Nullable>enable</Nullable>
    <TreatWarningsAsErrors>true</TreatWarningsAsErrors>
  </PropertyGroup>

  <ItemGroup>
    <PackageReference
      Include="Microsoft.EntityFrameworkCore.SqlServer" Version="7.0.0"
/>
  </ItemGroup>

  <ItemGroup>
    <ProjectReference Include="..\Northwind.Common.EntityModels
.SqlServer\Northwind.Common.EntityModels.SqlServer.csproj" />
```

```
    </ItemGroup>

  </Project>
```

**Warning!** The path to the project reference should not have a line break in your project file.

3. In the `Northwind.Common.DataContext.SqlServer` project, delete the `Class1.cs` file.

4. Build the `Northwind.Common.DataContext.SqlServer` project.

5. Move the `NorthwindContext.cs` file from the `Northwind.Common.EntityModels.SqlServer` project/folder to the `Northwind.Common.DataContext.SqlServer` project/folder.

6. In the `Northwind.Common.DataContext.SqlServer` project, in `NorthwindContext.cs`, remove the compiler warning about the connection string.

7. In the `Northwind.Common.DataContext.SqlServer` project, add a class named `NorthwindContextExtensions.cs`, and modify its contents to define an extension method that adds the Northwind database context to a collection of dependency services, as shown in the following code:

```csharp
using Microsoft.EntityFrameworkCore; // UseSqlServer
using Microsoft.Extensions.DependencyInjection; // IServiceCollection

namespace Packt.Shared;

public static class NorthwindContextExtensions
{
  /// <summary>
  /// Adds NorthwindContext to the specified IServiceCollection. Uses the
SqlServer database provider.
  /// </summary>
  /// <param name="services"></param>
  /// <param name="connectionString">Set to override the default.</param>
  /// <returns>An IServiceCollection that can be used to add more
services.</returns>
  public static IServiceCollection AddNorthwindContext(
    this IServiceCollection services,
    string connectionString = "Data Source=.;Initial Catalog=Northwind;"
+
      "Integrated
Security=true;MultipleActiveResultsets=true;Encrypt=false")
  {
    services.AddDbContext<NorthwindContext>(options =>
    {
      options.UseSqlServer(connectionString);
```

```
        options.LogTo(Console.WriteLine,
          new[] { Microsoft.EntityFrameworkCore
            .Diagnostics.RelationalEventId.CommandExecuting });
      });

    return services;
    }
  }
```

8.  Build the two class libraries and fix any compiler errors.

 **Good Practice:** We have provided an optional argument for the `AddNorthwindContext` method so that we can override the SQL Server database connection string. This will allow us more flexibility, for example, to load these values from a configuration file.

# Calculated properties on entity creation

EF Core 7 adds an `IMaterializationInterceptor` interface that allows interception before and after an entity is created, and when properties are initialized. This is useful for calculated values.

For example, when a service or client app requests entities to show to the user, it might want to cache a copy of the entity for a period of time. To do this, it needs to know when the entity was last refreshed. It would be useful if this information was automatically generated and stored with each entity.

To achieve this goal, we must complete four steps:

1.  First, define an interface with the extra property.
2.  Next, at least one entity model class must implement the interface.
3.  Then, define a class that implements the interceptor interface with a method named `InitializedInstance` that will execute on any entity, and if that entity implements the custom interface with the extra property, then it will set its value.
4.  Finally, we must create an instance of the interceptor and register it in the data context class.

Now let's implement this for Northwind `Employee` entities:

1.  In the `Northwind.Common.EntityModels.SqlServer` project, add a new file named `IHasLastRefreshed.cs`, and modify its contents to define the interface, as shown in the following code:

```
namespace Packt.Shared;

public interface IHasLastRefreshed
{
  DateTimeOffset LastRefreshed { get; set; }
}
```

2.   In the `Northwind.Common.EntityModels.SqlServer` project, in `Employee.cs`, implement the interface, as shown highlighted in the following code:

```
public partial class Employee : IHasLastRefreshed
{
  ...

  [NotMapped]
  public DateTimeOffset LastRefreshed { get; set; }
}
```

3.   In the `Northwind.Common.DataContext.SqlServer` project, add a new file named `SetLastRefreshedInterceptor.cs`, and modify its contents to define the interceptor, as shown in the following code:

```
// IMaterializationInterceptor, MaterializationInterceptionData
using Microsoft.EntityFrameworkCore.Diagnostics;

namespace Packt.Shared;

public class SetLastRefreshedInterceptor : IMaterializationInterceptor
{
  public object InitializedInstance(
    MaterializationInterceptionData materializationData,
    object entity)
  {
    if (entity is IHasLastRefreshed entityWithLastRefreshed)
    {
      entityWithLastRefreshed.LastRefreshed = DateTimeOffset.UtcNow;
    }
    return entity;
  }
}
```

4.   In the `Northwind.Common.DataContext.SqlServer` project, in `NorthwindContext.cs`, register the interceptor, as shown highlighted in the following code:

```
public partial class NorthwindContext : DbContext
{
  private static readonly SetLastRefreshedInterceptor
    setLastRefreshedInterceptor = new();
...
  protected override void OnConfiguring(DbContextOptionsBuilder
optionsBuilder)
  {
    if (!optionsBuilder.IsConfigured)
    {
      optionsBuilder.UseSqlServer("...");
```

```
    }
    optionsBuilder.AddInterceptors(setLastRefreshedInterceptor);
  }
  ...
}
```

5. Save changes.

# Creating a test project to check the integration of the class libraries

Since we will not be creating a client project in this chapter that uses the EF Core model, we should create a test project to make sure the database context and entity models integrate correctly:

1. Use your preferred coding tool to add a new **xUnit Test Project [C#]**/xunit project named Northwind.Common.EntityModels.Tests to the Chapter02 workspace/solution.

2. In Northwind.Common.EntityModels.Tests.csproj, modify the configuration to treat warnings as errors and to add an item group with a project reference to the Northwind.Common.DataContext.SqlServer project, as shown in the following markup:

```
<ItemGroup>
  <ProjectReference Include="..\Northwind.Common.DataContext
.SqlServer\Northwind.Common.DataContext.SqlServer.csproj" />
</ItemGroup>
```

 **Warning!** The path to the project reference should not have a line break in your project file.

3. Build the Northwind.Common.EntityModels.Tests project.

# Writing unit tests for entity models

A well-written unit test will have three parts:

- **Arrange:** This part will declare and instantiate variables for input and output.
- **Act:** This part will execute the unit that you are testing. In our case, that means calling the method that we want to test.
- **Assert:** This part will make one or more assertions about the output. An assertion is a belief that, if not true, indicates a failed test. For example, when adding 2 and 2, we would expect the result to be 4.

Now, we will write some unit tests for the NorthwindContext and entity model classes:

1. Rename the file UnitTest1.cs to NorthwindEntityModelsTests.cs and then open it.

2. In Visual Studio Code, rename the class to `NorthwindEntityModelsTests`. (Visual Studio prompts you to rename the class when you rename the file.)

3. Modify the `NorthwindEntityModelsTests` class to import the `Packt.Shared` namespace and have some test methods for ensuring the context class can connect, ensuring the provider is SQL Server, and ensuring the first product is named `Chai`, as shown in the following code:

```
using Packt.Shared;

namespace Northwind.Common.EntityModels.Tests
{
  public class NorthwindEntityModelsTests
  {
    [Fact]
    public void CanConnectIsTrue()
    {
      using (NorthwindContext db = new()) // arrange
      {
        bool canConnect = db.Database.CanConnect(); // act

        Assert.True(canConnect); // assert
      }
    }

    [Fact]
    public void ProviderIsSqlServer()
    {
      using (NorthwindContext db = new())
      {
        string? provider = db.Database.ProviderName;

        Assert.Equal("Microsoft.EntityFrameworkCore.SqlServer",
provider);
      }
    }

    [Fact]
    public void ProductId1IsChai()
    {
      using(NorthwindContext db = new())
      {
        Product product1 = db.Products.Single(p => p.ProductId == 1);

        Assert.Equal("Chai", product1.ProductName);
      }
    }
```

```
    [Fact]
    public void EmployeeHasLastRefreshedIn10sWindow()
    {
      using (NorthwindContext db = new())
      {
        Employee employee1 = db.Employees.Single(p => p.EmployeeId == 1);

        DateTimeOffset now = DateTimeOffset.UtcNow;

        Assert.InRange(actual: employee1.LastRefreshed,
          low: now.Subtract(TimeSpan.FromSeconds(5)),
          high: now.AddSeconds(5));
      }
    }
  }
}
```

# Running unit tests using Visual Studio 2022

Now we are ready to run the unit tests and see the results:

1.  In Visual Studio 2022, navigate to **Test | Run All Tests**.
2.  In **Test Explorer**, note that the results indicate that some tests ran, and all passed.

# Running unit tests using Visual Studio Code

Now we are ready to run the unit tests and see the results:

1.  In Visual Studio Code, in the `Northwind.Common.EntityModels.Tests` project's **TERMINAL** window, run the tests, as shown in the following command:

```
dotnet test
```

2.  In the output, note that the results indicate that some tests ran, and all passed.

 As an optional task, can you think of other tests you could write to make sure the database context and entity models are correct?

# Cleaning up data resources

When you are done with a SQL Server database, you can clean up the resources used.

## Removing Azure resources

You can now remove the resources used by SQL Database to save costs:

**Warning!** If you do not remove the resources used by an Azure SQL Database, then you will incur costs.

1. In the Azure portal, find the resource group named `apps-services-net7`.
2. Click **Delete**.
3. Enter the name of the resource group.
4. Click **Delete**.

## Removing Docker resources

You could now remove the resources used by Docker, but many of the other chapters in this book will need to connect to a Northwind database in SQL Server.

If you have completed all the chapters in the book, or plan to use full SQL Server or Azure SQL Database, and now want to remove all the Docker resources, then follow these steps:

1. At the command prompt or terminal, stop the `azuresqledge` container, as shown in the following command:

```
docker stop azuresqledge
```

2. At the command prompt or terminal, remove the `azuresqledge` container, as shown in the following command:

```
docker rm azuresqledge
```

 Removing the container will delete all data inside it.

3. At the command prompt or terminal, remove the `azure-sql-edge` image to release its disk space, as shown in the following command:

```
docker rmi mcr.microsoft.com/azure-sql-edge
```

## Practicing and exploring

Test your knowledge and understanding by answering some questions, getting some hands-on practice, and exploring this chapter's topics with deeper research.

# Exercise 2.1 – Test your knowledge

Answer the following questions:

1. Which NuGet package should you reference in a .NET project to get the best performance when working with data in SQL Server?
2. What is the safest way to define a database connection string for SQL Server?
3. What must T-SQL parameters and variables be prefixed with?
4. What must you do before reading an output parameter of a command executed using `ExecuteReader`?
5. What can the `dotnet-ef` tool be used for?
6. What type would you use for the property that represents a table, for example, the `Products` property of a data context?
7. What type would you use for the property that represents a one-to-many relationship, for example, the `Products` property of a `Category` entity?
8. What is the EF Core convention for primary keys?
9. Why might you choose the Fluent API in preference to annotation attributes?
10. Why might you implement the `IMaterializationInterceptor` interface in an entity type?

# Exercise 2.2 – Practice benchmarking ADO.NET against EF Core

In the `Chapter02` solution/workspace, create a console app named `Ch02Ex02_ADONETvsEFCore` that uses Benchmark.NET to compare retrieving all the products from the Northwind database using ADO.NET (`SqlClient`) and using EF Core.

 You can learn how to use Benchmark.NET by reading *Chapter 4, Benchmarking Performance, Multitasking, and Concurrency*.

# Exercise 2.3 – Explore topics

Use the links on the following page to learn more details about the topics covered in this chapter:

```
https://github.com/markjprice/apps-services-net7/blob/main/book-links.md#chapter-2---
managing-relational-data-using-sql-server
```

# Exercise 2.4 – Explore Dapper

Dapper is an alternative ORM to EF Core. It is more efficient because it extends the low-level ADO.NET `IDbConnection` interface with very basic functionality.

In the `Northwind.Console.SqlClient` project, add a package reference for `Dapper`, and then add a class to represent a supplier, as shown in the following code:

```
public class Supplier
{
  public int SupplierId { get; set; }
  public string? CompanyName { get; set; }
  public string? City { get; set; }
  public string? Country { get; set; }
}
```

In `Program.cs`, add statements to retrieve `Supplier` entities in Germany, as shown in the following code:

```
IEnumerable<Supplier> suppliers = connection.Query<Supplier>(
  sql: "SELECT * FROM Suppliers WHERE Country=@Country",
  param: new { Country = "Germany" });

foreach (Supplier supplier in suppliers)
{
  WriteLine("{0}: {1}, {2}, {3}",
    supplier.SupplierId, supplier.CompanyName,
    supplier.City, supplier.Country);
}
```

You can learn more about Dapper at the following link:

```
https://github.com/DapperLib/Dapper/blob/main/Readme.md
```

 I am considering adding a section about Dapper to the next edition of this book. Please let me know if this if something that I should prioritize. Thanks!

## Summary

In this chapter, you learned:

- How to connect to an existing SQL Server database.
- How to execute a simple query and process the results using fast and low-level ADO.NET.
- How to execute a simple query and process the results using the slower but more object-oriented EF Core.
- How to configure and decide between three mapping strategies for type hierarchies.
- How to implement calculated properties on entity creation.

In the next chapter, you will learn how to use cloud-native data storage with Azure Cosmos DB.

# 3

# Managing NoSQL Data Using Azure Cosmos DB

This chapter is about managing NoSQL data by using Azure Cosmos DB. You will learn some of the key concepts about Cosmos DB like its APIs, ways to model your data, and throughput provisioning, which influences costs. You will create some Cosmos DB resources using the local emulator and in the Azure cloud. Then you will learn how to work with more traditional data using Core (SQL) API. Finally, you will learn how to work with graph data using Gremlin API (online section).

This chapter will cover the following topics:

- Understanding NoSQL databases
- Creating Cosmos DB resources
- Manipulating data with Core (SQL) API
- Manipulating graph data with Gremlin API (online section)
- Cleaning up Azure resources

## Understanding NoSQL databases

Two of the most common places to store data are in a **Relational Database Management System** (**RDBMS**) such as SQL Server, PostgreSQL, MySQL, and SQLite, or in a **NoSQL** database such as Azure Cosmos DB, Redis, MongoDB, and Apache Cassandra.

Relational databases were invented in the 1970s. They are queried with **Structured Query Language** (**SQL**). At the time, data storage costs were high, so relational databases were designed to reduce data duplication as much as possible. Data is stored in tabular structures with rows and columns that are tricky to refactor once in production. They can be difficult and expensive to scale.

NoSQL does not just mean "no SQL"; it can also mean "not only SQL". NoSQL databases were invented in the 2000s, after the internet and the web had become popular and adopted many of the learnings from that era of software.

They are designed for massive scalability, high performance, and to make programming easier by providing maximum flexibility and allowing schema changes at any time because they do not enforce a structure.

## Cosmos DB and its APIs

Azure Cosmos DB is a NoSQL data store that supports multiple APIs. Its native API is SQL-based. It also supports alternative APIs like MongoDB, Cassandra, and Gremlin.

Azure Cosmos DB stores data in **atom-record-sequence** (**ARS**) format. You interact with this data via an API that you choose when you create the database:

- The **API for MongoDB** supports the MongoDB wire protocol versions 3.2, 3.6, 4.0, and 4.2, which allow existing clients to work with the data as if they are interacting with an actual MongoDB database. Tools like `mongodump` and `mongorestore` can be used to move any existing data into Azure Cosmos DB. You can find the latest MongoDB support at the following link: `https://docs.microsoft.com/en-us/azure/cosmos-db/mongodb/mongodb-introduction#how-the-api-works`.

- The **API for Cassandra** supports the **Cassandra Query Language** (**CQL**) wire protocol version 4, which allows existing clients to work with the data as if they are interacting with an actual Cassandra database.

- For a new project, sometimes known as a "greenfield " project, Microsoft recommends **Core (SQL) API**.

- For existing projects that use alternative APIs like Azure Table, you could choose to use the appropriate API so that your clients and tools do not need to be updated while gaining the benefits of data stored in Azure Cosmos DB. This reduces migration costs.

- If the relationships between data items have metadata that needs analyzing, then using **Gremlin API for Cosmos DB** to treat Cosmos DB as a graph data store is a good choice.

 **Good Practice:** If you are unsure which API to choose, select Core (SQL) as the default.

In this book, we will first use the native Core (SQL) API for Cosmos DB. This allows the developer to query JSON documents using a language like SQL. Core (SQL) API uses JSON's type system and JavaScript's function system.

Later in this chapter, we will use the Azure Cosmos DB graph API, which uses the Gremlin API.

## Document modeling

A typical JSON document representing a product from the Northwind database, the example database that we used in *Chapter 2, Managing Relational Data Using SQL Server*, when stored in Azure Cosmos DB might look like the following:

```json
{
  "id": "1",
  "productId": "1",
  "productName": "Chai",
  "supplier": {
    "supplierId": 1,
    "companyName": "Exotic Liquids",
    "contactName": "Charlotte Cooper",
    "Address": "49 Gilbert St.",
    "City": "London",
    "Country": "UK",
    "Phone": "(171) 555-2222"
  },
  "category": {
    "categoryId": 1,
    "categoryName": "Beverages",
    "description": "Soft drinks, coffees, teas, beers, and ales",
    "image": "https://myaccount.blob.core.windows.net/categories/beverages.png"
  },
  "quantityPerUnit": "10 boxes x 20 bags",
  "unitPrice": 18.0000,
  "unitsInStock": 39,
  "unitsOnOrder": 0,
  "reorderLevel": 10,
  "discontinued": false
}
```

Unlike with a relational database model, it is common to **embed** related data. That means duplicating data, like the category and supplier information, in many products. This is good practice if the related data is bounded.

For example, for a product there will only ever be one supplier and one category, so those relationships are bounded to one. If we were modeling a category and decided to embed its related products, then that could be poor practice because having all the product details as an array would be unbounded. Instead, we might choose to only store a unique identifier for each product and reference the product details stored elsewhere.

You should also consider how frequently the related data is updated. The more frequently it needs to be updated, the more you should avoid embedding it. If related data is unbounded but infrequently updated, then embedding might still be a good choice.

Deliberately but carefully denormalizing parts of your data model means you will need to execute fewer queries and updates for common operations, reducing cost both in money and performance.

Use embedding (denormalized data) when:

- The relationships are contained, like property owned by a person, or the children of a parent.
- The relationships are one-to-one or one-to-few, i.e., the related data is bounded.

- The related data needs infrequent updates.
- The related data often or always needs to be included in query results.

 **Good Practice:** Denormalized data models provide better read performance but worse write performance.

Imagine that you want to model an article and its comments on a popular news website. The comments are unbounded and for an engaging article would frequently be added to, especially during the hours or days after it is published while it is topical news. Or imagine an investor with stock they trade. The current price of that stock would be frequently updated.

In these scenarios, you would want to **normalize** the related data either wholly or partially. For example, you could choose to embed the most liked comments that will be shown at the top of the list directly under the article. Other comments could be stored separately and referenced using their primary keys. You could choose to embed stock information for long-term investments that are held for many years, like the price the investment was purchased at and the price at on the first day of each month since then (but not the current live price), but reference stock information for short-term investments for day trading.

Use referencing (normalized data) when:

- The relationships are one-to-many or many-to-many and unbounded.
- The related data needs frequent updates.

 **Good Practice:** Normalized data models require more queries, which worsens read performance but provides better write performance.

 You can read more about modeling documents in Azure Cosmos DB at the following link: `https://docs.microsoft.com/en-us/azure/cosmos-db/sql/modeling-data`.

## Consistency levels

Azure Cosmos DB is distributed globally and scales elastically. It relies on replication to provide low latency and high availability all over the world. To achieve this, you must accept and choose tradeoffs.

To ease the life of a programmer, you want total consistency of data. If data is modified anywhere in the world, then any subsequent read operation should see that change. The best consistency is known as **linearizability**. Linearizability increases the latency of write operations and reduces the availability of read operations because Azure Cosmos DB must wait for replication to occur globally.

A more relaxed consistency level improves latency and availability at the cost of potentially increased complexity for the programmer because data might be inconsistent.

Most NoSQL databases only offer two levels of consistency: strong and eventual. Azure Cosmos DB offers five to provide exactly the level of consistency that suits your project.

You choose the level of data consistency, and this will be guaranteed by the Service Level Agreement (SLA), as shown in the following list, ordered from the strongest to the weakest:

- **Strong** consistency guarantees linearizability across all regions globally. All other consistency levels are collectively known as "relaxed".

- **Bounded staleness** consistency guarantees the ability to read your own write within the write region, monotonic read within the region, and consistent prefix, and the staleness of read data is restricted to a specific number of versions for which the reads lag behind the writes within a specified time interval. For example, the time interval might be ten minutes and the number of versions might be three. That would mean that a maximum of three writes can be made in any ten-minute period before a read operation must reflect those changes.

- **Session** consistency guarantees the ability to read your own write within the write region, monotonic read, and consistent prefix.

- **Consistent prefix** consistency only guarantees the order that writes can then be read.

- **Eventual** consistency does not guarantee that the order of writes will match the order of reads. When writes pause, reads will eventually catch up as the replicas synchronize. It is possible for a client to read values older than the ones it read before. **Probabilistic Bounded Staleness (PBS)** is a measurement that shows how eventual your consistency is currently. You can monitor it in the Azure portal.

 You can read more details about consistency levels at the following link: `https://docs.microsoft.com/en-us/azure/cosmos-db/consistency-levels`.

## Hierarchy of components

The hierarchy of components for Azure Cosmos DB are:

- **Account:** You can create up to 50 accounts via the Azure portal.

- **Database:** You can have an unlimited number of databases per account. We will create a database named `Northwind`.

- **Container:** You can have an unlimited number of containers per database. We will create a container named `Products`.

- **Partition:** These are created and managed automatically within a container, and you can have an unlimited number. Partitions are either logical or physical. A **logical partition** contains items with the same partition key and defines the scope for transactions. Multiple logical partitions are mapped to a **physical partition**. Small containers may only need one physical partition.

You should not concern yourself with physical partitions since you have no control over them. Focus on deciding what your partition key should be, because that defines the items stored in a logical partition.

- **Item:** A stored entity in a container. We will add items that represent each product, like chai tea.

"Item" is a deliberately generic term and is used by Core (SQL) API to refer to a JSON document, but can also be used for the other APIs. The other APIs also have their own more specific terms:

- Cassandra uses **row**.
- MongoDB uses **document**.
- Graph databases like Gremlin use **vertex** and **edge**.

# Throughput provisioning

Throughput is measured as **request units per second (RU/s)**. A single **request unit (RU)** is the cost of performing a GET request for a 1KB document using its unique identifier. Creating, updating, and deleting cost more RUs; for example, a query might cost 46.54 RUs, or a delete operation might cost 14.23 RUs.

Throughput must be provisioned in advance, although you can scale up and down at any time in increments or decrements of 100 RU/s. You will be billed per hour.

You can discover how much a request costs in RUs by getting the RequestCharge property. You can learn more at the following link: https://docs.microsoft.com/en-us/azure/cosmos-db/sql/find-request-unit-charge.

You must provision throughput to run CRUD operations (reads, writes, updates, and deletes). You must estimate throughput by calculating the number of operations you'll need to support throughout the year. For example, a commerce website might need to expect much greater throughput at Thanksgiving in the US or Singles Day in China.

Most throughput settings are applied at the container level, or you can do so at the database level and have the settings shared across all containers. Throughput is distributed equally among partitions.

Once provisioned throughput is exhausted, Cosmos DB will start rate limiting access requests, and your code will have to wait and retry later. Luckily, we will use the .NET SDK for Cosmos DB, which automatically reads the retry-after response header and retries after that time limit.

Using the Azure portal, you can provision between 400 RU/s and 250,000 RU/s. At the time of writing, the 400 RU/s minimum would cost about US$35 per month. You would then also need to add the cost of storage depending on how many GBs you want to store, for example, US$5 for a few GBs.

The free tier of Cosmos DB allows up to 1,000 RU/s and 25 GB of storage. You can use a calculator at the following link: https://cosmos.azure.com/capacitycalculator/.

Factors that affect RUs:

- **Item size**: A 2KB document costs twice as much as a 1KB document.
- **Indexed properties**: Indexing all item properties costs more than indexing a subset of properties.
- **Consistency**: Strict consistency costs twice as many RUs as looser consistency.
- **Query complexity**: The number of predicates (where filters), the number of results, the number of custom functions, projections, the size of the dataset, and so on, all increase the cost in RUs.

# Partition strategies

A good partition strategy allows a Cosmos DB database to grow and efficiently run queries and transactions. A good partition strategy is about choosing a suitable **partition key**. It is set for a container and cannot be changed.

The partition key should be chosen to evenly distribute operations across the database to avoid hot partitions, meaning a partition that handles more requests, so it is busier than other partitions.

A property that will be unique for an item and will often be used to look up an item might be a good choice. For example, for US citizens, a person's social security number. However, partition keys do not have to be unique. The partition key value will be combined with an item ID to uniquely identify an item.

Partitions are automatically created by Cosmos DB when needed. There is no negative impact on your applications and services from the automatic creation and deletion of partitions. Each partition can grow up to a maximum of 20 GB. Cosmos DB will automatically split partitions when needed.

A container should have a partition key that possess these attributes:

- High cardinality so that items are distributed evenly across partitions
- Evenly distributed requests across partitions
- Evenly distributed storage across partitions

# Data storage design

With relational databases, the schemas are rigid and inflexible. The Northwind database's products are all food-related so the schema might not change much. But if you are building a commerce system for a company that sells everything from clothes to electronic equipment to books, then a semi-structured data store like the following would be better:

- Clothing: Sizes like S, M L, XL; brand; color.
- Shoes: Sizes like 7, 8, 9; brand; color.
- Televisions: Sizes like 40", 52"; screen technology like OLED, LCD; brand.
- Books: Number of pages; author; publisher.

Being schema-less, Azure Cosmos DB can add new types of products with different structure and properties simply by adding a new product with that structure to a container.

## Migrating data to Cosmos DB

The open-source **Azure Cosmos DB Data Migration tool** can import data into Azure Cosmos DB from many different sources, including Azure Table Storage, SQL databases, MongoDB, text files in JSON and CSV formats, HBase, and more. The tool has both a command-line version and a GUI version.

> We will not use this migration tool in this book, so if you think it will be useful to you, then you can learn how to use it at the following link: `https://docs.microsoft.com/en-us/azure/cosmos-db/import-data`.

# Creating Cosmos DB resources

To see Azure Cosmos DB in action, first, we must create Cosmos DB resources. We can manually create them in the cloud using the Azure portal or programmatically create them using the Azure Cosmos DB .NET SDK. Azure Cosmos DB resources created in the cloud have a cost unless you use a trial or free account.

You can also create Azure Cosmos DB resources locally using an emulator, which will cost you nothing. At the time of writing, the Azure Cosmos DB Emulator only supports Windows. If you want to use Linux or macOS, then you can try to use the Linux Emulator that is currently in preview, or you could host the emulator in a Windows virtual machine.

## Using an emulator on Windows to create Azure Cosmos DB resources

Let's use the Azure Cosmos DB emulator on Windows to create Azure Cosmos DB resources like a database and container:

1. Download and install the latest version of Azure Cosmos DB Emulator on your local Windows computer from the following link (direct to the MSI installer file): `https://aka.ms/cosmosdb-emulator`.

2. Make sure the Azure Cosmos DB Emulator is running.

3. The Azure Cosmos DB Emulator user interface should start automatically but if not, start your favorite browser and navigate to `https://localhost:8081/_explorer/index.html`.

4. Note that the Azure Cosmos DB Emulator is running, hosted at `localhost` on port `8081`, with a **Primary Key** that you will need to securely connect to the service, as shown in *Figure 3.1*:

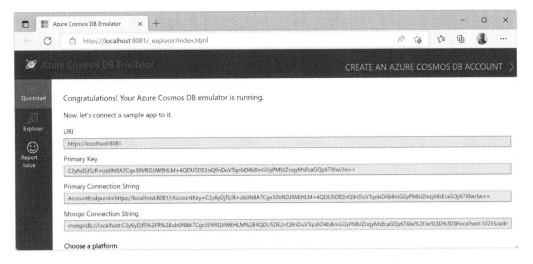

*Figure 3.1: The Azure Cosmos DB Emulator user interface on Windows*

 The default primary key for the emulator is the same value for everyone. You can specify your own key value by starting the emulator at the command line with the /key switch. You can learn about starting the emulator at the command line at the following link: https://docs.microsoft.com/en-us/azure/cosmos-db/emulator-command-line-parameters.

5.  In the navigation bar on the left, click **Explorer.**

6.  Click **New Container,** as shown in *Figure 3.2:*

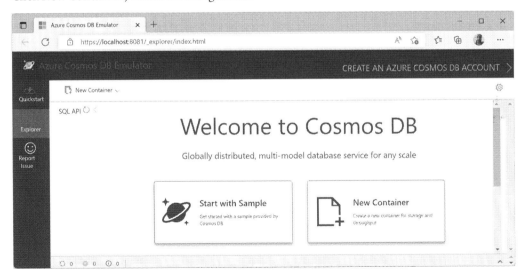

*Figure 3.2: Azure Cosmos DB data explorer*

7.   Complete the following information:

  •   For **Database id**, select **Create new** and enter Northwind. Leave the **Share throughput across containers** check box selected.

  •   For **Database throughput**, select **Autoscale**, and leave **Database max RU/s** as 4000. This will use a minimum of 400 RU/s and autoscale up to 4,000 RU/s when needed.

  •   For **Container id**, enter Products.

  •   For **Partition key**, enter /productId.

8.   Click **OK**.

9.   Expand the **Northwind** database, expand the **Products** container, and select **Items,** as shown in *Figure 3.3*:

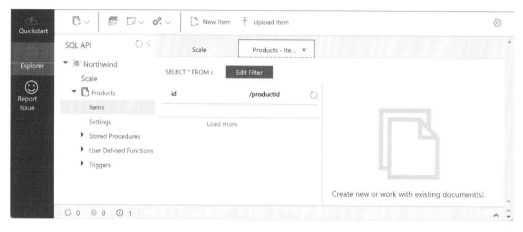

*Figure 3.3: The empty items in the Products container in the Northwind database*

10.  In the toolbar, click **New Item**.

11.  Replace the contents of the editor window with a JSON document that represents a product named Chai, as shown in the following JSON:

```
{
  "productId": 1,
  "productName": "Chai",
  "supplier": {
    "supplierId": 1,
    "companyName": "Exotic Liquids",
    "contactName": "Charlotte Cooper",
    "Address": "49 Gilbert St.",
    "City": "London",
    "Country": "UK",
    "Phone": "(171) 555-2222"
  },
  "category": {
    "categoryId": 1,
```

```
        "categoryName": "Beverages",
        "description": "Soft drinks, coffees, teas, beers, and ales"
    },
    "quantityPerUnit": "10 boxes x 20 bags",
    "unitPrice": 18,
    "unitsInStock": 39,
    "unitsOnOrder": 0,
    "reorderLevel": 10,
    "discontinued": false
}
```

12. Click **Save**, and note the extra properties that are automatically added to any item, including id, _etag, and _ts, as shown highlighted in the following JSON:

```
{
    "productId": 1,
    "productName": "Chai",
    "supplier": {
        "supplierId": 1,
        "companyName": "Exotic Liquids",
        "contactName": "Charlotte Cooper",
        "Address": "49 Gilbert St.",
        "City": "London",
        "Country": "UK",
        "Phone": "(171) 555-2222"
    },
    "category": {
        "categoryId": 1,
        "categoryName": "Beverages",
        "description": "Soft drinks, coffees, teas, beers, and ales"
    },
    "quantityPerUnit": "10 boxes x 20 bags",
    "unitPrice": 18,
    "unitsInStock": 39,
    "unitsOnOrder": 0,
    "reorderLevel": 10,
    "discontinued": false,
    "id": "2ad4c71d-d0e4-4ebd-a146-bcf052f8d7d6",
    "_rid": "bmAuAJ9o6I8BAAAAAAAAAA==",
    "_self": "dbs/bmAuAA==/colls/bmAuAJ9o6I8=/docs/
bmAuAJ9o6I8BAAAAAAAAAA==/",
    "_etag": "\"00000000-0000-0000-8fc2-ec4d49ea01d8\"",
    "_attachments": "attachments/",
    "_ts": 1656952035
}
```

13. Click **New Item**.

14. Replace the contents of the editor window with a JSON document that represents a product named Chang, as shown in the following JSON:

```json
{
    "productId": 2,
    "productName": "Chang",
    "supplier": {
        "supplierId": 1,
        "companyName": "Exotic Liquids",
        "contactName": "Charlotte Cooper",
        "Address": "49 Gilbert St.",
        "City": "London",
        "Country": "UK",
        "Phone": "(171) 555-2222"
    },
    "category": {
        "categoryId": 1,
        "categoryName": "Beverages",
        "description": "Soft drinks, coffees, teas, beers, and ales"
    },
    "quantityPerUnit": "24 - 12 oz bottles",
    "unitPrice": 19,
    "unitsInStock": 17,
    "unitsOnOrder": 40,
    "reorderLevel": 25,
    "discontinued": false
}
```

15. Click **Save**.

16. Click **New Item**.

17. Replace the contents of the editor window with a JSON document that represents a product named Aniseed Syrup, as shown in the following JSON:

```json
{
    "productId": 3,
    "productName": "Aniseed Syrup",
    "supplier": {
        "supplierId": 1,
        "companyName": "Exotic Liquids",
        "contactName": "Charlotte Cooper",
        "Address": "49 Gilbert St.",
        "City": "London",
        "Country": "UK",
        "Phone": "(171) 555-2222"
    },
```

```
    "category": {
      "categoryId": 2,
      "categoryName": "Condiments",
      "description": "Sweet and savory sauces, relishes, spreads, and
  seasonings"
    },
    "quantityPerUnit": "12 - 550 ml bottles",
    "unitPrice": 10,
    "unitsInStock": 13,
    "unitsOnOrder": 70,
    "reorderLevel": 25,
    "discontinued": false
  }
```

18. Click **Save**.

19. Click the first item in the list and note that all the items have been automatically assigned GUID values for their id properties, as shown in *Figure 3.4*:

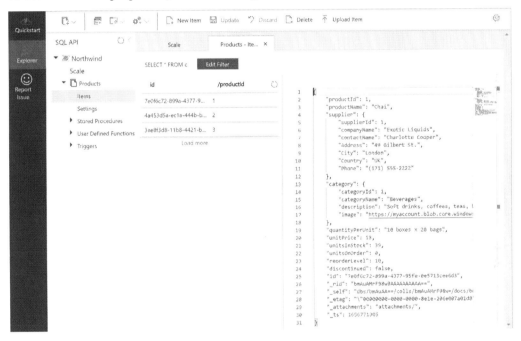

*Figure 3.4: A saved JSON document item in the Azure Cosmos DB Emulator*

20. In the toolbar, click **New SQL Query**, and note the default query text is SELECT * FROM c.

21. Modify the query text to return all products supplied by Exotic Liquids, and note that all three products are included in the array of results, as shown in *Figure 3.5* and in the following query:

```
SELECT * FROM c WHERE c.supplier.companyName = "Exotic Liquids"
```

*Figure 3.5: A query to return all products supplied by Exotic Liquids*

 Words are case-insensitive so WHERE is treated the same as Where or where. Property names are case-sensitive so CompanyName is different from companyName, and will return zero results.

22. Modify the query text to return all products in category 2, as shown in the following query:

```
SELECT * FROM c WHERE c.category.categoryId = 2
```

23. Execute the query and note that one product is included in the array of results.

# Using the Azure portal to create Azure Cosmos DB resources

 If you would prefer to only use the Azure Cosmos DB Emulator to avoid any costs, then feel free to skip this section, or just read through it without completing the steps yourself.

Now, let's use the Azure portal to create Azure Cosmos DB resources like an account, database, and container in the cloud:

1. If you do not have an Azure account, then you can sign up for one for free at the following link: https://azure.microsoft.com/free/.

2. Navigate to the Azure portal and sign in: https://portal.azure.com/.

3. In the Azure portal menu, click **+ Create a resource**.

4. In the **Create a resource** page, search for or click **Azure Cosmos DB**.

5.  In the **Core (SQL) - Recommended** box, click the **Create** button, as shown in *Figure 3.6*:

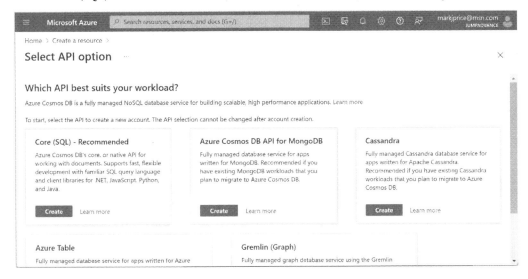

*Figure 3.6: Selecting an API option for Azure Cosmos DB in the cloud*

6.  On the **Basics** tab:

    •   Select your **Subscription**. Mine is named Pay-As-You-Go.

    •   Select a **Resource Group** or create a new one. I used the name apps-services-net7.

    •   Enter an Azure Cosmos DB **Account Name**. I used apps-services-net7.

    •   Select a **Location**. I chose **(Europe) UK West** as it is the closest to me.

    •   Leave **Capacity mode** set to **Provisioned throughput**.

    •   Leave **Apply Free Tier Discount** set to **Do not apply**. Only change this option if you want this account to be the only account within your subscription to be on the free tier. You might be better off saving this discount for another account that you might use for a real project, rather than a temporary learning account while reading this book.

> With Azure Cosmos DB free tier, you will get the first 1,000 RU/s and 25 GB of storage for free in an account. You can only enable free tier on one account per subscription. Microsoft estimates this has a value of a $64/month.

    •   Leave the **Limit total account throughput** check box selected.

7.  Click the **Next: Global Distribution** button and review the options, but leave them at their defaults.

8.  Click the **Next: Networking** button and review the options, but leave them at their defaults.

9.  Click the **Next: Backup Policy** button and review the options, but leave them at their defaults.

10. Click the **Next: Encryption** button and review the options, but leave them at their defaults.

11. Click the **Review + create** button.

12. Note the **Validation Success** message, review the summary, and then click the **Create** button, as shown in *Figure 3.7*:

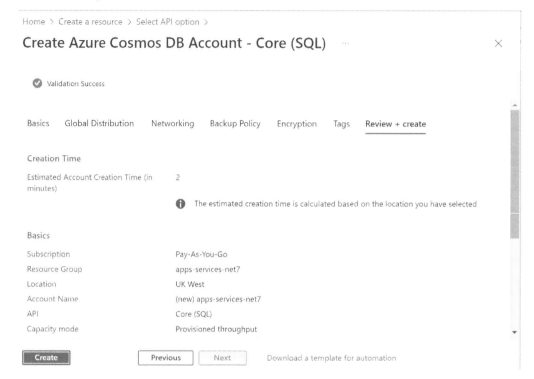

*Figure 3.7: A summary of the Azure Cosmos DB account about to be created in the cloud*

13. Wait for deployment to complete. This will take a few minutes.

14. Click the **Go to resource** button, and note that you are probably directed to the **Quick Start** page with steps to follow to create a container and so on, depending on if this is the first time that you have created an Azure Cosmos DB account.

15. In the left navigation, click **Overview**, and note the information about your Azure Cosmos DB account, as shown in *Figure 3.8*:

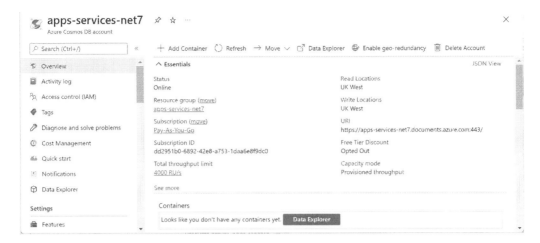

*Figure 3.8: Azure Cosmos DB account Overview page*

16. In the navigation on the left, click **Keys**, and note the **URI** and **Primary Key** needed to programmatically work with this Azure Cosmos DB account, as shown in *Figure 3.9*:

*Figure 3.9: Keys to programmatically work with the Azure Cosmos DB account*

17. In the navigation on the left, click **Data Explorer**, and close the video popup window.

18. In the toolbar, click **New Container**.

19. Complete the steps listed in the emulator section, *Using an emulator on Windows to create Azure Cosmos DB resources*, starting at *step 7* and going up to the end of that section.

# Using a .NET app to create Azure Cosmos DB resources

Next, we will create a console app project for creating the same Azure Cosmos DB resources in either the local emulator or in the cloud, depending on which URI and primary key that you choose to use:

1. Use your preferred code editor to create a new solution/workspace named Chapter03.

2.  Add a console app project, as defined in the following list:

    - Project template: **Console App**/console
    - Workspace/solution file and folder: Chapter03
    - Project file and folder: Northwind.CosmosDb.SqlApi

3.  In the project file, treat warnings as errors, add a package reference for Azure Cosmos, add a project reference to the Northwind data context project that you created in *Chapter 2*, *Managing Relational Data Using SQL Server*, and import the Console class statically and globally, as shown highlighted in the following markup:

```xml
<Project Sdk="Microsoft.NET.Sdk">

  <PropertyGroup>
    <OutputType>Exe</OutputType>
    <TargetFramework>net7.0</TargetFramework>
    <ImplicitUsings>enable</ImplicitUsings>
    <Nullable>enable</Nullable>
    <TreatWarningsAsErrors>true</TreatWarningsAsErrors>
  </PropertyGroup>

  <ItemGroup>
    <PackageReference Include="Microsoft.Azure.Cosmos" Version="3.26.1" />
  </ItemGroup>

  <ItemGroup>
    <ProjectReference Include="..\..\Chapter02\Northwind.Common.DataContext.SqlServer\Northwind.Common.DataContext.SqlServer.csproj" />
  </ItemGroup>

  <ItemGroup>
    <Using Include="System.Console" Static="true" />
  </ItemGroup>

</Project>
```

4.  Build the Northwind.CosmosDb.SqlApi project at the command line or terminal using the following command: dotnet build.

5.  Add a class file named Program.Helpers.cs.

6.  Modify its contents, as shown in the following code:

```csharp
partial class Program
{
  static void SectionTitle(string title)
  {
```

```
        ConsoleColor previousColor = ForegroundColor;
        ForegroundColor = ConsoleColor.DarkYellow;
        WriteLine("*");
        WriteLine($"* {title}");
        WriteLine("*");
        ForegroundColor = previousColor;
    }
}
```

7. Add a class file named `Program.Methods.cs`.

8. In `Program.Methods.cs`, add statements to import the namespace for working with Azure Cosmos. Then, define a method for the `Program` class that creates a Cosmos client and uses it to create a database named `Northwind` and a container named `Products`, in either the local emulator or in the cloud, as shown in the following code:

```csharp
// CosmosClient, DatabaseResponse, Database, IndexingPolicy, and so on
using Microsoft.Azure.Cosmos;

using System.Net; // HttpStatusCode

partial class Program
{
    // to use Azure Cosmos DB in the local emulator
    private static string endpointUri = "https://localhost:8081/";
    private static string primaryKey = "C2y6yDjf5/
R+ob0N8A7Cgv30VRDJIWEHLM+4QDU5DE2nQ9nDuVTqobD4b8mGGyPMbIZnqyMsEcaGQy67XIw/
Jw==";

    /*
    // to use Azure Cosmos DB in the cloud
    private static string account = "apps-services-net7"; // use your
account
    private static string endpointUri =
       $"https://{account}.documents.azure.com:443/";
    private static string primaryKey = "LGrx7H...gZw=="; // use your key
    */

    static async Task CreateCosmosResources()
    {
        SectionTitle("Creating Cosmos resources");

        try
        {
            using (CosmosClient client = new(
                accountEndpoint: endpointUri,
                authKeyOrResourceToken: primaryKey))
```

```
      {
        DatabaseResponse dbResponse = await client
          .CreateDatabaseIfNotExistsAsync(
            "Northwind", throughput: 400 /* RU/s */);

        string status = dbResponse.StatusCode switch
        {
          HttpStatusCode.OK => "exists",
          HttpStatusCode.Created => "created",
          _ => "unknown",
        };

        WriteLine("Database Id: {0}, Status: {1}.",
          arg0: dbResponse.Database.Id, arg1: status);

        IndexingPolicy indexingPolicy = new()
        {
          IndexingMode = IndexingMode.Consistent,
          Automatic = true, // items are indexed unless explicitly
excluded
          IncludedPaths = { new IncludedPath { Path = "/*" } }
        };

        ContainerProperties containerProperties = new("Products",
          partitionKeyPath: "/productId")
        {
          IndexingPolicy = indexingPolicy
        };

        ContainerResponse containerResponse = await dbResponse.Database
          .CreateContainerIfNotExistsAsync(
            containerProperties, throughput: 1000 /* RU/s */);

        status = dbResponse.StatusCode switch
        {
          HttpStatusCode.OK => "exists",
          HttpStatusCode.Created => "created",
          _ => "unknown",
        };

        WriteLine("Container Id: {0}, Status: {1}.",
          arg0: containerResponse.Container.Id, arg1: status);

        Container container = containerResponse.Container;

        ContainerProperties properties = await container.
```

```
ReadContainerAsync();
        WriteLine($"  PartitionKeyPath: {properties.PartitionKeyPath}");
        WriteLine($"  LastModified: {properties.LastModified}");
        WriteLine("  IndexingPolicy.IndexingMode: {0}",
          arg0: properties.IndexingPolicy.IndexingMode);
        WriteLine("  IndexingPolicy.IncludedPaths: {0}",
          arg0: string.Join(",", properties.IndexingPolicy
            .IncludedPaths.Select(path => path.Path)));
        WriteLine($"  IndexingPolicy: {properties.IndexingPolicy}");
      }
    }
    catch (HttpRequestException ex)
    {
      WriteLine("Error: {0}", arg0: ex.Message);
      WriteLine("Hint: Make sure the Azure Cosmos Emulator is running.");
    }
    catch (Exception ex)
    {
      WriteLine("Error: {0} says {1}",
        arg0: ex.GetType(),
        arg1: ex.Message);
    }
  }
}
```

Note the following in the preceding code:

- When using the emulator, the endpointUri and primaryKey are the same for everyone.
- The constructor for a CosmosClient requires the endpointUri and primaryKey.
- When creating a database, you must specify a name and throughput in RUs per second.
- When creating a container, you must specify a name and partition key path, and you can optionally set an indexing policy and override the throughput, which defaults to the database throughput.
- The response to a request to create an Azure Cosmos DB resource includes an HTTP status code like 200 OK if the resource already exists, or 201 Created if the resource did not exist but has now been successfully created. The response also includes information about the resource like its Id.

1. In Program.cs, delete the existing statements, and then add a statement to call the method to create Azure Cosmos resources, as shown in the following code:

```
await CreateCosmosResources();
```

2. Run the console app and note the results, as shown in the following output:

```
*
* Creating Cosmos resources
```

```
*
Database Id: Northwind, Status: exists.
Container Id: Products, Status: exists.
  PartitionKeyPath: /productId
  LastModified: 04/07/2022 11:11:31
  IndexingPolicy.IndexingMode: Consistent
  IndexingPolicy.IncludedPaths: /*
```

3.  In Azure Cosmos DB Emulator or Azure portal, use **Data Explorer** to delete the Northwind database. You will be prompted to enter its name to confirm deletion because this operation cannot be undone.

> It is important to delete the Northwind database at this point. Later in this chapter, you will programmatically add the 77 products from the SQL Server Northwind database to the Cosmos DB Northwind database. If you still have the three sample products in its Products container, then you will have issues.

4.  Run the console app and note that because we have just deleted the database, the code we have executed has (re)created the database, as shown in the following output:

```
*
* Creating Cosmos resources
*
Database Id: Northwind, Status: created.
Container Id: Products, Status: created.
  PartitionKeyPath: /productId
  LastModified: 04/07/2022 11:11:31
  IndexingPolicy.IndexingMode: Consistent
  IndexingPolicy.IncludedPaths: /*
```

# Manipulating data with Core (SQL) API

The most common API for working with data in Azure Cosmos DB is Core (SQL).

> The full documentation for Core (SQL) API can be found at the following link: https://docs.microsoft.com/en-us/azure/cosmos-db/sql/.

# Performing CRUD operations with Cosmos SQL API

You can perform CRUD operations on JSON documents in Cosmos with SQL API by calling the following most common overloads of methods on an instance of the Microsoft.Azure.Cosmos.Container class:

*   ReadItemAsync<T>(id, partitionKey): Where T is the item type to get, id is its unique identifier, and partitionKey is its partition key value.

- ReadManyItemsAsync<T>(idsAndPartitionKeys): Where T is the item type to get, and idsAndPartitionKeys are the unique identifiers and partition key values of a read-only list of items to retrieve.
- CreateItemAsync(object): Where object is an instance of the item type to insert.
- DeleteItemAsync<T>(id, partitionKey): Where T is the item type to delete, id is its unique identifier, and partitionKey is its partition key value.
- PatchItemAsync<T>(id, partitionKey, patchOperations): Where T is the item type to update, id is its unique identifier, partitionKey is its partition key value, and patchOperations is a read-only list of property changes.
- ReplaceItemAsync<T>(object, id): Where T is the item type to replace, id is its unique identifier, and object is an instance of the item type to replace it with.
- UpsertItemAsync<T>(object, id): Where T is the item type to either insert or replace, id is its unique identifier, and object is an instance of the item type to insert or replace the existing item with.

Each method returns a response that has the following common properties:

- Resource: The item that was retrieved/created/deleted/updated.
- RequestCharge: A double value indicating the request charge measured in RUs.
- StatusCode: An HTTP status code value; for example, 404 when a ReadItemAsync<T> request fails to find the item.
- Headers: A dictionary of HTTP response headers.
- Diagnostics: Useful information for diagnostics.
- ActivityId: A GUID value that is useful for tracking this activity through multi-tiered services.

Let's copy all the products from the Northwind database in SQL Server to Cosmos.

Since the entity classes in the EF Core for SQL Server class libraries are designed for the normalized data structure in Northwind SQL database, we will create new classes to represent items in Cosmos that have embedded related data. They will use JSON casing conventions since they represent JSON documents:

1. In the Northwind.CosmosDb.SqlApi project, add a class file named CategoryCosmos.cs.
2. Modify its content to define a CategoryCosmos class, as shown in the following code:

```
namespace Northwind.CosmosDb.Items;

public class CategoryCosmos
{
  public int categoryId { get; set; }
  public string categoryName { get; set; } = null!;
  public string? description { get; set; }
}
```

3. In the Northwind.CosmosDb.SqlApi project, add a class file named SupplierCosmos.cs.

4. Modify its content to define a `SupplierCosmos` class, as shown in the following code:

```
namespace Northwind.CosmosDb.Items;

public class SupplierCosmos
{
  public int supplierId { get; set; }
  public string companyName { get; set; } = null!;
  public string? contactName { get; set; }
  public string? contactTitle { get; set; }
  public string? address { get; set; }
  public string? city { get; set; }
  public string? region { get; set; }
  public string? postalCode { get; set; }
  public string? country { get; set; }
  public string? phone { get; set; }
  public string? fax { get; set; }
  public string? homePage { get; set; }
}
```

5. In the `Northwind.CosmosDb.SqlApi` project, add a class file named `ProductCosmos.cs`.

6. Modify its content to define a `ProductCosmos` class, as shown in the following code:

```
namespace Northwind.CosmosDb.Items;

public class ProductCosmos
{
  public string id { get; set; } = null!;
  public string productId { get; set; } = null!;
  public string productName { get; set; } = null!;
  public string? quantityPerUnit { get; set; }
  public decimal? unitPrice { get; set; }
  public short? unitsInStock { get; set; }
  public short? unitsOnOrder { get; set; }
  public short? reorderLevel { get; set; }
  public bool discontinued { get; set; }
  public CategoryCosmos? category { get; set; }
  public SupplierCosmos? supplier { get; set; }
}
```

**Good Practice:** All JSON document items in Cosmos must have an `id` property. To control the value, it is good practice to explicit define that property in the model. Otherwise, the system will assign a GUID value, as you saw earlier in this chapter when using **Data Explorer** to manually add a new item.

7. In `Program.Methods.cs`, add statements to import namespaces for the Northwind data context and entities types, the Northwind Cosmos types, and EF Core extensions, as shown in the following code:

```
using Packt.Shared; // NorthwindContext, Product, Category, and so on
using Northwind.CosmosDb.Items; // ProductCosmos, CategoryCosmos, and so
on
using Microsoft.EntityFrameworkCore; // Include extension method
```

8. In `Program.Methods.cs`, add statements to define a method to get all the products in the Northwind SQL database, including their related category and supplier, and then insert them as new items in the `Products` container in Cosmos, as shown in the following code:

```
static async Task CreateProductItems()
{
  SectionTitle("Creating product items");

  double totalCharge = 0.0;

  try
  {
    using (CosmosClient client = new(
      accountEndpoint: endpointUri,
      authKeyOrResourceToken: primaryKey))
    {
      Container container = client.GetContainer(
        databaseId: "Northwind", containerId: "Products");

      using (NorthwindContext db = new())
      {
        ProductCosmos[] products = db.Products

          // get the related data for embedding
          .Include(p => p.Category)
          .Include(p => p.Supplier)

          // filter any products with null category or supplier
          // to avoid null warnings
          .Where(p => (p.Category != null) && (p.Supplier != null))

          // project the EF Core entities into Cosmos JSON types
          .Select(p => new ProductCosmos
          {
            id = p.ProductId.ToString(),
            productId = p.ProductId.ToString(),
            productName = p.ProductName,
```

```
                quantityPerUnit = p.QuantityPerUnit,
                category = new CategoryCosmos
                {
                  categoryId = p.Category.CategoryId,
                  categoryName = p.Category.CategoryName,
                  description = p.Category.Description
                },
                supplier = new SupplierCosmos
                {
                  supplierId = p.Supplier.SupplierId,
                  companyName = p.Supplier.CompanyName,
                  contactName = p.Supplier.ContactName,
                  contactTitle = p.Supplier.ContactTitle,
                  address = p.Supplier.Address,
                  city = p.Supplier.City,
                  country = p.Supplier.Country,
                  postalCode = p.Supplier.PostalCode,
                  region = p.Supplier.Region,
                  phone = p.Supplier.Phone,
                  fax = p.Supplier.Fax,
                  homePage = p.Supplier.HomePage
                },
                unitPrice = p.UnitPrice,
                unitsInStock = p.UnitsInStock,
                reorderLevel = p.ReorderLevel,
                unitsOnOrder = p.UnitsOnOrder,
                discontinued = p.Discontinued,
            })
            .ToArray();

        foreach (ProductCosmos product in products)
        {
          try
          {
            ItemResponse<ProductCosmos> productResponse =
              await container.ReadItemAsync<ProductCosmos>(
              id: product.id, new PartitionKey(product.productId));

            WriteLine("Item with id: {0} exists. Query consumed {1}
RUs.",
              productResponse.Resource.id, productResponse.
RequestCharge);

            totalCharge += productResponse.RequestCharge;
          }
        catch (CosmosException ex)
```

```
                     when (ex.StatusCode == HttpStatusCode.NotFound)
                {
                  ItemResponse<ProductCosmos> productResponse =
                    await container.CreateItemAsync(product);

                  WriteLine("Created item with id: {0}. Insert consumed {1}
    RUs.",
                    productResponse.Resource.id, productResponse.
    RequestCharge);

                  totalCharge += productResponse.RequestCharge;
                }
              catch (Exception ex)
                {
                  WriteLine("Error: {0} says {1}",
                    arg0: ex.GetType(),
                    arg1: ex.Message);
                }
              }
            }
          }
        }
      catch (HttpRequestException ex)
      {
        WriteLine("Error: {0}", arg0: ex.Message);
        WriteLine("Hint: Make sure the Azure Cosmos Emulator is running.");
      }
      catch (Exception ex)
      {
        WriteLine("Error: {0} says {1}",
          arg0: ex.GetType(),
          arg1: ex.Message);
      }

      WriteLine("Total requests charge: {0:N2} RUs", totalCharge);
    }
```

9. In `Program.cs`, comment out the call to create the Azure Cosmos resources, and then add a statement to call the method to insert all the products, as shown in the following code:

```
await CreateProductItems();
```

10. Run the console app and note the results, which should be 77 product items inserted, as shown in the following partial output:

```
*
* Creating product items
*
```

```
Created item with id: 1. Insert consumed 14.29 RUs.
Created item with id: 2. Insert consumed 14.29 RUs.
Created item with id: 3. Insert consumed 14.29 RUs.
...
Created item with id: 76. Insert consumed 14.29 RUs.
Created item with id: 77. Insert consumed 14.48 RUs.
Total requests charge: 1,114.58 RUs
```

11. Run the console app again and note the results, which should show that the product items already exist, as shown in the following partial output:

```
*
* Creating product items
*
Item with id: 1 exists. Query consumed 1 RUs.
Item with id: 2 exists. Query consumed 1 RUs.
Item with id: 3 exists. Query consumed 1 RUs.
...
Item with id: 76 exists. Query consumed 1 RUs.
Item with id: 77 exists. Query consumed 1 RUs.
Total requests charge: 77.00 RUs
```

12. In the Azure Cosmos DB Emulator or Azure portal **Data Explorer**, confirm that there are 77 product items in the Products container.

13. In Program.Methods.cs, add statements to define a method to list all the items in the Products container in Cosmos, as shown in the following code:

```
static async Task ListProductItems(string sqlText = "SELECT * FROM c")
{
  SectionTitle("Listing product items");

  try
  {
    using (CosmosClient client = new(
      accountEndpoint: endpointUri,
      authKeyOrResourceToken: primaryKey))
    {
      Container container = client.GetContainer(
        databaseId: "Northwind", containerId: "Products");

      WriteLine("Running query: {0}", sqlText);

      QueryDefinition query = new(sqlText);

      using FeedIterator<ProductCosmos> resultsIterator =
        container.GetItemQueryIterator<ProductCosmos>(query);
```

```
      if (!resultsIterator.HasMoreResults)
      {
        WriteLine("No results found.");
      }

      while (resultsIterator.HasMoreResults)
      {
        FeedResponse<ProductCosmos> products =
          await resultsIterator.ReadNextAsync();

        WriteLine("Status code: {0}, Request charge: {1} RUs.",
          products.StatusCode, products.RequestCharge);

        WriteLine("{0} products found.", arg0: products.Count);

        foreach (ProductCosmos product in products)
        {
          WriteLine("id: {0}, productName: {1}, unitPrice: {2}",
            arg0: product.id, arg1: product.productName,
            arg2: product.unitPrice);
        }
      }
    }
    catch (HttpRequestException ex)
    {
      WriteLine("Error: {0}", arg0: ex.Message);
      WriteLine("Hint: Make sure the Azure Cosmos Emulator is running.");
    }
    catch (Exception ex)
    {
      WriteLine("Error: {0} says {1}",
        arg0: ex.GetType(),
        arg1: ex.Message);
    }
  }
```

14. In `Program.cs`, comment out the call to create the product items, and then add a statement to call the method to list the product items, as shown in the following code:

```
await ListProductItems();
```

15. Run the console app and note the results, which should be 77 product items, as shown in the following partial output:

```
*
* Listing product items
*
```

```
Running query: SELECT * FROM c
Status code: OK, Request charge: 3.93 RUs.
77 products found.
id: 1, productName: Chai, unitPrice: 18
id: 2, productName: Chang, unitPrice: 19
id: 3, productName: Aniseed Syrup, unitPrice: 10
...
id: 76, productName: Lakkalikööri, unitPrice: 18
id: 77, productName: Original Frankfurter grüne Soße, unitPrice: 13
```

16. In `Program.Methods.cs`, add statements to define a method to delete all the items in the Products container in Cosmos, as shown in the following code:

```
static async Task DeleteProductItems()
{
  SectionTitle("Deleting product items");

  double totalCharge = 0.0;

  try
  {
    using (CosmosClient client = new(
      accountEndpoint: endpointUri,
      authKeyOrResourceToken: primaryKey))
    {
      Container container = client.GetContainer(
        databaseId: "Northwind", containerId: "Products");

      string sqlText = "SELECT * FROM c";

      WriteLine("Running query: {0}", sqlText);

      QueryDefinition query = new(sqlText);

      using FeedIterator<ProductCosmos> resultsIterator =
        container.GetItemQueryIterator<ProductCosmos>(query);

      while (resultsIterator.HasMoreResults)
      {
        FeedResponse<ProductCosmos> products =
          await resultsIterator.ReadNextAsync();

        foreach (ProductCosmos product in products)
        {
          WriteLine("Delete id: {0}, productName: {1}",
            arg0: product.id, arg1: product.productName);
```

```
            ItemResponse<ProductCosmos> response =
              await container.DeleteItemAsync<ProductCosmos>(
              id: product.id, partitionKey: new(product.id));

            WriteLine("Status code: {0}, Request charge: {1} RUs.",
              response.StatusCode, response.RequestCharge);

            totalCharge += response.RequestCharge;
          }
        }
      }
    }
  }
  catch (HttpRequestException ex)
  {
    WriteLine("Error: {0}", arg0: ex.Message);
    WriteLine("Hint: Make sure the Azure Cosmos Emulator is running.");
  }
  catch (Exception ex)
  {
    WriteLine("Error: {0} says {1}",
      arg0: ex.GetType(),
      arg1: ex.Message);
  }

  WriteLine("Total requests charge: {0:N2} RUs", totalCharge);
}
```

17. In `Program.cs`, comment out the call to list the product items, and then add a statement to call the method to delete the product items, as shown in the following code:

```
await DeleteProductItems();
```

18. Run the console app and note the results, which should be 77 product items deleted, as shown in the following partial output:

```
*
* Deleting product items
*
Running query: SELECT * FROM c
Delete id: 1, productName: Chai
Status code: NoContent, Request charge: 14.29 RUs.
...
Delete id: 77, productName: Original Frankfurter grüne Soße
Status code: NoContent, Request charge: 14.48 RUs.
Total requests charge: 1,128.87 RUs
```

19. In the Azure Cosmos DB Emulator or Azure portal **Data Explorer**, confirm that the `Products` container is empty.

## Understanding SQL queries

The following keywords and more are available when writing SQL queries for Azure Cosmos DB:

- SELECT to select from item properties. Supports * for all and TOP for limiting the results to the first specific number of items.

- AS to define aliases.

- FROM to define the items to select from. Some of the previous queries used FROM c, where c is an implied alias for the items in the container. Since a SQL query is executed within the context of a container like Products, you can use any alias you like, so FROM Items c or FROM p would work equally well.

- WHERE to define a filter.

- LIKE to use pattern matching. % means zero, one, or more characters. _ means a single character. [a-f] or [aeiou] means a single character within the defined range or set. [^aeiou] means not in the range or set.

- IN, BETWEEN are range and set filters.

- AND, OR, NOT for Boolean logic.

- ORDER BY to sort the results.

- DISTINCT to remove duplicates.

- COUNT, AVG, SUM, and other aggregate functions.

To query the Products container using Core (SQL) API, you might write the following code:

```
SELECT p.id, p.productName, p.unitPrice FROM Items p
```

Let's try executing a SQL query against our product items:

1. In Program.cs, uncomment the call to (re)create the product items and modify the call to ListProductItems to pass a SQL query that filters the products to only show the products in the beverages category and only their ID, name, and unit price, as shown in the following code:

```
//await CreateCosmosResources();
await CreateProductItems();
await ListProductItems("SELECT p.id, p.productName, p.unitPrice FROM
Items p WHERE p.category.categoryName = 'Beverages'");
//await DeleteProductItems();
```

2. Run the console app and note the results, which should be the 12 product items in the beverages category, as shown in the following output:

```
*
* Listing product items
*
Running query: SELECT p.id, p.productName, p.unitPrice FROM Items p WHERE
p.category.categoryName = 'Beverages'
```

```
Status code: OK, Request charge: 3.19 RUs.
12 products found.
id: 1, productName: Chai, unitPrice: 18
id: 2, productName: Chang, unitPrice: 19
id: 24, productName: Guaraná Fantástica, unitPrice: 4.5
id: 34, productName: Sasquatch Ale, unitPrice: 14
id: 35, productName: Steeleye Stout, unitPrice: 18
id: 38, productName: Côte de Blaye, unitPrice: 263.5
id: 39, productName: Chartreuse verte, unitPrice: 18
id: 43, productName: Ipoh Coffee, unitPrice: 46
id: 67, productName: Laughing Lumberjack Lager, unitPrice: 14
id: 70, productName: Outback Lager, unitPrice: 15
id: 75, productName: Rhönbräu Klosterbier, unitPrice: 7.75
id: 76, productName: Lakkalikööri, unitPrice: 18
```

3.   In the Azure Cosmos DB Emulator or Azure portal **Data Explorer**, create a new SQL query, use the same SQL text, and execute it, as shown in *Figure 3.10*:

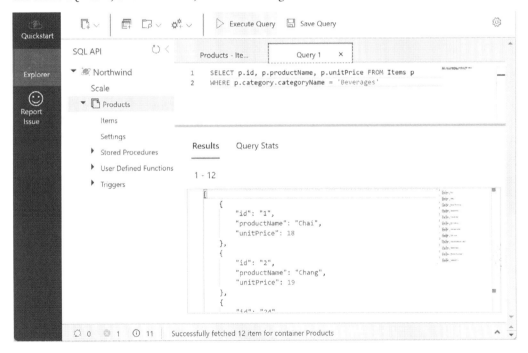

*Figure 3.10: Executing a SQL query in Data Explorer*

1.  Click **Query Stats**, and note the request charge (3.19 RUs), the number of records (12), and the output document size (752 bytes), as shown in *Figure 3.11*:

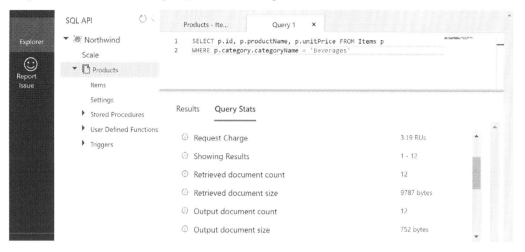

*Figure 3.11: Query statistics in Data Explorer*

Other useful query statistics include:

*   Index hit document count
*   Index lookup time
*   Document load time
*   Query engine execution time
*   Document write time

Try executing the following queries:

```
SELECT p.id, p.productName, p.unitPrice FROM Items p
WHERE p.unitPrice > 50

SELECT DISTINCT p.category FROM Items p

SELECT DISTINCT p.category.categoryName FROM Items p
WHERE p.discontinued = true

SELECT p.productName, p.supplier.city FROM Items p
WHERE p.supplier.country = 'Germany'

SELECT COUNT(p.id) AS HowManyProductsComeFromGermany FROM Items p
WHERE p.supplier.country = 'Germany'

SELECT AVG(p.unitPrice) AS AverageUnitPrice FROM Items p
```

# Understanding server-side programming

Azure Cosmos DB server-side programming consists of **stored procedures** and **user defined functions** (**UDFs**) written in JavaScript.

Stored procedures are the only way to ensure **ACID** (**Atomic, Consistent, Isolated, Durable**) transactions that combine multiple discrete activities into a single action that can be committed or rolled back. You cannot use client-side code to implement transactions. Server-side programming also provides improved performance, since the code executes where the data is stored.

UDFs can only be called from within a query, and they implement custom business logic like calculating tax.

Let's define a UDF to calculate the sales tax of products:

1.  In the Azure Cosmos DB Emulator or Azure portal **Data Explorer**, create a new user defined function (UDF), as shown in *Figure 3.12*:

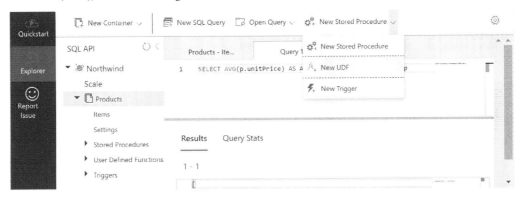

*Figure 3.12: Creating a new UDF*

2.  For the **User Defined Function Id**, enter salesTax.

3.  In the editor, enter JavaScript to define the salesTax function, as shown in the following code:

```
function salesTax(unitPrice){
    return unitPrice * 0.2;
}
```

4.  Create a new SQL query and enter SQL text to return the unit price and sales tax for products that cost more than 100, as shown in the following query:

```
SELECT p.unitPrice cost, udf.salesTax(p.unitPrice) AS tax
FROM Items p WHERE p.unitPrice > 100
```

5.  Click the **Save Query** button.

 If you are using cloud resources instead of the emulator, then for compliance reasons, Microsoft saves queries in a container in your Azure Cosmos account in a separate database called "___Cosmos". The estimated additional cost is $0.77 daily.

6. Execute the query and note the results, as shown in the following output:

```
[
    {
        "cost": 123.79,
        "tax": 24.758000000000003
    },
    {
        "cost": 263.5,
        "tax": 52.7
    }
]
```

 Note that **AS** to alias a property is optional. I prefer to specify **AS** for improved legibility.

# Manipulating graph data with Gremlin API

This is a bonus section for the chapter that is available online at https://github.com/markjprice/apps-services-net7/tree/main/docs/gremlin-api

# Cleaning up Azure resources

When you are done with an Azure Cosmos DB account, you must clean up the resources used, or you will incur costs for as long as those resources exist. You can delete resources individually or delete the resource group to delete the entire set of resources. If you delete an Azure Cosmos DB account, then all the databases and containers within it are also deleted:

1. In the Azure portal, navigate to **All Resources**.
2. In your apps-services-net7 resource group, click your Azure Cosmos DB account.
3. Click **Overview**, and then in the toolbar, click **Delete Account**.
4. In the **Confirm the Account Name** box, enter your account name.
5. Click the **Delete** button.

# Practicing and exploring

Test your knowledge and understanding by answering some questions, getting some hands-on practice, and exploring this chapter's topics with deeper research.

## Exercise 3.1 – Test your knowledge

Answer the following questions:

1. What are the APIs supported by Azure Cosmos DB?
2. At what level do you select the API: account, database, container, or partition?

3.  What does *embed* mean regarding data modeling with Cosmos DB?

4.  What is the unit of measurement for throughput for Cosmos DB and what does 1 unit represent?

5.  What package should you reference to programmatically work with Cosmos DB resources?

6.  What language do you use to write Cosmos DB Core (SQL) API user-defined functions and stored procedures?

7.  What is the difference between a vertex and an edge in a graph database?

8.  What package should you reference to programmatically execute Gremlin scripts?

9.  What Gremlin command returns all vertices that have a label of product and have a property named unitsInStock with more than 10 units in stock?

10. Why do some edges have weights?

## Exercise 3.2 – Practice data modeling and partitioning

Microsoft documentation has an extensive example of modeling and partitioning Azure Cosmos DB:

`https://docs.microsoft.com/en-us/azure/cosmos-db/sql/how-to-model-partition-example`

## Exercise 3.3 – Explore topics

Use the links on the following page to learn more detail about the topics covered in this chapter:

`https://github.com/markjprice/apps-services-net7/blob/main/book-links.md#chapter-3---managing-nosql-data-using-azure-cosmos-db`

## Exercise 3.4 – Explore NoSQL databases

This chapter focused on Azure Cosmos DB. If you wish to learn more about NoSQL databases such as MongoDB, and how to use them with EF Core, then I recommend the following links:

*   **Use NoSQL databases as a persistence infrastructure:** `https://docs.microsoft.com/en-us/dotnet/standard/microservices-architecture/microservice-ddd-cqrs-patterns/nosql-database-persistence-infrastructure`
*   **Document Database Providers for Entity Framework Core:** `https://github.com/BlueshiftSoftware/EntityFrameworkCore`

## Exercise 3.5 – Download cheat sheets

Download query cheat sheets for the four Azure Cosmos DB APIs and review them:

`https://docs.microsoft.com/en-us/azure/cosmos-db/sql/query-cheat-sheet`

## Exercise 3.6 – Read a Gremlin guide

To gain more experience with Gremlin graph API, you could read the following online book:

`https://kelvinlawrence.net/book/Gremlin-Graph-Guide.html`

# Summary

In this chapter, you learned:

- How to store flexibly structured data in Azure Cosmos DB.
- How to use the Cosmos SQL API.
- How to use the Cosmos Gremlin graph API (online section).

In the next chapter, you will use the `Task` type to improve the performance of your applications.

# 4

# Benchmarking Performance, Multitasking, and Concurrency

This chapter is about allowing multiple actions to occur at the same time to improve performance, scalability, and user productivity for the applications that you build.

In this chapter, we will cover the following topics:

- Understanding processes, threads, and tasks
- Monitoring performance and resource usage
- Running tasks asynchronously
- Synchronizing access to shared resources
- Understanding async and await

## Understanding processes, threads, and tasks

A **process**, with one example being each of the console applications we have created, has resources like memory and threads allocated to it.

A **thread** executes your code, statement by statement. By default, each process only has one thread, and this can cause problems when we need to do more than one task at the same time. Threads are also responsible for keeping track of things like the currently authenticated user and any internationalization rules that should be followed for the current language and region.

Windows and most other modern operating systems use **preemptive multitasking**, which simulates the parallel execution of tasks. It divides the processor time among the threads, allocating a **time slice** to each thread one after another. The current thread is suspended when its time slice finishes. The processor then allows another thread to run for a time slice.

When Windows switches from one thread to another, it saves the context of the thread and reloads the previously saved context of the next thread in the thread queue. This takes both time and resources to complete.

As a developer, if you have a small number of complex pieces of work and you want complete control over them, then you could create and manage individual `Thread` instances. If you have one main thread and multiple small pieces of work that can be executed in the background, then you can use the `ThreadPool` class to add delegate instances that point to those pieces of work implemented as methods to a queue, and they will be automatically allocated to threads in the thread pool.

In this chapter, we will use the `Task` type to manage threads at a higher abstraction level.

Threads may have to compete for and wait for access to shared resources, such as variables, files, and database objects. There are types for managing this that you will see in action later in this chapter.

Depending on the task, doubling the number of threads (workers) to perform a task does not halve the number of seconds that it will take to complete that task. In fact, it can increase the duration of the task, as shown in *Figure 4.1*:

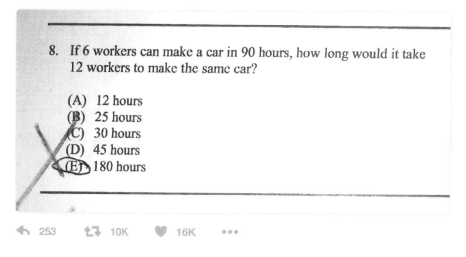

Figure 4.1: A tweet about tasks in the real world

**Good Practice:** Never assume that more threads will improve performance! Run performance tests on a baseline code implementation without multiple threads, and then again on a code implementation with multiple threads. You should also perform performance tests in a staging environment that is as close as possible to the production environment.

# Monitoring performance and resource usage

Before we can improve the performance of any code, we need to be able to monitor its speed and efficiency to record a baseline that we can then measure improvements against.

# Evaluating the efficiency of types

What is the best type to use for a scenario? To answer this question, we need to carefully consider what we mean by "best," and through this, we should consider the following factors:

- **Functionality:** This can be decided by checking whether the type provides the features you need.
- **Memory size:** This can be decided by the number of bytes of memory the type takes up.
- **Performance:** This can be decided by how fast the type is.
- **Future needs:** This depends on the changes in requirements and maintainability.

There will be scenarios, such as when storing numbers, where multiple types have the same functionality, so we will need to consider memory and performance to make a choice.

If we need to store millions of numbers, then the best type to use would be the one that requires the fewest bytes of memory. But if we only need to store a few numbers, yet we need to perform lots of calculations on them, then the best type to use would be the one that runs fastest on a specific CPU.

The `sizeof()` function shows the number of bytes that a single instance of a type uses in memory. When we are storing many values in more complex data structures, such as arrays and lists, then we need a better way of measuring memory usage.

You can read lots of advice online and in books, but the only way to know for sure what the best type would be for your code is to compare the types yourself.

In the next section, you will learn how to write code to monitor the actual memory requirements and performance when using different types.

Today a `short` variable might be the best choice, but it might be an even better choice to use an `int` variable, even though it takes twice as much space in the memory. This is because we might need a wider range of values to be stored in the future.

As listed above, there is an important metric that developers often forget: maintenance. This is a measure of how much effort another programmer would have to put in to understand and modify your code. If you make a nonobvious choice of type without explaining that choice with a helpful comment, then it might confuse the programmer who comes along later and needs to fix a bug or add a feature.

# Monitoring performance and memory using diagnostics

The `System.Diagnostics` namespace has lots of useful types for monitoring your code. The first useful type that we will look at is the `Stopwatch` type:

1. Use your preferred coding tool to create a class library project, as defined in the following list:

   - Project template: **Class Library** / `classlib`
   - Workspace/solution file and folder: `Chapter04`
   - Project file and folder: `MonitoringLib`

2.  Add a console app project, as defined in the following list:

    - Project template: **Console App**/console
    - Workspace/solution file and folder: Chapter04
    - Project file and folder: MonitoringApp

3.  Use your preferred coding tool to set which project is active:

    - If you are using Visual Studio 2022, set the startup project for the solution to the current selection.
    - If you are using Visual Studio Code, set MonitoringApp as the active OmniSharp project.

4.  In the MonitoringLib project, rename the Class1.cs file to Recorder.cs.

5.  In the MonitoringLib project, globally and statically import the System.Console class.

6.  In the MonitoringApp project, globally and statically import the System.Console class and add a project reference to the MonitoringLib class library, as shown in the following markup:

```
<ItemGroup>
  <Using Include="System.Console" Static="true" />
</ItemGroup>

<ItemGroup>
  <ProjectReference
    Include="..\MonitoringLib\MonitoringLib.csproj" />
</ItemGroup>
```

7.  Build the MonitoringApp project.

## Useful members of the Stopwatch and Process types

The Stopwatch type has some useful members, as shown in the following table:

| Member | Description |
|---|---|
| Restart method | This resets the elapsed time to zero and then starts the timer. |
| Stop method | This stops the timer. |
| Elapsed property | This is the elapsed time stored as a TimeSpan format (for example, hours:minutes:seconds). |
| ElapsedMilliseconds property | This is the elapsed time in milliseconds stored as an Int64 value. |

The Process type has some useful members, as shown in the following table:

| Member | Description |
|---|---|
| VirtualMemorySize64 | This displays the amount of virtual memory, in bytes, allocated for the process. |

| WorkingSet64 | This displays the amount of physical memory, in bytes, allocated for the process. |
|---|---|

## Implementing a Recorder class

We will create a `Recorder` class that makes it easy to monitor time and memory resource usage. To implement our `Recorder` class, we will use the `Stopwatch` and `Process` classes:

1. In `Recorder.cs`, change its contents to use a `Stopwatch` instance to record timings and the current `Process` instance to record memory usage, as shown in the following code:

```
using System.Diagnostics; // Stopwatch

using static System.Diagnostics.Process; // GetCurrentProcess()

namespace Packt.Shared;

public static class Recorder
{
  private static Stopwatch timer = new();

  private static long bytesPhysicalBefore = 0;
  private static long bytesVirtualBefore = 0;

  public static void Start()
  {
    // force some garbage collections to release memory that is
    // no longer referenced but has not been released yet
    GC.Collect();
    GC.WaitForPendingFinalizers();
    GC.Collect();
    GC.WaitForPendingFinalizers();
    GC.Collect();

    // store the current physical and virtual memory use
    bytesPhysicalBefore = GetCurrentProcess().WorkingSet64;
    bytesVirtualBefore = GetCurrentProcess().VirtualMemorySize64;

    timer.Restart();
  }

  public static void Stop()
  {
    timer.Stop();

    long bytesPhysicalAfter =
      GetCurrentProcess().WorkingSet64;
```

```
        long bytesVirtualAfter =
          GetCurrentProcess().VirtualMemorySize64;

      WriteLine("{0:N0} physical bytes used.",
        bytesPhysicalAfter - bytesPhysicalBefore);

      WriteLine("{0:N0} virtual bytes used.",
        bytesVirtualAfter - bytesVirtualBefore);

      WriteLine("{0} time span elapsed.", timer.Elapsed);

      WriteLine("{0:N0} total milliseconds elapsed.",
        timer.ElapsedMilliseconds);
    }
  }
```

 The Start method of the Recorder class uses the GC type (garbage collector) to ensure that any currently allocated but not referenced memory is collected before recording the amount of used memory. This is an advanced technique that you should almost never use in application code, because the GC understands memory usage better than a programmer would and should be trusted to make decisions about when to collect unused memory itself. Our need to take control in this scenario is exceptional.

2.  In Program.cs, delete the existing statements and then add statements to start and stop the Recorder while generating an array of 10,000 integers, as shown in the following code:

```
using Packt.Shared; // Recorder

WriteLine("Processing. Please wait...");
Recorder.Start();

// simulate a process that requires some memory resources...
int[] largeArrayOfInts = Enumerable.Range(
  start: 1, count: 10_000).ToArray();

// ...and takes some time to complete
Thread.Sleep(new Random().Next(5, 10) * 1000);
Recorder.Stop();
```

3.  Run the code and view the result, as shown in the following output:

```
Processing. Please wait...
827,392 physical bytes used.
131,072 virtual bytes used.
00:00:06.0123934 time span elapsed.
```

```
6,012 total milliseconds elapsed.
```

Remember that the time elapsed is randomly between 5 and 10 seconds. Your results will vary even between multiple subsequent runs on the same machine. For example, when run on my Mac mini M1, less physical memory but more virtual memory was used, as shown in the following output:

```
Processing. Please wait...
294,912 physical bytes used.
10,485,760 virtual bytes used.
00:00:06.0074221 time span elapsed.
6,007 total milliseconds elapsed.
```

## Measuring the efficiency of processing strings

Now that you've seen how the Stopwatch and Process types can be used to monitor your code, we will use them to evaluate the best way to process string variables:

1.  In the MonitoringApp project, add a new class file named Program.Helpers.cs.

2.  In Program.Helpers.cs, define a partial Program class with a method to output a section title in dark yellow color, as shown in the following code:

    ```
    partial class Program
    {
      static void SectionTitle(string title)
      {
        ConsoleColor previousColor = ForegroundColor;
        ForegroundColor = ConsoleColor.DarkYellow;
        WriteLine("*");
        WriteLine($"* {title}");
        WriteLine("*");
        ForegroundColor = previousColor;
      }
    }
    ```

3.  In Program.cs, comment out the previous statements by wrapping them in multi-line comment characters: /* */.

4.  Add statements to create an array of 50,000 int variables and then concatenate them with commas as separators using a string and StringBuilder class, as shown in the following code:

    ```
    int[] numbers = Enumerable.Range(
      start: 1, count: 50_000).ToArray();

    SectionTitle("Using StringBuilder");
    Recorder.Start();

    System.Text.StringBuilder builder = new();
    ```

```
for (int i = 0; i < numbers.Length; i++)
{
  builder.Append(numbers[i]);
  builder.Append(", ");
}

Recorder.Stop();
WriteLine();

SectionTitle("Using string with +");
Recorder.Start();

string s = string.Empty; // i.e. ""

for (int i = 0; i < numbers.Length; i++)
{
  s += numbers[i] + ", ";
}

Recorder.Stop();
```

5.  Run the code and view the result, as shown in the following output:

```
*
* Using StringBuilder
*
1,150,976 physical bytes used.
0 virtual bytes used.
00:00:00.0010796 time span elapsed.
1 total milliseconds elapsed.


*
* Using string with +
*
11,849,728 physical bytes used.
1,638,400 virtual bytes used.
00:00:01.7754252 time span elapsed.
1,775 total milliseconds elapsed.
```

We can summarize the results as follows:

*   The StringBuilder class used about 1 MB of physical memory, zero virtual memory, and took about 1 millisecond.
*   The string class with the + operator used about 11 MB of physical memory, 1.5 MB of virtual memory, and took 1.7 seconds.

In this scenario, StringBuilder is more than 1,000 times faster and about 10 times more memory-efficient when concatenating text! This is because string concatenation creates a new string each time you use it because string values are immutable so they can be safely pooled for reuse. StringBuilder creates a single buffer in memory while it appends more characters.

 **Good Practice:** Avoid using the String.Concat method or the + operator inside loops. Use StringBuilder instead.

Now that you've learned how to measure the performance and resource efficiency of your code using types built into .NET, let's learn about a NuGet package that provides more sophisticated performance measurements.

## Monitoring performance and memory using Benchmark.NET

There is a popular benchmarking NuGet package for .NET that Microsoft uses in its blog posts about performance improvements, so it is good for .NET developers to know how it works and use it for their own performance testing. Let's see how we could use it to compare performance between string concatenation and StringBuilder:

1.  Use your preferred code editor to add a new console app to the Chapter04 solution/workspace named Benchmarking.

    *   In Visual Studio Code, select Benchmarking as the active OmniSharp project.

2.  In the Benchmarking project, add a package reference to Benchmark.NET, remembering that you can find out the latest version and use that instead of the version I used, as shown in the following markup:

    ```
    <ItemGroup>
      <PackageReference Include="BenchmarkDotNet" Version="0.13.1" />
    </ItemGroup>
    ```

3.  Build the project to restore packages.

4.  Add a new class file named StringBenchmarks.cs.

5.  In StringBenchmarks.cs, add statements to define a class with methods for each benchmark you want to run, in this case, two methods that both combine twenty numbers comma-separated using either string concatenation or StringBuilder, as shown in the following code:

    ```
    using BenchmarkDotNet.Attributes; // [Benchmark]

    public class StringBenchmarks
    {
      int[] numbers;

      public StringBenchmarks()
    ```

```csharp
  {
    numbers = Enumerable.Range(
      start: 1, count: 20).ToArray();
  }

  [Benchmark(Baseline = true)]
  public string StringConcatenationTest()
  {
    string s = string.Empty; // e.g. ""

    for (int i = 0; i < numbers.Length; i++)
    {
      s += numbers[i] + ", ";
    }

    return s;
  }

  [Benchmark]
  public string StringBuilderTest()
  {
    System.Text.StringBuilder builder = new();

    for (int i = 0; i < numbers.Length; i++)
    {
      builder.Append(numbers[i]);
      builder.Append(", ");
    }

    return builder.ToString();
  }
}
```

6.  In `Program.cs`, delete the existing statements and then import the namespace for running benchmarks and add a statement to run the benchmarks class, as shown in the following code:

```csharp
using BenchmarkDotNet.Running;

BenchmarkRunner.Run<StringBenchmarks>();
```

7.  Use your preferred coding tool to run the console app with its release configuration:

    •   In Visual Studio 2022, in the toolbar, set **Solution Configurations** to **Release**, and then navigate to **Debug** | **Start Without Debugging**.

    •   In Visual Studio Code, in a terminal, use the `dotnet run --configuration Release` command.

8. Note the results, including some artifacts like report files, and the most important, a summary table that shows that `string` concatenation took a mean of 412.990 ns and `StringBuilder` took a mean of 275.082 ns, as shown in the following partial output:

```
// ***** BenchmarkRunner: Finish  *****

// * Export *
  BenchmarkDotNet.Artifacts\results\StringBenchmarks-report.csv
  BenchmarkDotNet.Artifacts\results\StringBenchmarks-report-github.md
  BenchmarkDotNet.Artifacts\results\StringBenchmarks-report.html

// * Detailed results *
StringBenchmarks.StringConcatenationTest: DefaultJob
Runtime = .NET 7.0.0 (7.0.22.22904), X64 RyuJIT; GC = Concurrent
Workstation
Mean = 412.990 ns, StdErr = 2.353 ns (0.57%), N = 46, StdDev = 15.957 ns
Min = 373.636 ns, Q1 = 413.341 ns, Median = 417.665 ns, Q3 = 420.775 ns,
Max = 434.504 ns
IQR = 7.433 ns, LowerFence = 402.191 ns, UpperFence = 431.925 ns
ConfidenceInterval = [404.708 ns; 421.273 ns] (CI 99.9%), Margin = 8.282
ns (2.01% of Mean)
Skewness = -1.51, Kurtosis = 4.09, MValue = 2
------------------- Histogram -------------------
[370.520 ns ; 382.211 ns) | @@@@@
[382.211 ns ; 394.583 ns) | @
[394.583 ns ; 411.300 ns) | @@
[411.300 ns ; 422.990 ns) | @@@@@@@@@@@@@@@@@@@@@@@@@@@@@@@@@@
[422.990 ns ; 436.095 ns) | @@@@@
-------------------------------------------------

StringBenchmarks.StringBuilderTest: DefaultJob
Runtime = .NET 7.0.0 (7.0.22.22904), X64 RyuJIT; GC = Concurrent
Workstation
Mean = 275.082 ns, StdErr = 0.558 ns (0.20%), N = 15, StdDev = 2.163 ns
Min = 271.059 ns, Q1 = 274.495 ns, Median = 275.403 ns, Q3 = 276.553 ns,
Max = 278.030 ns
IQR = 2.058 ns, LowerFence = 271.409 ns, UpperFence = 279.639 ns
ConfidenceInterval = [272.770 ns; 277.394 ns] (CI 99.9%), Margin = 2.312
ns (0.84% of Mean)
Skewness = -0.69, Kurtosis = 2.2, MValue = 2
------------------- Histogram -------------------
[269.908 ns ; 278.682 ns) | @@@@@@@@@@@@@@@
-------------------------------------------------

// * Summary *

BenchmarkDotNet=v0.13.1, OS=Windows 10.0.22000
```

```
11th Gen Intel Core i7-1165G7 2.80GHz, 1 CPU, 8 logical and 4 physical
cores
.NET SDK=7.0.100
  [Host]     : .NET 7.0.0 (7.0.22.22904), X64 RyuJIT
  DefaultJob : .NET 7.0.0 (7.0.22.22904), X64 RyuJIT


|                       Method |      Mean |   Error |    StdDev | Ratio |
RatioSD |
|----------------------- |---------:|--------:|---------:|------:|-----
---:|
| StringConcatenationTest | 413.0 ns | 8.28 ns | 15.96 ns |  1.00 |
0.00 |
|       StringBuilderTest | 275.1 ns | 2.31 ns |  2.16 ns |  0.69 |
0.04 |


// * Hints *
Outliers
  StringBenchmarks.StringConcatenationTest: Default -> 7 outliers
were removed, 14 outliers were detected (376.78 ns..391.88 ns, 440.79
ns..506.41 ns)
  StringBenchmarks.StringBuilderTest: Default      -> 2 outliers were
detected (274.68 ns, 274.69 ns)


// * Legends *
  Mean    : Arithmetic mean of all measurements
  Error   : Half of 99.9% confidence interval
  StdDev  : Standard deviation of all measurements
  Ratio   : Mean of the ratio distribution ([Current]/[Baseline])
  RatioSD : Standard deviation of the ratio distribution ([Current]/
[Baseline])
  1 ns    : 1 Nanosecond (0.000000001 sec)


// ***** BenchmarkRunner: End *****
// ** Remained 0 benchmark(s) to run **


Run time: 00:01:13 (73.35 sec), executed benchmarks: 2
Global total time: 00:01:29 (89.71 sec), executed benchmarks: 2
// * Artifacts cleanup *
```

The Outliers section is especially interesting because it shows that not only is string concatenation slower than StringBuilder, but it is also more inconsistent in how long it takes. Your results will vary, of course. Note that there might not be Hints and Outliers sections if there are no outliers when you run your benchmarks!

You have now seen two ways to measure performance. Now let's see how we can run tasks asynchronously to potentially improve performance.

# Running tasks asynchronously

To understand how multiple tasks can be run **simultaneously** (at the same time), we will create a console app that needs to execute three methods.

There will be three methods that need to be executed: the first takes 3 seconds, the second takes 2 seconds, and the third takes 1 second. To simulate that work, we can use the Thread class to tell the current thread to go to sleep for a specified number of milliseconds.

## Running multiple actions synchronously

Before we make the tasks run simultaneously, we will run them **synchronously**, that is, one after the other:

1.  Use your preferred code editor to add a new console app to the Chapter04 solution/workspace named WorkingWithTasks.

    •   In Visual Studio Code, select WorkingWithTasks as the active OmniSharp project.

2.  In the WorkingWithTasks project, globally and statically import the System.Console class.

3.  In the WorkingWithTasks project, add a new class file named Program.Helpers.cs.

4.  In Program.Helpers.cs, define a partial Program class with methods to output a section title, a task title, and information about the current thread, each in different colors to make them easier to identify in output, as shown in the following code:

```
partial class Program
{
  static void SectionTitle(string title)
  {
    ConsoleColor previousColor = ForegroundColor;
    ForegroundColor = ConsoleColor.DarkYellow;
    WriteLine("*");
    WriteLine($"* {title}");
    WriteLine("*");
    ForegroundColor = previousColor;
  }

  static void TaskTitle(string title)
  {
    ConsoleColor previousColor = ForegroundColor;
    ForegroundColor = ConsoleColor.Green;
    WriteLine($"{title}");
    ForegroundColor = previousColor;
  }

  static void OutputThreadInfo()
  {
    Thread t = Thread.CurrentThread;
```

```
    ConsoleColor previousColor = ForegroundColor;
    ForegroundColor = ConsoleColor.DarkCyan;

    WriteLine(
      "Thread Id: {0}, Priority: {1}, Background: {2}, Name: {3}",
      t.ManagedThreadId, t.Priority, t.IsBackground, t.Name ?? "null");

    ForegroundColor = previousColor;
  }
}
```

5.  In the `WorkingWithTasks` project, add a new class file named `Program.Methods.cs`.

6.  In `Program.Methods.cs`, add three methods that simulate work, as shown in the following code:

```
partial class Program
{
  static void MethodA()
  {
    TaskTitle("Starting Method A...");
    OutputThreadInfo();
    Thread.Sleep(3000); // simulate three seconds of work
    TaskTitle("Finished Method A.");
  }

  static void MethodB()
  {
    TaskTitle("Starting Method B...");
    OutputThreadInfo();
    Thread.Sleep(2000); // simulate two seconds of work
    TaskTitle("Finished Method B.");
  }

  static void MethodC()
  {
    TaskTitle("Starting Method C...");
    OutputThreadInfo();
    Thread.Sleep(1000); // simulate one second of work
    TaskTitle("Finished Method C.");
  }
}
```

7.  In `Program.cs`, delete the existing statements and then add statements to call the helper method to output information about the thread, define and start a stopwatch, call the three simulated work methods, and then output the milliseconds elapsed, as shown in the following code:

```
using System.Diagnostics; // Stopwatch
```

```
OutputThreadInfo();
Stopwatch timer = Stopwatch.StartNew();

SectionTitle("Running methods synchronously on one thread.");
MethodA();
MethodB();
MethodC();

WriteLine($"{timer.ElapsedMilliseconds:#,##0}ms elapsed.");
```

8. Run the code, view the result, and note that when there is only one unnamed foreground thread doing the work, the total time required is just over 6 seconds, as shown in the following output:

```
Thread Id: 1, Priority: Normal, Background: False, Name: null
*
* Running methods synchronously on one thread.
*
Starting Method A...
Thread Id: 1, Priority: Normal, Background: False, Name: null
Finished Method A.
Starting Method B...
Thread Id: 1, Priority: Normal, Background: False, Name: null
Finished Method B.
Starting Method C...
Thread Id: 1, Priority: Normal, Background: False, Name: null
Finished Method C.
6,028ms elapsed.
```

# Running multiple actions asynchronously using tasks

The Thread class has been available since the first version of .NET in 2002 and can be used to create new threads and manage them, but it can be tricky to work with directly.

.NET Framework 4.0 introduced the Task class in 2010, which represents an asynchronous operation. A task is a higher-level abstraction around the operating system thread that performs the operation, and the Task enables easier creation and management. Managing multiple threads wrapped in tasks will allow our code to execute at the same time, aka **asynchronously**.

Each Task has a Status property and a CreationOptions property. A Task has a ContinueWith method that can be customized with the TaskContinuationOptions enum, and it can be managed with the TaskFactory class.

## Starting tasks

We will look at three ways to start the methods using Task instances. There are links in the GitHub repository to articles that discuss the pros and cons.

Each has a slightly different syntax, but they all define a `Task` and start it:

1.  In `Program.cs`, add statements to create and start three tasks, one for each method, as shown highlighted in the following code:

```
SectionTitle("Running methods asynchronously on multiple threads.");
timer.Restart();

Task taskA = new(MethodA);
taskA.Start();
Task taskB = Task.Factory.StartNew(MethodB);
Task taskC = Task.Run(MethodC);

WriteLine($"{timer.ElapsedMilliseconds:#,##0}ms elapsed.");
```

2.  Run the code, view the result, and note that the elapsed milliseconds appear almost immediately. This is because each of the three methods is now being executed by three new background worker threads allocated from the thread pool, as shown in the following output:

```
*
* Running methods asynchronously on multiple threads.
*
Starting Method A...
Thread Id: 4, Priority: Normal, Background: True, Name: .NET ThreadPool
Worker
Starting Method C...
Thread Id: 7, Priority: Normal, Background: True, Name: .NET ThreadPool
Worker
Starting Method B...
Thread Id: 6, Priority: Normal, Background: True, Name: .NET ThreadPool
Worker
6ms elapsed.
```

 It is even likely that the console app will end before one or even all of the tasks have a chance to start and write to the console!

# Waiting for tasks

Sometimes, you need to wait for a task to complete before continuing. To do this, you can use the `Wait` method on a `Task` instance, or the `WaitAll` or `WaitAny` static methods on an array of tasks, as described in the following table:

| Method | Description |
|---|---|
| `t.Wait()` | This waits for the task instance named `t` to complete execution. |

| `Task.WaitAny(Task[])` | This waits for any of the tasks in the array to complete execution. |
| --- | --- |
| `Task.WaitAll(Task[])` | This waits for all the tasks in the array to complete execution. |

## Using wait methods with tasks

Let's see how we can use these wait methods to fix the problem with our console app:

1. In `Program.cs`, after creating the three tasks and before outputting the elapsed time, add statements to combine references to the three tasks into an array and pass them to the `WaitAll` method, as shown in the following code:

   ```
   Task[] tasks = { taskA, taskB, taskC };
   Task.WaitAll(tasks);
   ```

2. Run the code and view the result, and note the original thread will pause on the call to `WaitAll`, waiting for all three tasks to finish before outputting the elapsed time, which is a little over 3 seconds, as shown in the following output:

   ```
   Starting Method A...
   Starting Method B...
   Thread Id: 4, Priority: Normal, Background: True, Name: .NET ThreadPool
   Worker
   Thread Id: 6, Priority: Normal, Background: True, Name: .NET ThreadPool
   Worker
   Starting Method C...
   Thread Id: 7, Priority: Normal, Background: True, Name: .NET ThreadPool
   Worker
   Finished Method C.
   Finished Method B.
   Finished Method A.
   3,013ms elapsed.
   ```

The three new threads execute their code simultaneously, and they can potentially start in any order. `MethodC` should finish first because it takes only 1 second, then `MethodB`, which takes 2 seconds, and finally `MethodA`, because it takes 3 seconds.

However, the actual CPU used has a big effect on the results. It is the CPU that allocates time slices to each process to allow them to execute their threads. You have no control over when the methods run.

## Continuing with another task

If all three tasks can be performed at the same time, then waiting for all tasks to finish will be all we need to do. However, often a task is dependent on the output from another task. To handle this scenario, we need to define **continuation tasks**.

We will create some methods to simulate a call to a web service that returns a monetary amount, which then needs to be used to retrieve how many products cost more than that amount in a database. The result returned from the first method needs to be fed into the input of the second method.

This time, instead of waiting for fixed amounts of time, we will use the Random class to wait for a random interval between 2 and 4 seconds for each method call to simulate the work:

1.  In Program.Methods.cs, add two methods that simulate calling a web service and a database stored procedure, as shown in the following code:

```
static decimal CallWebService()
{
  TaskTitle("Starting call to web service...");
  OutputThreadInfo();
  Thread.Sleep((new Random()).Next(2000, 4000));
  TaskTitle("Finished call to web service.");
  return 89.99M;
}

static string CallStoredProcedure(decimal amount)
{
  TaskTitle("Starting call to stored procedure...");
  OutputThreadInfo();
  Thread.Sleep((new Random()).Next(2000, 4000));
  TaskTitle("Finished call to stored procedure.");
  return $"12 products cost more than {amount:C}.";
}
```

2.  In Program.cs, add statements to start a task to call the web service and then pass its return value to a task that starts the database stored procedure, as shown in the following code:

```
SectionTitle("Passing the result of one task as an input into another.");
timer.Restart();

Task<string> taskServiceThenSProc = Task.Factory
  .StartNew(CallWebService) // returns Task<decimal>
  .ContinueWith(previousTask => // returns Task<string>
    CallStoredProcedure(previousTask.Result));

WriteLine($"Result: {taskServiceThenSProc.Result}");

WriteLine($"{timer.ElapsedMilliseconds:#,##0}ms elapsed.");
```

3.  Run the code and view the result, as shown in the following output:

```
Starting call to web service...
Thread Id: 4, Priority: Normal, Background: True, Name: .NET ThreadPool
Worker
Finished call to web service.
Starting call to stored procedure...
Thread Id: 6, Priority: Normal, Background: True, Name: .NET ThreadPool
Worker
```

```
Finished call to stored procedure.
Result: 12 products cost more than £89.99.
5,463ms elapsed.
```

You might see two different threads running the web service and stored procedure calls as in the output above (for examples, threads 4 and 6), or the same thread might be reused since it is no longer busy.

## Nested and child tasks

As well as defining dependencies between tasks, you can define nested and child tasks. A **nested task** is a task that is created inside another task. A **child task** is a nested task that must finish before its parent task is allowed to finish.

Let's explore how these types of tasks work:

1. In `Program.Methods.cs`, add two methods, one of which starts a task to run the other, as shown in the following code:

```
static void OuterMethod()
{
  TaskTitle("Outer method starting...");
  Task innerTask = Task.Factory.StartNew(InnerMethod);
  TaskTitle("Outer method finished.");
}

static void InnerMethod()
{
  TaskTitle("Inner method starting...");
  Thread.Sleep(2000);
  TaskTitle("Inner method finished.");
}
```

2. In `Program.cs`, add statements to start a task to run the outer method and wait for it to finish before stopping, as shown in the following code:

```
SectionTitle("Nested and child tasks");

Task outerTask = Task.Factory.StartNew(OuterMethod);
outerTask.Wait();
WriteLine("Console app is stopping.");
```

3. Run the code and view the result, as shown in the following output:

```
Outer method starting...
Inner method starting...
Outer method finished.
Console app is stopping.
```

Although we wait for the outer task to finish, its inner task does not have to finish as well. In fact, the outer task might finish, and the console app could end, before the inner task even starts!

4.  To link these nested tasks as parent and child, we must use a special option. Modify the existing code that defines the inner task to add a `TaskCreationOption` value of `AttachedToParent`, as shown highlighted in the following code:

```
Task innerTask = Task.Factory.StartNew(InnerMethod,
  TaskCreationOptions.AttachedToParent);
```

5.  Run the code, view the result, and note that the inner task must finish before the outer task can, as shown in the following output:

```
Outer method starting...
Inner method starting...
Outer method finished.
Inner method finished.
Console app is stopping.
```

 The `OuterMethod` can finish before the `InnerMethod`, as shown by its writing to the console, but its task must wait, as shown by the console not stopping until both the outer and inner tasks finish.

# Wrapping tasks around other objects

Sometimes you might have a method that you want to be asynchronous, but the result to be returned is not itself a task. You can wrap the return value in a successfully completed task, return an exception, or indicate that the task was canceled by using one of the `Task` static methods, shown in the following table:

| Method | Description |
|---|---|
| `FromResult<TResult>(TResult)` | Creates a `Task<TResult>` object whose `Result` property is the non-task result and whose `Status` property is `RanToCompletion`. |
| `FromException<TResult>(Exception)` | Creates a `Task<TResult>` that's completed with a specified exception. |
| `FromCanceled<TResult>(CancellationToken)` | Creates a `Task<TResult>` that's completed due to cancellation with a specified cancellation token. |

These methods are useful when you need to:

*   Implement an interface that has asynchronous methods, but your implementation is synchronous. This is common for websites and services.

- Mock asynchronous implementations during unit testing.

Imagine that you need to create a method to validate XML input and the method must conform to an interface that requires a `Task<T>` to be returned, as shown in the following code:

```
public interface IValidation
{
  Task<bool> IsValidXmlTagAsync(this string input);
}
```

We could use these helpful `FromX` methods to return the results wrapped in a task, as shown in the following code:

```
using System.Text.RegularExpressions;

namespace Packt.Shared;

public static class StringExtensions : IValidation
{
  public static Task<bool> IsValidXmlTagAsync(this string input)
  {
    if (input == null)
    {
      return Task.FromException<bool>(
        new ArgumentNullException($"Missing {nameof(input)} parameter"));
    }

    if (input.Length == 0)
    {
      return Task.FromException<bool>(
        new ArgumentException($"{nameof(input)} parameter is empty."));
    }

    return Task.FromResult(Regex.IsMatch(input,
      @"^<([a-z]+)([^<]+)*(?:>(.*)<\/\1>|\s+\/>)$"));
  }
}
```

If the method you need to implement returns a `Task` (equivalent to `void` in a synchronous method) then you can return a predefined completed `Task` object, as shown in the following code:

```
public Task DeleteCustomerAsync()
{
  // ...
  return Task.CompletedTask;
}
```

# Synchronizing access to shared resources

When you have multiple threads executing at the same time, there is a possibility that two or more of the threads may access the same variable or another resource at the same time, and as a result, may cause a problem. For this reason, you should carefully consider how to make your code **thread-safe**.

The simplest mechanism for implementing thread safety is to use an object variable as a flag or traffic light to indicate when a shared resource has an exclusive lock applied.

In William Golding's *Lord of the Flies*, Piggy and Ralph spot a conch shell and use it to call a meeting. The boys impose a "rule of the conch" on themselves, deciding that no one can speak unless they're holding the conch.

I like to name the object variable I use for implementing thread-safe code the "conch." When a thread has the conch, no other thread should access the shared resource(s) represented by that conch. Note that I say *should*. Only code that respects the conch enables synchronized access. A conch is *not* a lock.

We will explore a couple of types that can be used to synchronize access to shared resources:

- `Monitor`: An object that can be used by multiple threads to check if they should access a shared resource within the same process.
- `Interlocked`: An object for manipulating simple numeric types at the CPU level.

## Accessing a resource from multiple threads

Let's create a console app to explore sharing resources between multiple threads:

1. Use your preferred code editor to add a new console app to the `Chapter04` solution/workspace named `SynchronizingResourceAccess`.

    - In Visual Studio Code, select `SynchronizingResourceAccess` as the active OmniSharp project.

2. Globally and statically import the `System.Console` class.

3. Add a new class file named `SharedObjects.cs`.

4. In `SharedObjects.cs`, define a static class with a field to store a message that is a shared resource, as shown in the following code:

    ```
    static class SharedObjects
    {
      public static string? Message; // a shared resource
    }
    ```

5. Add a new class file named `Program.Methods.cs`.

6. In `Program.Methods.cs`, define two methods that both loop five times, waiting for a random interval of up to two seconds and appending either A or B to the shared message resource, as shown in the following code:

    ```
    partial class Program
    ```

```
{
  static void MethodA()
  {
    for (int i = 0; i < 5; i++)
    {
      Thread.Sleep(Random.Shared.Next(2000));
      SharedObjects.Message += "A";
      Write(".");
    }
  }

  static void MethodB()
  {
    for (int i = 0; i < 5; i++)
    {
      Thread.Sleep(Random.Shared.Next(2000));
      SharedObjects.Message += "B";
      Write(".");
    }
  }
}
```

7.  In `Program.cs`, delete the existing statements. Add statements to import the namespace for diagnostic types like `Stopwatch`, and statements to execute both methods on separate threads using a pair of tasks, and wait for them to complete before outputting the elapsed milliseconds, as shown in the following code:

```
using System.Diagnostics; // Stopwatch

WriteLine("Please wait for the tasks to complete.");
Stopwatch watch = Stopwatch.StartNew();
Task a = Task.Factory.StartNew(MethodA);
Task b = Task.Factory.StartNew(MethodB);

Task.WaitAll(new Task[] { a, b });
WriteLine();
WriteLine($"Results: {SharedObjects.Message}.");
WriteLine($"{watch.ElapsedMilliseconds:N0} elapsed milliseconds.");
```

8.  Run the code and view the result, as shown in the following output:

```
Please wait for the tasks to complete.
..........
Results: BABABAABBA.
5,753 elapsed milliseconds.
```

This shows that both threads were modifying the message concurrently. In an actual application, this could be a problem. But we can prevent concurrent access by applying a mutually exclusive lock to a conch object, as well as adding code to the two methods to voluntarily check the conch before modifying the shared resource, which we will do in the following section.

## Applying a mutually exclusive lock to a conch

Now, let's use a conch to ensure that only one thread accesses the shared resource at a time:

1. In `SharedObjects.cs`, declare and instantiate an `object` variable to act as a conch, as shown in the following code:

   ```
   public static object Conch = new();
   ```

2. In `Program.Methods.cs`, in both `MethodA` and `MethodB`, add a `lock` statement for the conch around the `for` statements, as shown highlighted in the following code:

   ```
   lock (SharedObjects.Conch)
   {
     for (int i = 0; i < 5; i++)
     {
       Thread.Sleep(Random.Shared.Next(2000));
       SharedObjects.Message += "A";
       Write(".");
     }
   }
   ```

    **Good Practice:** Note that since checking the conch is voluntary, if you only use the `lock` statement in one of the two methods, the shared resource will continue to be accessed by both methods. Make sure that all methods that access a shared resource respect the conch.

3. Run the code and view the result, as shown in the following output:

   ```
   Please wait for the tasks to complete.
   ..........
   Results: BBBBBAAAAA.
   10,345 elapsed milliseconds.
   ```

Although the time elapsed was longer, only one method at a time could access the shared resource. Either `MethodA` or `MethodB` can start first. Once a method has finished its work on the shared resource, then the conch gets released, and the other method has the chance to do its work.

## Understanding the lock statement

You might wonder what the `lock` statement does when it "locks" an object variable (hint: it does not lock the object!), as shown in the following code:

```
lock (SharedObjects.Conch)
```

```
{
  // work with shared resource
}
```

The C# compiler changes the lock statement into a try-finally statement that uses the Monitor class to *enter* and *exit* the conch object (I like to think of it as *taking* and *releasing* the conch object), as shown in the following code:

```
try
{
  Monitor.Enter(SharedObjects.Conch);
  // work with shared resource
}
finally
{
  Monitor.Exit(SharedObjects.Conch);
}
```

When a thread calls Monitor.Enter on a reference type, it checks to see if some other thread has already taken the conch. If it has, the thread waits. If it has not, the thread takes the conch and gets on with its work on the shared resource. Once the thread has finished its work, it calls Monitor.Exit, releasing the conch. If another thread was waiting, it can now take the conch and do its work. This requires all threads to respect the conch by calling Monitor.Enter and Monitor.Exit appropriately.

> **Good Practice:** You cannot use value types (struct type) as a conch. Monitor.Enter requires a reference type because it locks the memory address.

## Avoiding deadlocks

Knowing how the lock statement is translated by the compiler to method calls on the Monitor class is also important because using the lock statement can cause a deadlock.

Deadlocks can occur when there are two or more shared resources (each with a conch to monitor which thread is currently doing work on each shared resource), and the following sequence of events happens:

- Thread X "locks" conch A and starts working on shared resource A.
- Thread Y "locks" conch B and starts working on shared resource B.
- While still working on resource A, thread X needs to also work with resource B, and so it attempts to "lock" conch B but is blocked because thread Y already has conch B.
- While still working on resource B, thread Y needs to also work with resource A, and so it attempts to "lock" conch A but is blocked because thread X already has conch A.

One way to prevent deadlocks is to specify a timeout when attempting to get a lock. To do this, you must manually use the `Monitor` class instead of using the `lock` statement:

1. In `Program.Methods.cs`, modify your code to replace the `lock` statements with code that tries to enter the conch with a timeout and outputs an error and then exits the monitor, allowing other threads to enter the monitor, as shown highlighted in the following code:

```
try
{
    if (Monitor.TryEnter(SharedObjects.Conch, TimeSpan.FromSeconds(15)))
    {
        for (int i = 0; i < 5; i++)
        {
            Thread.Sleep(Random.Shared.Next(2000));
            SharedObjects.Message += "A";
            Write(".");
        }
    }
    else
    {
        WriteLine("Method A timed out when entering a monitor on conch.");
    }
}
finally
{
    Monitor.Exit(SharedObjects.Conch);
}
```

2. Run the code and view the result, which should return the same results as before (although either A or B could grab the conch first) but is better code because it will prevent potential deadlocks.

 **Good Practice:** Only use the `lock` keyword if you can write your code such that it avoids potential deadlocks. If you cannot avoid potential deadlocks, then always use the `Monitor.TryEnter` method instead of `lock`, in combination with a `try-finally` statement, so that you can supply a timeout and one of the threads will back out of a deadlock if it occurs. You can read more about good threading practices at the following link: `https://docs.microsoft.com/en-us/dotnet/standard/threading/managed-threading-best-practices`.

## Synchronizing events

.NET events are not thread-safe, so you should avoid using them in multithreaded scenarios.

After learning that .NET events are not thread-safe, some developers attempt to use exclusive locks when adding and removing event handlers or when raising an event, as shown in the following code:

```
// event delegate field
public event EventHandler? Shout;

// conch
private object eventConch = new();

// method
public void Poke()
{
  lock (eventConch) // bad idea
  {
    // if something is listening...
    if (Shout != null)
    {
      // ...then call the delegate to raise the event
      Shout(this, EventArgs.Empty);
    }
  }
}
```

> **Good Practice:** Is it good or bad that some developers do this? It depends on complex factors, so I cannot give a value judgment. You can read more about events and thread safety at the following link: `https://docs.microsoft.com/en-us/archive/blogs/cburrows/field-like-events-considered-harmful`.
>
> But it is complicated, as explained by Stephen Cleary in the following blog post: `https://blog.stephencleary.com/2009/06/threadsafe-events.html`.

## Making CPU operations atomic

Atomic is from the Greek word **atomos**, which means *undividable*. It is important to understand which operations are atomic in multithreading because if they are not atomic, then they could be interrupted by another thread partway through their operation. Is the C# increment operator atomic, as shown in the following code?

```
int x = 3;
x++; // is this an atomic CPU operation?
```

It is not atomic! Incrementing an integer requires the following three CPU operations:

1. Load a value from an instance variable into a register.
2. Increment the value.
3. Store the value in the instance variable.

A thread could be interrupted after executing the first two steps. A second thread could then execute all three steps. When the first thread resumes execution, it will overwrite the value in the variable, and the effect of the increment or decrement performed by the second thread will be lost!

There is a type named `Interlocked` that can perform atomic actions like `Add`, `Increment`, `Decrement`, `Exchange`, `CompareExchange`, `And`, `Or`, and `Read` on the following integer types:

- `System.Int32` (int), `System.UInt32` (uint)
- `System.Int64` (long), `System.UInt64` (ulong)

`Interlocked` does not work on numeric types like `byte`, `sbyte`, `short`, `ushort`, and `decimal`.

`Interlocked` can perform atomic operations like `Exchange` and `CompareExchange` that swap values in memory on the following types:

- `System.Single` (float), `System.Double` (double)
- `nint`, `nuint`
- `T`, `System.Object` (object)

Let's see it in action:

1. Declare another field in the `SharedObjects` class that will count how many operations have occurred, as shown in the following code:

   ```
   public static int Counter; // another shared resource
   ```

2. In `Program.Methods.cs`, in both methods A and B, inside the `for` statement and after modifying the `string` value, add a statement to safely increment the counter, as shown in the following code:

   ```
   Interlocked.Increment(ref SharedObjects.Counter);
   ```

3. In `Program.cs`, after outputting the elapsed time, write the current value of the counter to the console, as shown in the following code:

   ```
   WriteLine($"{SharedObjects.Counter} string modifications.");
   ```

4. Run the code and view the result, as shown highlighted in the following output:

   ```
   Please wait for the tasks to complete.
   ..........
   Results: BBBBBAAAAA.
   13,531 elapsed milliseconds.
   10 string modifications.
   ```

Observant readers will realize that the existing conch object protects all shared resources accessed within a block of code locked by the conch, and therefore it is unnecessary to use `Interlocked` in this specific example. But if we had not already been protecting another shared resource like `Message`, then using `Interlocked` would be necessary.

## Applying other types of synchronization

`Monitor` and `Interlocked` are mutually exclusive locks that are simple and effective, but sometimes, you need more advanced options to synchronize access to shared resources, as shown in the following table:

| Type | Description |
|------|-------------|
| ReaderWriterLock, ReaderWriterLockSlim | These allow multiple threads to be in **read mode**, one thread to be in **write mode** with exclusive ownership of the write lock, and one thread that has read access to be in **upgradeable read mode**, from which the thread can upgrade to write mode without having to relinquish its read access to the resource. |
| Mutex | Like Monitor, this provides exclusive access to a shared resource, except it is used for inter-process synchronization. |
| Semaphore, SemaphoreSlim | These limit the number of threads that can access a resource or pool of resources concurrently by defining slots. This is known as **resource throttling** rather than **resource locking**. |
| AutoResetEvent, ManualResetEvent | Event wait handles allow threads to synchronize activities by signaling each other and by waiting for each other's signals. |

# Understanding async and await

C# 5 introduced two C# keywords when working with the Task type. They are especially useful for the following:

- Implementing multitasking for a **graphical user interface (GUI)**.
- Improving the scalability of web applications and web services.

In *Chapter 18, Building Mobile and Desktop Apps Using .NET MAUI*, we will see how the async and await keywords can implement multitasking for a GUI.

But for now, let's learn the theory of why these two C# keywords were introduced, and then later you will see them used in practice.

## Improving responsiveness for console apps

One of the limitations with console apps is that you can only use the await keyword inside methods that are marked as async, but C# 7 and earlier do not allow the Main method to be marked as async! Luckily, a new feature introduced in C# 7.1 was support for async in Main:

1. Use your preferred code editor to add a new console app to the Chapter04 solution/workspace named AsyncConsole.

   - In Visual Studio Code, select AsyncConsole as the active OmniSharp project.

2. In Program.cs, delete the existing statements, statically import Console, and then add statements to create an HttpClient instance, make a request for Apple's home page, and output how many bytes it has, as shown in the following code:

```
using static System.Console;

HttpClient client = new();
```

```
HttpResponseMessage response =
  await client.GetAsync("http://www.apple.com/");

WriteLine("Apple's home page has {0:N0} bytes.",
  response.Content.Headers.ContentLength);
```

3. Build the project and note that it builds successfully. In .NET 5 and earlier, the project template created an explicit `Program` class with a non-async `Main` method, so you would have seen an error message, as shown in the following output:

```
Program.cs(14,9): error CS4033: The 'await' operator can only be used
within an async method. Consider marking this method with the 'async'
modifier and changing its return type to 'Task'. [/Users/markjprice/apps-
services-net7/ Chapter04/AsyncConsole/AsyncConsole.csproj]
```

4. You would have had to add the `async` keyword to the `Main` method and change its return type to `Task`. With .NET 6 and later, the console app project template uses the top-level program feature to automatically define the `Program` class with an asynchronous `<Main>$` method for you.

5. Run the code and view the result, which is likely to have a different number of bytes since Apple changes its home page frequently, as shown in the following output:

```
Apple's home page has 40,252 bytes.
```

# Working with async streams

With .NET Core 3.0, Microsoft introduced the asynchronous processing of streams.

 You can complete a tutorial about async streams at the following link: `https://docs.microsoft.com/en-us/dotnet/csharp/tutorials/generate-consume-asynchronous-stream`.

Before C# 8.0 and .NET Core 3.0, the `await` keyword only worked with tasks that return scalar values. Async stream support in .NET Standard 2.1 allows an `async` method to return one value after another asynchronously.

Let's see a simulated example that returns three random integers as an async stream:

1. Use your preferred code editor to add a new console app to the `Chapter04` solution/workspace named `AsyncEnumerable`.

   • In Visual Studio Code, select `AsyncEnumerable` as the active OmniSharp project.

2. Globally and statically import the `System.Console` class.

3. In `Program.cs`, delete the existing statements and then at the bottom of `Program.cs`, create a method that uses the `yield` keyword to return a random sequence of three numbers asynchronously, as shown in the following code:

```
async static IAsyncEnumerable<int> GetNumbersAsync()
```

```
{
  Random r = Random.Shared;

  // simulate work
  await Task.Delay(r.Next(1500, 3000));
  yield return r.Next(0, 1001);

  await Task.Delay(r.Next(1500, 3000));
  yield return r.Next(0, 1001);
  await Task.Delay(r.Next(1500, 3000));
  yield return r.Next(0, 1001);
}
```

4.  Above `GetNumbersAsync`, add statements to enumerate the sequence of numbers, as shown in the following code:

```
await foreach (int number in GetNumbersAsync())
{
  WriteLine($"Number: {number}");
}
```

5.  Run the code and view the result, as shown in the following output:

```
Number: 509
Number: 813
Number: 307
```

# Improving responsiveness for GUI apps

So far in this book, we have only built console apps. Life for a programmer gets more complicated when building web applications, web services, and apps with GUIs such as Windows desktop and mobile apps.

One reason for this is that for a GUI app, there is a special thread: the **user interface** (UI) thread.

There are two rules for working in GUIs:

- Do not perform long-running tasks on the UI thread.
- Do not access UI elements on any thread except the UI thread.

To handle these rules, programmers used to have to write complex code to ensure that long-running tasks were executed by a non-UI thread, but once complete, the results of the task were safely passed to the UI thread to present to the user. It could quickly get messy!

Luckily, with C# 5 and later, you have the use of `async` and `await`. They allow you to continue to write your code as if it is synchronous, which keeps your code clean and easy to understand, but underneath, the C# compiler creates a complex state machine and keeps track of running threads. It's kind of magical! The combination of these two keywords makes the asynchronous method run on a worker thread and, when complete, return the results on the UI thread.

Let's see an example. We will build a Windows desktop app using WPF that gets employees from the Northwind database in a SQL Server database using low-level types like SqlConnection, SqlCommand, and SqlDataReader.

The Northwind database has a medium complexity and a decent number of sample records. You used it extensively in *Chapter 2, Managing Relational Data Using SQL Server*, where it was introduced and set up.

**Warning!** You will only be able to complete this task if you have Microsoft Windows and the Northwind database stored in Microsoft SQL Server. This is the only section in this book that is not cross-platform and modern (WPF is 17 years old!). You can use either Visual Studio 2022 or Visual Studio Code.

At this point, we are focusing on making a GUI app responsive. You will learn about XAML and building cross-platform GUI apps in *Chapter 18, Building Mobile and Desktop Apps Using .NET MAUI*. Since this book does not cover WPF elsewhere, I thought this task would be a good opportunity to at least see an example app built using WPF even if we do not look at it in detail.

Let's go!

1.  If you are using Visual Studio 2022 for Windows, add a new **WPF Application [C#]** project named WpfResponsive to the Chapter04 solution. If you are using Visual Studio Code, use the following command: dotnet new wpf, and make this the active OmniSharp project.

2.  Add a package reference for Microsoft.Data.SqlClient to the project.

3.  In the project file, note the output type is a Windows EXE, the target framework is .NET 7 for Windows (it will not run on other platforms like macOS and Linux), and the project uses WPF, as shown in the following markup:

```xml
<Project Sdk="Microsoft.NET.Sdk">

  <PropertyGroup>
    <OutputType>WinExe</OutputType>
    <TargetFramework>net7.0-windows</TargetFramework>
    <Nullable>enable</Nullable>
    <UseWPF>true</UseWPF>
  </PropertyGroup>

  <ItemGroup>
    <PackageReference Include="Microsoft.Data.SqlClient" Version="5.0.0"
/>
  </ItemGroup>

</Project>
```

4. Build the `WpfResponsive` project to restore packages.

5. In `MainWindow.xaml`, in the `<Grid>` element, add elements to define two buttons, a text box and a list box, laid out vertically in a stack panel, as shown in the following markup:

```xml
<StackPanel>
  <Button Name="GetEmployeesSyncButton"
          Click="GetEmployeesSyncButton_Click">

    Get Employees Synchronously</Button>
  <Button Name="GetEmployeesAsyncButton"
          Click="GetEmployeesAsyncButton_Click">
    Get Employees Asynchronously</Button>
  <TextBox HorizontalAlignment="Stretch" Text="Type in here" />
  <ListBox Name="EmployeesListBox" Height="350" />
</StackPanel>
```

 Visual Studio 2022 for Windows has good support for building WPF apps and will provide IntelliSense as you edit code and XAML markup. Visual Studio Code does not.

6. In `MainWindow.xaml.cs`, import the `System.Diagnostics` and `Microsoft.Data.SqlClient` namespaces.

7. In the `MainWindow` class, create two `string` constants for the database connection string and SQL statement, as shown in the following code:

```
private const string connectionString =
  "Data Source=.;" +
  "Initial Catalog=Northwind;" +
  "Integrated Security=true;" +
  "Encrypt=false;" +
  "MultipleActiveResultSets=true;";

private const string sql =
  "WAITFOR DELAY '00:00:05';" +
  "SELECT EmployeeId, FirstName, LastName FROM Employees";
```

8. Create event handlers for clicking on the two buttons. They must use the `string` constants to open a connection to the Northwind database and then populate the list box with the IDs and names of all employees, as shown in the following code:

```
private void GetEmployeesSyncButton_Click(object sender, RoutedEventArgs
e)
{
  Stopwatch timer = Stopwatch.StartNew();
```

```csharp
  using (SqlConnection connection = new(connectionString))
  {
    try
    {
      connection.Open();

      SqlCommand command = new(sql, connection);
      SqlDataReader reader = command.ExecuteReader();

      while (reader.Read())
      {
        string employee = string.Format("{0}: {1} {2}",
          reader.GetInt32(0), reader.GetString(1), reader.GetString(2));

        EmployeesListBox.Items.Add(employee);
      }

      reader.Close();
      connection.Close();
    }
    catch (Exception ex)
    {
      MessageBox.Show(ex.Message);
    }
  }
  EmployeesListBox.Items.Add($"Sync: {timer.ElapsedMilliseconds:N0}ms");
}

private async void GetEmployeesAsyncButton_Click(
  object sender, RoutedEventArgs e)
{
  Stopwatch timer = Stopwatch.StartNew();

  using (SqlConnection connection = new(connectionString))
  {
    try
    {
      await connection.OpenAsync();

      SqlCommand command = new(sql, connection);
      SqlDataReader reader = await command.ExecuteReaderAsync();

      while (await reader.ReadAsync())
```

```
          {
            string employee = string.Format("{0}: {1} {2}",
              await reader.GetFieldValueAsync<int>(0),
              await reader.GetFieldValueAsync<string>(1),
              await reader.GetFieldValueAsync<string>(2));

            EmployeesListBox.Items.Add(employee);
          }
          await reader.CloseAsync();
          await connection.CloseAsync();
        }
        catch (Exception ex)
        {
          MessageBox.Show(ex.Message);
        }
      }
      EmployeesListBox.Items.Add($"Async: {timer.ElapsedMilliseconds:N0}ms");
    }
```

Note the following:

- Defining an async void method is generally bad practice because it is "fire and forget". You will not be notified when it is completed and there is no way to cancel it because it does not return a Task or Task<T> that can be used to control it.

- The SQL statement uses the SQL Server command WAITFOR DELAY to simulate processing that takes five seconds. It then selects three columns from the Employees table.

- The GetEmployeesSyncButton_Click event handler uses synchronous methods to open a connection and fetch the employee rows.

- The GetEmployeesAsyncButton_Click event handler is marked as async and uses asynchronous methods with the await keyword to open a connection and fetch the employee rows.

- Both event handlers use a stopwatch to record the number of milliseconds the operation takes and add it to the list box.

9. Start the WPF app without debugging.

10. Click in the text box, enter some text, and note the GUI is responsive.

11. Click the **Get Employees Synchronously** button.

12. Try to click in the text box, and note the GUI is not responsive.

13. Wait for at least five seconds until the list box is filled with employees.

14. Click in the text box, enter some text, and note the GUI is responsive again.

15. Click the **Get Employees Asynchronously** button.

16. Click in the text box, enter some text, and note the GUI is still responsive while it performs the operation. Continue typing until the list box is filled with the employees, as shown in *Figure 4.2*:

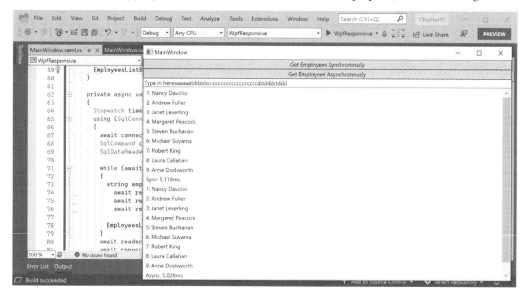

Figure 4.2: Loading employees into a WPF app synchronously and asynchronously

17. Note the difference in timings for the two operations. The UI is blocked when fetching data synchronously, while the UI remains responsive when fetching data asynchronously.

18. Close the WPF app.

# Improving scalability for web applications and web services

The `async` and `await` keywords can also be applied on the server side when building websites, applications, and services. From the client application's point of view, nothing changes (or they might even notice a small increase in the time taken for a request to return). So, from a single client's point of view, the use of `async` and `await` to implement multitasking on the server side makes their experience worse!

On the server side, additional, cheaper worker threads are created to wait for long-running tasks to finish so that expensive I/O threads can handle other client requests instead of being blocked. This improves the overall scalability of a web application or service. More clients can be supported simultaneously.

# Common types that support multitasking

There are many common types that have asynchronous methods that you can await, as shown in the following table:

| Type | Methods |
|---|---|
| DbContext<T> | AddAsync, AddRangeAsync, FindAsync, and SaveChangesAsync |

| DbSet<T> | AddAsync, AddRangeAsync, ForEachAsync, SumAsync, ToListAsync ToDictionaryAsync, AverageAsync, and CountAsync |
|---|---|
| HttpClient | GetAsync, PostAsync, PutAsync, DeleteAsync, and SendAsync |
| StreamReader | ReadAsync, ReadLineAsync, and ReadToEndAsync |
| StreamWriter | WriteAsync, WriteLineAsync, and FlushAsync |

**Good Practice:** Any time you see a method that ends in the suffix Async, check to see whether it returns Task or Task<T>. If it does return Task or Task<T>, then you could use it instead of the synchronous non-Async suffixed method. Remember to call it using await and decorate your method with async.

## Using await in catch blocks

When async and await were first introduced in C# 5, it was only possible to use the await keyword in a try block, but not in a catch block. In C# 6 and later, it is now possible to use await in both try and catch blocks.

# Practicing and exploring

Test your knowledge and understanding by answering some questions, getting some hands-on practice, and exploring this chapter's topics with deeper research.

## Exercise 4.1 – Test your knowledge

Answer the following questions:

1. What information can you find out about a process?
2. How accurate is the Stopwatch class?
3. By convention, what suffix should be applied to a method that returns Task or Task<T>?
4. To use the await keyword inside a method, what keyword must be applied to the method declaration?
5. How do you create a child task?
6. Why should you avoid the lock keyword?
7. When should you use the Interlocked class?
8. When should you use the Mutex class instead of the Monitor class?
9. What is the benefit of using async and await in a website or web service?
10. Can you cancel a task? If so, how?

## Exercise 4.2 – Explore topics

Use the links on the following GitHub page to learn more about the topics covered in this chapter:

https://github.com/markjprice/apps-services-net7/blob/main/book-links.md#chapter-4---improving-performance-and-scalability-using-multitasking

## Exercise 4.3 – Read more about parallel programming

Packt has a book that goes deeper into the topics in this chapter, *Parallel Programming and Concurrency with C# 10 and .NET 6: A modern approach to building faster, more responsive, and asynchronous .NET applications using C#*, by Alvin Ashcraft.

```
https://www.packtpub.com/product/parallel-programming-and-concurrency-with-c-10-and-
net-6/9781803243672
```

# Summary

In this chapter, you learned:

- How to define and start a task.
- How to wait for one or more tasks to finish.
- How to control task completion order.
- How to synchronize access to shared resources.
- The magic behind `async` and `await`.

In the next chapter, you will learn how to use some popular third-party libraries.

# 5

# Implementing Popular Third-Party Libraries

This chapter is about some popular third-party libraries for .NET that enable you to perform actions that either are not possible with the core .NET libraries or are better than the built-in functionality. These actions include manipulating images with ImageSharp, logging with Serilog, mapping objects to other objects with AutoMapper, making unit test assertions with FluentAssertions, validating data with FluentValidation, and generating PDFs with QuestPDF.

This chapter covers the following topics:

- Which third-party libraries are most popular?
- Working with images
- Logging with Serilog
- Mapping between objects
- Making fluent assertions in unit testing
- Validating data
- Generating PDFs

## Which third-party libraries are most popular?

To help me to decide which third-party libraries to include in this book, I researched which are downloaded most frequently at `https://www.nuget.org/stats`, and, as shown in the following table, they are:

| Rank | Package | Downloads |
|------|---------------|-------------|
| 1 | `newtonsoft.json` | 106,664,914 |
| 2 | `serilog` | 25,706,263 |
| 3 | `castle.core` | 18,426,836 |

| 4 | `newtonsoft.json.bson` | 18,018,770 |
| 5 | `awssdk.core` | 15,655,292 |
| 6 | `swashbuckle.aspnetcore.swagger` | 15,049,359 |
| 7 | `swashbuckle.aspnetcore.swaggergen` | 14,984,145 |
| 8 | `moq` | 13,864,846 |
| 9 | `automapper` | 13,390,653 |
| 10 | `serilog.sinks.file` | 13,043,367 |
| 12 | `polly` | 12,612,215 |
| 24 | `serilog.sinks.console` | 11,271,774 |
| 38 | `fluentvalidation` | 8,906,145 |
| 41 | `fluentassertions` | 8,419,263 |
| 100 | `nodatime` | 2,981,780 |

## What is covered in my books

My book, *C# 11 and .NET 7 – Modern Cross-Platform Development Fundamentals*, introduces processing JSON using `Newtonsoft.Json` and documenting web services using `Swashbuckle`. For now, using Castle Core to generate dynamic proxies and typed dictionaries, or deploying to and integrating with **Amazon Web Services (AWS)**, is out of scope for this book.

As well as raw download numbers, questions from readers and the usefulness of the library also contributed to my decision to include a library in this chapter, as summarized in the following list:

- Most popular library for manipulating images: **ImageSharp**
- Most popular library for logging: **Serilog**
- Most popular library for object mapping: **AutoMapper**
- Most popular library for unit test assertions: **FluentAssertions**
- Most popular library for data validation: **FluentValidation**
- Open-source library for generating PDFs: **QuestPDF**

## What could be covered in my books

In future editions, I plan to add other libraries. Please let me know which libraries would be most important for your needs. Currently, the following are most likely to be included in the next edition:

- Most popular library for handling dates and times: **NodaTime**, `https://nodatime.org/`
- Most popular library for generating dynamic proxies and typed dictionaries: **Castle Core**, `https://github.com/castleproject/Core`
- Most popular library for scheduling jobs: **Quartz.NET**, `https://www.quartz-scheduler.net/`

- Most popular library for resilience and transient fault handling: **Polly**, `https://github.com/App-vNext/Polly`
- Most popular library for mocking in unit tests: **Moq**, `https://github.com/moq/moq`

# Working with images

**ImageSharp** is a third-party cross-platform 2D graphics library. When .NET Core 1.0 was in development, there was negative feedback from the community about the missing `System.Drawing` namespace for working with 2D images. The ImageSharp project was started to fill that gap for modern .NET applications.

In their official documentation for `System.Drawing`, Microsoft says, "The `System.Drawing` namespace is not recommended for new development due to not being supported within a Windows or ASP.NET service, and it is not cross-platform. ImageSharp and SkiaSharp are recommended as alternatives."

 SixLabors released ImageSharp 2.0 on February 7, 2022, with WebP, Tiff, and Pbm format support, more efficient and faster memory pooling and allocation, and massive performance improvements for their JPEG and PNG formats. You can read the announcement at the following link: `https://sixlabors.com/posts/announcing-imagesharp-200/`.

## Generating grayscale thumbnails

Let's see what can be achieved with ImageSharp:

1.  Use your preferred code editor to add a new console app named `WorkingWithImages` to a `Chapter05` solution/workspace.

2.  In the `WorkingWithImages` project, create an images folder and download to it the nine images from the following link: `https://github.com/markjprice/apps-services-net7/tree/master/images/Categories`.

3.  If you are using Visual Studio 2022, then the images folder and its files must be copied to the `WorkingWithImages\bin\Debug\net7` folder:

    1.  In **Solution Explorer**, select all nine images.
    2.  In **Properties**, set **Copy To Output Directory** to **Copy Always**.
    3.  Open the project file and note the `<ItemGroup>` entries that will copy the nine images to the correct folder, as partially shown in the following markup:

        ```
        <ItemGroup>
          <None Update="images\categories.jpeg">
            <CopyToOutputDirectory>Always</CopyToOutputDirectory>
          </None>
        ```

```
    <None Update="images\category1.jpeg">
      <CopyToOutputDirectory>Always</CopyToOutputDirectory>
    </None>
  ...
```

4. In the `WorkingWithImages` project, globally and statically import the `System.Console` class and add a package reference for `SixLabors.ImageSharp`, as shown in the following markup:

```
<ItemGroup>
  <Using Include="System.Console" Static="true" />
</ItemGroup>

<ItemGroup>
  <PackageReference Include="SixLabors.ImageSharp" Version="2.1.0" />
</ItemGroup>
```

5. Build the `WorkingWithImages` project.

6. In `Program.cs`, delete the existing statements and then import some namespaces for working with images, as shown in the following code:

```
using SixLabors.ImageSharp; // Image
using SixLabors.ImageSharp.Processing; // Mutate extension method
```

7. In `Program.cs`, enter statements to convert all the files in the `images` folder into grayscale thumbnails at one-tenth size, as shown in the following code:

```
string imagesFolder = Path.Combine(
  Environment.CurrentDirectory, "images");

WriteLine($"I will look for images in the following folder:\
n{imagesFolder}");
WriteLine();

if (!Directory.Exists(imagesFolder))
{
  WriteLine();
  WriteLine("Folder does not exist!");
  return;
}

IEnumerable<string> images =
  Directory.EnumerateFiles(imagesFolder);
```

```
foreach (string imagePath in images)
{
  if (Path.GetFileNameWithoutExtension(imagePath).EndsWith("-thumbnail"))
  {
    WriteLine($"Skipping:\n  {imagePath}");
    WriteLine();
    continue; // this file has already been converted
  }

  string thumbnailPath = Path.Combine(
    Environment.CurrentDirectory, "images",
    Path.GetFileNameWithoutExtension(imagePath)
    + "-thumbnail" + Path.GetExtension(imagePath));

  using (Image image = Image.Load(imagePath))
  {
    WriteLine($"Converting:\n  {imagePath}");
    WriteLine($"To:\n  {thumbnailPath}");
    image.Mutate(x => x.Resize(image.Width / 10, image.Height / 10));
    image.Mutate(x => x.Grayscale());
    image.Save(thumbnailPath);
    WriteLine();
  }
}

WriteLine("Image processing complete. View the images folder.");
```

8. Run the console app and note the images should be converted into grayscale thumbnails, as shown in the following partial output:

```
I will look for images in the following folder:
C:\apps-services-net7\Chapter05\WorkingWithImages\bin\Debug\net7.0\images

Converting:
  C:\apps-services-net7\Chapter05\WorkingWithImages\bin\Debug\net7.0\
images\categories.jpeg
To:
  C:\apps-services-net7\Chapter05\WorkingWithImages\bin\Debug\net7.0\
images\categories-thumbnail.jpeg
```

```
Converting:
  C:\apps-services-net7\Chapter05\WorkingWithImages\bin\Debug\net7.0\
images\category1.jpeg
To:
  C:\apps-services-net7\Chapter05\WorkingWithImages\bin\Debug\net7.0\
images\category1-thumbnail.jpeg
...

Converting:
  C:\apps-services-net7\Chapter05\WorkingWithImages\bin\Debug\net7.0\
images\category8.jpeg
To:
  C:\apps-services-net7\Chapter05\WorkingWithImages\bin\Debug\net7.0\
images\category8-thumbnail.jpeg

Image processing complete. View the images folder.
```

9.  In the filesystem, open the images folder and note the much-smaller-in-bytes grayscale thumbnails, as shown in *Figure 5.1*:

*Figure 5.1: Images after processing*

## ImageSharp packages for drawing and the web

ImageSharp also has NuGet packages for programmatically drawing images and working with images on the web, as shown in the following list:

- SixLabors.ImageSharp.Drawing
- SixLabors.ImageSharp.Web

**More Information:** Learn more details at the following link: `https://docs.sixlabors.com/`.

# Logging with Serilog

Although .NET includes logging frameworks, third-party logging providers give more power and flexibility by using **structured event data**. Serilog is the most popular.

## Structured event data

Most systems write plain text messages to their logs.

Serilog can be told to write serialized structured data to the log. The @ symbol prefixing a parameter tells Serilog to serialize the object passed in, instead of just the result of calling the `ToString` method.

Later, that complex object can be queried for improved search and sort capabilities in the logs.

For example:

```
var lineitem = new { ProductId = 11, UnitPrice = 25.49, Quantity = 3 };


log.Information("Added {@LineItem} to shopping cart.", lineitem);
```

 You can learn more about how Serilog handles structured data at the following link: `https://github.com/serilog/serilog/wiki/Structured-Data`.

## Serilog sinks

All logging systems need to record the log entries somewhere. That could be to the console output, a file, or a more complex data store like a relational database or cloud data store. Serilog calls these **sinks**.

Serilog has hundreds of official and third-party sink packages for all the possible places you might want to record your logs. To use them, just include the appropriate package. The most popular are shown in the following list:

- `serilog.sinks.file`
- `serilog.sinks.console`
- `serilog.sinks.periodicbatching`
- `serilog.sinks.debug`
- `serilog.sinks.rollingfile` (deprecated; use `serilog.sinks.file` instead)
- `serilog.sinks.applicationinsights`
- `serilog.sinks.mssqlserver`

There are more than 390 packages currently listed on Microsoft's public NuGet feed: https://www.nuget.org/packages?q=serilog.sinks.

## Logging to the console and a rolling file with Serilog

Let's start:

1.  Use your preferred code editor to add a new console app named `Serilogging` to a `Chapter05` solution/workspace:

    *   In Visual Studio 2022, set the startup project to the current selection.
    *   In Visual Studio Code, select `Serilogging` as the active OmniSharp project.

2.  In the `Serilogging` project, globally and statically import the `System.Console` class and add a package reference for `Serilog`, including sinks for `console` and `file` (which also supports rolling files), as shown in the following markup:

    ```xml
    <ItemGroup>
      <Using Include="System.Console" Static="true" />
    </ItemGroup>

    <ItemGroup>
      <PackageReference Include="Serilog" Version="2.10.0" />
      <PackageReference Include="Serilog.Sinks.Console" Version="4.0.1" />
      <PackageReference Include="Serilog.Sinks.File" Version="5.0.0" />
    </ItemGroup>
    ```

3.  Build the `Serilogging` project.

4.  In the `Serilogging` project, in the `Models` folder, add a new class file named `ProductPageView.cs`, and modify its contents, as shown in the following code:

    ```csharp
    namespace Serilogging.Models;

    public class ProductPageView
    {
      public int ProductId { get; set; }
      public string? PageTitle { get; set; }
      public string? SiteSection { get; set; }
    }
    ```

5. In `Program.cs`, delete the existing statements and then import some namespaces for working with Serilog, as shown in the following code:

```
using Serilog; // Log, LoggerConfiguration, RollingInterval
using Serilog.Core; // Logger
using Serilogging.Models; // ProductPageView
```

6. In `Program.cs`, create a logger configuration that will write to the console as well as configuring a rolling interval that means a new file is created each day, and write various levels of log entries, as shown in the following code:

```
using Logger log = new LoggerConfiguration()
    .WriteTo.Console()
    .WriteTo.File("log.txt", rollingInterval: RollingInterval.Day)
    .CreateLogger();

Log.Logger = log;
Log.Information("The global logger has been configured.");

Log.Warning("Danger, Serilog, danger!");
Log.Error("This is an error!");
Log.Fatal("Fatal problem!");

ProductPageView pageView = new() {
  PageTitle = "Chai",
  SiteSection = "Beverages",
  ProductId = 1 };

Log.Information("{@PageView} occurred at {Viewed}",
  pageView, DateTimeOffset.UtcNow);

// just before ending an application
Log.CloseAndFlush();
```

7. Run the console app and note the messages, as shown in the following output:

```
[07:09:43 INF] The global logger has been configured.
[07:09:43 WRN] Danger, Serilog, danger!
[07:09:43 ERR] This is an error!
[07:09:43 FTL] Fatal problem!
[07:09:43 INF] {"ProductId": 1, "PageTitle": "Chai", "SiteSection":
"Beverages", "$type": "ProductPageView"} occurred at 09/07/2022 15:08:44
+00:00
```

8.  Open the `logYYYYMMDD.txt` file, where YYYY is the year, MM is the month, and DD is the day, and note it contains the same messages.

 **More Information:** Learn more details at the following link: `https://serilog.net/`.

# Mapping between objects

One of the most boring parts of being a programmer is mapping between objects. It is common to need to integrate systems or components that have conceptually similar objects but with different structures.

Models for data are different for different parts of an application. Models that represent data in storage are often called **entity models**. Models that represent data that must be passed between layers are often called **data transfer objects** (DTO). Models that represent only the data that must be presented to a user are often called **view models**. All these models are likely to have commonalities but different structures.

AutoMapper is a popular package for mapping objects because it has conventions that make the work as easy as possible. For example, if you have a source member called `CompanyName`, it will be mapped to a destination member with the name `CompanyName`.

 AutoMapper's creator, Jimmy Bogard, has written an article about its design philosophy that is worth reading, available at the following link: `https://jimmybogard.com/automappers-design-philosophy/`.

Let's see an example of AutoMapper in action. You will create four projects:

- A class library for the entity and view models.
- A class library to create mapper configurations for reuse in unit tests and actual projects.
- A unit test project to test the mappings.
- A console app to perform a live mapping.

We will construct an example object model that represents a customer and their shopping cart with a couple of items, and then map it to a summary view model to present to the user.

## Testing an AutoMapper configuration

It is good practice to always validate your configuration for mappings before using them, so we will start by defining some models and a mapping between them, and then create a unit test for the mappings:

1.  Use your preferred code editor to add a new **Class Library**/`classlib` project named `MappingObjects.Models` to the `Chapter05` solution/workspace.

2. In the MappingObjects.Models project, delete the file named Class1.cs.

3. In the MappingObjects.Models project, add a new class file named Customer.cs and modify its contents, as shown in the following code:

```
namespace Packt.Entities;

public record class Customer(
    string FirstName,
    string LastName
);
```

4. In the MappingObjects.Models project, add a new class file named LineItem.cs and modify its contents, as shown in the following code:

```
namespace Packt.Entities;

public record class LineItem(
    string ProductName,
    decimal UnitPrice,
    int Quantity
);
```

5. In the MappingObjects.Models project, add a new class file named Cart.cs and modify its contents, as shown in the following code:

```
namespace Packt.Entities;

public record class Cart(
    Customer Customer,
    List<LineItem> Items
);
```

6. In the MappingObjects.Models project, add a new class file named Summary.cs and modify its contents, as shown in the following code:

```
namespace Packt.ViewModels;

public class Summary
{
    public string? FullName { get; set; }
    public decimal Total { get; set; }
}
```

For the entity models, we used records because they will be immutable. But an instance of **Summary** will be created and then its members populated automatically by AutoMapper, so it must be a normal mutable class with public properties that can be set.

7.  Use your preferred code editor to add a new **Class Library**/classlib project named MappingObjects.Mappers to the Chapter05 solution/workspace.

8.  In the MappingObjects.Mappers project, treat warnings as errors, add a reference to the latest AutoMapper package, and add a reference to the models project, as shown highlighted in the following markup:

```xml
<Project Sdk="Microsoft.NET.Sdk">

  <PropertyGroup>
    <TargetFramework>net7.0</TargetFramework>
    <ImplicitUsings>enable</ImplicitUsings>
    <Nullable>enable</Nullable>
    <TreatWarningsAsErrors>true</TreatWarningsAsErrors>
  </PropertyGroup>

  <ItemGroup>
    <PackageReference Include="AutoMapper" Version="11.0.1" />
  </ItemGroup>

  <ItemGroup>
    <ProjectReference Include=
      "..\MappingObjects.Models\MappingObjects.Models.csproj" />
  </ItemGroup>

</Project>
```

9.  Build the MappingObjects.Mappers project to restore packages and compile referenced projects.

10. In the MappingObjects.Mappers project, delete the file named Class1.cs.

11. In the MappingObjects.Mappers project, add a new class file named CartToSummaryMapper. cs and modify its contents to create a mapper configuration that maps the FullName of the Summary to a combination of the FirstName and LastName from Customer, as shown in the following code:

```csharp
using AutoMapper; // MapperConfiguration
using AutoMapper.Internal; // Internal() extension method
using Packt.Entities; // Cart
```

```csharp
using Packt.ViewModels; // Summary

namespace MappingObjects.Mappers;

public static class CartToSummaryMapper
{
  public static MapperConfiguration GetMapperConfiguration()
  {
    MapperConfiguration config = new(cfg =>
    {
      // fix issue with .NET 7 and its new MaxInteger method
      // https://github.com/AutoMapper/AutoMapper/issues/3988
      cfg.Internal().MethodMappingEnabled = false;

      // configure mapper using projections

      cfg.CreateMap<Cart, Summary>()

        // FullName
        .ForMember(dest => dest.FullName, opt => opt.MapFrom(src =>
          string.Format("{0} {1}",
            src.Customer.FirstName,
            src.Customer.LastName)
        ));
    });

    return config;
  }
};
```

12. Use your preferred code editor to add a new **xUnit Test Project**/xunit named MappingObjects. Tests to the Chapter05 solution/workspace.

13. In the MappingObjects.Tests project, add a package reference to AutoMapper, as shown highlighted in the following markup:

```xml
<ItemGroup>
  <PackageReference Include="AutoMapper" Version="11.0.1" />
  <PackageReference Include="Microsoft.NET.Test.Sdk" Version="17.0.0" />
```

14. In the `MappingObjects.Tests` project, add project references to `MappingObjects.Models` and `MappingObjects.Mappers`, as shown in the following markup:

```xml
<ItemGroup>
  <ProjectReference Include=
    "..\MappingObjects.Mappers\MappingObjects.Mappers.csproj" />
  <ProjectReference Include=
    "..\MappingObjects.Models\MappingObjects.Models.csproj" />
</ItemGroup>
```

15. Build the `MappingObjects.Tests` project.

16. In the `MappingObjects.Tests` project, rename `UnitTest1.cs` to `TestAutoMapperConfig.cs`.

17. Modify the contents of `TestAutoMapperConfig.cs` to get the mapper and then assert that the mapping is complete, as shown in the following code:

```csharp
using AutoMapper; // MapperConfiguration
using MappingObjects.Mappers; // CartToSummaryMapper

namespace MappingObjects.Tests;

public class TestAutoMapperConfig
{
  [Fact]
  public void TestSummaryMapping()
  {
    MapperConfiguration config =
      CartToSummaryMapper.GetMapperConfiguration();

    config.AssertConfigurationIsValid();
  }
}
```

18. Run the test:

    • In Visual Studio 2022, navigate to **Test** | **Run All Tests**.

    • In Visual Studio Code, in **Terminal**, enter dotnet test.

19. Note the test fails because the `Total` member of the `Summary` view model is unmapped, as shown in *Figure 5.2*:

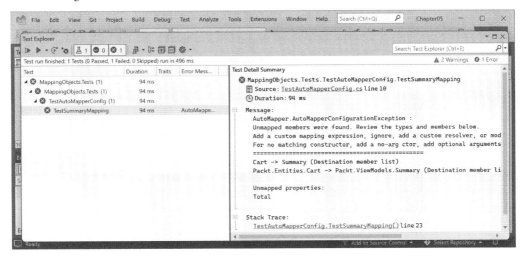

*Figure 5.2: The test fails because the Total member is unmapped*

20. In the `MappingObjects.Mappers` project, in the mapper configuration, add a mapping for the `Total` member, as shown highlighted in the following code:

```
MapperConfiguration config = new(cfg =>
{
  // fix issue with .NET 7 and its new MaxInteger method
  // https://github.com/AutoMapper/AutoMapper/issues/3988
  cfg.Internal().MethodMappingEnabled = false;

  // configure mapper using projections

  cfg.CreateMap<Cart, Summary>()

    // FullName
    .ForMember(dest => dest.FullName, opt => opt.MapFrom(src =>
      string.Format("{0} {1}",
        src.Customer.FirstName, src.Customer.LastName)
    ))

    // Total
    .ForMember(dest => dest.Total, opt => opt.MapFrom(
      src => src.Items.Sum(item => item.UnitPrice * item.Quantity)));
});
```

21.  Run the test and note that this time it passes.

# Performing live mappings between models

Now that we have validated the configuration of our mapping, we can use it in a live app:

1.  Use your preferred code editor to add a new **Console App**/console project named MappingObjects to the Chapter05 solution/workspace.

2.  In the MappingObjects project, globally and statically import the System.Console class, add a project reference for the two class libraries, and add a package reference for AutoMapper, as shown in the following markup:

```xml
<ItemGroup>
  <Using Include="System.Console" Static="true" />
</ItemGroup>

<ItemGroup>
  <ProjectReference Include=
    "..\MappingObjects.Mappers\MappingObjects.Mappers.csproj" />
  <ProjectReference Include=
    "..\MappingObjects.Models\MappingObjects.Models.csproj" />
</ItemGroup>

<ItemGroup>
  <PackageReference Include="AutoMapper" Version="11.0.1" />
</ItemGroup>
```

3.  Build the MappingObjects project:

    •   In Visual Studio Code, select MappingObjects as the active OmniSharp project.

4.  In Program.cs, delete the existing statements and then add some statements to construct an example object model that represents a customer and their shopping cart with a couple of items, and then map it to a summary view model to present to the user, as shown in the following code:

```csharp
using AutoMapper; // MapperConfiguration, IMapper
using MappingObjects.Mappers; // CartToSummaryMapper
using Packt.Entities; // Customer, Cart, LineItem
using Packt.ViewModels; // Summary

// Create an object model from "entity" model types that
// might have come from a data store.
```

```
Cart cart = new(
  Customer: new(
    FirstName: "John",
    LastName: "Smith"
  ),
  Items: new()
  {
    new(ProductName: "Apples", UnitPrice: 0.49M, Quantity: 10),
    new(ProductName: "Bananas", UnitPrice: 0.99M, Quantity: 4)
  }
);

WriteLine($"{cart.Customer}");
foreach (LineItem item in cart.Items)
{
  WriteLine($"  {item}");
}

// Get the mapper configuration for converting a Cart to a Summary.

MapperConfiguration config = CartToSummaryMapper.GetMapperConfiguration();

// Create a mapper using the configuration.

IMapper mapper = config.CreateMapper();

// Perform the mapping.

Summary summary = mapper.Map<Cart, Summary>(cart);

// Output the result.

WriteLine($"Summary: {summary.FullName} spent {summary.Total}.");
```

5.  Run the console app and note the successful result, as shown in the following code:

```
Customer { FirstName = John, LastName = Smith }
  LineItem { ProductName = Apples, UnitPrice = 0.49, Quantity = 10 }
  LineItem { ProductName = Bananas, UnitPrice = 0.99, Quantity = 4 }
Summary: John Smith spent 8.86.
```

**Good Practice:** There is a debate about when AutoMapper should be used that you can read about in an article (which has more links at the bottom) at the following link: `https://www.anthonysteele.co.uk/AgainstAutoMapper.html`.

**More Information:** Learn more details about AutoMapper at the following link: `https://automapper.org/`.

# Making fluent assertions in unit testing

**FluentAssertions** are a set of extension methods that make writing and reading the code in unit tests and the error messages of failing tests more similar to a natural human language like English.

It works with most unit testing frameworks, including xUnit. When you add a package reference for a test framework, FluentAssertions will automatically find the package and use it for throwing exceptions.

After importing the `FluentAssertions` namespace, call the `Should()` extension method on a variable and then one of the hundreds of other extension methods to make assertions in a human-readable way. You can chain multiple assertions using the `And()` extension method or have separate statements, each calling `Should()`.

## Making assertions about strings

Let's start by making assertions about a single `string` value:

1.  Use your preferred code editor to add a new **xUnit Test Project**/xunit named `FluentTests` to a `Chapter05` solution/workspace.

    *   In Visual Studio Code, select `FluentTests` as the active OmniSharp project.

2.  In the `FluentTests` project, add a package reference to `FluentAssertions`, as shown highlighted in the following markup:

    ```
    <ItemGroup>
      <PackageReference Include="FluentAssertions" Version="6.6.0" />
      <PackageReference Include="Microsoft.NET.Test.Sdk" Version="17.0.0" />
    ```

3.  Build the `FluentTests` project.

4.  Rename `UnitTest1.cs` to `FluentExamples.cs`.

5.  In `FluentExamples.cs`, import the namespace to make the fluent assertions extension methods available and write a test method for a `string` value, as shown in the following code:

    ```
    using FluentAssertions;
    ```

```
namespace FluentTests
{
  public class FluentExamples
  {
    [Fact]
    public void TestString()
    {
      string city = "London";
      string expectedCity = "London";

      city.Should().StartWith("Lo")
        .And.EndWith("on")
        .And.Contain("do")
        .And.HaveLength(6);

      city.Should().NotBeNull()
        .And.Be("London")
        .And.BeSameAs(expectedCity)
        .And.BeOfType<string>();

      city.Length.Should().Be(6);
    }
  }
}
```

6. Run the test:

   - In Visual Studio 2022, navigate to **Test | Run All Tests**.
   - In Visual Studio Code, in **Terminal**, enter dotnet test.

7. Note the test passes.

8. In the TestString method, in the expectedCity variable, delete the last n in London.

9. Run the test and note it fails, as shown in the following output:

   ```
   Expected city "Londo" to end with "on".
   ```

10. Add the n back in London.

11. Run the test again to confirm the fix.

# Making assertions about collections and arrays

Now let's continue by making assertions about collections and arrays:

1. In `FluentExamples.cs`, add a test method to explore collection assertions, as shown in the following code:

```
[Fact]
public void TestCollections()
{
  string[] names = new[] { "Alice", "Bob", "Charlie" };

  names.Should().HaveCountLessThan(4,
    "because the maximum items should be 3 or fewer");

  names.Should().OnlyContain(name => name.Length <= 6);
}
```

2. Run the tests and note the collections test fails, as shown in the following output:

```
Expected names to contain only items matching (name.Length <= 6), but
{"Charlie"} do(es) not match.
```

3. Change `Charlie` to `Charly`.

4. Run the tests and note they succeed.

# Making assertions about dates and times

Let's start by making assertions about date and time values:

1. In `FluentExamples.cs`, import the namespace for adding extension methods for named months and other useful date/time-related functionality, as shown in the following code:

```
using FluentAssertions.Extensions; // February, March extension methods
```

2. Add a test method to explore date/time assertions, as shown in the following code:

```
[Fact]
public void TestDateTimes()
{
  DateTime when = new(
    hour: 9, minute: 30, second: 0,
    day: 25, month: 3, year: 2022);

  when.Should().Be(25.March(2022).At(9, 30));
```

```
when.Should().BeOnOrAfter(23.March(2022));

when.Should().NotBeSameDateAs(12.February(2022));

when.Should().HaveYear(2022);

DateTime due = new(
    hour: 11, minute: 0, second: 0,
    day: 25, month: 3, year: 2022);

when.Should().BeAtLeast(2.Hours()).Before(due);
}
```

3. Run the tests and note the date/time test fails, as shown in the following output:

```
Expected when <2022-03-25 09:30:00> to be at least 2h before <2022-03-25
11:00:00>, but it is behind by 1h and 30m.
```

4. For the due variable, change the hour from 11 to 13.
5. Run the tests and note the date/time test succeeds.

 **More Information:** Learn more details at the following link: `https://fluentassertions.com/`.

# Validating data

**FluentValidation** allows you to define strongly typed validation rules in a human-readable way.

You create a validator for a type by inheriting from `AbstractValidator<T>`, where `T` is the type that you want to validate. In the constructor, you call the `RuleFor` method to define one or more rules. If a rule should run only in specified scenarios, then you call the `When` method.

## Understanding the built-in validators

FluentValidation ships with lots of useful built-in validator extension methods for defining rules, as shown in the following partial list:

- `Null`, `NotNull`, `Empty`, `NotEmpty`
- `Equal`, `NotEqual`
- `Length`, `MaxLength`, `MinLength`
- `LessThan`, `LessThanOrEqualTo`, `GreaterThan`, `GreaterThanOrEqualTo`

- InclusiveBetween, ExclusiveBetween
- ScalePrecision
- Must (aka predicate)
- Matches (aka regular expression), EmailAddress, CreditCard
- IsInEnum, IsEnumName

# Performing custom validation

The easiest way to create custom rules is to use Predicate to write a custom validation function. You can also call the Custom method to get maximum control.

# Customizing validation messages

There are a few extension methods that are used to customize the validation messages output when data fails to pass the rules:

- WithName: Change the name used for a property in the message.
- WithSeverity: Change the default severity from Error to Warning or some other level.
- WithErrorCode: Assign an error code that can be output in the message.
- WithState: Add some state that can be used in the message.
- WithMessage: Customize the format of the default message.

# Defining a model and validator

Let's see an example of FluentValidation in action. You will create three projects:

- A class library for a model to validate that represents an order made by a customer
- A class library for the validator for the model
- A console app to perform a live validation

Let's start:

1. Use your preferred code editor to add a new **Class Library**/classlib project named FluentValidation.Models to the Chapter05 solution/workspace.
2. In the FluentValidation.Models project, delete the file named Class1.cs.
3. In the FluentValidation.Models project, add a new class file named CustomerLevel.cs and modify its contents to define an enum with three customer levels, Bronze, Silver, and Gold, as shown in the following code:

```
namespace FluentValidation.Models;

public enum CustomerLevel
{
  Bronze,
```

```
    Silver,
    Gold
}
```

4.  In the FluentValidation.Models project, add a new class file named Order.cs and modify its contents, as shown in the following code:

```
namespace FluentValidation.Models;

public class Order
{
    public long OrderId { get; set; }
    public string? CustomerName { get; set; }
    public string? CustomerEmail { get; set; }
    public CustomerLevel CustomerLevel { get; set; }
    public decimal Total { get; set; }
    public DateTime OrderDate { get; set; }
    public DateTime ShipDate { get; set; }
}
```

5.  Use your preferred code editor to add a new **Class Library**/classlib project named FluentValidation.Validators to the Chapter05 solution/workspace.

6.  In the FluentValidation.Validators project, add a project reference to the models project and a package reference to the FluentValidation package, as shown in the following markup:

```
<ItemGroup>
  <PackageReference Include="FluentValidation" Version="10.4.0" />
</ItemGroup>

<ItemGroup>
  <ProjectReference Include=
    "..\FluentValidation.Models\FluentValidation.Models.csproj" />
</ItemGroup>
```

7.  Build the FluentValidation.Validators project.

8.  In the FluentValidation.Validators project, delete the file named Class1.cs.

9.  In the FluentValidation.Validators project, add a new class file named OrderValidator.cs and modify its contents, as shown in the following code:

```
using FluentValidation.Models;

namespace FluentValidation.Validators;
```

```csharp
public class OrderValidator : AbstractValidator<Order>
{
  public OrderValidator()
  {
    RuleFor(order => order.OrderId)
      .NotEmpty(); // not default(long)

    RuleFor(order => order.CustomerName)
      .NotNull()
      .WithName("Name");

    RuleFor(order => order.CustomerName)
      .MinimumLength(5)
      .WithSeverity(Severity.Warning);

    RuleFor(order => order.CustomerEmail)
      .NotEmpty()
      .EmailAddress();

    RuleFor(order => order.CustomerLevel)
      .IsInEnum();

    RuleFor(order => order.Total)
      .GreaterThan(0);

    RuleFor(order => order.ShipDate)
      .GreaterThan(order => order.OrderDate);

    When(order => order.CustomerLevel == CustomerLevel.Gold, () =>
    {
      RuleFor(order => order.Total).LessThan(50M);
      RuleFor(order => order.Total).GreaterThanOrEqualTo(20M);
    }).Otherwise(() =>
    {
      RuleFor(order => order.Total).LessThan(20M);
    });
  }
}
```

# Testing the validator

Now we are ready to create a console app to test the validator on the model:

1. Use your preferred code editor to add a new console app named `FluentValidation.App` to a `Chapter05` solution/workspace.

    - In Visual Studio Code, select `FluentValidation.App` as the active OmniSharp project.

2. In the `FluentValidation.App` project, globally and statically import the `System.Console` class and add project references for `FluentValidation.Validators` and `FluentValidation.Models`, as shown in the following markup:

```xml
<ItemGroup>
  <Using Include="System.Console" Static="true" />
</ItemGroup>

<ItemGroup>
  <ProjectReference Include=
    "..\FluentValidation.Models\FluentValidation.Models.csproj" />
  <ProjectReference Include=
    "..\FluentValidation.Validators\FluentValidation.Validators.csproj"
/>
</ItemGroup>
```

3. Build the `FluentValidation.App` project.

4. In `Program.cs`, delete the existing statements and then add statements to create an order and validate it, as shown in the following code:

```csharp
using FluentValidation.Models; // Order
using FluentValidation.Results; // ValidationResult
using FluentValidation.Validators; // OrderValidator

Order order = new()
{
  // start with an invalid order
};

OrderValidator validator = new();

ValidationResult result = validator.Validate(order);

WriteLine($"CustomerName: {order.CustomerName}");
```

```
WriteLine($"CustomerEmail: {order.CustomerEmail}");
WriteLine($"CustomerLevel: {order.CustomerLevel}");
WriteLine($"OrderId:       {order.OrderId}");
WriteLine($"OrderDate:     {order.OrderDate}");
WriteLine($"ShipDate:      {order.ShipDate}");
WriteLine($"Total:         {order.Total}");
WriteLine();
WriteLine($"IsValid:  {result.IsValid}");
foreach (var item in result.Errors)
{
  WriteLine($"  {item.Severity}: {item.ErrorMessage}");
}
```

5.  Run the console app and note the failed rules, as shown in the following output:

```
CustomerName:
CustomerEmail:
CustomerLevel: Bronze
OrderId:       0
OrderDate:     01/01/0001 00:00:00
ShipDate:      01/01/0001 00:00:00
Total:         0

IsValid:  False
  Error: 'Order Id' must not be empty.
  Error: 'Name' must not be empty.
  Error: 'Customer Email' must not be empty.
  Error: 'Total' must be greater than '0'.
  Error: 'Ship Date' must be greater than '01/01/0001 00:00:00'.
```

 The text of the error messages will be automatically localized into your operating system's native language.

6.  Set some property values for the order, as shown highlighted in the following code:

```
Order order = new()
{
  OrderId = 10001,
  CustomerName = "Abc",
  CustomerEmail = "abc&example.com",
```

```
    CustomerLevel = (CustomerLevel)4,
    OrderDate = new(2022, 12, 1),
    ShipDate = new(2022, 11, 5),
    Total = 49.99M
};
```

7. Run the console app and note the failed rules, as shown in the following output:

```
CustomerName:  Abc
CustomerEmail: abc&example.com
CustomerLevel: 4
OrderId:       10001
OrderDate:     01/12/2022 00:00:00
ShipDate:      05/11/2022 00:00:00
Total:         49.99


IsValid:  False
  Warning: The length of 'Customer Name' must be at least 5 characters.
You entered 3 characters.
  Error: 'Customer Email' is not a valid email address.
  Error: 'Customer Level' has a range of values which does not include
'4'.
  Error: 'Ship Date' must be greater than '01/12/2022 00:00:00'.
  Error: 'Total' must be less than '20'.
```

8. Modify some property values for the order, as shown highlighted in the following code:

```
Order order = new()
{
  OrderId = 10001,
  CustomerName = "Abcdef",
  CustomerEmail = "abc@example.com",
  CustomerLevel = CustomerLevel.Gold,
  OrderDate = new(2022, 12, 1),
  ShipDate = new(2022, 12, 5),
  Total = 49.99M
};
```

9. Run the console app and note the order is now valid, as shown in the following output:

```
CustomerName:  Abcdef
CustomerEmail: abc@example.com
CustomerLevel: Gold
```

```
OrderId:        10001
OrderDate:      01/12/2022 00:00:00
ShipDate:       05/12/2022 00:00:00
Total:          49.99

IsValid:  True
```

## Integrating with ASP.NET Core

For automatic validation with ASP.NET Core, FluentValidation supports .NET Core 3.1 and later.

 **More Information:** Learn more details at the following link: `https://cecilphillip.com/fluent-validation-rules-with-asp-net-core/`.

# Generating PDFs

One of the most common requests I get when teaching C# and .NET is, "What open-source library is available to generate PDF files?"

There are many licensed libraries for generating PDF files, but over the years it has been difficult to find cross-platform open-source ones. QuestPDF is the latest example.

 QuestPDF uses SkiaSharp and that has implementations for Windows, Mac, and Linux operating systems. The console app that you create in this section to generate PDFs is therefore cross-platform. But on an Apple Silicon Mac, like my Mac mini M1, I had to install the x64 version of .NET 7 and start the project using `dotnet run -a x64`. This tells the .NET SDK to use the x64 architecture, otherwise the SkiaSharp libraries give an error because they have not yet been built to target Arm64.

## Creating class libraries to generate PDF documents

Let's see an example of QuestPDF in action. You will create three projects:

- A class library for a model that represents a catalog of product categories with names and images.
- A class library for the document template.
- A console app to perform a live generation of a PDF file.

Let's start:

1.  Use your preferred code editor to add a new **Class Library**/classlib project named GeneratingPdf.Models to the Chapter05 solution/workspace.
2.  In the GeneratingPdf.Models project, delete the file named Class1.cs.

3.  In the `GeneratingPdf.Models` project, add a new class file named `Category.cs` and modify its contents to define a class with two properties for the name and identifier of a category, as shown in the following code:

    ```
    namespace GeneratingPdf.Models;

    public class Category
    {
      public int CategoryId { get; set; }
      public string CategoryName { get; set; } = null!;
    }
    ```

 Later, you will create an `images` folder with filenames that use the pattern `categoryN.jpeg`, where N is a number from 1 to 8 that matches the `CategoryId` values.

4.  In the `GeneratingPdf.Models` project, add a new class file named `Catalog.cs` and modify its contents to define a class with a property to store the eight categories, as shown in the following code:

    ```
    namespace GeneratingPdf.Models;

    public class Catalog
    {
      public List<Category> Categories { get; set; } = null!;
    }
    ```

5.  Use your preferred code editor to add a new **Class Library**/`classlib` project named `GeneratingPdf.Document` to the `Chapter05` solution/workspace.

6.  In the `GeneratingPdf.Document` project, add a package reference for `QuestPDF` and a project reference for the models class library, as shown in the following markup:

    ```
    <ItemGroup>
      <PackageReference Include="QuestPDF" Version="2022.4.1" />
    </ItemGroup>

    <ItemGroup>
      <ProjectReference Include=
        "..\GeneratingPdf.Models\GeneratingPdf.Models.csproj" />
    </ItemGroup>
    ```

7.  Build the `GeneratingPdf.Document` project.

8.  In the `GeneratingPdf.Document` project, delete the file named `Class1.cs`.

9.  In the `GeneratingPdf.Document` project, add a new class file named `CatalogDocument.cs`.

10. In `CatalogDocument.cs`, define a class that implements the `IDocument` interface to define a template with a header and a footer, and then output the eight categories, including name and image, as shown in the following code:

```csharp
using GeneratingPdf.Models; // Catalog
using QuestPDF.Drawing; // DocumentMetadata
using QuestPDF.Fluent; // Page
using QuestPDF.Helpers; // Colors
using QuestPDF.Infrastructure; // IDocument, IDocumentContainer

namespace GeneratingPdf.Document;

public class CatalogDocument : IDocument
{
  public Catalog Model { get; }

  public CatalogDocument(Catalog model)
  {
    Model = model;
  }

  public void Compose(IDocumentContainer container)
  {
    container
      .Page(page =>
      {
        page.Margin(50 /* points */);

        page.Header()
          .Height(100).Background(Colors.Grey.Lighten1)
          .AlignCenter().Text("Catalogue")
          .Style(TextStyle.Default.FontSize(20));

        page.Content()
          .Background(Colors.Grey.Lighten3)
          .Table(table =>
```

```
      {
        table.ColumnsDefinition(columns =>
        {
          columns.ConstantColumn(100);
          columns.RelativeColumn();
        });

        foreach (var item in Model.Categories)
        {
          table.Cell().Text(item.CategoryName);

          string imagePath = Path.Combine(
            Environment.CurrentDirectory, "images",
            $"category{item.CategoryId}.jpeg");

          table.Cell().Image(imagePath);
        }
      });

    page.Footer()
      .Height(50).Background(Colors.Grey.Lighten1)
      .AlignCenter().Text(x =>
      {
        x.CurrentPageNumber();
        x.Span(" of ");
        x.TotalPages();
      });
    });
  }

  public DocumentMetadata GetMetadata() => DocumentMetadata.Default;
}
```

## Creating a console app to generate PDF documents

Now we can create a console app project that will use the class libraries to generate a PDF document:

1.  Use your preferred code editor to add a new console app named GeneratingPdf.App to a Chapter05 solution/workspace.

    *   In Visual Studio Code, select GeneratingPdf.App as the active OmniSharp project.

2.  In the `GeneratingPdf.App` project, create an images folder and download to it the eight category images 1 to 8 from the following link: `https://github.com/markjprice/apps-services-net7/tree/master/images/Categories`.

3.  If you are using Visual Studio 2022, then the images folder and its files must be copied to the `GeneratingPdf.App\bin\Debug\net7` folder:

    1.  In **Solution Explorer**, select all the images.

    2.  In **Properties**, set **Copy To Output Directory** to **Copy Always**.

    3.  Open the project file and note the `<ItemGroup>` entries that will copy the nine images to the correct folder, as partially shown in the following markup:

    ```
    <ItemGroup>
      <None Update="images\category1.jpeg">
        <CopyToOutputDirectory>Always</CopyToOutputDirectory>
      </None>
    ...
    ```

4.  In the `GeneratingPdf.App` project, globally and statically import the `System.Console` class and add a project reference for the document template class library, as shown in the following markup:

    ```
    <ItemGroup>
      <Using Include="System.Console" Static="true" />
    </ItemGroup>

    <ItemGroup>
      <ProjectReference Include=
        "..\GeneratingPdf.Document\GeneratingPdf.Document.csproj" />
    </ItemGroup>
    ```

5.  Build the `GeneratingPdf.App` project.

6.  In `Program.cs`, delete the existing statements and then add statements to create a catalog model, pass it to a catalog document, generate a PDF file, and then attempt to open the file using the appropriate operating system command, as shown in the following code:

    ```
    using GeneratingPdf.Document; // CatalogDocument
    using GeneratingPdf.Models; // Catalog, Category
    using QuestPDF.Fluent; // GeneratePdf extension method

    string filename = "catalog.pdf";

    Catalog model = new()
    ```

```
{
  Categories = new()
  {
    new() { CategoryId = 1, CategoryName = "Beverages"},
    new() { CategoryId = 2, CategoryName = "Condiments"},
    new() { CategoryId = 3, CategoryName = "Confections"},
    new() { CategoryId = 4, CategoryName = "Dairy Products"},
    new() { CategoryId = 5, CategoryName = "Grains/Cereals"},
    new() { CategoryId = 6, CategoryName = "Meat/Poultry"},
    new() { CategoryId = 7, CategoryName = "Produce"},
    new() { CategoryId = 8, CategoryName = "Seafood"},
  }
};

CatalogDocument document = new(model);
document.GeneratePdf(filename);

WriteLine($"PDF catalog has been created: {filename}");

try
{
  if (OperatingSystem.IsWindows())
  {
    System.Diagnostics.Process.Start("explorer.exe", filename);
  }
  else
  {
    WriteLine("Open the file manually.");
  }
}
catch (Exception ex)
{
  WriteLine($"{ex.GetType()} says {ex.Message}");
}
```

The Process class and its Start method should also be able to start processes on Mac and Linux, but getting the paths right can be tricky, so I've left that as an optional exercise for the reader. You can learn more about the Process class and its Start method at the following link: https://docs.microsoft.com/en-us/dotnet/api/system.diagnostics.process.start.

7.  Run the console app and note the PDF file generated, as shown in *Figure 5.3*:

*Figure 5.3: A PDF file generated from C# code*

 **More Information:** Learn more details at the following link: `https://www.questpdf.com/`.

# Practicing and exploring

Test your knowledge and understanding by answering some questions, getting some hands-on practice, and doing deeper research into the topics in this chapter.

## Exercise 5.1 — Test your knowledge

Use the web to answer the following questions:

1.  What is the most downloaded third-party NuGet package of all time?
2.  What method do you call on the ImageSharp `Image` class to make a change like resizing the image or replacing colors with grayscale?
3.  What is a key benefit of using Serilog for logging?
4.  What is a Serilog sink?
5.  Should you always use a package like AutoMapper to map between objects?
6.  Which FluentAssertions method should you call to start a fluent assertion on a value?
7.  Which FluentAssertions method should you call to assert that all items in a sequence conform to a condition, like a `string` item must have less than six characters?
8.  Which FluentValidation class should you inherit from to define a custom validator?

9. With FluentValidation, how can you set a rule to only apply in certain conditions?

10. With QuestPDF, which interface must you implement to define a document for a PDF, and what methods of that interface must you implement?

## Exercise 5.2 – Explore topics

Use the links on the following page to learn more detail about the topics covered in this chapter:

```
https://github.com/markjprice/apps-services-net7/blob/main/book-links.md#chapter-5---
using-popular-third-party-libraries
```

## Summary

In this chapter, you explored some third-party libraries that are popular with .NET developers to perform functions including:

- Manipulating images using a Microsoft-recommended third-party library named ImageSharp.
- Logging structured data with Serilog.
- Mapping between objects, for example, entity models to view models.
- Making fluent assertions in unit testing.
- Validating data in an English language-readable way.
- Generating a PDF file.

In the next chapter, we will look at advanced features of the C# compiler.

# 6

# Observing and Modifying Code Execution Dynamically

This chapter is about some common types that are included with .NET for performing code reflection and applying and reading attributes, working with expression trees, and creating source generators.

This chapter covers the following topics:

- Working with reflection and attributes
- Working with expression trees
- Creating source generators

## Working with reflection and attributes

**Reflection** is a programming feature that allows code to understand and manipulate itself. An assembly is made up of up to four parts:

- **Assembly metadata and manifest**: Name, assembly, file version, referenced assemblies, and so on.
- **Type metadata**: Information about the types, their members, and so on.
- **IL code**: Implementation of methods, properties, constructors, and so on.
- **Embedded resources** (optional): Images, strings, JavaScript, and so on.

The metadata comprises items of information about your code. The metadata is generated automatically from your code (for example, information about the types and members) or applied to your code using attributes.

Attributes can be applied at multiple levels: to assemblies, to types, and to their members, as shown in the following code:

```
// an assembly-level attribute
[assembly: AssemblyTitle("Working with reflection and attributes")]
```

```
// a type-level attribute
[Serializable]
public class Person
{
  // a member-level attribute
  [Obsolete("Deprecated: use Run instead.")]
  public void Walk()
  {
...
```

Attribute-based programming is used a lot in app models like ASP.NET Core to enable features like routing, security, and caching.

# Versioning of assemblies

Version numbers in .NET are a combination of three numbers, with two optional additions. If you follow the rules of semantic versioning, the three numbers denote the following:

- **Major**: Breaking changes.
- **Minor**: Non-breaking changes, including new features, and often, bug fixes.
- **Patch**: Non-breaking bug fixes.

Optionally, a version can include these:

- **Prerelease**: Unsupported preview releases.
- **Build number**: Nightly builds.

 **Good Practice:** Follow the rules of semantic versioning, as described at the following link: `http://semver.org`.

# Reading assembly metadata

Let's explore working with attributes:

1. Use your preferred code editor to add a new **Console App**/console project named WorkingWithReflection to a Chapter06 solution/workspace:

    - In Visual Studio 2022, set the startup project to the current selection.
    - In Visual Studio Code, select WorkingWithReflection as the active OmniSharp project.

2. In the project file, statically and globally import the Console class, as shown in the following markup:

```
<ItemGroup>
  <Using Include="System.Console" Static="true" />
</ItemGroup>
```

3.  In `Program.cs`, import the namespace for reflection, and add statements to get the console app's assembly, output its name and location, and get all assembly-level attributes and output their types, as shown in the following code:

```
using System.Reflection; // Assembly

WriteLine("Assembly metadata:");
Assembly? assembly = Assembly.GetEntryAssembly();

if (assembly is null)
{
  WriteLine("Failed to get entry assembly.");
  return;
}

WriteLine($"  Full name: {assembly.FullName}");
WriteLine($"  Location: {assembly.Location}");
WriteLine($"  Entry point: {assembly.EntryPoint?.Name}");

IEnumerable<Attribute> attributes = assembly.GetCustomAttributes();
WriteLine($"  Assembly-level attributes:");
foreach (Attribute a in attributes)
{
  WriteLine($"    {a.GetType()}");
}
```

4.  Run the code and view the result, as shown in the following output:

```
Assembly metadata:
  Full name: WorkingWithReflection, Version=1.0.0.0, Culture=neutral,
PublicKeyToken=null
  Location: C:\apps-services-net7\Chapter06\WorkingWithReflection\bin\
Debug\net7.0\WorkingWithReflection.dll
  Entry point: <Main>$
  Assembly-level attributes:
    System.Runtime.CompilerServices.CompilationRelaxationsAttribute
    System.Runtime.CompilerServices.RuntimeCompatibilityAttribute
    System.Diagnostics.DebuggableAttribute
    System.Runtime.Versioning.TargetFrameworkAttribute
    System.Reflection.AssemblyCompanyAttribute
    System.Reflection.AssemblyConfigurationAttribute
    System.Reflection.AssemblyFileVersionAttribute
    System.Reflection.AssemblyInformationalVersionAttribute
    System.Reflection.AssemblyProductAttribute
    System.Reflection.AssemblyTitleAttribute
```

Note that because the full name of an assembly must uniquely identify the assembly, it is a combination of the following:

- **Name**, for example, `WorkingWithReflection`
- **Version**, for example, `1.0.0.0`
- **Culture**, for example, `neutral`
- **Public key token**, although this can be `null`

Now that we know some of the attributes decorating the assembly, we can ask for them specifically.

5. Add statements to get the `AssemblyInformationalVersionAttribute` and `AssemblyCompanyAttribute` classes and then output their values, as shown in the following code:

```
AssemblyInformationalVersionAttribute? version = assembly
  .GetCustomAttribute<AssemblyInformationalVersionAttribute>();

WriteLine($"  Version: {version?.InformationalVersion}");

AssemblyCompanyAttribute? company = assembly
  .GetCustomAttribute<AssemblyCompanyAttribute>();

WriteLine($"  Company: {company?.Company}");
```

6. Run the code and view the result, as shown in the following output:

```
Version: 1.0.0
Company: WorkingWithReflection
```

Hmmm, unless you set the version, it defaults to `1.0.0`, and unless you set the company, it defaults to the name of the assembly.

Let's explicitly set this information. The legacy .NET Framework way to set these values was to add attributes in the C# source code file, as shown in the following code:

```
[assembly: AssemblyCompany("Packt Publishing")]
[assembly: AssemblyInformationalVersion("1.3.0")]
```

The Roslyn compiler used by .NET sets these attributes automatically, so we can't use the old way. Instead, they must be set in the project file.

7. Edit the `WorkingWithReflection.csproj` project file to add elements for version and company, as shown highlighted in the following markup:

```
<Project Sdk="Microsoft.NET.Sdk">

  <PropertyGroup>
    <OutputType>Exe</OutputType>
    <TargetFramework>net7.0</TargetFramework>
```

```
<Nullable>enable</Nullable>
<ImplicitUsings>enable</ImplicitUsings>
<Version>7.0.1</Version>
<Company>Packt Publishing</Company>
</PropertyGroup>
```

8.  Run the code and view the result, as shown in the following partial output:

```
Assembly metadata:
  Full name: WorkingWithReflection, Version=7.0.1.0, Culture=neutral,
PublicKeyToken=null

  ...
  Version: 7.0.1
  Company: Packt Publishing
```

# Creating custom attributes

You can define your own attributes by inheriting from the Attribute class:

1.  Add a class file to your project named CoderAttribute.cs.

2.  In CoderAttribute.cs, define an attribute class that can decorate either classes or methods with two properties to store the name of a coder and the date they last modified some code, as shown in the following code:

```csharp
namespace Packt.Shared;

[AttributeUsage(AttributeTargets.Class | AttributeTargets.Method,
  AllowMultiple = true)]
public class CoderAttribute : Attribute
{
  public string Coder { get; set; }
  public DateTime LastModified { get; set; }

  public CoderAttribute(string coder, string lastModified)
  {
    Coder = coder;
    LastModified = DateTime.Parse(lastModified);
  }
}
```

3.  Add a class file to your project named Animal.cs.

4.  In Animal.cs, add a class with a method, and decorate the method with the Coder attribute with data about two coders, as shown in the following code:

```csharp
namespace Packt.Shared;

public class Animal
{
  [Coder("Mark Price", "22 August 2022")]
```

```
  [Coder("Johnni Rasmussen", "13 September 2022")]
  public void Speak()
  {
    WriteLine("Woof...");
  }
}
```

5.  In `Program.cs`, import namespaces for working with your custom attribute, as shown in the following code:

```
using Packt.Shared; // CoderAttribute
```

6.  In `Program.cs`, add code to get the types in the current assembly, enumerate their members, read any `Coder` attributes on those members, and output the information, as shown in the following code:

```
WriteLine();
WriteLine($"* Types:");
Type[] types = assembly.GetTypes();

foreach (Type type in types)
{
  WriteLine();
  WriteLine($"Type: {type.FullName}");
  MemberInfo[] members = type.GetMembers();

  foreach (MemberInfo member in members)
  {
    WriteLine("{0}: {1} ({2})",
      member.MemberType, member.Name,
      member.DeclaringType?.Name);

    IOrderedEnumerable<CoderAttribute> coders =
      member.GetCustomAttributes<CoderAttribute>()
      .OrderByDescending(c => c.LastModified);

    foreach (CoderAttribute coder in coders)
    {
      WriteLine("-> Modified by {0} on {1}",
        coder.Coder, coder.LastModified.ToShortDateString());
    }
  }
}
```

7.  Run the code and view the result, as shown in the following partial output:

```
* Types:
...
Type: Packt.Shared.Animal
```

```
Method: Speak (Animal)
-> Modified by Johnni Rasmussen on 13/09/2022
-> Modified by Mark Price on 22/08/2022
Method: GetType (Object)
Method: ToString (Object)
Method: Equals (Object)
Method: GetHashCode (Object)
Constructor: .ctor (Program)
...
Type: Program+<>c
Method: GetType (Object)
Method: ToString (Object)
Method: Equals (Object)
Method: GetHashCode (Object)
Constructor: .ctor (<>c)
Field: <>9 (<>c)
Field: <>9__0_0 (<>c)
```

# Understanding compiler-generated types and members

What is the `Program+<>c` type and its strangely named fields?

It is a compiler-generated **display class**. `<>` indicates compiler-generated and `c` indicates a display class. They are undocumented implementation details of the compiler and could change at any time. You can ignore them, so as an optional challenge, add statements to your console app to filter compiler-generated types by skipping types decorated with `CompilerGeneratedAttribute`.

Hint: Import the namespace for working with compiler-generated code, as shown in the following code:

```
using System.Runtime.CompilerServices; // CompilerGeneratedAttribute
```

# Making a type or member obsolete

Over time, you might decide to refactor your types and their members while maintaining backward compatibility. To encourage developers who use your types to use the newer implementations, you can decorate the old types and members with the [`Obsolete`] attribute.

Let's see an example:

1.  In `Animal.cs`, add a new method and mark the old method as obsolete, as shown highlighted in the following code:

```
[Coder("Mark Price", "22 August 2022")]
[Coder("Johnni Rasmussen", "13 September 2022")]
[Obsolete($"use {nameof(SpeakBetter)} instead.")]
public void Speak()
{
    WriteLine("Woof...");
}
```

```
public void SpeakBetter()
{
  WriteLine("Wooooooooof...");
}
```

2.  In `Program.cs`, modify the statements to detect obsolete methods, as shown highlighted in the following code:

```
foreach (MemberInfo member in members)
{
  ObsoleteAttribute? obsolete =
    member.GetCustomAttribute<ObsoleteAttribute>();

  WriteLine("{0}: {1} ({2}) {3}",
    member.MemberType, member.Name,
    member.DeclaringType?.Name,
    obsolete is null ? "" : $"Obsolete! {obsolete.Message}");
```

3.  Run the code and view the result, as shown in the following output:

```
Type: Packt.Shared.Animal
Method: Speak (Animal) Obsolete! use SpeakBetter instead.
-> Modified by Johnni Rasmussen on 13/09/2022
-> Modified by Mark Price on 22/08/2022
Method: SpeakBetter (Animal)
Method: GetType (Object)
Method: ToString (Object)
Method: Equals (Object)
Method: GetHashCode (Object)
Constructor: .ctor (Animal)
```

# Dynamically loading assemblies and executing methods

Normally, if a .NET project needs to execute in another .NET assembly, you reference the package or project, and then at compile time, the compiler knows the assemblies that will be loaded into the memory of the calling codebase during start up at runtime. But sometimes you may not know the assemblies that you need to call until runtime. For example, a word processor does not need to have the functionality to perform a mail merge loaded all the time. The mail merge feature could be implemented as a separate assembly that is only loaded into memory when it is activated by the user. Another example would be an application that allows custom plugins, perhaps even created by other developers.

You can dynamically load a set of assemblies into an `AssemblyLoadContext`, execute methods in them, and then unload the `AssemblyLoadContext`, which unloads the assemblies too. A side effect of this is reduced memory usage.

In .NET 7, the overhead of using reflection to invoke a member of a type, like calling a method or setting, or getting a property, has been made up to four times faster when it is done more than once on the same member.

Let's see how to dynamically load an assembly and then instantiate a class and interact with its members:

1.  Use your preferred code editor to add a new **Class Library**/classlib project named DynamicLoadAndExecute.Library to the Chapter06 solution/workspace.

2.  In the project file, treat warnings as errors, statically and globally import the Console class, and globally import the namespace for working with reflection, as shown highlighted in the following markup:

    ```xml
    <Project Sdk="Microsoft.NET.Sdk">

      <PropertyGroup>
        <TargetFramework>net7.0</TargetFramework>
        <ImplicitUsings>enable</ImplicitUsings>
        <Nullable>enable</Nullable>
        <TreatWarningsAsErrors>true</TreatWarningsAsErrors>
      </PropertyGroup>

      <ItemGroup>
        <Using Include="System.Reflection" />
        <Using Include="System.Console" Static="true" />
      </ItemGroup>

    </Project>
    ```

3.  Rename Class1.cs to Dog.cs.

4.  In Dog.cs, define a Dog class with a Speak method that writes a simple message to the console based on a string parameter passed to the method, as shown in the following code:

    ```csharp
    namespace DynamicLoadAndExecute.Library;

    public class Dog
    {
      public void Speak(string? name)
      {
        WriteLine($"{name} says Woof!");
      }
    }
    ```

5.  Use your preferred code editor to add a new **Console App**/console project named DynamicLoadAndExecute.Console to the Chapter06 solution/workspace.

6.  In the project file, treat warnings as errors, statically and globally import the Console class, and globally import the namespace for working with reflection, as shown highlighted in the following markup:

```xml
<Project Sdk="Microsoft.NET.Sdk">

  <PropertyGroup>
    <OutputType>Exe</OutputType>
    <TargetFramework>net7.0</TargetFramework>
    <ImplicitUsings>enable</ImplicitUsings>
    <Nullable>enable</Nullable>
    <TreatWarningsAsErrors>true</TreatWarningsAsErrors>
  </PropertyGroup>

  <ItemGroup>
    <Using Include="System.Reflection" />
    <Using Include="System.Console" Static="true" />
  </ItemGroup>

</Project>
```

7.  Build the DynamicLoadAndExecute.Library project to create the assembly in its bin folder structure.

8.  Build the DynamicLoadAndExecute.Console project to create its bin folder structure.

9.  Copy the three files from the DynamicLoadAndExecute.Library project's bin\Debug\net7.0 folder to the equivalent folder in the DynamicLoadAndExecute.Console project, as shown in the following list:

    *   DynamicLoadAndExecute.Library.deps.json
    *   DynamicLoadAndExecute.Library.dll
    *   DynamicLoadAndExecute.Library.pdb

10. In the DynamicLoadAndExecute.Console project, add a new class file named Program.Helpers. cs and modify its contents to define a method to output information about an assembly and its types, as shown in the following code:

```csharp
partial class Program
{
  static void OutputAssemblyInfo(Assembly a)
  {
    WriteLine("FullName: {0}", a.FullName);
    WriteLine("Location: {0}", Path.GetDirectoryName(a.Location));
    WriteLine("IsCollectible: {0}", a.IsCollectible);
    WriteLine("Defined types:");
    foreach (TypeInfo info in a.DefinedTypes)
    {
      if (!info.Name.EndsWith("Attribute"))
```

```
      {
        WriteLine("  Name: {0}, Members: {1}",
          info.Name, info.GetMembers().Count());
      }
    }
    WriteLine();
  }
}
```

11. In the `DynamicLoadAndExecute.Console` project, add a new class file named `DemoAssemblyLoadContext.cs`, and modify its contents to load a named assembly into the current context at runtime using an assembly dependency resolver, as shown in the following code:

```
using System.Runtime.Loader; // AssemblyDependencyResolver

internal class DemoAssemblyLoadContext : AssemblyLoadContext
{
  private AssemblyDependencyResolver _resolver;

  public DemoAssemblyLoadContext(string mainAssemblyToLoadPath)
    : base(isCollectible: true)
  {
    _resolver = new AssemblyDependencyResolver(mainAssemblyToLoadPath);
  }
}
```

12. In `Program.cs`, delete the existing statements. Then, use the load context class to load the class library and output information about it, and then dynamically create an instance of the Dog class and call its Speak method, as shown in the following code:

```
Assembly? thisAssembly = Assembly.GetEntryAssembly();

if (thisAssembly is null)
{
  WriteLine("Could not get the entry assembly.");
  return;
}

OutputAssemblyInfo(thisAssembly);

WriteLine("Creating load context for:\n {0}\n",
  Path.GetFileName(thisAssembly.Location));

DemoAssemblyLoadContext loadContext = new(thisAssembly.Location);

string assemblyPath = Path.Combine(
  Path.GetDirectoryName(thisAssembly.Location) ?? "",
```

```
    "DynamicLoadAndExecute.Library.dll");

WriteLine("Loading:\n  {0}\n",
  Path.GetFileName(assemblyPath));

Assembly dogAssembly = loadContext.LoadFromAssemblyPath(assemblyPath);

OutputAssemblyInfo(dogAssembly);

Type? dogType = dogAssembly.GetType("DynamicLoadAndExecute.Library.Dog");

if (dogType is null)
{
  WriteLine("Could not get the Dog type.");
  return;
}

MethodInfo? method = dogType.GetMethod("Speak");

if (method != null)
{
  object? dog = Activator.CreateInstance(dogType);

  for (int i = 0; i < 10; i++)
  {
    method.Invoke(dog, new object[] { "Fido" });
  }
}

WriteLine();
WriteLine("Unloading context and assemblies.");
loadContext.Unload();
```

13. Start the console app and note the results, as shown in the following output:

```
FullName: DynamicLoadAndExecute.Console, Version=1.0.0.0,
Culture=neutral, PublicKeyToken=null
Location: C:\apps-services-net7\Chapter06\DynamicLoadAndExecute.Console\
bin\Debug\net7.0
IsCollectible: False
Defined types:
  Name: DemoAssemblyLoadContext, Members: 29
  Name: Program, Members: 5

Creating load context for:
  DynamicLoadAndExecute.Console.dll
```

```
Loading:
  DynamicLoadAndExecute.Library.dll

FullName: DynamicLoadAndExecute.Library, Version=1.0.0.0,
Culture=neutral, PublicKeyToken=null
Location: C:\apps-services-net7\Chapter06\DynamicLoadAndExecute.Console\
bin\Debug\net7.0
IsCollectible: True
Defined types:
  Name: Dog, Members: 6

Fido says Woof!
Fido says Woof!
Fido says Woof!
Fido says Woof!
Fido says Woof!
Fido says Woof!
Fido says Woof!
Fido says Woof!
Fido says Woof!
Fido says Woof!

Unloading context and assemblies.
```

 Note that the entry assembly (the console app) is not **collectible**, meaning that it cannot be removed from memory, but the dynamically loaded class library is collectible.

## Doing more with reflection

This is just a taster of what can be achieved with reflection. Reflection can also do the following:

- **Inspect assembly contents using MetadataLoadContext**: https://docs.microsoft.com/en-us/dotnet/standard/assembly/inspect-contents-using-metadataloadcontext
- **Dynamically generate new code and assemblies**: https://docs.microsoft.com/en-us/dotnet/api/system.reflection.emit.assemblybuilder

# Working with expression trees

Expression trees represent code as a structure that you can examine or execute. Expression trees are immutable so you cannot change one, but you can create a copy with the changes you want.

If you compare expression trees to functions, then although functions have flexibility in the parameter values passed to them, the structure of the function, what it does with those values, and how are all fixed. Expression trees provide a structure that can dynamically change, so what and how a function is implemented can be dynamically changed at runtime.

Expression trees are also used to represent an expression in an abstract way, so instead of being expressed using C# code, the expression is expressed as a data structure in memory. This then allows that data structure to be expressed in other ways, using other languages.

When you write a LINQ expression for the EF Core database provider, it is represented by an expression tree that is then translated into an SQL statement. But even the simplest C# statement can be represented as an expression tree.

Let's look at a simple example, adding two numbers:

```
int three = 1 + 2;
```

This statement would be represented as the tree in *Figure 6.1*:

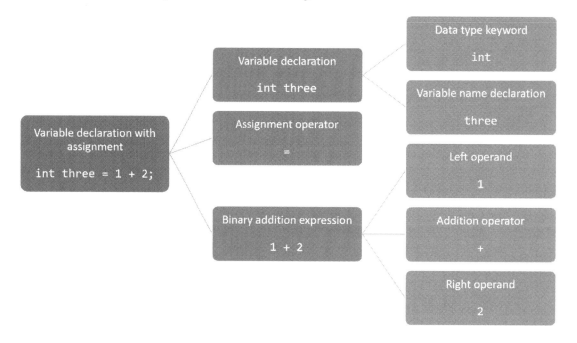

*Figure 6.1: An expression tree of a simple statement adding two numbers*

## Understanding components of expression trees

The `System.Linq.Expressions` namespace contains types for representing the components of an expression tree. For example:

| Type | Description |
|------|-------------|
| BinaryExpression | An expression with a binary operator. |
| BlockExpression | A block containing a sequence of expressions where variables can be defined. |
| CatchBlock | A catch statement in a try block. |

| ConditionalExpression | An expression that has a conditional operator. |
|---|---|
| LambdaExpression | A lambda expression. |
| MemberAssignment | Assigning to a field or property. |
| MemberExpression | Accessing a field or property. |
| MethodCallExpression | A call to a method. |
| NewExpression | A call to a constructor. |

Only expression trees that represent lambda expressions can be executed.

## Executing the simplest expression tree

Let's see how to construct, compile, and execute an expression tree:

1. Use your preferred code editor to add a new **Console App**/console project named WorkingWithExpressionTrees to the Chapter06 solution/workspace.

2. In the project file, statically and globally import the Console class, as shown in the following markup:

```
<ItemGroup>
  <Using Include="System.Console" Static="true" />
</ItemGroup>
```

3. In Program.cs, delete the existing statements and then define an expression tree and execute it, as shown in the following code:

```
using System.Linq.Expressions; // Expression and so on

ConstantExpression one = Expression.Constant(1, typeof(int));
ConstantExpression two = Expression.Constant(2, typeof(int));
BinaryExpression add = Expression.Add(one, two);

Expression<Func<int>> expressionTree = Expression.Lambda<Func<int>>(add);

Func<int> compiledTree = expressionTree.Compile();

WriteLine($"Result: {compiledTree()}");
```

4. Run the console app and note the result, as shown in the following output:

```
Result: 3
```

## Creating source generators

Source generators were introduced with C# 9 and .NET 5. They allow a programmer to get a compilation object that represents all the code being compiled, dynamically generate additional code files, and compile those too. Source generators are like code analyzers that can add more code to the compilation process.

A great example is the System.Text.Json source generator. The classic method for serializing JSON uses reflection at runtime to dynamically analyze an object model, but this is slow. The better method uses source generators to create source code that is then compiled to give improved performance.

> You can read more about the System.Text.Json source generator at the following link: https://devblogs.microsoft.com/dotnet/try-the-new-system-text-json-source-generator/.

## Implementing the simplest source generator

We will create a source generator that programmatically creates a code file that adds a method to the Program class, as shown in the following code:

```
// source-generated code
static partial class Program
{
  static partial void Message(string message)
  {
    System.Console.WriteLine($"Generator says: '{message}'");
  }
}
```

This method can then be called in the Program.cs file of the project that uses this source generator.

Let's see how to do this:

1.  Use your preferred code editor to add a new **Console App**/console project named GeneratingCodeApp to the Chapter06 solution/workspace.

2.  In the project file, statically and globally import the Console class, as shown in the following markup:

    ```
    <ItemGroup>
      <Using Include="System.Console" Static="true" />
    </ItemGroup>
    ```

3.  Add a new class file name Program.Methods.cs.

4.  In Program.Methods.cs, define a partial Program class with a partial method with a string parameter, as shown in the following code:

    ```
    partial class Program
    {
      static partial void Message(string message);
    }
    ```

5.  In Program.cs, delete the existing statements and then call the partial method, as shown in the following code:

    ```
    Message("Hello from some source generator code.");
    ```

6. Use your preferred code editor to add a new **Class Library**/classlib project named GeneratingCodeLib that targets .NET Standard 2.0 to the Chapter06 solution/workspace.

> Currently, source generators must target .NET Standard 2.0. The default C# version used for class libraries that target .NET Standard 2.0 is C# 7.3, as shown at the following link: https://docs.microsoft.com/en-us/dotnet/csharp/language-reference/configure-language-version#defaults.

7. In the project file, set the C# language version to 10 or later (to support global using statements), statically and globally import the Console class, and add the NuGet packages Microsoft.CodeAnalysis.Analyzers and Microsoft.CodeAnalysis.CSharp, as shown highlighted in the following markup:

```xml
<Project Sdk="Microsoft.NET.Sdk">

  <PropertyGroup>
    <TargetFramework>netstandard2.0</TargetFramework>
    <LangVersion>10</LangVersion>
  </PropertyGroup>

  <ItemGroup>
    <Using Include="System.Console" Static="true" />
  </ItemGroup>

  <ItemGroup>
    <PackageReference Include="Microsoft.CodeAnalysis.Analyzers"
                      Version="3.3.3">
      <PrivateAssets>all</PrivateAssets>
      <IncludeAssets>runtime; build; native; contentfiles; analyzers;
                     buildtransitive</IncludeAssets>
    </PackageReference>
    <PackageReference Include="Microsoft.CodeAnalysis.CSharp"
                      Version="4.1.0" />
  </ItemGroup>

</Project>
```

> This project does not enable null warnings because the <Nullable>enable</Nullable> element is missing. If you add it, then you will see some null warnings later.

8. Build the GeneratingCodeLib project.

9. Rename Class1.cs as MessageSourceGenerator.cs.

10. In the `GeneratingCodeLib` project, in `MessageSourceGenerator.cs`, define a class that implements `ISourceGenerator` and is decorated with the `[Generator]` attribute, as shown in the following code:

```
using Microsoft.CodeAnalysis; // [Generator],
GeneratorInitializationContext
                              // ISourceGenerator,
GeneratorExecutionContext

namespace Packt.Shared;

[Generator]
public class MessageSourceGenerator : ISourceGenerator
{
  public void Execute(GeneratorExecutionContext execContext)
  {
    IMethodSymbol mainMethod = execContext.Compilation
      .GetEntryPoint(execContext.CancellationToken);

    string sourceCode = $@"// source-generated code
static partial class {mainMethod.ContainingType.Name}
{{
  static partial void Message(string message)
  {{
    System.Console.WriteLine($""Generator says: '{{message}}'"");
  }}
}}
";
    string typeName = mainMethod.ContainingType.Name;
    execContext.AddSource($"{typeName}.Methods.g.cs", sourceCode);
  }

  public void Initialize(GeneratorInitializationContext initContext)
  {
    // this source generator does not need any initialization
  }
}
```

 **Good Practice:** Include `.g.` or `.generated.` in the filename of source-generated files.

11. In the `GeneratingCodeApp` project, in the project file, add a reference to the class library project, as shown in the following markup:

```
<ItemGroup>
```

```
    <ProjectReference Include="..\GeneratingCodeLib\GeneratingCodeLib.
csproj"
                       OutputItemType="Analyzer"
                       ReferenceOutputAssembly="false" />
</ItemGroup>
```

 **Good Practice:** It is sometimes necessary to restart Visual Studio 2022 to see the results of working with source generators.

Build the GeneratingCodeApp project and note the auto-generated class file:

- In Visual Studio 2022, in **Solution Explorer**, expand the **Dependencies | Analyzers | GeneratingCodeLib | Packt.Shared.MessageSourceGenerator** nodes to find the Program.Methods.g.cs file, as shown in *Figure 6.2*:

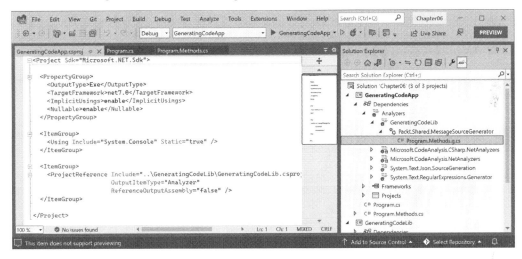

*Figure 6.2: The source-generated Program.Methods.g.cs file*

 Visual Studio Code does not automatically run analyzers. We must add an extra entry in the project file to enable the automatic generation of the source generator file.

- In Visual Studio Code, in the GeneratingCodeApp project, in the project file, in the `<PropertyGroup>`, add an entry to enable the generation of the code file, as shown in the following markup:

```
<EmitCompilerGeneratedFiles>true</EmitCompilerGeneratedFiles>
```

- In Visual Studio Code, in **Terminal**, build the GeneratingCodeApp project.

- In Visual Studio Code, in the obj/Debug/net7.0 folder, note the generated folder and its subfolder GeneratingCodeLib/Packt.Shared.MessageSourceGenerator, and the auto-generated file named Program.Methods.g.cs.

12. Open the Program.Methods.g.cs file and note its contents, as shown in the following code:

```
// source-generated code
static partial class Program
{
  static partial void Message(string message)
  {
    System.Console.WriteLine($"Generator says: '{message}'");
  }
}
```

13. Run the console app and note the message, as shown in the following output:

```
Generator says: 'Hello from some source generator code.'
```

 You can control the path for automatically generated code files by adding a <CompilerG eneratedFilesOutputPath> element.

## Doing more with source generators

Source generators are a massive topic.

To learn more, use the following links:

- Source generators design specification: https://github.com/dotnet/roslyn/blob/main/docs/features/source-generators.md
- Source generators samples: https://github.com/dotnet/roslyn-sdk/tree/main/samples/CSharp/SourceGenerators
- Source generators cookbook: https://github.com/dotnet/roslyn/blob/main/docs/features/source-generators.cookbook.md

# Practicing and exploring

Test your knowledge and understanding by answering some questions, getting some hands-on practice, and exploring with deeper research into the topics in this chapter.

## Exercise 6.1 – Test your knowledge

Use the web to answer the following questions:

1. What are the four parts of a .NET assembly and which are optional?
2. What can an attribute be applied to?

3. What are the names of the parts of a version number and what do they mean if they follow the rules of semantic versioning?

4. How do you get a reference to the assembly for the currently executing console app?

5. How do you get all the attributes applied to an assembly?

6. How should you create a custom attribute?

7. What class do you inherit from to enable dynamic loading of assemblies?

8. What is an expression tree?

9. What is a source generator?

10. Which interface must a source generator class implement and what methods are part of that interface?

## Exercise 6.2 — Explore topics

Use the links on the following page to learn more detail about the topics covered in this chapter:

```
https://github.com/markjprice/apps-services-net7/blob/main/book-links.md#chapter-6---
controlling-the-roslyn-compiler-reflection-and-expression-trees
```

## Summary

In this chapter, you:

- Reflected on code and attributes.
- Constructed, compiled, and executed a simple expression tree.
- Built a source generator and used it in a console app project.

In the next chapter, we will learn how to work with data stored in SQL Server.

## Join our book's Discord space

Join the book's Discord workspace for *Ask me Anything* sessions with the author.

```
https://packt.link/apps_and_services_dotnet7
```

# 7

# Handling Dates, Times, and Internationalization

This chapter is about some common types that are included with .NET. These include types for manipulating dates and times and implementing internationalization, which includes globalization and localization.

When writing code to handle times, it is especially important to consider time zones. Bugs are often introduced because two times are compared in different time zones without taking that into account. It is important to understand the concept of **Coordinated Universal Time (UTC)** and to convert time values into UTC before performing time manipulation. You should also be aware of any **Daylight Saving Time (DST)** adjustments that might be needed.

This chapter covers the following topics:

- Working with dates and times
- Working with time zones
- Working with cultures

## Working with dates and times

After numbers and text, the next most popular types of data to work with are dates and times. The two main types are as follows:

- `DateTime`: Represents a combined date and time value for a fixed point in time.
- `TimeSpan`: Represents a duration of time.

These two types are often used together. For example, if you subtract one `DateTime` value from another, the result is a `TimeSpan`. If you add a `TimeSpan` to a `DateTime`, then the result is a `DateTime` value.

# Specifying date and time values

A common way to create a date and time value is to specify individual values for the date and time components like day and hour, as described in the following table:

| Date/time parameter | Value range |
|---|---|
| year | 1 to 9,999 |
| month | 1 to 12 |
| day | 1 to the number of days in that month |
| hour | 0 to 23 |
| minute | 0 to 59 |
| second | 0 to 59 |
| millisecond | 0 to 999 |
| microsecond | 0 to 999 |

An alternative is to provide the value as a string to be parsed, but this can be misinterpreted depending on the default culture of the thread. For example, in the UK, dates are specified as day/month/year, compared to the US, where dates are specified as month/day/year.

Let's see what you might want to do with dates and times:

1.  Use your preferred code editor to create a new project, as defined in the following list:

    -   Project template: **Console App**/console
    -   Project file and folder: WorkingWithTime
    -   Workspace/solution file and folder: Chapter07

    In Visual Studio Code, select WorkingWithTime as the active OmniSharp project.

2.  In the project file, add an element to statically and globally import the System.Console class.

3.  Add a new class file named Program.Helpers.cs and modify its contents, as shown in the following code:

```
partial class Program
{
  static void SectionTitle(string title)
  {
    ConsoleColor previousColor = ForegroundColor;
    ForegroundColor = ConsoleColor.DarkYellow;
    WriteLine("*");
    WriteLine($"* {title}");
    WriteLine("*");
    ForegroundColor = previousColor;
  }
}
```

4.  In `Program.cs`, delete the existing statements and then add statements to initialize some special date/time values, as shown in the following code:

```
SectionTitle("Specifying date and time values");

WriteLine($"DateTime.MinValue:   {DateTime.MinValue}");
WriteLine($"DateTime.MaxValue:   {DateTime.MaxValue}");
WriteLine($"DateTime.UnixEpoch: {DateTime.UnixEpoch}");
WriteLine($"DateTime.Now:        {DateTime.Now}");
WriteLine($"DateTime.Today:      {DateTime.Today}");
```

5.  Run the code and note the results, as shown in the following output:

```
DateTime.MinValue:   01/01/0001 00:00:00
DateTime.MaxValue:   31/12/9999 23:59:59
DateTime.UnixEpoch: 01/01/1970 00:00:00
DateTime.Now:        23/03/2022 13:50:30
DateTime.Today:      23/03/2022 00:00:00
```

> The date and time formats output are determined by the culture settings of your console app; for example, mine uses *English (Great Britain)* culture. Optionally, to see the same output as mine, add a statement to the top of your `Program.cs`, as shown in the following code:
>
> ```
> Thread.CurrentThread.CurrentCulture =
>   System.Globalization.CultureInfo.GetCultureInfo("en-GB");
> ```

# Formatting date and time values

You have just seen that dates and times have default formats based on the current culture. You can take control of date and time formatting using custom format codes:

1.  Add statements to define Christmas Day in 2024 and display it in various ways, as shown in the following code:

```
DateTime xmas = new(year: 2024, month: 12, day: 25);
WriteLine($"Christmas (default format): {xmas}");
WriteLine($"Christmas (custom format): {xmas:dddd, dd MMMM yyyy}");
WriteLine($"Christmas is in month {xmas.Month} of the year.");
WriteLine($"Christmas is day {xmas.DayOfYear} of the year 2024.");
WriteLine($"Christmas {xmas.Year} is on a {xmas.DayOfWeek}.");
```

2.  Run the code and note the results, as shown in the following output:

```
Christmas (default format): 25/12/2024 00:00:00
Christmas (custom format): Wednesday, 25 December 2024
Christmas is in month 12 of the year.
Christmas is day 360 of the year 2024.
Christmas 2024 is on a Wednesday.
```

# Date and time calculations

Now, let's try performing simple calculations on date and time values:

1. Add statements to perform addition and subtraction with Christmas 2024, as shown in the following code:

```
SectionTitle("Date and time calculations");

DateTime beforeXmas = xmas.Subtract(TimeSpan.FromDays(12));
DateTime afterXmas = xmas.AddDays(12);

// :d means format as short date only without time
WriteLine($"12 days before Christmas: {beforeXmas:d}");
WriteLine($"12 days after Christmas: {afterXmas:d}");

TimeSpan untilXmas = xmas - DateTime.Now;

WriteLine($"Now: {DateTime.Now}");
WriteLine("There are {0} days and {1} hours until Christmas 2024.",
  arg0: untilXmas.Days, arg1: untilXmas.Hours);

WriteLine("There are {0:N0} hours until Christmas 2024.",
  arg0: untilXmas.TotalHours);
```

2. Run the code and note the results, as shown in the following output:

```
12 days before Christmas: 13/12/2024
12 days after Christmas: 06/01/2025
Now: 23/03/2022 16:16:02
There are 1007 days and 7 hours until Christmas 2024.
There are 24,176 hours until Christmas 2024.
```

3. Add statements to define the time on Christmas Day that your children (or dog? Or cat? Or iguana?) might wake up to open presents, and display it in various ways, as shown in the following code:

```
DateTime kidsWakeUp = new(
  year: 2024, month: 12, day: 25,
  hour: 6, minute: 30, second: 0);

WriteLine($"Kids wake up: {kidsWakeUp}");

WriteLine("The kids woke me up at {0}",
  arg0: kidsWakeUp.ToShortTimeString());
```

4. Run the code and note the results, as shown in the following output:

```
Kids wake up: 25/12/2024 06:30:00
```

```
The kids woke me up at 06:30
```

# Microseconds and nanoseconds

In earlier versions of .NET, the smallest unit of time measurement was a tick. A tick is 100 nanoseconds, so developers used to have to do the calculations themselves. .NET 7 introduces milli- and microsecond parameters to constructors, and micro- and nanosecond properties to the `DateTime`, `DateTimeOffset`, `TimeSpan`, and `TimeOnly` types.

Let's see some examples:

1.  Add statements to construct a date and time value with more precision than was possible and to display its value, as shown in the following code:

    ```
    SectionTitle("Milli-, micro-, and nanoseconds");

    DateTime preciseTime = new(
      year: 2022, month: 11, day: 8,
      hour: 12, minute: 0, second: 0,
      millisecond: 6, microsecond: 999);

    WriteLine("Millisecond: {0}, Microsecond: {1}, Nanosecond: {2}",
      preciseTime.Millisecond, preciseTime.Microsecond, preciseTime.Nanosecond);

    preciseTime = DateTime.UtcNow;

    // Nanosecond value will be 0 to 900 in 100 nanosecond increments.
    WriteLine("Millisecond: {0}, Microsecond: {1}, Nanosecond: {2}",
      preciseTime.Millisecond, preciseTime.Microsecond, preciseTime.Nanosecond);
    ```

2.  Run the code and note the results, as shown in the following output:

    ```
    *
    * Milli-, micro-, and nanoseconds
    *
    Millisecond: 6, Microsecond: 999, Nanosecond: 0
    Millisecond: 243, Microsecond: 958, Nanosecond: 400
    ```

# Globalization with dates and times

The current culture controls how dates and times are formatted and parsed:

1.  At the top of `Program.cs`, import the namespace for working with globalization, as shown in the following code:

    ```
    using System.Globalization; // CultureInfo
    ```

2.  Add statements to show the current culture that is used to display date and time values, and then parse the United States' Independence Day and display it in various ways, as shown in the following code:

```
SectionTitle("Globalization with dates and times");

// same as Thread.CurrentThread.CurrentCulture
WriteLine($"Current culture is: {CultureInfo.CurrentCulture.Name}");

string textDate = "4 July 2024";
DateTime independenceDay = DateTime.Parse(textDate);

WriteLine($"Text: {textDate}, DateTime: {independenceDay:d MMMM}");

textDate = "7/4/2024";
independenceDay = DateTime.Parse(textDate);

WriteLine($"Text: {textDate}, DateTime: {independenceDay:d MMMM}");

independenceDay = DateTime.Parse(textDate,
  provider: CultureInfo.GetCultureInfo("en-US"));

WriteLine($"Text: {textDate}, DateTime: {independenceDay:d MMMM}");
```

 **Good Practice:** Although you can create a `CultureInfo` instance using its constructor, unless you need to make changes to it, you should get a read-only shared instance by calling the `GetCultureInfo` method.

3.  Run the code and note the results, as shown in the following output:

```
Current culture is: en-GB
Text: 4 July 2024, DateTime: 4 July
Text: 7/4/2024, DateTime: 7 April
Text: 7/4/2024, DateTime: 4 July
```

 On my computer, the current culture is *English (Great Britain)*. If a date is given as 4 July 2021, then it is correctly parsed regardless of whether the current culture is British or American. But if the date is given as 7/4/2024, then it is wrongly parsed as 7 April. You can override the current culture by specifying the correct culture as a provider when parsing, as shown in the third example above.

4.  Add statements to loop from the year 2022 to 2028, displaying if the year is a leap year and how many days there are in February, and then show if Christmas and Independence Day are during DST, as shown in the following code:

```
for (int year = 2022; year <= 2028; year++)
{
  Write($"{year} is a leap year: {DateTime.IsLeapYear(year)}. ");
  WriteLine("There are {0} days in February {1}.",
    arg0: DateTime.DaysInMonth(year: year, month: 2), arg1: year);
}

WriteLine("Is Christmas daylight saving time? {0}",
  arg0: xmas.IsDaylightSavingTime());

WriteLine("Is July 4th daylight saving time? {0}",
  arg0: independenceDay.IsDaylightSavingTime());
```

5.   Run the code and note the results, as shown in the following output:

```
2022 is a leap year: False. There are 28 days in February 2022.
2023 is a leap year: False. There are 28 days in February 2023.
2024 is a leap year: True. There are 29 days in February 2024.
2025 is a leap year: False. There are 28 days in February 2025.
2026 is a leap year: False. There are 28 days in February 2026.
2027 is a leap year: False. There are 28 days in February 2027.
2028 is a leap year: True. There are 29 days in February 2028.
Is Christmas daylight saving time? False
Is July 4th daylight saving time? True
```

 DST is not used in all countries; it is also determined by hemisphere, and politics plays a role. For example, the United States is currently debating if they should make DST permanent. They might decide to leave the decision up to individual states. It could all get extra confusing for Americans over the next few years.

## Localizing the DayOfWeek enum

DayOfWeek is an enum so it cannot be localized as you might expect. Its string values are hardcoded in English, as shown in the following code:

```
namespace System
{
  public enum DayOfWeek
  {
    Sunday = 0,
    Monday = 1,
    Tuesday = 2,
    Wednesday = 3,
    Thursday = 4,
    Friday = 5,
    Saturday = 6
  }
}
```

There are two solutions to this problem. First, you could apply the dddd date format code to a whole date value. For example:

```
WriteLine($"The day of the week is {0:dddd}.", DateTime.Now);
```

Second, you can use a helper method of the DateTimeFormatInfo class to convert a DayOfWeek value into a localized string for output as text.

Let's see an example of the problem and solution:

1. Add statements to explicitly set the current culture to Danish and then output the current day of the week in that culture, as shown in the following code:

```
SectionTitle("Localizing the DayOfWeek enum");

CultureInfo previousCulture = Thread.CurrentThread.CurrentCulture;

// explicitly set culture to Danish (Denmark)
Thread.CurrentThread.CurrentCulture =
  CultureInfo.GetCultureInfo("da-DK");

WriteLine("Culture: {0}, DayOfWeek: {1}",
  Thread.CurrentThread.CurrentCulture.NativeName,
  DateTime.Now.DayOfWeek);

WriteLine("Culture: {0}, DayOfWeek: {1:dddd}",
  Thread.CurrentThread.CurrentCulture.NativeName,
  DateTime.Now);

WriteLine("Culture: {0}, DayOfWeek: {1}",
  Thread.CurrentThread.CurrentCulture.NativeName,
  DateTimeFormatInfo.CurrentInfo.GetDayName(DateTime.Now.DayOfWeek));

Thread.CurrentThread.CurrentCulture = previousCulture;
```

2. Run the code and note the results, as shown in the following output:

```
*
* Localizing the DayOfWeek enum
*
Culture: dansk (Danmark), DayOfWeek: Thursday
Culture: dansk (Danmark), DayOfWeek: torsdag
Culture: dansk (Danmark), DayOfWeek: torsdag
```

# Working with only a date or a time

.NET 6 introduced some new types for working with only a date value or only a time value, named DateOnly and TimeOnly.

These are better than using a `DateTime` value with a zero time to store a date-only value because it is type-safe and avoids misuse. `DateOnly` also maps better to database column types, for example, a date column in SQL Server. `TimeOnly` is good for setting alarms and scheduling regular meetings or the opening hours for an organization, and it maps to a time column in SQL Server.

Let's use them to plan the coronation of the new King of England, Charles III, probably during the spring of 2023:

1.  Add statements to define the King's coronation, and a time for it to start, and then combine the two values to make a calendar entry so that we don't miss it, as shown in the following code:

    ```
    SectionTitle("Working with only a date or a time");

    DateOnly coronation = new(year: 2023, month: 5, day: 6);
    WriteLine($"The King's Coronation is on {coronation.ToLongDateString()}.");

    TimeOnly starts = new(hour: 11, minute: 30);
    WriteLine($"The King's Coronation starts at {starts}.");

    DateTime calendarEntry = coronation.ToDateTime(starts);
    WriteLine($"Add to your calendar: {calendarEntry}.");
    ```

2.  Run the code and note the results, as shown in the following output:

    ```
    The King's Coronation is on Saturday, 6 May 2023.
    The King's Coronation starts at 11:30.
    Add to your calendar: 06/05/2023 11:30:00.
    ```

# Working with time zones

In the code example about the King's coronation, using a `TimeOnly` was not actually a good idea because the time-only value does not include information about time zone. It is only useful if you are in the correct time zone. `TimeOnly` is therefore a poor choice for an event. For events, we need to understand and handle time zones.

## Understanding DateTime and TimeZoneInfo

The `DateTime` class has many useful members related to time zones, as shown in the following table:

| Member | Description |
| --- | --- |
| `Now` property | A `DateTime` value that represents the current date and time in the local time zone |
| `UtcNow` property | A `DateTime` value that represents the current date and time in the UTC time zone |
| `Kind` property | A `DateTimeKind` value that indicates if the `DateTime` value is `Unspecified`, `Utc`, or `Local` |

| IsDaylightSavingTime method | A bool that indicates if the DateTime value is during DST |
|---|---|
| ToLocalTime method | Converts a UTC DateTime value to the equivalent local time |
| ToUniversalTime method | Converts a local DateTime value to the equivalent UTC time |

The TimeZoneInfo class has many useful members, as shown in the following table:

| Member | Description |
|---|---|
| Id property | A string that uniquely identifies the time zone. |
| Local property | A TimeZoneInfo value that represents the current local time zone. Varies depending on where the code executes. |
| Utc property | A TimeZoneInfo value that represents the UTC time zone. |
| StandardName property | A string for the name of the time zone when Daylight Saving is not active. |
| DaylightName property | A string for the name of the time zone when Daylight Saving is active. |
| DisplayName property | A string for the general name of the time zone. |
| BaseUtcOffset property | A TimeSpan that represents the difference between this time zone and the UTC time zone, ignoring any potential Daylight Saving adjustments. |
| SupportsDaylightSavingTime property | A bool that indicates if this time zone has Daylight Saving adjustments. |
| ConvertTime method | Converts a DateTime value to another DateTime value in a different time zone. You can specific the source and destination time zones. |
| ConvertTimeFromUtc method | Converts a DateTime value in the UTC time zone to a DateTime value in a specified time zone. |
| ConvertTimeToUtc method | Converts a DateTime value in a specified time zone to a DateTime value in the UTC time zone. |
| IsDaylightSavingTime method | Returns a bool indicating if the DateTime value is in Daylight Saving. |
| GetSystemTimeZones method | Returns a collection of time zones registered with the operating system. |

# Exploring DateTime and TimeZoneInfo

Use the TimeZoneInfo class to work with time zones:

1. Use your preferred code editor to add a new console app named `WorkingWithTimeZones` to the `Chapter07` solution/workspace:

    • In Visual Studio 2022, set the **Startup Project** to **Current selection**.
    • In Visual Studio Code, select `WorkingWithTimeZones` as the active OmniSharp project.

2. Statically and globally import the `System.Console` class.

3. Add a new class file named `Program.Helpers.cs`.

4. Modify its contents to define some helper methods to output a section title in a visually different way, output a list of all time zones in the current system, and output details about a `DateTime` or `TimeZoneInfo` object, as shown in the following code:

```
using System.Collections.ObjectModel; // ReadOnlyCollection<T>

partial class Program
{
  static void SectionTitle(string title)
  {
    ConsoleColor previousColor = ForegroundColor;
    ForegroundColor = ConsoleColor.DarkYellow;
    WriteLine("*");
    WriteLine($"* {title}");
    WriteLine("*");
    ForegroundColor = previousColor;
  }

  static void OutputTimeZones()
  {
    // get the time zones registered with the OS
    ReadOnlyCollection<TimeZoneInfo> zones =
      TimeZoneInfo.GetSystemTimeZones();

    WriteLine("*");
    WriteLine($"* {zones.Count} time zones:");
    WriteLine("*");

    // order the time zones by Id instead of DisplayName
    foreach (TimeZoneInfo zone in zones.OrderBy(z => z.Id))
```

```
    {
      WriteLine($"{zone.Id}");
    }
  }

  static void OutputDateTime(DateTime dateTime, string title)
  {
    SectionTitle(title);
    WriteLine($"Value: {dateTime}");
    WriteLine($"Kind: {dateTime.Kind}");
    WriteLine($"IsDaylightSavingTime: {dateTime.IsDaylightSavingTime()}");
    WriteLine($"ToLocalTime(): {dateTime.ToLocalTime()}");
    WriteLine($"ToUniversalTime(): {dateTime.ToUniversalTime()}");
  }

  static void OutputTimeZone(TimeZoneInfo zone, string title)
  {
    SectionTitle(title);
    WriteLine($"Id: {zone.Id}");
    WriteLine("IsDaylightSavingTime(DateTime.Now): {0}",
      zone.IsDaylightSavingTime(DateTime.Now));
    WriteLine($"StandardName: {zone.StandardName}");
    WriteLine($"DaylightName: {zone.DaylightName}");
    WriteLine($"BaseUtcOffset: {zone.BaseUtcOffset}");
  }

  static string GetCurrentZoneName(TimeZoneInfo zone, DateTime when)
  {
    // time zone names change if Daylight Saving time is active
    // e.g. GMT Standard Time becomes GMT Summer Time
    return zone.IsDaylightSavingTime(when) ?
      zone.DaylightName : zone.StandardName;
  }
}
```

5.  In `Program.cs`, delete the existing statements. Add statements to output the current date and
    time in the local and UTC time zones, and then output details about the local and UTC time
    zones, as shown in the following code:

```
OutputTimeZones();

OutputDateTime(DateTime.Now, "DateTime.Now");
OutputDateTime(DateTime.UtcNow, "DateTime.UtcNow");

OutputTimeZone(TimeZoneInfo.Local, "TimeZoneInfo.Local");
OutputTimeZone(TimeZoneInfo.Utc, "TimeZoneInfo.Utc");
```

6. Run the console app and note the results, including the time zones registered on your operating system (there are 141 on my Windows 11 laptop), and that it is currently 4:17pm on 31 May 2022 in England, meaning I am in the GMT Standard Time zone. However, because DST is active, it is currently known as GMT Summer Time, which is one hour ahead of UTC, as shown in the following output:

```
*
* 141 time zones:
*
Afghanistan Standard Time
Alaskan Standard Time
...
West Pacific Standard Time
Yakutsk Standard Time
Yukon Standard Time
*
* DateTime.Now
*
Value: 31/05/2022 16:17:03
Kind: Local
IsDaylightSavingTime: True
ToLocalTime(): 31/05/2022 16:17:03
ToUniversalTime(): 31/05/2022 15:17:03
*
* DateTime.UtcNow
*
Value: 31/05/2022 15:17:03
Kind: Utc
IsDaylightSavingTime: False
ToLocalTime(): 31/05/2022 16:17:03
ToUniversalTime(): 31/05/2022 15:17:03
*
* TimeZoneInfo.Local
*
Id: GMT Standard Time
IsDaylightSavingTime(DateTime.Now): True
StandardName: GMT Standard Time
DaylightName: GMT Summer Time
BaseUtcOffset: 00:00:00
*
* TimeZoneInfo.Utc
*
Id: UTC
IsDaylightSavingTime(DateTime.Now): False
StandardName: Coordinated Universal Time
```

```
DaylightName: Coordinated Universal Time
BaseUtcOffset: 00:00:00
```

 The `BaseUtcOffset` of the **GMT Standard Time** zone is zero because normally Daylight Saving is not active. That is why it is prefixed `Base`.

7.  In `Program.cs`, add statements to prompt the user to enter a time zone (using Eastern Standard Time as a default), get that time zone, output details about it, and then compare a time entered by the user with the equivalent time in the other time zone, and catch potential exceptions, as shown in the following code:

```csharp
Write("Enter a time zone or press Enter for US East Coast: ");
string zoneId = ReadLine()!;

if (string.IsNullOrEmpty(zoneId))
{
  zoneId = "Eastern Standard Time";
}

try
{
  TimeZoneInfo otherZone = TimeZoneInfo.FindSystemTimeZoneById(zoneId);
  OutputTimeZone(otherZone,
    $"TimeZoneInfo.FindSystemTimeZoneById(\"{zoneId}\")");

  SectionTitle($"What's the time in {zoneId}?");

  Write("Enter a local time or press Enter for now: ");
  string? timeText = ReadLine();
  DateTime localTime;
  if ((string.IsNullOrEmpty(timeText)) ||
    (!DateTime.TryParse(timeText, out localTime)))
  {
    localTime = DateTime.Now;
  }

  DateTime otherZoneTime = TimeZoneInfo.ConvertTime(
    dateTime: localTime, sourceTimeZone: TimeZoneInfo.Local,
    destinationTimeZone: otherZone);

  WriteLine("{0} {1} is {2} {3}.",
    localTime, GetCurrentZoneName(TimeZoneInfo.Local, localTime),
    otherZoneTime, GetCurrentZoneName(otherZone, otherZoneTime));
}
```

```
catch (TimeZoneNotFoundException)
{
  WriteLine($"The {zoneId} zone cannot be found on the local system.");
}
catch (InvalidTimeZoneException)
{
  WriteLine($"The {zoneId} zone contains invalid or missing data.");
}
catch (System.Security.SecurityException)
{
  WriteLine("The application does not have permission to read time zone
information.");
}
catch (OutOfMemoryException)
{
  WriteLine($"Not enough memory is available to load information on the
{zoneId} zone.");
}
```

8.  Run the console app, press *Enter* for US East Coast, and then enter 12:30pm for the local time, and note the results, as shown in the following output:

```
Enter a time zone or press Enter for US East Coast:
*
* TimeZoneInfo.FindSystemTimeZoneById("Eastern Standard Time")
*
Id: Eastern Standard Time
IsDaylightSavingTime(DateTime.Now): True
StandardName: Eastern Standard Time
DaylightName: Eastern Summer Time
BaseUtcOffset: -05:00:00
*
* What's the time in Eastern Standard Time?
*
Enter a local time or press Enter for now: 12:30pm
31/05/2022 12:30:00 GMT Summer Time is 31/05/2022 07:30:00 Eastern Summer
Time.
```

 My local time zone is GMT Standard Time so there is currently a five-hour time difference between me and the US East Coast. Your local time zone will be different.

9.  Run the console app, copy one of the time zones to the clipboard and paste it at the prompt, and then press *Enter* for the local time. Note the results, as shown in the following output:

```
Enter a time zone or press Enter for US East Coast: AUS Eastern Standard
Time
```

```
*
* TimeZoneInfo.FindSystemTimeZoneById("AUS Eastern Standard Time")
*
Id: AUS Eastern Standard Time
IsDaylightSavingTime(DateTime.Now): False
StandardName: AUS Eastern Standard Time
DaylightName: AUS Eastern Summer Time
BaseUtcOffset: 10:00:00
*
* What's the time in AUS Eastern Standard Time?
*
Enter a local time or press Enter for now:
31/05/2022 17:00:04 GMT Summer Time is 01/06/2022 02:00:04 AUS Eastern
Standard Time.
```

 Sydney, Australia, is currently nine hours ahead, so at 5pm for me, it is 2am on the following day for them.

# Working with cultures

Internationalization is the process of enabling your code to correctly run all over the world. It has two parts, **globalization** and **localization**, and both of them are about working with cultures.

**Globalization** is about writing your code to accommodate multiple languages and region combinations. The combination of a language and a region is known as a culture. It is important for your code to know both the language and region because, for example, the date and currency formats are different in Quebec and Paris, despite them both using the French language.

There are **International Organization for Standardization (ISO)** codes for all culture combinations. For example, in the code da-DK, da indicates the Danish language and DK indicates the Denmark region, and in the code fr-CA, fr indicates the French language and CA indicates the Canada region.

 ISO is not an acronym. ISO is a reference to the Greek word *isos* (which means equal). You can see a list of ISO culture codes at the following link: https://lonewolfonline.net/list-net-culture-country-codes/.

**Localization** is about customizing the user interface to support a language, for example, changing the label of a button to be Close (en) or Fermer (fr). Since localization is more about the language, it doesn't always need to know about the region, although ironically enough, standardization (en-US) and standardisation (en-GB) suggest otherwise.

> **Good Practice:** I am not a professional translator of software user interfaces, so take all examples in this chapter as general guidance. My research into French user interface labeling common practice led me to the following links, but it would be best to hire a professional if you are not a native language speaker: `https://french.stackexchange.com/questions/12969/translation-of-it-terms-like-close-next-search-etc` and `https://www.linguee.com/english-french/translation/close+button.html`.

## Detecting and changing the current culture

Internationalization is a huge topic on which thousand-page books have been written. In this section, you will get a brief introduction to the basics using the `CultureInfo` and `RegionInfo` types in the `System.Globalization` namespace.

Let's write some code:

1. Use your preferred code editor to add a new console app named `WorkingWithCultures` to the `Chapter07` solution/workspace.

   • In Visual Studio Code, select `WorkingWithCultures` as the active OmniSharp project.

2. In the project file, statically and globally import the `System.Console` class and globally import the `System.Globalization` namespace so that we can use the `CultureInfo` class, as shown in the following markup:

```
<ItemGroup>
  <Using Include="System.Console" Static="true" />
  <Using Include="System.Globalization" />
</ItemGroup>
```

3. Add a new class file named `Program.Helpers.cs`, and modify its contents to add a method to the partial `Program` class that will output information about the cultures used for globalization and localization, as shown in the following code:

```
partial class Program
{
  static void OutputCultures(string title)
  {
    ConsoleColor previousColor = ForegroundColor;
    ForegroundColor = ConsoleColor.DarkYellow;

    WriteLine("*");
    WriteLine($"* {title}");
    WriteLine("*");

    // get the cultures from the current thread
    CultureInfo globalization = CultureInfo.CurrentCulture;
```

```
        CultureInfo localization = CultureInfo.CurrentUICulture;

        WriteLine("The current globalization culture is {0}: {1}",
          globalization.Name, globalization.DisplayName);

        WriteLine("The current localization culture is {0}: {1}",
          localization.Name, localization.DisplayName);

        WriteLine("Days of the week: {0}",
          string.Join(", ", globalization.DateTimeFormat.DayNames));

        WriteLine("Months of the year: {0}",
          string.Join(", ", globalization.DateTimeFormat.MonthNames
          // some calendars have 13 months; most have 12 and the last is empty
          .TakeWhile(month => !string.IsNullOrEmpty(month))));

        WriteLine("1st day of this year: {0}",
          new DateTime(year: DateTime.Today.Year, month: 1, day: 1)
          .ToString("D", globalization));

        WriteLine("Number group separator: {0}",
          globalization.NumberFormat.NumberGroupSeparator);

        WriteLine("Number decimal separator: {0}",
          globalization.NumberFormat.NumberDecimalSeparator);

        RegionInfo region = new RegionInfo(globalization.LCID);

        WriteLine("Currency symbol: {0}", region.CurrencySymbol);

        WriteLine("Currency name: {0} ({1})",
          region.CurrencyNativeName, region.CurrencyEnglishName);

        WriteLine("IsMetric: {0}", region.IsMetric);

        WriteLine();

        ForegroundColor = previousColor;
    }
}
```

4. In `Program.cs`, delete the existing statements and add statements to set the output encoding of the `Console` to support Unicode. Then, output information about the globalization and localization cultures. Then, prompt the user to enter a new culture code and show how that affects the formatting of common values such as dates and currency, as shown in the following code:

```
// to enable special characters like €
OutputEncoding = System.Text.Encoding.Unicode;

OutputCultures("Current culture");

WriteLine("Example ISO culture codes:");

string[] cultureCodes = new[] {
  "da-DK", "en-GB", "en-US", "fa-IR",
  "fr-CA", "fr-FR", "he-IL", "pl-PL", "sl-SI" };

foreach (string code in cultureCodes)
{
  CultureInfo culture = CultureInfo.GetCultureInfo(code);
  WriteLine("  {0}: {1} / {2}",
    culture.Name, culture.EnglishName, culture.NativeName);
}

WriteLine();

Write("Enter an ISO culture code: ");
string? cultureCode = ReadLine();

if (string.IsNullOrWhiteSpace(cultureCode))
{
  cultureCode = "en-US";
}

CultureInfo ci;

try
{
  ci = CultureInfo.GetCultureInfo(cultureCode);
}
catch (CultureNotFoundException)
{
  WriteLine($"Culture code not found: {cultureCode}");
  WriteLine("Exiting the app.");
  return;
}

// change the current cultures on the thread
CultureInfo.CurrentCulture = ci;
CultureInfo.CurrentUICulture = ci;

OutputCultures("After changing the current culture");
```

```
Write("Enter your name: ");
string? name = ReadLine();
if (string.IsNullOrWhiteSpace(name))
{
  name = "Bob";
}

Write("Enter your date of birth: ");
string? dobText = ReadLine();

if (string.IsNullOrWhiteSpace(dobText))
{
  // if they do not enter a DOB then use
  // sensible defaults for their culture
  dobText = ci.Name switch
    {
       "en-US" or "fr-CA" => "1/27/1990",
       "da-DK" or "fr-FR" or "pl-PL" => "27/1/1990",
       "fa-IR" => "1990/1/27",
       _ => "1/27/1990"
    };
}

Write("Enter your salary: ");
string? salaryText = ReadLine();

if (string.IsNullOrWhiteSpace(salaryText))
{
  salaryText = "34500";
}

DateTime dob = DateTime.Parse(dobText);
int minutes = (int)DateTime.Today.Subtract(dob).TotalMinutes;
decimal salary = decimal.Parse(salaryText);

WriteLine(
  "{0} was born on a {1:dddd}. {0} is {2:N0} minutes old. {0} earns {3:C}.",
  name, dob, minutes, salary);
```

When you run an application, it automatically sets its thread to use the culture of the operating system. I am running my code in London, UK, so the thread is set to English (Great Britain).

The code prompts the user to enter an alternative ISO code. This allows your applications to replace the default culture at runtime.

The application then uses standard format codes to output the day of the week using format code dddd, the number of minutes with thousand separators using format code N0, and the salary with the currency symbol. These adapt automatically, based on the thread's culture.

5. Run the code and enter en-US for the ISO code (or press *Enter*) and then enter some sample data including a date in a format valid for US English, as shown in the following output:

```
*
* Current culture
*
The current globalization culture is en-GB: English (United Kingdom)
The current localization culture is en-GB: English (United Kingdom)
Days of the week: Sunday, Monday, Tuesday, Wednesday, Thursday, Friday,
Saturday
Months of the year: January, February, March, April, May, June, July,
August, September, October, November, December
1st day of this year: 01 January 2022
Number group separator: ,
Number decimal separator: .
Currency symbol: £
Currency name: British Pound (British Pound)
IsMetric: True

Example ISO culture codes:
   da-DK: Danish (Denmark) / dansk (Danmark)
   en-GB: English (United Kingdom) / English (United Kingdom)
   en-US: English (United States) / English (United States)
   fa-IR: Persian (Iran) / فارسی (ایران)
   fr-CA: French (Canada) / français (Canada)
   fr-FR: French (France) / français (France)
   he-IL: Hebrew (Israel) / עברית (ישראל)
   pl-PL: Polish (Poland) / polski (Polska)
   sl-SI: Slovenian (Slovenia) / slovenščina (Slovenija)

Enter an ISO culture code: en-US
*
* After changing the current culture
*
The current globalization culture is en-US: English (United States)
The current localization culture is en-US: English (United States)
Days of the week: Sunday, Monday, Tuesday, Wednesday, Thursday, Friday,
Saturday
Months of the year: January, February, March, April, May, June, July,
August, September, October, November, December
1st day of this year: Saturday, January 1, 2022
Number group separator: ,
Number decimal separator: .
```

```
Currency symbol: $
Currency name: US Dollar (US Dollar)
IsMetric: False

Enter your name: Alice
Enter your date of birth: 3/30/1967
Enter your salary: 34500
Alice was born on a Thursday. Alice is 28,938,240 minutes old. Alice
earns $34,500.00
```

6.  Run the code again and try Danish in Denmark (da-DK), as shown in the following output:

```
Enter an ISO culture code: da-DK
*
* After changing the current culture
*

The current globalization culture is da-DK: dansk (Danmark)
The current localization culture is da-DK: dansk (Danmark)
Days of the week: søndag, mandag, tirsdag, onsdag, torsdag, fredag,
lørdag
Months of the year: januar, februar, marts, april, maj, juni, juli,
august, september, oktober, november, december
1st day of this year: lørdag den 1. januar 2022
Number group separator: .
Number decimal separator: ,
Currency symbol: kr.
Currency name: dansk krone (Danish Krone)
IsMetric: True

Enter your name: Mikkel
Enter your date of birth: 16/3/1980
Enter your salary: 65000
Mikkel was born on a søndag. Mikkel is 22.119.840 minutes old. Mikkel
earns 65.000,00 kr.
```

In this example, only the date and salary are globalized into Danish. The rest of the text is hardcoded as English. Later, we will translate that English text into other languages. For now, let's see some other differences between cultures:

7.  Run the code again and try Polish in Poland (pl-PL), and note the grammar rules in Polish make the day number possessive for the month name, so the month styczeń becomes stycznia, as shown in the following output:

```
The current globalization culture is pl-PL: polski (Polska)
...
Months of the year: styczeń, luty, marzec, kwiecień, maj, czerwiec,
lipiec, sierpień, wrzesień, październik, listopad, grudzień
1st day of this year: sobota, 1 stycznia 2022
...
```

```
Enter your name: Bob
Enter your date of birth: 1972/4/16
Enter your salary: 50000
Bob was born on a niedziela. Bob is 26 398 080 minutes old. Bob earns 50
000,00 zł.
```

8.  Run the code again and try Persian in Iran (fa-IR), and note that dates in Iran must be specified as year/month/day, and that this year (2022) is the year 1400 in the Persian calendar, as shown in the following output:

```
The current globalization culture is fa-IR: فارسی (ایران)
The current localization culture is fa-IR: فارسی (ایران)
Days of the week: یکشنبه, دوشنبه, سه‌شنبه, چهارشنبه, پنجشنبه, جمعه, شنبه
Months of the year: فروردین, اردیبهشت, خرداد, تیر, مرداد, شهریور, مهر, آبان, آذر, دی, بهمن, اسفند
1st day of this year: شنبه 11, دی 1400
Number group separator: ,
Number decimal separator: ,
Currency symbol: ریال
Currency name: ریال ایران (Iranian Rial)
IsMetric: True

Enter your name: Cyrus
Enter your date of birth: 1372/4/16
Enter your salary: 50000
Cyrus was born on a درد. Cyrus is 15,242,400 minutes old. Cyrus earns
50,000.
```

 Although I tried to confirm with a Persian reader if this example is correct, due to factors like right-to-left languages being tricky to work with in console apps and copying and pasting from a console window into a word processor, I apologize in advance to my Persian readers if this example is all messed up!

# Temporarily using the invariant culture

Sometimes you might need to temporarily use a different culture without actually switching the current thread to that culture. For example, when automatically generating documents, queries, and commands that include data values, you might need to ignore your current culture and use a standard culture. For this purpose, you can use the invariant culture that is based on US English.

For example, you might need to generate a JSON document with a decimal number value and format the number with two decimal places, as shown in the following code:

```csharp
decimal price = 54321.99M;
string document = $$"""
  {
    "price": "{{price:N2}}"
  }
  """;
```

If you were to execute this on a Slovenian computer, you would get the following output:

```
{
  "price": "54.321,99"
}
```

If you then tried to insert this JSON document into a cloud database, then it would fail because it would not understand the number format that uses commas for decimals and dots for groups.

So, you can override the current culture and specify the invariant culture when outputting the number as a string value, as shown in the following code:

```
decimal price = 54321.99M;
string document = $$"""
  {
    "price": "{{price.ToString("N2", CultureInfo.InvariantCulture)}}"
  }
  """;
```

If you were to execute this on a Slovenian (or any other culture) computer, you would now get the following output that would be successfully recognized by a cloud database and not throw exceptions:

```
{
  "price": "54,321.99"
}
```

Now let's see how to translate text from one language to another so that the label prompts are in the correct language for the current culture.

# Localizing your user interface

A localized application is divided into two parts:

- An assembly containing code that is the same for all locales and contains resources for when no other resource file is found.
- One or more assemblies that contain the user interface resources that are different for different locales. These are known as **satellite assemblies**.

This model allows the initial application to be deployed with default invariant resources and, over time, additional satellite assemblies can be deployed as the resources are translated.

User interface resources include any text for messages, logs, dialog boxes, buttons, labels, or even file-names of images, videos, and so on. Resource files are XML files with the .resx extension. The filename includes a culture code, for example, PacktResources.en-GB.resx or PacktResources.da-DK.resx.

The automatic culture fallback search path for resources goes from specific culture (language and region) to neutral culture (language only) to invariant culture (supposed to be independent but basically US English).

If the current thread culture is en-AU (Australian English), then it will search for the resource file in the following order:

1. Australian English: `PacktResources.en-AU.resx`
2. Neutral English: `PacktResources.en.resx`
3. Invariant: `PacktResources.resx`

# Defining and loading resources

To load resources from these satellite assemblies, we use some standard .NET types named `IStringLocalizer<T>` and `IStringLocalizerFactory`. Implementations of these are loaded from the .NET generic host as dependency services:

1. In the `WorkingWithCultures` project, add package references to Microsoft extensions for working with generic hosting and localization, as shown in the following markup:

```
<ItemGroup>
  <PackageReference Include="Microsoft.Extensions.Hosting"
                    Version="7.0.0" />
  <PackageReference Include="Microsoft.Extensions.Localization"
                    Version="7.0.0" />
</ItemGroup>
```

2. Build the `WorkingWithCultures` project to restore packages.

3. In the project folder, create a new folder named `Resources`.

4. In the `Resources` folder, add a new XML file named `PacktResources.resx`, and modify the contents to contain default invariant language resources (usually equivalent to US English), as shown in the following markup:

```
<?xml version="1.0" encoding="utf-8"?>
<root>
  <data name="EnterYourDob" xml:space="preserve">
    <value>Enter your date of birth: </value>
  </data>
  <data name="EnterYourName" xml:space="preserve">
    <value>Enter your name: </value>
  </data>
  <data name="EnterYourSalary" xml:space="preserve">
    <value>Enter your salary: </value>
  </data>
  <data name="PersonDetails" xml:space="preserve">
    <value>{0} was born on a {1:dddd}. {0} is {2:N0} minutes old. {0}
earns {3:C}.</value>
  </data>
</root>
```

5.  In the `WorkingWithCultures` project folder, add a new class file named `PacktResources.cs` that will load text resources for the user interface, as shown in the following code:

```csharp
using Microsoft.Extensions.Localization; // IStringLocalizer,
LocalizedString

public class PacktResources
{
  private readonly IStringLocalizer<PacktResources> localizer = null!;

  public PacktResources(IStringLocalizer<PacktResources> localizer)
  {
    this.localizer = localizer;
  }

  public string? GetEnterYourNamePrompt()
  {
    string resourceStringName = "EnterYourName";

    // 1. get the LocalizedString object
    LocalizedString localizedString = localizer[resourceStringName];

    // 2. check if the resource string was found
    if (localizedString.ResourceNotFound)
    {
      ConsoleColor previousColor = ForegroundColor;
      ForegroundColor = ConsoleColor.Red;
      WriteLine($"Error: resource string \"{resourceStringName}\" not
found."
        + Environment.NewLine
        + $"Search path: {localizedString.SearchedLocation}");
      ForegroundColor = previousColor;

      return $"{localizedString}: ";
    }
    // 3. return the found resource string
    return localizedString;
  }

  public string? GetEnterYourDobPrompt()
  {
    // LocalizedString has an implicit cast to string
    // that falls back to the key if the resource string is not found
    return localizer["EnterYourDob"];
  }
```

```
    public string? GetEnterYourSalaryPrompt()
    {
      return localizer["EnterYourSalary"];
    }

    public string? GetPersonDetails(
      string name, DateTime dob, int minutes, decimal salary)
    {
      return localizer["PersonDetails", name, dob, minutes, salary];
    }
}
```

For the `GetEnterYourNamePrompt` method, I broke the implementation down into steps to get useful information like checking if the resource string is found and showing the search path if not. The other method implementations use a simplified fallback to the key name for the resource string if they are not found.

6.  In `Program.cs`, at the top, import the namespaces for working with hosting and dependency injection, and then configure a host that enables localization and the `PacktResources` service, as shown in the following code:

```
using Microsoft.Extensions.Hosting; // IHost, Host

// AddLocalization, AddTransient<T>
using Microsoft.Extensions.DependencyInjection;

using IHost host = Host.CreateDefaultBuilder(args)
  .ConfigureServices(services =>
  {
    services.AddLocalization(options =>
    {
      options.ResourcesPath = "Resources";
    });

    services.AddTransient<PacktResources>();
  })
  .Build();
```

**Good Practice:** By default, `ResourcesPath` is an empty string, meaning it looks for `.resx` files in the current directory. We are going to make the project tidier by putting resources into a subfolder.

7.  After changing the current culture, add a statement to get the `PacktResources` service and use it to output localized prompts for the user to enter their name, date of birth, and salary, and then output their details, as highlighted in the following code:

```
OutputCultures("After changing the current culture");

PacktResources resources =
    host.Services.GetRequiredService<PacktResources>();

Write(resources.GetEnterYourNamePrompt());
string? name = ReadLine();
if (string.IsNullOrWhiteSpace(name))
{
  name = "Bob";
}

Write(resources.GetEnterYourDobPrompt());
string? dobText = ReadLine();

if (string.IsNullOrWhiteSpace(dobText))
{
  // if they do not enter a DOB then use
  // sensible defaults for their culture
  dobText = ci.Name switch
    {
      "en-US" or "fr-CA" => "1/27/1990",
      "da-DK" or "fr-FR" or "pl-PL" => "27/1/1990",
      "fa-IR" => "1990/1/27",
      _ => "1/27/1990"
    };
}

Write(resources.GetEnterYourSalaryPrompt());
string? salaryText = ReadLine();

if (string.IsNullOrWhiteSpace(salaryText))
{
  salaryText = "34500";
}

DateTime dob = DateTime.Parse(dobText);
int minutes = (int)DateTime.Today.Subtract(dob).TotalMinutes;
decimal salary = decimal.Parse(salaryText);

WriteLine(resources.GetPersonDetails(name, dob, minutes, salary));
```

# Testing globalization and localization

Now we can run the console app and see the resources being loaded:

1.  Run the console app and enter da-DK for the ISO code. Note that the prompts are in US English because we currently only have invariant culture resources.

 To save time and to make sure you have the correct structure, you can copy, paste, and rename the .resx files instead of creating empty new ones.

2.  In the Resources folder, add a new XML file named PacktResources.da.resx, and modify the contents to contain non-region-specific Danish language resources, as shown in the following markup:

```xml
<?xml version="1.0" encoding="utf-8"?>
<root>
  <data name="EnterYourDob" xml:space="preserve">
    <value>Indtast din fødselsdato: </value>
  </data>
  <data name="EnterYourName" xml:space="preserve">
    <value>Indtast dit navn: </value>
  </data>
  <data name="EnterYourSalary" xml:space="preserve">
    <value>Indtast din løn: </value>
  </data>
  <data name="PersonDetails" xml:space="preserve">
    <value>{0} blev født på en {1:dddd}. {0} er {2:N0} minutter gammel.
{0} tjener {3:C}.</value>
  </data>
</root>
```

3.  In the Resources folder, add a new XML file named PacktResources.fr.resx, and modify the contents to contain non-region-specific French language resources, as shown in the following markup:

```xml
<?xml version="1.0" encoding="utf-8"?>
<root>
  <data name="EnterYourDob" xml:space="preserve">
    <value>Entrez votre date de naissance: </value>
  </data>
  <data name="EnterYourName" xml:space="preserve">
    <value>Entrez votre nom: </value>
  </data>
  <data name="EnterYourSalary" xml:space="preserve">
    <value>Entrez votre salaire: </value>
  </data>
```

```
        <data name="PersonDetails" xml:space="preserve">
          <value>{0} est né un {1:dddd}. {0} a {2:N0} minutes. {0} gagne
{3:C}.</value>
        </data>
      </root>
```

4.  In the Resources folder, add a new XML file named `PacktResources.fr-CA.resx`, and modify the contents to contain French language in Canada region resources, as shown in the following markup:

```
        <?xml version="1.0" encoding="utf-8"?>
        <root>
          <data name="EnterYourDob" xml:space="preserve">
            <value>Entrez votre date de naissance / Enter your date of birth:
            </value>
          </data>
          <data name="EnterYourName" xml:space="preserve">
            <value>Entrez votre nom / Enter your name: </value>
          </data>
          <data name="EnterYourSalary" xml:space="preserve">
            <value>Entrez votre salaire / Enter your salary: </value>
          </data>
          <data name="PersonDetails" xml:space="preserve">
            <value>{0} est né un {1:dddd}. {0} a {2:N0} minutes. {0} gagne
{3:C}.</value>
          </data>
        </root>
```

5.  In the Resources folder, add a new XML file named `PacktResources.pl-PL.resx`, and modify the contents to contain Polish language in Poland region resources, as shown in the following markup:

```
        <?xml version="1.0" encoding="utf-8"?>
        <root>
          <data name="EnterYourDob" xml:space="preserve">
            <value>Wpisz swoją datę urodzenia: </value>
          </data>
          <data name="EnterYourName" xml:space="preserve">
            <value>Wpisz swoje imię i nazwisko: </value>
          </data>
          <data name="EnterYourSalary" xml:space="preserve">
            <value>Wpisz swoje wynagrodzenie: </value>
          </data>
          <data name="PersonDetails" xml:space="preserve">
            <value>{0} urodził się na {1:dddd}. {0} ma {2:N0} minut. {0} zarabia
{3:C}.</value>
          </data>
        </root>
```

6. In the Resources folder, add a new XML file named `PacktResources.fa-IR.resx`, and modify the contents to contain Farsi language in Iranian region resources, as shown in the following markup:

```xml
<?xml version="1.0" encoding="utf-8"?>
<root>
  <data name="EnterYourDob" xml:space="preserve">
    <value>تاریخ تولد خود را وارد کنید / Enter your date of birth:
    </value>
  </data>
  <data name="EnterYourName" xml:space="preserve">
    <value>اسمت را وارد کن / Enter your name: </value>
  </data>
  <data name="EnterYourSalary" xml:space="preserve">
    <value>حقوق خود را وارد کنید / Enter your salary: </value>
  </data>
  <data name="PersonDetails" xml:space="preserve">
    <value>{0} دقیقه است. {0} {2:N0} هبه دنیا آمد. رد {1:dddd} {0}
{3:C}.</value>
  </data>
</root>
```

7. Run the code and enter `da-DK` for the ISO code. Note that the prompts are in Danish, as shown in the following output:

```
The current localization culture is da-DK: dansk (Danmark)
...
Indtast dit navn: Bob
Indtast din fødselsdato: 3/4/1987
Indtast din løn: 45449
Bob blev født på en fredag. Bob er 18.413.280 minutter gammel. Bob tjener
45.449,00 kr.
```

8. Run the code and enter `fr-FR` for the ISO code. Note that the prompts are in French only, as shown in the following output:

```
The current localization culture is fr-FR: français (France)
...
Entrez votre nom: Monique
Entrez votre date de naissance: 2/12/1990
Entrez votre salaire: 45000
Monique est né un Dimanche. Monique a 16 485 120 minutes. Monique gagne
45 000,00 €.
```

9. Run the code and enter `fr-CA` for the ISO code. Note that the prompts are in French and English because Canada might have a requirement to support both as official languages, as shown in the following output:

```
The current localization culture is fr-CA: français (Canada)
```

```
...
Entrez votre nom / Enter your name: Sophie
Entrez votre date de naissance / Enter your date of birth: 4/5/2001
Entrez votre salaire / Enter your salary: 65000
Sophie est né un jeudi. Sophie a 11 046 240 minutes. Sophie gagne 65
000,00 $ CA.
```

10. Run the code and enter `fa-IR` for the ISO code. Note that the prompts are in Persian/Farsi and English, and there is the additional complication of a right-to-left language, as shown in the following output:

```
The current localization culture is fa-IR: (ناری ا) یسر اف
...
اسمت را و ارد کن / Enter your name: Hoshyar
تاریخ تولد خود را و ارد کنید / Enter your date of birth: 1370/3/6
حقوق خود را و ارد کنید / Enter your salary: 90000
Hoshyar در چهارشنبه آ نیا د مد. Hoshyar 11,190,240 دقیقه است. Hoshyar
ری ال90,000.
```

 If you need to work with Persian dates then there are NuGet packages with open-source GitHub repositories that you can try, although I cannot vouch for their correctness, like `https://github.com/VahidN/DNTPersianUtils.Core` and `https://github.com/imanabidi/PersianDate.NET`.

11. In the `Resources` folder, in `PacktResources.da.resx`, modify the contents to deliberately change the key for the prompt to enter your name by appending `Wrong`, as shown highlighted in the following markup:

```
<?xml version="1.0" encoding="utf-8"?>
<root>
  <data name="EnterYourDob" xml:space="preserve">
    <value>Indtast din fødselsdato: </value>
  </data>
  <data name="EnterYourNameWrong" xml:space="preserve">
    <value>Indtast dit navn: </value>
  </data>
  <data name="EnterYourSalary" xml:space="preserve">
    <value>Indtast din løn: </value>
  </data>
  <data name="PersonDetails" xml:space="preserve">
    <value>{0} blev født på en {1:dddd}. {0} er {2:N0} minutter gammel.
{0} tjener {3:C}.</value>
  </data>
</root>
```

12. Run the code and enter da-DK for the ISO code. Note that the prompts are in Danish, except for the enter your name prompt in English, due to it falling back to the default resource file, as shown in the following output:

```
The current localization culture is da-DK: dansk (Danmark)
...
Enter your name: Bob
Indtast din fødselsdato: 3/4/1987
Indtast din løn: 45449
Bob blev født på en fredag. Bob er 18.413.280 minutter gammel. Bob tjener
45.449,00 kr.
```

13. In the Resources folder, in PacktResources.resx, modify the contents to deliberately change the key for the prompt to enter your name by appending Wrong.

14. Run the code and enter da-DK for the ISO code. Note that the prompts are in Danish, except for the enter your name prompt, which shows an error and uses the key name as a last resort fallback, as shown in the following output:

```
The current localization culture is da-DK: dansk (Danmark)
...
Error: resource string "EnterYourName" not found.
Search path: WorkingWithCultures.Resources.PacktResources
EnterYourName: Bob
Indtast din fødselsdato: 3/4/1987
Indtast din løn: 45449
Bob blev født på en fredag. Bob er 18.413.280 minutter gammel. Bob tjener
45.449,00 kr.
```

15. Remove the Wrong suffix in both resource files.

16. In **File Explorer**, open the WorkingWithCultures project folder, and select the bin/Debug/net7.0/da folder, as shown in *Figure 7.1*:

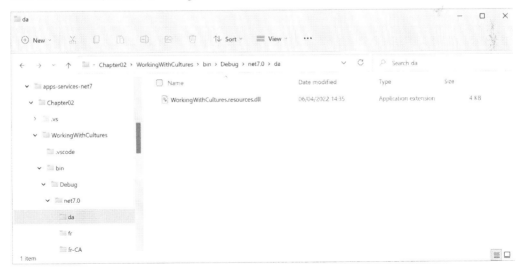

*Figure 7.1: The satellite assembly folders for culture resources*

17. Note the satellite assembly named `WorkingWithCultures.resources.dll` for the neutral Danish resources.

Any other culture resource assemblies are named the same but stored in folders that match the appropriate culture code. You can use tools like ResX Resource Manager, found at `https://dotnetfoundation.org/projects/resx-resource-manager`, to create many more `.resx` files, compile them into satellite assemblies, and then deploy them to users without needing to recompile the original console app.

**Good Practice:** Consider whether your application needs to be internationalized and plan for that before you start coding! Think about all the data that will need to be globalized (date formats, number formats, and sorting text behavior). Write down all the pieces of text in the user interface that will need to be localized.

Microsoft has an online tool (found at the following link: `https://www.microsoft.com/en-us/Language/`) that can help you translate text in your user interfaces:

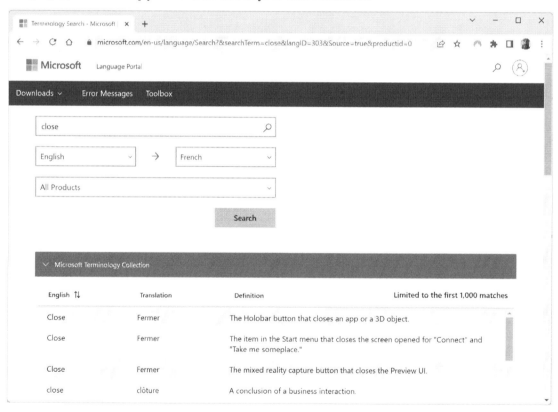

*Figure 7.2: Microsoft user interface online text translation tool*

# Practicing and exploring

Test your knowledge and understanding by answering some questions, getting some hands-on practice, and exploring the topics in this chapter with deeper research.

## Exercise 7.1 – Test your knowledge

Use the web to answer the following questions:

1. What is the difference between localization, globalization, and internationalization?
2. What is the smallest measurement of time available in .NET?
3. How long is a "tick" in .NET?
4. In what scenario might you use a `DateOnly` value instead of a `DateTime` value?
5. For a time zone, what does its `BaseUtcOffset` property tell you?
6. How can you get information about the local time zone in which your code is executing?
7. For a `DateTime` value, what does its `Kind` property tell you?
8. How can you control the current culture for your executing code?
9. What is the ISO culture code for Welsh?
10. How do localization resource file fallbacks work?

## Exercise 7.2 – Explore topics

Use the links on the following page to learn more detail about the topics covered in this chapter:

`https://github.com/markjprice/apps-services-net7/blob/main/book-links.md#chapter-7---handling-dates-times-and-internationalization`

## Exercise 7.3 – Learn from expert Jon Skeet

Jon Skeet is a world-renowned expert on internationalization. Watch him present *Working with Time is Easy* at the following link: `https://www.youtube.com/watch?v=saeKBuPewcU`.

Read about NodaTime, Jon's library that provides a better date and time API for .NET: `https://nodatime.org/`.

# Summary

In this chapter, you:

- Explored dates and times.
- Learned how to handle time zones.
- Learned how to internationalize your code using globalization and localization.

In the next chapter, you will learn how to protect data and files using hashing, signing, encryption, authentication, and authorization.

# 8

# Protecting Your Data and Applications

This chapter is about protecting your data from being viewed or manipulated by malicious users. You will learn how to protect your data using encryption, hashing, and signing. You will also learn how to properly generate random numbers for use with cryptographic operations, and how to implement basic authentication and authorization for users.

This chapter covers the following topics:

- Understanding the vocabulary of protection
- Encrypting and decrypting data
- Hashing data
- Signing data
- Generating random numbers
- Authenticating and authorizing users

**Warning!** The code in this chapter covers security primitives for basic educational purposes only. You must not use any of the code in this chapter for production libraries and apps. It is good practice to use libraries implemented by security professionals that are built using these security primitives and that have been hardened for real-world use following the latest best security practices. In *Chapter 9, Building and Securing Web Services Using Minimal APIs*, you will learn higher-level practical techniques for protecting and securing your apps and services. At the end of this chapter, you will find links to Microsoft good practices that you must follow if you do intend to implement yourself what you have learned in this chapter.

# Understanding the vocabulary of protection

There are many techniques to protect your data; below, we'll briefly introduce some of the most popular ones, and you will see more detailed explanations and practical implementations throughout this chapter:

- **Encrypting** and **decrypting**: This is a two-way process to convert your data from cleartext into ciphertext and back again. **Cleartext** is the original text that you want to protect. **Ciphertext** is the result of encrypting the cleartext.

- **Hashing**: This is a one-way process to generate a digest. **Hash** is the verb; **digest** is the noun. No matter the size of the input, the digest is of fixed length, for example, a fixed-size byte array. Digests can be used to securely store passwords or to detect malicious changes or corruption of your data. Simple hashing algorithms should not be used for passwords. You should use PBKDF2, bcrypt, or scrypt because these algorithms can guarantee that there cannot be two inputs that generate the same digest when used properly.

- **Signing**: This technique is used to ensure that data has come from a claimed source by validating a signature that has been applied to some data against someone's public key. For example, messages can be authenticated and validated by a receiver.

- **Authenticating**: This technique is used to identify someone by checking their credentials.

- **Authorizing**: This technique is used to ensure that someone has permission to perform an action or work with some data by checking the roles or groups they belong to.

 **Good Practice:** If security is important to you (and it should be!), then hire an experienced security expert for guidance rather than relying on advice found online. It is very easy to make small mistakes and leave your applications and data vulnerable without realizing it until it is too late!

# Keys and key sizes

Protection algorithms often use a **key**. Keys are represented by byte arrays of varying sizes. Keys are used for various purposes, as shown in the following list:

- Encrypting and decrypting: AES, 3DES, RC2, Rijndael, and RSA
- Signing and verifying: RSA, ECDSA, and DSA
- Message authenticating and validating: HMAC
- Key agreement, aka safe encryption key exchange: Diffie-Hellman, Elliptical Curve Diffie-Hellman

 **Good Practice:** Choose a bigger key size for stronger protection. This is an oversimplification because some RSA implementations support up to 16,384-bit keys that can take days to generate and would be overkill in most scenarios. A 2048-bit key should be sufficient until the year 2030, at which point you should upgrade to 3,192-bit keys.

Keys for encryption and decryption can be **symmetric** (also known as **shared** or **secret** because the same key is used to encrypt and decrypt and therefore must be kept safe) or **asymmetric** (a public-private key pair where the public key is used to encrypt and only the private key can be used to decrypt).

> **Good Practice:** Symmetric key encryption algorithms are fast and can encrypt large amounts of data using a stream. Asymmetric key encryption algorithms are slow and can only encrypt small byte arrays. The most common uses of asymmetric keys are signature creation and validation.

In the real world, get the best of both worlds by using a symmetric key to encrypt your data, and an asymmetric key to share the symmetric key. This is how **Secure Sockets Layer** (**SSL**) 2.0 encryption on the internet worked in 1995. Today, what is still often called SSL is **Transport Layer Security** (**TLS**), which uses key agreement rather than RSA-encrypted session keys.

## IVs and block sizes

When encrypting large amounts of data, there are likely to be repeating sequences. For example, in an English document, in the sequence of characters, the would appear frequently, and each time it might get encrypted as hQ2. A good cracker would use this knowledge to make it easier to crack the encryption, as shown in the following output:

```
When the wind blew hard the umbrella broke.
5:s4&hQ2aj#D f9d1d£8fh"&hQ2s0)an DF8SFd#][1
```

We can avoid repeating sequences by dividing data into **blocks**. After encrypting a block, a byte array value is generated from that block, and this value is fed into the next block to adjust the algorithm. The next block is encrypted so the output is different even for the same input as the preceding block. To encrypt the first block, we need a byte array to feed in. This is called the **initialization vector** (**IV**).

An IV:

- Should be generated randomly along with every encrypted message.
- Should be transmitted along with the encrypted message.
- Is not itself a secret.

## Salts

A **salt** is a random byte array that is used as an additional input to a one-way hash function. If you do not use a salt when generating digests, then when many of your users register with 123456 as their password (about 8% of users still did this in 2016!), they will all have the same digest, and their accounts will be vulnerable to a rainbow table attack that uses precalculated digests.

When a user registers, the salt should be randomly generated and concatenated with their chosen password before being hashed. The generated digest (but not the original password) is stored with the salt in the database.

Then, when the user next logs in and enters their password, you look up their salt, concatenate it with the entered password, regenerate a digest, and then compare its value with the digest stored in the database. If they are the same, you know they entered the correct password.

Even salting passwords is not enough for truly secure storage. You should do a lot more work, like PBKDF2, bcrypt, or scrypt. But that work is beyond the scope of this book.

## Generating keys and IVs

Keys and IVs are byte arrays. Both of the two parties that want to exchange encrypted data need the key and IV values, but byte arrays can be difficult to exchange reliably.

You can reliably generate a key or IV using a **password-based key derivation function (PBKDF2)**. A good one is the `Rfc2898DeriveBytes` class, which takes a password, a salt, an iteration count, and a hash algorithm (the default is SHA-1, which is no longer recommended). It then generates keys and IVs by making calls to its `GetBytes` method. The iteration count is the number of times that the password is hashed during the process. The more iterations, the harder it will be to crack.

Although the `Rfc2898DeriveBytes` class can be used to generate the IV as well as the key, the IV should be randomly generated each time and transmitted with the encrypted message as plaintext because it does not need to be secret.

> **Good Practice:** The salt size should be 8 bytes or larger, and the iteration count should be a value that takes about 100ms to generate a key and IV for the encryption algorithm on the target machine. This value will increase over time as CPUs improve. In the example code you write below, we use 150,000, but that value will already be too low for some computers by the time you read this.

## Encrypting and decrypting data

In .NET, there are multiple encryption algorithms you can choose from.

In legacy .NET Framework, some algorithms are implemented by the OS and their names are suffixed with `CryptoServiceProvider` or `Cng`. Some algorithms are implemented in the .NET BCL and their names are suffixed with `Managed`.

In modern .NET, all algorithms are implemented by the operating system. If the OS algorithms are certified by the **Federal Information Processing Standards (FIPS)**, then .NET uses FIPS-certified algorithms rather than implementing the algorithm in the .NET base class library.

> Cryptographic operations are performed by operating system implementations so that when an OS has a security vulnerability fixed, then .NET apps benefit immediately. But this means that those .NET apps can only use features that an OS supports. You can read about which features are supported by which OS at the following link: `https://docs.microsoft.com/en-us/dotnet/standard/security/cross-platform-cryptography`.

Generally, you will always use an abstract class like `Aes` and its `Create` factory method to get an instance of an algorithm, so you will not need to know if you are using `CryptoServiceProvider` or `Managed` anyway.

Some algorithms use symmetric keys, and some use asymmetric keys. The main asymmetric encryption algorithm is RSA. Ron Rivest, Adi Shamir, and Leonard Adleman described the algorithm in 1977. A similar algorithm was designed in 1973 by Clifford Cocks, an English mathematician working for GCHQ, the British intelligence agency, but it was not declassified until 1997 so Rivest, Shamir, and Adleman got the credit and had their names immortalized in the RSA acronym.

Symmetric encryption algorithms use `CryptoStream` to encrypt or decrypt large amounts of bytes efficiently. Asymmetric algorithms can only handle small amounts of bytes, stored in a byte array instead of a stream.

The most common symmetric encryption algorithms derive from the abstract class named `SymmetricAlgorithm` and are shown in the following list:

- AES
- DESCryptoServiceProvider
- TripleDES
- RC2CryptoServiceProvider
- RijndaelManaged

If you need to write code to decrypt some data sent by an external system, then you will have to use whatever algorithm the external system used to encrypt the data. Or if you need to send encrypted data to a system that can only decrypt using a specific algorithm, again you will not have a choice of algorithm.

If your code will both encrypt and decrypt, then you can choose the algorithm that best suits your requirements for strength, performance, and so on.

 **Good Practice:** Choose the **Advanced Encryption Standard (AES)**, which is based on the Rijndael algorithm, for symmetric encryption. Choose RSA for asymmetric encryption. Do not confuse RSA with DSA. **Digital Signature Algorithm (DSA)** cannot encrypt data. It can only generate and verify signatures.

# Encrypting symmetrically with AES

To make it easier to reuse your protection code in multiple projects, we will create a static class named `Protector` in its own class library and then reference it in a console app.

Let's go!

1. Use your preferred code editor to create a new console app project, as defined in the following list:

   - Project template: **Console App**/`console`

- Workspace/solution file and folder: `Chapter08`
- Project file and folder: `EncryptionApp`

2. Add a new **Class Library**/`classlib` named `CryptographyLib` to the `Chapter08` solution/workspace:

   - If you are using Visual Studio 2022, set the startup project for the solution to the current selection.

   - If you are using Visual Studio Code, select `EncryptionApp` as the active OmniSharp project.

3. In the `CryptographyLib` project, rename the `Class1.cs` file to `Protector.cs`.

4. In the `CryptographyLib` project, globally and statically import the `System.Console` class.

5. In the `EncryptionApp` project, add a project reference to the `CryptographyLib` library, and globally and statically import the `System.Console` class, as shown in the following markup:

```
<ItemGroup>
  <Using Include="System.Console" Static="true" />
</ItemGroup>

<ItemGroup>
  <ProjectReference
    Include="..\CryptographyLib\CryptographyLib.csproj" />
</ItemGroup>
```

6. Build the `EncryptionApp` project and make sure there are no compile errors.

7. In `Protector.cs`, define a static class named `Protector` with fields for storing a salt byte array and a large number of iterations, and methods to `Encrypt` and `Decrypt`, as shown in the following code:

```
using System.Diagnostics; // Stopwatch
using System.Security.Cryptography; // Aes, Rfc2898DeriveBytes, etc.
using System.Text; // Encoding

using static System.Convert; // ToBase64String, FromBase64String

namespace Packt.Shared;

public static class Protector
{
  // salt size must be at least 8 bytes, we will use 16 bytes
  private static readonly byte[] salt =
```

```csharp
    Encoding.Unicode.GetBytes("7BANANAS");

// Default iterations for Rfc2898DeriveBytes is 1000.
// Iterations should be high enough to take at least 100ms to
// generate a Key and IV on the target machine. 150,000 iterations
// takes 139ms on my 11th Gen Intel Core i7-1165G7 @ 2.80GHz.
private static readonly int iterations = 150_000;

public static string Encrypt(
  string plainText, string password)
{
  byte[] encryptedBytes;
  byte[] plainBytes = Encoding.Unicode.GetBytes(plainText);

  using (Aes aes = Aes.Create()) // abstract class factory method
  {
    // record how long it takes to generate the Key and IV
    Stopwatch timer = Stopwatch.StartNew();

    using (Rfc2898DeriveBytes pbkdf2 = new(
      password, salt, iterations, HashAlgorithmName.SHA256))
    {
      WriteLine("PBKDF2 algorithm: {0}, Iteration count: {1:N0}",
        pbkdf2.HashAlgorithm, pbkdf2.IterationCount);

      aes.Key = pbkdf2.GetBytes(32); // set a 256-bit key
      aes.IV = pbkdf2.GetBytes(16); // set a 128-bit IV
    }

    timer.Stop();

    WriteLine("{0:N0} milliseconds to generate Key and IV.",
      arg0: timer.ElapsedMilliseconds);

    WriteLine("Encryption algorithm: {0}-{1}, {2} mode with {3} padding.",
      "AES", aes.KeySize, aes.Mode, aes.Padding);

    using (MemoryStream ms = new())
```

```
      {
        using (ICryptoTransform transformer = aes.CreateEncryptor())
        {
          using (CryptoStream cs = new(
            ms, transformer, CryptoStreamMode.Write))
          {
            cs.Write(plainBytes, 0, plainBytes.Length);

            if (!cs.HasFlushedFinalBlock)
            {
              cs.FlushFinalBlock();
            }
          }
        }
        encryptedBytes = ms.ToArray();
      }
    }

    return ToBase64String(encryptedBytes);
  }

  public static string Decrypt(
    string cipherText, string password)
  {
    byte[] plainBytes;
    byte[] cryptoBytes = FromBase64String(cipherText);

    using (Aes aes = Aes.Create())
    {
      using (Rfc2898DeriveBytes pbkdf2 = new(
        password, salt, iterations, HashAlgorithmName.SHA256))
      {
        aes.Key = pbkdf2.GetBytes(32);
        aes.IV = pbkdf2.GetBytes(16);
      }

      using (MemoryStream ms = new())
      {
        using (ICryptoTransform transformer = aes.CreateDecryptor())
```

```
        {
          using (CryptoStream cs = new(
            ms, aes.CreateDecryptor(), CryptoStreamMode.Write))
          {
            cs.Write(cryptoBytes, 0, cryptoBytes.Length);

            if (!cs.HasFlushedFinalBlock)
            {
              cs.FlushFinalBlock();
            }
          }
        }
        plainBytes = ms.ToArray();
      }
    }

    return Encoding.Unicode.GetString(plainBytes);
  }
}
```

Note the following points about the preceding code:

- Although the salt and iteration count can be hardcoded (but preferably stored in the message itself), the password must be passed as a parameter at runtime when calling the Encrypt and Decrypt methods.

- In .NET 7, five constructors for the Rfc2898DeriveBytes class have been deprecated, including the one that I used in previous editions of this book. The preferred constructors now require a HashAlgorithmName to be specified. We specify SHA256, which is better than the old default of SHA1.

- We use a Stopwatch to record how long it takes to generate the key and IV so that we can make sure that it is at least 100ms.

- We use a temporary MemoryStream type to store the results of encrypting and decrypting, and then call ToArray to turn the stream into a byte array.

- It is important to flush the final block if it has not already been flushed.

- We convert the encrypted byte arrays to and from a Base64 encoding to make them easier to read for humans.

 **Good Practice:** Never hardcode a password in your source code because, even after compilation, the password can be read in the assembly by using disassembler tools.

8.  In the `EncryptionApp` project, in `Program.cs`, delete the existing statements, and then import the namespace for the `Protector` class and the namespace for the `CryptographicException` class, as shown in the following code:

    ```
    using System.Security.Cryptography; // CryptographicException
    using Packt.Shared; // Protector
    ```

     In a real project, you might statically import the `Packt.Shared.Protector` class so that you can call its methods like `Encrypt` without prefixing them with a class name like `Protector.Encrypt`. In this learning project, I want to make sure that you know where the methods are coming from.

9.  In `Program.cs`, add statements to prompt the user for a message and a password, and then encrypt and decrypt, as shown in the following code:

    ```
    Write("Enter a message that you want to encrypt: ");
    string? message = ReadLine();

    Write("Enter a password: ");
    string? password = ReadLine();

    if ((password is null) || (message is null))
    {
      WriteLine("Message or password cannot be null.");
      return;
    }

    string cipherText = Protector.Encrypt(message, password);

    WriteLine($"Encrypted text: {cipherText}");

    Write("Enter the password: ");
    string? password2Decrypt = ReadLine();

    if (password2Decrypt is null)
    {
     WriteLine("Password to decrypt cannot be null.");
     return;
    }

    try
    ```

```
{
  string clearText = Protector.Decrypt(cipherText, password2Decrypt);
  WriteLine($"Decrypted text: {clearText}");
}
catch (CryptographicException)
{
  WriteLine("You entered the wrong password!");
}
catch (Exception ex)
{
  WriteLine("Non-cryptographic exception: {0}, {1}",
    arg0: ex.GetType().Name,
    arg1: ex.Message);
}
```

10. Run the code, try entering a message and password to encrypt, enter the same password to decrypt, and view the result, as shown in the following output:

```
Enter a message that you want to encrypt: Hello Bob
Enter a password: secret
PBKDF2 algorithm: SHA256, Iteration count: 150,000
139 milliseconds to generate Key and IV.
Encryption algorithm: AES-256, CBC mode with PKCS7 padding.
Encrypted text: eWt8sgL7aSt5DC9g74ONEPO7mjd55lXB/MmCZpUsFE0=
Enter the password: secret
Decrypted text: Hello Bob
```

 If your output shows the number of milliseconds at less than 100, then adjust the number of iterations higher until it is greater than 100. Note that a different number of iterations will affect the encrypted text, so it will look different from the above output.

11. Run the console app and try entering a message and password to encrypt, but this time enter the password incorrectly to decrypt, and view the result, as shown in the following output:

```
Enter a message that you want to encrypt: Hello Bob
Enter a password: secret
PBKDF2 algorithm: SHA256, Iteration count: 150,000
134 milliseconds to generate Key and IV.
Encryption algorithm: AES-256, CBC mode with PKCS7 padding.
Encrypted text: eWt8sgL7aSt5DC9g74ONEPO7mjd55lXB/MmCZpUsFE0=
Enter the password: 123456
You entered the wrong password!
```

**Good Practice:** To support future encryption upgrades like switching to an improved algorithm or upgrading to a larger key size, record information about what choices you made: for example, AES-256, CBC mode with PKCS#7 padding, and PBKDF2 and its hash algorithm and iteration count. This good practice is known as **cryptographic agility**.

# Hashing data

In .NET, there are multiple hash algorithms you can choose from. Some do not use any key, some use symmetric keys, and some use asymmetric keys.

There are two important factors to consider when choosing a hash algorithm:

- **Collision resistance:** How rare is it to find two inputs that share the same hash?
- **Preimage resistance:** For a hash, how difficult would it be to find another input that shares the same hash?

Some common non-keyed hashing algorithms are shown in the following table:

| Algorithm | Hash size | Description |
|---|---|---|
| MD5 | 16 bytes | This is commonly used because it is fast, but it is not collision-resistant. |
| SHA1 | 20 bytes | The use of SHA1 on the internet has been deprecated since 2011. |
| SHA256, SHA384, SHA512 | 32 bytes, 48 bytes, 64 bytes | These are the **Secure Hashing Algorithm 2nd generation (SHA2)** algorithms with different hash sizes. |

**Good Practice:** Avoid MD5 and SHA1 because they have known weaknesses. Choose a larger hash size to reduce the possibility of repeated hashes. The first publicly known MD5 collision happened in 2010. The first publicly known SHA1 collision happened in 2017. You can read more at the following link: `https://arstechnica.co.uk/information-technology/2017/02/at-deaths-door-for-years-widely-used-sha1-function-is-now-dead/`.

# Hashing with the commonly used SHA256

We will now add a class to represent a user stored in memory, a file, or a database. We will use a dictionary to store multiple users in memory:

1.  In the `CryptographyLib` class library project, add a new class file named `User.cs`, and define a record with three properties for storing a user's name, a random salt value, and their salted and hashed password, as shown in the following code:

    ```
    namespace Packt.Shared;
    ```

```
public record class User(string Name, string Salt,
    string SaltedHashedPassword);
```

2.  In `Protector.cs`, add statements to declare a dictionary to store users and define two methods, one to register a new user and one to validate their password when they subsequently log in, as shown in the following code:

```
private static Dictionary<string, User> Users = new();

public static User Register(
    string username, string password)
{
    // generate a random salt
    RandomNumberGenerator rng = RandomNumberGenerator.Create();
    byte[] saltBytes = new byte[16];
    rng.GetBytes(saltBytes);
    string saltText = ToBase64String(saltBytes);

    // generate the salted and hashed password
    string saltedhashedPassword = SaltAndHashPassword(password, saltText);

    User user = new(username, saltText, saltedhashedPassword);

    Users.Add(user.Name, user);

    return user;
}

// check a user's password that is stored
// in the private static dictionary Users
public static bool CheckPassword(string username, string password)
{
    if (!Users.ContainsKey(username))
    {
        return false;
    }

    User u = Users[username];

    return CheckPassword(password,
```

```
      u.Salt, u.SaltedHashedPassword);
  }

  // check a password using salt and hashed password
  public static bool CheckPassword(string password,
    string salt, string hashedPassword)
  {
    // re-generate the salted and hashed password
    string saltedhashedPassword = SaltAndHashPassword(
      password, salt);

    return (saltedhashedPassword == hashedPassword);
  }

  private static string SaltAndHashPassword(string password, string salt)
  {
    using (SHA256 sha = SHA256.Create())
    {
      string saltedPassword = password + salt;
      return ToBase64String(sha.ComputeHash(
        Encoding.Unicode.GetBytes(saltedPassword)));
    }
  }
}
```

3. Use your preferred code editor to add a new console app named HashingApp to the Chapter08 solution/workspace.

   • In Visual Studio Code, select HashingApp as the active OmniSharp project.

4. In the HashingApp project, add a project reference to CryptographyLib, and globally and statically import the System.Console class.

5. Build the HashingApp project and make sure there are no compile errors.

6. In the HashingApp project, in Program.cs, delete the existing statements, and then add statements to register a user and prompt to register a second user. Then, prompt to log in as one of those users and validate the password, as shown in the following code:

```
using Packt.Shared;

WriteLine("Registering Alice with Pa$$w0rd:");
User alice = Protector.Register("Alice", "Pa$$w0rd");

WriteLine($"  Name: {alice.Name}");
```

```
WriteLine($"  Salt: {alice.Salt}");
WriteLine("  Password (salted and hashed): {0}",
  arg0: alice.SaltedHashedPassword);
WriteLine();

Write("Enter a new user to register: ");
string? username = ReadLine();
if (string.IsNullOrEmpty(username))
{
  username = "Bob";
}

Write($"Enter a password for {username}: ");
string? password = ReadLine();
if (string.IsNullOrEmpty(password))
{
  password = "Pa$$w0rd";
}

WriteLine("Registering a new user:");
User newUser = Protector.Register(username, password);
WriteLine($"  Name: {newUser.Name}");
WriteLine($"  Salt: {newUser.Salt}");
WriteLine("  Password (salted and hashed): {0}",
  arg0: newUser.SaltedHashedPassword);
WriteLine();

bool correctPassword = false;

while (!correctPassword)
{
  Write("Enter a username to log in: ");
  string? loginUsername = ReadLine();
  if (string.IsNullOrEmpty(loginUsername))
  {
    WriteLine("Login username cannot be empty.");
    Write("Press Ctrl+C to end or press ENTER to retry.");
    ReadLine();
    continue;
  }
```

```
Write("Enter a password to log in: ");
string? loginPassword = ReadLine();
if (string.IsNullOrEmpty(loginPassword))
{
  WriteLine("Login password cannot be empty.");
  Write("Press Ctrl+C to end or press ENTER to retry.");
  ReadLine();
  continue;
}

correctPassword = Protector.CheckPassword(
  loginUsername, loginPassword);

if (correctPassword)
{
  WriteLine($"Correct! {loginUsername} has been logged in.");
}
else
{
  WriteLine("Invalid username or password. Try again.");
}
}
```

7.  Run the code, register a new user with the same password as Alice, and view the result, as shown in the following output:

```
Registering Alice with Pa$$w0rd:
  Name: Alice
  Salt: I1I1dzIjkd7EYDf/6jaf4w==
  Password (salted and hashed): pIoadjE4W/
XaRFkqS3br3UuAuPv/3LVQ8kzj6mvcz+s=

Enter a new user to register: Bob
Enter a password for Bob: Pa$$w0rd
Registering a new user:
  Name: Bob
  Salt: 1X7ym/UjxTiuEWBC/vIHpw==
  Password (salted and hashed):
DoBFtDhKeN0aaaLVdErtrZ3mpZSvpWDQ9TXDosTq0sQ=

Enter a username to log in: Alice
```

```
Enter a password to log in: secret
Invalid username or password. Try again.
Enter a username to log in: Bob
Enter a password to log in: secret
Invalid username or password. Try again.
Enter a username to log in: Bob
Enter a password to log in: Pa$$w0rd
Correct! Bob has been logged in.
```

 Even if two users register with the same password, they have randomly generated salts so that their salted and hashed passwords are different.

# Signing data

To prove that some data has come from someone we trust, it can be signed. You do not sign the data itself; instead, you sign a *hash* of the data, because all the signature algorithms first hash the data as an implementation step. They also allow you to shortcut this step and provide the data already hashed.

We will be using the SHA256 algorithm for generating the hash, combined with the RSA algorithm for signing the hash.

We could use DSA for both hashing and signing. DSA is faster than RSA for generating a signature, but it is slower than RSA for validating a signature. Since a signature is generated once but validated many times, it is best to have faster validation than generation.

 **Good Practice:** DSA is rarely used today. The improved equivalent is **Elliptic Curve DSA (ECDSA)**. Although ECDSA is slower than RSA, it generates a shorter signature with the same level of security.

## Signing with SHA256 and RSA

Let's explore signing data and checking the signature with a public key:

1. In the `Protector` class, add statements to declare a field to store a public key as a `string` value, and two methods to generate and validate a signature, as shown in the following code:

```
public static string? PublicKey;

public static string GenerateSignature(string data)
{
  byte[] dataBytes = Encoding.Unicode.GetBytes(data);
  SHA256 sha = SHA256.Create();
```

```
  byte[] hashedData = sha.ComputeHash(dataBytes);
  RSA rsa = RSA.Create();

  PublicKey = rsa.ToXmlString(false); // exclude private key

  return ToBase64String(rsa.SignHash(hashedData,
    HashAlgorithmName.SHA256, RSASignaturePadding.Pkcs1));
}

public static bool ValidateSignature(
  string data, string signature)
{
  if (PublicKey is null) return false;

  byte[] dataBytes = Encoding.Unicode.GetBytes(data);
  SHA256 sha = SHA256.Create();

  byte[] hashedData = sha.ComputeHash(dataBytes);
  byte[] signatureBytes = FromBase64String(signature);

  RSA rsa = RSA.Create();
  rsa.FromXmlString(PublicKey);

  return rsa.VerifyHash(hashedData, signatureBytes,
    HashAlgorithmName.SHA256, RSASignaturePadding.Pkcs1);
}
```

Note the following from the preceding code:

- Only the public part of the public-private key pair needs to be made available to the code that is checking the signature so that we can pass `false` when we call the `ToXmlString` method. The private part is required to sign data and must be kept secret because anyone with the private part can sign data as if they are you!
- The hash algorithm used to generate the hash from the data by calling the `SignHash` method must match the hash algorithm set when calling the `VerifyHash` method. In the preceding code, we used `SHA256`.

Now we can test signing some data and checking its signature.

2. Use your preferred code editor to add a new console app named `SigningApp` to the `Chapter08` solution/workspace.

- In Visual Studio Code, select `SigningApp` as the active OmniSharp project.

3.  In the `SigningApp` project, add a project reference to `CryptographyLib`, and globally and statically import the `System.Console` class.

4.  Build the `SigningApp` project and make sure there are no compile errors.

5.  In `Program.cs`, delete the existing statements and then import the `Packt.Shared` namespace. Add statements to prompt the user to enter some text, sign it, check its signature, then modify the data, and check the signature again to deliberately cause a mismatch, as shown in the following code:

```csharp
using Packt.Shared;

Write("Enter some text to sign: ");
string? data = ReadLine();

if (string.IsNullOrEmpty(data))
{
  WriteLine("You must enter some text.");
  return;
}

string signature = Protector.GenerateSignature(data);

WriteLine($"Signature: {signature}");
WriteLine("Public key used to check signature:");
WriteLine(Protector.PublicKey);

if (Protector.ValidateSignature(data, signature))
{
  WriteLine("Correct! Signature is valid. Data has not been
manipulated.");
}
else
{
  WriteLine("Invalid signature or the data has been manipulated.");
}

// simulate manipulated data by replacing the
// first character with an X or Y
string manipulatedData = data.Replace(data[0], 'X');
if (manipulatedData == data)
{
    manipulatedData = data.Replace(data[0], 'Y');
```

```
    }

    if (Protector.ValidateSignature(manipulatedData, signature))
    {
      WriteLine("Correct! Signature is valid. Data has not been manipulated.
    ");
    }
    else
    {
      WriteLine("Invalid signature or manipulated data: {0} " ,
        manipulatedData);
    }
```

6.  Run the code and enter some text, as shown in the following output (edited for length):

```
Enter some text to sign: The cat sat on the mat.
Signature: BXSTdM...4Wrg==
Public key used to check signature:
<RSAKeyValue>
    <Modulus>nHtwl3...mw3w==</Modulus>
    <Exponent>AQAB</Exponent>
</RSAKeyValue>
Correct! Signature is valid. Data has not been manipulated.
Invalid signature or manipulated data: Xhe cat sat on the mat.
```

# Generating random numbers

Sometimes you need to generate random numbers, perhaps in a game that simulates rolls of a die, or for use with cryptography in encryption or signing. There are a couple of classes that can generate random numbers in .NET.

## Generating random numbers for games and similar apps

In scenarios that don't need truly random numbers, like games, you can use a shared instance of the Random class or create an instance of the Random class, as shown in the following code example:

```
Random r1 = Random.Shared; // Thread-safe
Random r2 = new(); // NOT thread-safe
```

Random has a constructor with a parameter for specifying a seed value used to initialize its pseudo-random number generator, as shown in the following code:

```
Random r = new(Seed: 46378);
```

> **Good Practice:** Shared seed values act as a secret key, so if you use the same random number generation algorithm with the same seed value in two applications, then they can generate the same "random" sequences of numbers. Sometimes this is necessary, for example, when synchronizing a GPS receiver with a satellite, or when a game needs to randomly generate the same level. But usually, you want to keep your seed secret.

Once you have a Random object, you can call its methods to generate random numbers, as shown in the following code examples:

```
// minValue is an inclusive lower bound i.e. 1 is a possible value
// maxValue is an exclusive upper bound i.e. 7 is not a possible value
int dieRoll = r.Next(minValue: 1, maxValue: 7); // returns 1 to 6

double randomReal = r.NextDouble(); // returns 0.0 to less than 1.0

byte[] arrayOfBytes = new byte[100];
r.NextBytes(arrayOfBytes); // 100 random bytes (values 0 to 255) in an array
```

The Next method takes two parameters: minValue and maxValue. But maxValue is not the maximum value that the method returns! It is an *exclusive upper bound*, meaning it is one more than the maximum value. In a similar way, the value returned by the NextDouble method is greater than or equal to 0.0 and less than 1.0.

## Generating random numbers for cryptography

The Random class generates cryptographically weak **pseudo-random** numbers. This is not good enough for cryptography. If the random numbers are not truly random, then they are predictable, and a cracker can break your protection.

For cryptographically strong pseudo-random numbers, you must use a RandomNumberGenerator-derived type, such as those created by calling the RandomNumberGenerator.Create factory method either with a named algorithm or using its default implementation.

We will now create a method to generate a truly random byte array that can be used in algorithms like encryption for key and IV values:

1. In the Protector class, add statements to define a method to get a random key or IV for use in encryption, as shown in the following code:

```
public static byte[] GetRandomKeyOrIV(int size)
{
  RandomNumberGenerator r = RandomNumberGenerator.Create();

  byte[] data = new byte[size];
```

```
    r.GetBytes(data);

    // data is an array now filled with
    // cryptographically strong random bytes
    return data;
}
```

Now we can test the random bytes generated for a truly random encryption key or IV.

2.  Use your preferred code editor to add a new console app named `RandomizingApp` to the `Chapter08` solution/workspace.

    •   In Visual Studio Code, select `RandomizingApp` as the active OmniSharp project.

3.  In the `RandomizingApp` project, add a project reference to `CryptographyLib`, and globally and statically import the `System.Console` class.

4.  Build the `RandomizingApp` project and make sure there are no compile errors.

5.  In `Program.cs`, delete the existing statements and then import the `Packt.Shared` namespace. Add statements to prompt the user to enter a size of byte array and then generate random byte values and write them to the console, as shown in the following code:

```
using Packt.Shared;

Write("How big do you want the key (in bytes): ");
string? size = ReadLine();

if (string.IsNullOrEmpty(size))
{
  WriteLine("You must enter a size for the key.");
  return;
}

byte[] key = Protector.GetRandomKeyOrIV(int.Parse(size));

WriteLine($"Key as byte array:");
for (int b = 0; b < key.Length; b++)
{
  Write($"{key[b]:x2} ");
  if (((b + 1) % 16) == 0) WriteLine();
}
WriteLine();
```

6. Run the code, enter a typical size for the key, such as 256, and view the randomly generated key, as shown in the following output:

```
How big do you want the key (in bytes): 256
Key as byte array:
f1 57 3f 44 80 e7 93 dc 8e 55 04 6c 76 6f 51 b9
e8 84 59 e5 8d eb 08 d5 e6 59 65 20 b1 56 fa 68
...
```

# Authenticating and authorizing users

**Authentication** is the process of verifying the identity of a user by validating their credentials against some authority. Credentials include a username and password combination, or a fingerprint or face scan. Once authenticated, the authority can make **claims** about the user, for example, what their email address is, and what groups or roles they belong to.

**Authorization** is the process of verifying membership of groups or roles before allowing access to resources such as application functions and data. Although authorization can be based on individual identity, it is good security practice to authorize based on group or role membership (which can be indicated via claims) even when there is only one user in the role or group. This is because that allows the user's membership to change in the future without reassigning the user's individual access rights.

For example, instead of assigning access rights to Buckingham Palace to *Charles Philip Arthur George Windsor* (a user), you would assign access rights to the *Monarch of the United Kingdom of Great Britain and Northern Ireland and other realms and territories* (a role) and then add Charles as the only member of that role. Then, at some point in the future, you do not need to change any access rights for the *Monarch* role; you just remove Charles and add the next person in the line of succession. And, of course, you would implement the line of succession as a queue.

## Authentication and authorization mechanisms

There are multiple authentication and authorization mechanisms to choose from. They all implement a pair of interfaces in the System.Security.Principal namespace: IIdentity and IPrincipal.

### Identifying a user

IIdentity represents a user, so it has a Name property and an IsAuthenticated property to indicate if they are anonymous or if they have been successfully authenticated from their credentials, as shown in the following code:

```
namespace System.Security.Principal
{
  public interface IIdentity
  {
    string? AuthenticationType { get; }
```

```
    bool IsAuthenticated { get; }
    string? Name { get; }
  }
}
```

A common class that implements this interface is `GenericIdentity`, which inherits from `ClaimsIdentity`, as shown in the following code:

```
namespace System.Security.Principal
{
  public class GenericIdentity : ClaimsIdentity
  {
    public GenericIdentity(string name);
    public GenericIdentity(string name, string type);
    protected GenericIdentity(GenericIdentity identity);
    public override string AuthenticationType { get; }
    public override IEnumerable<Claim> Claims { get; }
    public override bool IsAuthenticated { get; }
    public override string Name { get; }
    public override ClaimsIdentity Clone();
  }
}
```

The `Claim` objects have a `Type` property that indicates if the claim is for their name, their membership of a role or group, their date of birth, and so on, as shown in the following code:

```
namespace System.Security.Claims
{
  public class Claim
  {
    // various constructors

    public string Type { get; }
    public ClaimsIdentity? Subject { get; }
    public IDictionary<string, string> Properties { get; }
    public string OriginalIssuer { get; }
    public string Issuer { get; }
    public string ValueType { get; }
    public string Value { get; }
    protected virtual byte[]? CustomSerializationData { get; }
    public virtual Claim Clone();
    public virtual Claim Clone(ClaimsIdentity? identity);
    public override string ToString();
```

```
    public virtual void WriteTo(BinaryWriter writer);
    protected virtual void WriteTo(BinaryWriter writer, byte[]? userData);
  }


  public static class ClaimTypes
  {
    public const string Actor = "http://schemas.xmlsoap.org/ws/2009/09/
identity/claims/actor";
    public const string NameIdentifier = "http://schemas.xmlsoap.org/
ws/2005/05/identity/claims/nameidentifier";
    public const string Name = "http://schemas.xmlsoap.org/ws/2005/05/identity/
claims/name";
    public const string PostalCode = "http://schemas.xmlsoap.org/ws/2005/05/
identity/claims/postalcode";

    // ...many other string constants

    public const string MobilePhone = "http://schemas.xmlsoap.org/ws/2005/05/
identity/claims/mobilephone";
    public const string Role = "http://schemas.microsoft.com/ws/2008/06/
identity/claims/role";
    public const string Webpage = "http://schemas.xmlsoap.org/ws/2005/05/
identity/claims/webpage";
  }
}
```

## User membership

IPrincipal is used to associate an identity with the roles and groups that they are members of, so it can be used for authorization purposes, as shown in the following code:

```
namespace System.Security.Principal
{
  public interface IPrincipal
  {
    IIdentity? Identity { get; }
    bool IsInRole(string role);
  }
}
```

The current thread executing your code has a CurrentPrincipal property that can be set to any object that implements IPrincipal, and it will be checked when permission is needed to perform a secure action.

The most common class that implements this interface is `GenericPrincipal`, which inherits from `ClaimsPrincipal`, as shown in the following code:

```
namespace System.Security.Principal
{
  public class GenericPrincipal : ClaimsPrincipal
  {
    public GenericPrincipal(IIdentity identity, string[]? roles);
    public override IIdentity Identity { get; }
    public override bool IsInRole([NotNullWhen(true)] string? role);
  }
}
```

# Implementing authentication and authorization

Let's explore authentication and authorization by implementing a custom authentication and authorization mechanism:

1.  In the `CryptographyLib` project, add a property to the `User` record to store an array of roles, as highlighted in the following code:

    ```
    public record class User(string Name, string Salt,
      string SaltedHashedPassword, string[]? Roles);
    ```

2.  Modify the `Register` method in the `Protector` class to allow an array of roles to be passed as an optional parameter, as shown highlighted in the following code:

    ```
    public static User Register(string username,
      string password, string[]? roles = null)
    ```

3.  In the `Register` method, add a parameter to set the array of roles in the new `User` object, as shown highlighted in the following code:

    ```
    User user = new(username, saltText,
      saltedhashedPassword, roles);
    ```

4.  Import the namespace for working with the user identity, as shown in the following code:

    ```
    using System.Security.Principal; // GenericIdentity, GenericPrincipal
    ```

5.  Add statements to the `Protector` class to define a `LogIn` method to log in a user, and if the username and password are valid, then create a generic identity and principal and assign them to the current thread, indicating that the type of authentication was a custom one named `PacktAuth`, as shown in the following code:

    ```
    public static void LogIn(string username, string password)
    {
      if (CheckPassword(username, password))
    ```

```
    {
      GenericIdentity gi = new(
        name: username, type: "PacktAuth");

      GenericPrincipal gp = new(
        identity: gi, roles: Users[username].Roles);

      // set the principal on the current thread so that
      // it will be used for authorization by default
      Thread.CurrentPrincipal = gp;

    }
  }
```

6. Use your preferred code editor to add a new console app named SecureApp to the Chapter08 solution/workspace.

    • In Visual Studio Code, select SecureApp as the active OmniSharp project.

7. In the SecureApp project, add a project reference to CryptographyLib, and globally and statically import the System.Console class.

8. Build the SecureApp project and make sure there are no compile errors.

9. In the SecureApp project, in Program.cs, delete the existing statements, and then import required namespaces for working with authentication and authorization, as shown in the following code:

```
using Packt.Shared; // Protector
using System.Security.Principal; // IPrincipal
using System.Security.Claims; // ClaimsPrincipal, Claim
```

10. In Program.cs, add statements to register three users, named Alice, Bob, and Eve, in various roles, prompt the user to log in, and then output information about them, as shown in the following code:

```
Protector.Register("Alice", "Pa$$w0rd", roles: new[] { "Admins" });

Protector.Register("Bob", "Pa$$w0rd",
  roles: new[] { "Sales", "TeamLeads" });

// Eve is not a member of any roles
Protector.Register("Eve", "Pa$$w0rd");

// prompt user to enter username and password to login
// as one of these three users
```

```
Write($"Enter your username: ");
string? username = ReadLine()!;

Write($"Enter your password: ");
string? password = ReadLine()!;

Protector.LogIn(username, password);

if (Thread.CurrentPrincipal == null)
{
  WriteLine("Log in failed.");
  return;
}

IPrincipal p = Thread.CurrentPrincipal;

WriteLine($"IsAuthenticated: {p.Identity?.IsAuthenticated}");
WriteLine(
  $"AuthenticationType: {p.Identity?.AuthenticationType}");
WriteLine($"Name: {p.Identity?.Name}");
WriteLine($"IsInRole(\"Admins\"): {p.IsInRole("Admins")}");
WriteLine($"IsInRole(\"Sales\"): {p.IsInRole("Sales")}");

if (p is ClaimsPrincipal)
{
  WriteLine($"{p.Identity?.Name} has the following claims:");

  IEnumerable<Claim>? claims = (p as ClaimsPrincipal)?.Claims;

  if (claims is not null)
  {
    foreach (Claim claim in claims)
    {
      WriteLine($"{claim.Type}: {claim.Value}");
    }
  }
}
```

11. Run the code, log in as `Alice` with `Pa$$word`, and view the results, as shown in the following output:

```
Enter your username: Alice
Enter your password: Pa$$w0rd
IsAuthenticated: True
AuthenticationType: PacktAuth
Name: Alice
IsInRole("Admins"): True
IsInRole("Sales"): False
Alice has the following claims:
http://schemas.xmlsoap.org/ws/2005/05/identity/claims/name: Alice
http://schemas.microsoft.com/ws/2008/06/identity/claims/role: Admins
```

12. Run the code, log in as `Alice` with `secret`, and view the results, as shown in the following output:

```
Enter your username: Alice
Enter your password: secret
Log in failed.
```

13. Run the code, log in as `Bob` with `Pa$$word`, and view the results, as shown in the following output:

```
Enter your username: Bob
Enter your password: Pa$$w0rd
IsAuthenticated: True
AuthenticationType: PacktAuth
Name: Bob
IsInRole("Admins"): False
IsInRole("Sales"): True
Bob has the following claims:
http://schemas.xmlsoap.org/ws/2005/05/identity/claims/name: Bob
http://schemas.microsoft.com/ws/2008/06/identity/claims/role: Sales
http://schemas.microsoft.com/ws/2008/06/identity/claims/role: TeamLeads
```

## Protecting application functionality

Now let's explore how we can use authorization to prevent some users from accessing some features of an application:

1. At the top of `Program.cs`, add a statement to import the namespace for security exceptions, as shown in the following code:

```
using System.Security; // SecurityException
```

2.  At the bottom of `Program.cs`, add a method that is secured by checking for permission in the method, and throw appropriate exceptions if the user is anonymous or not a member of the `Admins` role, as shown in the following code:

```
static void SecureFeature()
{
  if (Thread.CurrentPrincipal == null)
  {
    throw new SecurityException(
      "A user must be logged in to access this feature.");
  }

  if (!Thread.CurrentPrincipal.IsInRole("Admins"))
  {
    throw new SecurityException(
      "User must be a member of Admins to access this feature.");
  }

  WriteLine("You have access to this secure feature.");
}
```

3.  Above the `SecureFeature` method, add statements to call the `SecureFeature` method in a `try` statement, as shown in the following code:

```
try
{
  SecureFeature();
}
catch (Exception ex)
{
  WriteLine($"{ex.GetType()}: {ex.Message}");
}
```

4.  Run the code, log in as `Alice` with `Pa$$word`, and view the result, as shown in the following output:

```
You have access to this secure feature.
```

5.  Run the code, log in as `Bob` with `Pa$$word`, and view the result, as shown in the following output:

```
System.Security.SecurityException: User must be a member of Admins to
access this feature.
```

# Real-world authentication and authorization

Although it is valuable to see some examples of how authentication and authorization can work, in the real world you should not build your own security systems because it is too likely that you might introduce flaws.

Instead, you should look at commercial or open-source implementations. These usually implement standards like OAuth 2.0 and OpenID Connect. A popular open-source one is **IdentityServer4** but it will only be maintained until November 2022. A semi-commercial option is Duende IdentityServer.

Microsoft's official position is that "Microsoft already has a team and a product in that area, Azure Active Directory, which allows 500,000 objects for free." You can read more at the following link: `https://devblogs.microsoft.com/aspnet/asp-net-core-6-and-authentication-servers/`.

You will learn more about web security in *Chapter 9, Building and Securing Web Services Using Minimal APIs*.

# Practicing and exploring

Test your knowledge and understanding by answering some questions, getting some hands-on practice, and exploring the topics covered in this chapter with deeper research.

## Exercise 8.1 – Test your knowledge

Answer the following questions:

1. Of the encryption algorithms provided by .NET, which is the best choice for symmetric encryption?
2. Of the encryption algorithms provided by .NET, which is the best choice for asymmetric encryption?
3. What is a rainbow attack?
4. For encryption algorithms, is it better to have a larger or smaller block size?
5. What is a cryptographic hash?
6. What is a cryptographic signature?
7. What is the difference between symmetric and asymmetric encryption?
8. What does RSA stand for?
9. Why should passwords be salted before being stored?
10. SHA1 is a hashing algorithm designed by the United States National Security Agency. Why should you never use it?

# Exercise 8.2 – Practice protecting data with encryption and hashing

In the `Chapter08` solution/workspace, add a console app named `Ch08Ex02_EncryptData` that protects sensitive data like a credit card number or password stored in an XML file, such as the following example:

```xml
<?xml version="1.0" encoding="utf-8" ?>
<customers>
  <customer>
    <name>Bob Smith</name>
    <creditcard>1234-5678-9012-3456</creditcard>
    <password>Pa$$w0rd</password>
  </customer>
  ...
</customers>
```

The customer's credit card number and password are currently stored in cleartext. The credit card number must be encrypted so that it can be decrypted and used later, and the password must be salted and hashed.

 **Good Practice:** You should not store credit card numbers in your applications. This is just an example of a secret that you might want to protect. If you have to store credit card numbers, then there is a lot more you must do to be Payment Card Industry (PCI)-compliant.

# Exercise 8.3 – Practice protecting data with decryption

In the `Chapter08` solution/workspace, add a console application named `Ch08Ex03_DecryptData` that opens the XML file that you protected in the preceding code and decrypts the credit card number.

# Exercise 8.4 – Explore topics

Use the links on the following page to learn more detail about the topics covered in this chapter:

`https://github.com/markjprice/apps-services-net7/blob/main/book-links.md#chapter-3---protecting-your-data-and-applications`

# Exercise 8.5 – Review Microsoft encryption recommendations

Use the following link to review Microsoft recommendations and best practices for using encryption. The document is based on Microsoft's internal standards for their **Security Development Lifecycle (SDL)**:

`https://docs.microsoft.com/en-us/security/sdl/cryptographic-recommendations`

# Summary

In this chapter, you learned how to:

- Encrypt and decrypt using symmetric encryption.
- Generate a salted hash.
- Sign data and check the signature on the data.
- Generate truly random numbers.
- Use authentication and authorization to protect the features of your applications.

In the next chapter, you will learn how to build web services using the ASP.NET Core Minimal API and how to secure and protect them.

# 9

# Building and Securing Web Services Using Minimal APIs

This chapter is about building and securing web services using ASP.NET Core Minimal APIs. This includes implementing techniques to protect a web service from attacks as well as authentication and authorization.

This chapter will cover the following topics:

- Building web services using ASP.NET Core Minimal APIs
- Relaxing the same origin security policy using CORS
- Preventing denial-of-service attacks using rate limiting
- Understanding identity services

## Building web services using ASP.NET Core Minimal APIs

In earlier versions of ASP.NET Core, implementing even a simple web service required a lot of boiler-plate code. For example, the ASP.NET Core Web API project template in ASP.NET Core 5 implements a simple weather service using four code files (controller, model, program, and startup class files), with a total 139 lines of code:

- `WeatherForecastController.cs` has 39 lines of code
- `WeatherForecast.cs` has 15 lines of code
- `Program.cs` has 26 lines of code
- `Startup.cs` has 59 lines of code

Compare that to a minimal Hello World web service implementation using Express.js, as shown in the following code:

```
const express = require('express')
```

```
const app = express()
const port = 3000

app.get('/', (req, res) => {
  res.send('Hello World!')
})

app.listen(port, () => {
  console.log(`Example app listening on port ${port}`)
})
```

Introduced in ASP.NET Core 6, Minimal APIs reduce the code needed to implement a web service. Combined with other .NET 6 features like global implicit namespace imports and top-level programs, the amount of code needed has been significantly reduced.

The minimal Hello World web service implementation equivalent of the Express.js example using ASP.NET Core 6 or later Minimal APIs is now only 5 lines of code and 6 lines of configuration, as shown in the following two statement blocks:

```
int port = 3000;
var app = WebApplication.Create();
app.MapGet("/", () => "Hello World!");
Console.WriteLine($"Example app listening on port {port}");
await app.RunAsync($"https://localhost:{port}/");
```

The platform is specified in the project file, and the implicit using statements SDK feature does some heavy lifting. It is enabled by default, as shown highlighted in the following markup:

```
<Project Sdk="Microsoft.NET.Sdk.Web">
  <PropertyGroup>
    <TargetFramework>net7.0</TargetFramework>
    <ImplicitUsings>enable</ImplicitUsings>
  </PropertyGroup>
</Project>
```

The Web API template in ASP.NET Core 7 that implements the same weather service only needs Program.cs with 46 lines of code and 6 lines of configuration. That is a two-thirds reduction compared to the old project template.

## Understanding Minimal APIs route mappings

The WebApplication instance has methods that you can call to map a route to a lambda expression or statement:

- MapGet: Map a route to a GET request to retrieve an entity.
- MapPost: Map a route to a POST request to insert an entity.

- **MapPut**: Map a route to a PUT request to update an entity.
- **MapPatch**: Map a route to a PATCH request to update an entity.
- **MapDelete**: Map a route to a DELETE request to delete an entity.
- **MapMethods**: Map a route to any other HTTP method or methods, for example, CONNECT or HEAD.

For example, you might want to map an HTTP GET request for the relative path api/customers to a delegate defined by a lambda expression or a function that returns a JSON document containing a list of customers, as shown in the following code:

```
app.MapGet("api/customers", () => GetListOfCustomersAsJson());
```

You might want to map an HTTP CONNECT request for the relative path api/customers to a lambda statement block, as shown in the following code:

```
app.MapMethods("api/customers", new[] { "CONNECT" }, () =>
  {
    // Do something.
  });
```

## Understanding parameter mapping

The delegate can have parameters defined that can be set automatically. Although most mappings can be configured without explicitly being specified, you can optionally use attributes to define where ASP.NET Core Minimal APIs should set the parameter values from:

- [FromServices]: The parameter will be set from the registered dependency services.
- [FromRoute]: The parameter will be set from a matching named route segment.
- [FromQuery]: The parameter will be set from a matching named query string parameter.
- [FromBody]: The parameter will be set from the body of the HTTP request.

For example, to update an entity in a database, you would need a database context to be retrieved from the registered dependency services, an identifier passed as a query string or route segment, and the new entity in the body of the request, as shown in the following code:

```
app.MapPut("api/customers/{id}", async (
  [FromServices] NorthwindContext db,
  [FromRoute] string id, // or [FromQuery] string id,
  [FromBody] Customer customer) =>
{
  Customer? existingCustomer = await db.Customers.FindAsync(id);
  ...
});
```

# Understanding return values

A Minimal API's service can return data in some common formats:

| Type | Lambda |
|------|--------|
| Plain text | `() => "Hello World!"`<br>`() => Results.Text("Hello World!")` |
| JSON document | `() => new { FirstName = "Bob", LastName = "Jones" }`<br>`() => Results.Json(new { FirstName = "Bob", LastName = "Jones" })` |
| IResult with status codes | `() => Results.Ok(new { FirstName = "Bob", LastName = "Jones" })`<br>`() => Results.NoContent()`<br>`() => Results.Redirect("new/path")`<br>`() => Results.NotFound()`<br>`() => Results.BadRequest()`<br>`() => Results.Problem()`<br>`() => Results.StatusCode(405)` |
| File | `() => Results.File("/path/filename.ext")` |

# Documenting a Minimal APIs service

You can call additional methods to specify what return types and status codes can be expected from an endpoint:

- `Produces<T>(StatusCodes.Status200OK)`: When successful, this route returns a response containing a type `T` and status code `200`.
- `Produces(StatusCodes.Status404NotFound)`: When no match for the route is found, this route returns an empty response and status code `404`.

# Setting up an ASP.NET Core Web API project

First, we will create a simple ASP.NET Core Web API project that we will later protect using various techniques, including rate limiting, CORS, and authentication and authorization.

The API for this web service is defined as shown in the following table:

| Method | Path | Request body | Response body | Success code |
|--------|------|--------------|---------------|--------------|
| GET | / | None | Hello World! | 200 |
| GET | /api/products | None | Array of in-stock Product objects | 200 |
| GET | /api/products/outofstock | None | Array of out-of-stock Product objects | 200 |

| GET | /api/products/ discontinued | None | Array of discontinued Product objects | 200 |
|------|------|------|------|------|
| GET | /api/products/{id} | None | Product object | 200 |
| GET | /api/products/{name} | None | Array of Product objects that contain the name | 200 |
| POST | /api/products | Product object (no Id value) | Product object | 201 |
| PUT | /api/products/{id} | Product object | None | 204 |
| DELETE | /api/products/{id} | None | None | 204 |

Let's go:

1. Use your preferred code editor to create a new solution/workspace named `Chapter09`.

2. Add a Web API project, as defined in the following list:

    - Project template: **ASP.NET Core Web API**/`webapi --use-minimal-apis`
    - Workspace/solution file and folder: `Chapter09`
    - Project file and folder: `Northwind.WebApi.Service`
    - **Authentication type:** None
    - **Configure for HTTPS:** Selected
    - **Enable Docker:** Cleared
    - **Use controllers (uncheck to use minimal APIs):** Cleared
    - **Enable OpenAPI support:** Selected
    - **Do not use top-level statements:** Cleared

 To create a Web API project using Minimal APIs with `dotnet new`, you must use either the `-minimal` switch or the `--use-minimal-apis` switch.

3. Add a project reference to the Northwind database context project for SQL Server that you created in *Chapter 2, Managing Relational Data Using SQL Server*, as shown in the following markup:

```
<ItemGroup>
  <ProjectReference Include="..\..\Chapter02\Northwind.Common.DataContext
.SqlServer\Northwind.Common.DataContext.SqlServer.csproj" />
</ItemGroup>
```

The path cannot have a line break. If you did not complete the task to create the class libraries in *Chapter 2*, then download the solution projects from the GitHub repository.

4.  At the command line or terminal, build the `Northwind.WebApi.Service` project to make sure the entity model class library projects outside the current solution are properly compiled, as shown in the following command:

```
dotnet build
```

5.  In the `Properties` folder, in `launchSettings.json`, modify the `applicationUrl` of the profile named `https` to use port `5091`, as shown highlighted in the following configuration:

```
"profiles": {
  ...
  "https": {
    "commandName": "Project",
    "dotnetRunMessages": true,
    "launchBrowser": true,
    "launchUrl": "swagger",
    "applicationUrl": "https://localhost:5091",
    "environmentVariables": {
      "ASPNETCORE_ENVIRONMENT": "Development"
    }
```

6.  In `Program.cs`, delete the statements about the weather service and replace them with statements to configure responses to all the HTTP requests documented in the API table, as shown highlighted in the following code:

```
using Microsoft.AspNetCore.Http.HttpResults; // Results
using Microsoft.AspNetCore.Mvc; // [FromServices]
using Microsoft.AspNetCore.OpenApi; // WithOpenApi
using Packt.Shared; // AddNorthwindContext extension method

var builder = WebApplication.CreateBuilder(args);

// Add services to the container.
// Learn more about configuring Swagger/OpenAPI at https://aka.ms/
aspnetcore/swashbuckle
builder.Services.AddEndpointsApiExplorer();
builder.Services.AddSwaggerGen();

builder.Services.AddNorthwindContext();

var app = builder.Build();
```

```
// Configure the HTTP request pipeline.
if (app.Environment.IsDevelopment())
{
  app.UseSwagger();
  app.UseSwaggerUI();
}

app.UseHttpsRedirection();

app.MapGet("/", () => "Hello World!");

int pageSize = 10;

app.MapGet("api/products", (
  [FromServices] NorthwindContext db,
  [FromQuery] int? page) =>
  db.Products.Where(product =>
    (product.UnitsInStock > 0) && (!product.Discontinued))
    .Skip(((page ?? 1) - 1) * pageSize).Take(pageSize)
  )
  .WithName("GetProducts")
  .WithOpenApi(operation =>
  {
    operation.Description =
      "Get products with UnitsInStock > 0 and Discontinued = false.";
    operation.Summary = "Get in-stock products that are not
discontinued.";
    return operation;
  })
  .Produces<Product[]>(StatusCodes.Status200OK);

app.MapGet("api/products/outofstock", ([FromServices] NorthwindContext
db) =>
  db.Products.Where(product =>
    (product.UnitsInStock == 0) && (!product.Discontinued)))
  .WithName("GetProductsOutOfStock")
  .WithOpenApi()
  .Produces<Product[]>(StatusCodes.Status200OK);

app.MapGet("api/products/discontinued", ([FromServices] NorthwindContext
db) =>
  db.Products.Where(product => product.Discontinued))
  .WithName("GetProductsDiscontinued")
  .WithOpenApi()
```

```csharp
  .Produces<Product[]>(StatusCodes.Status200OK);

app.MapGet("api/products/{id:int}",
  async Task<Results<Ok<Product>, NotFound>> (
  [FromServices] NorthwindContext db,
  [FromRoute] int id) =>
    await db.Products.FindAsync(id) is Product product ?
      TypedResults.Ok(product) : TypedResults.NotFound())
  .WithName("GetProductById")
  .WithOpenApi()
  .Produces<Product>(StatusCodes.Status200OK)
  .Produces(StatusCodes.Status404NotFound);

app.MapGet("api/products/{name}", (
  [FromServices] NorthwindContext db, [FromRoute] string name) =>
    db.Products.Where(p => p.ProductName.Contains(name)))
  .WithName("GetProductsByName")
  .WithOpenApi()
  .Produces<Product[]>(StatusCodes.Status200OK);

app.MapPost("api/products", async ([FromBody] Product product,
  [FromServices] NorthwindContext db) =>
{
  db.Products.Add(product);
  await db.SaveChangesAsync();
  return Results.Created($"api/products/{product.ProductId}", product);
}).WithOpenApi()
  .Produces<Product>(StatusCodes.Status201Created);

app.MapPut("api/products/{id:int}", async (
  [FromRoute] int id,
  [FromBody] Product product,
  [FromServices] NorthwindContext db) =>
{
  Product? foundProduct = await db.Products.FindAsync(id);

  if (foundProduct is null) return Results.NotFound();
```

```
    foundProduct.ProductName = product.ProductName;
    foundProduct.CategoryId = product.CategoryId;
    foundProduct.SupplierId = product.SupplierId;
    foundProduct.QuantityPerUnit = product.QuantityPerUnit;
    foundProduct.UnitsInStock = product.UnitsInStock;
    foundProduct.UnitsOnOrder = product.UnitsOnOrder;
    foundProduct.ReorderLevel = product.ReorderLevel;
    foundProduct.UnitPrice = product.UnitPrice;
    foundProduct.Discontinued = product.Discontinued;

  await db.SaveChangesAsync();

  return Results.NoContent();
}).WithOpenApi()
  .Produces(StatusCodes.Status404NotFound)
  .Produces(StatusCodes.Status204NoContent);

app.MapDelete("api/products/{id:int}", async (
  [FromRoute] int id,
  [FromServices] NorthwindContext db) =>
{
  if (await db.Products.FindAsync(id) is Product product)
  {
    db.Products.Remove(product);
    await db.SaveChangesAsync();
    return Results.NoContent();
  }
  return Results.NotFound();
}).WithOpenApi()
  .Produces(StatusCodes.Status404NotFound)
  .Produces(StatusCodes.Status204NoContent);

app.Run();
```

7. Start the website project using the `https` profile (`dotnet run --launch-profile https`) and note the Swagger documentation, as shown in *Figure 9.1*:

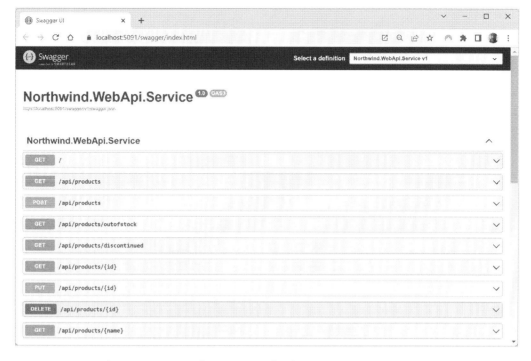

*Figure 9.1: Swagger documentation for the Northwind Web API service*

8. Click **GET /api/products** to expand that section.

9. Click the **Try it out** button, note the optional query string parameter named **page**, and then click the **Execute** button.

10. Note the response includes the first ten products that are in stock and not discontinued: 1, 2, 3, 4, 6, 7, 8, 10, 11, and 12.

11. For the **page** parameter, enter 3, and then click the **Execute** button.

12. Note the response includes the third page of ten products that are in stock and are not discontinued: 25, 26, 27, 30, 32, 33, 34, 35, 36, and 37.

13. Click **GET /api/products** to collapse that section.

14. Try executing the **GET /api/products/outofstock** path and note it returns one product, **31 Gorgonzola Telino**, that has zero units in stock and is not discontinued.

15. Try executing the **GET /api/products/discontinued** path and note it returns eight products: 5, 9, 17, 24, 28, 29, 42, and 53, which all have their `Discontinued` properties set to `true`.

16. Click **GET /api/products/{id}** to expand that section.

17. Click **Try it out**, enter the required **id** parameter as 77, click **Execute**, and note the response contains the product named **Original Frankfurter grüne Soße**, as shown in the following JSON document:

```json
{
    "productId": 77,
    "productName": "Original Frankfurter grüne Soße",
    "supplierId": 12,
    "categoryId": 2,
    "quantityPerUnit": "12 boxes",
    "unitPrice": 13,
    "unitsInStock": 32,
    "unitsOnOrder": 0,
    "reorderLevel": 15,
    "discontinued": false,
    "category": null,
    "supplier": null,
    "orderDetails": []
}
```

18. Click **GET /api/products/{id}** to collapse that section.

19. Click **GET /api/products/{name}** to expand that section.

20. Click **Try it out**, enter the required **name** parameter as man, click **Execute**, and note the response contains the products named **Queso Manchego La Pastora** and **Manjimup Dried Apples**.

21. Leave the web service running.

# Testing web services using Visual Studio Code extensions

Using the Swagger user interface to test web services can quickly get clumsy. A better tool is the Visual Studio Code extension named **REST Client**:

1. If you have not already installed REST Client by Huachao Mao (`humao.rest-client`), then install it in Visual Studio Code now.

2. In your preferred code editor, start the `Northwind.WebApi.Service` project using the `https` profile (if it is not already running) and leave it running.

3. In Visual Studio Code, in the `apps-services-net7` folder, if it does not already exist create a `RestClientTests` folder, and then open that folder.

4. In the `RestClientTests` folder, create a file named `webapi-get-products.http`, and modify its contents to contain a request to get all products, as shown in the following code:

```
### Get first page of 10 products that are in stock and not discontinued
GET https://localhost:5091/api/products/
```

5.  Click **Send Request**, and note the response is the same as what was returned by Swagger, a JSON document response containing the first ten products that are in stock and not discontinued, as shown in *Figure 9.2*:

Figure 9.2: REST Client getting the products from the Web API service

6.  In `webapi-get-products.http`, add more requests separated by ###, as shown in the following file:

```
### Get third page of 10 products that are in stock and not discontinued
GET https://localhost:5091/api/products?page=3

### Get products that are out-of-stock but not discontinued
GET https://localhost:5091/api/products/outofstock

### Get products that are discontinued
GET https://localhost:5091/api/products/discontinued

### Get product 77
GET https://localhost:5091/api/products/77

### Get products that contain "man"
GET https://localhost:5091/api/products/man
```

7.  Note that you can execute an HTTP request by clicking **Send Request** above each query, or by navigating to **View | Command Palette** and selecting the **Rest Client: Send Request** command or using its keyboard shortcut for your operating system.

8.  In the `RestClientTests` folder, create a file named `webapi-insert-product.http`, and modify its contents to contain a POST request to insert a new product, as shown in the following code:

```
POST https://localhost:5091/api/products/
Content-Type: application/json

{
  "productName": "Harry's Hamburgers",
  "supplierId": 7,
```

```
    "categoryId": 6,
    "quantityPerUnit": "6 per box",
    "unitPrice": 24.99,
    "unitsInStock": 0,
    "unitsOnOrder": 20,
    "reorderLevel": 10,
    "discontinued": false
}
```

9. Click **Send Request**, and note the response indicates that the new product was added successfully because the status code is 201, and its location includes its product ID, as shown in *Figure 9.3*:

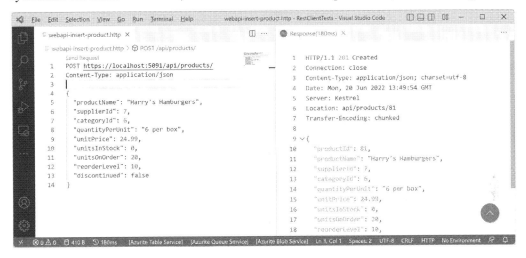

*Figure 9.3: REST Client inserting a new product by calling the Web API service*

 Originally, there are 77 products in the Northwind database. The next product ID
would be 78. The actual product ID assigned automatically will depend on if you
have previously added any other products. In *Figure 9.3*, you can see that 81 was assigned. You could re-execute the SQL script to drop and then recreate the database.

10. In the RestClientTests folder, create a file named webapi-update-product.http, and modify
    its contents to contain a PUT request to update the product with ID 81 with a different quantity
    per unit, unit price, and units in stock, as shown in the following code:

```
PUT https://localhost:5091/api/products/81
Content-Type: application/json

{
    "productName": "Harry's Hamburgers",
    "supplierId": 7,
    "categoryId": 6,
    "quantityPerUnit": "12 per box",
```

```
    "unitPrice": 44.99,
    "unitsInStock": 50,
    "unitsOnOrder": 20,
    "reorderLevel": 10,
    "discontinued": false
  }
```

11. Send the request and note you should get a 204 status code in the response, meaning a successful update.

12. Confirm the product was updated by executing a GET request for the product ID.

13. In the RestClientTests folder, create a file named webapi-delete-product.http, and modify its contents to contain a DELETE request for the new product, as shown in the following code:

```
DELETE https://localhost:5091/api/products/81
```

14. Note the successful response, as shown in *Figure 9.4*:

*Figure 9.4: Deleting a product using the Web API service*

15. Send the request again and note the response contains a 404 status code because the product has now been deleted.

16. Shut down the web server.

# Excluding paths from OpenAPI documentation

Sometimes you want to have a path that works but is not shown in the Swagger documentation:

1. In Program.cs, for the root path that returns Hello World!, exclude it from the OpenAPI documentation, as shown highlighted in the following code:

```
app.MapGet("/", () => "Hello World!")
  .ExcludeFromDescription();
```

2. Start the Northwind.WebApi.Service project using the https profile and note the path is now not documented.

We now have a working web service implemented using ASP.NET Core Minimal APIs. Now let's attack it! (So that we can learn how to prevent those attacks!)

# Relaxing the same origin security policy using CORS

Modern web browsers support multiple tabs so users can visit multiple websites at the same time efficiently. If code executing in one tab could access resources in another tab, then that could become a method of attack.

All web browsers implement a security feature called the **same origin policy**. This means that only requests that come from the same origin are allowed. For example, if a block of JavaScript is served from the same origin that hosts a web service or served an <iframe>, then that JavaScript can call the service and access the data in the <iframe>. If a request is made from a different origin, then the request fails.

An origin is defined by the following:

- **Scheme** aka protocol, for example, HTTP or HTTPS
- **Port** (if specified)
- **Host/domain/subdomain**, for example, www.example.com, www.example.net, example.com

If the origin is http://www.example.com/about-us/, then the following are NOT the same origin:

- Different scheme: https://www.example.com/about-us/
- Different host/domain: http://www.example.co.uk/about-us/
- Different subdomain: http://careers.example.com/about-us/
- Different port: http://www.example.com:8000/about-us/

It is the web browser that sets the Origin header automatically when making an HTTP request. This cannot be overridden. The same origin policy does *not* apply to any HTTP requests that come from a non-web browser, because in those cases the programmer could change the Origin header anyway. If you create a console app or even an ASP.NET Core project that uses .NET classes like HttpClient to make a request, the same origin policy does not apply unless you explicitly set the Origin header.

Let's see some examples of calling the web service from a web page with a different origin and from a .NET app.

## Configuring HTTP logging for the web service

First, let's enable HTTP logging for the web service and configure it to show the origin of requests:

1. In the Northwind.WebApi.Service project, in Program.cs, import the namespace for controlling which HTTP fields are logged, as shown in the following code:

   ```
   using Microsoft.AspNetCore.HttpLogging; // HttpLoggingFields
   ```

2. In Program.cs, before the call to builder.Build(), add a statement to add HTTP logging including the Origin header and all fields including the response body, as shown in the following code:

   ```
   builder.Services.AddHttpLogging(options =>
   {
   ```

```
    // Add the Origin header so it will not be redacted.
    options.RequestHeaders.Add("Origin");

    // By default, the response body is not included.
    options.LoggingFields = HttpLoggingFields.All;
});
```

3. In `Program.cs`, after the call to `UseHttpsRedirection()`, add a statement to use HTTP logging, as shown in the following code:

```
app.UseHttpLogging();
```

4. In `appsettings.Development.json`, add an entry to set the level for HTTP logging to `Information`, as shown highlighted in the following configuration:

```
{
  "Logging": {
    "LogLevel": {
      "Default": "Information",
      "Microsoft.AspNetCore": "Warning",
      "Microsoft.AspNetCore.HttpLogging": "Information"
    }
  }
}
```

# Creating a web page JavaScript client

Next, let's create a web page client that will attempt to use JavaScript on a different port to call the web service:

1. Use your preferred code editor to add a new project, as defined in the following list:

    1. Project template: **ASP.NET Core Web App (Model-View-Controller)**/`mvc`
    2. Workspace/solution file and folder: `Chapter09`
    3. Project file and folder: `Northwind.WebApi.Client.Mvc`
    4. Other Visual Studio 2022 options:

        • **Authentication Type:** None
        • **Configure for HTTPS:** Selected
        • **Enable Docker:** Cleared
        • **Do not use top-level statements:** Cleared

    In Visual Studio 2022, set the startup project to the current selection.

    In Visual Studio Code, select `Northwind.WebApi.Client.Mvc` as the active OmniSharp project.

2. In the `Northwind.WebApi.Client.Mvc` project, in the `Properties` folder, in `launchSettings.json`, change the `applicationUrl` for the `https` profile to use port `5092`, as shown in the following markup:

```
"applicationUrl": "https://localhost:5092",
```

3. In the `Views/Home` folder, in `Index.cshtml`, replace the existing markup with the markup below, which has a link to a route that has not been defined yet. This will also define a text box and button, and a JavaScript block that makes a call to the web service to get products that contain a partial name, as shown in the following code:

```
@{
    ViewData["Title"] = "Products using JavaScript";
}
<div class="text-center">
    <h1 class="display-4">@ViewData["Title"]</h1>
    <div>
        Go to <a href="/home/products">Products using .NET</a>
    </div>
    <div>
        <input id="productName" placeholder="Enter part of a product name" />
        <input id="getProductsButton" type="button" value="Get Products" />
    </div>
    <div>
        <table id="productsTable" class="table">
            <thead>
                <tr>
                    <th scope="col">Product Name</th>
                </tr>
            </thead>
            <tbody id="tableBody">

            </tbody>
        </table>
    </div>
    <script>
        var baseaddress = "https://localhost:5091/";

        function xhr_load() {
            console.log(this.responseText);

            var products = JSON.parse(this.responseText);

            var out = "";
            var i;
```

```
            for (i = 0; i < products.length; i++) {
                out += '<tr><td><a href="' + baseaddress + 'api/products/' +
                    products[i].productId + '">' +
                    products[i].productName + '</a></td></tr>';
            }
            document.getElementById("tableBody").innerHTML = out;
        }

        function getProductsButton_click() {
            xhr.open("GET", baseaddress + "api/products/" +
              document.getElementById("productName").value);

            xhr.send();
        }

        document.getElementById("getProductsButton")
          .addEventListener("click", getProductsButton_click);

        var xhr = new XMLHttpRequest();
        xhr.addEventListener("load", xhr_load);
    </script>
</div>
```

4.  Start the `Northwind.WebApi.Service` project using the `https` profile without debugging.
5.  Start the `Northwind.WebApi.Client.Mvc` project using the `https` profile without debugging.

 If you are using Visual Studio Code, then the web browser will not start automatically. Start Chrome, and then navigate to `https://localhost:5092`.

6.  In Chrome, show **Developer Tools** and the **Console**.
7.  In the text box, enter man, click the **Get Products** button, and note the error, as shown in the following output and in *Figure 9.5*:

```
Access to XMLHttpRequest at 'https://localhost:5091/api/products/man'
from origin 'https://localhost:5092' has been blocked by CORS policy:
No 'Access-Control-Allow-Origin' header is present on the requested
resource.
GET https://localhost:5091/api/products/man net::ERR_FAILED 200
```

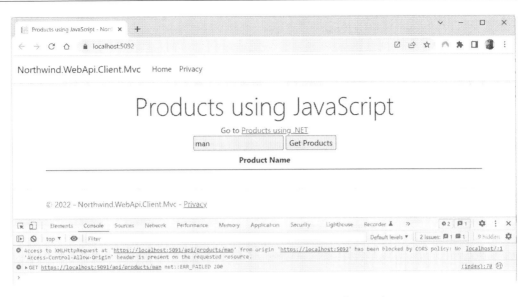

*Figure 9.5: CORS error in the Developer Tools console*

8.  At the command prompt or terminal for the Northwind.WebApi.Service project, note the HTTP log for the request and that the Host is on a different port number to the Origin so they do not have the same origin, as shown highlighted in the following output:

```
info: Microsoft.AspNetCore.HttpLogging.HttpLoggingMiddleware[1]
      Request:
      Protocol: HTTP/2
      Method: GET
      Scheme: https
      PathBase:
      Path: /api/products/man
      Accept: */*
      Host: localhost:5091
      User-Agent: Mozilla/5.0 (Windows NT 10.0; Win64; x64)
AppleWebKit/537.36 (KHTML, like Gecko) Chrome/102.0.0.0 Safari/537.36
      Accept-Encoding: gzip, deflate, br
      Accept-Language: en-US,en;q=0.9,sv;q=0.8
      Origin: https://localhost:5092
      Referer: [Redacted]
      sec-ch-ua: [Redacted]
      sec-ch-ua-mobile: [Redacted]
      sec-ch-ua-platform: [Redacted]
      sec-fetch-site: [Redacted]
      sec-fetch-mode: [Redacted]
      sec-fetch-dest: [Redacted]
```

9.  Also note the output shows that the web service did execute the database query and return the products in a JSON document response to the browser, as shown in the following output:

```
info: Microsoft.AspNetCore.HttpLogging.HttpLoggingMiddleware[2]
      Response:
      StatusCode: 200
      Content-Type: application/json; charset=utf-8
info: Microsoft.AspNetCore.HttpLogging.HttpLoggingMiddleware[4]
      ResponseBody: [{"productId":12,"productName":"Queso Manchego La
Pastora","supplierId":5,"categoryId":4,"quantityPerUnit":"10 - 500 g
pkgs.",
"unitPrice":38.0000,"unitsInStock":86,"unitsOnOrder":0,"reorderLevel"
:0,"discontinued":false,"category":null,"supplier":null,"orderDetails":[]},
{"productId":51,"productName":"Manjimup Dried Apples","supplierId":24,
"categoryId":7,"quantityPerUnit":"50 - 300 g pkgs.","unitPrice":53.0000,
"unitsInStock":20,"unitsOnOrder":0,"reorderLevel":10,"discontinued":false,
"category":null,"supplier":null,"orderDetails":[]}]
```

 It is the browser that enforces the same origin policy by refusing to reveal the HTTP response to the JavaScript.

10.  Close the browser(s) and shut down the web servers.

## Creating a .NET client

Next, let's create a .NET client to the web service to see that the same origin policy does not apply:

1.  In the `Northwind.WebApi.Client.Mvc` project, add a reference to the entity models project so that we can use the `Product` class, as shown in the following markup:

```
<ItemGroup>
  <ProjectReference Include="..\..\Chapter02\Northwind.Common.
EntityModels.SqlServer\Northwind.Common.EntityModels.SqlServer.csproj" />
</ItemGroup>
```

2.  Build the `Northwind.WebApi.Client.Mvc` project at the command line.

3.  In `Program.cs`, import the namespace for working with HTTP headers, as shown in the following code:

```
using System.Net.Http.Headers; // MediaTypeWithQualityHeaderValue
```

4.  In `Program.cs`, before the call the `builder.Build()` call, add statements to configure an HTTP client factory to web service, as shown in the following code:

```
builder.Services.AddHttpClient(name: "Northwind.WebApi.Service",
  configureClient: options =>
```

```
    {
      options.BaseAddress = new("https://localhost:5091/");
      options.DefaultRequestHeaders.Accept.Add(
        new MediaTypeWithQualityHeaderValue(
          "application/json", 1.0));
    });
```

5.  In the `Controllers` folder, in `HomeController.cs`, import the namespace for the entity models, as shown in the following code:

    ```
    using Packt.Shared; // Product
    ```

6.  In `HomeController.cs`, add statements to store the registered HTTP client factory in a private readonly field, as shown highlighted in the following code:

    ```
    private readonly ILogger<HomeController> _logger;
    private readonly IHttpClientFactory clientFactory;

    public HomeController(ILogger<HomeController> logger,
      IHttpClientFactory httpClientFactory)
    {
      _logger = logger;
      clientFactory = httpClientFactory;
    }
    ```

7.  In `HomeController.cs`, add an asynchronous action method named `Products` that will use the HTTP factory to request products whose name contains a value entered as an optional name parameter in a custom MVC route, as shown in the following code:

    ```
    [Route("home/products/{name?}")]
    public async Task<IActionResult> Products(string? name)
    {
      HttpClient client = clientFactory.CreateClient(
        name: "Northwind.WebApi.Service");

      HttpRequestMessage request = new(
        method: HttpMethod.Get, requestUri: $"api/products/{name}");

      HttpResponseMessage response = await client.SendAsync(request);

      IEnumerable<Product>? model = await response.Content
        .ReadFromJsonAsync<IEnumerable<Product>>();

      ViewData["baseaddress"] = client.BaseAddress;

      return View(model);
    }
    ```

8.  In the `Views/Home` folder, add a new view file named `Products.cshtml`.

9.  In `Products.cshtml`, modify its contents to output a table of products that match part of a product name entered in a text box, as shown in the following markup:

```
@using Packt.Shared
@model IEnumerable<Product>?
@{
  ViewData["Title"] = "Products using .NET";
}
<div class="text-center">
  <h1 class="display-4">@ViewData["Title"]</h1>
  <div>
    Go to <a href="/">Products using JavaScript</a>
  </div>
  <form action="/home/products">
    <input name="name" placeholder="Enter part of a product name" />
    <input type="submit" value="Get Products" />
  </form>
  <div>
    <table class="table">
      <thead>
        <tr>
          <th scope="col">Product Name</th>
        </tr>
      </thead>
      <tbody>
        @if (Model is not null)
        {
          @foreach (Product p in Model)
          {
            <tr><td><a href="@(ViewData["baseaddress"])api/products/
@p.ProductId">@p.ProductName</a></td></tr>
          }
        }
      </tbody>
    </table>
  </div>
</div>
```

10. Start the `Northwind.WebApi.Service` project without debugging.

11. Start the `Northwind.WebApi.Client.Mvc` project without debugging.

12. On the home page, click the link to go to **Products using .NET**, and note the first ten products are shown in the table.

13. In the text box, enter man, click **Get Products**, and note that two products are shown in the table, as shown in *Figure 9.6*:

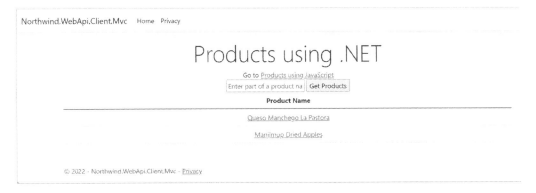

Figure 9.6: Getting two products from a web service using .NET

 It is the .NET HTTP client that is calling the web service, so the same origin policy does not apply. If you were to check the logs at the command line or terminal as you did before, you would see the ports are different, but it does not matter.

14. Click one of the product names to make a direct request to the web service for an individual product and note the response, as shown in the following document:

```
{"productId":12,"productName":"Queso Manchego La Pastora","supplierId":5,
"categoryId":4,"quantityPerUnit":"10 - 500 g pkgs.","unitPrice":38.0000,
"unitsInStock":86,"unitsOnOrder":0,"reorderLevel"
:0,"discontinued":false,"category":null,"supplier":null,"orderDetails":[]}
```

15. Close the browser and shut down the web servers.

# Understanding CORS

**Cross Origin Resource Sharing** (**CORS**) is a HTTP-header-based feature that disables the same origin security policy in specific scenarios. The HTTP headers indicate which additional origins are allowed.

Let's enable CORS in the web service so that it can send extra headers to indicate to the browser that it is allowed to access resources from a different origin:

1. In the `Northwind.WebApi.Service` project, in `Program.cs`, after creating the `builder`, add statements to define a named CORS policy that allows the MVC project as an origin, as shown in the following code:

```
string northwindMvc = "Northwind.Mvc.Policy";
```

```
builder.Services.AddCors(options =>
{
  options.AddPolicy(name: northwindMvc,
    policy =>
    {
      policy.WithOrigins("https://localhost:5092");
    });
});
```

2.  In `Program.cs`, after the call to `UseHttpLogging`, add a statement to use the CORS policy, as shown in the following code:

    ```
    app.UseCors(policyName: northwindMvc);
    ```

3.  Start the `Northwind.WebApi.Service` project without debugging.

4.  Start the `Northwind.WebApi.Client.Mvc` project without debugging.

5.  Show **Developer Tools** and its **Console**.

6.  On the home page, in the text box, enter man, click **Get Products**, and note that the console shows the JSON document returned from the web service and the table is filled with the two products, as shown in *Figure 9.7*:

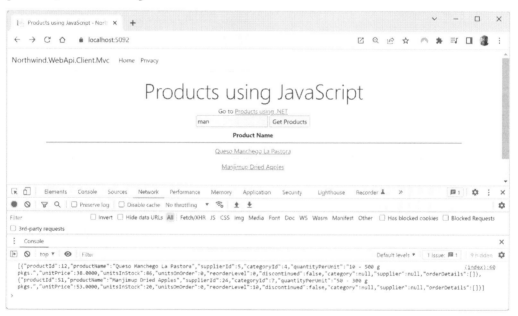

*Figure 9.7: A successful cross origin request to the web service using JavaScript*

7.  Close the browser and shut down the web servers.

# Enabling CORS for specific endpoints

In the previous example, we enabled the same CORS policy for the whole web service. You might need finer control at the endpoint level:

1. In the `Northwind.WebApi.Service` project, in `Program.cs`, change the call to `UseCors` to not specify the policy name, as shown in the following code:

```
// app.UseCors(policyName: northwindMvc);

// without a named policy the middleware is added but not active
app.UseCors();
```

2. At the end of the call to `MapGet` that gets a product using a product ID, add a call to `RequiresCors`, as shown highlighted in the following code:

```
app.MapGet("api/products/{id:int}",
    async Task<Results<Ok<Product>, NotFound>> (
    [FromServices] NorthwindContext db,
    [FromRoute] int id) =>
        await db.Products.FindAsync(id) is Product product ?
            TypedResults.Ok(product) : TypedResults.NotFound())
    .WithName("GetProductById")
    .WithOpenApi()
    .Produces<Product>(StatusCodes.Status200OK)
    .Produces(StatusCodes.Status404NotFound)
    .RequireCors(policyName: northwindMvc);
```

3. Start the `Northwind.WebApi.Service` project without debugging.

4. Start the `Northwind.WebApi.Client.Mvc` project without debugging.

5. Show **Developer Tools** and its **Console**.

6. On the home page, in the text box, enter cha, click **Get Products**, and note the console shows a CORS error because we enabled CORS for the wrong endpoint!

7. Close the browser and shut down the web servers.

8. At the end of the call to `MapGet` that gets products that contain part of a product name, add a call to `RequiresCors`, as shown highlighted in the following code:

```
app.MapGet("api/products/{name}", (
    [FromServices] NorthwindContext db,
    [FromRoute] string name) =>
        db.Products.Where(p => p.ProductName.Contains(name)))
    .WithName("GetProductsByName")
    .WithOpenApi()
    .Produces<Product[]>(StatusCodes.Status200OK)
    .RequireCors(policyName: northwindMvc);
```

9. Start the `Northwind.WebApi.Service` project without debugging.

10. Start the `Northwind.WebApi.Client.Mvc` project without debugging.

11. Show **Developer Tools** and its **Console**.

12. On the home page, in the text box, enter cha, click **Get Products**, and note that the console shows the JSON document returned from the web service and the table is filled with three products.

13. Close the browser and shut down the web servers.

## Understanding other CORS policy options

You can control the following:

- Allowed origins, for example, `https://*.example.com/`.

- Allowed HTTP methods, for example, `GET`, `POST`, `DELETE`, and so on.

- Allowed HTTP request headers, for example, `Content-Type`, `Content-Language`, `x-custom-header`, and so on.

- Exposed HTTP response headers, meaning which headers to include unredacted in a response (because by default response headers are redacted), for example, `x-custom-header`.

 You can learn more about options for CORS policies at the following link: `https://docs.microsoft.com/en-us/aspnet/core/security/cors#cors-policy-options`.

# Preventing denial-of-service attacks using rate limiting

A **denial-of-service** (**DoS**) attack is a malicious attempt to disrupt a web service by overwhelming it with requests. If the requests all came from the same place, it would be relatively easy to cut them off as soon as the attack is detected. These attacks are often implemented as **distributed DoS** (**DDoS**) attacks from many locations so you cannot separate attackers from genuine clients.

Genuine clients should only make the minimum requests they need. How many is reasonable will depend on your service. One way to prevent DDoS attacks would be to limit how many requests are allowed from any client per minute. This technique is not just useful to prevent attacks. Even genuine clients might accidentally make too many requests, or for a commercial web service you might want to charge different amounts for different rates, like when controlling a subscription.

When a client makes requests over a set rate limit, the client should receive either 429 Too Many Requests or 503 Service Unavailable responses.

## Rate limiting using the AspNetCoreRateLimit package

`AspNetCoreRateLimit`, a third-party package, provides flexible rate-limiting middleware based on IP address or client ID:

1. In the `Northwind.WebApi.Service` project, add a reference to the `AspNetCoreRateLimit` package, as shown in the following markup:

   ```
   <PackageReference Include="AspNetCoreRateLimit" Version="4.0.2" />
   ```

2. In `appsettings.Development.json`, add configuration for default rate limit options and client-specific policies, as shown highlighted in the following configuration:

```json
{
    "Logging": {
      "LogLevel": {
        "Default": "Information",
        "Microsoft.AspNetCore": "Warning",
        "Microsoft.AspNetCore.HttpLogging": "Information"
      }
    },
    "ClientRateLimiting": {
      "EnableEndpointRateLimiting": false,
      "StackBlockedRequests": false,
      "ClientIdHeader": "X-Client-Id",
      "HttpStatusCode": 429,
      "EndpointWhitelist": [ "get:/api/license", "*:/api/status" ],
      "ClientWhitelist": [ "dev-id-1", "dev-id-2" ],
      "GeneralRules": [
        {
          "Endpoint": "*",
          "Period": "10s",
          "Limit": 2
        },
        {
          "Endpoint": "*",
          "Period": "12h",
          "Limit": 100
        }
      ]
    },
    "ClientRateLimitPolicies": {
      "ClientRules": [
        {
          "ClientId": "console-client-abc123",
          "Rules": [
            {
              "Endpoint": "*",
              "Period": "10s",
              "Limit": 5
            },
            {
              "Endpoint": "*",
              "Period": "12h",
              "Limit": 250
            }
```

```
            ]
          }
        ]
      }
    }
```

Note the following:

- `EnableEndpointRateLimiting` is `false`, meaning all endpoints will share the same rules.
- If a client needs to identify itself, it can set a header named `X-Client-Id` to a unique string value.
- If a rate limit is reached for a client, the service will start returning 429 status code responses to that client.
- Two endpoints will be excluded from the rate limits: one for getting a license and one for checking the status of the service. We will not actually implement these features.
- Two client IDs named `dev-id-1` and `dev-id-2` will be excluded from the rate limits. These could be special client accounts for internal developers.
- Two general (default) rules are configured: the first sets a rate limit of 2 requests every 10 seconds, and the second sets a rate limit of 100 requests every 12 hours.
- Two client-specific rules are configured: for the client ID named `console-client-abc123`, it is allowed to make up to 5 requests every 10 seconds, and up to 250 requests every 12 hours.

3. Build the `Northwind.WebApi.Service` project.

4. In `Program.cs`, import the namespace for working with rate-limiting options, as shown in the following code:

```
using AspNetCoreRateLimit; // ClientRateLimitOptions,
ClientRateLimitPolicies
```

5. In `Program.cs`, declare and set a variable that controls the built-in ASP.NET Core rate limiting to `false`, as shown in the following code:

```
bool useMicrosoftRateLimiting = false;
```

6. In `Program.cs`, after creating the `builder`, add statements to load the rate-limiting configuration from the app settings and set the rate-limiting options, as shown in the following code:

```
// Configure AspNetCoreRateLimit rate limiting middleware.
if (!useMicrosoftRateLimiting)
{
  // Add services to store rate limit counters and rules.
  builder.Services.AddMemoryCache();
  builder.Services.AddInMemoryRateLimiting();

  // Load default rate limit options from appsettings.json.
  builder.Services.Configure<ClientRateLimitOptions>(
```

```
builder.Configuration.GetSection("ClientRateLimiting"));

// Load client-specific policies from appsettings.json.
builder.Services.Configure<ClientRateLimitPolicies>(
  builder.Configuration.GetSection("ClientRateLimitPolicies"));

// Register the configuration.
builder.Services.AddSingleton
  <IRateLimitConfiguration, RateLimitConfiguration>();
}
```

7.  In `Program.cs`, in the call to configure HTTP logging, add a statement to allow two rate-limiting headers to not be redacted, as shown highlighted in the following code:

```
builder.Services.AddHttpLogging(options =>
{
  // Add the Origin header so it will not be redacted.
  options.RequestHeaders.Add("Origin");

  // Add the rate limiting headers so they will not be redacted.
  options.RequestHeaders.Add("X-Client-Id");
  options.ResponseHeaders.Add("Retry-After");

  // By default, the response body is not included.
  options.LoggingFields = HttpLoggingFields.All;
});
```

8.  In `Program.cs`, after building the app object, add statements to seed the client policy store (which just means loading the policies from the configuration), as shown in the following code:

```
if (!useMicrosoftRateLimiting)
{
  using (IServiceScope scope = app.Services.CreateScope())
  {
    IClientPolicyStore clientPolicyStore = scope.ServiceProvider
      .GetRequiredService<IClientPolicyStore>();

    await clientPolicyStore.SeedAsync();
  }
}
```

9.  In `Program.cs`, after calling `UseHttpLogging`, add a call to use client rate limiting, as shown in the following code:

```
if (!useMicrosoftRateLimiting)
{
  app.UseClientRateLimiting();
}
```

## Creating a rate-limited console client

Now we can create a console app that will be a client to the web service:

1.  Use your preferred code editor to add a new console app to the `Chapter09` solution/workspace named `Northwind.WebApi.Client.Console`.

    -   In Visual Studio Code, select `Northwind.WebApi.Client.Console` as the active OmniSharp project.

2.  In the `Northwind.WebApi.Client.Console` project, globally and statically import the `System.Console` class, and add a reference to the entity models project, as shown in the following markup:

    ```
    <ItemGroup>
      <Using Include="System.Console" Static="true" />
    </ItemGroup>

    <ItemGroup>
      <ProjectReference Include="..\..\Chapter02\Northwind.Common.
    EntityModels.SqlServer\Northwind.Common.EntityModels.SqlServer.csproj" />
    </ItemGroup>
    ```

3.  In `Program.cs`, delete the existing statements. Add statements to prompt the user for a client name to identify it, and then create an HTTP client to make a request to get the first page of products from the web service once per second until the user presses *Ctrl* + *C* to stop the console app, as shown in the following code:

    ```csharp
    using Packt.Shared; // Product
    using System.Net.Http.Json; // ReadFromJsonAsync<T>

    Write("Enter a client name: ");
    string? clientName = ReadLine();

    if (string.IsNullOrEmpty(clientName))
    {
      clientName = $"console-client-{Guid.NewGuid()}";
    }

    WriteLine($"X-Client-Id will be: {clientName}");

    HttpClient client = new();

    client.BaseAddress = new("https://localhost:5091");

    client.DefaultRequestHeaders.Accept.Clear();
    ```

```csharp
client.DefaultRequestHeaders.Accept.Add(new("application/json"));

// specify rate limiting client id
client.DefaultRequestHeaders.Add("X-Client-Id", clientName);

ConsoleColor previousColor;

while (true)
{
  previousColor = ForegroundColor;
  ForegroundColor = ConsoleColor.DarkGreen;
  Write("{0:hh:mm:ss}: ", DateTime.UtcNow);
  ForegroundColor = previousColor;

  int waitFor = 1; // seconds

  try
  {
    HttpResponseMessage response = await client.GetAsync("api/products");

    if (response.IsSuccessStatusCode)
    {
      Product[]? products =
        await response.Content.ReadFromJsonAsync<Product[]>();

      if (products != null)
      {
        foreach (Product product in products)
        {
          Write(product.ProductName);
          Write(", ");
        }
        WriteLine();
      }
    }
    else
    {
      previousColor = ForegroundColor;
      ForegroundColor = ConsoleColor.DarkRed;
      WriteLine($"{(int)response.StatusCode}: {await response.Content.
ReadAsStringAsync()}");
      ForegroundColor = previousColor;
    }
  }
  catch (Exception ex)
```

```
    {
        WriteLine(ex.Message);
    }

    await Task.Delay(TimeSpan.FromSeconds(waitFor));
}
```

4.  Start the `Northwind.WebApi.Service` project using the `https` profile without debugging.

5.  Start the `Northwind.WebApi.Client.Console` project without debugging.

6.  In the console app, press *Enter* to generate a GUID-based client ID.

7.  Start the `Northwind.WebApi.Client.Console` project without debugging again so we have two clients.

8.  In the console app, press *Enter* to generate a GUID-based client ID.

9.  Note that each client can make two requests before it starts to receive 429 status codes, as shown in the following output:

```
Enter a client name:
X-Client-Id will be: console-client-d54c61ba-66bb-4e39-9c1a-7af6e2bf647e
07:32:18: Chai, Chang, Aniseed Syrup, Chef Anton's Cajun Seasoning,
Grandma's Boysenberry Spread, Uncle Bob's Organic Dried Pears, Northwoods
Cranberry Sauce, Ikura, Queso Cabrales, Queso Manchego La Pastora,
07:32:20: Chai, Chang, Aniseed Syrup, Chef Anton's Cajun Seasoning,
Grandma's Boysenberry Spread, Uncle Bob's Organic Dried Pears, Northwoods
Cranberry Sauce, Ikura, Queso Cabrales, Queso Manchego La Pastora,
07:32:21: 429: API calls quota exceeded! maximum admitted 2 per 10s.
07:32:22: 429: API calls quota exceeded! maximum admitted 2 per 10s.
07:32:23: 429: API calls quota exceeded! maximum admitted 2 per 10s.
07:32:24: 429: API calls quota exceeded! maximum admitted 2 per 10s.
07:32:25: 429: API calls quota exceeded! maximum admitted 2 per 10s.
07:32:26: 429: API calls quota exceeded! maximum admitted 2 per 10s.
07:32:27: 429: API calls quota exceeded! maximum admitted 2 per 10s.
07:32:28: Chai, Chang, Aniseed Syrup, Chef Anton's Cajun Seasoning,
Grandma's Boysenberry Spread, Uncle Bob's Organic Dried Pears, Northwoods
Cranberry Sauce, Ikura, Queso Cabrales, Queso Manchego La Pastora,
07:32:29: Chai, Chang, Aniseed Syrup, Chef Anton's Cajun Seasoning,
Grandma's Boysenberry Spread, Uncle Bob's Organic Dried Pears, Northwoods
Cranberry Sauce, Ikura, Queso Cabrales, Queso Manchego La Pastora,
07:32:30: 429: API calls quota exceeded! maximum admitted 2 per 10s.
07:32:31: 429: API calls quota exceeded! maximum admitted 2 per 10s.
07:32:32: 429: API calls quota exceeded! maximum admitted 2 per 10s.
```

10.  Stop the two console apps.

11. In the command line for the web service, note the HTTP logs that show each request from the console client with its client ID sent as a header named X-Client-Id, the request being blocked because that client has exceeded its quota, and a response that contains a header named Retry-After containing the number of seconds the client should wait before retrying, as shown highlighted in the following output:

```
info: Microsoft.AspNetCore.HttpLogging.HttpLoggingMiddleware[1]
      Request:
      Protocol: HTTP/1.1
      Method: GET
      Scheme: https
      PathBase:
      Path: /api/products
      Accept: application/json
      Host: localhost:5091
      X-Client-Id: console-client-d54c61ba-66bb-4e39-9c1a-7af6e2bf647e
info: AspNetCoreRateLimit.ClientRateLimitMiddleware[0]
      Request get:/api/products from ClientId console-client-d54c61ba-
66bb-4e39-9c1a-7af6e2bf647e has been blocked, quota 2/10s exceeded by 3.
Blocked by rule *, TraceIdentifier 0HMIKGNJQEK5P:0000000E. MonitorMode:
False
info: Microsoft.AspNetCore.HttpLogging.HttpLoggingMiddleware[2]
      Response:
      StatusCode: 429
      Content-Type: text/plain
      Retry-After: 6
info: Microsoft.AspNetCore.HttpLogging.HttpLoggingMiddleware[4]
      ResponseBody: API calls quota exceeded! maximum admitted 2 per 10s.
```

12. In the Northwind.WebApi.Client.Console project, in Program.cs, add statements to read the Retry-After header to get the number of seconds to wait for, as shown highlighted in the following code:

```
previousColor = ForegroundColor;
ForegroundColor = ConsoleColor.DarkRed;
WriteLine($"{(int)response.StatusCode}: {await response.Content.
ReadAsStringAsync()}");

string retryAfter = response.Headers
  .GetValues("Retry-After").ToArray()[0];

if (int.TryParse(retryAfter, out waitFor))
{
  WriteLine($"Retry after {waitFor} seconds.");
}
ForegroundColor = previousColor;
```

13. Start the `Northwind.WebApi.Client.Console` project without debugging.

14. In the console app, press *Enter* to generate a GUID-based client ID.

15. Note the console app will now sensibly wait for the suggested number of seconds before making its next call to the service, as shown in the following output:

```
Enter a client name:
X-Client-Id will be: console-client-add7613f-51a9-4c4a-8ec7-0244203d2e19
07:45:01: Chai, Chang, Aniseed Syrup, Chef Anton's Cajun Seasoning,
Grandma's Boysenberry Spread, Uncle Bob's Organic Dried Pears, Northwoods
Cranberry Sauce, Ikura, Queso Cabrales, Queso Manchego La Pastora,
07:45:02: Chai, Chang, Aniseed Syrup, Chef Anton's Cajun Seasoning,
Grandma's Boysenberry Spread, Uncle Bob's Organic Dried Pears, Northwoods
Cranberry Sauce, Ikura, Queso Cabrales, Queso Manchego La Pastora,
07:45:03: 429: API calls quota exceeded! maximum admitted 2 per 10s.
Retry after 8 seconds.
07:45:11: Chai, Chang, Aniseed Syrup, Chef Anton's Cajun Seasoning,
Grandma's Boysenberry Spread, Uncle Bob's Organic Dried Pears, Northwoods
Cranberry Sauce, Ikura, Queso Cabrales, Queso Manchego La Pastora,
07:45:12: Chai, Chang, Aniseed Syrup, Chef Anton's Cajun Seasoning,
Grandma's Boysenberry Spread, Uncle Bob's Organic Dried Pears, Northwoods
Cranberry Sauce, Ikura, Queso Cabrales, Queso Manchego La Pastora,
07:45:13: 429: API calls quota exceeded! maximum admitted 2 per 10s.
Retry after 8 seconds.
```

16. Start the `Northwind.WebApi.Client.Console` project without debugging.

17. In the console app, enter the name `dev-id-1`, and note that the rate limit does not apply to this console app client.

18. Start the `Northwind.WebApi.Client.Console` project without debugging.

19. In the console app, enter the name `console-client-abc123`, and note that the rate limit is different for this console app client ID, as shown in the following output:

```
info: AspNetCoreRateLimit.ClientRateLimitMiddleware[0]
      Request get:/api/products from ClientId console-client-abc123
has been blocked, quota 2/10s exceeded by 1. Blocked by rule *,
TraceIdentifier 0HMIKGS1TPSHJ:00000006. MonitorMode: False
```

# Rate limiting using ASP.NET Core middleware

ASP.NET Core 7 introduces its own rate-limiting middleware, distributed as a separate NuGet package:

1. In the `Northwind.WebApi.Service` project, add a reference to the `Microsoft.AspNetCore.RateLimiting` package, as shown highlighted in the following markup:

```
<ItemGroup>
  <PackageReference Include="AspNetCoreRateLimit" Version="4.0.2" />
  <PackageReference Include="Microsoft.AspNetCore.OpenApi"
Version="7.0.0" />
  <PackageReference Include="Microsoft.AspNetCore.RateLimiting"
               Version="7.0.0" />
```

```
  <PackageReference Include="Swashbuckle.AspNetCore" Version="6.2.3" />
</ItemGroup>
```

2. Build the `Northwind.WebApi.Service` project.

3. In `Program.cs`, import the namespaces for working with rate limiting, as shown in the following code:

```
using Microsoft.AspNetCore.RateLimiting; // RateLimiterOptions
using System.Threading.RateLimiting; // FixedWindowRateLimiterOptions
```

4. At the top of `Program.cs`, after importing namespaces, change the variable to control if we want to use the built-in rate-limiting feature, as shown in the following code:

```
bool useMicrosoftRateLimiting = true;
```

5. In the statement that maps the `GET` endpoint for products, require that it use a rate-limiting policy named `fixed5per10seconds`, as shown highlighted in the following code:

```
app.MapGet("api/products", (
  [FromServices] NorthwindContext db,
  [FromQuery] int? page) =>
  db.Products.Where(product =>
    (product.UnitsInStock > 0) && (!product.Discontinued))
    .Skip(((page ?? 1) - 1) * pageSize).Take(pageSize)
  )
  .WithName("GetProducts")
  .WithOpenApi(operation =>
  {
    operation.Description =
      "Get products with UnitsInStock > 0 and Discontinued = false.";
    operation.Summary = "Get in-stock products that are not
discontinued.";
    return operation;
  })
  .Produces<Product[]>(StatusCodes.Status200OK)
  .RequireRateLimiting("fixed5per10seconds");
```

6. At the bottom of `Program.cs`, before running the host, add statements to define a policy named `fixed5per10seconds` to control rate limiting, as shown in the following code:

```
// Configure ASP.NET Core rate limiting middleware.
if (useMicrosoftRateLimiting)
{
  RateLimiterOptions rateLimiterOptions = new();

  rateLimiterOptions.AddFixedWindowLimiter(
    policyName: "fixed5per10seconds", options =>
    {
      options.PermitLimit = 5;
```

```
        options.QueueProcessingOrder = QueueProcessingOrder.OldestFirst;
        options.QueueLimit = 2;
        options.Window = TimeSpan.FromSeconds(10);
    });

    app.UseRateLimiter(rateLimiterOptions);
}
```

7.  Start the `Northwind.WebApi.Service` project without debugging.

8.  Start the `Northwind.WebApi.Client.Console` project without debugging.

9.  In the console app, press *Enter* to generate a GUID-based client ID.

10. Note the console app will now make up to five requests in each 10-second window but then have to pause until that window has passed, as shown in the following output:

```
Enter a client name:
X-Client-Id will be: console-client-16b15d15-f3f3-4e28-a6b7-692c76673e0c
01:40:19: Chai, Chang, Aniseed Syrup, Chef Anton's Cajun Seasoning,
Grandma's Boysenberry Spread, Uncle Bob's Organic Dried Pears, Northwoods
Cranberry Sauce, Ikura, Queso Cabrales, Queso Manchego La Pastora,
01:40:20: Chai, Chang, Aniseed Syrup, Chef Anton's Cajun Seasoning,
Grandma's Boysenberry Spread, Uncle Bob's Organic Dried Pears, Northwoods
Cranberry Sauce, Ikura, Queso Cabrales, Queso Manchego La Pastora,
01:40:21: Chai, Chang, Aniseed Syrup, Chef Anton's Cajun Seasoning,
Grandma's Boysenberry Spread, Uncle Bob's Organic Dried Pears, Northwoods
Cranberry Sauce, Ikura, Queso Cabrales, Queso Manchego La Pastora,
01:40:22: Chai, Chang, Aniseed Syrup, Chef Anton's Cajun Seasoning,
Grandma's Boysenberry Spread, Uncle Bob's Organic Dried Pears, Northwoods
Cranberry Sauce, Ikura, Queso Cabrales, Queso Manchego La Pastora,
01:40:23: Chai, Chang, Aniseed Syrup, Chef Anton's Cajun Seasoning,
Grandma's Boysenberry Spread, Uncle Bob's Organic Dried Pears, Northwoods
Cranberry Sauce, Ikura, Queso Cabrales, Queso Manchego La Pastora,
01:40:28: Chai, Chang, Aniseed Syrup, Chef Anton's Cajun Seasoning,
Grandma's Boysenberry Spread, Uncle Bob's Organic Dried Pears, Northwoods
Cranberry Sauce, Ikura, Queso Cabrales, Queso Manchego La Pastora,
01:40:29: Chai, Chang, Aniseed Syrup, Chef Anton's Cajun Seasoning,
Grandma's Boysenberry Spread, Uncle Bob's Organic Dried Pears, Northwoods
Cranberry Sauce, Ikura, Queso Cabrales, Queso Manchego La Pastora,
01:40:30: Chai, Chang, Aniseed Syrup, Chef Anton's Cajun Seasoning,
Grandma's Boysenberry Spread, Uncle Bob's Organic Dried Pears, Northwoods
Cranberry Sauce, Ikura, Queso Cabrales, Queso Manchego La Pastora,
01:40:31: Chai, Chang, Aniseed Syrup, Chef Anton's Cajun Seasoning,
Grandma's Boysenberry Spread, Uncle Bob's Organic Dried Pears, Northwoods
Cranberry Sauce, Ikura, Queso Cabrales, Queso Manchego La Pastora,
01:40:32: Chai, Chang, Aniseed Syrup, Chef Anton's Cajun Seasoning,
Grandma's Boysenberry Spread, Uncle Bob's Organic Dried Pears, Northwoods
Cranberry Sauce, Ikura, Queso Cabrales, Queso Manchego La Pastora,
01:40:38: Chai, Chang, Aniseed Syrup, Chef Anton's Cajun Seasoning,
Grandma's Boysenberry Spread, Uncle Bob's Organic Dried Pears, Northwoods
Cranberry Sauce, Ikura, Queso Cabrales, Queso Manchego La Pastora,
```

You can learn more about the different types of built-in rate limiter at the following link: https://docs.microsoft.com/en-us/aspnet/core/performance/rate-limit.

# Understanding identity services

Identity services are used to authenticate and authorize users. It is important for these services to implement open standards so that you can integrate disparate systems. Common standards include **OpenID Connect** and **OAuth 2.0**.

Microsoft has no plans to officially support third-party authentication servers like **IdentityServer4** because "creating and sustaining an authentication server is a full-time endeavor, and Microsoft already has a team and a product in that area, Azure Active Directory, which allows 500,000 objects for free."

## JWT bearer authorization

**JSON Web Token** (JWT) is a standard that defines a compact and secure method to transmit information as a JSON object. The JSON object is digitally signed so it can be trusted. The most common scenario for using JWT is authorization.

A user logs in to a trusted party using credentials like a username and password, a biometric scan, or two-factor authentication, and the trusted party issues a JWT. This is then sent with every request to the secure web service.

In its compact form, JWTs consist of three parts separated by dots. These parts are the header, payload, and signature, as shown in the following format: `aaa.bbb.ccc`. The header and payload are Base64 encoded.

## Authenticating service clients using JWT bearer authentication

During local development, the `dotnet user-jwts` command-line tool is used to create and manage local JWTs. The values are stored in a JSON file in the local machine's user profile folder.

Let's secure the web service using JWT bearer authentication and test it with a local token:

1. In the `Northwind.WebApi.Service` project, add a reference to the package for JWT bearer authentication, as shown in the following markup:

   ```
   <PackageReference Include="Microsoft.AspNetCore.Authentication.JwtBearer"
                     Version="7.0.0" />
   ```

2. Build the `Northwind.WebApi.Service` project.

3. In `Program.cs`, import the namespace for security claims, as shown in the following code:

   ```
   using System.Security.Claims; // ClaimsPrincipal
   ```

4.  In `Program.cs`, after creating the `builder`, add statements to add authorization and authentication using JWT, as shown highlighted in the following code:

```
var builder = WebApplication.CreateBuilder(args);

builder.Services.AddAuthorization();
builder.Services.AddAuthentication(defaultScheme: "Bearer")
  .AddJwtBearer();
```

5.  In `Program.cs`, after building the app, add a statement to use authorization, as shown highlighted in the following code:

```
var app = builder.Build();

app.UseAuthorization();
```

6.  In `Program.cs`, after mapping a HTTP GET request for the root path to return a plain text Hello World response, add a statement to map an HTTP GET request for the secret path to return the authenticated user's name if they are authorized, as shown in the following code:

```
app.MapGet("/", () => "Hello World!")
  .ExcludeFromDescription();

app.MapGet("/secret", (ClaimsPrincipal user) =>
  $"Welcome, {user.Identity?.Name ?? "secure user"}. The secret
ingredient is love.")
  .RequireAuthorization();
```

7.  In the `Northwind.WebApi.Service` project folder, at the command prompt or terminal, create a local JWT, as shown in the following command:

```
dotnet user-jwts create
```

8.  Note the automatically assigned `ID`, `Name`, and `Token`, as shown in the following partial output:

```
New JWT saved with ID 'd7e22000'.
Name: markjprice

Token: eyJhbGciOiJIUzI1NiIsInR5cCI6IkpXVCJ9.
eyJ1bmlxdWVfbmFtZSI6Im1hcmtqcHJpY2UiLCJzdWIiOiJtYXJran...lci1qd3RzIn0.
pGEbYKRjU98dEjxLSx7GAEm41LXMS0J80iIjuZbqrj4
```

9.  At the command prompt or terminal, print all the information for the ID that was assigned, as shown in the following command:

```
dotnet user-jwts print d7e22000 --show-all
```

10. Note the scheme is `Bearer` so the token must be sent with every request, the audience(s) lists the authorized client domains and port numbers, the token expires after three months, the JSON objects that represent the header and payload, and finally, the compact token with its Base64 encoded three parts separated by dots, as shown in the following partial output:

```
Found JWT with ID 'd7e22000'.
ID: d7e22000
Name: markjprice
Scheme: Bearer
Audience(s): http://localhost:30225, https://localhost:44344, http://
localhost:5090, https://localhost:5091
Not Before: 2022-09-26T10:58:18.0000000+00:00
Expires On: 2022-12-26T10:58:18.0000000+00:00
Issued On: 2022-09-26T10:58:19.0000000+00:00
Scopes: none
Roles: [none]
Custom Claims: [none]
Token Header: {"alg":"HS256","typ":"JWT"}
Token Payload: {"unique_
name":"markjprice","sub":"markjprice","jti":"d7e22000","aud":["http://
localhost:30225","https://localhost:44344","http://
localhost:5090","https://localhost:5091"],"nbf":1664189898,"exp":16720522
98,"iat":1664189899,"iss":"dotnet-user-jwts"}
Compact Token: eyJhbGciOiJIUzI1NiIsInR5cCI6IkpXVCJ9.
eyJ1bmlxdWVfbmFtZSI6Im1hcmtqcHJpY2UiLCJzdWIiOiJtYXJranByaWNl...
uZXQtdXNlci1qd3RzIn0.pGEbYKRjU98dEjxLSx7GAEm41LXMS0J80iIjuZbqrj4
```

11. In the `Northwind.WebApi.Service` project, in `appsettings.Development.json`, note the new section named `Authentication`, as shown highlighted in the following configuration:

```
{
  "Logging": {
    "LogLevel": {
      "Default": "Information",
      "Microsoft.AspNetCore": "Warning",
      "Microsoft.AspNetCore.HttpLogging": "Information"
    }
  },
  "Authentication": {
    "Schemes": {
      "Bearer": {
        "ValidAudiences": [
          "http://localhost:30225",
          "https://localhost:44344",
          "http://localhost:5090"
          "https://localhost:5091"
        ],
        "ValidIssuer": "dotnet-user-jwts"
      }
    }
  }
}
```

12. Start the `Northwind.WebApi.Service` project using the `https` profile without debugging.

13. In the browser, change the relative path to `/secret` and note the response is rejected with a `401` status code.

14. Start Visual Studio Code and open the `RestClientTests` folder.

15. In the `RestClientTests` folder, create a file named `webapi-secure-request.http`, and modify its contents to contain a request to get the secret ingredient, as shown in the following code (but use your bearer token, of course):

```
### Get the secret ingredient.
GET https://localhost:5091/secret/
Authorization: Bearer eyJhbGciOiJIUzI1NiIsInR5cCI6IkpXVCJ9.
eyJ1bmlxdWVfbmFtZSI6Im1hcmtqcHJpY2UiLCJzdWIiOiJtYXJranByaWNl...
uZXQtdXNlci1qd3RzIn0.pGEbYKRjU98dEjxLSx7GAEm41LXMS0J80iIjuZbqrj4
```

16. Click **Send Request**, and note the response, as shown in the following output:

```
Welcome, secure user. The secret ingredient is love.
```

17. Close the browser and shut down the web service.

# Practicing and exploring

Test your knowledge and understanding by answering some questions, getting some hands-on practice, and exploring this chapter's topics with deeper research.

## Exercise 9.1 – Test your knowledge

Answer the following questions:

1. List six method names that can be specified in an HTTP request.

2. List six status codes and their descriptions that can be returned in an HTTP response.

3. How is the ASP.NET Core Minimal APIs service technology different from the ASP.NET Core Web APIs service technology?

4. With the ASP.NET Core Minimal APIs service technology, how do you map an HTTP `PUT` request to `api/customers` to a lambda statement block?

5. With the ASP.NET Core Minimal APIs service technology, how do you map a method or lambda parameter to a value in a route, query string, or the body of the request?

6. Does enabling CORS increase security for a web service?

7. You have added statements to `Program.cs` to enable HTTP logging but HTTP requests and responses are not being logged. What is the most likely reason and how can you fix it?

8. How do you limit the rate of requests for a specific client using the `AspNetCoreRateLimit` package?

9. How do you limit the rate of requests for a specific endpoint using the `Microsoft.AspNetCore.RateLimiting` package?

10. What does JWT mean?

## Exercise 9.2 – Review Microsoft HTTP API design policy

Microsoft has internal HTTP/REST API design guidelines. Microsoft teams reference this document when designing their HTTP APIs. They are a great starting point for your own standards for HTTP APIs. You can review them here:

```
https://github.com/microsoft/api-guidelines
```

The guidelines have a section specific to CORS:

```
https://github.com/microsoft/api-guidelines/blob/vNext/Guidelines.md#8-cors
```

## Exercise 9.3 – Explore topics

Use the links in the following GitHub repository to learn more about the topics covered in this chapter:

```
https://github.com/markjprice/apps-services-net7/blob/main/book-links.md#chapter-9---
building-and-securing-web-services-using-minimal-apis
```

## Summary

In this chapter, you learned how to:

- Build a web service that implements the REST architectural style using Minimal APIs.
- Relax the same origin security policy for specified domains and ports using CORS.
- Implement two different rate-limiting packages to prevent denial-of-service attacks.
- Secure services using JWT bearer authorization.

In the next chapter, you will learn how to expose data using OData.

# 10

# Exposing Data via the Web Using OData

In this chapter, you will be introduced to OData, a standard that makes it easy to expose data via the Web to make it accessible to any client that can make an HTTP request.

This chapter will cover the following topics:

- Understanding OData
- Building a web service that supports OData
- Testing OData services using Visual Studio Code extensions
- Versioning OData controllers
- Enabling entity inserts, updates, and deletes
- Building clients for OData services

## Understanding OData

One of the most common uses of a web service is to expose a database to clients that do not understand how to work directly with the native database. Another common use is to provide a simplified or abstracted API that exposes an authenticated interface to a subset of the data to control access.

In *Chapter 2, Managing Relational Data Using SQL Server*, you learned how to create an EF Core model to expose an SQL Server database to any .NET project. But what about non-.NET projects? I know it's crazy to imagine, but not every developer uses .NET!

Luckily, all development platforms support HTTP, so all development platforms can call web services, and ASP.NET Core has a package for making that easy and powerful using a standard named OData.

# Understanding the OData standard

OData (Open Data Protocol) is an ISO/IEC-approved, OASIS standard that defines a set of best practices for building and consuming RESTful APIs. Microsoft created it in 2007 and released versions 1.0, 2.0, and 3.0 under its Microsoft Open Specification Promise. Version 4.0 was then standardized at OASIS and released in 2014. OData is based on HTTP and has multiple endpoints to support multiple versions and entity sets.

 ASP.NET Core OData implements OData version 4.0.

# Understanding OData queries

Unlike traditional Web APIs where the service defines all the methods and what gets returned, OData uses **URL query strings** to define its queries. This enables the client to have more control over what is returned and minimizes round trips. Of course, the OData service controls the scope of those queries, but within that scope, the client has complete control.

For example, when querying the Northwind database that we created in *Chapter 2* for SQL Server, a client might only need two fields of data, ProductName and Cost, and the related Supplier object, and only for products where the ProductName contains the word burger and the cost is less than 4.95, with the results sorted by country and then cost. The client would construct their query as a URL query string using standard named parameters, as shown in the following request:

```
GET https://example.com/v1/products?$filter=contains(ProductName,
'burger') and UnitPrice lt 4.95&$orderby=Shipper/
Country,UnitPrice&$select=ProductName,UnitPrice&$expand=Supplier
```

# Building a web service that supports OData

There is no dotnet new project template for ASP.NET Core OData, but it uses controller classes, so we will use the ASP.NET Core Web API project template and then add package references to add the OData capabilities:

1. Use your preferred code editor to add a new project, as defined in the following list:

    • Project template: **ASP.NET Core Web API**/webapi
    • Workspace/solution file and folder: Chapter10
    • Project file and folder: Northwind.OData.Service
    • Other Visual Studio options: **Authentication Type:** None, **Configure for HTTPS:** Selected, **Enable Docker:** Cleared, **Use controllers (uncheck to use minimal APIs):** Checked, **Enable OpenAPI support:** Selected, **Do not use top-level statements:** Cleared.

    In Visual Studio Code, select Northwind.OData.Service as the active OmniSharp project.

2. Configure the project to treat warnings as errors and add a package reference for ASP.NET Core OData alongside the existing package references for OpenApi and Swashbuckle, as shown highlighted in the following markup:

```
<Project Sdk="Microsoft.NET.Sdk.Web">

  <PropertyGroup>
    <TargetFramework>net7.0</TargetFramework>
    <Nullable>enable</Nullable>
    <ImplicitUsings>enable</ImplicitUsings>
    <TreatWarningsAsErrors>true</TreatWarningsAsErrors>
  </PropertyGroup>

  <ItemGroup>
    <PackageReference Include="Microsoft.AspNetCore.OData"
                      Version="8.0.10" />
    <PackageReference Include="Microsoft.AspNetCore.OpenApi"
                      Version="7.0.0" />
    <PackageReference Include="Swashbuckle.AspNetCore"
                      Version="6.2.3" />
  </ItemGroup>

</Project>
```

**Good Practice:** The version numbers of the NuGet packages above are likely to increase after the book is published. As a general guide, you will want to use the latest package version.

Although it is the most popular downloaded package for OData, do *not* reference Microsoft.Data.OData because it only supports versions 1 to 3 and it is not being maintained. The other popular packages for OData are Microsoft.OData.Core and Microsoft.OData.Edm, which are both dependencies of the package you just referenced so they will be included in your project automatically.

3. Add a project reference to the Northwind database context project for SQL Server that you created in *Chapter 2, Managing Relational Data Using SQL Server*, as shown in the following markup:

```
<ItemGroup>
  <ProjectReference Include="..\..\Chapter02\Northwind.Common.DataContext
.SqlServer\Northwind.Common.DataContext.SqlServer.csproj" />
</ItemGroup>
```

If you did not complete the task to create the class libraries in *Chapter 2*, then download the solution projects from the GitHub repository.

4.  At the command line or terminal, build the `Northwind.OData.Service` project to make sure the two projects outside the current solution are properly compiled, as shown in the following command:

```
dotnet build
```

 If you are using Visual Studio 2022, if you try to build the OData project using the **Build** menu then you will get the following error: `error  NU1105:` `Unable to find project information for 'C:\apps-services-net7\` `Chapter02\Northwind.Common.DataContext.SqlServer\Northwind.Common.` `DataContext.SqlServer.csproj'. If you are using Visual Studio, this` `may be because the project is unloaded or not part of the current` `solution so run a restore from the command-line.`

5.  In the `Northwind.OData.Service` folder, delete `WeatherForecast.cs`.
6.  In the `Controllers` folder, delete `WeatherForecastController.cs`.

## Defining OData models for the EF Core models

The first task is to define what we want to expose as OData models in the web service. You have complete control, so if you have an existing EF Core model as we do for Northwind, you do not have to expose all of it.

You do not even have to use EF Core models. The data source can be anything. In this book, we will only look at using it with EF Core because that is the most common use for .NET developers.

Let's define two OData models: one to expose the Northwind product catalog, i.e., the categories and products tables; and one to expose the customers, their orders, and related tables:

1.  Add a new class file named `Program.Methods.cs`.
2.  In `Program.Methods.cs`, import some namespaces for working with OData and our entity models, and then add a method to define and return an OData model for the Northwind catalog that will only expose the entity sets, i.e., tables for `Categories`, `Products`, and `Suppliers`, as shown in the following code:

```
using Microsoft.OData.Edm; // IEdmModel
using Microsoft.OData.ModelBuilder; // ODataConventionModelBuilder
using Packt.Shared; // NorthwindContext and entity models

partial class Program
```

```
{
    static IEdmModel GetEdmModelForCatalog()
    {
        ODataConventionModelBuilder builder = new();
        builder.EntitySet<Category>("Categories");
        builder.EntitySet<Product>("Products");
        builder.EntitySet<Supplier>("Suppliers");
        return builder.GetEdmModel();
    }
}
```

3. Add a method to define an OData model for the Northwind customer orders, and note that the same entity set can appear in multiple OData models like `Products` does, as shown in the following code:

```
static IEdmModel GetEdmModelForOrderSystem()
{
    ODataConventionModelBuilder builder = new();
    builder.EntitySet<Customer>("Customers");
    builder.EntitySet<Order>("Orders");
    builder.EntitySet<Employee>("Employees");
    builder.EntitySet<Product>("Products");
    builder.EntitySet<Shipper>("Shippers");
    return builder.GetEdmModel();
}
```

4. In `Program.cs`, import the namespace for working with OData and the namespace for the database context registration extension method, as shown in the following code:

```
using Microsoft.AspNetCore.OData; // AddOData extension method
using Packt.Shared; // AddNorthwindContext extension method
```

5. In the services configuration section, before the call to `AddControllers`, add a statement to register the `Northwind` database context, as shown in the following code:

```
builder.Services.AddNorthwindContext();
```

6. In the services configuration section, after the call to `AddControllers`, chain a call to the `AddOData` extension method to define two OData models and enable features like projection, filtering, and sorting, as shown highlighted in the following code:

```
builder.Services.AddControllers()
  .AddOData(options => options
    // register OData models
    .AddRouteComponents(routePrefix: "catalog",
      model: GetEdmModelForCatalog())

    .AddRouteComponents(routePrefix: "ordersystem",
      model: GetEdmModelForOrderSystem())
```

```
    // enable query options
    .Select() // enable $select for projection
    .Expand() // enable $expand to navigate to related entities
    .Filter() // enable $filter
    .OrderBy() // enable $orderby
    .SetMaxTop(100) // enable $top
    .Count() // enable $count
);
```

7.  In the `Properties` folder, open `launchSettings.json`.

8.  In the `Northwind.OData.Service` profile, modify the `applicationUrl` to use port `5101` for HTTPS, as shown in the following markup:

    ```
    "applicationUrl": "https://localhost:5101",
    ```

## Testing the OData models

Now we can check that the OData models have been defined correctly:

1.  Start the `Northwind.OData.Service` project.

2.  Start Chrome if it does not start automatically.

3.  Navigate to `https://localhost:5101/swagger` and note the `Northwind.OData.Service v1` service is documented, as shown in *Figure 10.1*:

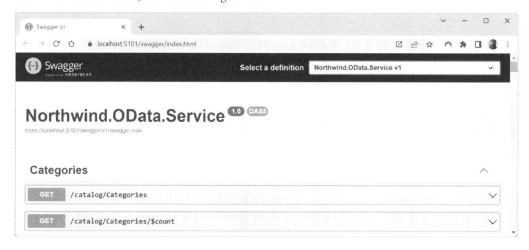

*Figure 10.1: Swagger documentation for the Northwind.OData.Service project*

4.  In the **Metadata** section, click **GET /catalog**, click **Try it out**, click **Execute**, and note the response body that shows the names and URLs of the three entity sets in the catalog OData model, as shown in the following output:

    ```
    {
      "@odata.context": "https://localhost:5101/catalog/$metadata",
      "value": [
    ```

```json
    {
      "name": "Categories",
      "kind": "EntitySet",
      "url": "Categories"
    },
    {
      "name": "Products",
      "kind": "EntitySet",
      "url": "Products"
    },
    {
      "name": "Suppliers",
      "kind": "EntitySet",
      "url": "Suppliers"
    }
  ]
}
```

5. Click **GET /catalog** to collapse that section.
6. Click **GET /catalog/$metadata**, click **Try it out**, click **Execute**, and note the model describes the entities like `Category` in detail with properties and keys, including navigation properties for the products in each category, as shown in *Figure 10.2*:

Figure 10.2: OData model metadata for the Northwind catalog

7. Click **GET /catalog/$metadata** to collapse that section.
8. Close Chrome and shut down the web server.

## Creating and testing OData controllers

Next, we must create OData controllers, one for each type of entity, to retrieve data:

1. In the `Controllers` folder, add an empty controller class file named `CategoriesController.cs`.

2.  Modify its contents to inherit from `ODataController`, get an instance of the Northwind database context using constructor parameter injection, and define two `Get` methods to retrieve all categories or one category using a unique key, as shown in the following code:

```
using Microsoft.AspNetCore.Mvc; // IActionResult
using Microsoft.AspNetCore.OData.Query; // [EnableQuery]
using Microsoft.AspNetCore.OData.Routing.Controllers; // ODataController
using Packt.Shared; // NorthwindContext

namespace Northwind.OData.Service.Controllers;

public class CategoriesController : ODataController
{
  protected readonly NorthwindContext db;

  public CategoriesController(NorthwindContext db)
  {
    this.db = db;
  }

  [EnableQuery]
  public IActionResult Get()
  {
    return Ok(db.Categories);
  }

  [EnableQuery]
  public IActionResult Get(int key)
  {
    return Ok(db.Categories.Where(
      category => category.CategoryId == key));
  }
}
```

3.  Repeat the above step for `Products` and `Suppliers`.

 I will leave it as an optional task for the reader to do the same for the other entities to enable the order system OData model if you choose. Note the `CustomerId` is a string instead of an `int`.

4.  Start the `Northwind.OData.Service` web service.

5.  Start Chrome, navigate to `https://localhost:5101/swagger`, and note the **Categories**, **Products**, and **Suppliers** entity sets are now documented because you created OData controllers for them, as shown in *Figure 10.3*:

*Figure 10.3: The Categories entity set is now documented*

6.  Click **GET /catalog/Categories**, click **Try it out**, click **Execute**, and note the response body that shows a JSON document containing all categories in the entity set, as partially shown in the following output:

```
{
  "@odata.context": "https://localhost:5101/
catalog/$metadata#Categories",
  "value": [
    {
      "CategoryId": 1,
      "CategoryName": "Beverages",
      "Description": "Soft drinks, coffees, teas, beers, and ales",
      "Picture": "FRwvAAIAAAANAA4AFAAhAP////9CaX..."
    },
    {
      "CategoryId": 2,
      "CategoryName": "Condiments",
      "Description": "Sweet and savory sauces, relishes, spreads, and
seasonings",
      "Picture": "FRwvAAIAAAANAA4AFAAhAP////9CaX..."
    },
    ...
  ]
}
```

7.  At the command prompt or terminal, note the output from logging the SQL command that was executed, as shown in the following output:

```
info: Microsoft.EntityFrameworkCore.Infrastructure[10403]
      Entity Framework Core 7.0.0 initialized 'NorthwindContext' using
provider 'Microsoft.EntityFrameworkCore.SqlServer:7.0.0' with options:
None
dbug: 22/05/2022 15:07:15.131 RelationalEventId.CommandExecuting[20100]
(Microsoft.EntityFrameworkCore.Database.Command)
      Executing DbCommand [Parameters=[], CommandType='Text',
CommandTimeout='30']
      SELECT [c].[CategoryId], [c].[CategoryName], [c].[Description],
[c].[Picture]
```

```
FROM [Categories] AS [c]
```

 We are noting the SQL statement now so that you can see that all columns and all rows are requested by the OData service when it receives a GET request to the catalog/categories path. Later, we will use EF Core logs again to see how OData queries are automatically translated into efficient SQL queries. OData services do not have to return all columns and rows from the database to the service and then perform the filtering inside the service.

8.   Close Chrome and shut down the web server.

# Testing OData services using Visual Studio Code extensions

Using the Swagger user interface to test OData controllers can quickly get clumsy. A better tool is the Visual Studio Code extension named **REST Client**:

1.   If you have not already installed REST Client by Huachao Mao (humao.rest-client), then install it in Visual Studio Code now.

 If you have only been using Visual Studio 2022 up to this point, you must install Visual Studio Code now, even if you only use it to run this useful REST Client extension.

2.   In your preferred code editor, start the Northwind.OData.Service project web service and leave it running.

3.   In Visual Studio Code, in the apps-services-net7 folder, if it does not already exist, create a RestClientTests folder, and then open the folder.

4.   In the RestClientTests folder, create a file named odata-catalog.http and modify its contents to contain a request to get all categories, as shown in the following code:

```
GET https://localhost:5101/catalog/categories/ HTTP/1.1
```

 **Good Practice:** Specifying the HTTP version at the end of the request is optional because REST Client will default to using 1.1. To avoid clutter, I will not specify it in future requests. The GET verb is also optional because REST Client will default to making a GET request.

5.   Click **Send Request**, and note the response is the same as what was returned by Swagger, a JSON document containing all categories, as shown in *Figure 10.4*:

*Figure 10.4: REST Client getting the categories from the OData service*

6.  In odata-catalog.http, add more requests separated by ###, as shown in the following table:

| Request | Response |
|---------|----------|
| https://localhost:5101/<br>catalog/categories(3) | {<br>    "@odata.context":<br>"https://localhost:5101/catalog/$metadata#Catego<br>ries/$entity",<br>    "CategoryId": 3,<br>    "CategoryName": "Confections",<br>    "Description": "Desserts, candies, and sweet<br>breads",<br>    "Picture": "FRwvAA..."<br>} |
| https://localhost:5101/<br>catalog/categories/3 | Same as above |
| https://localhost:5101/<br>catalog/categories/$count | 8 |
| https://localhost:5101/<br>catalog/products | JSON document containing all products |
| https://localhost:5101/<br>catalog/products/$count | 77 |

| https://localhost:5101/<br>catalog/products(2) | {<br>  "@odata.context": "https://localhost:5101/cat<br>alog/$metadata#Products/$entity",<br>  "ProductId": 2,<br>  "ProductName": "Chang",<br>  "SupplierId": 1,<br>  "CategoryId": 1,<br>  "QuantityPerUnit": "24 - 12 oz bottles",<br>  "UnitPrice": 19.0000,<br>  "UnitsInStock": 17,<br>  "UnitsOnOrder": 40,<br>  "ReorderLevel": 25,<br>  "Discontinued": false<br>} |
|---|---|
| https://localhost:5101/<br>catalog/suppliers | JSON document containing all suppliers |
| https://localhost:5101/<br>catalog/suppliers/$count | 29 |

7.  Note that you can execute an HTTP request by clicking **Send Request** above each query, or by navigating to **View** | **Command Palette** and selecting the **Rest Client: Send Request** command or using its keyboard shortcut for your operating system, as shown in *Figure 10.5*:

*Figure 10.5: Queries in REST Client*

# Querying OData services using REST Client

To execute arbitrary queries against an OData model, we earlier enabled selecting, filtering, and ordering.

 For the official documentation of OData URL conventions and standard queries, see the following link: `http://docs.oasis-open.org/odata/odata/v4.01/odata-v4.01-part2-url-conventions.html#_Toc31360954`.

# Understanding OData standard query options

One of the benefits of OData is that it defines standard query options, as shown in the following table:

| Option | Description | Example |
|---|---|---|
| $select | Selects properties for each entity. | $select=CategoryId,CategoryName |
| $expand | Selects related entities via navigation properties. | $expand=Products |
| $filter | The expression is evaluated for each resource, and only entities where the expression is true are included in the response. | $filter=startswith(ProductName, 'ch') or (UnitPrice gt 50) |
| $orderby | Sorts the entities by the properties listed in ascending (default) or descending order. | $orderby=UnitPrice desc,ProductName |
| $skip<br><br>$top | Skips the specified number of items.<br>Takes the specified number of items. | $skip=40&$top=10 |

 For performance reasons, batching with $skip and $top is disabled by default.

# Understanding OData operators

OData has operators for use with the $filter option, as shown in the following table:

| Operator | Description |
|---|---|
| eq | Equals |
| ne | Not equals |
| lt | Less than |
| gt | Greater than |
| le | Less than or equal to |
| ge | Greater than or equal to |
| and | And |
| or | Or |
| not | Not |
| add | Arithmetic add for numbers and date/time values |
| sub | Arithmetic subtract for numbers and date/time values |

| `mul` | Arithmetic multiply for numbers |
| `div` | Arithmetic division for numbers |
| `mod` | Arithmetic modulus division for numbers |

# Understanding OData functions

OData has functions for use with the `$filter` option, as shown in the following table:

| Operator | Description |
| --- | --- |
| `startswith(stringToSearch, string)` | Text values that start with the specified value |
| `endswith(stringToSearch, string)` | Text values that end with the specified value |
| `concat(string1, string2)` | Concatenate two text values |
| `contains(stringToSearch, string)` | Text values that contain the specified value |
| `indexof(stringToSearch, string)` | Returns the position of a text value |
| `length(string)` | Returns the length of a text value |
| `substring(string, index, length)` | Extracts a substring from a text value |
| `tolower(string)` | Converts to lower case |
| `toupper(string)` | Converts to upper case |
| `trim(string)` | Trims whitespace before and after text value |
| `now` | The current date and time |
| `day(datetime)`, `month(datetime)`, `year(datetime)` | Extracts date components |
| `hour(datetime)`, `minute(datetime)`, `second(datetime)` | Extracts time components |

# Exploring OData queries

Let's experiment with some OData queries:

1.  In the `RestClientTests` folder, create a file named `odata-catalog-queries.http`, and modify its contents to contain a request to get all categories, as shown in the following code:

    ```
    GET https://localhost:5101/catalog/categories/
      ?$select=CategoryId,CategoryName
    ```

 **Good Practice:** Put the query string part on a new line to make the queries easier to read, as shown in the previous example.

2.   Click **Send Request** and note that the response is a JSON document containing all categories, but only the ID and name properties.

3.   Separated by ###, add and send a request to get products with names that start with Ch, like Chai and Chef Anton's Gumbo Mix, or have a unit price of more than 50, like Mishi Kobe Niku or Sir Rodney's Marmalade, as shown in the following request:

```
GET https://localhost:5101/catalog/products/
  ?$filter=startswith(ProductName,'Ch') or (UnitPrice gt 50)
```

4.   Add and send a request to get products sorted with most expensive at the top, and then sorted within a price by product name, and only include the ID, name, and price properties, as shown in the following request:

```
GET https://localhost:5101/catalog/products/
  ?$orderby=UnitPrice desc,ProductName
  &$select=ProductId,ProductName,UnitPrice
```

5.   Add and send a request to get a specific product, and only include the ID, name, and price properties, as shown in the following request:

```
GET https://localhost:5101/catalog/products(77)/
  ?$select=ProductId,ProductName,UnitPrice
```

6.   Add and send a request to get categories and their related products, as shown in the following request:

```
GET https://localhost:5101/catalog/categories/
  ?$select=CategoryId,CategoryName
  &$expand=Products
```

7.   Add and send a request to get a specific category and its related products, as shown in the following request:

```
GET https://localhost:5101/catalog/categories(8)/
  ?$select=CategoryId,CategoryName
  &$expand=Products
```

8.   Shut down the web server.

## Using logs to review the efficiency of OData requests

How does OData querying work? Let's find out by using the logging in the Northwind database context to see the actual SQL statements that are executed:

1.   Start the Northwind.OData.Service web service.

2.   Start Chrome and navigate to https://localhost:5101/catalog/products/?$filter=starts with(ProductName,'Ch')or(UnitPrice gt 50)&$select=ProductId,ProductName,UnitPrice.

3.  In Chrome, note the result, as shown in the following output:

```
{"@odata.context":"https://localhost:5101/catalog/$metadata#Products
(ProductId,ProductName,UnitPrice)","value":
[{"ProductId":1,"ProductName":"Chai","UnitPrice":18.0000},{"ProductId":2,
"ProductName":"Chang","UnitPrice":19.0000},{"ProductId":4,"ProductName":
"Chef Anton's Cajun Seasoning","UnitPrice":22.0000},{"ProductId":5,
"ProductName":"Chef Anton's Gumbo
Mix","UnitPrice":21.3500},{"ProductId":9,
"ProductName":"Mishi Kobe Niku","UnitPrice":97.0000},{"ProductId":18,
"ProductName":"Carnarvon Tigers","UnitPrice":62.5000},{"ProductId":20,
"ProductName":"Sir Rodney's
Marmalade","UnitPrice":81.0000},{"ProductId":29,
"ProductName":"Th\u00fcringer Rostbratwurst","UnitPrice":123.7900},
{"ProductId":38,"ProductName":"C\u00f4te de Blaye","UnitPrice":263.5000},
{"ProductId":39,"ProductName":"Chartreuse verte","UnitPrice":18.0000},
{"ProductId":48,"ProductName":"Chocolade",
"UnitPrice":12.7500},{"ProductId":51,"ProductName":"Manjimup Dried
Apples",
"UnitPrice":53.0000},{"ProductId":59,"ProductName":"Raclette
Courdavault",
"UnitPrice":55.0000}]}
```

4.  At the command prompt or terminal, note the logged SQL statement that was executed, as shown in the following output:

```
info: Microsoft.EntityFrameworkCore.Database.Command[20101]
      Executed DbCommand (57ms) [Parameters=[@__TypedProperty_0='?'
(Size = 4000), @__TypedProperty_0_1='?' (Size = 40), @__TypedProperty_1=
'?' (Precision = 2) (DbType = Decimal)], CommandType='Text',
CommandTimeout
='30']
      SELECT [p].[ProductId], [p].[ProductName], [p].[UnitPrice]
      FROM [Products] AS [p]
      WHERE @__TypedProperty_0 = N'' OR LEFT([p].[ProductName],
LEN(@__TypedProperty_0_1)) = @__TypedProperty_0 OR [p].[UnitPrice] >
@__TypedProperty_1
```

> It might look like the Get action method on the ProductsController returns the entire Products table, but it actually returns an IQueryable<Products> object. In other words, it returns a LINQ query, not yet the results. We decorated the Get action method with the [EnableQuery] attribute. This enables OData to extend the LINQ query with filters, projections, sorting, and so on, and only then does it execute the query, serialize the results, and return them to the client. This makes OData services as flexible *and* efficient as possible when it translates from its query language to LINQ and then into SQL statements.

5.  Close the browser and shut down the web server.

# Versioning OData controllers

It is good practice to plan for future versions of your OData models that might have different schemas and behavior.

To maintain backward compatibility, you can use OData URL prefixes to specify a version number:

1. In the `Northwind.OData.Service` project, in `Program.cs`, in the services configuration section, after adding the two OData models for `catalog` and `orders`, add a third OData model that has a version number and uses the same `GetEdmModelForCatalog` method, as shown highlighted in the following code:

```
.AddRouteComponents(routePrefix: "catalog",
  model: GetEdmModelForCatalog())
.AddRouteComponents(routePrefix: "ordersystem",
  model: GetEdmModelForOrderSystem())
.AddRouteComponents(routePrefix: "catalog/v{version}",
  model: GetEdmModelForCatalog())
```

2. In `ProductsController.cs`, modify the `Get` methods to add a `string` parameter named `version` that defaults to `"1"`, and use it to change the behavior of the methods if version 2 is specified in a request, as shown highlighted in the following code:

```
[EnableQuery]
public IActionResult Get(string version = "1")
{
  Console.WriteLine($"*** ProductsController version {version}.");
  return Ok(db.Products);
}

[EnableQuery]
public IActionResult Get(int key, string version = "1")
{
  Console.WriteLine($"*** ProductsController version {version}.");

  IQueryable<Product> products = db.Products.Where(
    product => product.ProductId == key);

  Product? p = products.FirstOrDefault();

  if ((products is null) || (p is null))
  {
    return NotFound($"Product with id {key} not found.");
  }

  if (version == "2")
  {
    p.ProductName += " version 2.0";
```

```
    }

    return Ok(p);
}
```

3.  In your preferred code editor, start the `Northwind.OData.Service` project web service.

4.  In Visual Studio Code, in `odata-catalog-queries.http`, add a request to get the product with ID 50 using the v2 OData model, as shown in the following code:

    ```
    GET https://localhost:5101/catalog/v2/products(50)
    ```

5.  Click **Send Request**, and note the response is the product with its name appended with **version 2.0**, as shown highlighted in the following output:

    ```
    {
        "@odata.context": "https://localhost:5101/
    v2/$metadata#Products/$entity",
        "ProductId": 50,
        "ProductName": "Valkoinen suklaa version 2.0",
        "SupplierId": 23,
        "CategoryId": 3,
        "QuantityPerUnit": "12 - 100 g bars",
        "UnitPrice": 16.2500,
        "UnitsInStock": 65,
        "UnitsOnOrder": 0,
        "ReorderLevel": 30,
        "Discontinued": false
    }
    ```

6.  At the command prompt or terminal, note version 2 is used, as shown in the following output:

    ```
    *** ProductsController version 2.
    ```

7.  In `odata-catalog-queries.http`, add a request to get the product with ID 50 using the default (v1) OData model, as shown in the following code:

    ```
    GET https://localhost:5101/catalog/products(50)
    ```

8.  Click **Send Request**, and note the response is the product with its name unmodified.

9.  At the command prompt or terminal, note version 1 is used, as shown in the following output:

    ```
    *** ProductsController version 1.
    ```

10. Shut down the web server.

# Enabling entity inserts, updates, and deletes

Although the most common use for OData is to provide a Web API that supports custom queries, you might also want to support CRUD operations like inserts. Let's see how to do that:

1. In `ProductsController.cs`, add an action method to respond to POST requests, as shown in the following code:

```
public IActionResult Post([FromBody] Product product)
{
  db.Products.Add(product);
  db.SaveChanges();
  return Created(product);
}
```

2. Set a breakpoint on the open brace of the method.

3. Start the OData web service with debugging.

4. In Visual Studio Code, in the `RestClientTests` folder, create a new file named `odata-catalog-insert-product.http`, as shown in the following HTTP request:

```
POST https://localhost:5101/catalog/products
Content-Type: application/json
Content-Length: 234


{
  "ProductName": "Impossible Burger",
  "SupplierId": 7,
  "CategoryId": 6,
  "QuantityPerUnit": "Pack of 4",
  "UnitPrice": 40.25,
  "UnitsInStock": 50,
  "UnitsOnOrder": 0,
  "ReorderLevel": 30,
  "Discontinued": false
}
```

5. Click **Send Request**.

6.  In your code editor, note the breakpoint is hit, and you can use the debugging tools to see the product parameter successfully deserialized from the body of the HTTP POST request, as shown in *Figure 10.6*:

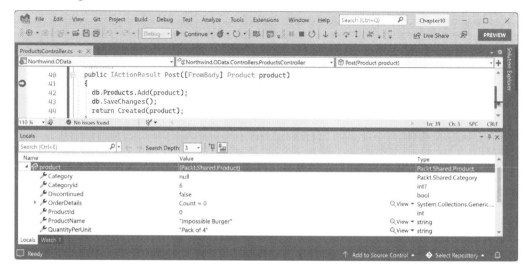

*Figure 10.6: Debugging the OData POST request method handler*

7.  Allow the code to continue executing.

8.  In Visual Studio Code, note the successful response, as shown in the following output:

```
HTTP/1.1 201 Created
Connection: close
Content-Type: application/json; odata.metadata=minimal; odata.
streaming=true
Date: Sun, 22 May 2022 15:13:11 GMT
Server: Kestrel
Location: https://localhost:5101/catalog/Products(78)
Transfer-Encoding: chunked
OData-Version: 4.0

{
  "@odata.context": "https://localhost:5101/
catalog/$metadata#Products/$entity",
  "ProductId": 78,
  "ProductName": "Impossible Burger",
  "SupplierId": 7,
  "CategoryId": 6,
  "QuantityPerUnit": "Pack of 4",
  "UnitPrice": 40.25,
  "UnitsInStock": 50,
  "UnitsOnOrder": 0,
  "ReorderLevel": 30,
```

```
        "Discontinued": false
    }
```

9. Optionally, implement two more methods to enable updates using an HTTP PUT request and deletes using an HTTP DELETE request.

# Building clients for OData services

Finally, let's see how a .NET client might call the OData web service. Let's review how clients interact with an OData service.

If we want to query the OData service for products that start with the letters Cha, then we would need to send a GET request with a relative URL path similar to the following:

```
catalog/products/?$filter=startswith(ProductName,
'Cha')&$select=ProductId,ProductName,UnitPrice
```

OData returns data in a JSON document with a property named value that contains the resulting products as an array, as shown in the following JSON document:

```
{
    "@odata.context": "https://localhost:5101/catalog/$metadata#Products",
    "value": [
    {
        "ProductId": 1,
        "ProductName": "Chai",
        "SupplierId": 1,
        "CategoryId": 1,
        "QuantityPerUnit": "10 boxes x 20 bags",
        "UnitPrice": 18,
        "UnitsInStock": 39,
        "UnitsOnOrder": 0,
        "ReorderLevel": 10,
        "Discontinued": false
    },
```

We will create an ASP.NET Core website project to act as a client, and a model class to make it easy to deserialize the HTTP response:

1. Use your preferred code editor to add an MVC website project, as defined in the following list:

    - Project template: **ASP.NET Core Web App (Model-View-Controller) [C#]**/mvc
    - Project file and folder: Northwind.OData.Client.Mvc
    - Workspace/solution file and folder: Chapter10
    - Additional information - Authentication type: **None**
    - For Visual Studio, leave all other options as their defaults.

2. If you are using Visual Studio 2022, set the startup project to the current selection. If you are using Visual Studio Code, select Northwind.OData.Client.Mvc as the active OmniSharp project.

3.  Add a project reference to the `Northwind.Common.EntityModels.SqlServer` project in the `Chapter02` folder, as shown in the following markup:

    ```
    <ItemGroup>
      <ProjectReference Include="..\..\Chapter02\Northwind.Common.
    EntityModels.SqlServer\Northwind.Common.EntityModels.SqlServer.csproj" />
    </ItemGroup>
    ```

4.  Build the `Northwind.OData.Client.Mvc` project.

5.  In the `Properties` folder, open `launchSettings.json`.

6.  In the `Northwind.OData.Client.Mvc` profile, modify the `applicationUrl` to use port 5102 for HTTPS, as shown in the following markup:

    ```
    "applicationUrl": "https://localhost:5102",
    ```

7.  In the `Northwind.OData.Client.Mvc` project, in the `Models` folder, add a new class file named `ODataProducts.cs`, as shown in the following code:

    ```
    using Packt.Shared; // Product

    namespace Northwind.OData.Client.Mvc.Models;

    public class ODataProducts
    {
      public Product[]? Value { get; set; }
    }
    ```

8.  In `Program.cs`, add a statement to import the namespace for setting media types in an HTTP header, as shown in the following code:

    ```
    using System.Net.Http.Headers; // MediaTypeWithQualityHeaderValue
    ```

9.  In `Program.cs`, after the call to `AddControllersWithViews`, add statements to register an HTTP client for the OData service that will request JSON for the response data format, as shown in the following code:

    ```
    builder.Services.AddHttpClient(name: "Northwind.OData",
      configureClient: options =>
      {
        options.BaseAddress = new Uri("https://localhost:5101/");
        options.DefaultRequestHeaders.Accept.Add(
          new MediaTypeWithQualityHeaderValue(
          "application/json", 1.0));
      });
    ```

# Calling services in the Northwind MVC website

Next, we will call the service on the home page:

1. In the `Controllers` folder, in `HomeController.cs`, declare a field to store the registered HTTP client factory service, as shown in the following code:

```
protected readonly IHttpClientFactory clientFactory;
```

2. In the class constructor, add statements to pass and store the registered HTTP client factory service, as shown highlighted in the following code:

```
public HomeController(ILogger<HomeController> logger,
  IHttpClientFactory clientFactory)
{
  _logger = logger;
  this.clientFactory = clientFactory;
}
```

3. Make the `Index` method asynchronous, and then add statements that call the OData service to get products that start with `Cha` and store the result in the `ViewData` dictionary, as shown highlighted in the following code:

```
public async Task<IActionResult> Index(string startsWith = "Cha")
{
  try
  {
    HttpClient client = clientFactory.CreateClient(
      name: "Northwind.OData");

    HttpRequestMessage request = new(
      method: HttpMethod.Get, requestUri:
      "catalog/products/?$filter=startswith(ProductName, " +
      $"'{startsWith}')&$select=ProductId,ProductName,UnitPrice");

    HttpResponseMessage response = await client.SendAsync(request);

    ViewData["startsWith"] = startsWith;
    ViewData["products"] = (await response.Content
      .ReadFromJsonAsync<ODataProducts>())?.Value;
  }
  catch (Exception ex)
  {
    _logger.LogWarning($"Northwind.OData service exception: {ex.
Message}");
  }

  return View();
}
```

4.  In Views/Home, in Index.cshtml, delete its existing markup and then add markup to render the products with a form for the visitor to enter the start of a product name, as shown in the following markup:

```
@using Packt.Shared
@{
   ViewData["Title"] = "Home Page";
   Product[]? products = ViewData["products"] as Product[];
}
<div class="text-center">
   <h1 class="display-4">@ViewData["Title"]</h1>
   @if (products is not null)
   {
      <h2>Products that start with '@ViewData["startsWith"]' using OData</
h2>
      <p>
        @if (products.Length == 0)
        {
          <span class="badge rounded-pill bg-danger">No products found.</
span>
        }
        else
        {
          @foreach (Product p in products)
          {
            <span class="badge rounded-pill bg-info text-dark">
              @p.ProductId
              @p.ProductName
              @(p.UnitPrice is null ? "" : p.UnitPrice.Value.ToString("c"))
            </span>
          }
        }
      </p>
   }
   <form method="get">
     Product name starts with:
     <input name="startsWith" value="@ViewData["startsWith"]" />
     Press ENTER to search.
   </form>
</div>
```

5.  Start the Northwind.OData.Service project without debugging.

6.  Start the Northwind.OData.Client.Mvc project without debugging.

7.  Start Chrome and navigate to https://localhost:5102/.

8.  Note that three products are returned from the OData service, as shown in *Figure 10.7*:

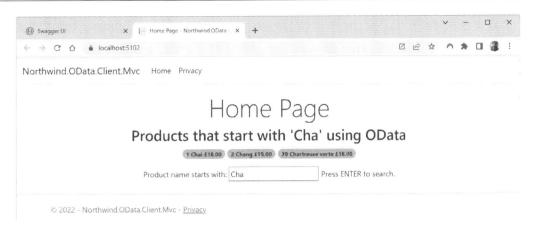

*Figure 10.7: Three product names starting with Cha returned from the OData service*

9.  At the command line or terminal for the OData service, note the SQL command used, as shown in the following output:

```
info: Microsoft.EntityFrameworkCore.Database.Command[20101]
      Executed DbCommand (28ms) [Parameters=[@__TypedProperty_0='?' (Size
= 4000), @__TypedProperty_0_1='?' (Size = 40)], CommandType='Text',
CommandTimeout='30']
      SELECT [p].[ProductId], [p].[ProductName], [p].[UnitPrice]
      FROM [Products] AS [p]
      WHERE @__TypedProperty_0 = N'' OR LEFT([p].[ProductName],
LEN(@__TypedProperty_0_1)) = @__TypedProperty_0
```

10. At the command line or terminal for the MVC website, note the HTTP request made and its response, as shown in the following output:

```
info: System.Net.Http.HttpClient.Northwind.OData.Service.
LogicalHandler[100]
      Start processing HTTP request GET https://localhost:5101/catalog/
products/?$filter=startswith(ProductName,'Cha')&$select=ProductId,
ProductName,UnitPrice
info: System.Net.Http.HttpClient.Northwind.OData.Service.
ClientHandler[100]
      Sending HTTP request GET https://localhost:5101/catalog/
products/?$filter=startswith(ProductName,'Cha')&$select=ProductId,
ProductName,UnitPrice
info: System.Net.Http.HttpClient.Northwind.OData.Service.
ClientHandler[101]
      Received HTTP response headers after 998.5241ms - 200
info: System.Net.Http.HttpClient.Northwind.OData.Service.
LogicalHandler[101]
      End processing HTTP request after 1004.9182ms - 200
```

11. Type b in the text box, press *Enter*, and note the results only include the one product that starts with the letter b, **Boston Crab Meat**.

12. Type d in the text box, press *Enter*, and note the error message saying that no products were found.

13. Close Chrome and shut down both the web servers.

## Revisiting the introductory query

At the start of this chapter, I introduced an example of a query you could run against an OData service. Let's see if it works with our service:

1. In Visual Studio Code, in the RestClientTests folder, create a new file named odata-final-query.http, as shown in the following HTTP request:

```
GET https://localhost:5101/catalog/products
  ?$filter=contains(ProductName, 'ch') and UnitPrice lt 44.95
  &$orderby=Supplier/Country,UnitPrice
  &$select=ProductName,UnitPrice
  &$expand=Supplier
```

2. Click **Send Request** and note the response contains products and their suppliers, sorted by country first and then, within each country, sorted by unit price, as shown in the following partial output:

 The parts of the output that I clipped out to save space are indicated with ellipses (...).

```
HTTP/1.1 200 OK
Connection: close
Content-Type: application/json; odata.metadata=minimal; odata.
streaming=true
Date: Thu, 21 Jul 2022 20:34:34 GMT
Server: Kestrel
Transfer-Encoding: chunked
OData-Version: 4.0

{
  "@odata.context": "https://localhost:5101/
catalog/$metadata#Products(ProductName,UnitPrice,Supplier())",
  "value": [
    ...
    {
      "ProductName": "Chartreuse verte",
      "UnitPrice": 18.0000,
      "Supplier": {
        ...
```

```
        "Country": "France",
        ...
      }
    },
    ...
    {
      "ProductName": "Gnocchi di nonna Alice",
      "UnitPrice": 38.0000,
      "Supplier": {
        ...
        "Country": "Italy",
        ...
      }
    },
    {
      "ProductName": "Chocolade",
      "UnitPrice": 12.7500,
      "Supplier": {
        ...
        "Country": "Netherlands",
        ...
      }
    },
    ...
    {
      "ProductName": "Chai",
      "UnitPrice": 18.0000,
      "Supplier": {
        ...
        "Country": "UK",
        ...
      }
    },
    {
      "ProductName": "Chang",
      "UnitPrice": 19.0000,
      "Supplier": {
        ...
        "Country": "UK",
        ...
      }
    },
    ...
  ]
}
```

# Practicing and exploring

Test your knowledge and understanding by answering some questions, getting some hands-on practice, and exploring this chapter's topics with deeper research.

## Exercise 10.1 – Test your knowledge

Answer the following questions:

1. What transport protocol does an OData service use?
2. Why is an OData service more flexible than a traditional ASP.NET Core Web API service?
3. What must you do to an action method in an OData controller to enable query strings to customize what it returns?
4. What URL path would return customers in Germany who have made more than one order?
5. How do you get related entities?

## Exercise 10.2 – Explore topics

Use the links on the following page to learn more detail about the topics covered in this chapter:

```
https://github.com/markjprice/apps-services-net7/blob/main/book-links.md#chapter-10--
-exposing-data-via-the-web-using-odata
```

# Summary

In this chapter, you learned:

- The concepts around OData services.
- How to build an OData service using ASP.NET Core and a Microsoft NuGet package.
- How to query an OData service.
- How to perform data modifications.
- How to build an OData client.

In the next chapter, you will learn about GraphQL, another standard that enables client control over the data returned from a service.

# 11

# Combining Data Sources Using GraphQL

In this chapter, you will be introduced to GraphQL, a service technology that provides a more modern approach to combining data from various sources and then providing a standard way to query that data.

This chapter will cover the following topics:

- Understanding GraphQL
- Building a service that supports GraphQL
- Defining GraphQL queries for EF Core models
- Building a .NET client for a GraphQL service
- Implementing GraphQL mutations

## Understanding GraphQL

As you saw in *Chapter 10, Exposing Data via the Web Using OData*, OData is a possible choice for combining data from different stores and exposing it via a common protocol like HTTP. OData also has a built-in query language for the client to control what data they want returned. But OData has a rather old-fashioned approach and is tied to the HTTP standard, for example, using query strings in an HTTP request.

If you would prefer to use a more modern and flexible technology for combining and exposing your data as a service, then a good alternative is **GraphQL**.

Like OData, GraphQL is a standard for describing your data and then querying it that gives the client control over exactly what they need. It was developed internally by Facebook in 2012 before being open sourced in 2015, and is now managed by the GraphQL Foundation.

Some of the key benefits of GraphQL over OData are:

- GraphQL does not require HTTP because it is transport-agnostic, so you could use alternative transport protocols like WebSockets or TCP.

- GraphQL has more client libraries for different platforms than OData has.
- GraphQL has a single endpoint, usually simply /graphql.

OData does have the advantage that it is more mature.

# GraphQL query document format

GraphQL uses its own document format for its queries, which are a bit like JSON, but GraphQL queries do not require commas between field names, as shown in the following query:

```
{
  product (productId: 23) {
    productId
    productName
    cost
    supplier {
      companyName
      country
    }
  }
}
```

 The official media type for GraphQL query documents is application/graphql.

# Requesting fields

The most basic GraphQL query requests one or more fields from a type, for example, requesting three fields for each customer entity, as shown in the following code:

```
# The query keyword is optional.
query {
  customer {
    customerId
    companyName
    country
  }
}
```

Comments are prefixed with the # symbol.

The response is in JSON format, for example, an array of customer objects, as shown in the following document:

```
{
  "data": [
    {
```

```
      "customerId": "ALFKI",
      "companyName": "Alfreds Futterkiste",
      "country": "Germany"
    },
    ...
  ]
}
```

## Specifying filters and arguments

With an HTTP or REST-style API, the caller is limited to only passing parameters when the API pre-defines that. With GraphQL, you can set parameters anywhere in the query, as shown in the following code:

```
query getOrdersByDateAndCountry {
  order(orderDate: "23/04/1998") {
    orderId
    orderDate
    customer(country: "UK") {
      companyName
      country
    }
  }
}
```

You would want to pass values for named parameters instead of hardcoding them, as shown in the following code:

```
query getOrdersByDateAndCountry($country: String, $orderDate: String) {
  order(orderDate: $orderDate) {
    orderId
    orderDate
    customer(country: $country) {
      companyName
      country
    }
  }
}
```

 You can learn more about the GraphQL query language at the following link: https://graphql.org/learn/queries/.

# Understanding other GraphQL capabilities

As well as queries, other standard GraphQL features are mutations and subscriptions:

- **Mutations** enable creating, updating, and deleting resources.
- **Subscriptions** enable a client to get notified when resources change. They work best with additional communication technologies like WebSockets.

# Understanding the ChilliCream GraphQL platform

In the sixth edition of my book, *C# 10 and .NET 6 – Modern Cross-Platform Development*, I included an example of implementing a GraphQL service using a platform named GraphQL.NET. At the time, this was the most popular platform for implementing GraphQL with .NET.

 You can learn about GraphQL.NET at the following link: `https://graphql-dotnet.github.io/`.

However, soon after publishing, the developer made breaking changes that broke the code, with a lack of documentation on how to migrate. In my opinion, GraphQL.NET also requires too much configuration for even the most basic example, and the documentation is frustrating. I have a feeling that, although it is powerful, it implements the GraphQL specification in a one-to-one manner instead of rethinking how a .NET platform could make it easier to get started. So, for this book, I looked for alternatives, and I found exactly what I was looking for.

ChilliCream is a company that has created a platform to work with GraphQL:

- **Hot Chocolate** enables you to create GraphQL services for .NET.
- **Strawberry Shake** enables you to create GraphQL clients for .NET.
- **Banana Cake Pop** enables you to run queries and explore a GraphQL endpoint using a Monaco-based GraphQL IDE.
- **Green Donut** enables better performance when loading data.

Unlike some other packages that can be used to add support for GraphQL, ChilliCream packages are designed to be as easy to implement as possible, using conventions and simple POCO classes instead of complex types and special schemas. It works the way Microsoft would have built a GraphQL platform for .NET, with sensible defaults and conventions rather than lots of boilerplate code and configuration.

As ChilliCream says on their home page, "We at ChilliCream build the ultimate GraphQL platform. Most of our code is open-source and will forever remain open-source."

 The GitHub repository for Hot Chocolate is at the following link: `https://github.com/ChilliCream/hotchocolate`.

# Building a service that supports GraphQL

There is no dotnet new project template for GraphQL, so we will use the ASP.NET Core Empty project template. Even though GraphQL does not have to be hosted in a web server because it is not tied to HTTP, it is a sensible choice to get started. We will then add a package reference for GraphQL support:

1.  Use your preferred code editor to add a new project, as defined in the following list:

    1.  Project template: **ASP.NET Core Empty**/web
    2.  Workspace/solution file and folder: Chapter11
    3.  Project file and folder: Northwind.GraphQL
    4.  Other Visual Studio 2022 options:

        *   **Authentication Type:** None
        *   **Configure for HTTPS:** Selected
        *   **Enable Docker:** Cleared
        *   **Enable OpenAPI support:** Cleared

2.  In Visual Studio Code, select Northwind.GraphQL as the active OmniSharp project.

3.  Add a package reference for Hot Chocolate hosted in ASP.NET Core, as shown in the following markup:

    ```
    <ItemGroup>
      <PackageReference Include="HotChocolate.AspNetCore" Version="13.0.0" />
    </ItemGroup>
    ```

     I recommend that you go to the following link and then reference the latest version: https://www.nuget.org/packages/HotChocolate.AspNetCore/.

4.  In the Properties folder, in launchSettings.json, modify the applicationUrl to use port 5111 for https and port 5112 for http, and change the launchUrl to graphql, as shown highlighted in the following configuration:

    ```
    "profiles": {
      "http": {
        "commandName": "Project",
        "dotnetRunMessages": true,
        "launchBrowser": true,
        "launchUrl": "graphql",
        "applicationUrl": "http://localhost:5112",
        "environmentVariables": {
          "ASPNETCORE_ENVIRONMENT": "Development"
        }
      },
    ```

```
"https": {
    "commandName": "Project",
    "dotnetRunMessages": true,
    "launchBrowser": true,
    "launchUrl": "graphql",
    "applicationUrl": "https://localhost:5111;http://localhost:5112",
    "environmentVariables": {
      "ASPNETCORE_ENVIRONMENT": "Development"
    }
},
```

5.  Build the `Northwind.GraphQL` project.

# Defining the GraphQL schema for Hello World

The first task is to define what we want to expose as GraphQL models in the web service.

Let's define a GraphQL query for the most basic Hello World example, which will return a simple greeting when a request for a greeting is made:

1.  In the `Northwind.GraphQL` project/folder, add a class file named `Query.cs`.

2.  Modify the class to have a method named `GetGreeting` that returns the plain text `"Hello, World!"`, as shown in the following code:

```
namespace Northwind.GraphQL;

public class Query
{
    public string GetGreeting() => "Hello, World!";
}
```

3.  In `Program.cs`, import the namespace where we defined the `Query` class, as shown in the following code:

```
using Northwind.GraphQL; // Query
```

4.  In the section for configuring services, after the call to `CreateBuilder`, add a statement to add GraphQL server-side support and add the query type to the collection of registered services, as shown in the following code:

```
builder.Services
    .AddGraphQLServer()
    .AddQueryType<Query>();
```

5. Modify the statement that maps a GET request to return a more useful plain text message, as shown in the following code:

```
app.MapGet("/", () => "Navigate to: https://localhost:5111/graphql");
```

6. In the section for configuring the HTTP pipeline, before the call to Run, add a statement to map GraphQL as an endpoint, as shown in the following code:

```
app.MapGraphQL();
```

7. Start the Northwind.GraphQL project using the https profile without debugging.

   • If you are using Visual Studio 2022, then select the **https** profile, start the project without debugging, and note the browser starts automatically.

   • If you are using Visual Studio Code, then enter the following command: dotnet run --launch-profile https, start Chrome manually, and navigate to https://localhost:5111/graphql.

8. Note the **BananaCakePop** user interface, as shown in *Figure 11.1*:

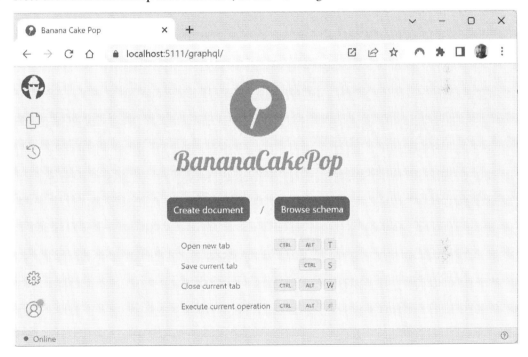

*Figure 11.1: BananaCakePop home page*

9. Click the **Browse schema** button.

10. In **Connection Settings**, confirm that the **Schema Endpoint** is correct, note the **Subscription Endpoint** uses the WebSocket protocol (**wss**), and then click **Cancel**, as shown in *Figure 11.2*:

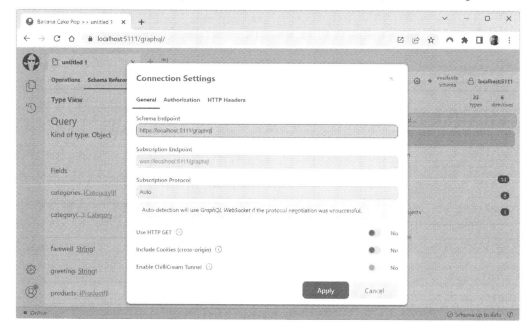

*Figure 11.2: Reviewing the BananaCakePop connection settings*

11. In the **Schema Reference**, note the special Query object is the entry point for all other queries, and it has a field named greeting that returns a string value.

12. Click the **Schema Definition** tab, scroll down to the bottom, and note there is only one type defined, the special Query object with its greeting field that is a string value, as shown in the following code:

```
type Query {
  greeting: String!
}
```

The exclamation mark indicates the string value will not be null.

# Writing and executing GraphQL queries

Now we know the schema, we can write and run a query:

1. In **Banana Cake Pop**, click the **Operations** tab.

2. On the left-hand side, type an open curly brace {, and note that a close curly brace } is written for you.

3. Type the letter g and note the autocomplete shows it recognizes the greeting field, as shown in *Figure 11.3*:

*Figure 11.3: Autocomplete for the greeting field*

4. Press *Enter* to accept the autocomplete suggestion.
5. Click the **Run** button and note the response, as shown in *Figure 11.4* and the following output:

```
{
  "data": {
    "greeting": "Hello, World!"
  }
}
```

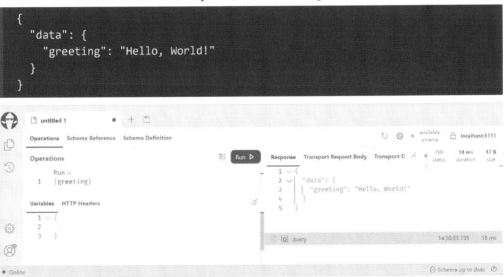

*Figure 11.4: Using the GraphQL playground to execute a greet query*

6. Close Chrome and shut down the web server.

## Naming GraphQL queries

The query that we wrote was unnamed. We could also have created it as a named query, as shown in the following code:

```
query QueryNameGoesHere {
  greeting
}
```

Named queries allow clients to identify queries and responses for telemetry purposes, for example, when hosting in Microsoft Azure cloud services and monitoring using Application Insights.

## Understanding field conventions

The method we created in the Query class was named GetGreeting, but when querying it we used greeting. The Get prefix on method names that represent fields in GraphQL is optional. Let's see some more examples:

1.  In Query.cs, add two more methods without the Get prefix, as shown highlighted in the following code:

    ```
    namespace Northwind.GraphQL;

    public class Query
    {
      public string GetGreeting() => "Hello, World!";
      public string Farewell() => "Ciao! Ciao!";
      public int RollTheDie() => Random.Shared.Next(1, 7);
    }
    ```

2.  Start the Northwind.GraphQL project using the https profile without debugging.
3.  In **Banana Cake Pop**, note the pop-up message saying it has updated the schema.
4.  Click the **Schema Definition** tab, and note the updated schema, as shown in the following code:

    ```
    type Query {
      greeting: String!
      farewell: String!
      rollTheDie: Int!
    }
    ```

     C# methods use TitleCase. GraphQL fields use camelCase.

5.  Click the **Operations** tab, and modify the query to specify a name and to request the rollTheDie field, as shown in the following code:

    ```
    query getNumber {
    ```

```
    rollTheDie
}
```

6. Either click the **Run** button again or click **Execute** above the query multiple times. Note that the responses contain a random number between 1 and 6, and a history of requests and responses is stored for the current browser session, as shown in *Figure 11.5*:

*Figure 11.5: Executing a named query and the history of requests and responses*

7. Close Chrome and shut down the web server.

# Defining GraphQL queries for EF Core models

Now that we have a basic GraphQL service operating successfully, let's extend it to enable querying the Northwind database.

## Adding support for EF Core

We must add another Hot Chocolate package to allow easy dependency service integration of our EF Core database context with GraphQL query classes:

1. Add a package reference for Hot Chocolate integration with EF Core and a project reference to the Northwind database context project, as shown highlighted in the following markup:

```xml
<ItemGroup>
  <PackageReference Include="HotChocolate.AspNetCore" Version="13.0.0" />
  <PackageReference Include="HotChocolate.Data.EntityFramework"
                    Version="13.0.0" />
</ItemGroup>

<ItemGroup>
  <ProjectReference Include="..\..\Chapter02\Northwind.Common.DataContext
.SqlServer\Northwind.Common.DataContext.SqlServer.csproj" />
</ItemGroup>
```

 The path to the project must not have a line break. All Hot Chocolate packages must have the same version number.

2.  Build the `Northwind.GraphQL` project at the command line or terminal using `dotnet build`.

 When you reference a project outside of the current solution, you must build the project at least once at the command line or terminal before you can use the Visual Studio 2022 **Build** menu to compile it.

3.  In `Program.cs`, import the namespace for working with our EF Core model for the Northwind database, as shown in the following code:

```
using Packt.Shared; // AddNorthwindContext extension method
```

4.  Add a statement after the `CreateBuilder` method to register the `Northwind` database context class, and add a statement after adding the GraphQL server support to register the `NorthwindContent` class for dependency injection, as shown highlighted in the following code:

```
builder.Services.AddNorthwindContext();

builder.Services
  .AddGraphQLServer()
  .RegisterDbContext<NorthwindContext>()
  .AddQueryType<Query>();
```

5.  In `Query.cs`, add statements to define an object graph type that has some types of queries to return a list of categories, a single category, products for a category, and all products, as shown highlighted in the following code:

```
using Microsoft.EntityFrameworkCore; // Include extension method
using Packt.Shared; // NorthwindContext

namespace Northwind.GraphQL;

public class Query
{
  public string GetGreeting() => "Hello, World!";
  public string Farewell() => "Ciao! Ciao!";
  public int RollTheDie() => Random.Shared.Next(1, 7);

  public IQueryable<Category> GetCategories(NorthwindContext db) =>
    db.Categories.Include(c => c.Products);

  public Category? GetCategory(NorthwindContext db, int categoryId)
  {
    Category? category = db.Categories.Find(categoryId);
    if (category == null) return null;
    db.Entry(category).Collection(c => c.Products).Load();
    return category;
```

```
    }

    public IQueryable<Product> GetProducts(NorthwindContext db) =>
      db.Products.Include(p => p.Category);

    public IQueryable<Product> GetProductsInCategory(
      NorthwindContext db, int categoryId) =>
        db.Products.Where(p => p.CategoryId == categoryId);
    }
```

# Exploring GraphQL queries with Northwind

Now we can test writing GraphQL queries for the categories and products in the Northwind database:

1.  Start the `Northwind.GraphQL` service project using the `https` profile without debugging.

2.  In **Banana Cake Pop**, click the **Schema Definition** tab, and note the query and type definitions for `Category`, as partially shown in *Figure 11.6*:

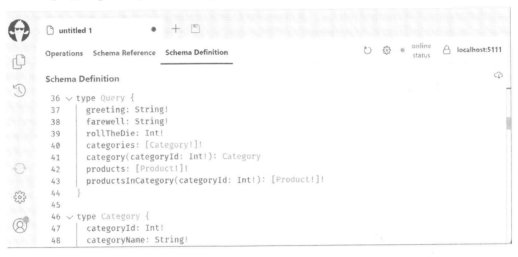

*Figure 11.6: Schema for querying the Northwind categories and products using GraphQL*

3.  Note the full definitions in the following code:

```
type Query {
  greeting: String!
  farewell: String!
  rollTheDie: Int!
  categories: [Category!]!
  category(categoryId: Int!): Category
  products: [Product!]!
  productsInCategory(categoryId: Int!): [Product!]!
}

type Category {
```

```
      categoryId: Int!
      categoryName: String!
      description: String
      picture: [Byte!]
      products: [Product!]!
    }

    type Product {
      productId: Int!
      productName: String!
      supplierId: Int
      categoryId: Int
      quantityPerUnit: String
      unitPrice: Decimal
      unitsInStock: Short
      unitsOnOrder: Short
      reorderLevel: Short
      discontinued: Boolean!
      category: Category
      supplier: Supplier
      orderDetails: [OrderDetail!]!
    }
```

4.   Click the **Operations** tab, and write a named query to request the ID, name, and description fields for all categories, as shown in the following markup:

```
query AllCategories {
  categories {
    categoryId
    categoryName
    description
  }
}
```

5.   Click **Execute** or the **Run** button, and note the response, as shown in *Figure 11.7* and the following partial output:

```
{
  "data": {
    "categories": [
      {
        "categoryId": 1,
        "categoryName": "Beverages",
        "description": "Soft drinks, coffees, teas, beers, and ales"
      },
      {
        "categoryId": 2,
        "categoryName": "Condiments",
```

```
        "description": "Sweet and savory sauces, relishes, spreads, and
seasonings"
        },
        ...
```

*Figure 11.7: Getting all categories*

6.  Click the + to open a new tab, and write a query to request the category with ID 2, including the ID, name, and price of its products, as shown in the following markup:

```
query Condiments {
  category (categoryId: 2) {
    categoryId
    categoryName
    products {
      productId
      productName
      unitPrice
    }
  }
}
```

> Make sure that the I in `categoryId` is uppercase.

7.  Click **Execute** or the **Run** button, and note the response, as shown in the following partial output:

```
{
  "data": {
    "category": {
      "categoryId": 2,
      "categoryName": "Condiments",
      "products": [
```

```
{
    "productId": 3,
    "productName": "Aniseed Syrup",
    "unitPrice": 10
},
{
    "productId": 4,
    "productName": "Chef Anton's Cajun Seasoning",
    "unitPrice": 22
},
...
```

8.  Click the + tab to open a new tab, and write a query to request the ID, name, and units in stock of the products in the category with ID 1, as shown in the following markup:

```
query BeverageProducts {
    productsInCategory (categoryId: 1) {
        productId
        productName
        unitsInStock
    }
}
```

9.  Click **Execute** or the **Run** button, and note the response, as shown in the following partial output:

```
{
    "data": {
        "productsInCategory": [
            {
                "productId": 1,
                "productName": "Chai",
                "unitsInStock": 39
            },
            {
                "productId": 2,
                "productName": "Chang",
                "unitsInStock": 17
            },
            ...
```

10. Click the + tab to open a new tab, and write a query to request the ID, name, and units in stock of products along with their category names, as shown in the following markup:

```
query productsWithCategoryNames {
    products {
        productId
        productName
        category {
            categoryName
```

```
        }
      unitsInStock
    }
  }
```

11. Click **Execute** or the **Run** button, and note the response, as shown in the following partial output:

```
{
  "data": {
    "products": [
      {
        "productId": 1,
        "productName": "Chai",
        "category": {
          "categoryName": "Beverages"
        },
        "unitsInStock": 39
      },
      {
        "productId": 2,
        "productName": "Chang",
        "category": {
          "categoryName": "Beverages"
        },
        "unitsInStock": 17
      },
      ...
```

12. Click the + tab to open a new tab, and write a query to request the ID and name of a category, select the category by specifying its category ID, and include the ID and name for each of its products. The ID of the category will be set using a variable, as shown in the following markup:

```
query categoryAndItsProducts($id: Int!){
  category(categoryId: $id) {
    categoryId
    categoryName
    products {
      productId
      productName
    }
  }
}
```

13. In the **Variables** section, define a value for the variable, as shown in the following code and in *Figure 11.8*:

```
{
  "id": 1
}
```

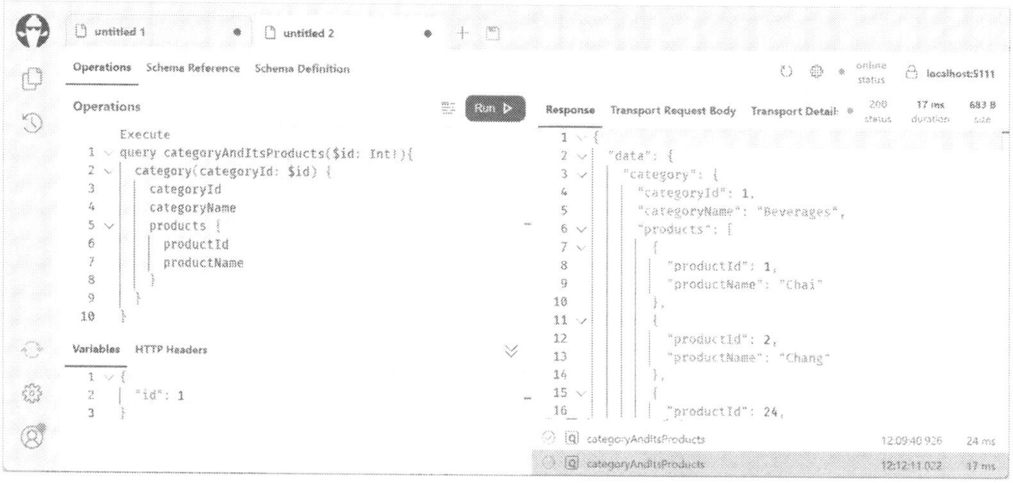

*Figure 11.8: Executing a GraphQL query with a variable*

14. Click **Execute** or the **Run** button, and note the response, as shown in the following partial output:

```
{
  "data": {
    "category": {
      "categoryId": 1,
      "categoryName": "Beverages",
      "products": [
        {
          "productId": 1,
          "productName": "Chai"
        },
        {
          "productId": 2,
          "productName": "Chang"
        },
        ...
      ]
    }
  }
}
```

15. Close Chrome and shut down the web server.

# Building a .NET client for a GraphQL service

Now that we have explored some queries with the **Banana Cake Pop** tool, let's see how a client could call the GraphQL service. Although the **Banana Cake Pop** tool is convenient, it runs in the same domain as the service, so some issues might not become apparent until we create a separate client.

Most GraphQL services process GET and POST requests in either the application/graphql or application/json media formats. An application/graphql request would only contain a query document. The benefit of using application/json is that as well as the query document, you can specify operations when you have more than one, and define and set variables, as shown in the following code:

```
{
   "query": "...",
   "operationName": "...",
   "variables": { "variable1": "value1", ... }
}
```

We will use the application/json media format.

## Understanding GraphQL responses

A GraphQL service should return a JSON document containing the expected data object and maybe some errors in an array, with the following structure:

```
{
   "data": { ... },
   "errors": [ ... ]
}
```

The errors array should only be in the document if there are errors.

## Using REST Client as a GraphQL client

Before we write code as a client to the GraphQL service, it would be good to test it with the Visual Studio Code extension named **REST Client**. This is so that if our .NET client app does not work, we know the problem is in our client code rather than the service:

1. If you have not already installed REST Client by Huachao Mao (humao.rest-client), then install it in Visual Studio Code now.

2. In your preferred code editor, start the Northwind.GraphQL project web service using the https profile without debugging and leave it running.

3. In Visual Studio Code, in the RestClientTests folder, create a file named graphql-seafood-products.http, and modify its contents to contain a request to get products in the seafood category, as shown in the following code:

```
POST https://localhost:5111/graphql
Content-Type: application/json
Content-Length: 90

{
   "query" : "{productsInCategory(categoryId:8){productId productName
unitsInStock}}"
}
```

4. Above the POST, click **Send Request**, and note the response, as shown in *Figure 11.9*:

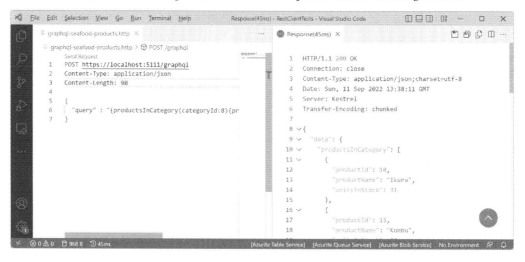

*Figure 11.9: Requesting seafood products using REST Client*

5. In the RestClientTests folder, create a file named graphql-all-categories.http, and modify its contents to contain a request to get the ID, name, and description of all categories, as shown in the following code:

```
POST https://localhost:5111/graphql
Content-Type: application/json
Content-Length: 69

{
   "query" : "{categories{categoryId categoryName description}}"
}
```

6. Above the POST, click **Send Request**, and note the response contains the eight categories in a data property.

7. In the query document, change categoryId to id and the Content-Length to 61.

8. Send the request and note the response contains an errors array, as shown in the following response:

```
HTTP/1.1 400 Bad Request
Connection: close
Content-Type: application/json; charset=utf-8
Date: Mon, 30 May 2022 06:07:55 GMT
Server: Kestrel
Transfer-Encoding: chunked

{
   "errors": [
```

```
          {
              "message": "The field \u0060id\u0060 does not exist on the type \
          u0060Category\u0060.",
              "locations": [
                {
                    "line": 1,
                    "column": 13
                }
              ],
              "path": [
                "categories"
              ],
              "extensions": {
                "type": "Category",
                "field": "id",
                "responseName": "id",
                "specifiedBy": "http://spec.graphql.org/October2021/#sec-Field-
          Selections-on-Objects-Interfaces-and-Unions-Types"
              }
            }
          ]
        }
```

9.  In the `RestClientTests` folder, create a file named graphql-category-products.http, and modify its contents to contain a request to get the ID and name of a category specified by a parameter for its ID, along with the ID and name of each of its products, as shown in the following code:

```
POST https://localhost:5111/graphql
Content-Type: application/json
Content-Length: 168

{
  "query": "query categoryAndItsProducts($id: Int!){category(categoryId:
$id){categoryId categoryName products{productId productName}}}",
  "variables": {"id":1}
}
```

10. Above the `POST`, click **Send Request**, and note the response contains category 1, Beverages, with its products in a data property.

11. Change the ID to 4, send the request, and note the response contains category 4, Dairy Products, with its products in a data property.

12. Close the files, the `RestClientTests` folder, and Visual Studio Code.

# Using an ASP.NET Core MVC project as a GraphQL client

We will create a model class to make it easy to deserialize the response:

1.  Use your preferred code editor to add a new project, as defined in the following list:

    1.  Project template: **ASP.NET Core Web App (Model-View-Controller)**/mvc
    2.  Workspace/solution file and folder: Chapter11
    3.  Project file and folder: Northwind.Mvc.GraphQLClient
    4.  Other Visual Studio 2022 options:

        *   **Authentication Type:** None
        *   **Configure for HTTPS:** Selected
        *   **Enable Docker:** Cleared
        *   **Do not use top-level statements:** Cleared

2.  In Visual Studio 2022, set the startup project to the current selection. In Visual Studio Code, select Northwind.Mvc.GraphQLClient as the active OmniSharp project.

3.  In the Northwind.Mvc.GraphQLClient project, add a project reference to the Northwind entity models project, as shown in the following markup:

    ```
    <ItemGroup>
      <ProjectReference Include="..\..\Chapter02\Northwind.Common.EntityModels
    .SqlServer\Northwind.Common.EntityModels.SqlServer.csproj" />
    </ItemGroup>
    ```

     The path to the project must not have a line break.

4.  Build the Northwind.Mvc.GraphQLClient project.

5.  In the Properties folder, in launchSettings.json, modify the applicationUrl to use port 5113 for https and port 5114 for http, as shown highlighted in the following configuration:

    ```
    "profiles": {
      "http": {
        "commandName": "Project",
        "dotnetRunMessages": true,
        "launchBrowser": true,
        "applicationUrl": "http://localhost:5114",
        "environmentVariables": {
          "ASPNETCORE_ENVIRONMENT": "Development"
        }
      },
      "https": {
    ```

```
      "commandName": "Project",
      "dotnetRunMessages": true,
      "launchBrowser": true,
      "applicationUrl": "https://localhost:5113;http://localhost:5114",
      "environmentVariables": {
        "ASPNETCORE_ENVIRONMENT": "Development"
      }
    },
```

6.  In the Northwind.Mvc.GraphQLClient project, in the Models folder, add a new class file named ResponseErrors.cs, as shown in the following code:

```csharp
namespace Northwind.Mvc.GraphQLClient.Models;

public class ResponseErrors
{
  public Error[]? Errors { get; set; }
}

public class Error
{
  public string Message { get; set; } = null!;
  public Location[] Locations { get; set; } = null!;
  public string[] Path { get; set; } = null!;
}

public class Location
{
  public int Line { get; set; }
  public int Column { get; set; }
}
```

7.  In the Models folder, add a new class file named ResponseProducts.cs, as shown in the following code:

```csharp
using Packt.Shared; // Product

namespace Northwind.Mvc.GraphQLClient.Models;

public class ResponseProducts
{
  public class DataProducts
  {
    public Product[]? ProductsInCategory { get; set; }
  }

  public DataProducts? Data { get; set; }
}
```

8.  In the `Models` folder, add a new class file named `ResponseCategories.cs`, as shown in the following code:

```
using Packt.Shared; // Category

namespace Northwind.Mvc.GraphQLClient.Models;

public class ResponseCategories
{
  public class DataCategories
  {
    public Category[]? Categories { get; set; }
  }

  public DataCategories? Data { get; set; }
}
```

9.  In the `Models` folder, add a new class file named `IndexViewModel.cs` that will have properties to store all the data that we might want to show in the view, as shown in the following code:

```
using Packt.Shared; // Product
using System.Net; // HttpStatusCode

namespace Northwind.Mvc.GraphQLClient.Models;

public class IndexViewModel
{
  public HttpStatusCode Code { get; set; }
  public string? RawResponseBody { get; set; }
  public Product[]? Products { get; set; }
  public Category[]? Categories { get; set; }
  public Error[]? Errors { get; set; }
}
```

10. In `Program.cs`, import the namespace for setting HTTP headers, as shown in the following code:

```
using System.Net.Http.Headers; // MediaTypeWithQualityHeaderValue
```

11. In `Program.cs`, after the `CreateBuilder` method call, add statements to register an HTTP client for the GraphQL service, as shown in the following code:

```
builder.Services.AddHttpClient(name: "Northwind.GraphQL",
  configureClient: options =>
  {
    options.BaseAddress = new Uri("https://localhost:5111/");
    options.DefaultRequestHeaders.Accept.Add(
      new MediaTypeWithQualityHeaderValue(
      "application/json", 1.0));
  });
```

12. In the `Controllers` folder, in `HomeController.cs`, import the namespace for working with text encodings and for our Northwind entity models, as shown in the following code:

```
using System.Text; // Encoding
```

13. Define a field to store the registered HTTP client factory, and set it in the constructor, as shown in the following code:

```
protected readonly IHttpClientFactory clientFactory;

public HomeController(ILogger<HomeController> logger,
  IHttpClientFactory clientFactory)
{
  _logger = logger;
  this.clientFactory = clientFactory;
}
```

14. In the `Index` action method, modify the method to be asynchronous. Then, add statements to call the GraphQL service, and note the HTTP request is a `POST`, the media type is for an `application/json` document that contains a GraphQL query, and the query requests the ID, name, and number of units in stock for all products in a given category passed as a parameter named `id`, as shown in the following code:

```
public async Task<IActionResult> Index(string id = "1")
{
  IndexViewModel model = new();

  try
  {
    HttpClient client = clientFactory.CreateClient(
      name: "Northwind.GraphQL");

    // first, try a simple GET request to service root

    HttpRequestMessage request = new(
      method: HttpMethod.Get, requestUri: "/");

    HttpResponseMessage response = await client.SendAsync(request);

    if (!response.IsSuccessStatusCode)
    {
      model.Code = response.StatusCode;
      model.Errors = new[] { new Error { Message =
        "Service is not successfully responding to GET requests." } };
      return View(model);
    }

    // next, make a request to the GraphQL endpoint
```

```
      request = new(
        method: HttpMethod.Post, requestUri: "graphql");

      request.Content = new StringContent(content: $$$"""
        {
          "query": "{productsInCategory(categoryId:{{{id}}}){productId
productName unitsInStock}}"
        }
        """,
        encoding: Encoding.UTF8,
        mediaType: "application/json");

      response = await client.SendAsync(request);

      model.Code = response.StatusCode;
      model.RawResponseBody = await response.Content.ReadAsStringAsync();

      if (response.IsSuccessStatusCode)
      {
        model.Products = (await response.Content
          .ReadFromJsonAsync<ResponseProducts>())?.Data?.ProductsInCategory;
      }
      else
      {
        model.Errors = (await response.Content
          .ReadFromJsonAsync<ResponseErrors>())?.Errors;
      }
    }
    catch (Exception ex)
    {
      _logger.LogWarning(
        $"Northwind.GraphQL service exception: {ex.Message}");

      model.Errors = new[] { new Error { Message = ex.Message } };
    }

    return View(model);
}
```

**Good Practice:** To set the content of our request, we use the C# 11 raw interpolated string literal syntax of three dollar signs and three double quotes. This allows us to embed the `id` variable using three curly braces that do not get confused with the two curly braces after `unitsInStock` that end the query itself.

15. In the `Views/Home` folder, in `Index.cshtml`, delete its existing markup and then add markup

to render the seafood products, as shown in the following markup:

```
@using Packt.Shared
@using Northwind.Mvc.GraphQLClient.Models @* for VS Code only *@
@model IndexViewModel
@{
  ViewData["Title"] = "Products from GraphQL service";
}
<div class="text-center">
  <h1 class="display-4">@ViewData["Title"]</h1>
  <div class="card card-body">
    <form>
      Enter a category id
      <input name="id" value="1" />
      <input type="submit" />
    </form>
  </div>
  @if (Model.Errors is not null)
  {
    <div class="alert alert-danger" role="alert">
      <table class="table table-striped">
        <thead>
        <tr>
          <td>Message</td>
          <td>Path</td>
          <td>Locations</td>
        </tr>
        </thead>
        <tbody>
          @foreach (Error error in Model.Errors)
          {
            <tr>
              <td>@error.Message</td>
              <td>
                @if (error.Path is not null)
                {
                  @foreach (string path in error.Path)
                  {
                    <span class="badge bg-danger">@path</span>
                  }
                }
              </td>
              <td>
                @if (error.Locations is not null)
                {
                  @foreach (Location location in error.Locations)
```

```razor
                    {
                      <span class="badge bg-danger">
                        @location.Line, @location.Column
                      </span>
                    }
                  }
                </td>
              </tr>
            }
          </tbody>
        </table>
      </div>
    }
    @if (Model.Categories is not null)
    {
      <div>
        <p class="alert alert-success" role="alert">
          There are @Model.Categories.Count() products.</p>
        <p>
          @foreach (Category category in Model.Categories)
          {
            <span class="badge bg-dark">
              @category.CategoryId
              @category.CategoryName
            </span>
          }
        </p>
      </div>
    }
    @if (Model.Products is not null)
    {
      <div>
        <p class="alert alert-success" role="alert">
          There are @Model.Products.Count() products.</p>
        <p>
          @foreach (Product p in Model.Products)
          {
            <span class="badge bg-dark">
              @p.ProductId
              @p.ProductName
              -
              @(p.UnitsInStock is null ? "0" : p.UnitsInStock.Value) in
stock
            </span>
          }
        </p>
```

```
      </div>
    }
    <p>
      <a class="btn btn-primary" data-bs-toggle="collapse"
         href="#collapseExample" role="button"
         aria-expanded="false" aria-controls="collapseExample">
        Show/Hide Details
      </a>
    </p>
    <div class="collapse" id="collapseExample">
      <div class="card card-body">
        Status code @((int)Model.Code): @Model.Code
        <hr />
        @Model.RawResponseBody
      </div>
    </div>
  </div>
```

# Testing the .NET client

Now we can test our .NET client:

1.  Start the `Northwind.GraphQL` project using its `https` profile without debugging.
2.  Start the `Northwind.Mvc.GraphQLClient` project using its `https` profile.
3.  Note that products are successfully retrieved using GraphQL, as shown in *Figure 11.10*:

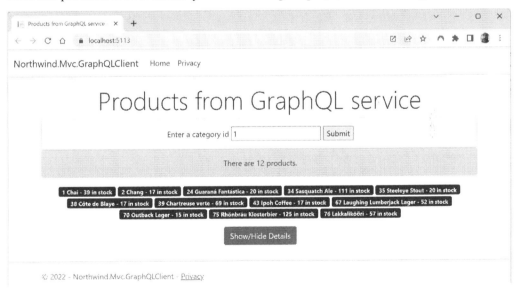

*Figure 11.10: Products in the Beverages category from the GraphQL service*

4.  Enter another category ID that exists, for example, 4.
5.  Enter a category ID that is out of range, for example, 13, and note there are 0 products returned.

6.  Close Chrome and shut down the web server for the `Northwind.Mvc.GraphQLClient` project.

7.  In `HomeController.cs`, modify the query to make a deliberate mistake, like changing `productId` to `productid`.

8.  Start the `Northwind.Mvc.GraphQLClient` project using the `https` profile without debugging.

9.  Click the **Show/Hide Details** button and note the error message and response details, as shown in *Figure 11.11*:

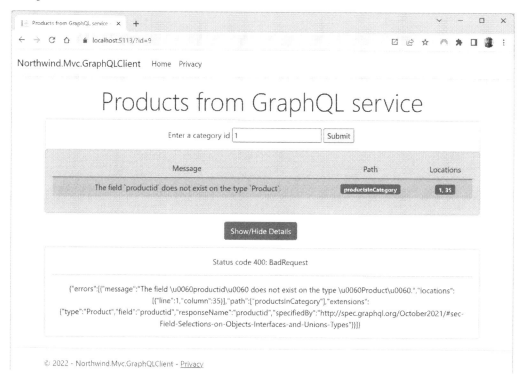

*Figure 11.11: Showing error details*

10. Close Chrome and shut down both web servers.

# Understanding Strawberry Shake

Instead of using ordinary HTTP clients, ChilliCream has a GraphQL client library to more easily build .NET clients to GraphQL services. You can learn more about it at the following link:

```
https://chillicream.com/docs/strawberryshake
```

# Creating a console app client

Now let's create another client using Strawberry Shake so that you can see the benefits:

1.  Use your preferred code editor to add a new **Console App**/console project named `Northwind.GraphQL.Client.Console`.

2. At the command line or terminal for the project folder, create a tools manifest file, as shown in the following command:

```
dotnet new tool-manifest
```

3. At the command line or terminal, install the Strawberry Shake tools, as shown in the following command:

```
dotnet tool install StrawberryShake.Tools --local
```

4. In the project, treat warnings as errors, add references to NuGet packages for Microsoft extensions for dependency injection and HTTP, and for Strawberry Shake code generation and HTTP transport, and globally and statically import the Console class, as shown highlighted in the following markup:

```xml
<Project Sdk="Microsoft.NET.Sdk">

  <PropertyGroup>
    <OutputType>Exe</OutputType>
    <TargetFramework>net7.0</TargetFramework>
    <ImplicitUsings>enable</ImplicitUsings>
    <Nullable>enable</Nullable>
    <TreatWarningsAsErrors>true</TreatWarningsAsErrors>
  </PropertyGroup>

  <ItemGroup>
    <PackageReference Include="Microsoft.Extensions.DependencyInjection"
                      Version="7.0.0" />
    <PackageReference Include="Microsoft.Extensions.Http"
                      Version="7.0.0" />
    <PackageReference Include=
                      "StrawberryShake.CodeGeneration.CSharp.Analyzers"
                      Version="13.0.0" />
    <PackageReference Include="StrawberryShake.Transport.Http"
                      Version="13.0.0" />
  </ItemGroup>

  <ItemGroup>
    <Using Include="System.Console" Static="true" />
  </ItemGroup>

</Project>
```

 At the time of writing, the versions of the two Strawberry Shake packages were 12.14.0. By the time this book is published I expect them to be 13.0.0 or later, but if they have not reached general availability yet, then use the older version number.

5. Build the `Northwind.GraphQL.Client.Console` project.

6. Start the GraphQL service using the `https` profile without debugging.

7. At the command line or terminal, add a client for your GraphQL service, as shown in the following command:

```
dotnet graphql init https://localhost:5111/graphql/ -n NorthwindClient
```

8. In the `Northwind.GraphQL.Client.Console` project, in the `.graphqlrc.json` file, add an entry to control the C# namespace used during code generation, as shown highlighted in the following markup:

```
{
  "schema": "schema.graphql",
  "documents": "**/*.graphql",
  "extensions": {
    "strawberryShake": {
      "name": "NorthwindClient",
      "namespace": "Northwind.GraphQL.Client.Console",
      "url": "https://localhost:5111/graphql/",
      "dependencyInjection": true,
      "strictSchemaValidation": true,
      "hashAlgorithm": "md5",
      "useSingleFile": true,
      "requestStrategy": "Default",
      "outputDirectoryName": "Generated",
      "noStore": false,
      "emitGeneratedCode": true,
      "razorComponents": false,
      "records": {
        "inputs": false,
        "entities": false
      },
      "transportProfiles": [
        {
          "default": "Http",
          "subscription": "WebSocket"
        }
      ]
    }
  }
}
```

9. Add a new file named `seafoodProducts.graphql` that defines a query to get seafood products, as shown in the following document:

```
query seafoodProducts {
  productsInCategory(categoryId:8) {
```

```
      productId
      productName
      unitsInStock
  }
}
```

Query files used by Strawberry Shake must be named.

10. Build the `Northwind.GraphQL.Client.Console` project.

11. Note the **Generated** folder that was autogenerated and the file in it, as shown in *Figure 11.12*:

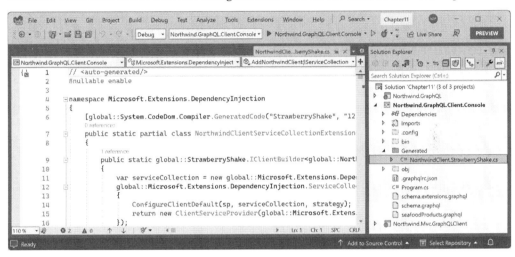

*Figure 11.12: The generated class file for the Northwind GraphQL service*

12. In `Program.cs`, delete the existing statements. Add statements to create a new service collection, add the autogenerated `NorthwindClient` to it with the correct URL for the service, and then get and use the dependency service to fetch the seafood products, as shown in the following code:

```csharp
using Microsoft.Extensions.DependencyInjection; // ServiceCollection
using Northwind.GraphQL.Client.Console; // INorthwindClient
using StrawberryShake; // EnsureNoErrors extension method

ServiceCollection serviceCollection = new();

serviceCollection
  .AddNorthwindClient()
  .ConfigureHttpClient(client =>
    client.BaseAddress = new Uri("https://localhost:5111/graphql"));

IServiceProvider services = serviceCollection.BuildServiceProvider();
```

```
INorthwindClient client = services.GetRequiredService<INorthwindClient>();

var result = await client.SeafoodProducts.ExecuteAsync();
result.EnsureNoErrors();

if (result.Data is null)
{
  WriteLine("No data!");
  return;
}

foreach (var product in result.Data.ProductsInCategory)
{
  WriteLine("{0}: {1}",
    product.ProductId, product.ProductName);
}
```

13. Run the console app and note the results, as shown in the following output:

```
10: Ikura
13: Konbu
18: Carnarvon Tigers
30: Nord-Ost Matjeshering
36: Inlagd Sill
37: Gravad lax
40: Boston Crab Meat
41: Jack's New England Clam Chowder
45: Rogede sild
46: Spegesild
58: Escargots de Bourgogne
73: Röd Kaviar
```

# Implementing GraphQL mutations

Most services need to modify data as well as query it. GraphQL calls these **mutations**. A mutation has three related components:

- The mutation itself, which defines the change that will be made to the graph. It should be named using a verb, a noun, and use camel casing, for example, addProduct.

- The **input** is the input for a mutation, and it should have the same name as the mutation with a suffix of Input, for example, AddProductInput. Although there is only one input, it is an object graph so can be as complex as you need.

- The **payload** is the returned document for a mutation, and it should have the same name as the mutation with a suffix of Payload, for example, AddProductPayload. Although there is only one payload, it is an object graph so can be as complex as you need.

Let's define mutations for adding, updating, and deleting products:

1. In the `Northwind.GraphQL` project/folder, add a class file named `Mutation.cs`.
2. In the class file, define a record and two classes to represent the three types needed to perform an `addProduct` mutation, as shown in the following code:

```csharp
using Packt.Shared; // Product

namespace Northwind.GraphQL;

public record AddProductInput(
    string ProductName,
    int? SupplierId,
    int? CategoryId,
    string QuantityPerUnit,
    decimal? UnitPrice,
    short? UnitsInStock,
    short? UnitsOnOrder,
    short? ReorderLevel,
    bool Discontinued);

public class AddProductPayload
{
    public AddProductPayload(Product product)
    {
        Product = product;
    }

    public Product Product { get; }
}

public class Mutation
{
    public async Task<AddProductPayload> AddProductAsync(
        AddProductInput input, NorthwindContext db)
    {
        Product product = new()
        {
            ProductName = input.ProductName,
            SupplierId = input.SupplierId,
            CategoryId = input.CategoryId,
            QuantityPerUnit = input.QuantityPerUnit,
            UnitPrice = input.UnitPrice,
            UnitsInStock = input.UnitsInStock,
            UnitsOnOrder = input.UnitsOnOrder,
            ReorderLevel = input.ReorderLevel,
            Discontinued = input.Discontinued
```

```
    };

    db.Products.Add(product);

    int affectedRows = await db.SaveChangesAsync();

    return new AddProductPayload(product);
  }
}
```

3. In `Program.cs`, add a call to the `AddMutationType<T>` method to register your `Mutation` class, as shown highlighted in the following code:

```
builder.Services
  .AddGraphQLServer()
  .RegisterDbContext<NorthwindContext>()
  .AddQueryType<Query>()
  .AddMutationType<Mutation>();
```

4. Start the `Northwind.GraphQL` service project using the `https` profile without debugging.

5. In **Banana Cake Pop**, click the **Schema Definition** tab, and note the mutation type, as partially shown in *Figure 11.13*:

*Figure 11.13: Schema for mutating a product using GraphQL*

6. Note the full schema definitions for the `addProduct` mutation and its related types in the following code:

```
type Mutation {
  addProduct(input: AddProductInput!): AddProductPayload!
}

type Product {
  productId: Int!
  productName: String!
  supplierId: Int
  categoryId: Int
  quantityPerUnit: String
```

```
    unitPrice: Decimal
    unitsInStock: Short
    unitsOnOrder: Short
    reorderLevel: Short
    discontinued: Boolean!
    category: Category
    supplier: Supplier
    orderDetails: [OrderDetail!]!
}

...

type AddProductPayload {
    product: Product!
}

input AddProductInput {
    productName: String!
    supplierId: Int
    categoryId: Int
    quantityPerUnit: String!
    unitPrice: Decimal
    unitsInStock: Short
    unitsOnOrder: Short
    reorderLevel: Short
    discontinued: Boolean!
}
```

7. Click the **Operations** tab and, if necessary, create a new blank document, and then enter a mutation to add a new product named `Tasty Burgers`, as shown in the following code:

```
mutation AddProduct {
  addProduct(
    input: {
      productName: "Tasty Burgers"
      supplierId: 1
      categoryId: 2
      quantityPerUnit: "6 per box"
      unitPrice: 40
      unitsInStock: 0
      unitsOnOrder: 0
      reorderLevel: 0
      discontinued: false
    }
  )
  {
    product {
```

```
        productId
        productName
      }
    }
  }
}
```

8. Click **Execute** or the **Run** button, and note the new product has been successfully added and assigned the next sequential number by the SQL Server database, as shown in the following output and in *Figure 11.14*:

```
{
  "data": {
    "addProduct": {
      "product": {
        "productId": 79,
        "productName": "Tasty Burgers"
      }
    }
  }
}
```

*Figure 11.14: Adding a new product using a GraphQL mutation*

9. Close the browser and shut down the web server.

# Practicing and exploring

Test your knowledge and understanding by answering some questions, getting some hands-on practice, and exploring this chapter's topics with deeper research.

# Exercise 11.1 — Test your knowledge

Answer the following questions:

1. What transport protocol does a GraphQL service use?
2. What media type does GraphQL use for its queries?
3. How can you parameterize GraphQL queries?
4. What are the benefits of using Strawberry Shake over a regular HTTP client for GraphQL queries?
5. How might you insert a new product into the Northwind database?

# Exercise 11.2 — Explore topics

Use the links on the following page to learn more details about the topics covered in this chapter:

```
https://github.com/markjprice/apps-services-net7/blob/main/book-links.md#chapter-11--
-combining-data-sources-using-graphql
```

# Exercise 11.3 — Practice building .NET clients

In `HomeController.cs`, add an action method named `Categories` and implement it to query the `categories` field with a variable for the id. On the page, allow the visitor to submit an id and see the category information and a list of its products.

# Summary

In this chapter, you learned:

- Some of the concepts around GraphQL.
- How to build a `Query` class with fields that represent entities that can be queried.
- How to use the Banana Cake Pop tool to explore a GraphQL service schema.
- How to use the REST Client extension to `POST` to a GraphQL service.
- How to create a .NET client for a GraphQL service.
- How to implement GraphQL mutations.

In the next chapter, you will learn about the gRPC service technology that can be used to implement very efficient microservices.

# Join our book's Discord space

Join the book's Discord workspace for *Ask me Anything* sessions with the author.

https://packt.link/apps_and_services_dotnet7

# 12

# Building Efficient Microservices Using gRPC

In this chapter, you will be introduced to gRPC, which enables a developer to build highly efficient services across most platforms. However, web browsers do not have full support for programmatic access to all features of HTTP/2, which is required by gRPC. This makes gRPC most useful for implementing intermediate tier-to-tier services and microservices because they must perform a lot of communication between multiple microservices to achieve a complete task.

Improving the efficiency of that communication is vital to success for the scalability and performance of microservices. A monolithic, two-tier, client-to-service style service could get away with being less efficient because there is only one layer of communication. The more tiers and therefore the more layers of communication there are between microservices, the more important efficient communication between those layers becomes, as shown in *Figure 12.1*:

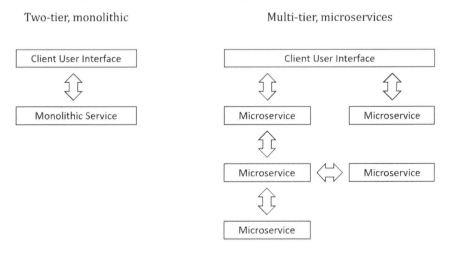

*Figure 12.1: Comparing a two-tier monolithic service with multi-tier microservices*

This chapter will cover the following topics:

- Understanding gRPC
- Building a gRPC service and client
- Implementing gRPC for an EF Core model
- Implementing gRPC JSON transcoding

# Understanding gRPC

gRPC is a modern open-source high-performance **Remote Procedure Call** (**RPC**) framework that can run in any environment. An RPC is when one computer calls a procedure in another process or on another computer over a network as if it were calling a local procedure. It is an example of a client-server architecture.

 You can learn more about the RPCs at the following link: `https://en.wikipedia.org/ wiki/Remote_procedure_call`.

## How gRPC works

A gRPC service developer defines a service interface for the methods that can be called remotely, including defining the method parameters and return types. The service implements this interface and runs a gRPC server to handle client calls.

On the client, a strongly typed gRPC client provides the same methods as on the server.

## Defining gRPC contracts with .proto files

gRPC uses contract-first API development that supports language-agnostic implementations. A **contract** in this case is an agreement that a service will expose a defined list of methods with specified parameters and return types that implement a prescribed behavior. A client that wishes to call the service can be certain that the service will continue to conform to the contract over time. For example, although new methods might be added, existing ones will never change or be removed.

You write the contracts using `.proto` files that have their own language syntax, and then use tools to convert them into various languages, like C#. The `.proto` files are used by both the server and client to exchange messages in the correct format.

## gRPC benefits

gRPC minimizes network usage by using **Protobuf** binary serialization that is not human-readable, unlike JSON or XML used by web services.

gRPC requires HTTP/2, which provides significant performance benefits over earlier versions, like binary framing and compression, and multiplexing of HTTP/2 calls over a single connection.

Binary framing means how the HTTP messages are transferred between the client and server. HTTP/1.x uses newline delimited plaintext. HTTP/2 splits communication into smaller messages (frames) that are encoded in binary format. Multiplexing means combining multiple messages from different sources into a single message to more efficiently use a shared resource like a network transport.

## gRPC limitations

The main limitation of gRPC is that it cannot be used in web browsers because no browser provides the level of control required to support a gRPC client. For example, browsers do not allow a caller to require that HTTP/2 be used.

Another limitation for developers is that due to the binary format of the messages, it is harder to diagnose and monitor issues. Many tools do not understand the format and cannot show the messages in a human-readable format.

There is an initiative called **gRPC-Web** that adds an extra proxy layer, and the proxy forwards requests to the gRPC server. However, it only supports a subset of gRPC due to the listed limitations.

## Types of gRPC methods

gRPC has four types of method:

- **Unary** methods have structured request and response messages. A unary method completes when the response message is returned. Unary methods should be chosen in all scenarios that do not require a stream.
- **Streaming** methods are used when a large amount of data must be exchanged, and they do so using a stream of bytes. They have the `stream` keyword prefix for either an input parameter, an output parameter, or both:
  - **Server streaming** methods receive a request message from the client and return a stream. Multiple messages can be returned over the stream. A server streaming call ends when the server-side method returns, but the server-side method could run until it receives a cancellation token from the client.
  - **Client streaming** methods only receive a stream from the client without any message. The server-side method processes the stream until it is ready to return a response message. Once the server-side method returns its message, the client streaming call is done.
  - **Bi-directional streaming** methods only receive a stream from the client without any message and only return data via a second stream. The call is done when the server-side method returns. Once a bi-directional streaming method is called, the client and service can send messages to each other at any time.

In this book, we will only look at the details of unary methods. If you would like the next edition to cover streaming methods, please let me know.

## Microsoft's gRPC packages

Microsoft has invested in building a set of packages for .NET to work with gRPC and, since May 2021, it is Microsoft's recommended implementation of gRPC for .NET.

Microsoft's gRPC for .NET includes:

- `Grpc.AspNetCore` for hosting a gRPC service in ASP.NET Core.
- `Grpc.Net.Client` for adding gRPC client support to any .NET project by building on `HttpClient`.
- `Grpc.Net.ClientFactory` for adding gRPC client support to any .NET code base by building on `HttpClientFactory`.

 You can learn more at the following link: `https://github.com/grpc/grpc-dotnet`.

# Building a gRPC service and client

Let's see an example service and client for sending and receiving simple messages.

## Building a Hello World gRPC service

We will start by building the gRPC service using one of the project templates provided as standard:

1.  Use your preferred code editor to create a new project, as defined in the following list:

    - Project template: **ASP.NET Core gRPC Service**/grpc
    - Workspace/solution file and folder: `Chapter12`
    - Project file and folder: `Northwind.Grpc.Service`

     For working with `.proto` files in Visual Studio Code, you can install the extension **vscode-proto3** (`zxh404.vscode-proto3`).

2.  In the `Protos` folder, in `greet.proto`, note that it defines a service named `Greeter` with a method named `SayHello` that exchanges messages named `HelloRequest` and `HelloReply`, as shown in the following code:

    ```
    syntax = "proto3";

    option csharp_namespace = "Northwind.Grpc.Service";

    package greet;

    // The greeting service definition.
    service Greeter {
      // Sends a greeting
      rpc SayHello (HelloRequest) returns (HelloReply);
    }
    ```

```
// The request message containing the user's name.
message HelloRequest {
  string name = 1;
}

// The response message containing the greetings.
message HelloReply {
  string message = 1;
}
```

3. In `Northwind.Grpc.Service.csproj`, note that the `.proto` file is registered for use on the server-side and also note the package reference for implementing a gRPC service hosted in ASP.NET Core, as shown in the following markup:

```
<ItemGroup>
  <Protobuf Include="Protos\greet.proto" GrpcServices="Server" />
</ItemGroup>

<ItemGroup>
  <PackageReference Include="Grpc.AspNetCore" Version="2.48.0" />
</ItemGroup>
```

4. In the `Services` folder, in `GreeterService.cs`, note that it inherits from a class named `GreeterBase` and it asynchronously implements the `Greeter` service contract by having a `SayHello` method that accepts a `HelloRequest` input parameter and returns a `HelloReply`, as shown in the following code:

```
using Grpc.Core;
using Northwind.Grpc.Service;

namespace Northwind.Grpc.Service.Services
{
  public class GreeterService : Greeter.GreeterBase
  {
    private readonly ILogger<GreeterService> _logger;

    public GreeterService(ILogger<GreeterService> logger)
    {
      _logger = logger;
    }

    public override Task<HelloReply> SayHello(
      HelloRequest request, ServerCallContext context)
    {
      return Task.FromResult(new HelloReply
      {
        Message = "Hello " + request.Name
      });
```

```
        }
      }
    }
```

5.  If you are using Visual Studio 2022, in **Solution Explorer**, click **Show All Files**.

6.  In the `obj\Debug\net7.0\Protos` folder, note the two class files named `Greet.cs` and `GreetGrpc.cs` that are automatically generated from the `greet.proto` file, as shown in *Figure 12.2*:

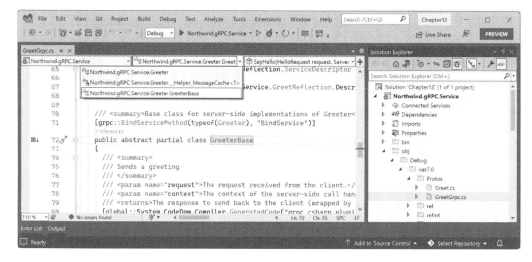

*Figure 12.2: The autogenerated class files from a .proto file for a gRPC service*

7.  In `GreetGrpc.cs`, note the `Greeter.GreeterBase` class that the `GreeterService` class inherited from. You do not need to understand how this base class is implemented, but you should know it is what handles all the details of gRPC's efficient communication.

8.  If you are using Visual Studio 2022, in **Solution Explorer**, expand **Dependencies**, expand **Packages**, expand **Grpc.AspNetCore**, and note that it has dependencies on Google's **Google.Protobuf** package, and Microsoft's **Grpc.AspNetCore.Server.ClientFactory** and **Grpc.Tools** packages, as shown in *Figure 12.3*:

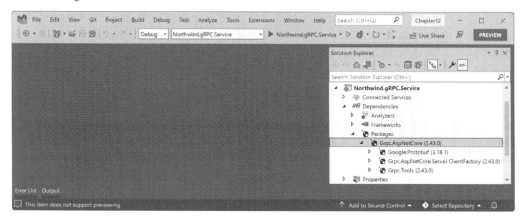

*Figure 12.3: The Grpc.AspNetCore package references the Grpc.Tools and Google.Protobuf packages*

The Grpc.Tools package generates the C# class files from the registered .proto files, and those class files use types defined in Google's package to implement the serialization to the Protobuf serialization format. The Grpc.AspNetCore.Server. ClientFactory package includes both server-side and client-side support for gRPC in a .NET project.

9. In Program.cs, in the section that configures services, note the call to add gRPC to the services collection, as shown in the following code:

```
builder.Services.AddGrpc();
```

10. In Program.cs, in the section for configuring the HTTP pipeline, note the call to map the Greeter service, as shown in the following code:

```
app.MapGrpcService<GreeterService>();
```

11. In the Properties folder, open launchSettings.json and modify the applicationUrl setting to use port 5121, as shown highlighted in the following markup:

```
{
  "profiles": {
    "Northwind.Grpc.Service": {
      "commandName": "Project",
      "dotnetRunMessages": true,
      "launchBrowser": false,
      "applicationUrl": "https://localhost:5121",
      "environmentVariables": {
        "ASPNETCORE_ENVIRONMENT": "Development"
      }
    }
  }
}
```

12. Build the Northwind.Grpc.Service project.

# Building a Hello World gRPC client

We will add an ASP.NET Core MVC website project and then add the gRPC client packages to enable it to call the gRPC service:

1. Use your preferred code editor to add a new project, as defined in the following list:

    • Project template: **ASP.NET Core Web App (Model-View-Controller)**/mvc

    • Workspace/solution file and folder: Chapter12

    • Project file and folder: Northwind.Grpc.Client.Mvc

    • If you are using Visual Studio 2022, set the startup project to the current selection.

2.  In the `Northwind.Grpc.Client.Mvc` project, add package references for Microsoft's gRPC client factory and tools, and Google's .NET library for Protocol Buffers, as shown in the following markup:

```
<ItemGroup>
  <PackageReference Include="Grpc.Net.ClientFactory" Version="2.48.0" />
  <PackageReference Include="Grpc.Tools" Version="2.48.0">
    <PrivateAssets>all</PrivateAssets>
    <IncludeAssets>runtime; build; native; contentfiles;
      analyzers; buildtransitive</IncludeAssets>
  </PackageReference>
  <PackageReference Include="Google.Protobuf" Version="3.21.5" />
</ItemGroup>
```

**Good Practice:** The `Grpc.Net.ClientFactory` package references the `Grpc.Net.Client` package that implements client-side support for gRPC in a .NET project, but it does not reference other packages like `Grpc.Tools` or `Google.Protobuf`. We must reference those packages explicitly. The `Grpc.Tools` package is only used during development, so it is marked as `PrivateAssets=all` to ensure that the tools are not published with the production website.

3.  In the `Properties` folder, open `launchSettings.json` and modify the `applicationUrl` setting to use port 5122, as shown highlighted in the following markup:

```
{
  "profiles": {
    "Northwind.Grpc.Client.Mvc": {
      "commandName": "Project",
      "dotnetRunMessages": true,
      "launchBrowser": false,
      "applicationUrl": "https://localhost:5122",
      "environmentVariables": {
        "ASPNETCORE_ENVIRONMENT": "Development"
      }
    }
  }
}
```

4.  Copy the `Protos` folder from the `Northwind.Grpc.Service` project/folder to the `Northwind.Grpc.Client.Mvc` project/folder.

In Visual Studio 2022, you can drag and drop to copy. In Visual Studio Code, drag and drop while holding the *Ctrl* or *Cmd* key.

5. In the `Northwind.Grpc.Client.Mvc` project, in the `Protos` folder, in `greet.proto`, modify the namespace to match the namespace for the current project so that the automatically generated classes will be in the same namespace, as shown in the following code:

```
option csharp_namespace = "Northwind.Grpc.Client.Mvc";
```

6. In the `Northwind.Grpc.Client.Mvc` project file, add or modify the item group that registers the `.proto` file to indicate that it is being used on the client side, as shown highlighted in the following markup:

```
<ItemGroup>
  <Protobuf Include="Protos\greet.proto" GrpcServices="Client" />
</ItemGroup>
```

 Visual Studio 2022 will have created the item group for you, but it will set the `GrpcServices` to `Server` by default, so you must manually change that to `Client`.

7. Build the `Northwind.Grpc.Client.Mvc` project to ensure that the automatically generated classes are created.

8. In the `obj\Debug\net7.0\Protos` folder, in `GreetGrpc.cs`, note the `Greeter.GreeterClient` class, as partially shown in the following code:

```
public static partial class Greeter
{
  ...
  public partial class GreeterClient : grpc::ClientBase<GreeterClient>
  {
```

9. In `Program.cs`, import the namespace for `Greeter.GreeterClient`, as shown in the following code:

```
using Northwind.Grpc.Client.Mvc; // Greeter.GreeterClient
```

10. In `Program.cs`, in the section of configuring services, and a statement to add the `GreeterClient` as a named gRPC client that will be communicating with a service that is listening on port 5121, as shown in the following code:

```
builder.Services.AddGrpcClient<Greeter.GreeterClient>("Greeter",
  options =>
  {
    options.Address = new Uri("https://localhost:5121");
  });
```

11. In the `Controllers` folder, in `HomeController.cs`, import the namespaces to work with gRPC channels and the gRPC client factory, as shown in the following code:

```
using Grpc.Net.Client; // GrpcChannel
```

```
using Grpc.Net.ClientFactory; // GrpcClientFactory
```

12. In the controller class, declare a field to store a greeter client instance and set it by using the client factory in the constructor, as shown highlighted in the following code:

```
public class HomeController : Controller
{
  private readonly ILogger<HomeController> _logger;
  protected readonly Greeter.GreeterClient greeterClient;

  public HomeController(ILogger<HomeController> logger,
    GrpcClientFactory factory)
  {
    _logger = logger;
    greeterClient = factory.CreateClient<Greeter.
GreeterClient>("Greeter");
  }
```

13. In the `Index` action method, make the method asynchronous, add a `string` parameter named name with a default value of `Henrietta`, and then add statements to use the gRPC client to call the `SayHelloAsync` method, passing a `HelloRequest` object and storing the `HelloReply` response in `ViewData`, while catching any exceptions, as shown highlighted in the following code:

```
public async Task<IActionResult> Index(string name = "Henrietta")
{
  try
  {
    HelloReply reply = await greeterClient.SayHelloAsync(
      new HelloRequest { Name = name });

    ViewData["greeting"] = "Greeting from gRPC service: " + reply.
Message;
  }
  catch (Exception ex)
  {
    _logger.LogWarning($"Northwind.Grpc.Service is not responding.");
    ViewData["exception"] = ex.Message;
  }

  return View();
}
```

14. In `Views/Home`, in `Index.cshtml`, after the Welcome heading, remove the existing `<p>` element and then add markup to render a form for the visitor to enter their name, and then if they submit and the gRPC service responds, to output the greeting, as shown in the following markup:

```
<div class="alert alert-secondary">
  <form>
```

```
      <input name="name" placeholder="Enter your name" />
      <input type="submit" />
   </form>
</div>
@if (ViewData["greeting"] is not null)
{
   <p class="alert alert-primary">@ViewData["greeting"]</p>
}
@if (ViewData["exception"] is not null)
{
   <p class="alert alert-danger">@ViewData["exception"]</p>
}
```

 If you clean a gRPC project, then you will lose the automatically generated types and see compile errors. To recreate them, simply make any change to a .proto file or close and reopen the project/solution.

## Testing a gRPC service and client

Now we can start the gRPC service and see if the MVC website can call it successfully:

1.  Start the `Northwind.Grpc.Service` project without debugging.
2.  Start the `Northwind.Grpc.Client.Mvc` project.
3.  If necessary, start a browser and navigate to the home page: `https://localhost:5122/`.
4.  Note the greeting on the home page, as shown in *Figure 12.4*:

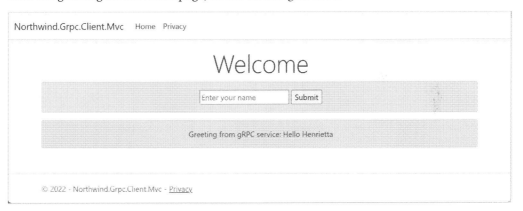

*Figure 12.4: Home page after calling the gRPC service to get a greeting*

5.  View the command prompt or terminal for the ASP.NET Core MVC project and note the info messages that indicate an HTTP/2 POST was processed by the `greet.Greeter/SayHello` endpoint in about 41 ms, as shown in the following output:

```
info: System.Net.Http.HttpClient.Greeter.LogicalHandler[100]
```

```
        Start processing HTTP request POST https://localhost:5121/greet.
Greeter/SayHello
info: System.Net.Http.HttpClient.Greeter.ClientHandler[100]
        Sending HTTP request POST https://localhost:5121/greet.Greeter/
SayHello
info: System.Net.Http.HttpClient.Greeter.ClientHandler[101]
        Received HTTP response headers after 60.5352ms - 200
info: System.Net.Http.HttpClient.Greeter.LogicalHandler[101]
        End processing HTTP request after 69.1623ms - 200
```

6.  Enter and submit another name in the page.

7.  Close the browser and shut down the web servers.

# Implementing gRPC for an EF Core model

Now we will add a service for working with the Northwind database to the gRPC project.

## Implementing the gRPC service

We will reference the EF Core model that you created in *Chapter 2*, *Managing Relational Data Using SQL Server*, then define a contract for the gRPC service using a .proto file, and finally implement the service:

1.  In the Northwind.Grpc.Service project, add a project reference to the Northwind database context project, as shown in the following markup:

    ```
    <ItemGroup>
      <ProjectReference Include="..\..\Chapter02\Northwind.Common.DataContext
    .SqlServer\Northwind.Common.DataContext.SqlServer.csproj" />
    </ItemGroup>
    ```

     The Include path must not have a line break.

2.  At the command line or terminal, build the Northwind.Grpc.Service project.

3.  In the Northwind.Grpc.Service project, in the Protos folder, add a new file (the item template is named **Protocol Buffer File** in Visual Studio 2022) named shipper.proto, as shown in the following code:

    ```
    syntax = "proto3";

    option csharp_namespace = "Northwind.Grpc.Service";

    package shipper;

    service Shipper {
      rpc GetShipper (ShipperRequest) returns (ShipperReply);
    ```

```
}

message ShipperRequest {
  int32 shipperId = 1;
}

message ShipperReply {
  int32 shipperId = 1;
  string companyName = 2;
  string phone = 3;
}
```

4. Open the project file and add an entry to include the shipper.proto file, as shown highlighted in the following markup:

```
<ItemGroup>
  <Protobuf Include="Protos\greet.proto" GrpcServices="Server" />
  <Protobuf Include="Protos\shipper.proto" GrpcServices="Server" />
</ItemGroup>
```

5. Build the Northwind.Grpc.Service project.

6. In the Services folder, add a new class file named ShipperService.cs, and modify its contents to define a shipper service that uses the Northwind database context to return shippers, as shown in the following code:

```
using Grpc.Core; // ServerCallContext
using Packt.Shared; // NorthwindContext
using ShipperEntity = Packt.Shared.Shipper;

namespace Northwind.Grpc.Service.Services;

public class ShipperService : Shipper.ShipperBase
{
  protected readonly ILogger<ShipperService> _logger;
  protected readonly NorthwindContext db;

  public ShipperService(ILogger<ShipperService> logger,
    NorthwindContext db)
  {
    _logger = logger;
    this.db = db;
  }

  public override async Task<ShipperReply?> GetShipper(
    ShipperRequest request, ServerCallContext context)
  {
    ShipperEntity? shipper = await db.Shippers.FindAsync(request.
ShipperId);
```

```
      if (shipper == null)
      {
        return null;
      }
      else
      {
        return ToShipperReply(shipper);
      }
    }

    private ShipperReply ToShipperReply(ShipperEntity shipper)
    {
      return new ShipperReply
      {
        ShipperId = shipper.ShipperId,
        CompanyName = shipper.CompanyName,
        Phone = shipper.Phone
      };
    }
}
```

 The .proto file generates classes that represent the messages sent to and from a gRPC service. We therefore cannot use the entity classes defined for the EF Core model. We need a helper method like **ToShipperReply** that can map an instance of an entity class to an instance of the .proto-generated classes like **ShipperReply**. This could be a good use for AutoMapper, although in this case the mapping is simple enough to hand-code.

7.   In Program.cs, import the namespace for the Northwind database context, as shown in the following code:

```
using Packt.Shared; // AddNorthwindContext extension method
```

8.   In the section that configures services, add a call to register the Northwind database context, as shown in the following code:

```
builder.Services.AddNorthwindContext();
```

9.   In the section that configures the HTTP pipeline, after the call to register GreeterService, add a statement to register ShipperService, as shown in the following code:

```
app.MapGrpcService<ShipperService>();
```

## Implementing the gRPC client

Now we can add client capabilities to the Northwind MVC website:

1. Copy the `shipper.proto` file from the `Protos` folder in the `Northwind.Grpc.Service` project to the `Protos` folder in the `Northwind.Grpc.Client.Mvc` project.

2. In the `Northwind.Grpc.Client.Mvc` project, in `shipper.proto`, modify the namespace to match the namespace for the current project so that the automatically generated classes will be in the same namespace, as shown in the following code:

```
option csharp_namespace = "Northwind.Grpc.Client.Mvc";
```

3. In the `Northwind.Grpc.Client.Mvc` project file, modify or add the entry to register the `.proto` file as being used on the client side, as shown highlighted in the following markup:

```
<ItemGroup>
  <Protobuf Include="Protos\greet.proto" GrpcServices="Client" />
  <Protobuf Include="Protos\shipper.proto" GrpcServices="Client" />
</ItemGroup>
```

4. In the `Northwind.Grpc.Client.Mvc` project file, in `Program.cs`, add a statement to register the `ShipperClient` class to connect to the gRPC service listening on port 5121, as shown in the following code:

```
builder.Services.AddGrpcClient<Shipper.ShipperClient>("Shipper",
  options =>
  {
    options.Address = new Uri("https://localhost:5121");
  });
```

5. In the `Controllers` folder, in `HomeController.cs`, declare a field to store a shipper client instance and set it by using the client factory in the constructor, as shown highlighted in the following code:

```
public class HomeController : Controller
{
  private readonly ILogger<HomeController> _logger;
  protected readonly Greeter.GreeterClient greeterClient;
  protected readonly Shipper.ShipperClient shipperClient;

  public HomeController(ILogger<HomeController> logger,
    GrpcClientFactory factory)
  {
    _logger = logger;
    greeterClient = factory.CreateClient<Greeter.GreeterClient>("Greeter");
    shipperClient = factory.CreateClient<Shipper.ShipperClient>("Shipper");
  }
```

6. In `HomeController.cs`, in the `Index` action method, add a parameter named `id` and statements to call the `Shipper` gRPC service to get a shipper with the matching `ShipperId`, as shown highlighted in the following code:

```
public async Task<IActionResult> Index(
  string name = "Henrietta", int id = 1)
{
  try
  {
    HelloReply reply = await greeterClient.SayHelloAsync(
      new HelloRequest { Name = name });

    ViewData["greeting"] = "Greeting from gRPC service: " + reply.
Message;

    ShipperReply shipperReply = await shipperClient.GetShipperAsync(
      new ShipperRequest { ShipperId = id });

    ViewData["shipper"] = "Shipper from gRPC service: " +
      $"ID: {shipperReply.ShipperId}, Name: {shipperReply.CompanyName},"
      + $" Phone: {shipperReply.Phone}.";
  }
  catch (Exception ex)
  {
    _logger.LogWarning($"Northwind.Grpc.Service is not responding.");
    ViewData["exception"] = ex.Message;
  }

  return View();
}
```

7. In `Views/Home`, in `Index.cshtml`, add code to render a form for the visitor to enter a shipper ID, and render the shipper details after the greeting, as shown highlighted in the following markup:

```
@{
  ViewData["Title"] = "Home Page";
}
<div class="text-center">
  <h1 class="display-4">Welcome</h1>
  <div class="alert alert-secondary">
    <form>
      <input name="name" placeholder="Enter your name" />
      <input type="submit" />
    </form>
    <form>
      <input name="id" placeholder="Enter a shipper id" />
      <input type="submit" />
```

```
      </form>
    </div>
    @if (ViewData["greeting"] is not null)
    {
      <p class="alert alert-primary">@ViewData["greeting"]</p>
    }
    @if (ViewData["exception"] is not null)
    {
      <p class="alert alert-danger">@ViewData["exception"]</p>
    }
    @if (ViewData["shipper"] is not null)
    {
      <p class="alert alert-primary">@ViewData["shipper"]</p>
    }
  </div>
```

8.  Start the `Northwind.Grpc.Service` project without debugging.
9.  Start the `Northwind.Grpc.Client.Mvc` project.
10. If necessary, start a browser and navigate to the home page: `https://localhost:5122/`.
11. Note the shipper information on the services page, as shown in *Figure 12.5*:

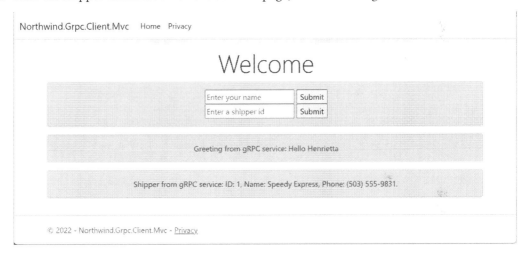

*Figure 12.5: Home page after calling the gRPC service to get a shipper*

12. There are three shippers in the Northwind database with IDs of 1, 2, and 3. Try entering their IDs to ensure they can all be retrieved, and try entering an ID that does not exist, like 4.
13. Close the browser and shut down the web servers.

## Getting request and response metadata

Formally defined request and response messages as part of a contract are not the only mechanism to pass data between client and service. You can also use metadata sent as headers and trailers. Both are simple dictionaries that are passed along with the messages.

Let's see how you can get metadata about a gRPC call:

1. In `HomeController.cs`, import the namespace to use the `AsyncUnaryCall<T>` class, as shown in the following code:

   ```
   using Grpc.Core; // AsyncUnaryCall<T>
   ```

2. In the `Index` method, comment out the statement that makes the call to the gRPC shipper service. Add statements that get the underlying `AsyncUnaryCall<T>` object, then use it to get the headers, output them to the log, and then get the response, as shown highlighted in the following code:

   ```
   // ShipperReply shipperReply = await shipperClient.GetShipperAsync(
   //   new ShipperRequest { ShipperId = id });

   // the same call as above but not awaited
   AsyncUnaryCall<ShipperReply> shipperCall = shipperClient.GetShipperAsync(
     new ShipperRequest { ShipperId = id });

   Metadata metadata = await shipperCall.ResponseHeadersAsync;

   foreach (Metadata.Entry entry in metadata)
   {
     // not really critical, just doing this to make it easier to see
     _logger.LogCritical($"Key: {entry.Key}, Value: {entry.Value}");
   }

   ShipperReply shipperReply = await shipperCall.ResponseAsync;

   ViewData["shipper"] = "Shipper from gRPC service: " +
     $"ID: {shipperReply.ShipperId}, Name: {shipperReply.CompanyName},"
     + $" Phone: {shipperReply.Phone}.";
   ```

3. Start the `Northwind.Grpc.Service` project without debugging.

4. Start the `Northwind.Grpc.Client.Mvc` project.

5. If necessary, start a browser and navigate to the home page: `https://localhost:5122/`.

6. Note the client successfully POSTing to the gRPC `Greeter` and `Shipper` services and the red critical messages outputting the two entries in the gRPC metadata for the call to `GetShipper`, with keys of `date` and `server`, as shown in *Figure 12.6*:

*Figure 12.6: Logging metadata from a gRPC call*

7.  Close the browser and shut down the web servers.

> The trailers equivalent of the `ResponseHeadersAsync` property is the `GetTrailers` method. It has a return value of `Metadata` that contains the dictionary of trailers. Trailers are accessible at the end of a call.

# Adding a deadline for higher reliability

Setting a deadline for a gRPC call is recommended practice because it controls the upper limit on how long a gRPC call can run for. It prevents gRPC services from potentially consuming too many server resources.

The deadline information is sent to the service, so the service has an opportunity to give up its work once the deadline has passed instead of continuing forever. Even if the server completes its work within the deadline, the client may give up before the response arrives at the client because the deadline has passed due to the overhead of communication.

Let's see an example:

1.  In the `Northwind.Grpc.Service` project, in the `Services` folder, in `ShipperService.cs`, in the `GetShipper` method, add a statement to pause for 5 seconds, as shown highlighted in the following code:

```
public override async Task<ShipperReply?> GetShipper(
  ShipperRequest request, ServerCallContext context)
{
  _logger.LogCritical(
    "This request has a deadline of {0:T}. It is now {1:T}.",
```

```
    context.Deadline, DateTime.UtcNow);

    await Task.Delay(TimeSpan.FromSeconds(5));

    return ToShipperReply(
      await db.Shippers.FindAsync(request.ShipperId));
}
```

2.  In `HomeController.cs`, in the `Index` method, set a deadline of 3 seconds when calling the `GetShipperAsync` method, as shown highlighted in the following code:

```
AsyncUnaryCall<ShipperReply> shipperCall = shipperClient.GetShipperAsync(
    new ShipperRequest { ShipperId = id },
    deadline: DateTime.UtcNow.AddSeconds(3)); // must be a UTC DateTime
```

3.  In `HomeController.cs`, in the `Index` method, before the existing `catch` block, add a `catch` block for an `RpcException` when the exception's status code matches the code for deadline exceeded, as shown highlighted in the following code:

```
catch (RpcException rpcex) when (rpcex.StatusCode ==
    global::Grpc.Core.StatusCode.DeadlineExceeded)
{
    _logger.LogWarning("Northwind.Grpc.Service deadline exceeded.");
    ViewData["exception"] = rpcex.Message;
}
catch (Exception ex)
{
    _logger.LogWarning($"Northwind.Grpc.Service is not responding.");
    ViewData["exception"] = ex.Message;
}
```

4.  In the `Northwind.Grpc.Service` project, in `appsettings.Development.json`, modify the logging level for ASP.NET Core from the default of `Warning` to `Information`, as shown highlighted in the following configuration:

```
{
  "Logging": {
    "LogLevel": {
      "Default": "Information",
      "Microsoft.AspNetCore": "Information"
    }
  }
}
```

5.  In the `Northwind.Grpc.Client.Mvc` project, in `appsettings.Development.json`, modify the logging level for ASP.NET Core from the default of `Warning` to `Information`, as shown highlighted in the following configuration:

```
{
  "Logging": {
    "LogLevel": {
      "Default": "Information",
      "Microsoft.AspNetCore": "Information"
    }
  }
}
```

6. Start the `Northwind.Grpc.Service` project without debugging.

7. Start the `Northwind.Grpc.Client.Mvc` project.

8. If necessary, start a browser and navigate to the home page: `https://localhost:5122/`.

9. At the command prompt or terminal for the gRPC service, note the request has a three second deadline, as shown in the following output:

```
crit: Northwind.Grpc.Service.Services.ShipperService[0]
      This request has a deadline of 14:56:30. It is now 14:56:27.
```

10. In the browser, note that after three seconds the home page shows a deadline exceeded exception, as shown in *Figure 12.7*:

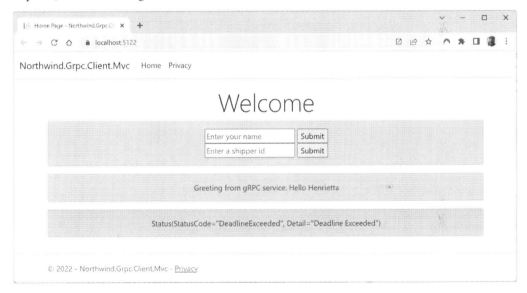

*Figure 12.7: A deadline has passed*

11. At the command prompt or terminal for the ASP.NET Core MVC client, note the logs that start at the point where a request is made to the `GetShipper` method on the gRPC service, but the deadline is exceeded, as shown in the following output:

```
info: System.Net.Http.HttpClient.Shipper.LogicalHandler[100]
      Start processing HTTP request POST https://localhost:5121/shipper.
Shipper/GetShipper
```

```
info: System.Net.Http.HttpClient.Shipper.ClientHandler[100]
      Sending HTTP request POST https://localhost:5121/shipper.Shipper/
GetShipper
warn: Grpc.Net.Client.Internal.GrpcCall[7]
      gRPC call deadline exceeded.
info: System.Net.Http.HttpClient.Shipper.ClientHandler[101]
      Received HTTP response headers after 3031.4299ms - 200
info: System.Net.Http.HttpClient.Shipper.LogicalHandler[101]
      End processing HTTP request after 3031.5469ms - 200
crit: Northwind.Grpc.Client.Mvc.Controllers.HomeController[0]
      Key: date, Value: Thu, 18 Aug 2022 15:14:17 GMT
crit: Northwind.Grpc.Client.Mvc.Controllers.HomeController[0]
      Key: server, Value: Kestrel
info: Grpc.Net.Client.Internal.GrpcCall[3]
      Call failed with gRPC error status. Status code:
'DeadlineExceeded', Message: 'Deadline Exceeded'.
warn: Northwind.Grpc.Client.Mvc.Controllers.HomeController[0]
      Northwind.Grpc.Service deadline exceeded.
```

12. Close the browser and shut down the web servers.

 **Good Practice:** The default is no deadline. Always set a deadline in the client call. In your service implementation, get the deadline and use it to automatically abandon the work if it is exceeded. Pass the cancellation token to any asynchronous calls so that work completes quickly on the server and frees up resources.

# Implementing gRPC JSON transcoding

JSON is the most popular format for services that return data to a browser or mobile device. It would be great if we could create a gRPC service and magically make it callable via non-HTTP/2 using JSON. Thankfully, there is a solution.

Microsoft has a new technology they have named **gRPC JSON transcoding**, which is an ASP.NET Core extension that creates HTTP endpoints with JSON for gRPC services, based on Google's HttpRule class for their gRPC Transcoding. You can read about that at the following link: https://cloud.google.com/dotnet/docs/reference/Google.Api.CommonProtos/latest/Google.Api.HttpRule.

# Enabling gRPC JSON transcoding

Let's see how to enable gRPC JSON transcoding in our gRPC service:

1. In the Northwind.Grpc.Service project, add a package reference for gRPC JSON transcoding, as shown highlighted in the following markup:

```
<ItemGroup>
  <PackageReference Include="Grpc.AspNetCore" Version="2.48.0" />
  <PackageReference Include="Microsoft.AspNetCore.Grpc.JsonTranscoding"
```

```
                            Version="7.0.0" />
  </ItemGroup>
```

2.  In `Program.cs`, add a call to add JSON transcoding after the call to add gRPC, as shown highlighted in the following code:

    ```
    builder.Services.AddGrpc().AddJsonTranscoding();
    ```

3.  In the `Northwind.Grpc.Service` project/folder, add a folder named `google`.

4.  In the `google` folder, add a folder named `api`.

5.  In the `api` folder, add two `.proto` files named `http.proto` and `annotations.proto`.

6.  Copy and paste the raw contents for the two files from the files found at the following link: `https://github.com/dotnet/aspnetcore/tree/main/src/Grpc/JsonTranscoding/test/testassets/Sandbox/google/api`.

7.  In the `Protos` folder, in `greet.proto`, import the annotations `.proto` file and use it to add an option to expose an endpoint to make an HTTP request to the `SayHello` method, as shown highlighted in the following code:

    ```
    syntax = "proto3";

    import "google/api/annotations.proto";

    option csharp_namespace = "Northwind.Grpc.Service";

    package greet;

    // The greeting service definition.
    service Greeter {
      // Sends a greeting
      rpc SayHello (HelloRequest) returns (HelloReply) {
        option (google.api.http) = {
          get: "/v1/greeter/{name}"
        };
      }
    }

    // The request message containing the user's name.
    message HelloRequest {
      string name = 1;
    }

    // The response message containing the greetings.
    message HelloReply {
      string message = 1;
    }
    ```

8.  In the `Protos` folder, in `shipper.proto`, import the annotations `.proto` file and use it to add an option to expose an endpoint to make an HTTP request to the `GetShipper` method, as shown in the following code:

```
syntax = "proto3";

import "google/api/annotations.proto";

option csharp_namespace = "Northwind.Grpc.Service";

package shipper;

service Shipper {
  rpc GetShipper (ShipperRequest) returns (ShipperReply) {
    option (google.api.http) = {
      get: "/v1/shipper/{shipperId}"
    };
  }
}

message ShipperRequest {
  int32 shipperId = 1;
}

message ShipperReply {
  int32 shipperId = 1;
  string companyName = 2;
  string phone = 3;
}
```

# Testing gRPC JSON transcoding

Now we can start the gRPC service and call it directly from any browser:

1.  Start the `Northwind.Grpc.Service` project.

2.  Start any browser, show the developer tools, and click the **Network** tab to start recording network traffic.

3.  Navigate to a URL to make a `GET` request that will call the `SayHello` method: `https://localhost:5121/v1/greeter/Bob`, and note the JSON response returned by the gRPC service, as shown in *Figure 12.8*:

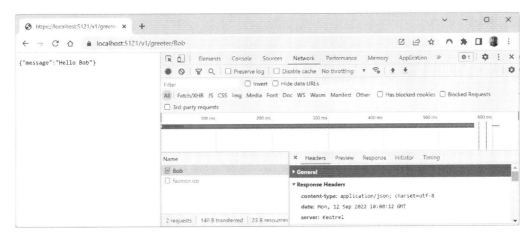

*Figure 12.8: Making an HTTP 1.1 GET request to a gRPC service and receiving a response in JSON*

4.   Navigate to a URL to make a GET request to call the GetShipper method: `https://localhost:5121/v1/shipper/2`, and note the JSON response returned by the gRPC service, as shown in *Figure 12.9*:

*Figure 12.9: Making an HTTP 1.1 GET request to a gRPC service and receiving a response in JSON*

5.   Close the browser and shut down the web server.

## Comparing with gRPC-Web

**gRPC-Web** is an alternative to gRPC JSON transcoding to allow gRPC services to be called from a browser. gRPC-Web achieves this by executing a gRPC-Web client inside the browser. This has the advantage that the communications between browser and gRPC service use Protobuf and therefore get all the performance and scalability benefits of true gRPC communication.

As you have seen, gRPC JSON transcoding allows browsers to call gRPC services as if they were HTTP APIs with JSON. The browser needs to know nothing about gRPC. The gRPC service is responsible for converting those HTTP API calls into calls to the actual gRPC service implementation.

To simplify and summarize:

- gRPC JSON transcoding happens on the server side.
- gRPC-Web happens on the client side.

 **Good Practice:** Add gRPC JSON transcoding support to all your gRPC services hosted in ASP.NET Core. This provides the best of both worlds. Clients that cannot use gRPC natively can call the Web API. Clients that can use gRPC natively can call it directly.

# Practicing and exploring

Test your knowledge and understanding by answering some questions, getting some hands-on practice, and exploring this chapter's topics with deeper research.

## Exercise 12.1 – Test your knowledge

Answer the following questions:

1. What are three benefits of gRPC that make it a good choice for implementing services?
2. How are contracts defined in gRPC?
3. Which of the following .NET types require extensions to be imported: `int`, `double`, and `DateTime`?
4. Why should you set a deadline when calling a gRPC method?
5. What are the benefits of enabling gRPC JSON transcoding to a gRPC service hosted in ASP.NET Core?

## Exercise 12.2 – Explore topics

Use the links on the following page to learn more detail about the topics covered in this chapter:

```
https://github.com/markjprice/apps-services-net7/blob/main/book-links.md#chapter-12--
-building-efficient-microservices-using-grpc
```

# Summary

In this chapter, you:

- Learned some concepts around gRPC services, how they work, and their benefits.
- Implemented a simple gRPC service.
- Implemented a gRPC service that uses an EF Core model.
- Learned how to set deadlines and read metadata sent as headers and trailers.

- Extended a gRPC service with support for being called as an HTTP service with JSON, to support clients that cannot work with gRPC natively.

In the next chapter, you will learn about SignalR, a technology for performing real-time communication between client and server.

# 13

# Broadcasting Real-Time Communication Using SignalR

In this chapter, you will be introduced to SignalR, a technology that enables a developer to create a service that can have multiple clients and broadcast messages to all of them or a subset of them live in real time. A canonical example is a group chat app. Other examples include notification systems and dashboards that need instantly up-to-date information like stock prices.

This chapter will cover the following topics:

- Understanding SignalR
- Building a live communication service using SignalR
- Building a web client using the SignalR JavaScript library
- Building a .NET console app client
- Streaming data using SignalR

## Understanding SignalR

The web is great for building general-purpose websites and services, but it was not designed for specialized scenarios that require a web page to be instantaneously updated with new information as it becomes available.

## The history of real-time communication on the web

To understand the benefits of SignalR, it helps to know the history of HTTP and how organizations worked to make it better for real-time communication between clients and servers.

In the early days of the web in the 1990s, browsers had to make a full-page HTTP GET request to the web server to get fresh information to show to the visitor.

In late 1999, Microsoft released Internet Explorer 5.0 with a component named **XMLHttpRequest** that could make asynchronous HTTP calls in the background. This alongside **dynamic HTML (DHTML)** allowed parts of the web page to be updated with fresh data smoothly.

The benefits of this technique were obvious, and soon all browsers added the same component.

# AJAX

Google took maximum advantage of this capability to build clever web applications such as Google Maps and Gmail. A few years later, the technique became popularly known as **Asynchronous JavaScript and XML (AJAX)**.

AJAX still uses HTTP to communicate, however, and that has limitations:

- First, HTTP is a request-response communication protocol, meaning that the server cannot push data to the client. It must wait for the client to make a request.

- Second, HTTP request and response messages have headers with lots of potentially unnecessary overhead.

# WebSocket

**WebSocket** is full duplex, meaning that either the client or server can initiate communicating new data. WebSocket uses the same TCP connection for the life cycle of the connection. It is also more efficient in the message sizes that it sends because they are minimally framed with 2 bytes.

WebSocket works over HTTP ports 80 and 443 so it is compatible with the HTTP protocol, and the WebSocket handshake uses the HTTP Upgrade header to switch from the HTTP protocol to the WebSocket protocol.

Modern web apps are expected to deliver up-to-date information. Live chat is the canonical example, but there are lots of potential applications, from stock prices to games.

Whenever you need the server to push updates to the web page, you need a web-compatible, real-time communication technology. WebSocket could be used, but it is not supported by all clients.

# Introducing SignalR

**ASP.NET Core SignalR** is an open-source library that simplifies adding real-time web functionality to apps by being an abstraction over multiple underlying communication technologies, which allows you to add real-time communication capabilities using C# code.

The developer does not need to understand or implement the underlying technology used, and SignalR will automatically switch between underlying technologies depending on what the visitor's web browser supports. For example, SignalR will use WebSocket when it's available, and gracefully falls back on other technologies such as AJAX long polling when it isn't, while your application code stays the same.

SignalR is an API for server-to-client **remote procedure calls** (**RPCs**). The RPCs call JavaScript functions on clients from server-side .NET code. SignalR has hubs to define the pipeline and handles the message dispatching automatically using two built-in hub protocols: JSON and a binary one based on MessagePack.

On the server side, SignalR runs everywhere that ASP.NET Core runs: Windows, macOS, or Linux servers. SignalR supports the following client platforms:

- JavaScript clients for current browsers including Chrome, Firefox, Safari, and Edge
- .NET clients including Blazor, .NET MAUI, and Xamarin for Android and iOS mobile apps
- Java 8 and later

# Azure SignalR Service

Earlier, I mentioned that it would be good practice to separate the SignalR service hosting project from the web project that uses the JavaScript library to act as a client. This is because a SignalR service potentially needs to handle lots of simultaneous client requests and respond quickly to them all.

Once you separate the SignalR hosting, you can take advantage of **Azure SignalR Service**. This offers global reach and a world-class data center and network, and it scales to millions of connections while meeting SLAs like providing compliance and high security.

 You can learn more about Azure SignalR Service at the following link: `https://docs.microsoft.com/en-us/azure/azure-signalr/signalr-overview`.

# Designing method signatures

In *Chapter 12, Building Efficient Microservices Using gRPC*, you learned that gRPC methods can only have a single message parameter. This limitation is to enforce good practice.

When designing the method signatures for a SignalR service, it is good practice to define methods with a single message parameter rather than multiple simple type parameters. Unlike gRPC, this good practice is not enforced by the technology with SignalR, so you will have to be disciplined.

For example, define a type with multiple properties to use as the single message parameter instead of passing multiple `string` values, as shown in the following code:

```
// bad practice
public void SendMessage(string to, string body)

// better practice
public class Message
{
  public string To { get; set; }
  public string Body { get; set; }
}

public void SendMessage(Message message)
```

The reason for this good practice is that it allows future changes like adding a message title. For the bad practice example, a third `string` parameter named `title` would need to be added and existing clients would get errors because they are not sending the extra `string` value. But using the good practice example will not break the method signature so existing clients can continue to call it as before the change. On the server side, the extra `title` property will just have a `null` value that can be checked for and perhaps set to a default value.

# Building a live communication service using SignalR

The SignalR server library is included in ASP.NET Core. But the JavaScript client library is not automatically included in the project. We will use the **Library Manager CLI** to get the client library from **unpkg**, a **content delivery network** (**CDN**) that can deliver anything found in Node Package Manager.

Let's add a SignalR server-side hub and client-side JavaScript to an ASP.NET Core MVC project to implement a chat feature that allows visitors to send messages to:

- Everyone currently using the website
- Dynamically defined groups
- A single specified user

 **Good Practice:** In a production solution, it would be better to host the SignalR hub in a separate web project so that it can be hosted and scaled independently from the rest of the website. Live communication can often put excessive load on a website.

## Defining some shared models

First, we will define two shared models that can be used on both the server-side and client-side .NET projects that will work with our chat service:

1.  Use your preferred code editor to create a new project, as defined in the following list:

    - Project template: **Class Library**/`classlib`
    - Workspace/solution file and folder: `Chapter13`
    - Project file and folder: `Northwind.Common`

2.  In the `Northwind.Common` project, rename the `Class1.cs` file to `UserModel.cs`.
3.  Modify its contents to define a model for registering a user's name, unique connection ID, and the groups that they belong to, as shown in the following code:

```
namespace Northwind.Chat.Models;

public class UserModel
{
  public string Name { get; set; } = null!;
  public string ConnectionId { get; set; } = null!;
  public string? Groups { get; set; } // comma-separated list
}
```

4. In the `Northwind.Common` project, add a class file named `MessageModel.cs`. Modify its contents to define a message model with properties for who the message is sent to, who the message was sent from, and the message body, as shown in the following code:

```
namespace Northwind.Chat.Models;

public class MessageModel
{
  public string From { get; set; } = null!;
  public string To { get; set; } = null!;
  public string? Body { get; set; }
}
```

# Enabling a server-side SignalR hub

Next, we will enable a SignalR hub on the server side in an ASP.NET Core MVC project:

1. Use your preferred code editor to add a new project, as defined in the following list:

    - Project template: **ASP.NET Core Web App (Model-View-Controller)**/mvc
    - Workspace/solution file and folder: Chapter13
    - Project file and folder: Northwind.SignalR.Service.Client.Mvc

2. In the `Northwind.SignalR.Service.Client.Mvc` project, add a project reference to the `Northwind.Common` project.

3. In the `Properties` folder, in `launchSettings.json`, for the `http` profile, modify the `applicationUrl` to use port 5132, and then in the `https` profile, modify the `applicationUrl` to use port 5131 for `https` and 5132 for `http`, as shown highlighted in the following configuration:

```
{
  "iisSettings": {
    "windowsAuthentication": false,
    "anonymousAuthentication": true,
    "iisExpress": {
      "applicationUrl": "http://localhost:34530",
      "sslPort": 44353
    }
  },
  "profiles": {
    "http": {
      "commandName": "Project",
      "dotnetRunMessages": true,
      "launchBrowser": true,
      "applicationUrl": "http://localhost:5132",
      "environmentVariables": {
        "ASPNETCORE_ENVIRONMENT": "Development"
      }
```

```
    },
    "https": {
      "commandName": "Project",
      "dotnetRunMessages": true,
      "launchBrowser": true,
      "applicationUrl": "https://localhost:5131;http://localhost:5132",
      "environmentVariables": {
        "ASPNETCORE_ENVIRONMENT": "Development"
      }
    },
    "IIS Express": {
      "commandName": "IISExpress",
      "launchBrowser": true,
      "environmentVariables": {
        "ASPNETCORE_ENVIRONMENT": "Development"
      }
    }
  }
}
```

4.  In the `Northwind.SignalR.Service.Client.Mvc` project, add a Hubs folder.

5.  In the Hubs folder, add a class file named `ChatHub.cs`. Modify its contents to inherit from the `Hub` class and implement two methods that can be called by a client, as shown in the following code:

```csharp
using Microsoft.AspNetCore.SignalR; // Hub
using Northwind.Chat.Models; // UserModel, MessageModel

namespace Northwind.SignalR.Service.Hubs;

public class ChatHub : Hub
{
  // a new instance of ChatHub is created to process each method so
  // we must store user names, connection IDs, and groups in a static
field
  private static Dictionary<string, UserModel> Users = new();

  public async Task Register(UserModel newUser)
  {
    UserModel user;
    string action = "registered as a new user";

    // try to get a stored user with a match on new user
    if (Users.ContainsKey(newUser.Name))
    {
      user = Users[newUser.Name];

      // remove any existing group registrations
```

```csharp
    if (user.Groups is not null)
    {
      foreach (string group in user.Groups.Split(','))
      {
        await Groups.RemoveFromGroupAsync(user.ConnectionId, group);
      }
    }
    user.Groups = newUser.Groups;

    // connection ID might have changed if the browser
    // refreshed so update it
    user.ConnectionId = Context.ConnectionId;

    action = "updated your registered user";
  }
  else
  {
    if (string.IsNullOrEmpty(newUser.Name))
    {
      // assign a GUID for name if they are anonymous
      newUser.Name = Guid.NewGuid().ToString();
    }
    newUser.ConnectionId = Context.ConnectionId;
    Users.Add(key: newUser.Name, value: newUser);
    user = newUser;
  }

  if (user.Groups is not null)
  {
    // a user does not have to belong to any groups
    // but if they do, register them with the Hub

    foreach (string group in user.Groups.Split(','))
    {
      await Groups.AddToGroupAsync(user.ConnectionId, group);
    }
  }

  // send a message to the registering user informing of success

  MessageModel message = new()
  {
    From = "SignalR Hub", To = user.Name,
    Body = string.Format(
      "You have successfully {0} with connection ID {1}.",
      arg0: action, arg1: user.ConnectionId)
```

```csharp
      };

      IClientProxy proxy = Clients.Client(user.ConnectionId);
      await proxy.SendAsync("ReceiveMessage", message);
    }

  public async Task SendMessage(MessageModel message)
  {
    IClientProxy proxy;

    if (string.IsNullOrEmpty(message.To))
    {
      message.To = "Everyone";
      proxy = Clients.All;
      await proxy.SendAsync("ReceiveMessage", message);
      return;
    }

    // if To has a value, then split it into a list of user and group
names
    string[] userAndGroupList = message.To.Split(',');

    // each item could be a user or group
    foreach (string userOrGroup in userAndGroupList)
    {
      if (Users.ContainsKey(userOrGroup))
      {
        // if the item is in Users then send the message to that user
        // by looking up their connection ID in the dictionary
        message.To = $"User: {Users[userOrGroup].Name}";
        proxy = Clients.Client(Users[userOrGroup].ConnectionId);
      }
      else // assume the item is a group name to send the message to
      {
        message.To = $"Group: {userOrGroup}";
        proxy = Clients.Group(userOrGroup);
      }
      await proxy.SendAsync("ReceiveMessage", message);
    }
  }
}
```

Note the following:

- ChatHub has a private field to store a list of registered users. It is a dictionary with name of registered users as a unique key.

- ChatHub has two methods that a client can call: Register and SendMessage.

- Register has a single parameter of type UserModel. The user's name, connection ID, and groups are stored in the static dictionary so that the user's name can be used to look up the connection ID later and send messages directly to that one user. After registering a new user or updating the registration of an existing user, a message is sent back to the client informing them of success.

- SendMessage has a single parameter of type MessageModel. The method branches based on the value of the To property. If To does not have a value, it calls the All property to get a proxy that will communicate with every client. If To has a value, the string is split using comma separators into an array. Each item in the array is checked to see if it matches a user in Users. If it matches, it calls the Client method to get a proxy that will communicate just with that one client. If it does not match, the item might be a group, so it calls the Group method to get a proxy that will communicate with just the members of that group. Finally, it sends the message asynchronously using the proxy.

6. In Program.cs, import the namespace for your SignalR hub, as shown in the following code:

```
using Northwind.SignalR.Service.Hubs; // ChatHub
```

7. In the section that configures services, add a statement to add support for SignalR to the services collection, as shown in the following code:

```
builder.Services.AddSignalR();
```

8. In the section that configures the HTTP pipeline, before the call to map controller routes, add a statement to map the relative URL path /chat to your SignalR hub, as shown in the following code:

```
app.MapHub<ChatHub>("/chat");
```

# Building a web client using the SignalR JavaScript library

Next, we will add the SignalR client-side JavaScript library so that we can use it on a web page:

1. Open a command prompt or terminal for the Northwind.SignalR.Service.Client.Mvc project/folder.

2. Install the Library Manager CLI tool, as shown in the following command:

```
dotnet tool install -g Microsoft.Web.LibraryManager.Cli
```

This tool might already be installed globally. To update it to the latest version, repeat the command but replace `install` with `update`, as shown highlighted in the following code:

```
PS C:\apps-services-net7\Chapter13\Northwind.SignalR.
Service.Client.Mvc> dotnet tool install -g Microsoft.Web.
LibraryManager.CliTool 'microsoft.web.librarymanager.cli'
is already installed.
PS C:\apps-services-net7\Chapter13\Northwind.SignalR.
Service.Client.Mvc> dotnet tool update -g Microsoft.Web.
LibraryManager.Cli
Tool 'microsoft.web.librarymanager.cli' was successfully
updated from version '2.1.113' to version '2.1.161'.
```

3. Enter a command to add the `signalr.js` and `signalr.min.js` libraries to the project from the unpkg source, as shown in the following command:

```
libman install @microsoft/signalr@latest -p unpkg -d wwwroot/js/signalr
--files dist/browser/signalr.js --files dist/browser/signalr.min.js
```

4. Note the success message, as shown in the following output:

```
Downloading file https://unpkg.com/@microsoft/signalr@latest/dist/
browser/signalr.js...
Downloading file https://unpkg.com/@microsoft/signalr@latest/dist/
browser/signalr.min.js...
wwwroot/js/signalr/dist/browser/signalr.js written to disk
wwwroot/js/signalr/dist/browser/signalr.min.js written to disk
Installed library "@microsoft/signalr@latest" to "wwwroot/js/signalr"
```

Visual Studio 2022 also has a GUI for adding client-side JavaScript libraries. To use it, right-click a web project and then navigate to **Add** | **Client Side Libraries**.

## Adding a chat page to the MVC website

Next, we will add chat functionality to the home page:

1. In `Views/Home`, in `Index.cshtml`, modify its contents, as shown in the following markup:

```
@using Northwind.Chat.Models
@{
  ViewData["Title"] = "SignalR Chat";
}
<div class="container">
  <h1>@ViewData["Title"]</h1>
  <hr />
```

```html
<div class="row">
  <div class="col">
    <h2>Register User</h2>
    <div class="mb-3">
      <label for="myName" class="form-label">My name</label>
      <input type="text" class="form-control"
             id="myName" value="Alice" required />
    </div>
    <div class="mb-3">
      <label for="myGroups" class="form-label">My groups</label>
      <input type="text" class="form-control"
             id="myGroups" value="Sales,IT" />
    </div>
    <div class="mb-3">
      <input type="button" class="form-control"
             id="registerButton" value="Register User" />
    </div>
  </div>
  <div class="col">
    <h2>Send Message</h2>
    <div class="mb-3">
      <label for="from" class="form-label">From</label>
      <input type="text" class="form-control"
             id="from" value="Alice" readonly />
    </div>
    <div class="mb-3">
      <label for="to" class="form-label">To</label>
      <input type="text" class="form-control" id="to" />
    </div>
    <div class="mb-3">
      <label for="body" class="form-label">Body</label>
      <input type="text" class="form-control" id="body" />
    </div>
    <div class="mb-3">
      <input type="button" class="form-control"
             id="sendButton" value="Send Message" />
    </div>
  </div>
</div>
<div class="row">
  <div class="col">
    <hr />
    <h2>Messages received</h2>
    <ul id="messages"></ul>
  </div>
</div>
```

```
</div>
<script src="~/js/signalr/dist/browser/signalr.js"></script>
<script src="~/js/chat.js"></script>
```

Note the following:

- There are three sections on the page: **Register User**, **Send Message**, and **Messages received**:

    - The **Register User** section has two inputs for the visitor's name and a comma-separated list of the groups that they want to be a member of, and a button to click to register.

    - The **Send Message** section has three inputs for the name of the user that the message is from, the names of users and groups that the message will be sent to, and the body of the message, and a button to click to send the message.

    - The **Messages received** section has a bullet-list element that will be dynamically populated with a list item when a message is received.

- There are two script elements for the SignalR JavaScript client-side library and the JavaScript implementation of the chat client.

2.  In `wwwroot/js`, add a new JavaScript file named `chat.js` and modify its contents, as shown in the following code:

```
"use strict";

var connection = new signalR.HubConnectionBuilder()
  .withUrl("/chat").build();

document.getElementById("registerButton").disabled = true;
document.getElementById("sendButton").disabled = true;

document.getElementById("myName").addEventListener("input",
  function () {
    document.getElementById("from").value =
      document.getElementById("myName").value;
  }
);

connection.start().then(function () {
  document.getElementById("registerButton").disabled = false;
  document.getElementById("sendButton").disabled = false;
}).catch(function (err) {
  return console.error(err.toString());
});

connection.on("ReceiveMessage", function (received) {
  var li = document.createElement("li");
```

```
        document.getElementById("messages").appendChild(li);
        // note the use of backtick ` to enable a formatted string
        li.textContent =
          `To ${received.to}, From ${received.from}: ${received.body}`;
    });

    document.getElementById("registerButton").addEventListener("click",
      function (event) {
        var registermodel = {
          name: document.getElementById("myName").value,
          groups: document.getElementById("myGroups").value
        };
        connection.invoke("Register", registermodel).catch(function (err) {
          return console.error(err.toString());
        });
        event.preventDefault();
    });

    document.getElementById("sendButton").addEventListener("click",
      function (event) {
        var messagemodel = {
          from: document.getElementById("from").value,
          to: document.getElementById("to").value,
          body: document.getElementById("body").value
        };
        connection.invoke("SendMessage", messagemodel).catch(function (err) {
          return console.error(err.toString());
        });
        event.preventDefault();
    });
```

Note the following:

- The script creates a SignalR hub connection builder specifying the relative URL path to the chat hub on the server /chat.

- The script disables the **Register** and **Send** buttons until the connection is successfully established to the server-side hub.

- An input event handler is added to the **My name** text box to keep it synchronized with the **From** text box.

- When the connection gets a ReceiveMessage call from the server-side hub, it adds a list item element to the messages bullet list. The content of the list item contains details of the message, like from, to, and body. For the two models that we defined in C#, note that JavaScript uses camelCasing compared to C#, which uses TitleCase.

- A click event handler is added to the **Register User** button that creates a register model with the user's name and their groups and then invokes the Register method on the server side.

- A `click` event handler is added to the **Send Message** button that creates a message model with the `from`, `to`, and body fields, and then invokes the `SendMessage` method on the server side.

## Testing the chat feature

Now we are ready to try sending chat messages between multiple website visitors:

1. Start the `Northwind.SignalR.Service.Client.Mvc` project website using the `https` profile.

    - If you are using Visual Studio 2022, then select the **https** profile in the toolbar, and then start the `Northwind.SignalR.Service.Client.Mvc` project without debugging.
    - If you are using Visual Studio Code, then at the command line or terminal, enter the following command:

    ```
    dotnet run --launch-profile https
    ```

2. Start Chrome and navigate to `https://localhost:5131/`.
3. Note that `Alice` is already entered for the name, and `Sales,IT` is already entered for the groups. Click **Register User**, and note the response back from the SignalR hub, as shown in *Figure 13.1*:

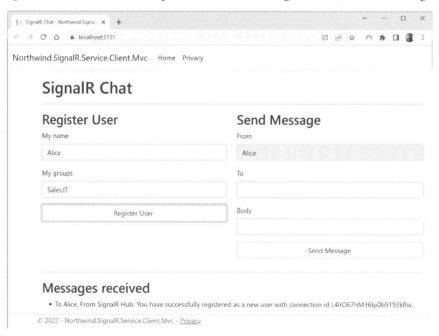

*Figure 13.1: Registering a new user in chat*

4. Open a new Chrome window or start another browser like Firefox or Edge.
5. Navigate to `https://localhost:5131/`.
6. Enter `Bob` for the name and `Sales` for the groups, and then click **Register User**.
7. Open a new Chrome window or start another browser like Firefox or Edge.

8. Navigate to `https://localhost:5131/`.

9. Enter `Charlie` for the name and `IT` for the groups, and then click **Register User**.

10. Arrange the browser windows so that you can see all three simultaneously.

 A great tool for arranging windows is PowerToys and its FancyZones feature. Learn more at the following link: `https://docs.microsoft.com/en-us/windows/powertoys/`.

11. In Alice's browser, in **To**, enter `Sales`; in **Body**, enter `Sell more!`; and then click **Send Message**.

12. Note that Alice and Bob receive the message, as shown in *Figure 13.2*:

*Figure 13.2: Alice sends a message to the Sales group*

13. In Bob's browser, in **To**, enter `IT`; in **Body**, enter `Fix more bugs!`; and then click **Send Message**.

14. Note that Alice and Charlie receive the message, as shown in *Figure 13.3*:

*Figure 13.3: Bob sends a message to the IT group*

15. In Alice's browser, in **To**, enter Bob; in **Body**, enter Bonjour Bob!; and then click **Send Message**.

16. Note that only Bob receives the message.

17. In Charlie's browser, leave **To** empty; in **Body**, enter Everybody dance now!; and then click **Send Message**.

18. Note that everyone receives the message, as shown in *Figure 13.4*:

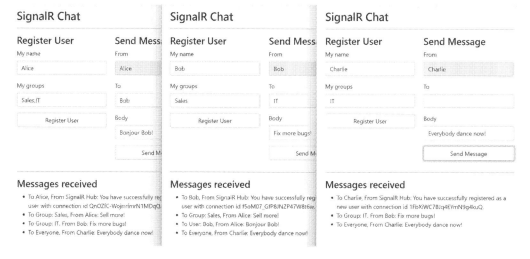

*Figure 13.4: Charlie sends a message to everyone*

19. In Charlie's browser, in **To**, enter HR,Alice; in **Body**, enter Is anyone in HR listening?; and then click **Send Message**.

20. Note that Alice receives the message sent directly to her, but since the HR group does not exist, no one receives the message sent to that group, as shown in *Figure 13.5*:

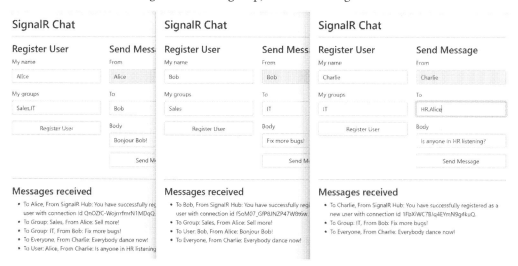

*Figure 13.5: Charlie sends a message to Alice and a group that does not exist*

21. Close the browsers and shut down the web server.

# Building a .NET console app client

You have just seen a .NET service hosting a SignalR hub, and a JavaScript client exchanging messages with other clients via that SignalR hub. Now, let's create a .NET client for SignalR.

## Creating a .NET client for SignalR

We will use a console app, although any .NET project type would need the same package reference and implementation code:

1.  Use your preferred code editor to add a new project, as defined in the following list:

    *   Project template: **Console Application**/console
    *   Workspace/solution file and folder: Chapter13
    *   Project file and folder: Northwind.SignalR.Client.Console

2.  Add a package reference for the ASP.NET Core SignalR client and a project reference for Northwind.Common, and globally and statically import the System.Console class, as shown in the following markup:

    ```
    <ItemGroup>
      <PackageReference Include="Microsoft.AspNetCore.SignalR.Client"
                        Version="7.0.0" />
    </ItemGroup>

    <ItemGroup>
      <ProjectReference
        Include="..\Northwind.Common\Northwind.Common.csproj" />
    </ItemGroup>

    <ItemGroup>
      <Using Include="System.Console" Static="true" />
    </ItemGroup>
    ```

3.  In Program.cs, delete the existing statements, import namespaces for working with SignalR as a client and the chat models, and then add statements to prompt the user to enter a username and groups to register with, create a hub connection, and finally listen for received messages, as shown in the following code:

    ```
    using Microsoft.AspNetCore.SignalR.Client; // HubConnection
    using Northwind.Chat.Models; // UserModel, MessageModel

    Write("Enter a username (required): ");
    string? username = ReadLine();

    if (string.IsNullOrEmpty(username))
    {
      WriteLine("You must enter a username to register with chat!");
    ```

```
      return;
  }

  Write("Enter your groups (optional): ");
  string? groups = ReadLine();

  HubConnection hubConnection = new HubConnectionBuilder()
      .WithUrl("https://localhost:5131/chat")
      .Build();

  hubConnection.On<MessageModel>("ReceiveMessage", message =>
  {
    WriteLine($"To {message.To}, From {message.From}: {message.Body}");
  });

  await hubConnection.StartAsync();

  WriteLine("Successfully started.");

  UserModel registration = new()
  {
    Name = username,
    Groups = groups
  };

  await hubConnection.InvokeAsync("Register", registration);

  WriteLine("Successfully registered.");
  WriteLine("Listening... (press ENTER to stop.)");
  ReadLine();
```

## Testing the .NET console app client

Let's start the SignalR service and call it from the console app:

1.  Start the `Northwind.SignalR.Service.Client.Mvc` project website using the `https` profile without debugging.

2.  Start Chrome and navigate to `https://localhost:5131/`.

3.  Click **Register User**.

4.  Start the `Northwind.SignalR.Client.Console` project.

5.  Enter your name and the groups `Sales,Admins`.

6.  Arrange the browser and console app windows so that you can see both simultaneously.

7.  In Alice's browser, in **To**, enter `Sales`; in **Body**, enter `Go team!`; click **Send Message**, and note that Alice and you receive the message, as shown in *Figure 13.6*:

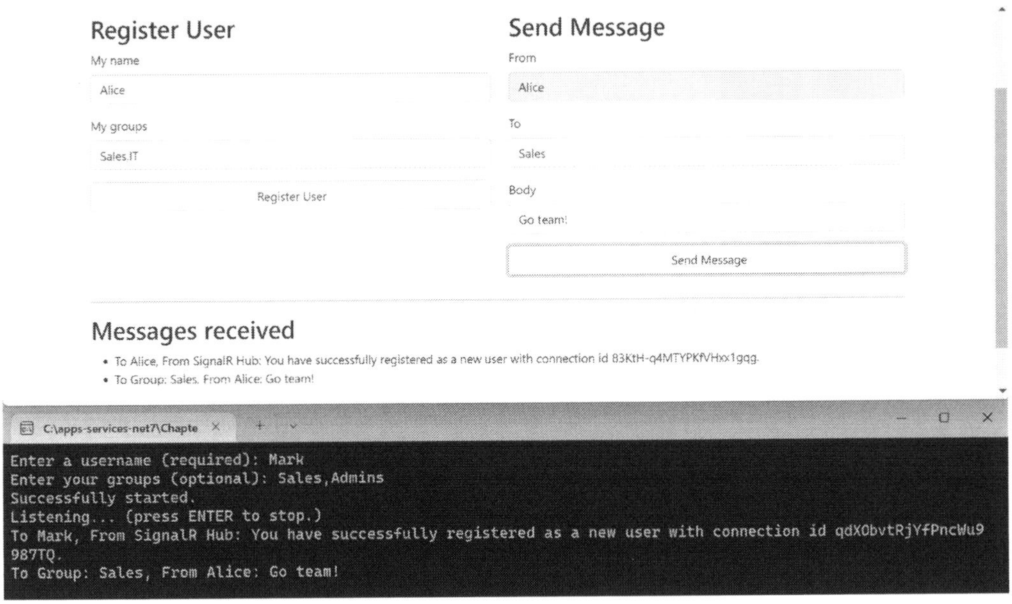

*Figure 13.6: Alice sends messages to different types of recipients*

8. In the console app, press *Enter* to stop it.

9. Close Chrome and shut down the web server.

# Streaming data using SignalR

So far, we have seen how SignalR can broadcast structured messages to one or more clients. This works well with data that is relatively small and structured and exists completely at a point in time. But what about data that comes in parts over time? **Streams** can be used for these scenarios. SignalR supports both service-to-client (downloading data from a stream) and client-to-service (uploading data to a stream).

To enable download streaming, a hub method must return `IAsyncEnumerable<T>` (only supported by C# 8 or later) or `ChannelReader<T>`.

To enable upload streaming, a hub method must accept a parameter of type `IAsyncEnumerable<T>` (only supported by C# 8 or later) or `ChannelReader<T>`.

## Defining a hub for streaming

Let's add some streaming methods to see how they work in action:

1. In the `Northwind.Common` project, add a new file named `StockPrice.cs` and modify its content to define a record for stock price data, as shown in the following code:

```
namespace Northwind.SignalR.Streams;

public record StockPrice(string Stock, double Price);
```

2.  Build the `Northwind.SignalR.Service.Client.Mvc` project to update its referenced projects.

3.  In the `Northwind.SignalR.Service.Client.Mvc` project, in the Hubs folder, add a new class named `StockPriceHub.cs`, and modify its contents to define a hub with two streaming methods, as shown in the following code:

```csharp
using Microsoft.AspNetCore.SignalR; // Hub
using System.Runtime.CompilerServices; // [EnumeratorCancellation]
using Northwind.SignalR.Streams; // StockPrice

namespace Northwind.SignalR.Service.Hubs;

public class StockPriceHub : Hub
{
  public async IAsyncEnumerable<StockPrice> GetStockPriceUpdates(
    string stock,
    [EnumeratorCancellation] CancellationToken cancellationToken)
  {
    double currentPrice = 267.10; // Simulated initial price.

    for (int i = 0; i < 10; i++)
    {
      // Check the cancellation token regularly so that the server will
      // stop producing items if the client disconnects.
      cancellationToken.ThrowIfCancellationRequested();

      // Increment or decrement the current price by a random amount.
      currentPrice += (Random.Shared.NextDouble() * 10.0) - 5.0;

      StockPrice stockPrice = new(stock, currentPrice);

      Console.WriteLine("[{0}] {1} at {2:C}",
        DateTime.UtcNow, stockPrice.Stock, stockPrice.Price);

      yield return stockPrice;

      await Task.Delay(4000, cancellationToken); // milliseconds
    }
  }

  public async Task UploadStocks(IAsyncEnumerable<string> stocks)
  {
    await foreach (string stock in stocks)
    {
      Console.WriteLine($"Uploading {stock}...");
    }
  }
}
```

4.  In the `Northwind.SignalR.Service.Client.Mvc` project, in `Program.cs`, register the stock price hub, as shown highlighted in the following code:

```
app.MapHub<ChatHub>("/chat");
app.MapHub<StockPriceHub>("/stockprice");
```

# Creating a .NET console app client for streaming

Now, we can create a simple client to download a stream of data from the SignalR hub and upload a stream of data to the SignalR hub:

1.  Use your preferred code editor to add a new project, as defined in the following list:

    *   Project template: **Console Application**/console
    *   Workspace/solution file and folder: `Chapter13`
    *   Project file and folder: `Northwind.SignalR.Client.Console.Streams`

2.  In the `Northwind.SignalR.Client.Console.Streams` project file, treat warnings as errors, add a package reference for the ASP.NET Core SignalR client, add a project reference to `Northwind.Common`, and globally and statically import the `System.Console` class, as shown highlighted in the following markup:

```xml
<Project Sdk="Microsoft.NET.Sdk">

  <PropertyGroup>
    <OutputType>Exe</OutputType>
    <TargetFramework>net7.0</TargetFramework>
    <ImplicitUsings>enable</ImplicitUsings>
    <Nullable>enable</Nullable>
    <TreatWarningsAsErrors>true</TreatWarningsAsErrors>
  </PropertyGroup>

  <ItemGroup>
    <PackageReference Include="Microsoft.AspNetCore.SignalR.Client"
                      Version="7.0.0" />
  </ItemGroup>

  <ItemGroup>
    <ProjectReference
      Include="..\Northwind.Common\Northwind.Common.csproj" />
  </ItemGroup>

  <ItemGroup>
    <Using Include="System.Console" Static="true" />
  </ItemGroup>

</Project>
```

3.  In the `Northwind.SignalR.Client.Console.Streams` project, add a new class file named `Program.Methods.cs`, and modify its content to define static methods in the partial `Program` class to generate 10 random four-letter stock codes asynchronously, as shown in the following code:

```
partial class Program
{
  static async IAsyncEnumerable<string> GetStocksAsync()
  {
    for (int i = 0; i < 10; i++)
    {
      // Return a random four-letter stock code.
      yield return $"{AtoZ()}{AtoZ()}{AtoZ()}{AtoZ()}";

      await Task.Delay(3000); // milliseconds
    }
  }

  static string AtoZ()
  {
    return char.ConvertFromUtf32(Random.Shared.Next(65, 91));
  }
}
```

4.  In the `Northwind.SignalR.Client.Console.Streams` project, in `Program.cs`, delete the existing statements. Import namespaces for working with SignalR as a client, and then add statements to prompt the user to enter a stock, create a hub connection, listen for received streams of stock prices, and then send an asynchronous stream of stocks to the service, as shown in the following code:

```
using Microsoft.AspNetCore.SignalR.Client; // HubConnection
using Northwind.SignalR.Streams; // StockPrice

Write("Enter a stock (press Enter for MSFT): ");
string? stock = ReadLine();

if (string.IsNullOrEmpty(stock))
{
  stock = "MSFT";
}

HubConnection hubConnection = new HubConnectionBuilder()
  .WithUrl("https://localhost:5131/stockprice")
  .Build();
```

```
await hubConnection.StartAsync();

try
{
  CancellationTokenSource cts = new();

  IAsyncEnumerable<StockPrice> stockPrices =
    hubConnection.StreamAsync<StockPrice>(
      "GetStockPriceUpdates", stock, cts.Token);

  await foreach (StockPrice sp in stockPrices)
  {
    WriteLine($"{sp.Stock} is now {sp.Price:C}.");

    Write("Do you want to cancel (y/n)? ");
    ConsoleKey key = ReadKey().Key;
    if (key == ConsoleKey.Y)
    {
      cts.Cancel();
    }
    WriteLine();
  }
}
catch (Exception ex)
{
  WriteLine($"{ex.GetType()} says {ex.Message}");
}
WriteLine();

WriteLine("Streaming download completed.");

await hubConnection.SendAsync("UploadStocks", GetStocksAsync());

WriteLine("Uploading stocks... (press ENTER to stop.)");
ReadLine();

WriteLine("Ending console app.");
```

## Testing the streaming service and client

Finally, we can test the streaming data functionality:

1.  Start the Northwind.SignalR.Service.Client.Mvc project website using the https profile.
2.  Start the Northwind.SignalR.Client.Console.Streams console app.

3.   Arrange the console windows for the ASP.NET Core MVC website and the client console app so that you can see both side by side.

4.   In the client console app, press *Enter* to use the Microsoft stock code, as shown in the following output:

```
Enter a stock (press Enter for MSFT):
MSFT is now £265.00.
Do you want to cancel (y/n)?
```

5.   In the website console window, wait for about 10 seconds, and note that several stock prices have been generated in the service, as shown in the following output:

```
info: Microsoft.Hosting.Lifetime[14]
      Now listening on: https://localhost:5131
info: Microsoft.Hosting.Lifetime[14]
      Now listening on: http://localhost:5132
info: Microsoft.Hosting.Lifetime[0]
      Application started. Press Ctrl+C to shut down.
info: Microsoft.Hosting.Lifetime[0]
      Hosting environment: Development
info: Microsoft.Hosting.Lifetime[0]
      Content root path: C:\apps-services-net7\Chapter13\Northwind.
SignalR.Service.Client.Mvc
[12/09/2022 17:52:26] MSFT at £265.00
[12/09/2022 17:52:30] MSFT at £260.78
[12/09/2022 17:52:34] MSFT at £264.86
[12/09/2022 17:52:38] MSFT at £262.10
```

6.   In the client console app, press *N* to receive the next updated price. Keep pressing *N* until the prices have been read, and then press *Y*, and note that a cancellation token is received by the SignalR service so it stops, and the client now starts uploading stocks, as shown in the following output:

```
MSFT is now £260.78.
Do you want to cancel (y/n)? n
MSFT is now £264.86.
Do you want to cancel (y/n)? n
MSFT is now £262.10.
Do you want to cancel (y/n)? y
System.Threading.Tasks.TaskCanceledException says A task was canceled.

Streaming download completed.
Uploading stocks... (press ENTER to stop.)
```

7.   In the website console window, note that the random stock codes are received, as shown in the following output:

```
Uploading PJON...
```

```
Uploading VWJD...
Uploading PDUY...
Uploading QZIX...
Uploading AFRW...
Uploading QGFV...
Uploading JQLA...
Uploading TRMC...
Uploading HMOJ...
Uploading QQMQ...
```

8.   Close both console windows.

# Practicing and exploring

Test your knowledge and understanding by answering some questions, getting some hands-on practice, and exploring this chapter's topics with deeper research.

## Exercise 13.1 – Test your knowledge

Answer the following questions:

1.   What transports does SignalR use, and which is the default?

2.   What is a good practice for RPC method signature design?

3.   What tool can you use to download the SignalR JavaScript library?

4.   What happens if you send a SignalR message to a client with a connection ID that does not exist?

5.   What are the benefits of separating a SignalR service from other ASP.NET Core components?

## Exercise 13.2 – Explore topics

Use the links on the following GitHub repository to learn more about the topics covered in this chapter:

```
https://github.com/markjprice/apps-services-net7/blob/main/book-links.md#chapter-13--
-broadcasting-real-time-communication-using-signalr
```

# Summary

In this chapter, you learned:

•   About the history of technologies before SignalR.

•   About the concepts and technologies that underpin SignalR.

•   How to implement chat functionality using SignalR, including building a hub hosted in a website project, and clients using JavaScript and a .NET console app.

•   Downloading and uploading streams of data using SignalR.

In the next chapter, you will learn about Azure Functions, which integrates nicely with Azure SignalR Service.

# 14

# Building Serverless Nanoservices Using Azure Functions

In this chapter, you will be introduced to functions implemented using Azure Functions, which can be configured to only require server-side resources while they execute. The functions execute when they are triggered by an activity like a message sent to a queue, a file uploaded to Azure Storage, or at a regularly scheduled interval.

This chapter will cover the following topics:

- Understanding Azure Functions
- Building an Azure Functions project
- Responding to timer and resource triggers
- Publishing an Azure Functions project to the cloud
- Cleaning up Azure Functions resources

## Understanding Azure Functions

**Azure Functions** is an event-driven serverless compute platform. You can build and debug locally and later deploy to the Microsoft Azure cloud. Functions can be implemented in many languages, not just C# and .NET. It has extensions for Visual Studio 2022 and Visual Studio Code and a command-line tool.

But first, you might be wondering, "How is it possible to have a service without a server?"

*Serverless* does not literally mean there is no server. What serverless means is a service without a *permanently running server*, and usually that means not running for most of the time or running with low resources and scaling up dynamically when needed. This can save a lot of costs.

For example, organizations often have business functions that only need to run once per hour, once per month, or on an ad hoc basis. Perhaps the organization prints checks (cheques in England) to pay its employees at the end of the month. Those checks might need the salary amounts converted to words to print on the check.

A function to convert numbers to words could be implemented as a serverless service. For a content management system, editors might upload new images, and those images might need to be processed in various ways, like generating thumbnails and other optimizations. This work can be added to a queue, or a function triggered when the file is uploaded to Blob Storage.

A function in Azure Functions can be much more than just a single function. They support complex, stateful workflows and event-driven solutions using **Durable Functions**.

 I do not cover Durable Functions in this book, so if you are interested, then you can learn more about it at the following link: `https://docs.microsoft.com/en-us/azure/azure-functions/durable/durable-functions-overview?tabs=csharp`.

Azure Functions has a programming model based on triggers and bindings that enable your serverless service to respond to events and connect to other services like data stores.

## Azure Functions triggers and bindings

**Triggers** and **bindings** are key concepts for Azure Functions.

Triggers are what cause a function to execute. Each function must have one and only one trigger. The most common triggers are shown in the following list:

- **HTTP**: This trigger responds to an incoming HTTP request, typically a GET or POST.
- **SignalR**: This trigger responds to messages sent from Azure SignalR Service.
- **Cosmos DB**: This trigger uses the Cosmos DB Change Feed to listen for inserts and updates.
- **Timer**: This trigger responds to a scheduled time occurring. It does not retry if a function fails. The function is not called again until the next time on the schedule.
- **Queue**: This trigger responds to a message arriving in a queue ready for processing.
- **Blob Storage**: This trigger responds to a new or updated **binary large object** (BLOB).
- **Event Grid**: This trigger responds when a predefined event occurs.

Bindings allow functions to have inputs and outputs. Each function can have zero, one, or more bindings. Some common bindings are shown in the following list:

- **Blob Storage**: Read or write to any file stored as a BLOB.
- **Cosmos DB**: Read or write documents to a cloud-scale data store.
- **SignalR**: Receive or make remote method calls.
- **Queue**: Write a message to a queue or read a message from a queue.
- **SendGrid**: Send an email message.
- **Twilio**: Send an SMS message.
- **IoT Hub**: Write to an internet-connected device.

You can see the full list of supported triggers and bindings at the following link: https://docs.microsoft.com/en-us/azure/azure-functions/functions-triggers-bindings?tabs=csharp#supported-bindings.

Triggers and bindings are configured differently for different languages. For C# and Java, you decorate methods and parameters with attributes. For the other languages, you configure a file named `function.json`.

## NCRONTAB expressions

The Timer trigger uses NCRONTAB expressions to define the frequency of the timer. The default time zone is **Coordinated Universal Time** (**UTC**), but this can be overridden.

If you are hosting an Azure Functions project in an App Service plan, then you can alternatively use a `TimeSpan`, but I recommend learning NCRONTAB expressions for flexibility.

An NCRONTAB expression consists of five (if seconds are not given) or six parts:

```
* * * * * *
- - - - - -
| | | | | |
| | | | | +--- day of week (0 - 6) (Sunday=0)
| | | | +----- month (1 - 12)
| | | +------- day of month (1 - 31)
| | +--------- hour (0 - 23)
| +----------- min (0 - 59)
+------------- sec (0 - 59)
```

A star * in the value field above means all legal values, as given in parentheses for that column. You can specify ranges using a hyphen, and a step value using /:

- 0 means at that value. For example, for hours, at midnight.
- 0,6,12,18 means at those listed values. For example, for hours, at midnight, 6 AM, 12 noon, and 6 PM.
- 3-7 means at that range of values. For example, for hours, at 3 AM, 4 AM, 5 AM, 6 AM, and 7 AM.
- 4/3 means a start value of 4 and a step value of 3. For example, for hours, at 4 AM, 7 AM, 10 AM, 1 PM, 4 PM, 7 PM, and 10 PM.

The following table shows some examples:

| Expression | Description |
|---|---|
| 0 5 * * * * | Once every hour of the day at minute 5 of each hour. |
| 0 0,10,30,40 * * * * | Four times an hour – at minutes 0, 10, 30, and 40 during every hour. |
| * * */2 * * * | Every 2 hours. |

| | |
|---|---|
| `0,15 * * * * *` | At 0 and 15 seconds every minute. |
| `0/15 * * * * *` | At 0, 15, 30, 45 seconds every minute, aka every 15 seconds. |
| `0-15 * * * * *` | At 0, 1, 2, 3, and so on up to 15 seconds past each minute, but not 16 to 59 seconds past each minute. |
| `0 30 9-16 * * *` | Eight times a day – at hours 9:30 AM, 10:30 AM, and so on up to 4:30 PM. |
| `0 */5 * * * *` | 12 times an hour – at second 0 of every 5th minute of every hour. |
| `0 0 */4 * * *` | 6 times a day – at minute 0 of every 4th hour of every day. |
| `0 30 9 * * *` | 9:30 AM every day. |
| `0 30 9 * * 1-5` | 9:30 AM every workday. |
| `0 30 9 * * Mon-Fri` | 9:30 AM every workday. |
| `0 30 9 * Jan Mon` | 9:30 AM every Monday in January. |

Now let's build a simple console app to test your understanding of NCRONTAB expressions:

1.  Use your preferred code editor to add a new console app named `NCrontab.Console` to a `Chapter14` solution/workspace.

2.  In the `NCrontab.Console` project, globally and statically import the `System.Console` class and add a package reference for `NCrontab.Signed`, as shown in the following markup:

    ```
    <ItemGroup>
      <Using Include="System.Console" Static="true" />
    </ItemGroup>

    <ItemGroup>
      <PackageReference Include="NCrontab.Signed" Version="3.3.2" />
    </ItemGroup>
    ```

     The NCRONTAB library is only for parsing expressions. It is not itself a scheduler. You can learn more about it in the GitHub repository at the following link: `https://github.com/atifaziz/NCrontab`.

3.  Build the `NCrontab.Console` project.

4.  In `Program.cs`, delete the existing statements. Add statements to define a date range for the year 2023, output a summary of NCRONTAB syntax, construct an NCRONTAB schedule, and then use it to output the next 40 occurrences that would occur in 2023, as shown in the following code:

    ```
    using NCrontab;

    DateTime start = new(2023, 1, 1);
    DateTime end = start.AddYears(1);
    ```

```
WriteLine($"Start at:    {start:ddd, dd MMM yyyy HH:mm:ss}");
WriteLine($"End at:      {end:ddd, dd MMM yyyy HH:mm:ss}");
WriteLine();

string sec = "0,30";
string min = "*";
string hour = "*";
string dayOfMonth = "*";
string month = "*";
string dayOfWeek = "*";

string expression = string.Format(
  "{0,-3} {1,-3} {2,-3} {3,-3} {4,-3} {5,-3}",
  sec, min, hour, dayOfMonth, month, dayOfWeek);

WriteLine($"Expression: {expression}");
WriteLine(@"          \ / \ / \ / \ / \ / \ /");
WriteLine($"           -   -   -   -   -   -");
WriteLine($"           |   |   |   |   |   |");
WriteLine($"           |   |   |   |   |   +--- day of week (0 - 6)
(Sunday=0)");
WriteLine($"           |   |   |   |   +------- month (1 - 12)");
WriteLine($"           |   |   |   +----------- day of month (1 -
31)");
WriteLine($"           |   |   +--------------- hour (0 - 23)");
WriteLine($"           |   +------------------- min (0 - 59)");
WriteLine($"           +----------------------- sec (0 - 59)");
WriteLine();

CrontabSchedule schedule = CrontabSchedule.Parse(expression,
  new CrontabSchedule.ParseOptions { IncludingSeconds = true });

IEnumerable<DateTime> occurrences = schedule.GetNextOccurrences(start,
end);

// Output the first 40 occurrences.
foreach (DateTime occurrence in occurrences.Take(40))
{
  WriteLine($"{occurrence:ddd, dd MMM yyyy HH:mm:ss}");
}
```

Note the following:

- The default potential time span for occurrences is the whole year of 2023.
- The default expression is 0,30 * * * * *, meaning at 0 and 30 seconds of every minute of every hour of every day of every week of every month.

- The formatting for the syntax help assumes each component will be three characters wide because -3 is used for output formatting. You could write a cleverer algorithm to dynamically adjust the arrows to point to variable width components, but I got lazy. I will leave that as an exercise for the reader.
- Our expression includes seconds, so when parsing, we must set that as an additional option.
- After defining the schedule, the schedule calls its GetNextOccurrences method to return a sequence of all the calculated occurrences.
- The loop only outputs the first 40 occurrences. That should be enough to understand how most expressions work.

5.  Start the console app without debugging, and note the occurrences are every 30 seconds, as shown in the following partial output:

```
Start at:   Sun, 01 Jan 2023 00:00:00
End at:     Mon, 01 Jan 2024 00:00:00

Expression: 0,30 *    *    *    *    *
            \ / \ / \ / \ / \ / \ /
             -   -   -   -   -   -
             |   |   |   |   |   |
             |   |   |   |   |   +--- day of week (0 - 6) (Sunday=0)
             |   |   |   |   +------- month (1 - 12)
             |   |   |   +----------- day of month (1 - 31)
             |   |   +--------------- hour (0 - 23)
             |   +------------------- min (0 - 59)
             +----------------------- sec (0 - 59)


Sun, 01 Jan 2023 00:00:30
Sun, 01 Jan 2023 00:01:00
Sun, 01 Jan 2023 00:01:30
...
Sun, 01 Jan 2023 00:14:30
Sun, 01 Jan 2023 00:15:00
```

 Note that although the start time is Sun, 01 Jan 2023 at 00:00:00, that value is excluded from the occurrences because it is not a "next" occurrence.

6.  Close the console app.
7.  In Program.cs, modify the components of the expression to test some of the examples in the table, or make up your own examples. Try the expression 0 0 */4 * * *, and note it should have the following partial output:

```
Start at:    Sun, 01 Jan 2023 00:00:00
End at:      Mon, 01 Jan 2024 00:00:00

Expression: 0    0    */4 *    *    *
                 \ / \ / \ / \ / \ / \ /
                 -  -  -  -  -  -
                 |  |  |  |  |  |
                 |  |  |  |  |  +--- day of week (0 - 6) (Sunday=0)
                 |  |  |  |  +------- month (1 - 12)
                 |  |  |  +---------- day of month (1 - 31)
                 |  |  +------------- hour (0 - 23)
                 |  +---------------- min (0 - 59)
                 +------------------- sec (0 - 59)

Sun, 01 Jan 2023 04:00:00
Sun, 01 Jan 2023 08:00:00
Sun, 01 Jan 2023 12:00:00
Sun, 01 Jan 2023 16:00:00
Sun, 01 Jan 2023 20:00:00
Mon, 02 Jan 2023 00:00:00
Mon, 02 Jan 2023 04:00:00
Mon, 02 Jan 2023 08:00:00
Mon, 02 Jan 2023 12:00:00
Mon, 02 Jan 2023 16:00:00
Mon, 02 Jan 2023 20:00:00
Tue, 03 Jan 2023 00:00:00
...
```

Note that although the start time is Sun, 01 Jan 2023 00:00:00, that value is excluded from the occurrences because it is not a "next" occurrence. So, Sunday only has five occurrences. Monday onward has the expected six occurrences per day.

## Azure Functions versions and languages

Azure Functions currently supports four versions of the runtime host and multiple languages, as shown in the following table:

| Language | v1 | v2 | v3 | v4 |
|---|---|---|---|---|
| C#, F# | .NET Framework 4.8 | .NET Core 2.1 | .NET Core 3.1, .NET 5.0[2] | .NET 7.0[2], .NET 6.0[3], .NET Framework 4.8[4] |
| JavaScript[1] | Node.js 6 | Node 8, 10 | Node 10, 12, 14 | Node 14, 16 |
| Java | - | Java 8 | Java 8, 11 | Java 8, 11 |

| PowerShell | - | PowerShell Core 6 | PowerShell 7, Core 6 | PowerShell 7 |
|---|---|---|---|---|
| Python | - | Python 3.6, 3.7 | Python 3.6, 3.7, 3.8, 3.9 | Python 3.7, 3.8, 3.9 |

[1] Azure Functions supports the TypeScript language via transpiling (transforming/compiling) to JavaScript.

[2] .NET 5.0 and .NET 7.0 are only supported in the isolated hosting model because they are **Standard Term Support (STS)** releases.

[3] .NET 6.0 supports both isolated and in-process hosting models because it is a **Long Term Support (LTS)** release. When .NET 8.0 LTS releases in November 2023, it will also support both hosting models. By then, there will be an Azure Functions v5 because each version can only have a single version of .NET.

[4] Support for .NET Framework 4.8 with v4 is in preview at the time of writing.

**Good Practice:** Microsoft recommends using v4 for functions in all languages. v1 and v2 are in maintenance mode and should be avoided.

In this book, we will only look at implementing Azure Functions v4 and only using C# and .NET 6.0 so that we can use the in-process hosting model and get long term support.

For advanced uses, you can even register a custom handler that would enable you to use any language you like for the implementation of a function. You can read more about Azure Functions custom handlers at the following link: `https://docs.microsoft.com/en-us/azure/azure-functions/functions-custom-handlers`.

## Azure Functions hosting models

Azure Functions has two hosting models, in-process and isolated, as described in the following list:

- **In-process:** Your function is implemented in a class library that runs in the same process as the host. Your functions are required to run on the same version of .NET as the Azure Functions runtime, which means your functions must run on LTS releases of .NET. The latest LTS release is .NET 6. The next LTS release will be .NET 8 in November 2023.
- **Isolated:** Your function is implemented in a console app that runs in its own process. Your function can therefore execute on STS releases like .NET 7.0 that are not supported by the Azure Functions runtime, which only allows LTS releases in-process.

Azure Functions only natively supports one LTS version of .NET per version. For example, for Azure Functions v3, your function must use .NET Core 3.1 to use the in-process hosting model. For Azure Functions v4, your function must use .NET 6.0 to use the in-process hosting model. If you create an isolated function, then you can choose any .NET version.

**Good Practice:** For the best performance and scalability, use the in-process hosting model.

# Azure Functions hosting plans

After testing locally, you must deploy your Azure Functions project to an Azure hosting plan. There are three Azure Functions plans to choose from, as described in the following list:

- **Consumption:** In this plan, host instances are dynamically added and removed based on activity. This plan is the closest to *serverless*. It scales automatically during periods of high load. The cost is only for compute resources when your functions are running. You can configure a timeout for function execution times to ensure that your functions do not run forever.

- **Premium:** This plan supports elastic scaling up and down, perpetually warm instances to avoid cold starts, unlimited execution duration, multicore instance sizes up to four cores, potentially more predictable costs, and high-density app allocation for multiple Azure Functions projects. The cost is based on the number of core seconds and memory allocated across instances. At least one instance must be allocated at all times, so there will always be a minimum monthly cost per active plan even if it never executes that month.

- **Dedicated:** Executes in the cloud equivalent of a server farm. Hosting is provided by an Azure App Service plan that controls the allocated server resources. Azure App Service plans include Basic, Standard, Premium, and Isolated. This plan can be an especially good choice if you already have an App Service plan used for other projects like ASP.NET Core MVC websites, gRPC, OData, GraphQL services, and so on. The cost is only for the App Service plan. You can host as many Azure Functions and other web apps in it as you like.

 **Warning!** Premium and Dedicated plans both run on Azure App Service plans. You must carefully select the correct App Service plan that works with your Azure Functions hosting plan. For example, for Premium, you should choose an Elastic Premium plan like `EP1`. If you choose an App Service plan like `P1V1`, then you are choosing a Dedicated plan that will not elastically scale!

 You can read more about your choices at the following link: `https://docs.microsoft.com/en-us/azure/azure-functions/functions-scale`.

# Azure Storage requirements

Azure Functions requires an Azure Storage account for storing information for some bindings and triggers. These Azure Storage services can also be used by your code for its implementation:

- **Azure Files:** Stores and runs your function app code in a Consumption or Premium plan.

- **Azure Blob Storage:** Stores state for bindings and function keys.
- **Azure Queue Storage:** Used for failure and retry handling by some triggers.
- **Azure Table Storage:** Task hubs in Durable Functions use Blob, Queue, and Table Storage.

# Testing locally with Azurite

Azurite is an open-source local environment for testing Azure Functions with its related Blob, Queue, and Table Storage. Azurite is cross-platform on Windows, Linux, and macOS. Azurite supersedes the older Azure Storage Emulator.

To install Azurite:

- For Visual Studio 2022, Azurite is included.
- For Visual Studio Code, search for and install the Azurite extension.
- For installation at the command line, you must have Node.js version 8.0 or later installed and then you can enter the following command:

```
npm install -g azurite
```

Once you have locally tested a function, you can switch to an Azure Storage account in the cloud.

 You can learn more about Azurite at the following link: `https://docs.microsoft.com/en-us/azure/storage/common/storage-use-azurite`.

# Azure Functions authorization levels

Azure Functions has three authorization levels that control if an API key is required:

- **Anonymous:** No API key is required.
- **Function:** A function-level key is required.
- **Admin:** The master key is required.

API keys are available through the Azure portal.

# Azure Functions support for dependency injection

Dependency injection in Azure Functions is built on the standard .NET dependency injection features, but there are implementation differences depending on your chosen host model.

To register dependency services, create a class that inherits from the `FunctionsStartup` class and override its `Configure` method. Add the `[FunctionsStartup]` assembly attribute to specify the class name registered for startup. Add services to the `IFunctionsHostBuilder` instance passed to the method. You will do this in a task later in this chapter.

Normally, the class that implements an Azure Functions function is static with a static method. The use of constructor injection means that you must use instance classes for injected services and for your function class implementation.

## Installing Azure Functions Core Tools

**Azure Functions Core Tools** provides the core runtime and templates for creating functions, which enable local development on Windows, macOS, and Linux using any code editor.

 Azure Functions Core Tools is included in the **Azure development** workload of Visual Studio 2022, so you might already have it installed.

You can install the latest version of Azure Functions Core Tools from the following link:

`https://www.npmjs.com/package/azure-functions-core-tools`

The page above has instructions for installing using MSI and winget on Windows, Homebrew on Mac, npm on any operating system, and common Linux distributions.

# Building an Azure Functions project

Now, we can create an Azure Functions project. Although they can be created in the cloud using the Azure portal, developers will have a better experience creating and running them locally first. You can then deploy to the cloud once you have tested your function on your own computer.

Each code editor has a slightly different experience to getting started with an Azure Functions project, so let's have a look at each, in turn, starting with Visual Studio 2022.

## Using Visual Studio 2022

If you prefer to use Visual Studio 2022, here are the steps to create an Azure Functions project:

1.  In Visual Studio 2022, create a new project, as defined in the following list:

    *   Project template: **Azure Functions**
    *   Workspace/solution file and folder: Chapter14
    *   Project file and folder: Northwind.AzureFunctions.Service

2.  Choose options as shown in the following list:

    *   **Functions worker: .NET 6**
    *   **Function: Http trigger**
    *   Select **Use Azurite for runtime storage account (AzureWebJobsStorage)**
    *   Clear **Enable Docker**

- Authorization level: **Anonymous**

3.   Click **Create**.

## Using Visual Studio Code

If you prefer to use Visual Studio Code, here are the steps to create an Azure Functions project:

1.   In Visual Studio Code, navigate to **Extensions** and search for Azure Functions (ms-azuretools. vscode-azurefunctions). It has dependencies on two other extensions: Azure account (ms-vscode.azure-account) and Azure resources (ms-azuretools.vscode-azureresourcegroups), so those will be installed too. Click the **Install** button to install the extension.

2.   Create a Chapter14 folder and save a workspace as Chapter14.code-workspace in it.

> If you followed the instructions for Visual Studio 2022, then you will already have a Chapter14 folder. Create one named Chapter14-vscode instead so that you can compare both ways if you like.

3.   Create a subfolder named Northwind.AzureFunctions.Service and add it to the Chapter14 workspace.

4.   Close the Chapter14 workspace because the next few steps only work outside a workspace.

5.   In Visual Studio Code, open the Northwind.AzureFunctions.Service folder.

6.   Navigate to **View** | **Command Palette**, and type azure f, as shown in *Figure 14.1*:

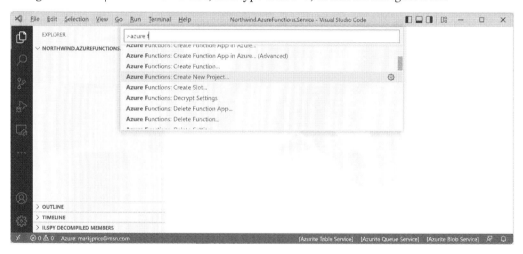

*Figure 14.1: Using Command Palette to select an Azure Functions command*

7.   In the list of **Azure Functions** commands, click **Azure Functions: Create New Project...**, and then select the Northwind.AzureFunctions.Service folder, as shown in *Figure 14.2*:

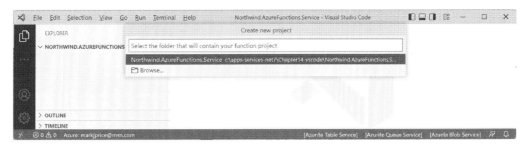

Figure 14.2: Selecting the folder for your Azure Functions project

8.  At the prompts, select the following:

    •   Select a language: **C#**

    •   Select a .NET runtime: **.NET 6**, as shown in *Figure 14.3*:

Figure 14.3: Selecting the target .NET runtime for your Azure Functions project

    •   Select a template for your project's first function: **HTTP trigger**

Figure 14.4: Selecting a trigger for the Azure Functions first function

    •   Provide a function name: NumbersToWordsFunction

    •   Provide a namespace: Northwind.AzureFunctions.Service

    •   Select the authorization level: **Anonymous**

9.  In the Visual Studio Code **File** menu, close the folder.

10. Open the Chapter14 workspace.

11. Navigate to **Terminal** | **New Terminal**.

12. At the command prompt, build the project, as shown in the following command:

```
dotnet build
```

## Using the func CLI

If you prefer to use the command line and some other code editor, here are the steps to create and start an Azure Functions project:

1. Create a `Chapter14` folder with a subfolder named `Northwind.AzureFunctions.Service`.

 If you followed the instructions for Visual Studio 2022 or Visual Studio Code, then you will already have a `Chapter14` folder. Create one named `Chapter14-cli` instead so that you can compare the three ways if you like.

2. In the command prompt or terminal, in the `Northwind.AzureFunctions.Service` folder, create a new Azure Functions project using C#, as shown in the following command:

```
func init --csharp
```

3. In the command prompt or terminal, in the `Northwind.AzureFunctions.Service` folder, create a new Azure Functions function using `HTTP trigger` that can be called anonymously, as shown in the following command:

```
func new --name NumbersToWordsFunction --template "HTTP trigger"
--authlevel "anonymous"
```

4. Optionally, you can start the function locally, as shown in the following command:

```
func start
```

 If you cannot find `func` at the command prompt or terminal, then try installing the Azure Functions Core Tools using Chocolatey, as described at the following link: `https://community.chocolatey.org/packages/azure-functions-core-tools`.

## Reviewing the Azure Functions project

Before we write a function, let's review what makes an Azure Functions project:

1. Open the project file, and note the Azure Functions version and the package references needed to implement a function that responds to HTTP requests, as shown in the following markup:

```
<Project Sdk="Microsoft.NET.Sdk">
  <PropertyGroup>
    <TargetFramework>net6.0</TargetFramework>
```

```
      <AzureFunctionsVersion>v4</AzureFunctionsVersion>
    </PropertyGroup>
    <ItemGroup>
      <PackageReference Include="Microsoft.NET.Sdk.Functions"
                        Version="4.1.1" />
    </ItemGroup>
    <ItemGroup>
      <None Update="host.json">
        <CopyToOutputDirectory>PreserveNewest</CopyToOutputDirectory>
      </None>
      <None Update="local.settings.json">
        <CopyToOutputDirectory>PreserveNewest</CopyToOutputDirectory>
        <CopyToPublishDirectory>Never</CopyToPublishDirectory>
      </None>
    </ItemGroup>
</Project>
```

2.  In host.json, note that logging to Application Insights is enabled but excludes Request types, as shown in the following markup:

```
{
    "version": "2.0",
    "logging": {
        "applicationInsights": {
            "samplingSettings": {
                "isEnabled": true,
                "excludedTypes": "Request"
            }
        }
    }
}
```

 Application Insights is Azure's monitoring and logging service. We will not be using it in this chapter.

3.  In local.settings.json, confirm that during local development, your project will use local development storage and an in-process hosting model, as shown in the following markup:

```
{
  "IsEncrypted": false,
  "Values": {
    "AzureWebJobsStorage": "UseDevelopmentStorage=true",
    "FUNCTIONS_WORKER_RUNTIME": "dotnet"
  }
}
```

4.  If the `AzureWebJobsStorage` setting is blank or missing, which might happen if you are using Visual Studio Code, then add it and set it to `UseDevelopmentStorage=true`, and then save changes.

> `FUNCTIONS_WORKER_RUNTIME` is the language being used by your project. `dotnet` means a .NET class library; `dotnet-isolated` would mean a .NET console app. Other values include `java`, `node`, `powershell`, and `python`.

## Implementing a simple function

We will write a function to convert numbers into words.

> Our implementation is borrowed from "Convert A Number into Words" by Richard Carr, published at the following link: `http://www.blackwasp.co.uk/numbertowords.aspx`.

Let's implement the function to convert numbers into words:

1.  Add a new class file named `NumbersToWords.cs`.
2.  To save typing almost 200 lines of code, copy the code for this class from the following link: `https://github.com/markjprice/apps-services-net7/blob/main/vs4win/Chapter14/Northwind.AzureFunctions.Service/NumbersToWords.cs`.

    *   If you are using Visual Studio 2022, in the `Northwind.AzureFunctions.Service` project, right-click `Function1.cs` and rename it to `NumbersToWordsFunction.cs`.

3.  In `NumbersToWordsFunction.cs`, modify the contents to implement a function to convert an amount as a number into words, as shown in the following code:

```
// IActionResult, OkObjectResult, BadRequestObjectResult
using Microsoft.AspNetCore.Mvc;
using Microsoft.Azure.WebJobs; // [FunctionName], [HttpTrigger]
using Microsoft.Azure.WebJobs.Extensions.Http; // AuthorizationLevel
using Microsoft.AspNetCore.Http; // HttpRequest
using Microsoft.Extensions.Logging; // ILogger
using System.Numerics; // BigInteger
using Packt.Shared; // ToWords extension method
using System.Threading.Tasks; // Task<T>

namespace Northwind.AzureFunctions.Service;

public static class NumbersToWordsFunction
{
  [FunctionName(nameof(NumbersToWordsFunction))]
  public static async Task<IActionResult> Run(
```

```
    [HttpTrigger(AuthorizationLevel.Anonymous,
      "get", "post", Route = null)] HttpRequest req,
    ILogger log)
  {
    log.LogInformation("C# HTTP trigger function processed a request.");

    string amount = req.Query["amount"];

    if (BigInteger.TryParse(amount, out BigInteger number))
    {
      return await Task.FromResult(new OkObjectResult(number.ToWords()));
    }
    else
    {
      return new BadRequestObjectResult($"Failed to parse: {amount}");
    }
  }
}
```

# Testing a simple function

Now we can test the function in our local development environment:

1. Start the `Northwind.AzureFunctions.Service` project.

   - If you are using Visual Studio Code, you will need to navigate to the **Run and Debug** pane, make sure that **Attach to .NET Functions** is selected, and then click the **Run** button.

   - On Windows, if you see a **Windows Security Alert** from **Windows Defender Firewall**, then click **Allow access**.

2. Note that **Azure Functions Core Tools** hosts your function by default on port 7071, as shown in the following output and *Figure 14.5*:

```
Azure Functions Core Tools
Core Tools Version:       4.0.4544 Commit hash:
44e84987044afc45f0390191bd5d70680a1c544e   (64-bit)
Function Runtime Version: 4.3.2.18186

[2022-06-03T11:27:13.041Z] Found C:\apps-services-net7\Chapter14\
Northwind.AzureFunctions.Service\Northwind.AzureFunctions.Service.csproj.
Using for user secrets file configuration.

Functions:

        NumbersToWordsFunction: [GET,POST] http://localhost:7071/api/
NumbersToWordsFunction

For detailed output, run func with --verbose flag.
```

```
[2022-06-03T11:27:21.937Z] Host lock lease acquired by instance ID '00000
00000000000000011150C3D'.
```

*Figure 14.5: Azure Functions Core Tools hosting a function*

3. Select the URL for your function and copy it to the clipboard.

4. Start Chrome.

5. Paste the URL into the address box, append the query string `?amount=123456`, and note the successful response in the browser of **one hundred and twenty three thousand, four hundred and fifty six**, as shown in *Figure 14.6*:

*Figure 14.6: A successful call to the function running locally*

6. In the command prompt or terminal, note the function was called successfully, as shown in the following output:

```
[2022-06-03T11:32:51.574Z] Executing 'NumbersToWordsFunction'
(Reason='This function was programmatically called via the host APIs.',
Id=234d3122-ff3d-4896-94b3-db3c8b5013d8)
[2022-06-03T11:32:51.603Z] C# HTTP trigger function processed a request.
[2022-06-03T11:32:51.629Z] Executed 'NumbersToWordsFunction' (Succeeded,
Id=234d3122-ff3d-4896-94b3-db3c8b5013d8, Duration=96ms)
```

7. Try calling the function without an amount in the query string, or a non-integer value for the amount, and note the function returns a `400` status code indicating a bad request, as shown in *Figure 14.7*:

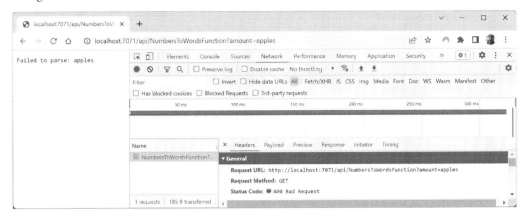

*Figure 14.7: A bad request to the Azure Function running locally*

8. Close Chrome and shut down the web server (or in Visual Studio Code, stop debugging).

# Responding to timer and resource triggers

Now that you have seen an Azure Functions function that responds to an HTTP request, let's build some that respond to other types of triggers.

Support for HTTP and timer triggers is built in. Support for other bindings is implemented as extension packages.

## Implementing a timer triggered function

First, we will make a function that runs every hour and requests a page from amazon.com for the sixth edition of my book, *C# 10 and .NET 6 – Modern Cross-Platform Development*, so that I can keep track of its Best Sellers Rank in the United States.

The function will need to make HTTP `GET` requests so we should inject the HTTP client factory. To do that, we will need to add some extra package references and create a special startup class:

1. In the `Northwind.AzureFunctions.Service` project, add package references for working with Azure Functions extensions, HTTP extensions, and if necessary, update the version of the `Microsoft.NET.Sdk.Functions` package reference to the latest, as shown highlighted in the following markup:

```xml
<ItemGroup>
  <PackageReference Include="Microsoft.Azure.Functions.Extensions"
                    Version="1.1.0" />
  <PackageReference Include="Microsoft.Extensions.Http" Version="6.0.0" />
  <PackageReference Include="Microsoft.NET.Sdk.Functions"
```

```
                          Version="4.1.1" />
    </ItemGroup>
```

2. Build the `Northwind.AzureFunctions.Service` project.

3. In the `Northwind.AzureFunctions.Service` project, add a class file named `AzureFunctionsStartup.cs` to inject the HTTP client factory.

4. Modify its contents, as shown in the following code:

```
// [FunctionsStartup], FunctionsStartup, IFunctionsHostBuilder
using Microsoft.Azure.Functions.Extensions.DependencyInjection;

// AddHttpClient extension method
using Microsoft.Extensions.DependencyInjection;

// MediaTypeWithQualityHeaderValue
using System.Net.Http.Headers;

[assembly: FunctionsStartup(typeof(
  Northwind.AzureFunctions.Service.AzureFunctionsStartup))]
namespace Northwind.AzureFunctions.Service;

public class AzureFunctionsStartup : FunctionsStartup
{
  public override void Configure(IFunctionsHostBuilder builder)
  {
    builder.Services.AddHttpClient(name: "Amazon",
      configureClient: options =>
    {
      options.BaseAddress = new System.Uri("https://www.amazon.com");

      // pretend to be Chrome in US English

      options.DefaultRequestHeaders.Accept.Add(
        new MediaTypeWithQualityHeaderValue("text/html"));
      options.DefaultRequestHeaders.Accept.Add(
        new MediaTypeWithQualityHeaderValue("application/xhtml+xml"));
      options.DefaultRequestHeaders.Accept.Add(
        new MediaTypeWithQualityHeaderValue("application/xml", 0.9));
      options.DefaultRequestHeaders.Accept.Add(
        new MediaTypeWithQualityHeaderValue("image/avif"));
      options.DefaultRequestHeaders.Accept.Add(
        new MediaTypeWithQualityHeaderValue("image/webp"));
      options.DefaultRequestHeaders.Accept.Add(
        new MediaTypeWithQualityHeaderValue("image/apng"));
      options.DefaultRequestHeaders.Accept.Add(
        new MediaTypeWithQualityHeaderValue("*/*", 0.8));
```

```
      options.DefaultRequestHeaders.AcceptLanguage.Add(
        new StringWithQualityHeaderValue("en-US"));
      options.DefaultRequestHeaders.AcceptLanguage.Add(
        new StringWithQualityHeaderValue("en-GB",0.9));
      options.DefaultRequestHeaders.AcceptLanguage.Add(
        new StringWithQualityHeaderValue("en",0.8));

      options.DefaultRequestHeaders.UserAgent.Add(
        new(productName: "Chrome", productVersion: "102.0.0.0"));
    });
  }
}
```

5.  Add a class file named `ScrapeAmazonFunction.cs`.

6.  Modify its contents to implement a function that requests the page for the sixth edition of my book on the Amazon website and process the response, which is compressed using GZIP, to extract the book's Best Seller Rank, as shown in the following code:

```
using Microsoft.Azure.WebJobs; // [FunctionName], [TimerTrigger]
using Microsoft.Extensions.Logging; // ILogger
using System.IO; // Stream, StreamReader
using System.IO.Compression; // GZipStream, CompressionMode
using System.Net.Http; // IHttpClientFactory, HttpClient
using System.Threading.Tasks; // Task<T>

namespace Northwind.AzureFunctions.Service;

public class ScrapeAmazonFunction
{
  private const string relativePath =
    "10-NET-Cross-Platform-Development-websites/dp/1801077363/";

  private readonly IHttpClientFactory clientFactory;

  public ScrapeAmazonFunction(IHttpClientFactory clientFactory)
  {
    this.clientFactory = clientFactory;
  }

  [FunctionName(nameof(ScrapeAmazonFunction))]
  public async Task Run( // every hour
    [TimerTrigger("0 0 * * * *")] TimerInfo timer,
    ILogger log)
  {
    log.LogInformation("C# Timer trigger function executed at {0}.",
      System.DateTime.UtcNow);
```

```csharp
      log.LogInformation(
        "C# Timer trigger function next three occurrences at: " +
        $"{timer.FormatNextOccurrences(3, System.DateTime.UtcNow)}.");

      HttpClient client = clientFactory.CreateClient("Amazon");
      HttpResponseMessage response = await client.GetAsync(relativePath);
      log.LogInformation($"Request: GET {client.BaseAddress}{relativePath}");

      if (response.IsSuccessStatusCode)
      {
        log.LogInformation($"Successful HTTP request.");

        // read the content from a GZIP stream into a string
        Stream stream = await response.Content.ReadAsStreamAsync();
        GZipStream gzipStream = new(stream, CompressionMode.Decompress);
        StreamReader reader = new(gzipStream);
        string page = reader.ReadToEnd();

        // extract the Best Sellers Rank
        int posBsr = page.IndexOf("Best Sellers Rank");
        string bsrSection = page.Substring(posBsr, 45);

        // bsrSection will be something like:
        //    "Best Sellers Rank: </span> #22,258 in Books ("

        // get the position of the # and the following space
        int posHash = bsrSection.IndexOf("#") + 1;
        int posSpaceAfterHash = bsrSection.IndexOf(" ", posHash);

        // get the BSR number as text
        string bsr = bsrSection.Substring(
          posHash, posSpaceAfterHash - posHash);
        bsr = bsr.Replace(",", null); // remove commas

        // parse the text into a number
        if (int.TryParse(bsr, out int bestSellersRank))
        {
          log.LogInformation($"Best Sellers Rank #{bestSellersRank:N0}.");
        }
        else
        {
          log.LogError($"Failed to extract BSR number from: {bsrSection}.");
        }
      }
      else
```

```
        {
            log.LogError($"Bad HTTP request.");
        }
    }
}
```

# Testing the Timer triggered function

Information about a function can be retrieved by making an HTTP GET request in the following format:

```
http://locahost:7071/admin/functions/<functionname>
```

Now we can test the Timer function in our local development environment:

1. Start the `Northwind.AzureFunctions.Service` project.

    • If you are using Visual Studio Code, you will need to make sure you have the Azurite extension installed and the Azurite services running. Navigate to the **Run and Debug** pane, make sure that **Attach to .NET Functions** is selected, and then click the **Run** button.

2. Note there are now two functions, as shown in the following partial output:

```
Functions:

        NumbersToWordsFunction: [GET,POST] http://localhost:7071/api/
NumbersToWordsFunction

        ScrapeAmazonFunction: timerTrigger
```

3. Start Visual Studio Code.
4. Open the `RestClientTests` folder.
5. Add a new file named `azurefunctions-scrapeamazon.http`.
6. Modify its contents, as shown in the following code:

```
### Get information about the NumbersToWordsFunction function
GET http://localhost:7071/admin/functions/NumbersToWordsFunction
### Get information about the ScrapeAmazonFunction function
GET http://localhost:7071/admin/functions/ScrapeAmazonFunction
```

7. Send the first request and note that a JSON document is returned with information about the `NumbersToWordsFunction` function, as shown in the following response:

```
HTTP/1.1 200 OK
Content-Length: 918
Connection: close
Content-Type: application/json; charset=utf-8
Date: Sat, 04 Jun 2022 13:32:11 GMT
Server: Kestrel
```

```json
{
  "name": "NumbersToWordsFunction",
  "script_root_path_href": "http://localhost:7071/admin/vfs/
NumbersToWordsFunction/",
  "script_href": "http://localhost:7071/admin/vfs/bin/Northwind.
AzureFunctions.Service.dll",
  "config_href": "http://localhost:7071/admin/vfs/NumbersToWordsFunction/
function.json",
  "test_data_href": null,
  "href": "http://localhost:7071/admin/functions/NumbersToWordsFunction",
  "invoke_url_template": "http://localhost:7071/api/
numberstowordsfunction",
  "language": "DotNetAssembly",
  "config": {
    "generatedBy": "Microsoft.NET.Sdk.Functions.Generator-4.1.1",
    "configurationSource": "attributes",
    "bindings": [
      {
        "type": "httpTrigger",
        "methods": [
          "get",
          "post"
        ],
        "authLevel": "anonymous",
        "name": "req"
      }
    ],
    "disabled": false,
    "scriptFile": "../bin/Northwind.AzureFunctions.Service.dll",
    "entryPoint": "Northwind.AzureFunctions.Service.
NumbersToWordsFunction.Run"
  },
  "files": null,
  "test_data": null,
  "isDisabled": false,
  "isDirect": true,
  "isProxy": false
}
```

8. Send the second request and note that a JSON document is returned with information about the `ScrapeAmazonFunction` function. The most interesting information for this function is the bindings type and schedule, as shown in the following partial response:

```json
"bindings": [
  {
    "type": "timerTrigger",
    "schedule": "0 0 * * * *",
    "useMonitor": true,
```

```
        "runOnStartup": false,
        "name": "timer"
    }
  ],
```

9. Add a third request that will trigger the Timer function manually without having to wait for the hour mark by POSTing an empty JSON document to its admin endpoint, as shown in the following code:

```
### Make a manual request to the Timer function
POST http://localhost:7071/admin/functions/ScrapeAmazonFunction
Content-Type: application/json

{}
```

10. Send the third request and note that it was successfully accepted, as shown in the following response:

```
HTTP/1.1 202 Accepted
Content-Length: 0
Connection: close
Date: Sat, 04 Jun 2022 13:42:57 GMT
Server: Kestrel
```

11. Remove the {} in the body of the request, send it again, and note the client error response from which we can deduce that an empty JSON document is required, as shown in the following response:

```
HTTP/1.1 400 Bad Request
Content-Length: 0
Connection: close
Date: Sat, 04 Jun 2022 14:03:42 GMT
Server: Kestrel
```

12. Add the empty JSON document back.

13. At the command line or terminal, note that the function was triggered by our call; it output the time it was triggered (1:42 PM) and the times of its next three occurrences in its normal schedule (2 PM, 3 PM, and 4 PM, all in the UTC time zone) if I were to leave the service running, as shown in the following output:

```
[2022-06-04T13:42:58.471Z] Executing 'ScrapeAmazonFunction' (Reason='This
function was programmatically called via the host APIs.', Id=2b2bc297-
1870-4ee7-a289-beb0910c54db)
[2022-06-04T13:42:58.473Z] C# Timer trigger function executed at
06/04/2022 13:42:58.
[2022-06-04T13:42:58.474Z] C# Timer trigger function next three
occurrences at: 06/04/2022 14:00:00Z (06/04/2022 14:00:00Z)
[2022-06-04T13:42:58.475Z] 06/04/2022 15:00:00Z (06/04/2022 15:00:00Z)
[2022-06-04T13:42:58.476Z] 06/04/2022 16:00:00Z (06/04/2022 16:00:00Z)
```

```
[2022-06-04T13:42:58.478Z] .
[2022-06-04T13:43:00.133Z] Request: GET https://www.amazon.com/10-NET-
Cross-Platform-Development-websites/dp/1801077363/
[2022-06-04T13:43:00.137Z] Successful HTTP request.
[2022-06-04T13:43:00.185Z] Best Sellers Rank #22,258.
[2022-06-04T13:43:00.187Z] Executed 'ScrapeAmazonFunction' (Succeeded,
Id=2b2bc297-1870-4ee7-a289-beb0910c54db, Duration=1726ms)
```

14. Optionally, wait until the hour mark and note that the next occurrence triggers, as shown in the following output:

```
[2022-06-04T14:00:00.005Z] Executing 'ScrapeAmazonFunction'
(Reason='Timer fired at 2022-06-04T15:00:00.0043305+01:00', Id=2d3d3233-
5a51-4e20-b9e6-2462b0058593)
[2022-06-04T14:00:00.008Z] C# Timer trigger function executed at
06/04/2022 14:00:00.
[2022-06-04T14:00:00.011Z] C# Timer trigger function next three
occurrences at: 06/04/2022 15:00:00Z (06/04/2022 15:00:00Z)
[2022-06-04T14:00:00.013Z] 06/04/2022 16:00:00Z (06/04/2022 16:00:00Z)
[2022-06-04T14:00:00.014Z] 06/04/2022 17:00:00Z (06/04/2022 17:00:00Z)
[2022-06-04T14:00:00.016Z] .
[2022-06-04T14:00:01.835Z] Request: GET https://www.amazon.com/10-NET-
Cross-Platform-Development-websites/dp/1801077363/
[2022-06-04T14:00:01.836Z] Successful HTTP request.
[2022-06-04T14:00:01.868Z] Best Sellers Rank #22,258.
[2022-06-04T14:00:01.872Z] Executed 'ScrapeAmazonFunction' (Succeeded,
Id=2d3d3233-5a51-4e20-b9e6-2462b0058593, Duration=1867ms)
```

15. If I were to stop the service running, wait for more than an hour, and then start the service, it would immediately run the function because it is past due, as shown highlighted in the following output:

```
[2022-06-04T16:19:31.367Z] Executing 'ScrapeAmazonFunction'
(Reason='Timer fired at 2022-06-04T17:19:31.3297218+01:00', Id=8adb3675-
d677-4a7b-9a77-e0fb1c3e0fee)
[2022-06-04T16:19:31.369Z] Trigger Details: UnscheduledInvocationReason:
IsPastDue, OriginalSchedule: 2022-06-04T16:00:00.0000000+01:00
[2022-06-04T16:19:31.383Z] C# Timer trigger function executed at
06/04/2022 16:19:31.
[2022-06-04T16:19:31.384Z] C# Timer trigger function next three
occurrences at: 06/04/2022 17:00:00Z (06/04/2022 17:00:00Z)
[2022-06-04T16:19:31.385Z] 06/04/2022 18:00:00Z (06/04/2022 18:00:00Z)
[2022-06-04T16:19:31.386Z] 06/04/2022 19:00:00Z (06/04/2022 19:00:00Z)
[2022-06-04T16:19:31.387Z] .
[2022-06-04T16:19:33.694Z] Request: GET https://www.amazon.com/10-NET-
Cross-Platform-Development-websites/dp/1801077363/
[2022-06-04T16:19:33.698Z] Successful HTTP request.
[2022-06-04T16:19:33.720Z] Best Sellers Rank #24,412.
[2022-06-04T16:19:33.732Z] Executed 'ScrapeAmazonFunction' (Succeeded,
```

```
Id=8adb3675-d677-4a7b-9a77-e0fb1c3e0fee, Duration=2394ms)
```

16. Stop the service.

## Implementing a function that works with queues and BLOBs

The HTTP triggered function responded directly to the GET request with plain text. We will now extend that function to bind to Queue Storage and add a message to a queue to indicate that an image needs to be generated and uploaded to Blob Storage. This can then be printed as a check.

When running the service locally, we want to generate the image of the check BLOB in the local filesystem to make it easier to ensure it is working correctly. We will set a custom environment variable only in local settings to detect that condition.

We need a font that looks like handwriting. Google has a useful website where you can search for, preview, and download fonts. The one we will use is Caveat, as shown at the following link:

```
https://fonts.google.com/specimen/Caveat?category=Handwriting&preview.text=one%20
hundred%20and%20twenty%20three%20thousand,%20four%20hundred%20and%20fifty%20six&preview.
text_type=custom#standard-styles
```

Let's go:

1.  Download the font at the link above, extract the ZIP file, and copy the files into a folder named fonts, as shown in *Figure 14.8*:

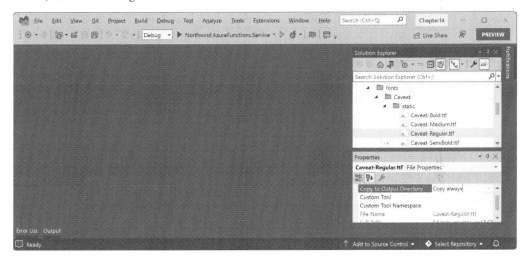

*Figure 14.8: The fonts folder with the Caveat font files*

2.  Select the Caveat-Regular.ttf font file.

3.  In **Properties**, set **Copy to Output Directory** to **Copy always**, as shown in *Figure 14.8*. This adds an entry to the project file, as shown highlighted in the following markup:

```
<ItemGroup>
  <None Update="fonts\Caveat\static\Caveat-Regular.ttf">
    <CopyToOutputDirectory>Always</CopyToOutputDirectory>
```

```
  </None>
  <None Update="host.json">
    <CopyToOutputDirectory>PreserveNewest</CopyToOutputDirectory>
  </None>
  <None Update="local.settings.json">
    <CopyToOutputDirectory>PreserveNewest</CopyToOutputDirectory>
    <CopyToPublishDirectory>Never</CopyToPublishDirectory>
  </None>
</ItemGroup>
```

4.  In the `Northwind.AzureFunctions.Service` project, add package references for working with Azure Storage extensions and drawing with ImageSharp, as shown highlighted in the following markup:

```
<ItemGroup>
  <PackageReference Include="Microsoft.Azure.Functions.Extensions"
                    Version="1.1.0" />
  <PackageReference Include="Microsoft.Azure.WebJobs.Extensions.Storage"
                    Version="5.0.1" />
  <PackageReference Include="SixLabors.ImageSharp" Version="2.1.3" />
  <PackageReference Include="SixLabors.ImageSharp.Drawing"
                    Version="1.0.0-*" />
  <PackageReference Include="Microsoft.Extensions.Http" Version="6.0.0"
/>
  <PackageReference Include="Microsoft.NET.Sdk.Functions"
                    Version="4.1.1" />
</ItemGroup>
```

 The `Microsoft.Azure.WebJobs.Extensions.Storage` package references the packages for Blob and Queue Storage. If you also need Table Storage, then add a reference to `Microsoft.Azure.WebJobs.Extensions.Tables`.

5.  Build the project to restore packages.

6.  In the `Northwind.AzureFunctions.Service` project, in `NumbersToWordsFunction.cs`, decorate the class to specify the name of the Storage account, as shown highlighted in the following code:

```
[StorageAccount("AzureWebJobsStorage")]
public static class NumbersToWordsFunction
{
```

7.  In `NumbersToWordsFunction.cs`, add a statement to register the function with an output binding for Queue Storage so that it can write to a named queue, as shown highlighted in the following code:

```
public static async Task<IActionResult> Run(
    [HttpTrigger(AuthorizationLevel.Anonymous,
```

```
    "get", "post", Route = null)] HttpRequest req,
  [Queue("checksQueue")] ICollector<string> collector,
  ILogger log)
{
```

8.  In NumbersToWordsFunction.cs, modify the statements that run when the amount is success-
    fully parsed to add the words variable to the queue as well as return the words variable as an
    HTTP response, as shown highlighted in the following code:

```
if (BigInteger.TryParse(amount, out BigInteger number))
{
  string words = number.ToWords();
  collector.Add(words);
  return await Task.FromResult(new OkObjectResult(words));
}
else
{
  return new BadRequestObjectResult($"Failed to parse: {amount}");
}
```

9.  In local.settings.json, add an environment variable named IS_LOCAL with a value of true,
    as shown highlighted in the following configuration:

```
{
  "IsEncrypted": false,
  "Values": {
    "AzureWebJobsStorage": "UseDevelopmentStorage=true",
    "FUNCTIONS_WORKER_RUNTIME": "dotnet",
    "IS_LOCAL": true
  }
}
```

10. Add a class file named CheckGeneratorFunction.cs.

11. Modify its contents, as shown in the following code:

```
using Azure.Storage.Blobs; // BlobContainerClient
using Azure.Storage.Blobs.Models; // BlobContainerInfo
using Azure.Storage.Queues.Models; // QueueMessage
using Microsoft.Azure.WebJobs; // [FunctionName], [QueueTrigger]
using Microsoft.Extensions.Logging; // ILogger
using SixLabors.Fonts; // Font
using SixLabors.ImageSharp; // Image
using SixLabors.ImageSharp.Drawing; // IPath
using SixLabors.ImageSharp.Drawing.Processing; // IBrush, IPen
using SixLabors.ImageSharp.PixelFormats; // PixelColorBlendingMode
using SixLabors.ImageSharp.Processing; // Mutate extension method
using System.IO; // Stream, FileAccess
using System.Threading.Tasks; // Task<T>
```

```csharp
namespace Northwind.AzureFunctions.Service;

[StorageAccount("AzureWebJobsStorage")]
public static class CheckGeneratorFunction
{
  [FunctionName(nameof(CheckGeneratorFunction))]
  public static async Task Run(
    [QueueTrigger("checksQueue")] QueueMessage message,
    [Blob("checks-blob-container")] BlobContainerClient blobContainerClient,
    ILogger log)
  {
    // write some information about the message to the log
    log.LogInformation("C# Queue trigger function executed.");
    log.LogInformation($"MessageId: {message.MessageId}.");
    log.LogInformation($"InsertedOn: {message.InsertedOn}.");
    log.LogInformation($"ExpiresOn: {message.ExpiresOn}.");
    log.LogInformation($"Body: {message.Body}.");

    // create a new blank image with a white background
    using (Image<Rgba32> image = new(width: 1200, height: 600,
      backgroundColor: new Rgba32(r: 255, g: 255, b: 255, a: 100)))
    {
      // load the font file and create a large font
      FontCollection collection = new();
      FontFamily family = collection.Add(
        @"fonts\Caveat\static\Caveat-Regular.ttf");
      Font font = family.CreateFont(72);

      string amount = message.Body.ToString();

      DrawingOptions options = new()
      {
        GraphicsOptions = new()
        {
          ColorBlendingMode = PixelColorBlendingMode.Multiply
        }
      };

      // define some pens and brushes

      IPen blackPen = Pens.Solid(Color.Black, 2);
      IPen blackThickPen = Pens.Solid(Color.Black, 8);
      IPen greenPen = Pens.Solid(Color.Green, 3);
      IBrush redBrush = Brushes.Solid(Color.Red);
      IBrush blueBrush = Brushes.Solid(Color.Blue);
```

```csharp
      // define some paths and draw them

      IPath border = new RectangularPolygon(
        x: 50, y: 50, width: 1100, height: 500);

      image.Mutate(x => x.Draw(options, blackPen, border));

      IPath star = new Star(x: 150.0f, y: 150.0f,
        prongs: 5, innerRadii: 20.0f, outerRadii: 30.0f);

      image.Mutate(x => x.Fill(options, redBrush, star)
                          .Draw(options, greenPen, star));

      IPath line1 = new Polygon(new LinearLineSegment(
        new PointF(x: 100, y: 275), new PointF(x: 1050, y: 275)));

      image.Mutate(x => x.Draw(options, blackPen, line1));

      IPath line2 = new Polygon(new LinearLineSegment(
        new PointF(x: 100, y: 365), new PointF(x: 1050, y: 365)));

      image.Mutate(x => x.Draw(options, blackPen, line2));

      TextOptions textOptions = new(font)
      {
        Origin = new PointF(100, 200),
        WrappingLength = 1000,
        HorizontalAlignment = HorizontalAlignment.Left
      };

      image.Mutate(x => x.DrawText(
        textOptions, amount, blueBrush, blackPen));

      string blobName = $"{System.DateTime.UtcNow:yyyy-MM-dd-hh-mm-ss}.
png";
      log.LogInformation($"Blob name: {blobName}.");

      try
      {
        if (System.Environment.GetEnvironmentVariable("IS_LOCAL") ==
"true")
        {
          // create blob in the local filesystem

          string folder = $@"{System.Environment.CurrentDirectory}\
blobs";
```

```
            if (!Directory.Exists(folder))
            {
              Directory.CreateDirectory(folder);
            }
            log.LogInformation($"Blobs folder: {folder}");

            string blobPath = $@"{folder}\{blobName}";

            await image.SaveAsPngAsync(blobPath);
          }

          // create BLOB in Blob Storage via a memory stream

          Stream stream = new MemoryStream();

          await image.SaveAsPngAsync(stream);
          stream.Seek(0, SeekOrigin.Begin);

          blobContainerClient.CreateIfNotExists();

          BlobContentInfo info = await blobContainerClient.UploadBlobAsync(
            blobName, stream);

          log.LogInformation(
            $"Blob sequence number: {info.BlobSequenceNumber}.");
        }
        catch (System.Exception ex)
        {
          log.LogError(ex.Message);
        }
      }
    }
  }
```

Note the following:

- Decorating the class with [StorageAccount("AzureWebJobsStorage")] tells the function how to connect to Azure Storage, either locally or once deployed to the cloud.
- The [QueueTrigger("checksQueue")] QueueMessage message parameter means the function is triggered by a message being added to the checksQueue and the message is automatically passed to the parameter named message.
- The [Blob("checks-blob-container")] BlobContainerClient blobContainerClient parameter means we can access the checks-blob-container container via the blobContainerClient parameter.

- We use ImageSharp to create a 1200x600 image of a check.
- We use the current UTC date and time to name the BLOB to avoid duplicates. In a real implementation, you would need something more robust like GUIDs.
- If the `IS_LOCAL` environment variable is set to `true`, then we save the image as a PNG to the local filesystem in a `blobs` subfolder.
- We save the image as a PNG to a memory stream that is then uploaded to the BLOB container.

## Testing the function that works with queues and BLOBs

Now we can test the function that works with queues and BLOBs in our local development environment:

1. Start the `Northwind.AzureFunctions.Service` project.

    - If you are using Visual Studio Code, you will need to navigate to the **Run and Debug** pane, make sure that **Attach to .NET Functions** is selected, and then click the **Run** button.

2. Note there are now three functions, as shown in the following partial output:

```
Functions:

        NumbersToWordsFunction: [GET,POST] http://localhost:7071/api/
NumbersToWordsFunction

        CheckGeneratorFunction: queueTrigger

        ScrapeAmazonFunction: timerTrigger
```

3. Start Visual Studio Code.

4. Open the `RestClientTests` folder.

5. Add a new file named `azurefunctions-numberstowords.http`.

6. Modify its contents, as shown in the following code:

```
### Trigger the NumbersToWordsFunction function
GET http://localhost:7071/api/NumbersToWordsFunction?amount=123456
```

7. Send the request and note that a JSON document is returned with information about the `NumbersToWordsFunction` function, as shown in the following response and *Figure 14.9*:

```
HTTP/1.1 200 OK
Connection: close
Content-Type: text/plain; charset=utf-8
Date: Sun, 05 Jun 2022 07:04:05 GMT
Server: Kestrel
Transfer-Encoding: chunked
```

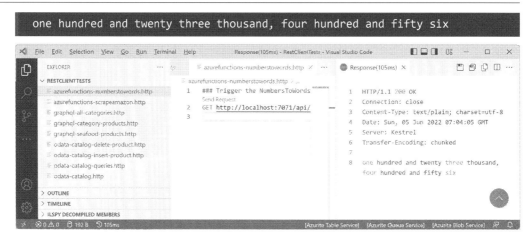

*Figure 14.9: Triggering the HTTP endpoint for NumbersToWordsFunction*

8. At the command line or terminal, note the function call was successful and a message was sent to the queue that then triggered the CheckGeneratorFunction, as shown in the following output:

```
[2022-06-05T07:04:06.353Z] Executing 'NumbersToWordsFunction'
(Reason='This function was programmatically called via the host APIs.',
Id=9eec6b0b-79e2-4b2a-82cb-bdc521bfbb18)
[2022-06-05T07:04:06.356Z] C# HTTP trigger function processed a request.
[2022-06-05T07:04:06.400Z] Executed 'NumbersToWordsFunction' (Succeeded,
Id=9eec6b0b-79e2-4b2a-82cb-bdc521bfbb18, Duration=73ms)
[2022-06-05T07:04:07.306Z] Executing 'CheckGeneratorFunction'
(Reason='New queue message detected on 'checksqueue'.', Id=900b14d8-e103-
4b95-b09b-62a9d2e7eeb6)
[2022-06-05T07:04:07.308Z] Trigger Details: MessageId: 526fed97-
741d-4d73-a488-37f77ec7283d, DequeueCount: 1, InsertedOn: 2022-06-
05T07:04:06.000+00:00
[2022-06-05T07:04:07.317Z] C# Queue trigger function executed.
[2022-06-05T07:04:07.319Z] MessageId: 526fed97-741d-4d73-a488-
37f77ec7283d.
[2022-06-05T07:04:07.322Z] InsertedOn: 05/06/2022 07:04:06 +00:00.
[2022-06-05T07:04:07.324Z] ExpiresOn: 12/06/2022 07:04:06 +00:00.
[2022-06-05T07:04:07.324Z] Body: one hundred and twenty three thousand,
four hundred and fifty six.
[2022-06-05T07:04:09.734Z] Blob name: 2022-06-05-07-04-09.png.
[2022-06-05T07:04:09.736Z] Blobs folder: C:\apps-services-net7\Chapter14\
Northwind.AzureFunctions.Service\bin\Debug\net6.0\blobs
```

9. In the filesystem, note the image created locally in the blobs folder, as shown in *Figure 14.10*:

*Figure 14.10: The check image generated in the blobs folder*

10. Note the check image, as shown in *Figure 14.11*:

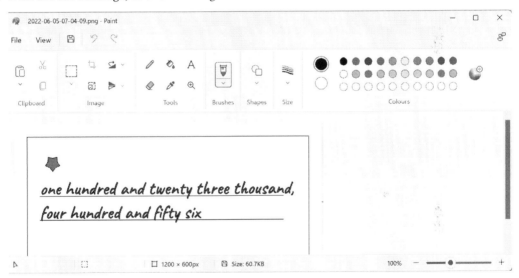

*Figure 14.11: The check image opened in Paint*

11. In Visual Studio Code, in the **AZURE** pane, note the BLOB created in Azurite.

# Publishing an Azure Functions project to the cloud

Now, let's create a function app and related resources in an Azure subscription, then deploy your functions to the cloud and run it there.

If you do not already have an Azure account, then you can sign up for a free one at the following link: https://azure.microsoft.com/en-us/free/.

# Using Visual Studio 2022 to publish

Visual Studio 2022 has a GUI to publish to Azure:

1. In **Solution Explorer**, right-click the `Northwind.AzureFunctions.Service` project and select **Publish**.

2. In the **Where are you publishing today?** dialog, for **Target**, select **Azure**, and then click **Next**.

3. Select **Azure Function App (Windows)** and click **Next**.

4. Sign in and enter your Azure credentials.

5. Select your subscription.

6. In the **Function Instance** section, click the + button that has a tooltip that says **Create a new Azure Function...**.

7. Complete the dialog box, as shown in *Figure 14.12*:

   - **Name:** This must be globally unique. It suggested `NorthwindAzureFunctionsServi ce20220605082816` based on the project name and the current date and time.

   - **Subscription name:** Your subscription. I have a subscription named **Pay-As-You-Go**.

   - **Resource group:** Select or create a new resource group to make it easier to delete everything later. I chose `apps-services-net7`.

   - **Plan Type: Consumption** (pay for only what you use).

   - **Location:** A data center nearest to you. I chose **UK South**.

   - **Azure Storage:** Create a new account named `northwindazurefunctions` (or something else that is globally unique) in a data center nearest to you and choose **Standard – Locally Redundant Storage** for the account type.

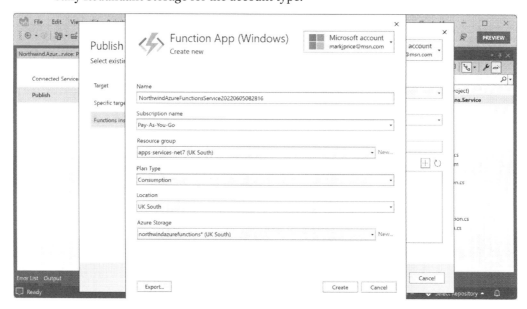

*Figure 14.12: Creating a new Azure Functions app*

8. Click **Create**. This process can take a minute or more.

9. In the **Publish** dialog, click **Finish** and then click **Close**.

10. In the **Publish** window, click the **Publish** button, as shown in *Figure 14.13*:

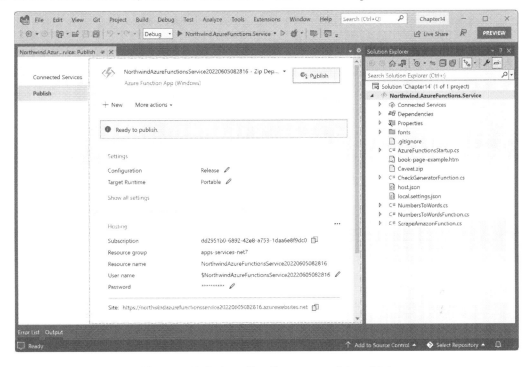

*Figure 14.13: An Azure Functions app ready to publish*

11. Review the output window, as shown in the following publishing output:

```
Build started...
1>------ Build started: Project: Northwind.AzureFunctions.Service,
Configuration: Release Any CPU ------
1>C:\Program Files\dotnet\sdk\7.0.100-preview.4.22252.9\Sdks\Microsoft.
NET.Sdk\targets\Microsoft.NET.RuntimeIdentifierInference.targets(216,5):
message NETSDK1057: You are using a preview version of .NET. See:
https://aka.ms/dotnet-support-policy
1>Northwind.AzureFunctions.Service -> C:\apps-services-net7\Chapter14\
Northwind.AzureFunctions.Service\bin\Release\net6.0\Northwind.
AzureFunctions.Service.dll
2>------ Publish started: Project: Northwind.AzureFunctions.Service,
Configuration: Release Any CPU ------
2>You are using a preview version of .NET. See: https://aka.ms/dotnet-
support-policy
2>Northwind.AzureFunctions.Service -> C:\apps-services-net7\Chapter14\
Northwind.AzureFunctions.Service\bin\Release\net6.0\Northwind.
AzureFunctions.Service.dll
2>Northwind.AzureFunctions.Service -> C:\apps-services-net7\Chapter14\
Northwind.AzureFunctions.Service\obj\Release\net6.0\PubTmp\Out\
```

```
2>Publishing C:\apps-services-net7\Chapter14\Northwind.
AzureFunctions.Service\obj\Release\net6.0\PubTmp\Northwind.
AzureFunctions.Service - 20220605083801718.zip to https://
northwindazurefunctionsservice20220605082816.scm.azurewebsites.net/api/
zipdeploy...
2>Zip Deployment succeeded.
========== Build: 1 succeeded, 0 failed, 0 up-to-date, 0 skipped
==========
========== Publish: 1 succeeded, 0 failed, 0 skipped ==========
Waiting for function app to be ready...
Function app is ready
```

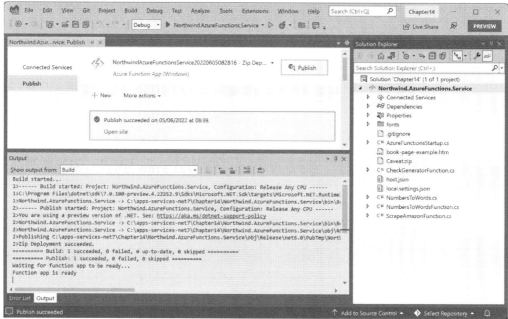

*Figure 14.14: Output window showing a successful deployment to Azure cloud*

12. Click **Open site** and note your Azure Functions v4 host site is ready, as shown in *Figure 14.15*:

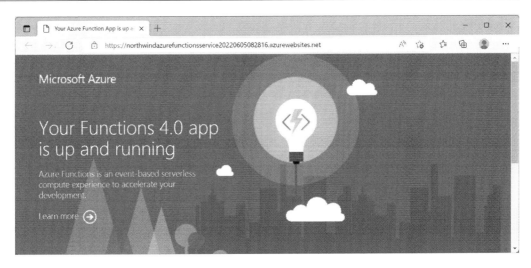

*Figure 14.15: An Azure Functions project deployed and ready for action*

13. Test the function in your browser by appending it to the address box, as shown in the following relative URL and *Figure 14.16*: /api/NumbersToWordsFunction?amount=987654321

*Figure 14.16: Calling the Azure Functions function in the cloud*

## Using Visual Studio Code to publish

You can learn how to publish using Visual Studio Code at the following link:

```
https://docs.microsoft.com/en-us/azure/azure-functions/functions-develop-vs-
code?tabs=csharp#sign-in-to-azure
```

## Cleaning up Azure Functions resources

You can use the following steps to delete the function app and its related resources to avoid incurring further costs:

1. In your browser, navigate to https://portal.azure.com/.
2. In the Azure portal, in your function app **Overview** blade, select the **Resource Group**.

3.  Confirm that it contains only resources that you want to delete; for example, there should be a **Storage account**, a **Function App**, and an **App Service plan**, as shown in *Figure 14.17*:

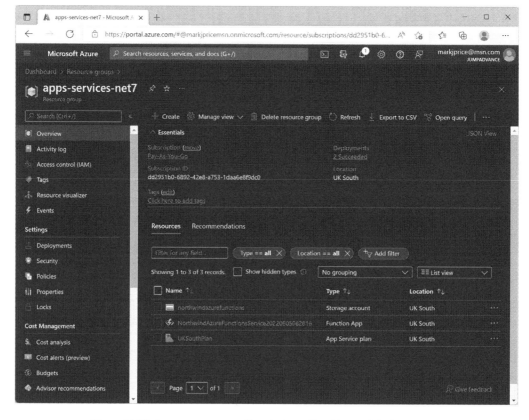

*Figure 14.17: A resource group with only Azure Functions-related resources*

4.  If you are sure you want to delete all the resources in the group, then click **Delete resource group** and accept any other confirmations. Alternatively, you can delete each resource individually.

# Practicing and exploring

Test your knowledge and understanding by answering some questions, getting some hands-on practice, and exploring this chapter's topics with deeper research.

## Exercise 14.1 – Test your knowledge

Answer the following questions:

1.  What is the difference between the in-process and isolated hosting models for Azure Functions?
2.  What attribute do you use to cause a function to trigger when a message arrives in a queue?
3.  What attribute do you use to make a queue available to send messages to?

4. What schedule does the following NCRONTAB expression define?

   ```
   0 0 */6 * 6 6
   ```

5. How can you configure a dependency service for use in a function?

## Exercise 14.2 – Explore topics

Use the links on the following page to learn more detail about the topics covered in this chapter:

```
https://github.com/markjprice/apps-services-net7/blob/main/book-links.md#chapter-14--
-building-serverless-nanoservices-using-azure-functions
```

## Summary

In this chapter, you learned:

- Some of the concepts around Azure Functions.
- How to build serverless services using Azure Functions.
- How to respond to HTTP, Timer, and Queue triggers.
- How to bind to Queue and Blob Storage.
- How to deploy an Azure Functions project to the cloud.

In the next chapter, you will review how to build websites using ASP.NET Core MVC.

# 15

# Building Web User Interfaces Using ASP.NET Core

This chapter is about building web user interfaces with ASP.NET Core. You will learn about ASP.NET Core MVC views, Razor syntax, HTML Helpers and Tag Helpers, internationalizing your website, and how to use Bootstrap for quick user interface prototyping.

This chapter will cover the following topics:

- Setting up an ASP.NET Core MVC website
- Defining web user interfaces with Razor views
- Localizing and globalizing with ASP.NET Core
- Defining web user interfaces with Tag Helpers

## Setting up an ASP.NET Core MVC website

The **Model-View-Controller** (**MVC**) design pattern allows a clean separation between technical concerns, as shown in the following list:

- **Models:** Classes that represent the data entities and view models used on the website.
- **Views:** Razor files, that is, .cshtml files, that render data in view models into HTML web pages. Blazor uses the .razor file extension, but do not confuse them with Razor files!
- **Controllers:** Classes that execute code when an HTTP request arrives at the web server. The controller methods usually create a view model that may contain entity models, and pass it to a view to generate an HTTP response to send back to the web browser or an other client.

## Creating an ASP.NET Core MVC website

You will use a project template to create an ASP.NET Core MVC website project that has a local database for authenticating and authorizing users. Visual Studio 2022 defaults to using SQL Server LocalDB for the accounts database. Visual Studio Code (or more accurately the dotnet CLI tool) uses SQLite by default and you can specify a switch to use SQL Server LocalDB instead.

Let's see it in action:

1.  Use your preferred code editor to create an ASP.NET Core MVC website project with authentication accounts stored in a database, as defined in the following list:

    *   Project template: **ASP.NET Core Web App (Model-View-Controller) [C#]**/mvc
    *   Project file and folder: `Northwind.Mvc`
    *   Workspace/solution file and folder: `Chapter15`
    *   **Additional information - Authentication type: Individual Accounts**/`--auth Individual`
    *   For Visual Studio 2022, leave all other options as their defaults.

    For Visual Studio Code, select `Northwind.Mvc` as the active OmniSharp project.

2.  Build the `Northwind.Mvc` project.

3.  If you created the MVC project using Visual Studio 2022, then the database for authentication and authorization will be stored in SQL Server LocalDB. But the database does not yet exist. At a command prompt or terminal, in the `Northwind.Mvc` folder, enter the command to run database migrations so that the database used to store credentials for authentication is created, as shown in the following command:

```
dotnet ef database update
```

 If you created the MVC project using `dotnet new`, then the database for authentication and authorization will be stored in SQLite and the file has already been created, named `app.db`.

4.  In the root folder for the MVC website project, in the `appsettings.json` file, note the connection string for the authentication database named `DefaultConnection`, as shown in the following configuration:

    *   Using SQL Server LocalDB:

        ```
        {
          "ConnectionStrings": {
            "DefaultConnection": "Server=(localdb)\\
        mssqllocaldb;Database=aspnet-Northwind.Mvc-...;Trusted_
        Connection=True;MultipleActiveResultSets=true"
          },
        ```

    *   Using SQLite:

        ```
        {
          "ConnectionStrings": {
            "DefaultConnection": "DataSource=app.db;Cache=Shared"
          },
        ```

# Exploring the default ASP.NET Core MVC website

Let's review the behavior of the default ASP.NET Core MVC website project template:

1. In the Northwind.Mvc project, expand the Properties folder, open the launchSettings.json file, and note the random port numbers (yours will be different) configured for the Kestrel-hosted project for http and https, as shown highlighted in the following settings:

```json
{
  "iisSettings": {
    "windowsAuthentication": false,
    "anonymousAuthentication": true,
    "iisExpress": {
      "applicationUrl": "http://localhost:11227",
      "sslPort": 44315
    }
  },
  "profiles": {
    "http": {
      "commandName": "Project",
      "dotnetRunMessages": true,
      "launchBrowser": true,
      "applicationUrl": "http://localhost:5047",
      "environmentVariables": {
        "ASPNETCORE_ENVIRONMENT": "Development"
      }
    },
    "https": {
      "commandName": "Project",
      "dotnetRunMessages": true,
      "launchBrowser": true,
      "applicationUrl": "https://localhost:7047;http://localhost:5047",
      "environmentVariables": {
        "ASPNETCORE_ENVIRONMENT": "Development"
      }
    },
    "IIS Express": {
      "commandName": "IISExpress",
      "launchBrowser": true,
      "environmentVariables": {
        "ASPNETCORE_ENVIRONMENT": "Development"
      }
    }
  }
}
```

2. For the `https` profile, for its `applicationUrl` setting, change the port numbers to `5151` for `https` and `5152` for `http`, as shown in the following setting:

```
"applicationUrl": "https://localhost:5151;http://localhost:5152",
```

3. Save the changes to the `launchSettings.json` file.

4. In your preferred code editor or at the command line, start the `Northwind.Mvc` project with the `https` profile and using Chrome as the browser:

   - If you are using Visual Studio 2022, then select the `https` profile as the **Startup Project**, and **Google Chrome** as the **Web Browser**, as shown in *Figure 15.1*:

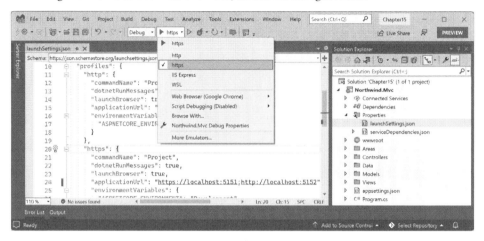

*Figure 15.1: Select the https profile to start the Northwind MVC project*

   - If you are using Visual Studio 2022, then start the `Northind.Mvc` website project without debugging.

   - If you are using Visual Studio Code, then at the command prompt or terminal, enter the following command:

```
dotnet run --launch-profile https
```

5. Start Chrome (if necessary) and open **Developer Tools**.

6. Navigate to `https://localhost:5151/` and note the following, as shown in *Figure 15.2*:

   - The top navigation menu with links to **Home**, **Privacy**, **Register**, and **Login**. If the viewport width is 575 pixels or less, then the navigation collapses into a hamburger menu.

   - The title of the website, **Northwind.Mvc**, shown in the header and footer:

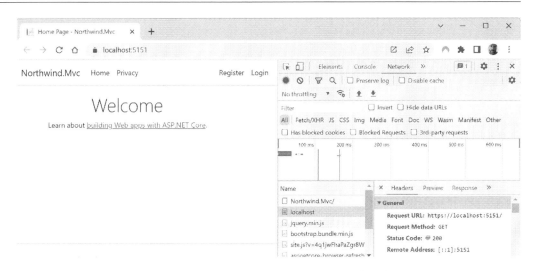

*Figure 15.2: The ASP.NET Core MVC project template website home page*

## Understanding visitor registration

By default, passwords must have at least one non-alphanumeric character, at least one digit (0-9), and at least one uppercase letter (A-Z). I use Pa$$w0rd in scenarios like this when I am just exploring.

The MVC project template follows best practice for **double-opt-in** (**DOI**), meaning that after filling in an email and password to register, an email is sent to the email address, and the visitor must click a link in that email to confirm that they want to register.

We have not yet configured an email provider to send that email, so we must simulate that step:

1. Close the **Developer Tools** pane.
2. In the top navigation menu, click **Register**.
3. Enter an email and password, and then click the **Register** button. (I used test@example.com and Pa$$w0rd.)
4. Click the link with the text **Click here to confirm your account** and note that you are redirected to a **Confirm email** web page that you could customize.
5. In the top navigation menu, click **Login**, enter your email and password (note that there is an optional checkbox to remember you, and there are links if the visitor has forgotten their password or they want to register as a new visitor), and then click the **Log in** button.
6. Click your email address in the top navigation menu. This will navigate to an account management page. Note that you can set a phone number, change your email address, change your password, enable two-factor authentication (if you add an authenticator app), and download and delete your personal data. This last feature is good for compliance with legal regulations like the European GDPR.
7. Close Chrome and press *Ctrl* + *C* to shut down the web server.

# Reviewing an MVC website project structure

In your code editor, in Visual Studio **Solution Explorer** (toggle on **Show All Files**) or in Visual Studio Code **EXPLORER**, review the structure of an MVC website project, as shown in *Figure 15.3*:

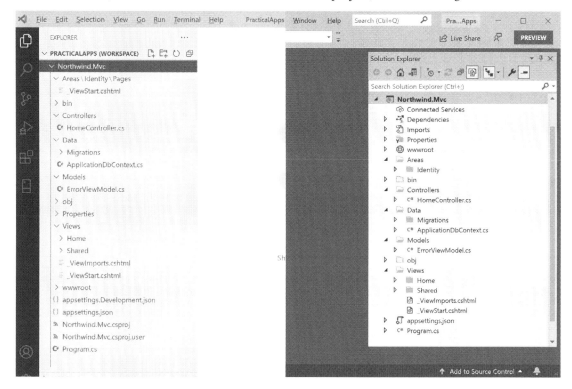

*Figure 15.3: The default folder structure of an ASP.NET Core MVC project*

We will look in more detail at some of these parts later, but for now, note the following:

- `Areas`: This folder contains nested folders and a file needed to integrate your website project with ASP.NET Core Identity, which is used for authentication.

- `bin`, `obj`: These folders contain temporary files needed during the build process and the compiled assemblies for the project.

- `Controllers`: This folder contains C# classes that have methods (known as **actions**) that fetch a model and pass it to a view, for example, `HomeController.cs`.

- `Data`: This folder contains Entity Framework Core migration classes used by the ASP.NET Core Identity system to provide data storage for authentication and authorization, for example, `ApplicationDbContext.cs`.

- `Models`: This folder contains C# classes that represent all the data gathered together by a controller and passed to a view, for example, `ErrorViewModel.cs`.

- `Properties`: This folder contains a configuration file for Kestrel (or IIS or IIS Express on Windows) named `launchSettings.json`, for launching the website during development. This file is only used on the local development machine and is not deployed to your production website.

- **Views**: This folder contains the `.cshtml` Razor files that combine HTML and C# code to dynamically generate HTML responses. The `_ViewStart` file sets the default layout and `_ViewImports` imports common namespaces used in all views like Tag Helpers:

    - **Home**: This subfolder contains Razor files for the home and privacy pages.
    - **Shared**: This subfolder contains Razor files for the shared layout, an error page, and two partial views for logging in and validation scripts.

- **wwwroot**: This folder contains static content used by the website, such as CSS for styling, libraries of JavaScript, JavaScript for this website project, and a `favicon.ico` file. You also put images and other static file resources like PDF documents in here. The project template includes Bootstrap and jQuery libraries.

- **app.db**: This is the SQLite database that stores registered visitors. (If you used SQL Server LocalDB, then it will not be needed.)

- **appsettings.json** and **appsettings.Development.json**: These files contain settings that your website can load at runtime, for example, the database connection string for the ASP.NET Core Identity system and logging levels.

- **Northwind.Mvc.csproj**: This file contains project settings like the use of the Web .NET SDK, an entry for SQLite to ensure that the `app.db` file is copied to the website's output folder, and a list of NuGet packages that your project requires like EF Core for your chosen database provider, including:

    - `Microsoft.AspNetCore.Diagnostics.EntityFrameworkCore`
    - `Microsoft.AspNetCore.Identity.EntityFrameworkCore`
    - `Microsoft.AspNetCore.Identity.UI`
    - `Microsoft.EntityFrameworkCore.Sqlite` or `Microsoft.EntityFrameworkCore.SqlServer`
    - `Microsoft.EntityFrameworkCore.Tools`

- **Program.cs**: This file defines a hidden `Program` class that contains the `<Main>$` entry point. It builds a pipeline for processing incoming HTTP requests and hosts the website using default options, like configuring the Kestrel web server and loading `appsettings`. It adds and configures services that your website needs, for example, ASP.NET Core Identity for authentication, SQLite or SQL Server for identity data storage, and so on, and routes for your application.

## Referencing an EF Core class library and registering a data context

We will reference the EF Core model that you created in *Chapter 2, Managing Relational Data Using SQL Server*:

1.  In the `Northwind.Mvc` project, add an element to `<PropertyGroup>` to treat warnings as errors, as shown in the following markup:

    ```
    <TreatWarningsAsErrors>true</TreatWarningsAsErrors>
    ```

2.  In the `Northwind.Mvc` project, add a project reference to the Northwind database context project, as shown in the following markup:

```
<ItemGroup>
  <ProjectReference Include="..\..\Chapter02\Northwind.Common.DataContext
.SqlServer\Northwind.Common.DataContext.SqlServer.csproj" />
</ItemGroup>
```

 The `Include` path must not have a line break.

3.  At the command line or terminal, build the `Northwind.Mvc` project.

# Defining web user interfaces with Razor views

Let's see how we can build the user interface of a web page in a modern ASP.NET Core MVC website.

## Understanding Razor views

In MVC, the V stands for *view*. The responsibility of a view is to transform a model into HTML or other formats.

There are multiple **view engines** that could be used to do this. The default view engine is called **Razor**, and it uses the @ symbol to indicate server-side code execution.

Let's review the home page view and how it uses a shared layout:

1.  In the `Views/Home` folder, open the `Index.cshtml` file and note the block of C# code wrapped in @{ }. This will execute first and can be used to store data that needs to be passed into a shared layout file, like the title of the web page, as shown in the following code:

```
@{
   ViewData["Title"] = "Home Page";
}
```

2.  Note the static HTML content in the `<div>` element that uses Bootstrap classes like `text-center` and `display-4` for styling.

3.  In the `Views` folder, open the `_ViewImports.cshtml` file and note that it imports some namespaces and then adds the ASP.NET Core Tag Helpers, as shown in the following code:

```
@using Northwind.Mvc
@using Northwind.Mvc.Models
@addTagHelper *, Microsoft.AspNetCore.Mvc.TagHelpers
```

4. In the `Views` folder, open the `_ViewStart.cshtml` file. It gets executed when the `View` method is called in a controller class. It is used to set defaults that apply to all views. For example, note that it sets the `Layout` property of all views to a shared layout file, as shown in the following markup:

```
@{
    Layout = "_Layout";
}
```

5. In the `Shared` folder, open the `_Layout.cshtml` file.

6. Note that the title is being read from the `ViewData` dictionary that was set earlier in the `Index.cshtml` view, as shown in the following markup:

```
<title>@ViewData["Title"] - Northwind.Mvc</title>
```

7. Note the rendering of links to support Bootstrap and a site stylesheet, where ~ means the `wwwroot` folder, as shown in the following markup:

```
<link rel="stylesheet"
    href="~/lib/bootstrap/dist/css/bootstrap.css" />
<link rel="stylesheet" href="~/css/site.css" asp-append-version="true" />
<link rel="stylesheet" href="~/Northwind.Mvc.styles.css"
    asp-append-version="true" />
```

8. Note the rendering of a navigation bar in the header, as shown in the following markup:

```
<body>
  <header>
    <nav class="navbar ...">
```

9. Note the rendering of a collapsible `<div>` containing a partial view for logging in, and hyperlinks to allow users to navigate between pages using ASP.NET Core Tag Helpers with attributes like `asp-controller` and `asp-action`, as shown in the following markup:

```
<div class=
    "navbar-collapse collapse d-sm-inline-flex justify-content-between">
    <ul class="navbar-nav flex-grow-1">
      <li class="nav-item">
        <a class="nav-link text-dark" asp-area=""
          asp-controller="Home" asp-action="Index">Home</a>
      </li>
      <li class="nav-item">
        <a class="nav-link text-dark"
          asp-area="" asp-controller="Home"
          asp-action="Privacy">Privacy</a>
      </li>
    </ul>
    <partial name="_LoginPartial" />
</div>
```

The `<a>` elements use Tag Helper attributes named `asp-controller` and `asp-action` to specify the controller name and action name that will execute when the link is clicked on. The `asp-area` attribute can be used to organize and group pages within large complex MVC websites. If you want to navigate to a feature in a Razor Class Library, then you can also use `asp-area` to specify the feature name.

10. Note the rendering of the body inside the `<main>` element, as shown in the following markup:

```
<div class="container">
  <main role="main" class="pb-3">
    @RenderBody()
  </main>
</div>
```

The `RenderBody` method injects the contents of a specific Razor view for a page like the `Index.cshtml` file at that point in the shared layout.

11. Note the rendering of `<script>` elements at the bottom of the page so that it does not slow down the display of the page, and that you can add your own script blocks into an optional defined section named `Scripts`, as shown in the following markup:

```
<script src="~/lib/jquery/dist/jquery.min.js"></script>
<script src="~/lib/bootstrap/dist/js/bootstrap.bundle.min.js">
</script>
<script src="~/js/site.js" asp-append-version="true"></script>
@await RenderSectionAsync("Scripts", required: false)
```

## Prototyping with Bootstrap

Bootstrap is the world's most popular framework for building responsive, mobile-first websites. It combines CSS stylesheets with JavaScript libraries to implement its functionality. It is a good choice for prototyping a website user interface, although before going public you might want to hire a web designer to build a custom Bootstrap theme or replace it with a completely custom set of CSS stylesheets to give your website a distinct brand.

Bootstrap can be divided into four parts: Layout, Content, Components, and Utilities. You can use only the parts you need.

## Breakpoints and containers

The first thing to understand about Bootstrap is its predefined **breakpoints**:

- X-Small (no inline suffix): <576 px
- Small (`sm`): >=576 px
- Medium (`md`): >=768 px

- Large (lg): >=992 px
- Extra large (xl): >=1,200 px
- Extra extra large (xxl): >=1,400 px

Containers are the foundation of the Bootstrap grid layout system. Imagine you have a `<div>` element that uses the Bootstrap `container` class, as shown in the following markup:

```
<div class="container">
   Some content.
</div>
```

As you can see in the table below, when the width of the browser is less than 576 pixels, the `<div>` will stretch to fill 100% of the available width. When the width of the browser is greater than or equal to 576 pixels, the width of the `<div>` becomes fixed at 540 pixels wide, until the width of browser is greater than or equal to 768 pixels, at which point the width of the `<div>` becomes fixed at 720 pixels wide. This repeats as the width of the browser increases; at each breakpoint, the fixed width of the `<div>` snaps to a larger value.

| | X-Small <576 px | Small >=576 px | Medium >=768 px | Large >=992 px | Extra large >=1,200 px | XXL >=1,400 px |
|---|---|---|---|---|---|---|
| `.container` | 100% | 540 px | 720 px | 960 px | 1,140 px | 1,320 px |
| `.container-sm` | 100% | 540 px | 720 px | 960 px | 1,140 px | 1,320 px |
| `.container-md` | 100% | 100% | 720 px | 960 px | 1,140 px | 1,320 px |
| `.container-lg` | 100% | 100% | 100% | 960 px | 1,140 px | 1,320 px |
| `.container-xl` | 100% | 100% | 100% | 100% | 1,140 px | 1,320 px |
| `.container-xxl` | 100% | 100% | 100% | 100% | 100% | 1,320 px |
| `.container-fluid` | 100% | 100% | 100% | 100% | 100% | 100% |

Imagine that you now have a `<div>` element that uses the `container-lg` class, as shown in the following markup:

```
<div class="container-lg">
   Some content.
</div>
```

As you can see in the table above, when the width of the browser is less than 992 pixels, the `<div>` will always take up 100% of the available browser width. At 992 pixels and above, the `<div>` width snaps to the breakpoints 960 px, 1,140 px, and 1,320 px.

If you use the class `container-fluid`, the `<div>` always takes up 100% of the available width.

## Rows and columns

A Bootstrap container can be divided into rows and columns, for example, one row with three columns, as shown in the following markup:

```
<div class="container">
  <div class="row">
    <div class="col">
      Column
    </div>
    <div class="col">
      Column
    </div>
    <div class="col">
      Column
    </div>
  </div>
</div>
```

If you use the col class, then each column will have equal width. But each row is also divided into 12 virtual columns. If you specify a number suffix between 1 and 12, then that column will use that number of twelfths and the others will divide the rest equally. For example, you could say the left column should use 2 twelfths, the right column should use 4 twelfths, and the middle column uses the rest, as shown in the following markup:

```
<div class="container">
  <div class="row">
    <div class="col-2">
      Column
    </div>
    <div class="col">
      Column
    </div>
    <div class="col-4">
      Column
    </div>
  </div>
</div>
```

 The grid system is powerful but can get complicated quickly. To learn more, you can visit the following link: https://getbootstrap.com/docs/5.2/layout/grid/.

## Color themes

Bootstrap has eight built-in color themes in addition to the default (black on white), as shown in the following list and *Figure 15.4*:

- `primary`: Bright blue theme. For example, white text on a bright blue background, or bright blue text and outline on a white background.
- `secondary`: Gray theme. For example, white text on a gray background, or grey text and outline on a white background.
- `success`: Green theme. For example, white text on a dark green background, or dark green text and outline on a white background.
- `danger`: Red theme. For example, white text on a red background, or red text and outline on a white background.
- `warning`: Yellow theme. For example, black text on a yellow background, or yellow text and outline on a white background.
- `info`: Light blue theme. For example, black text on a light blue background, or light blue text and outline on a white background.
- `light`: Light gray theme. For example, black text on a light gray background, or light grey text and outline on a white background.
- `dark`: Dark gray theme. For example, white text on a dark gray background, or dark grey text and outline on a white background.

*Figure 15.4: Bootstrap color themes*

## Tables

Bootstrap styles for tables are not automatically applied. You must opt-in by applying the `table` class. You can then apply additional style classes.

- `table`: Required to enable table styling.
- `table-primary`, `table-warning`, and so on: Alternative enabling of table styling with color theme.
- `table-sm`: To use half the default padding so the table is more compact.
- `table-striped`: Add zebra-striping to any table row within the `<tbody>`.
- `table-hover`: Enable a hover state to change highlights as the mouse moves over table rows within a `<tbody>`.
- `table-bordered`: Add a border on all sides of the table and its cells.

Let's see an example, as shown in the following markup:

```
<table class="table table-striped table-hover table-bordered">
  <thead>
    <tr>
      <th>
        ...
  </thead>
  <tbody>
    <tr>
      <td>
        ...
  </tbody>
</table>
```

The contents in cells in `<thead>` align to the bottom by default. The contents in cells in `<tbody>` align to the top by default. You can override these defaults and control other alignment by using the following classes:

- `align-top`: Align the contents of the row or cell to the top.
- `vertical-align-middle`: Align the contents of the row or cell to the middle vertically.
- `align-bottom`: Align the contents of the row or cell to the bottom.
- `align-left`: Align the contents of the row or cell to the left.
- `align-middle`: Align the contents of the row or cell to the middle horizontally.
- `align-right`: Align the contents of the row or cell to the right.

## Buttons and links

Bootstrap has button styles that can be applied to actual `<button>` and `<input type="button">` elements as well as hyperlinks, as shown in the following markup:

```
<button class="btn btn-primary" type="button">Click Me</button>
<input class="btn btn-primary" type="button" value="Click Me">
<a class="btn btn-primary" href="#" role="button">Click Me</a>
```

All three elements above would look like a bright blue button with the label **Click Me**.

If you do not want the text in the button label to wrap, add the `text-nowrap` class.

Use `btn-outline-primary` (or any of the other color themes) to have more subtle styling that uses the color for the outline and text with a white background until the mouse hovers over the button.

You can adjust the size of the button by adding `btn-sm` to make it smaller or `btn-lg` to make it larger.

## Badges

Badges are used to show small pieces of information, like the number of unread messages. For example:

```
<button type="button" class="btn btn-primary">
```

```
  Messages <span class="badge bg-secondary">@numberOfUnreadMessages</span>
</button>
```

You can reposition the badge and use the `rounded-pill` class to turn the default rectangle badge into a circular one like most apps do, to show the number of unread notifications or messages inside a red circle:

```
<button type="button" class="btn btn-primary position-relative">
  Messages
  <span class="position-absolute top-0 start-100 translate-middle
        badge rounded-pill bg-danger">
    @numberOfUnreadMessages <span class="visually-hidden">unread messages</span>
  </span>
</button>
```

You can use a more rounded corner to turn a badge into a pill, as shown in the following markup and in *Figure 15.5*:

```
<span class="badge rounded-pill bg-primary">Primary</span>
<span class="badge rounded-pill bg-secondary">Secondary</span>
<span class="badge rounded-pill bg-success">Success</span>
<span class="badge rounded-pill bg-danger">Danger</span>
<span class="badge rounded-pill bg-warning text-dark">Warning</span>
<span class="badge rounded-pill bg-info text-dark">Info</span>
<span class="badge rounded-pill bg-light text-dark">Light</span>
<span class="badge rounded-pill bg-dark">Dark</span>
```

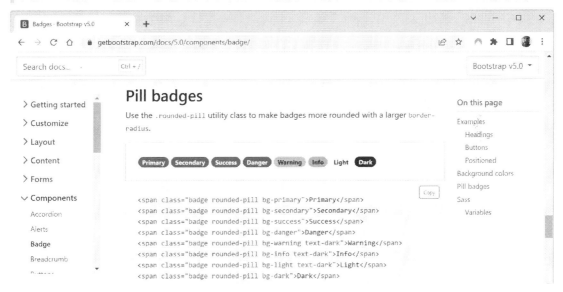

*Figure 15.5: Pill badges using Bootstrap*

## Alerts

You will often need to show messages to website visitors. Alerts must use one of the eight color themes. Any links within the alert element should use the `alert-link` class. The contents can be plain text or use additional elements like headings, as shown in the following markup:

```
<div class="alert alert-success" role="alert">
  <h4 class="alert-heading">Order was accepted.</h4>
  <p>To view the order, click <a href="#" class="alert-link">here</a>.</p>
</div>
```

> For more examples of alerts, for example, adding icons inside the alert, see the official documentation at the following link: `https://getbootstrap.com/docs/5.2/components/alerts/#icons`.

## Good practice for Bootstrap

Bootstrap is like Marmite. Some developers love it; some hate it.

Good reasons to use Bootstrap include:

- It saves time
- It is customizable
- It is open-source
- It is well documented officially and has lots of answers about it on sites like Stack Overflow.

But implementing Bootstrap without care has the following negatives:

- Your website will look generic
- It is heavy compared to a hand-crafted solution

> **Good Practice:** As well as defining your own styles, base your styles on a common library, such as Bootstrap, that implements responsive design. However, if you are building a website that needs a distinct identity or brand, make sure you use its theming support. Do not just accept the defaults.

## Understanding Razor syntax and expressions

Before we customize the home page view, let's review an example Razor file. The file has an initial Razor code block that instantiates an order with price and quantity and then outputs information about the order on the web page, as shown in the following markup:

```
@{
  Order order = new()
  {
    OrderId = 123,
```

```
      Product = "Sushi",
      Price = 8.49M,
      Quantity = 3
   };
}

<div>Your order for @order.Quantity of @order.Product has a total cost of $@
order.Price * @order.Quantity</div>
```

The preceding Razor file would result in the following incorrect output:

```
Your order for 3 of Sushi has a total cost of $8.49 * 3
```

Although Razor markup can include the value of any single property using the `@object.property` syntax, you should wrap expressions in parentheses, as shown in the following markup:

```
<div>Your order for @order.Quantity of @order.Product has a total cost of $@
(order.Price * order.Quantity)</div>
```

The preceding Razor expression results in the following correct output:

```
Your order for 3 of Sushi has a total cost of $25.47
```

## Understanding HTML Helper methods

While creating a view for ASP.NET Core MVC, you can use the `Html` object and its methods to generate markup. When Microsoft first introduced ASP.NET MVC in 2009, these HTML Helper methods were the way to programmatically render HTML. Modern ASP.NET Core retains these HTML Helper methods for backward compatibility and provides Tag Helpers that are usually easier to read and write in most scenarios. But there are notable situations where Tag Helpers cannot be used, like in Razor components. You will learn about Tag Helpers later in this chapter.

Some useful methods include the following:

*   `ActionLink`: Use this to generate an anchor `<a>` element that contains a URL path to the specified controller and action. For example, `Html.ActionLink(linkText: "Binding", actionName: "ModelBinding", controllerName: "Home")` would generate `<a href="/home/modelbinding">Binding</a>`.
*   `AntiForgeryToken`: Use this inside a `<form>` to insert a `<hidden>` element containing an anti-forgery token that can be validated when the form is submitted.
*   `Display` and `DisplayFor`: Use this to generate HTML markup for the expression relative to the current model using a display template. There are built-in display templates for .NET types and custom templates can be created in the `DisplayTemplates` folder. The folder name is case-sensitive on case-sensitive filesystems.
*   `DisplayForModel`: Use this to generate HTML markup for an entire model instead of a single expression.

- Editor and EditorFor: Use this to generate HTML markup for the expression relative to the current model using an editor template. There are built-in editor templates for .NET types that use `<label>` and `<input>` elements, and custom templates can be created in the EditorTemplates folder. The folder name is case-sensitive on case-sensitive filesystems.

- EditorForModel: Use this to generate HTML markup for an entire model instead of a single expression.

- Encode: Use this to safely encode an object or string into HTML. For example, the string value "`<script>`" would be encoded as "`&lt;script&gt;`". This is not normally necessary, since the Razor @ symbol encodes string values by default.

- Raw: Use this to render a string value *without* encoding as HTML.

- PartialAsync and RenderPartialAsync: Use these to generate HTML markup for a partial view. You can optionally pass a model and view data.

## Defining a strongly typed Razor view

To improve the IntelliSense when writing a view, you can define what type the view can expect using an @model directive at the top. Let's modify the home page to display a table of orders from the Northwind database:

1. In Program.cs, import the namespace to use the AddNorthwindContext extension method, as shown in the following code:

   ```
   using Packt.Shared; // AddNorthwindContext extension method
   ```

2. In the section that adds services to the container, add a statement that registers NorthwindContext as a service, as shown in the following code:

   ```
   builder.Services.AddNorthwindContext();
   ```

3. In the Controllers folder, in HomeController.cs, import the namespace for the Northwind entity models and EF Core features, as shown in the following code:

   ```
   using Packt.Shared; // Northwind entity models
   using Microsoft.EntityFrameworkCore; // Include extension method
   ```

4. In the controller class, define a field to store the Northwind data context and set it in the constructor, as shown highlighted in the following code:

   ```
   private readonly NorthwindContext db;

   public HomeController(ILogger<HomeController> logger, NorthwindContext db)
   {
     _logger = logger;
     this.db = db;
   }
   ```

5. In the `Index` action method, add statements to create a view model containing all the orders and their related order details, as shown highlighted in the following code:

```
public IActionResult Index()
{
  IEnumerable<Order> model = db.Orders
    .Include(order => order.Customer)
    .Include(order => order.OrderDetails)
    .OrderByDescending(order => order.OrderDetails
      .Sum(detail => detail.Quantity * detail.UnitPrice))
    .AsEnumerable();

  return View(model);
}
```

6. In the `Views` folder, in `_ViewImports.cshtml`, add a statement to import the EF Core entity models for all Razor views and pages, as shown in the following code:

```
@using Packt.Shared @* Northwind entity models *@
```

7. In the `Views\Home` folder, in `Index.cshtml`, at the top of the file, add a statement to set the model type to use a collection of orders, as shown in the following code:

```
@model IEnumerable<Order>
```

Now, whenever we type `Model` in this view, our code editor will know the correct type for the model and will provide IntelliSense for it.

> While entering code in a view, remember the following:
>
> - Declare the type for the model using @model (with a lowercase m)
> - Interact with the instance of the model using @Model (with an uppercase M)

8. In `Index.cshtml`, in the initial Razor code block, replace the existing content with an HTML table of the orders, as shown in the following markup:

```
@model IEnumerable<Order>
@{
  ViewData["Title"] = "Orders";
}

<div class="text-center">
  <h1 class="display-4">@ViewData["Title"]</h1>
  <table class="table table-bordered table-striped">
    <thead>
```

```
    <tr>
      <th>Order ID</th>
      <th>Order Date</th>
      <th>Company Name</th>
      <th>Country</th>
      <th>Item Count</th>
      <th>Order Total</th>
    </tr>
  </thead>
  <tbody>
    @foreach (Order order in Model)
    {
      <tr>
        <td>@order.OrderId</td>
        <td>@order.OrderDate?.ToString("D")</td>
        <td>@order.Customer?.CompanyName</td>
        <td>@order.Customer?.Country</td>
        <td>@order.OrderDetails.Count()</td>
        <td>@order.OrderDetails.Sum(detail => detail.Quantity * detail.
UnitPrice).ToString("C")</td>
      </tr>
    }
  </tbody>
  </table>
</div>
```

Let's see the result of our customized home page:

1. Start the `Northwind.Mvc` website project.
2. Note that the home page now shows a table of orders with the highest-value order sorted first, as shown in *Figure 15.6*:

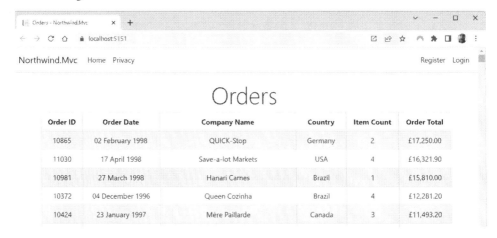

*Figure 15.6: The updated Northwind MVC website home page*

> I am running my web server on my local laptop, and its operating system, Windows 11, is configured to use United Kingdom culture for date, time, and currency values. Next, we will see how to localize the web page for the preferred culture of the visitor.

3.  Close Chrome and shut down the web server.

# Localizing and globalizing with ASP.NET Core

In *Chapter 7, Handling Dates, Times, and Internationalization*, you learned about working with dates, times, time zones, and how to globalize and localize a .NET codebase.

In this section, we will look specifically at how to localize a website that uses ASP.NET Core.

As well as localizing `string` values using `IStringLocalizer`, you can localize HTML values using `IHtmlLocalizer`, but this should be done with care. Usually, HTML markup should be the same for all locales. For views, you can use `IViewLocalizer`.

Let's create some resource files to localize the web user interface into American English, British English, and French, and then globalize the data like dates and currency values:

1.  In the `Northwind.Mvc` project, add a new folder named `Resources`. This is the default name for the folder that localizer services look in for `*.resx` resource files.

2.  In `Resources`, add a new folder named `Views`.

3.  In `Views`, add a new folder named `Home`.

## Creating resource files

How you can create resource files (`*.resx`) depends on your code editor.

### Using Visual Studio 2022

You can use a special project item type and editor:

1.  In `Home`, add a file type of **Resources File** named `Index.en-US.resx`.

2.  Use the editor to define names and values, as shown in *Figure 15.7*:

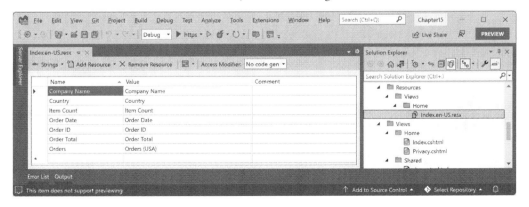

*Figure 15.7: Using the Resources File editor to define the localized labels*

3.   Close the editor.

4.   Copy and paste the file and rename it as `Index.en-GB.resx`.

5.   In `Index.en-GB.resx`, modify USA to UK. This is so we can see a difference.

6.   Close the editor.

7.   Copy and paste the file and rename it as `Index.fr-FR.resx`.

8.   In `Index.fr-FR.resx`, modify the value column to use French. (See the instructions for Visual Studio Code for the translations.)

9.   Copy and paste the file and rename it as `Index.fr.resx`.

10.  In `Index.fr.resx`, modify the last value to be `Commandes` `(Neutral French)`.

## Using Visual Studio Code

You will have to edit the file without a special editor:

1.   In `Home`, add a new file named `Index.en-US.resx`.

2.   Modify the contents to contain American English language resources, as shown in the following markup:

```xml
<?xml version="1.0" encoding="utf-8"?>
<root>
  <data name="Company Name" xml:space="preserve">
    <value>Company Name</value>
  </data>
  <data name="Country" xml:space="preserve">
    <value>Country</value>
  </data>
  <data name="Item Count" xml:space="preserve">
    <value>Item Count</value>
  </data>
  <data name="Order Date" xml:space="preserve">
    <value>Order Date</value>
  </data>
  <data name="Order ID" xml:space="preserve">
    <value>Order ID</value>
  </data>
  <data name="Order Total" xml:space="preserve">
    <value>Order Total</value>
  </data>
  <data name="Orders" xml:space="preserve">
    <value>Orders (USA)</value>
  </data>
</root>
```

3.   Copy and paste the file and rename it as `Index.en-GB.resx`.

4.   In `Index.en-GB.resx`, modify USA to UK. This is so we can see a difference.

5. Copy and paste the file and rename it as `Index.fr-FR.resx`.

6. In `Index.fr-FR.resx`, modify the value column to use French:

```xml
<?xml version="1.0" encoding="utf-8"?>
<root>
  <data name="Company Name" xml:space="preserve">
    <value>Nom de l'entreprise</value>
  </data>
  <data name="Country" xml:space="preserve">
    <value>Pays</value>
  </data>
  <data name="Item Count" xml:space="preserve">
    <value>Nombre d'éléments</value>
  </data>
  <data name="Order Date" xml:space="preserve">
    <value>Date de commande</value>
  </data>
  <data name="Order ID" xml:space="preserve">
    <value>Numéro de commande</value>
  </data>
  <data name="Order Total" xml:space="preserve">
    <value>Total de la commande</value>
  </data>
  <data name="Orders" xml:space="preserve">
    <value>Commandes (France)</value>
  </data>
</root>
```

7. Copy and paste the file and rename it as `Index.fr.resx`.

8. In `Index.fr.resx`, modify the last value to be `Commandes (Neutral French)`.

## Localizing Razor views with an injected view localizer

Now we can continue for both code editors:

1. In the `Views/Home` folder, in `Index.cshtml`, import the namespace for working with localization, inject the `IViewLocalizer` service, and make changes to use the labels in the view model, as shown highlighted in the following markup:

```razor
@using Microsoft.AspNetCore.Mvc.Localization
@model IEnumerable<Order>
@inject IViewLocalizer Localizer
@{
  ViewData["Title"] = Localizer["Orders"];
}

<div class="text-center">
```

```
<h1 class="display-4">@ViewData["Title"]</h1>
<table class="table table-bordered table-striped">
  <thead>
    <tr>
      <th>@Localizer["Order ID"]</th>
      <th>@Localizer["Order Date"]</th>
      <th>@Localizer["Company Name"]</th>
      <th>@Localizer["Country"]</th>
      <th>@Localizer["Item Count"]</th>
      <th>@Localizer["Order Total"]</th>
    </tr>
  </thead>
</table>
```

 **Good Practice:** The key values like `"Order ID"` are used to look up the localized values. If a value is missing, then it returns the key value as a default. It is good practice to therefore use key values that also work as a good fallback, which is why I used US English proper titles as the key values above.

2.  In `Program.cs`, before the call to `AddControllersWithViews`, add a statement to add localization and set the path to find resource files to the `Resources` folder, and after the call to `AddControllersWithViews`, append a call to add view localization, as shown highlighted in the following code:

```
builder.Services.AddLocalization(
  options => options.ResourcesPath = "Resources");

builder.Services.AddControllersWithViews().AddViewLocalization();
```

3.  In `Program.cs`, after the call to `Build` the app object, add statements to declare four cultures that we will support: US English, British English, neutral French, and French in France. Then, create a new localization options object and add those cultures as supported for both localization of user interfaces (`UICultures`) and for globalization of data values like dates and currency (`Cultures`), as shown in the following code:

```
string[] cultures = new[] { "en-US", "en-GB", "fr", "fr-FR" };

RequestLocalizationOptions localizationOptions = new();

// cultures[0] will be "en-US"
localizationOptions.SetDefaultCulture(cultures[0])
  .AddSupportedCultures(cultures) // globalization of data formats
  .AddSupportedUICultures(cultures); // localization of UI

app.UseRequestLocalization(localizationOptions);
```

Request localization means that the browser can request what culture it prefers by adding a query string parameter (for example, `?culture=en-US&ui-culture=en-US`), sending a cookie (for example, `c=en-US|uic=en-US`), or setting an HTTP header (for example, `Accept-Language: en-US,en;q=0.9,fr-FR;q=0.8,fr;q=0.7,en-GB;q=0.6`). Calling the `UseRequestLocalization` method tells ASP.NET Core to look for these requests and to change the current thread processing that request to use the appropriate culture to format data and load resource values.

4.  Start the `Northwind.Mvc` website project.

5.  In Chrome, navigate to **Settings**.

6.  In the **Search settings** box, type `lang`, and note you will find the **Languages** section, as shown in *Figure 15.8*:

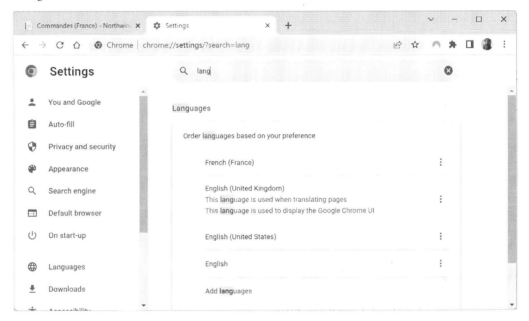

*Figure 15.8: Searching Chrome Settings for the Languages section*

**Warning!** If you are using a localized version of Chrome, in other words, its user interface is in your local language, like French, then you will need to search for the word "language" in your own language. (Although "language" in French is "langue", so entering "lang" will still work. But in Spanish you would need to search for "idioma".)

7.  Click **Add languages**, search for french, select both **French - français** and **French (France) -français (France)**, and then click **Add**, as shown in *Figure 15.9*:

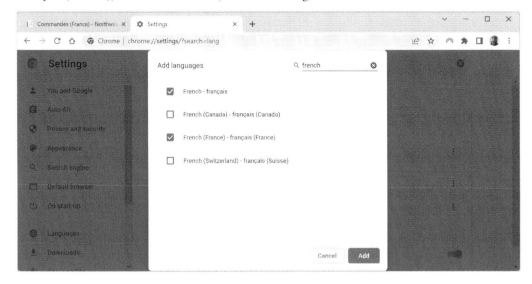

Figure 15.9: Adding neutral French and French in France languages to Chrome

 **Warning!** If you are using a localized version of Chrome, then you will need to search for the word "French" in your own language. For example, in Spanish, it would be "Francés", and in Welsh it would be "Ffrangeg".

8.   Add British English and US English.

9.   In the dots menu to the right of **French (France)**, click **Move to the top**, and confirm that it is at the top of your list of languages.

10.  Close the **Settings** tab.

11.  Hold down *Ctrl* and click the **Refresh** button, and note that the home page now uses localized labels and French formats for dates and currency, as shown in *Figure 15.10*:

*Figure 15.10: The Orders table localized and globalized into French*

12. Repeat the above steps for the other languages, for example, US English.

13. View **Developer Tools**, and note that the request headers have been set with US English first, as shown in *Figure 15.11*:

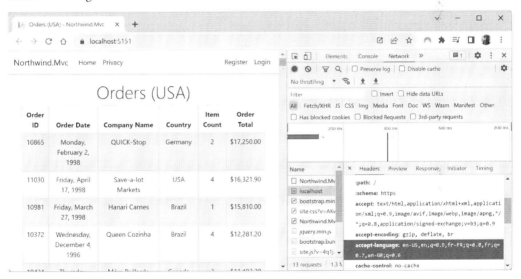

*Figure 15.11: The Orders table localized and globalized into US English due to the Accept-Language header*

## Understanding the Accept-Language header

You might wonder how the `Accept-Language` header works:

```
Accept-Language: en-US,en;q=0.9,fr-FR;q=0.8,fr;q=0.7,en-GB;q=0.6
```

The `Accept-Language` header uses commas as separators between culture codes. Each culture code can be neutral (just a language) or specific (language and region), and each can have a quality value between 0.0 and 1.0 (default). The values should therefore be read as follows:

- `en-US`: English language in United States ranked highest at 1.0.
- `en;q=0.9`: English language anywhere in the world ranked at 0.9.
- `fr-FR;q=0.8`: English language in France ranked at 0.8.
- `fr;q=0.7`: French language anywhere in the world ranked at 0.7.
- `en-GB;q=0.6`: English language in United Kingdom ranked lowest at 0.6.

# Defining web user interfaces with Tag Helpers

Tag Helpers make it easier to make static HTML elements dynamic. The markup is cleaner and easier to read, edit, and maintain than if you use HTML Helpers.

However, Tag Helpers do not replace HTML Helpers because there are some things that can only be achieved with HTML Helpers, like rendering output that contains multiple nested tags. Tag Helpers also cannot be used in Razor components. So, you must learn HTML Helpers and treat Tag Helpers as an optional choice that is better in some scenarios.

Tag Helpers are especially useful for **Front End** (**FE**) developers who primarily work with HTML, CSS, and JavaScript because the FE developer does not have to learn C# syntax. Tag Helpers just use what look like normal HTML attributes on elements. The attribute names and values can also be selected from IntelliSense if your code editor supports that; both Visual Studio 2022 and Visual Studio Code do.

## Comparing HTML Helpers and Tag Helpers

For example, to render a linkable hyperlink to a controller action, you could use an HTML Helper method, as shown in the following markup:

```
@Html.ActionLink("View our privacy policy.", "Privacy", "Index")
```

To make it clearer how it works, you could use named parameters:

```
@Html.ActionLink(linkText: "View our privacy policy.",
    action: "Privacy", controller: "Index")
```

But using a Tag Helper would be even clearer and cleaner for someone who works a lot with HTML:

```
<a asp-action="Privacy" asp-controller="Home">View our privacy policy.</a>
```

All three examples above generate the following rendered HTML element:

```
<a href="/home/privacy">View our privacy policy.</a>
```

In the next few sections, we will review some of the more common Tag Helpers:

- Anchor Tag Helper
- Cache Tag Helper
- Environment Tag Helper
- Image Tag Helper
- Forms-related Tag Helpers

## Exploring the Anchor Tag Helper

Let's see some examples of the Anchor Tag Helper. First, we will create three clickable hyperlinks styled as buttons to view the home page with all orders, the orders for a single customer, and the orders in a single country. This will allow us to see the basics of creating links to controllers and actions, as well as passing parameters using a route parameter and arbitrary query string parameters:

1.  In the Views folder, in _ViewImports.cshtml, note the @addTagHelper directive, which adds the ASP.NET Core Tag Helpers, as shown highlighted in the following code:

    ```
    @using Northwind.Mvc
    @using Northwind.Mvc.Models
    @addTagHelper *, Microsoft.AspNetCore.Mvc.TagHelpers
    ```

2.  In the Views/Home folder, in Privacy.cshtml, add markup to define a paragraph with clickable hyperlinks styled as buttons using the <a> tag, as shown in the following markup:

    ```
    <p>
      <a asp-controller="Home" asp-action="Index"
         class="btn btn-primary" role="button">Orders</a>

      <a asp-controller="Home"
         class="btn btn-outline-primary" role="button">This Page</a>

      <a asp-controller="Home" asp-action="Index" asp-route-id="ALFKI"
         class="btn btn-outline-primary" role="button">
         Orders for Alfreds Futterkiste</a>

      <a asp-controller="Home" asp-action="Index" asp-route-country="Brazil"
         class="btn btn-outline-primary" role="button">Orders in Brazil</a>
    </p>
    ```

If you set a controller name without an action name, then it defaults to the current action, in this case, Privacy. The asp-route-{parametername} attribute can use any arbitrary parameter name. In the code example above, we use id and country. id will map to the route parameter with the same name. country is not a route parameter, so it will be passed as a query string.

3.  In the `Controllers` folder, in `HomeController.cs`, modify the `Index` action method to define two optional parameters to pass a customer ID and the name of a country, and then modify the LINQ query to use them to filter the orders if they are set, as shown highlighted in the following code:

```
public IActionResult Index(string? id = null, string? country = null)
{
    IEnumerable<Order> model = db.Orders
        .Include(order => order.Customer)
        .Include(order => order.OrderDetails);

    if (id != null)
    {
        model = model.Where(order => order.Customer?.CustomerId == id);
    }

    if (country != null)
    {
        model = model.Where(order => order.Customer?.Country == country);
    }

    model = model
        .OrderByDescending(order => order.OrderDetails
            .Sum(detail => detail.Quantity * detail.UnitPrice))
        .AsEnumerable();

    return View(model);
}
```

4.  Start the `Northwind.Mvc` website project.

5.  View **Developer Tools** and click **Elements**.

6.  On the home page, click **Privacy** to navigate to that page, and note the buttons, including their raw HTML that shows the `href` attribute paths that were generated by the Anchor Tag Helper, as shown in Figure *15.12*:

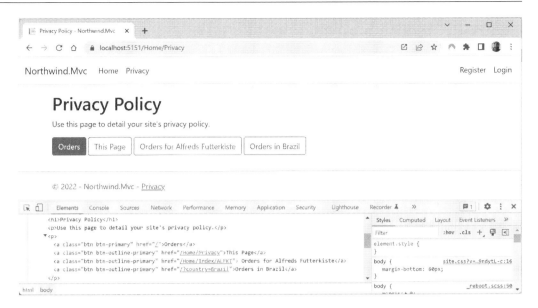

*Figure 15.12: Three hyperlinks styled as buttons generated by Anchor Tag Helper*

7.  Click each button and then come back to this page to make sure they work correctly.

8.  Shut down the web server and close the browser.

9.  In the Views/Home folder, in Index.cshtml, at the end of the table of orders, add an anchor tag
    to indicate the end of the orders table, as shown highlighted in the following markup:

    ```
    </table>
    <a id="endOfTable" />
    </div>
    ```

10. In the Views/Home folder, in Privacy.cshtml, after the existing anchor tags, add another one
    to link to the anchor with an id of endOfTable by setting the asp-fragment attribute, as shown
    in the following markup:

    ```
    <a asp-controller="Home" asp-action="Index" asp-fragment="endOfTable"
        class="btn btn-outline-primary">Orders (end of table)</a>
    ```

11. In the Views/Home folder, in Privacy.cshtml, modify the second anchor tag to explicitly set
    the protocol to use https, as shown highlighted in the following markup:

    ```
    <a asp-controller="Home" asp-protocol="https"
        class="btn btn-outline-primary">This Page</a>
    ```

12. In the Controllers folder, in HomeController.cs, add an action method named Shipper. Give
    it a parameter to receive a shipper entity passed as a query string and then pass it to the view,
    as shown in the following code:

    ```
    public IActionResult Shipper(Shipper shipper)
    {
    ```

```
    return View(shipper);
}
```

13. In the `Views/Home` folder, add an empty Razor view named `Shipper.cshtml`.

14. Modify the contents, as shown in the following markup:

```
@model Shipper
@{
    ViewData["Title"] = "Shippers";
}
<h1>@ViewData["Title"]</h1>
<div>
    <div class="mb-3">
        <label for="shipperIdInput" class="form-label">Shipper Id</label>
        <input type="number" class="form-control" id="shipperIdInput"
               value="@Model.ShipperId">
    </div>
    <div class="mb-3">
        <label for="companyNameInput" class="form-label">Company Name</label>
        <input class="form-control" id="companyNameInput"
               value="@Model.CompanyName">
    </div>
    <div class="mb-3">
        <label for="phoneInput" class="form-label">Phone</label>
        <input class="form-control" id="phoneInput" value="@Model.Phone">
    </div>
</div>
```

15. In the `Views/Home` folder, in `Privacy.cshtml`, at the top of the file, add code and markup to inject the Northwind database context. Then, use it to define a Razor function to create a dictionary with string values for both the key and value populated from the shippers table, as shown highlighted in the following code:

```
@inject NorthwindContext db
@{
    ViewData["Title"] = "Privacy Policy";
}
@functions {
    public async Task<IDictionary<string, string>> GetShipperData()
    {
        // first the first shipper
        Shipper? shipper = await db.Shippers.FindAsync(1);

        Dictionary<string, string> keyValuePairs = new();

        if (shipper != null)
        {
```

```
    keyValuePairs = new()
    {
        { "ShipperId", shipper.ShipperId.ToString() },
        { "CompanyName", shipper.CompanyName },
        { "Phone", shipper.Phone ?? string.Empty }
    };
    }

    return keyValuePairs;
    }
}
```

16. After the existing anchor tags, add another one to pass the dictionary to the current page, as shown in the following markup:

```
<a asp-controller="Home" asp-action="Shipper"
    asp-all-route-data="await GetShipperData()"
    class="btn btn-outline-primary">Shipper</a>
```

> Passing a complex object as a query string like this quickly hits the limit of about 1,000 characters for a URL. To send larger objects, you should use POST instead of GET by using a <form> element instead of an anchor tag <a>.

17. Start the Northwind.Mvc website project.

18. View **Developer Tools** and click **Elements**.

19. On the home page, click **Privacy** to navigate to that page and note the buttons, including their raw HTML that shows the href attribute paths that were generated by the Anchor Tag Helper, as shown in Figure 15.13:

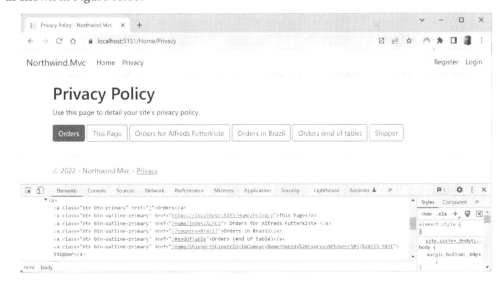

*Figure 15.13: Using a fragment and passing a complex object using query string parameters*

> A side benefit of specifying the protocol is that the generated URL must include the protocol, domain, and any port number, as well as the relative path, so it is a convenient way to get an absolute URL instead of the default relative path URL.

20. Click the **Orders (end of table)** button and note that the browser navigates to the home page and then jumps to the end of the orders table.

21. Go back to the **Privacy** page, click the **Shipper** button, and note the shipper details, as shown in *Figure 15.14*:

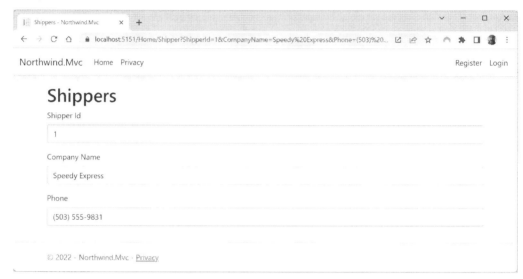

*Figure 15.14: A shipper passed using query string parameters*

22. Close the browser and shut down the web server.

# Exploring the Cache Tag Helpers

The Cache and Distributed Cache Tag Helpers improve the performance of your web pages by caching their content using the in-memory or registered distributed cache providers respectively.

An in-memory cache is best for a single web server or a web server farm with session affinity enabled. **Session affinity** means that subsequent requests from the same browser are served by the same web server.

A distributed cache is best for a web server farm or in a cloud provider like Azure. You can register providers for SQL Server, Redis, or NCache, or create your own custom provider.

> In this book, we will only look at in-memory caching, so if you want to learn more about distributed caching then you can use the following link: `https://docs.microsoft.com/en-us/aspnet/core/performance/caching/distributed`.

Attributes that can be applied to the Cache Tag Helper include:

- enabled: Default value is true. This exists so that you can include the <cache> element in the markup but decide at runtime if it should be enabled or not.
- expires-after: A TimeSpan value to expire after. The default is 00:20:00, meaning 20 minutes.
- expires-on: A DateTimeOffset value to expire at. No default.
- expires-sliding: A TimeSpan value to expire after if the value has not been accessed during that time. This is useful when storing database entities that cost a lot to create and have varied popularity. The popular entities will stay cached if they continue to be accessed. Less popular entities will drop out. No default.
- vary-by-{type}: These attributes allow multiple different cached versions based on differences in an HTTP header value, a user, route, cookie, or query string value, or a custom value.

Let's see an example of the Cache Tag Helper:

1. In the Views/Home folder, in Index.cshtml, immediately after the heading and before the table, add <div> elements to define a Bootstrap row with two columns that show the current UTC date and time twice, once live and then once cached, as shown in the following markup:

```
<div class="row">
  <div class="col">
    <h2>Live</h2>
    <p class="alert alert-info">
    UTC: @DateTime.UtcNow.ToLongDateString() at
        @DateTime.UtcNow.ToLongTimeString()
    </p>
  </div>
  <div class="col">
    <h2>Cached</h2>
    <p class="alert alert-secondary">
      <cache>
        UTC: @DateTime.UtcNow.ToLongDateString() at
             @DateTime.UtcNow.ToLongTimeString()
      </cache>
    </p>
  </div>
</div>
```

2. Start the Northwind.Mvc website project.

3.   Refresh the home page several times over several seconds and note the left-hand time is always refreshed to show the live time, and the right-hand time is cached (for 20 minutes by default), as shown in *Figure 15.15*:

*Figure 15.15: Live and cached UTC times*

4.   Close the browser and shut down the web server.

5.   In the Views/Home folder, in Index.cshtml, modify the `<cache>` element to expire after 10 seconds, as shown highlighted in the following markup:

```
<cache expires-after="@TimeSpan.FromSeconds(10)">
```

6.   Start the Northwind.Mvc website project.

7.   Refresh the home page several times over several seconds and note that the left-hand time is always refreshed to show the live time, and the right-hand time is cached for 10 seconds before it then refreshes.

8.   Close the browser and shut down the web server.

## Exploring the Environment Tag Helper

The Environment Tag Helper renders its content only if the current environment matches one of the values in a comma-separated list of names. This is useful if you want to render some content like instructions to a tester when hosted in a staging environment, or content like customer-specific information that developers and testers do not need to see while hosted in the production environment.

As well as a names attribute to set the comma-separated list of environments, you can also use include (works the same as names) and exclude (renders for all environments *except* the ones in the list).

Let's see an example:

1.   In the Views/Home folder, in Privacy.cshtml, inject the dependency service for the web host environment, as shown in the following code:

```
@inject IWebHostEnvironment webhost
```

2. After the heading, add two `<environment>` elements, the first to show output only for developers and testers, and the second to show output only for product visitors, as shown in the following markup:

```
<environment names="Development,Staging">
  <div class="alert alert-warning">
    <h2>Attention developers and testers</h2>
    <p>
      This is a warning that only developers and testers will see.
      Current environment:
      <span class="badge bg-warning">@webhost.EnvironmentName</span>
    </p>
  </div>
</environment>
<environment names="Production">
  <div class="alert alert-info">
    <h2>Welcome, visitor!</h2>
    <p>
      This is information that only a visitor to the production website
      will see. Current environment:
      <span class="badge bg-info">@webhost.EnvironmentName</span>
    </p>
  </div>
</environment>
```

3. Start the `Northwind.Mvc` website project.

4. Navigate to the **Privacy** page, and note the message for developers and testers, as shown in *Figure 15.16*:

*Figure 15.16: The Privacy page in the Development environment*

5. Close the browser and shut down the web server.

6.  In the `Properties` folder, in `launchSettings.json`, for the `https` profile, change the environment setting to `Production`, as shown highlighted in the following JSON:

```
"https": {
  "commandName": "Project",
  "dotnetRunMessages": true,
  "launchBrowser": true,
  "applicationUrl": "https://localhost:5151;http://localhost:5152",
  "environmentVariables": {
    "ASPNETCORE_ENVIRONMENT": "Production"
  }
},
```

7.  Start the `Northwind.Mvc` website project.

8.  Navigate to the **Privacy** page, and note the message for public visitors, as shown in *Figure 15.17*:

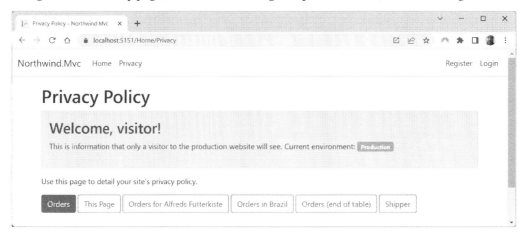

*Figure 15.17: The Privacy page in the Production environment*

9.  Close the browser and shut down the web server.

10. In the `Properties` folder, in `launchSettings.json`, for the `https` profile, change the environment setting back to `Development`.

## Understanding how cache busting with Tag Helpers works

When `asp-append-version` is specified with a `true` value in a `<link>`, `<img>`, or `<script>` element, the Tag Helper for that tag type is invoked.

They work by automatically appending a query string value named v that is generated from a SHA256 hash of the referenced source file, as shown in the following example generated output:

```
<script src="~/js/site.js? v=Kl_dqr9NVtnMdsM2MUg4qthUnWZm5T1fCEimBPWDNgM"></
script>
```

You can see this for yourself in the current project because the _Layout.cshtml file has the `<script src="~/js/site.js" asp-append-version="true"></script>` element.

If even a single byte within the site.js file changes, then its hash value will be different, and therefore if a browser or CDN is caching the script file, then it will bust the cached copy and replace it with the new version.

The src attribute must be set to a static file stored on the local web server, usually in the wwwroot folder but you can configure additional locations. Remote references are not supported.

## Exploring Forms-related Tag Helpers

The Form Tag Helper generates the `<form>` elements action attribute for a MVC controller action or named route. Like the Anchor Tag Helper, you can pass parameters using the asp-route-`<parametername>` attribute. It also generates a hidden verification token to prevent cross-site request forgery. You must apply the [ValidateAntiForgeryToken] attribute to the HTTP POST action method to properly use this feature.

The Label and Input Tag Helpers bind labels and inputs to properties on a model. They can then generate the id, name, and for attributes automatically, as well as add validation attributes and messages.

Let's see an example of a form for entering shipper information:

1. In the Views/Home folder, in Shipper.cshtml, duplicate the existing markup that outputs shipper details, wrap it in a `<form>` element that uses the Form Tag Helper, and modify the `<label>` and `<input>` elements to use the Label and Input Tag Helpers, as shown highlighted in the following markup:

```
@model Shipper
@{
  ViewData["Title"] = "Shippers";
}
<h1>@ViewData["Title"]</h1>
<h2>Without Form Tag Helper</h2>
<div>
  <div class="mb-3">
    <label for="shipperIdInput" class="form-label">Shipper ID</label>
    <input type="number" class="form-control" id="shipperIdInput"
           value="@Model.ShipperId">
  </div>
  <div class="mb-3">
    <label for="companyNameInput" class="form-label">Company Name</label>
    <input class="form-control" id="companyNameInput"
           value="@Model.CompanyName">
  </div>
```

```html
    <div class="mb-3">
      <label for="phoneInput" class="form-label">Phone</label>
      <input class="form-control" id="phoneInput" value="@Model.Phone">
    </div>
  </div>
  <h2>With Form Tag Helper</h2>
  <form asp-controller="Home" asp-action="ProcessShipper"
        class="form-horizontal" role="form">
    <div>
      <div class="mb-3">
        <label asp-for="ShipperId" class="form-label" />
        <input asp-for="ShipperId" class="form-control">
      </div>
      <div class="mb-3">
        <label asp-for="CompanyName" class="form-label" />
        <input asp-for="CompanyName" class="form-control">
      </div>
      <div class="mb-3">
        <label asp-for="Phone" class="form-label" />
        <input asp-for="Phone" class="form-control">
      </div>
      <div class="mb-3">
        <input type="submit" class="form-control">
      </div>
    </div>
  </form>
```

2. In the `Controllers` folder, in `HomeController.cs`, add an action method named `ProcessShipper`. Give it a parameter to receive a shipper entity passed as a query string and then return it as a JSON document using the `Json` method, as shown in the following code:

```csharp
[HttpPost]
[ValidateAntiForgeryToken]
public IActionResult ProcessShipper(Shipper shipper)
{
  return Json(shipper);
}
```

3. Start the `Northwind.Mvc` website project.

4. Navigate to the **Privacy** page, and then click the **Shipper** button.

5. In the **Shipper** page, right-click, select **View page source**, and note the different HTML output for the form generated by the Form, Input, and Label Tag Helpers, including a hidden element named __RequestVerificationToken, as shown in the following markup and in *Figure 15.18*:

```html
<h2>With Form Tag Helper</h2>
<form class="form-horizontal" role="form" action="/Home/ProcessShipper"
method="post">
```

```
    <div>
      <div class="mb-3">
        <label class="form-label" for="ShipperId" />
        <input class="form-control" type="number" data-val="true"
  data-val-required="The ShipperId field is required." id="ShipperId"
  name="ShipperId" value="1">
      </div>
      <div class="mb-3">
        <label class="form-label" for="CompanyName" />
        <input class="form-control" type="text" data-val="true" data-val-
  length="The field CompanyName must be a string with a maximum length
  of 40." data-val-length-max="40" data-val-required="The CompanyName
  field is required." id="CompanyName" maxlength="40" name="CompanyName"
  value="Speedy Express">
      </div>
      <div class="mb-3">
        <label class="form-label" for="Phone" />
        <input class="form-control" type="text" data-val="true" data-
  val-length="The field Phone must be a string with a maximum length of
  24." data-val-length-max="24" id="Phone" maxlength="24" name="Phone"
  value="(503) 555-9831">
      </div>
      <div class="mb-3">
        <input type="submit" class="form-control">
      </div>
    </div>
  <input name="__RequestVerificationToken" type="hidden"
  value="CfDJ8NTt08jabvBCqd1P4J-HCq3X9CDrTPjBphdDdVmG6UT0GFBJk1w7F1OLmNT-jE
  GjlGIjfV3kmNUaofOAxlGgiZJwbAR73g-QgFw8oFV_0vjlo45t9dL9E1l1hZzjLXtj8B7y
  sDkCYcm8W9zS0T7V3R0" /></form>
```

*Figure 15.18: A web form generated by the Form, Input, and Label Tag Helpers*

6. In the form, change the shipper ID and company name, noting that attributes like `maxlength="40"` prevent a company name longer than 40 characters, and `type="number"` only allows numbers for the shipper ID, as shown in *Figure 15.19*:

*Figure 15.19: A web form for a shipper*

7. Click the **Submit** button and note the JSON document returned, as shown in *Figure 15.20*:

*Figure 15.20: A processed shipper*

8. Close the browser and shut down the web server.

# Practicing and exploring

Test your knowledge and understanding by answering some questions, getting some hands-on practice, and exploring this chapter's topics with deeper research.

## Exercise 15.1 – Test your knowledge

Answer the following questions:

1. What is the advantage of declaring a strongly typed Razor view and how do you do it?
2. How do you enable Tag Helpers in a view?
3. What are the pros and cons of HTML Helper methods compared to Tag Helpers?
4. How can a browser request a preferred language for localization?
5. How do you localize text in a view?
6. What is the prefix for attributes recognized by Tag Helpers?
7. How can you pass a complex object as a query string parameter?
8. How can you control how long the contents of the `<cache>` element are cached for?

9. What is the `<environment>` element used for?

10. How does cache busting with Tag Helpers work?

## Exercise 15.2 – Practice building user interfaces with Bootstrap

Create a new ASP.NET Core MVC project named `Ch15Ex02_ExploringBootstrap`. Add views that implement the following Bootstrap features:

- Accordion: `https://getbootstrap.com/docs/5.2/components/accordion/`
- Cards: `https://getbootstrap.com/docs/5.2/components/card/`
- Carousel: `https://getbootstrap.com/docs/5.2/components/carousel/`
- NavBar: `https://getbootstrap.com/docs/5.2/components/navbar/`
- Popovers: `https://getbootstrap.com/docs/5.2/components/popovers/`
- Toast: `https://getbootstrap.com/docs/5.2/components/toasts/`
- Tooltips: `https://getbootstrap.com/docs/5.2/components/tooltips/`

## Exercise 15.3 – Explore topics

Use the links on the following page to learn more about the topics covered in this chapter:

`https://github.com/markjprice/apps-services-net7/blob/main/book-links.md#chapter-15---building-web-user-interfaces-using-aspnet-core`

## Summary

In this chapter, you learned how to build user interfaces using ASP.NET Core MVC. You learned about:

- ASP.NET Core Razor views and Razor syntax.
- Some common Bootstrap styles.
- Localizing and globalizing an ASP.NET Core website.
- HTML Helpers and Tag Helpers.

In the next chapter, you will learn how to build web user interface components using Blazor WebAssembly.

# 16

# Building Web Components Using Blazor WebAssembly

This chapter is about building web components using Blazor WebAssembly. These can be rich and interactive user interfaces that render as HTML and CSS to provide cross-platform browser support.

There are many advantages to using .NET for client-side web development. You can write 99% of your code using C# instead of JavaScript and interop with JavaScript modules for the other 1%. You can share business logic between server and client because Blazor implements .NET Standard as well as the latest .NET 7 libraries, so you can use the extensive older .NET libraries, both from Microsoft and third-parties.

This chapter will cover the following topics:

- Understanding Blazor
- Building Blazor components
- Building a Blazor data component
- Implementing caching using local storage
- Building Progressive Web Apps

## Understanding Blazor

Blazor is Microsoft's framework for web component development built on .NET.

## Blazor hosting models

Blazor has multiple hosting models to choose from:

- **Blazor WebAssembly**: The code executes in the web browser like other **single page application (SPA)** frameworks, for example, React and Angular. Your .NET assemblies and the .NET runtime are downloaded to the browser and cached for future use.

The nature of Blazor WebAssembly provides some key benefits, including the ability to run the app offline when not connected to the network, to host the app on a static website or serve it from a **content delivery network** (**CDN**), and to offload processing to the client, which increases scalability.

- **Blazor Server**: The code executes on the web server and user interface updates are sent to the browser using SignalR. The nature of Blazor Server provides some key benefits, including complete .NET API support, direct access to all server-side resources like databases, fast initial load time, and your code being protected because it never leaves the server.

- **Blazor Hybrid**: The code executes in a local web view hosted in a native client app. The app can be built using .NET MAUI if the app needs to be cross-platform, or Windows Presentation Foundation or Windows Forms if you are only targeting Windows. The main benefit of Blazor Hybrid compared to the other two hosting models is access to native client capabilities that can provide a better user experience.

Blazor WebAssembly and Blazor Server support the latest version of all four major web browsers, Chrome, Firefox, Edge, and Safari, on mobile and desktop platforms. Blazor Hybrid supports the latest web view components on the three major platforms, Chrome on Android, Safari on iOS and macOS, and Edge WebView2 on Windows.

> **More Information:** The official Blazor documentation has a useful table to help you choose between the hosting models. You can find it at the following link: `https://docs.microsoft.com/en-us/aspnet/core/blazor/hosting-models#which-blazor-hosting-model-should-i-choose`.

## Deployment choices for Blazor WebAssembly apps

There are two main ways to deploy a Blazor WebAssembly app:

- You can create and deploy just a Blazor WebAssembly app client project by placing its published files in any static hosting web server. For example, Azure Static Web Apps is a potential choice of host for a Blazor WebAssembly app. You can read more at the following link: `https://docs.microsoft.com/en-us/azure/static-web-apps/overview`.

- You can deploy a Blazor WebAssembly app server project, which references the client app and perhaps hosts services called by the Blazor WebAssembly app as well as the app itself. The Blazor WebAssembly app is placed in the `wwwroot` folder of the server website project, along with any other static assets.

> **More Information:** You can read more about these choices at the following link: `https://docs.microsoft.com/en-us/aspnet/core/blazor/host-and-deploy/webassembly`.

# The browser compatibility analyzer for Blazor WebAssembly

With .NET 6 and later, Microsoft has unified the .NET library for all workloads. However, although, in theory, this means that a Blazor WebAssembly app has full access to all .NET APIs, in practice, it runs inside a browser sandbox so there are limitations. If you call an unsupported API, this will throw a `PlatformNotSupportedException`.

To be forewarned about unsupported APIs, you can add a platform compatibility analyzer that will warn you when your code uses APIs that are not supported by browsers.

 **Blazor WebAssembly App** and **Razor Class Library** project templates automatically enable browser compatibility checks.

To manually activate browser compatibility checks, for example, in a **Class Library** project, add an entry to the project file, as shown in the following markup:

```
<ItemGroup>
  <SupportedPlatform Include="browser" />
</ItemGroup>
```

Microsoft decorates unsupported APIs, as shown in the following code:

```
[UnsupportedOSPlatform("browser")]
public void DoSomethingOutsideTheBrowserSandbox()
{
  ...
}
```

 **Good Practice:** If you create libraries that includes functionality that cannot be used in Blazor WebAssembly apps, then you should decorate your APIs in the same way.

# CSS and JavaScript isolation

Blazor components often need to provide their own CSS to apply styling or JavaScript for activities that cannot be performed purely in C#, like access to browser APIs. To ensure this does not conflict with site-level CSS and JavaScript, Blazor supports CSS and JavaScript isolation.

If you have a component named `Index.razor`, simply create a CSS file named `Index.razor.css`. The styles defined within this file will override any other styles in the project for this component, but not for the rest of the website.

For JavaScript isolation, you do not use a naming convention in the same way as with CSS. Instead, Blazor enables JavaScript isolation using JavaScript modules imported using the JavaScript interop feature of Blazor, as you will see later in this chapter.

You can read more about JavaScript isolation at the following link: `https://docs.`
`microsoft.com/en-us/aspnet/core/blazor/javascript-interoperability/call-`
`javascript-from-dotnet#javascript-isolation-in-javascript-modules`.

## Blazor components

Blazor is all about **components**. A component is a part of a web app, like a button, a grid, a form for gathering input from the visitor, or even a whole page. Components can be reused and nested to build more complex components.

A Blazor component usually consists of a Razor file with the file extension `.razor`. Just like Razor views in ASP.NET Core MVC or Razor Pages, Razor files used by Blazor components easily mix HTML and C# code. As well as the HTML elements that make up the user interface parts, and the CSS used to style them, the Razor file also has a code block to implement event handling, properties, and other statements to provide the functionality of the component.

For example, a Blazor component named `ProgressBar.razor` could implement a progress bar using Bootstrap. It might define parameters for a minimum, maximum, and the current value of the progress bar, and have Boolean parameters to enable animation style and show the current value as text, as shown in the following markup:

```
<div class="progress">
  <div class="progress-bar progress-bar-striped bg-info
            @(IsAnimated ? " progress-bar-animated" : "")"
      role="progressbar" aria-label="@LabelText" style="width: @Value%"
      aria-valuenow="@Value" aria-valuemin="@Minimum" aria-valuemax="@Maximum">
    @(ShowValue ? Value + "%" : "")
  </div>
</div>

@code {
  [Parameter]
  public int Value { get; set; } = 0;

  [Parameter]
  public int Minimum { get; set; } = 0;

  [Parameter]
  public int Maximum { get; set; } = 100;

  [Parameter]
  public bool IsAnimated { get; set; } = false;

  [Parameter]
```

```
    public bool ShowValue { get; set; } = false;

    [Parameter]
    public string? LabelText { get; set; } = "Progress bar";
}
```

To embed an instance of the component on a page, you use the component name as if it were an HTML element and set its parameters using HTML attributes, as shown in the following markup:

```
<ProgressBar Value="25" IsAnimated="true" ShowValue="true"
             LabelText="Progress of database deletion" />
```

# Blazor routing to page components

The Router component in the App.razor file enables routing to components, as shown in the following markup:

```
<Router AppAssembly="@typeof(App).Assembly">
  <Found Context="routeData">
    <RouteView RouteData="@routeData" DefaultLayout="@typeof(MainLayout)" />
    <FocusOnNavigate RouteData="@routeData" Selector="h1" />
  </Found>
  <NotFound>
    <PageTitle>Not found</PageTitle>
    <LayoutView Layout="@typeof(MainLayout)">
      <p role="alert">Sorry, there's nothing at this address.</p>
    </LayoutView>
  </NotFound>
</Router>
```

The Router component scans the assembly specifically in its AppAssembly parameter for components decorated with the [Route] attribute and registers their URL paths.

If a route match is found, then the context of the request is stored in a variable named routeData and passed to the matching Razor file. A default layout is set to use a file named MainLayout.razor. In the Razor file, the focus is set to the first <h1> element. If the Razor file contains a form, then you might want to set the first form input element like a textbox to have the focus. The FocusOnNavigate component has a Selector property that must be set to a valid CSS selector. This could be a tag selector like the default h1, or a more specific CSS selector that uses a CSS class or an ID. The setting is common across all components in your app so you will need to set one that works across all your components.

If a route match is not found, then the Razor markup specified in the <LayoutView> is rendered with the shared layout and its page title set to Not found.

For example, in a typical ASP.NET Core MVC project, an MVC controller could be decorated with the [Route] attribute, as shown in the following code:

```
[Route("customers")]
public class CustomersController
{
```

An HTTP GET request to the relative path /customers would be matched to the route.

To create an equivalent routable page component, add the @page directive to the top of a component's
.razor file, as shown in the following markup:

```
@page "customers"
```

A page component can have multiple @page directives to register multiple routes.

> If you were to write code that uses reflection to find the component class generated for
> you from the Razor markup file, then you would discover that it is decorated with the
> [Route] attribute due to the @page directive.

At runtime, the page component is merged with any specific layout that you have specified, just
like an MVC view or Razor Page would be. By default, Blazor project templates define a file named
MainLayout.razor as the layout for page components.

> **Good Practice:** By convention, put routable page Blazor components in the Pages folder
> and non-page components in a Components folder.

## How to pass route parameters

Blazor routes can include case-insensitive named parameters, and your code can most easily access
the passed values by binding the parameter to a property in the code block using the [Parameter]
attribute, as shown in the following markup:

```
@page "/employees/{country}"

<div>Country parameter as the value: @Country</div>

@code {
  [Parameter]
  public string Country { get; set; }
}
```

The recommended way to handle a parameter that should have a default value when it is missing is to
suffix the parameter in the route with ? and use the null coalescing operator in the OnParametersSet
method, as shown highlighted in the following markup:

```
@page "/employees/{country?}"

<div>Country parameter as the value: @Country</div>

@code {
```

```
[Parameter]
public string? Country { get; set; }

protected override void OnParametersSet()
{
    // if the automatically set property is null
    // set its value to USA
    Country = Country ?? "USA";
}
}
```

## Setting parameters from a query string

You can also set component properties using parameters from a query string, as shown in the following code:

```
[Parameter]
[SupplyParameterFromQuery(Name = "country")]
public string? Country { get; set; }
```

## Route constraints for parameters

Route constraints validate that the data type is correct for a passed parameter. If a potential request with a parameter value violates the constraint, then a match for that route is not made, and other routes will be evaluated instead. If no routes match, then a 404 is returned.

If you do not set constraints, then any value is acceptable as a route match, but a data type conversion exception may result when the value is converted into the C# method's expected data type.

| Constraint example | Description |
|---|---|
| {isanimated:bool} | The IsAnimated property must be set to a valid Boolean value, for example, TRUE or true. |
| {hiredate:datetime} | The HireDate property must be a valid date/time value. |
| {price:decimal} | The UnitPrice property must be a valid decimal value. |
| {shipweight:double} | The ShipWeight property must be a valid double value. |
| {shipwidth:float} | The ShipWidth property must be a valid float value. |
| {orderid:guid} | The OrderId property must be a valid Guid value. |
| {categoryid:int} | The CategoryId property must be a valid int value. |
| {nanoseconds:long} | The Nanoseconds property must be a valid long value. |

**Good Practice:** Route constraints assume invariant culture so your URLs must not be localized. For example, always use invariant culture formats to pass date and time parameter values.

## Base component classes

The OnParametersSet method is defined by the base class that components inherit from by default, named ComponentBase, as shown in the following code:

```
using Microsoft.AspNetCore.Components;

public abstract class ComponentBase : IComponent, IHandleAfterRender,
IHandleEvent
{
  // members not shown
}
```

ComponentBase has some useful methods that you can call and override, as shown in the following table:

| Method(s) | Description |
|---|---|
| InvokeAsync | Call this method to execute a function on the associated renderer's synchronization context. This avoids the requirement to write thread-synchronizing code when accessing shared resources. Multiple threads are not allowed to access the rendering process at the same time. The use of InvokeAsync means that only one thread will access components at any given moment, which eliminates the need to write thread-locking and synchronization code for shared state. |
| OnAfterRender, OnAfterRenderAsync | Override these methods to invoke code after each time the component has been rendered. |
| OnInitialized, OnInitializedAsync | Override these methods to invoke code after the component has received its initial parameters from its parent in the render tree. |
| OnParametersSet, OnParametersSetAsync | Override these methods to invoke code after the component has received parameters and the values have been assigned to properties. |
| ShouldRender | Override this method to indicate if the component should render. |
| StateHasChanged | Call this method to cause the component to re-render. |

Blazor components can have shared layouts in a similar way to MVC views and Razor Pages. You would create a .razor component file and make it explicitly inherit from LayoutComponentBase, as shown in the following markup:

```
@inherits LayoutComponentBase

<div>
  ...
  @Body
  ...
</div>
```

The base class has a property named Body that you can render in the markup at the correct place within the layout.

You can set a default layout for components in the `App.razor` file and its `Router` component. To explicitly set a layout for a component, use the `@layout` directive, as shown in the following markup:

```
@page "/employees"

@layout AlternativeLayout

<div>
  ...
</div>
```

## How to navigate Blazor routes to page components

Microsoft provides a dependency service named `NavigationManager` that understands Blazor routing and the `NavLink` component. The `NavigateTo` method is used to go to the specified URL.

In HTML, you use the `<a>` element to define navigation links, as shown in the following markup:

```
<a href="/employees">Employees</a>
```

In Blazor, use the `<NavLink>` component, as shown in the following markup:

```
<NavLink href="/employees">Employees</NavLink>
```

The `NavLink` component is better than an anchor element because it automatically sets its class to `active` if its `href` is a match with the current location URL. If your CSS uses a different class name, then you can set the class name in the `NavLink.ActiveClass` property.

By default, in the matching algorithm, the `href` is a path *prefix*, so if `NavLink` has an `href` of `/employees`, as shown in the preceding code example, then it would match all the following paths and set them all to have the `active` class style:

```
/employees
/employees/USA
/employees/UK/London
```

To ensure that the matching algorithm only performs matches on *all* of the text in the path – in other words, there is only a match when the whole complete text matches but not when just part of the path matches – then set the `Match` parameter to `NavLinkMatch.All`, as shown in the following code:

```
<NavLink href="/employees" Match="NavLinkMatch.All">Employees</NavLink>
```

If you set other attributes such as `target`, they are passed through to the underlying `<a>` element that is generated.

## Building Blazor components

With ASP.NET Core 7, Blazor introduces new project templates for starting from an empty project. They provide the minimum to run, without any example components. These include the old `Counter` component that has a button that increments a label that starts at one when clicked, or the `FetchData` component that calls a weather service and shows a table with five rows of random temperatures.

First, we will create a Blazor WebAssembly project that we will then add components to:

1.  Use your preferred code editor to create a new solution/workspace named `Chapter16`.

2.  Add a console app project, as defined in the following list:

    •   Project template: **Blazor WebAssembly App Empty**/`blazorwasm-empty`

    •   Workspace/solution file and folder: `Chapter16`

    •   Project file and folder: `Northwind.BlazorWasm`

    •   **Configure for HTTPS**: Selected

    •   **ASP.NET Core Hosted**: Selected or use the `--hosted` switch

    •   **Progressive Web App**: Selected or use the `--pwa` switch

3.  Note that three projects have been created named `Northwind.BlazorWasm.Client`, `Northwind.BlazorWasm.Server`, and `Northwind.BlazorWasm.Shared`. The `Client` project is the Blazor WebAssembly project, and it could be deployed on its own. The `Server` project is currently hosting the client app. We will also add a service to this project for the client to call. The `Shared` project is where you can put classes that will be used in both projects. It is referenced but not currently needed.

4.  Use your preferred coding tool to set which project is active:

    •   If you are using Visual Studio 2022, set the startup project for the solution to the `Northwind.BlazorWasm.Server` project.

    •   If you are using Visual Studio Code, set `Northwind.BlazorWasm.Server` as the active OmniSharp project.

5.  In the `Northwind.BlazorWasm.Server` project, in `Program.cs`, note that the statements enable a fairly standard ASP.NET Core HTTP pipeline, for example, enabling Razor Pages and MVC controllers and views, with some additions specifically to host a Blazor WebAssembly client app.

6.  In `Program.cs`, note that when running in the development environment, WebAssembly debugging tools are enabled, as shown highlighted in the following code:

    ```
    if (app.Environment.IsDevelopment())
    {
        app.UseWebAssemblyDebugging();
    }
    ```

7.  In `Program.cs`, note that the server project is configured to respond to requests for the Blazor WebAssembly framework files so they can be downloaded to a browser from the root of the website, as shown in the following code:

    ```
    app.UseBlazorFrameworkFiles();
    ```

8.  In `Program.cs`, note that if there are no matches for Razor Pages or MVC routes, then the website serves a static file named `index.html`, as shown in the following code:

    ```
    app.MapFallbackToFile("index.html");
    ```

The Server project does not have an index.html file. This file will be provided by the Client project.

9. In the Northwind.BlazorWasm.Server project, expand the Properties folder, open the launchSettings.json file, and note the random port numbers (yours will be different) configured for the Kestrel-hosted project for http and https, as shown highlighted in the following settings:

```
{
  "profiles": {
    "http": {
      "commandName": "Project",
      "launchBrowser": true,
      "environmentVariables": {
        "ASPNETCORE_ENVIRONMENT": "Development"
      },
      "dotnetRunMessages": true,
      "inspectUri": "{wsProtocol}://{url.hostname}:{url.port}/_framework/
debug/ws-proxy?browser={browserInspectUri}",
      "applicationUrl": "http://localhost:5170"
    },
    "https": {
      "commandName": "Project",
      "launchBrowser": true,
      "environmentVariables": {
        "ASPNETCORE_ENVIRONMENT": "Development"
      },
      "dotnetRunMessages": true,
      "inspectUri": "{wsProtocol}://{url.hostname}:{url.port}/_framework/
debug/ws-proxy?browser={browserInspectUri}",
      "applicationUrl": "https://localhost:7170;http://localhost:5170"
    },
    "IIS Express": {
```

10. For the https profile, for its applicationUrl setting, change the port numbers to 5161 for https and 5162 for http, as shown in the following setting:

```
"applicationUrl": "https://localhost:5161;http://localhost:5162",
```

11. For the http profile, for its applicationUrl setting, change the port number to 5162 for http, as shown in the following setting:

```
"applicationUrl": "http://localhost:5162",
```

12. Save the changes to the launchSettings.json file.

13. In the `Northwind.BlazorWasm.Client` project, expand the `wwwroot` folder, and then open the `index.html` file.

14. In `index.html`, note the `<link>` elements to reference a stylesheet and manifest, as shown in the following markup:

    ```
    <link href="css/app.css" rel="stylesheet" />
    <link href="manifest.json" rel="manifest" />
    ```

15. In `index.html`, note the `<div>` elements that show by default while loading the Blazor WebAssembly runtime and when errors occur, as shown in the following markup:

    ```
    <div id="app">Loading...</div>
    <div id="blazor-error-ui">
      An unhandled error has occurred.
      <a href="" class="reload">Reload</a>
      <a class="dismiss">✖</a>
    </div>
    ```

16. In `index.html`, note the `<script>` elements to enable Blazor WebAssembly and a service worker for this web page, as shown in the following markup:

    ```
    <script src="_framework/blazor.webassembly.js"></script>
    <script>navigator.serviceWorker.register('service-worker.js');</script>
    ```

17. In `index.html`, add markup to use the latest version of Bootstrap, including a `<meta>` element in the `<head>` to set the viewport and a `<script>` element at the bottom of the `<body>` to add support for advanced Bootstrap bundled features provided by Popper.js, as shown highlighted in the following markup:

    ```
    <!DOCTYPE html>
    <html lang="en">
    <head>
      <meta charset="utf-8" />
      <base href="/" />
      <link href="css/app.css" rel="stylesheet" />
      <link href="manifest.json" rel="manifest" />
      <meta name="viewport" content="width=device-width, initial-scale=1">
      <link href="https://cdn.jsdelivr.net/npm/bootstrap@5.2.0/
    dist/css/bootstrap.min.css" rel="stylesheet" integrity="sha384-
    gH2yIJqKdNHPEq0n4Mqa/HGKIhSkIHeL5AyhkYV8i59U5AR6csBvApHHN1/vI1Bx"
    crossorigin="anonymous">
    </head>
    <body>
      <div id="app">Loading...</div>
      <div id="blazor-error-ui">
        An unhandled error has occurred.
        <a href="" class="reload">Reload</a>
        <a class="dismiss">✖</a>
      </div>
    ```

```
<script src="_framework/blazor.webassembly.js"></script>
<script>navigator.serviceWorker.register('service-worker.js');</script>
<script src="https://cdn.jsdelivr.net/npm/bootstrap@5.2.0/dist/js/
bootstrap.bundle.min.js" integrity="sha384-A3rJD856KowSb7dwlZdYEkO39Gagi7
vIsF0jrRAoQmDKKtQBHUuLZ9AsSv4jD4Xa" crossorigin="anonymous"></script>
</body>
</html>
```

18. In `MainLayout.razor`, add markup to use Bootstrap grid classes to create a navigation area in a left column and render the body of the Blazor WebAssembly client app in the remaining space, as shown highlighted in the following markup:

```
@inherits LayoutComponentBase
<main>
  <div class="container">
    <div class="row">
      <div class="col-md-auto">
        <div class="alert alert-secondary">
            Navigation (coming soon)
        </div>
      </div>
      <div class="col">@Body</div>
    </div>
  </div>
</main>
```

19. In the `Pages` folder, in `Index.razor`, note the `@page` directive that configures a route for the root path to go to this page, and then change the heading, as shown highlighted in the following markup:

```
@page "/"

<h1>Hello, Blazor!</h1>
```

20. Start the `Northwind.BlazorWasm.Server` website project using its `https` profile without debugging:

    • If you are using Visual Studio 2022, then in **Solution Explorer**, select the `Northwind.BlazorWasm.Server` project to make it active. In the Visual Studio 2022 toolbar, select the `https` profile as the **Startup Project**, and **Google Chrome** as the **Web Browser**.

    • If you are using Visual Studio Code, then at the command line or terminal, enter the following command:

    ```
    dotnet run --launch-profile https
    ```

21. At the command prompt or terminal, note the ports used by the `Server` project website, as shown in the following output:

    ```
    info: Microsoft.Hosting.Lifetime[14]
    ```

```
        Now listening on: https://localhost:5161
info: Microsoft.Hosting.Lifetime[14]
        Now listening on: http://localhost:5162
info: Microsoft.Hosting.Lifetime[0]
        Application started. Press Ctrl+C to shut down.
info: Microsoft.Hosting.Lifetime[0]
        Hosting environment: Development
info: Microsoft.Hosting.Lifetime[0]
        Content root path: C:\apps-services-net7\Northwind.BlazorWasm\
Northwind.BlazorWasm\Server
```

22. In Chrome, note that the Server project hosts the Client app project because we started the Server project, and yet we can see the Blazor components that are in the Client project, and the <h1> element has the focus, as shown in *Figure 16.1*:

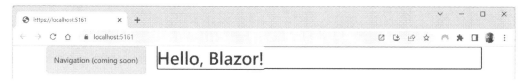

*Figure 16.1: A simple page implemented as a Blazor WebAssembly component*

23. Close the browser and shut down the web server.

# Building and testing a Blazor progress bar component

In this section, we will build a component to provide a progress bar. It will use Bootstrap classes to set a stripped light blue color, with options to animate the bar and show the current value of the progress as a percentage:

1. In the Northwind.BlazorWasm.Client project, add a new folder named Components.

2. In the Components folder, add a new file named ProgressBar.razor. In Visual Studio, the project item template is named **Razor Component**.

>  **Good Practice:** Component filenames must start with an uppercase letter, or you will have compile errors!

3. In ProgressBar.razor, add statements to render <div> elements that use Bootstrap classes to define a progress bar with bindable parameters to set various properties, as shown in the following markup:

```
<div class="progress">
  <div class="progress-bar progress-bar-striped bg-info
              @(IsAnimated ? " progress-bar-animated" : "")"
       role="progressbar" aria-label="@LabelText"
```

```
            style="width: @Value%" aria-valuenow="@Value"
            aria-valuemin="@Minimum" aria-valuemax="@Maximum">
      @(ShowValue ? Value + "%" : "")
    </div>
  </div>

  @code {
    [Parameter]
    public int Value { get; set; } = 0;

    [Parameter]
    public int Minimum { get; set; } = 0;

    [Parameter]
    public int Maximum { get; set; } = 100;

    [Parameter]
    public bool IsAnimated { get; set; } = false;

    [Parameter]
    public bool ShowValue { get; set; } = false;

    [Parameter]
    public string? LabelText { get; set; } = "Progress bar";
  }
```

4.  In _Imports.razor, add a statement to import the files in the Components folder for use in all
    Razor files, as shown in the following code:

    ```
    @using Northwind.BlazorWasm.Client.Components
    ```

    > The _Imports.razor file only applies to .razor files. If you use code-behind .cs
    > files to implement component code, then they must have namespaces imported
    > separately or use global usings to implicitly import the namespace.

5.  In the Pages folder, in Index.razor, add statements to define a Bootstrap row with two equal
    columns, and add a <ProgressBar> component set to 25%, as shown highlighted in the fol-
    lowing markup:

    ```
    @page "/"

    <h1>Hello, Blazor!</h1>

    <div class="row">
      <div class="col">
    ```

```
        <div class="alert alert-info">
            <h4>Progress of database deletion</h4>
            <ProgressBar Value="25" IsAnimated="true" ShowValue="true"
                         LabelText="Progress of database deletion" />
        </div>
    </div>
    <div class="col">
        More components coming soon.
    </div>
</div>
```

6.  In `App.razor`, comment out the `<FocusOnNavigate>` element so that the `<h1>` is not selected, as shown in the following markup:

```
@*<FocusOnNavigate RouteData="@routeData" Selector="h1" />*@
```

> A benefit of setting a focus on a navigate selector is that it ensures page navigations will be announced when using a screen reader, but it can look visually unappealing.

7.  Start the `Northind.BlazorWasm.Server` website project using its `https` profile without debugging.

8.  Note the progress bar that shows the progress of the (simulated!) database deletion, as shown in *Figure 16.2*:

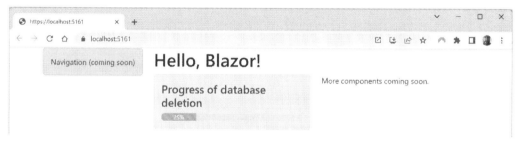

*Figure 16.2: Viewing the progress of a (simulated) database deletion*

9.  Close the browser and shut down the web server.

## Building and testing a Blazor dialog box component

In this section, we will build a component to provide a popup dialog box for interaction with the website visitor. It will use Bootstrap classes to define a button that, when clicked, shows a dialog box with two buttons with configurable labels.

The component will also define two event callbacks that can be handled by the parent to customize what code executes when the two buttons are clicked.

Let's go:

1. In the `Northwind.BlazorWasm.Client` project, in the `Components` folder, add a new file named `DialogBox.razor`. In Visual Studio, the project item template is named **Razor Component**.

2. In `DialogBox.razor`, add statements to render `<div>` elements that use Bootstrap classes to define a button and modal dialog box with bindable parameters to set various properties, as shown in the following markup:

```
<!-- Button to show the dialog box. -->
<button type="button" class="btn btn-primary"
        data-bs-toggle="modal" data-bs-target="#dialogBox">
  @DialogTitle
</button>

<!-- Dialog box to popup. -->
<div class="modal fade" id="dialogBox"
     data-bs-backdrop="static" data-bs-keyboard="false" tabindex="-1"
     aria-labelledby="dialogBoxLabel" aria-hidden="true">
  <div class="modal-dialog">
    <div class="modal-content">
      <div class="modal-header">
        <h5 class="modal-title" id="dialogBoxLabel">@DialogTitle</h5>
        <button type="button" class="btn-close"
                data-bs-dismiss="modal" aria-label="Close"></button>
      </div>
      <div class="modal-body">
        @ChildContent
      </div>
      <div class="modal-footer">
        <button type="button" class="btn btn-primary"
                @onclick="OnClickPrimary">
          @PrimaryButtonText
        </button>
        <button type="button" class="btn btn-secondary"
                data-bs-dismiss="modal" @onclick="OnClickSecondary">
          @SecondaryButtonText
        </button>
      </div>
    </div>
  </div>
</div>
@code {
  [Parameter]
  public string? DialogTitle { get; set; }

  // ChildContent is a special name that is set automatically by any
  // markup content within the component begin and end elements.
```

```
    [Parameter]
    public RenderFragment? ChildContent { get; set; }

    [Parameter]
    public string? PrimaryButtonText { get; set; } = "OK";

    [Parameter]
    public EventCallback<MouseEventArgs> OnClickPrimary { get; set; }

    [Parameter]
    public string? SecondaryButtonText { get; set; } = "Cancel";

    [Parameter]
    public EventCallback<MouseEventArgs> OnClickSecondary { get; set; }
}
```

Note the two buttons have default text values of OK and Cancel, and they both have event callback parameters that will have information about the mouse pointer passed as event arguments. Also note the button with class="btn-close" that visually appears as the **X** button in the top-right corner to close the dialog.

3.  In the Pages folder, in Index.razor, in the second column, remove the temporary "coming soon" message and then add statements to add a <DialogBox> component that sets the two button labels to Yes and No, as shown in the following markup:

```
<DialogBox DialogTitle="Delete Database"
           PrimaryButtonText="Yes" OnClickPrimary="Yes_Click"
           SecondaryButtonText="No" OnClickSecondary="No_Click">
    Are you sure you want to delete the entire database? Really?
</DialogBox>
```

Any content between the <DialogBox> and </DialogBox> elements is automatically set as the ChildContent property.

4.  In Index.razor, at the bottom of the file, add a Razor code block to define event handlers for the two click events that output which button was clicked and the current position of the mouse pointer, as shown in the following code:

```
@code {
    private void Yes_Click(MouseEventArgs e)
    {
        Console.WriteLine("User clicked 'Primary' button at ({0}, {1}).",
            arg0: e.ClientX, arg1: e.ClientY);
    }
```

```
    private void No_Click(MouseEventArgs e)
    {
      Console.WriteLine("User clicked 'Secondary' button at ({0}, {1}).",
        arg0: e.ClientX, arg1: e.ClientY);
    }
  }
```

5.  Start the Northwind.BlazorWasm.Server website project using its https profile without debugging.

6.  Click the **Delete Database** button and note the modal dialog box that pops up, as shown in *Figure 16.3*:

*Figure 16.3: A popup modal dialog box built using Blazor WebAssembly*

7.  Show **Developer Tools** and its **Console**.

8.  In the **Delete Database** dialog box, click the **Yes** button and **No** button a few times (clicking the **No** button or the **x** button will close the dialog, so click the **Delete Database** button again to reshow the dialog box), and note the messages written to the console, as shown in *Figure 16.4*:

*Figure 16.4: The dialog box component writing to the browser console*

9.  Close the browser and shut down the web server.

You can read more about the supported event arguments at the following link: https://docs.microsoft.com/en-us/aspnet/core/blazor/components/event-handling#event-arguments.

# Building and testing a Blazor alert component

In this section, we will build a component to provide alerts for showing messages to the website visitor. It will use Bootstrap classes to define a colorful area for the message, which can be dismissed. The message, title, icon, and color theme can be configured.

1. In the `Northwind.BlazorWasm.Shared` project, in the `SharedClass.cs` file, add statements to define some static classes with `string` constant values for common Bootstrap color themes and icons, as shown in the following code:

```csharp
namespace Packt.Shared;

public static class BootstrapColors
{
  public const string Primary = "primary";
  public const string Secondary = "secondary";
  public const string Danger = "danger";
  public const string Warning = "warning";
  public const string Success = "success";
  public const string Info = "info";
}

public static class BootstrapIcons
{
  public const string Alarm = "bi-alarm";
  public const string AlarmFill = "bi-alarm-fill";
  public const string Archive = "bi-archive";
  public const string ArchiveFill = "bi-archive-fill";
  public const string ArrowRepeat = "bi-arrow-repeat";
  public const string Bag = "bi-bag";
  public const string BagFill = "bi-bag-fill";
  public const string Bell = "bi-bell";
  public const string BellFill = "bi-bell-fill";
  public const string XCircle = "bi-x-circle";
  public const string XSquare = "bi-x-square";
  public const string XOctagon = "bi-x-octagon";
  public const string CheckSquare = "bi-check-square";
  public const string CheckCircle = "bi-check-circle";
  public const string Info = "bi-info";
  public const string InfoLarge = "bi-info-lg";
  public const string InfoCircle = "bi-info-circle";
  public const string InfoCircleFill = "bi-info-circle-fill";
  public const string InfoSquare = "bi-info-square";
  public const string InfoSquareFill = "bi-info-square-fill";
  public const string Exclamation = "bi-exclamation";
  public const string ExclamationLarge = "bi-exclamation-lg";
  public const string ExclamationCircle = "bi-exclamation-circle";
```

```
    public const string ExclamationCircleFill = "bi-exclamation-circle-fill";
    public const string ExclamationSquare = "bi-exclamation-square";
    public const string ExclamationSquareFill = "bi-exclamation-square-fill";
    public const string ExclamationTriangle = "bi-exclamation-triangle";
    public const string ExclamationTriangleFill = "bi-exclamation-triangle-
fill";
}
```

 The complete list of icons is searchable at the following link: `https://icons.getbootstrap.com/`.

2.   In the `Northwind.BlazorWasm.Client` project, in the `wwwroot` folder, in `index.html`, add a `<link>` element to the `<head>` to reference Bootstrap Icons, as shown in the following markup:

```
<link href="https://cdn.jsdelivr.net/npm/bootstrap-icons@1.9.1/font/
bootstrap-icons.css" rel="stylesheet">
```

3.   In the `Northwind.BlazorWasm.Client` project, in `_Imports.razor`, import the namespace for the static `BootstrapColors` and `BootstrapIcons` classes, as shown in the following code:

```
@using Packt.Shared
```

4.   In the `Northwind.BlazorWasm.Client` project, in the `Components` folder, add a new file named `Alert.razor`. In Visual Studio, the project item template is named **Razor Component**.

5.   In `Alert.razor`, add statements to render `<div>` elements that use Bootstrap classes to define a `<div>` with bindable parameters to set various properties, as shown in the following markup:

```
<div class="alert alert-@ColorTheme d-flex align-items-center
    @(IsDismissable ? " alert-dismissible fade show" : "")" role="alert">
  <div>
    <h4 class="alert-heading"><i class="@Icon"></i> @Title</h4>
    @Message
    @if (IsDismissable)
    {
      <button type="button" class="btn-close"
              data-bs-dismiss="alert" aria-label="Close"></button>
    }
  </div>
</div>

@code {
  [Parameter]
  public bool IsDismissable { get; set; } = true;
```

```
    [Parameter]
    public string ColorTheme { get; set; } = BootstrapColors.Primary;

    [Parameter]
    public string Icon { get; set; } = BootstrapIcons.InfoCircle;

    [Parameter]
    public string? Title { get; set; }

    [Parameter]
    public string? Message { get; set; }
  }
```

6.  In the Pages folder, in Index.razor, add a new Bootstrap container row and column with an Alert element, as shown in the following markup:

```
<div class="row">
  <div class="col">
    <Alert IsDismissable="true"
           Icon="@(BootstrapIcons.ExclamationTriangleFill)"
           ColorTheme="@(BootstrapColors.Warning)"
           Title="Warning"
           Message="Deleting the database cannot be undone." />
  </div>
</div>
```

7.  Start the Northwind.BlazorWasm.Server website project using its https profile without debugging.

8.  On the home page, note the warning alert, as shown in *Figure 16.5*:

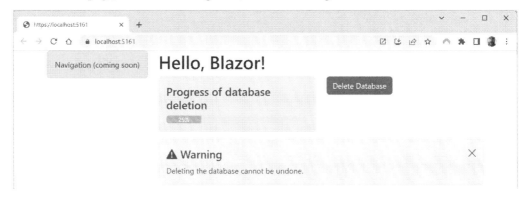

*Figure 16.5: The dialog box component writing to the browser console*

9.  Click the close button to dismiss the warning.

10. Close the browser and shut down the web server.

# Building a Blazor data component

In this section, we will build a component to list, create, and edit employees in the Northwind database.

We will build it over several steps:

1.  Make a Blazor component that renders the name of an employee set as a parameter.

2.  Make it work as a routable page as well as a component.

3.  Implement the functionality to perform CRUD operations on employees in a database.

4.  Build and call a Minimal API web service.

We will add the new component to the existing Blazor WebAssembly client project:

1.  In the `Northwind.BlazorWasm.Client` project, in the `Pages` folder, add a new file named `Employees.razor`. In Visual Studio, the project item template is named **Razor Component**.

2.  Add statements to output a heading for the `Employees` component and define a code block that defines a property to store the name of a country, as shown highlighted in the following markup:

```
<h3>Employees @(string.IsNullOrWhiteSpace(Country)
    ? "Worldwide" : "in " + Country)</h3>

@code {
  [Parameter]
  public string? Country { get; set; }
}
```

3.  In the `Pages` folder, in `Index.razor`, add statements to the bottom of the markup, before the `@code` block, to instantiate the `Employees` component twice: once setting USA as the `Country` parameter, and once without setting the country, as shown in the following markup:

```
<div class="row">
  <div class="col">
    <Employees Country="USA" />
    <Employees />
  </div>
</div>
```

4.  Start the `Northwind.BlazorWasm.Server` project using its `https` profile without debugging.

5.  Start Chrome, navigate to `https://localhost:5161/`, and note the `Employees` components, as shown in *Figure 16.6*:

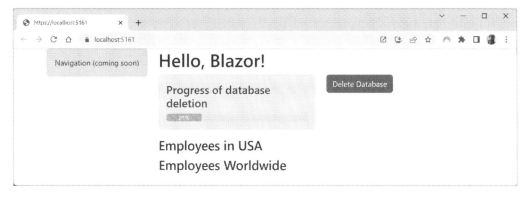

*Figure 16.6: The Employees component without any parameters set and with the Country parameter set to USA*

6.  Close the browser and shut down the web server.

## Making the component a routable page component

It is simple to turn this component into a routable page component with a route parameter for the country:

1.  In the `Pages` folder, in the `Index.razor` component, remove the two `<Employee>` elements because we will now use them as pages.

2.  In the `Pages` folder, in the `Employees.razor` component, add a statement at the top of the file to register `/employees` as its route with an optional country route parameter, as shown in the following markup:

    ```
    @page "/employees/{country?}"
    ```

3.  In the `Components` folder, add a new Razor component named `NavMenu.razor`.

4.  In `MainLayout.razor`, replace the temporary text message with a `NavMenu` element, as shown in the following markup:

    ```
    <NavMenu />
    ```

5.  In `NavMenu.razor`, add list item elements to navigate to the home page and to show employees worldwide and in the USA or UK, as shown in the following markup:

    ```
    <nav class="nav nav-pills flex-column">
      <div class="nav-item px-3">
        <NavLink class="nav-link" href="/" Match="NavLinkMatch.All">
          Home
        </NavLink>
      </div>
      <div class="nav-item px-3">
    ```

```
          <NavLink class="nav-link" href="employees" Match="NavLinkMatch.All">
            Employees Worldwide
          </NavLink>
        </div>
        <div class="nav-item px-3">
          <NavLink class="nav-link" href="employees/USA">
            Employees in USA
          </NavLink>
        </div>
        <div class="nav-item px-3">
          <NavLink class="nav-link" href="employees/UK">
            Employees in UK
          </NavLink>
        </div>
      </nav>
```

6. Start the `Northwind.BlazorWasm.Server` project using its `https` profile without debugging.

7. Start Chrome and navigate to `https://localhost:5161/`.

8. In the left navigation menu, click **Employees in USA**. Note that the country name is correctly passed to the page component and that the component uses the same shared layout as the other page components, like `Index.razor`. Also note the URL: `https://localhost:5161/employees/USA`.

9. Close Chrome and shut down the web server.

## Getting entities into a component by building a web service

Now that you have seen the minimum implementation of an entity component, we can add the functionality to fetch entities. In this case, we will use the Northwind database context to fetch employees from the database and expose it as a Minimal API web service:

1. In `Northwind.BlazorWasm.Server.csproj`, add a reference to the Northwind database context project for SQL Server, as shown in the following markup:

```
<ItemGroup>
  <ProjectReference Include="..\..\..\Chapter02\Northwind.Common.DataContext
.SqlServer\Northwind.Common.DataContext.SqlServer.csproj" />
</ItemGroup>
```

 **Warning!** Unlike previous projects, relative path references for shared projects like the entity models and the database are three levels up, for example, `"..\..\.."`, because we have additional depths of folders for `Server`, `Client`, and `Shared`.

2. Build the `Northwind.BlazorWasm.Server` project at the command line or terminal.

3.   In `Program.cs`, import namespaces for working with Minimal API attributes, registering the Northwind database context extension method, and serializing JSON, as shown in the following code:

```
using Microsoft.AspNetCore.Mvc; // [FromServices]
using Packt.Shared; // AddNorthwindContext extension method
using System.Text.Json.Serialization; // ReferenceHandler

// define an alias for the JsonOptions class
using HttpJsonOptions = Microsoft.AspNetCore.Http.Json.JsonOptions;
```

4.   In `Program.cs`, after the call to `CreateBuilder`, add a statement to configure the registered dependency service for JSON options and set its reference handler to preserve references, so that the reference between an employee and their manager does not cause a runtime exception due to circular references, as shown in the following code:

```
builder.Services.Configure<HttpJsonOptions>(options =>
{
  options.SerializerOptions.ReferenceHandler = ReferenceHandler.Preserve;
});
```

 Be careful to configure `Microsoft.AspNetCore.Http.Json.JsonOptions` and not `Microsoft.AspNetCore.Mvc.JsonOptions`! I have created an alias to make this explicit since we need to import the `Microsoft.AspNetCore.Mvc` namespace for other types.

5.   In `Program.cs`, before the call to `Build`, add a statement to register the Northwind database context in the dependency services collection, as shown in the following code:

```
builder.Services.AddNorthwindContext();
```

6.   In `Program.cs`, before the call to the `MapRazorPages` method, add statements to define some endpoints to GET and POST employees, as shown in the following code:

```
app.MapGet("api/employees", (
  [FromServices] NorthwindContext db) =>
    Results.Json(db.Employees))
  .WithName("GetEmployees")
  .Produces<Employee[]>(StatusCodes.Status200OK);

app.MapGet("api/employees/{id:int}", (
  [FromServices] NorthwindContext db,
  [FromRoute] int id) =>
  {
    Employee? employee = db.Employees.Find(id);
    if (employee == null)
```

```
    {
      return Results.NotFound();
    }
    else
    {
      return Results.Json(employee);
    }
  })
  .WithName("GetEmployeesById")
  .Produces<Employee>(StatusCodes.Status200OK)
  .Produces(StatusCodes.Status404NotFound);

app.MapGet("api/employees/{country}", (
  [FromServices] NorthwindContext db,
  [FromRoute] string country) =>
    Results.Json(db.Employees.Where(employee =>
    employee.Country == country)))
  .WithName("GetEmployeesByCountry")
  .Produces<Employee[]>(StatusCodes.Status200OK);

app.MapPost("api/employees", async ([FromBody] Employee employee,
  [FromServices] NorthwindContext db) =>
  {
    db.Employees.Add(employee);
    await db.SaveChangesAsync();
    return Results.Created($"api/employees/{employee.EmployeeId}",
employee);
  })
  .Produces<Employee>(StatusCodes.Status201Created);
```

 Due to the {id:int} constraint, a GET request to a path like api/employees/3 will map to the GetEmployeesById endpoint and a GET request to a path like api/employess/USA will map to the GetEmployeesByCountry endpoint. When POSTing to the api/employees endpoint, the response includes a URL to the newly created employee with its database-assigned ID.

## Getting entities into a component by calling the web service

Now we can add the functionality to the entity component to call the web service:

1. In Northwind.BlazorWasm.Client.csproj, add a reference to the latest preview or release version of the QuickGrid package, as shown in the following markup:

```
<PackageReference Include="Microsoft.AspNetCore.Components.QuickGrid"
                  Version="0.1.0-alpha.22351.1" />
```

**QuickGrid** is an experimental open-source basic grid Blazor component. You can learn more about it at the following link: `https://aspnet.github.io/quickgridsamples/`.

2.  In `Northwind.BlazorWasm.Client.csproj`, add a reference to the Northwind entities project for SQL Server, as shown in the following markup:

```
<ItemGroup>
    <ProjectReference Include="..\..\..\Chapter02\Northwind.Common.
EntityModels.SqlServer\Northwind.Common.EntityModels.SqlServer.csproj" />
</ItemGroup>
```

3.  Build the `Northwind.BlazorWasm.Client` project at the command line or terminal.

4.  In the project folder, in `Program.cs`, note that the Blazor project template configures an HTTP client for use in the `Client` project, and that it assumes the `Server` project is where any web services will be hosted, as shown in the following code:

```
builder.Services.AddHttpClient("Northwind.BlazorWasm.ServerAPI",
    client => client.BaseAddress = new Uri(builder.HostEnvironment.
BaseAddress));
```

5.  In the project folder, in `_Imports.razor`, import the namespaces for working with QuickGrid and serializing JSON, so that Blazor components that we build do not need to import the namespaces individually, as shown in the following markup:

```
@using Microsoft.AspNetCore.Components.QuickGrid
@using System.Text.Json
@using System.Text.Json.Serialization
```

6.  In the `Pages` folder, in `Employees.razor`, add statements to inject the HTTP client factory and then use it to output a grid of either all employees or employees in a specific country, as shown in the following code:

```
@page "/employees/{country?}"
@inject IHttpClientFactory httpClientFactory
<h3>
    Employees @(string.IsNullOrWhiteSpace(Country) ? "Worldwide" : "in " +
Country)
</h3>

<QuickGrid Items="@employees">
    <PropertyColumn Property="@(emp => emp.EmployeeId)" Sortable="true" />
    <PropertyColumn Property="@(emp => emp.FirstName)" Sortable="true" />
    <PropertyColumn Property="@(emp => emp.LastName)" Sortable="true" />
    <PropertyColumn Property="@(emp => emp.City)" Sortable="true" />
```

```
    <PropertyColumn Property="@(emp => emp.Country)" Sortable="true" />
    <PropertyColumn Property="@(emp => emp.BirthDate)"
                    Format="yyyy-MM-dd" Sortable="true" />
    <PropertyColumn Property="@(emp => emp.HireDate)"
                    Format="yyyy-MM-dd" Sortable="true" />
  </QuickGrid>

@code {
  [Parameter]
  public string? Country { get; set; }

  // QuickGrid works best if it binds to an IQueryable<T> sequence
  private IQueryable<Employee>? employees;

  protected override async Task OnParametersSetAsync()
  {
    Employee[]? employeesArray = null;

    // Employee entity has circular reference to itself so
    // we must control how references are handled.
    JsonSerializerOptions jsonOptions = new()
      {
        ReferenceHandler = ReferenceHandler.Preserve,
        PropertyNameCaseInsensitive = true
      };

    HttpClient client = httpClientFactory.CreateClient(
      "Northwind.BlazorWasm.ServerAPI");

    string path = "api/employees";

    try
    {
      employeesArray = (await client.GetFromJsonAsync<Employee[]?>(
        path, jsonOptions));
    }
    catch (Exception ex)
    {
      Console.WriteLine($"{ex.GetType()}: {ex.Message}");
    }

    if (employeesArray is not null)
    {
      employees = employeesArray.AsQueryable();

      if (!string.IsNullOrWhiteSpace(Country))
```

```
      {
        employees = employees.Where(emp => emp.Country == Country);
      }
    }
  }
}
```

 Although the web service has an endpoint that allows returning only employees in a specified country, later we will add caching for employees, so in this implementation we will request all employees and use client-side filtering for the bound data grid.

7.  Start the `Northwind.Blazor.Wasm.Server` project using its `https` profile without debugging.

8.  Start Chrome and navigate to `https://localhost:5161/`.

9.  In the left navigation menu, click **Employees in USA**, and note that the grid of employees loads from the web service and renders in the web page, as shown in *Figure 16.7*:

*Figure 16.7: The grid of employees in the USA*

10. Click the grid column headings to reorder the grid of employees by birth date, with the oldest employee at the top.

11. In the left navigation menu, click **Employees Worldwide**, and note that the grid of employees is unfiltered by country and sorted by birth date, as shown in *Figure 16.8*:

*Figure 16.8: Grid of worldwide employees sorted by birth date*

12. In the left navigation menu, click **Employees in UK**, and note that the grid of employees is filtered to only show employees in the UK.

13. Close Chrome and shut down the web server.

# Implementing caching using local storage

At the moment, while viewing an Employees page component, QuickGrid can sort the employees without making a call to the web service. But the Employees component must call the web service every time we navigate between pages because the component's data is stored in memory and its lifetime matches its page.

All modern browsers support two types of storage: local and session. **Session storage** is restricted to the current browser tab and current session. As soon as the tab closes, the storage is removed. **Local storage** is available across multiple tabs and sessions, but it is limited to the current domain, like example.com, so, for example, google.com cannot access it. Both are dictionaries that use string values for both the key and value, so we will need to parse types stored in them.

Blazor cannot directly access browser resources like storage. We must create JavaScript code to interoperate between .NET and the browser. Rather than adding JavaScript to the index.html page, modern browsers allow you to dynamically load JavaScript files as modules and then call their functions. To make it easier for Blazor developers to work with, it is common to create and register a dependency service to interop with JavaScript modules.

## Interop with JavaScript modules

Blazor defines an interface named IJSRuntime that enables interop with JavaScript. It can dynamically load a JavaScript module file using its InvokeAsync<IJSObjectReference> method. You must pass an instruction to import and the relative path to the JavaScript file, as shown in the following code:

```
await _jsRuntime.InvokeAsync<IJSObjectReference>(
  "import", "/js/MyJavaScriptModule.js")
```

The JavaScript file must use the export JavaScript keyword to make its functions available, as shown in the following code:

```
export function showAlert(message) {
  window.alert(message);
}
```

Interop with JavaScript happens asynchronously, so we must use lazy references to any JavaScript modules that we attempt to load and wait for them to be ready before calling them.

A Blazor dependency service that we define and register should implement the IAsyncDisposable interface and implement its DisposeAsync to release any resources, like references to JavaScript modules.

To call the functions, the IJSObjectReference interface that wraps the JavaScript module provides methods like InvokeAsync<T> and InvokeVoidAsync. The first parameter of these is the name of the function that you want to call. The rest of the parameters match the parameters of the JavaScript function.

# Building a local storage service

Let's extend the Employees component so that it uses local storage to cache the employees for a configurable number of minutes before then re-calling the web service to refresh the data. This will also help us to enable offline capabilities for our components if we want to in the future.

1.  In the Northwind.BlazorWasm.Client project, in the wwwroot folder, create a new folder named js.

2.  In the js folder, create a new JavaScript file named localStorageInterop.js.

3.  Modify the contents of the file to define some functions for working with local storage, as shown in the following code:

```javascript
export function get(key) {
  return window.localStorage.getItem(key);
}

export function set(key, value) {
  window.localStorage.setItem(key, value);
}

export function clear() {
  window.localStorage.clear();
}

export function remove(key) {
  window.localStorage.removeItem(key);
}
```

 You can learn more about the methods of the window.localStorage object at the following link: https://developer.mozilla.org/en-US/docs/Web/API/ Window/localStorage.

4.  In the Northwind.BlazorWasm.Client project, create a new folder named Services.

5.  In the Services folder, create a new C# class file named LocalStorageService.cs.

6.  Modify the contents of the file to define a service that has IJSRuntime as a dependency service passed using constructor parameter injection and a lazy reference to the loaded JavaScript module, with some asynchronous methods for working with local storage, as shown in the following code:

```csharp
using Microsoft.JSInterop;

namespace Northwind.BlazorWasm.Client.Services;

public class LocalStorageService : IAsyncDisposable
{
```

```
  private readonly IJSRuntime jsRuntime;
  private Lazy<IJSObjectReference> jsModule = new();

  public LocalStorageService(IJSRuntime jsRuntime)
  {
    this.jsRuntime = jsRuntime;
  }

  private async Task WaitForReference()
  {
    if (!jsModule.IsValueCreated)
    {
      jsModule = new(await jsRuntime.InvokeAsync<IJSObjectReference>(
        "import", "/js/LocalStorageInterop.js"));
    }
  }

  public async ValueTask DisposeAsync()
  {
    if (jsModule.IsValueCreated)
    {
      await jsModule.Value.DisposeAsync();
    }
  }

  public async Task<string> GetValueAsync(string key)
  {
    await WaitForReference();
    var result = await jsModule.Value.InvokeAsync<string>("get", key);
    return result;
  }

  public async Task SetValueAsync(string key, string value)
  {
    await WaitForReference();
    await jsModule.Value.InvokeVoidAsync("set", key, value);
  }

  public async Task ClearAsync()
  {
    await WaitForReference();
    await jsModule.Value.InvokeVoidAsync("clear");
  }

  public async Task RemoveAsync(string key)
  {
```

```
      await WaitForReference();
      await jsModule.Value.InvokeVoidAsync("remove", key);
    }
  }
```

7.  In `Program.cs`, import the namespace for your Blazor app services including the local storage service, as shown in the following code:

```
using Northwind.BlazorWasm.Client.Services; // LocalStorageService
```

8.  In `Program.cs`, before the call to build and run the Blazor app, add a statement to register the local storage service as a scoped service, as shown in the following code:

```
builder.Services.AddScoped<LocalStorageService>();
```

9.  In `_Imports.razor`, import the namespace for classes in the `Services` folder, as shown in the following markup:

```
@using Northwind.BlazorWasm.Client.Services
```

10. In the `Pages` folder, in `Employees.razor`, inject the local storage service, as shown in the following code:

```
@inject LocalStorageService localStorage
```

11. In `Employees.razor`, in the `@code` block, add statements to define a duration to cache for. Use the local storage service to store the JSON returned from the service. Use the cached copy if the duration has not expired instead of calling the web service again, as shown in the following code:

```
@code {
  private const string keyTS = "employeesLastGet";
  private const string keyData = "employeesArray";

  [Parameter]
  public TimeSpan CacheDuration { get; set; } = TimeSpan.FromMinutes(10);

  [Parameter]
  public string? Country { get; set; }

  // QuickGrid works best if it binds to an IQueryable<T> sequence
  private IQueryable<Employee>? employees;

  protected override async Task OnParametersSetAsync()
  {
    string employeesJson = "{}";
    Employee[]? employeesArray = null;

    // Employee entity has circular reference to itself so
    // we must control how references are handled.
    JsonSerializerOptions jsonOptions = new()
```

```csharp
  {
    ReferenceHandler = ReferenceHandler.Preserve,
    PropertyNameCaseInsensitive = true
  };

string lastGetText = await localStorage.GetValueAsync(keyTS);

bool isDate = DateTime.TryParse(lastGetText, out DateTime lastGet);

if ((isDate) && (lastGet.Add(CacheDuration) >= DateTime.UtcNow))
{
  employeesJson = await localStorage.GetValueAsync(keyData);
}
else
{
  // refresh the employees from the web service

  HttpClient client = httpClientFactory.CreateClient(
      "Northwind.BlazorWasm.ServerAPI");

  string path = "api/employees";

  try
  {
    employeesJson = await client.GetStringAsync(path);

    await localStorage.SetValueAsync(keyData, employeesJson);
    await localStorage.SetValueAsync(keyTS, DateTime.UtcNow.
ToString());
  }
  catch (Exception ex)
  {
    Console.WriteLine($"{ex.GetType()}: {ex.Message}");
  }
}

try
{
  employeesArray = JsonSerializer.Deserialize<Employee[]?>(
    employeesJson, jsonOptions);
}
catch (Exception ex)
{
  Console.WriteLine($"{ex.GetType()}: {ex.Message}");
}
```

```
    if (employeesArray is not null)
    {
      employees = employeesArray.AsQueryable();

      if (!string.IsNullOrWhiteSpace(Country))
      {
        employees = employees.Where(emp => emp.Country == Country);
      }
    }
  }
}
```

12. Start the `Northwind.Blazor.Wasm.Server` project using its `https` profile without debugging.

13. Start Chrome and navigate to `https://localhost:5161/`.

14. Show **Developer Tools** and the **Network** tab.

15. In the left navigation menu, click **Employees in USA**, and note that the grid of employees loads from the web service and renders in the web page, and a request was made to download the JavaScript module for interop with local storage, as shown in *Figure 16.9*:

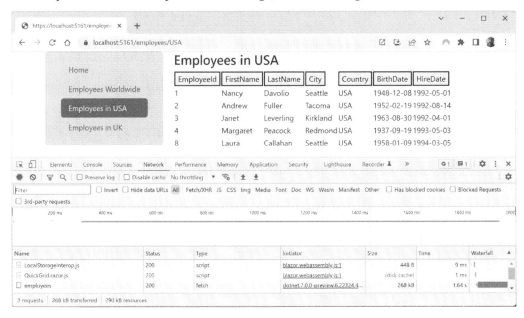

*Figure 16.9: Using JavaScript interop to work with the browser's local storage*

16. At the command prompt or terminal, note that the web service has queried the Northwind database, as shown in the following output:

```
info: Microsoft.EntityFrameworkCore.Infrastructure[10403]
      Entity Framework Core 7.0.0 initialized 'NorthwindContext' using
provider 'Microsoft.EntityFrameworkCore.SqlServer:7.0.0' with options:
None
```

```
dbug: 08/08/2022 15:54:58.616 RelationalEventId.CommandExecuting[20100]
(Microsoft.EntityFrameworkCore.Database.Command)
      Executing DbCommand [Parameters=[], CommandType='Text',
CommandTimeout='30']
      SELECT [e].[EmployeeId], [e].[Address], [e].[BirthDate], [e].
[City], [e].[Country], [e].[Extension], [e].[FirstName], [e].[HireDate],
[e].[HomePhone], [e].[LastName], [e].[Notes], [e].[Photo], [e].
[PhotoPath], [e].[PostalCode], [e].[Region], [e].[ReportsTo], [e].
[Title], [e].[TitleOfCourtesy]
      FROM [Employees] AS [e]
info: Microsoft.EntityFrameworkCore.Database.Command[20101]
      Executed DbCommand (68ms) [Parameters=[], CommandType='Text',
CommandTimeout='30']
      SELECT [e].[EmployeeId], [e].[Address], [e].[BirthDate], [e].
[City], [e].[Country], [e].[Extension], [e].[FirstName], [e].[HireDate],
[e].[HomePhone], [e].[LastName], [e].[Notes], [e].[Photo], [e].
[PhotoPath], [e].[PostalCode], [e].[Region], [e].[ReportsTo], [e].
[Title], [e].[TitleOfCourtesy]
      FROM [Employees] AS [e]
```

17. In **Developer Tools**, click the **Application** tab; in the **Storage** section, expand **Local Storage**, click **https://localhost:5161**, and note that all employees were downloaded and cached as a JSON document, and the timestamp is **2:54:59 PM** UTC, as shown in *Figure 16.10*:

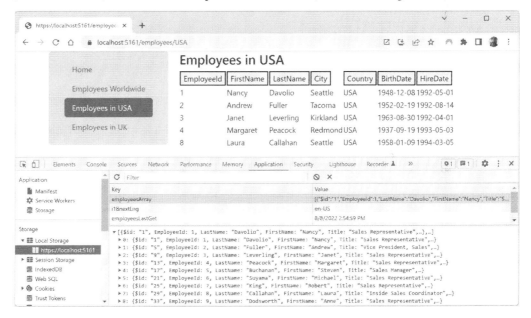

*Figure 16.10: The last request to the web service was at 2:54:59 PM UTC*

18. In the left navigation menu, click **Employees in UK**, and note that the grid of employees loads from local storage and renders in the web page.

19. At the command prompt or terminal, note that the web service was not called so it did not need to query the database.

20. Close the browser.

21. Restart Chrome and navigate to `https://localhost:5161`.

22. In the left navigation menu, click **Employees Worldwide**, and note that the grid of employees loads from local storage and renders in the grid on the web page.

23. At the command prompt or terminal, note that the web service was not called so it did not need to query the database.

24. In **Developer Tools**, click the **Application** tab; in the **Storage** section, expand **Local Storage**, click **https://localhost:5161**, and note the time that the employees were last refreshed.

25. Wait until that time plus 10 minutes have elapsed, click any of the items in the navigation menu, and note that the web service is called and so needs to execute a command to the Northwind database, as shown in *Figure 16.11*:

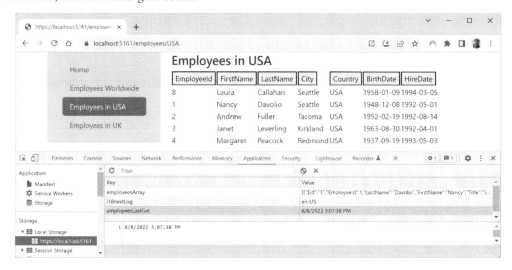

*Figure 16.11: More than 10 minutes have passed, so the local storage has been updated*

26. Close the browser and shut down the web server.

# Building Progressive Web Apps

**Progressive Web Apps** (**PWAs**) are SPAs that work like desktop apps. They can run in their own window instead of in a browser window, and then be started from the desktop or home screen on a mobile device. They automatically update in the background.

They are named "progressive" because they can first be used as a website, perhaps only once or rarely, and then be installed if the user finds they use them more frequently and want some of the benefits of a more integrated experience that works offline.

PWA support in Blazor WebAssembly projects means that the web app gains the following benefits:

- It acts as a normal web page until the visitor explicitly decides to progress to a full app experience, with better integrations with native platform features like notifications, full access to the filesystem, and so on.

- After the app is installed, it can be launched from the OS's start menu or desktop.
- It visually appears in its own app window instead of a browser tab.
- It works offline.
- It automatically updates.

When we created the projects for this chapter, we chose the PWA option so the Northwind.BlazorWasm.Client project already has PWA support. Now let's review what effect that choice had on the projects and the capabilities the Blazor app has:

1. In the Northwind.BlazorWasm.Client project, in the wwwroot folder, open the manifest.json file, and note that it is used to control things like the colors and icons used by the app, as shown in the following code:

```json
{
    "name": "Northwind.BlazorWasm",
    "short_name": "Northwind.BlazorWasm",
    "start_url": "./",
    "display": "standalone",
    "background_color": "#ffffff",
    "theme_color": "#03173d",
    "prefer_related_applications": false,
    "icons": [
      {
        "src": "icon-512.png",
        "type": "image/png",
        "sizes": "512x512"
      }
    ]
}
```

 You can learn more about the manifest.json file at the following link: https://developer.mozilla.org/en-US/docs/Web/Manifest.

2. Change the name to Northwind Blazor PWA and the short_name to Northwind PWA. The name is used for window titles and the short name might be used to label the icon on the desktop or phone home screen.

3. Start the Northwind.BlazorWasm.Server project using its https profile without debugging.

4. Start Chrome and navigate to https://localhost:5161/.

5.  In Chrome, in the address bar on the right, click the icon with the tooltip **Install Northwind Blazor PWA**, as shown in *Figure 16.12*:

*Figure 16.12: Chrome button to install the Northwind Blazor PWA as an app*

6.  Click the **Install** button, as shown in *Figure 16.13*:

*Figure 16.13: Chrome dialog box to install the Northwind Blazor PWA as an app*

7.  The app immediately appears in its own window. Close the app window and close Chrome.

8.  Launch the **Northwind Blazor PWA** app from your Windows Start menu or macOS Launchpad and note that it has a full app experience. Search for `northwind` if it does not appear in the recent apps list.

9.  On the right of the title bar, click the three dots menu and note that you can uninstall the app, as shown in *Figure 16.14*, but do not uninstall the app yet:

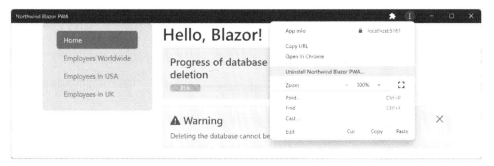

*Figure 16.14: App menu with the option to uninstall*

10. Navigate to **Developer Tools**. On Windows, you can press *F12* or *Ctrl* + *Shift* + *I*. On macOS, you can press *Cmd* + *Shift* + *I*.

11. Select the **Network** tab and then, in the **Throttling** dropdown, select the **Offline** preset.

12. In the left navigation menu, click **Home** and then click **Employees Worldwide**, and note the failure to load any employees and the error message at the bottom of the app window, as shown in *Figure 16.15*:

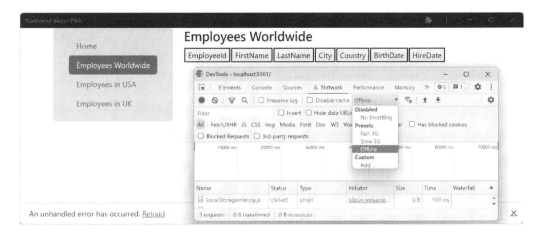

*Figure 16.15: Failure to load any employees when the network is offline*

13. In **Developer Tools**, set **Throttling** back to **Disabled: No throttling**.

14. Click the **Reload** link in the yellow error bar at the bottom of the app and note that functionality returns, as shown in *Figure 16.16*:

*Figure 16.16: Employees are loaded successfully when back online*

15. You could now uninstall the PWA app or just close it.

# Implementing offline support for PWAs

We could improve the experience by caching HTTP GET responses from the web API service locally, storing new, modified, or deleted customers locally, and then synchronizing with the server later by making the stored HTTP requests once network connectivity is restored. But that takes a lot of effort to implement well, and often changes in the architecture and design of an app, so it is beyond the scope of the 2022 editions of my books. I plan to add coverage of offline support in the second edition of my book *Apps and Services with .NET 8*, planned to be published in November 2023, if enough readers tell me they want that.

# Practicing and exploring

Test your knowledge and understanding by answering some questions, getting some hands-on practice, and exploring this chapter's topics with deeper research.

## Exercise 16.1 – Test your knowledge

Answer the following questions:

1. What are the three Blazor hosting models?
2. Does Blazor WebAssembly support all features of the latest .NET APIs?
3. What is the file extension for Blazor components?
4. How do you set the default layout for all Blazor page components?
5. How do you register a route for a Blazor page component?
6. When would you set the Match property of a `<NavLink>` component to `NavLinkMatch.All`?
7. You have imported a custom namespace in the _Imports.razor file, but when you try to use a class in that namespace in a code-behind file for the Blazor component, the class is not found. Why? How can you fix the issue?
8. What must you do to a property in a component class to have it set to a query string parameter automatically?
9. What is QuickGrid?
10. How can a Blazor component access browser features like local storage?

## Exercise 16.2 – Practice building Blazor components

Create a Blazor component named Carousel that wraps the Bootstrap classes for working with carousels as a component, and then use it to show the eight categories in the Northwind database, including images.

You can learn about the Bootstrap carousel at the following link: `https://getbootstrap.com/docs/5.2/components/carousel/`.

## Exercise 16.3 – Practice building an IndexedDB interop service

Browsers' local and session storage are okay for storing small amounts of data, but if you need more robust and capable storage in the browser, then you can use the IndexedDB API.

Create a Blazor service named IndexedDbService with a JavaScript module for interop with the IndexedDB API, and then use it to cache the employees.

You can learn more about the methods of the `window.indexedDB` object at the following link: `https://developer.mozilla.org/en-US/docs/Web/API/IndexedDB_API`.

## Exercise 16.4 – Explore topics

Use the links on the following page to learn more detail about the topics covered in this chapter:

`https://github.com/markjprice/apps-services-net7/blob/main/book-links.md#chapter-16--building-web-components-using-blazor-webassembly`

## Summary

In this chapter, you learned:

- About some important concepts surrounding Blazor WebAssembly, like hosting models, components, routing, and how to pass parameters.
- How to build Blazor components with settable parameters, child content, and custom events.
- How to build Blazor components that fetch data from a web service.
- How to interop with JavaScript to interact with browser features like local storage.

In the next chapter, you will learn how to use some common Blazor open-source components.

## Join our book's Discord space

Join the book's Discord workspace for *Ask me Anything* sessions with the author.

`https://packt.link/apps_and_services_dotnet7`

# 17

# Leveraging Open-Source Blazor Component Libraries

This chapter is about exploring open-source Blazor component libraries. We will look at Radzen Blazor in detail because it is free forever, and many of the other component libraries work in the same way. For example, they all include:

- A NuGet package to install.
- Themes, stylesheets, and JavaScript libraries to register, which often work like or integrate with Bootstrap.
- Namespaces to import, usually in _Imports.razor, so the components are available in your Razor files.
- Services that must be registered as scoped dependency services, and matching components that must be instantiated in shared layouts before you can use features like notifications and dialog boxes.

Once you have learned how one component library does this, the others are very similar.

This chapter will cover the following topics:

- Understanding open-source Blazor libraries
- Exploring Radzen Blazor components
- Building a web service for Northwind entities

## Understanding open-source Blazor component libraries

In *Chapter 16, Building Web Components Using Blazor WebAssembly*, you learned the key concepts around Blazor components and the practicalities of how to build them. Most of the time, you do not need to build your own components for common scenarios because there are plenty of Blazor component libraries, as shown in the following alphabetical list:

- Ant Design Blazor: `https://antblazor.com/`

- Blazored libraries and components: `https://github.com/Blazored`
- Blazorise: `https://blazorise.com/`
- BlazorStrap: `https://blazorstrap.io/`
- DevExpress Blazor Components: `https://www.devexpress.com/blazor/`
- MatBlazor: `https://www.matblazor.com/`
- MudBlazor: `https://mudblazor.com/`
- PanoramicData.Blazor: `https://panoramicdata.github.io/PanoramicData.Blazor/`
- Radzen Blazor: `https://blazor.radzen.com/`
- SyncFusion Blazor UI Components: `https://blazor.syncfusion.com/`
- Telerik UI for Blazor: `https://www.telerik.com/blazor-ui`

In this chapter, we will look at some of the components from the free open-source library named Radzen Blazor. You can then choose to investigate some of the others and whether you feel it is worth paying for their commercial licenses.

# Exploring Radzen Blazor components

First, we will create a Blazor WebAssembly project that we will then explore some of the Radzen Blazor components with:

1.  Use your preferred code editor to create a new solution/workspace named `Chapter17`.
2.  Add a console app project, as defined in the following list:

    - Project template: **Blazor WebAssembly App Empty**/`blazorwasm-empty`
    - Workspace/solution file and folder: `Chapter17`
    - Project file and folder: `Northwind.BlazorLibraries`
    - **Configure for HTTPS**: Selected
    - **ASP.NET Core hosted**: Selected or use the `--hosted` switch
    - **Progressive Web App**: Selected or use the `--pwa` switch

3.  Note that three projects have been created named `Northwind.BlazorLibraries.Client`, `Northwind.BlazorLibraries.Server`, and `Northwind.BlazorLibraries.Shared`.
4.  Use your preferred coding tool to set the `Server` project to be active:

    - If you are using Visual Studio 2022, make sure that the startup project for the solution is set to the `Northwind.BlazorLibraries.Server` project.
    - If you are using Visual Studio Code, set `Northwind.BlazorLibraries.Server` as the active OmniSharp project.

5.  In the `Northwind.BlazorLibraries.Server` project, expand the `Properties` folder, and open the `launchSettings.json` file.
6.  For the `https` profile, for its `applicationUrl` setting, change the port numbers to `5171` for https and `5172` for http, as shown in the following setting:

    ```
    "applicationUrl": "https://localhost:5171;http://localhost:5172",
    ```

7. For the `http` profile, for its `applicationUrl` setting, change the port number to 5172 for `http`, as shown in the following setting:

```
"applicationUrl": "http://localhost:5172",
```

8. Save the changes to the `launchSettings.json` file.

9. In the `Northwind.BlazorLibraries.Client` project, treat warnings as errors and add a reference to the Radzen Blazor package, as shown highlighted in the following markup:

```xml
<Project Sdk="Microsoft.NET.Sdk.BlazorWebAssembly">

  <PropertyGroup>
    <TargetFramework>net7.0</TargetFramework>
    <Nullable>enable</Nullable>
    <ImplicitUsings>enable</ImplicitUsings>
    <ServiceWorkerAssetsManifest>service-worker-assets.js</
ServiceWorkerAssetsManifest>
    <TreatWarningsAsErrors>true</TreatWarningsAsErrors>
  </PropertyGroup>


  <ItemGroup>
    <PackageReference Include="Microsoft.AspNetCore.Components.
WebAssembly"
                      Version="7.0.0" />
    <PackageReference Include="Microsoft.AspNetCore.Components.
WebAssembly.DevServer"
                      Version="7.0.0" PrivateAssets="all" />
    <PackageReference Include="Microsoft.Extensions.Http"
                      Version="7.0.0" />
    <PackageReference Include="Radzen.Blazor" Version="3.20.2" />
  </ItemGroup>

  <ItemGroup>
    <ProjectReference Include="..\Shared\Northwind.BlazorLibraries.
Shared.csproj" />
  </ItemGroup>

  <ItemGroup>
    <ServiceWorker Include="wwwroot\service-worker.js"
PublishedContent="wwwroot\service-worker.published.js" />
  </ItemGroup>

</Project>
```

10. In the `Northwind.BlazorLibraries.Client` project, in the `_Imports.razor` file, add a statement to import the Radzen Blazor namespace, as shown in the following code:

```
@using Radzen
```

```
@using Radzen.Blazor
```

11. In the `Northwind.BlazorLibraries.Client` project, in the `wwwroot` folder, open the `index.html` file.

12. In `index.html`, add markup in the `<head>` to set a blank favicon, and use the latest version of Bootstrap including a `<meta>` element in the `<head>` to set the viewport and to link to the default Radzen Blazor theme CSS file. At the bottom of the `<body>`, add a `<script>` element to add support for advanced features provided by Popper.js and Radzen Blazor, as shown highlighted in the following markup:

```
<!DOCTYPE html>
<html lang="en">
<head>
  <meta charset="utf-8" />
  <base href="/" />
  <link href="css/app.css" rel="stylesheet" />
  <link href="manifest.json" rel="manifest" />
  <link rel="icon" href="data:;base64,iVBORw0KGgo=">
  <meta name="viewport" content="width=device-width, initial-scale=1">
  <link href="https://cdn.jsdelivr.net/npm/bootstrap@5.2.0/
dist/css/bootstrap.min.css" rel="stylesheet" integrity="sha384-
gH2yIJqKdNHPEq0n4Mqa/HGKIhSkIHeL5AyhkYV8i59U5AR6csBvApHHNl/vI1Bx"
crossorigin="anonymous">
  <link rel="stylesheet" href="_content/Radzen.Blazor/css/default.css">
</head>
<body>
  <div id="app">Loading...</div>
  <div id="blazor-error-ui">
    An unhandled error has occurred.
    <a href="" class="reload">Reload</a>
    <a class="dismiss">✕</a>
  </div>
  <script src="_framework/blazor.webassembly.js"></script>
  <script>navigator.serviceWorker.register('service-worker.js');</script>
  <script src="https://cdn.jsdelivr.net/npm/bootstrap@5.2.0/dist/js/
bootstrap.bundle.min.js" integrity="sha384-A3rJD856KowSb7dwlZdYEkO39Gagi7
vIsF0jrRAoQmDKKtQBHUuLZ9AsSv4jD4Xa" crossorigin="anonymous"></script>
  <script src="_content/Radzen.Blazor/Radzen.Blazor.js"></script>
</body>
</html>
```

Some Radzen Blazor themes require Bootstrap. If you want to avoid Bootstrap, then you can reference the `_content/Radzen.Blazor/css/default-base.css` file instead, but you then can only use the base default theme without advanced layouts.

## Enabling the Radzen dialog, notification, context menu, and tooltip components

Let's enable some components that have related services that must be configured in the services collection and referenced in the main layout:

1. In the `Northwind.BlazorLibraries.Client` project, in `Program.cs`, import the namespace for working with Radzen services, as shown in the following code:

   ```
   using Radzen; // DialogService, NotificationService, and so on
   ```

2. In `Program.cs`, before the call to run the Blazor WebAssembly app, add statements to enable the dialog, notification, tooltip components, and context menu, as shown in the following code:

   ```
   builder.Services.AddScoped<DialogService>();
   builder.Services.AddScoped<NotificationService>();
   builder.Services.AddScoped<TooltipService>();
   builder.Services.AddScoped<ContextMenuService>();
   ```

3. In `MainLayout.razor`, add statements to embed the dialog, notification, context menu, and tooltip components. Add markup to use Bootstrap grid classes to create a navigation area in a left column and render the body of the Blazor WebAssembly client app in the remaining space, as shown highlighted in the following markup:

   ```
   @inherits LayoutComponentBase
   <RadzenDialog />
   <RadzenNotification />
   <RadzenContextMenu />
   <RadzenTooltip />
   <main>
     <div class="container">
       <div class="row">
         <div class="col-md-auto">
           <div class="alert alert-secondary">
               Navigation (coming soon)
           </div>
         </div>
         <div class="col">@Body</div>
       </div>
     </div>
   </main>
   ```

4. In `App.razor`, comment out the `<FocusOnNavigate>` element so that the `<h1>` is not selected, as shown in the following markup:

   ```
   @*<FocusOnNavigate RouteData="@routeData" Selector="h1" />*@
   ```

# Using the Radzen tooltip and context menu components

Let's use the context menu component to show a menu of shipping company items:

1.  In the Pages folder, in Index.razor, add statements to show a tooltip for the heading, show a context menu with shippers as items when the visitor right-clicks the heading, and then show what they clicked in the browser console, as shown in the following code:

```
@page "/"

@inject TooltipService tooltipService
@inject ContextMenuService contextMenuService

<h1 @ref="h1Element"
    @onmouseover="@(args => ShowTooltip(h1Element ,
      new TooltipOptions { Duration = 5000 }))"
    @oncontextmenu=@(args => ShowContextMenuWithItems(args))
    @oncontextmenu:preventDefault="true">
    Hello, Radzen Blazor!
</h1>

@code {
  ElementReference h1Element;

  void ShowTooltip(ElementReference elementReference,
    TooltipOptions? options = null)
  {
    tooltipService.Open(elementReference,
      "Right-click this heading to see shipping companies.",
      options);
  }

  void ShowContextMenuWithItems(MouseEventArgs args)
  {
    ContextMenuItem[] menuItems =
    {
      new() { Value = 1, Text = "Speedy Express" },
      new() { Value = 2, Text = "United Package" },
      new() { Value = 3, Text = "Federal Shipping" },
    };

    contextMenuService.Open(args, menuItems, OnMenuItemClick);
  }

  void OnMenuItemClick(MenuItemEventArgs args)
  {
    Console.WriteLine(
```

```
        $"Menu item clicked, Value={args.Value}, Text={args.Text}");

      contextMenuService.Close();
    }
  }
```

2.  Start the `Northwind.BlazorLibraries.Server` project without debugging.

    *   If you are using Visual Studio 2022, then in the Visual Studio 2022 toolbar, select the `https` profile as the **Startup Project**, and **Google Chrome** as the **Web Browser**.

    *   If you are using Visual Studio Code, then at the command line or terminal, enter the following command:

        ```
        dotnet run --launch-profile https
        ```

3.  In Chrome, show **Developer Tools** and its **Console**.

4.  On the home page, right-click the heading and note the menu items are the shipping companies, as shown in *Figure 17.1*:

*Figure 17.1: A context menu with shipping companies*

5.  Select a shipping company and note the output in the browser console, as shown in *Figure 17.2*:

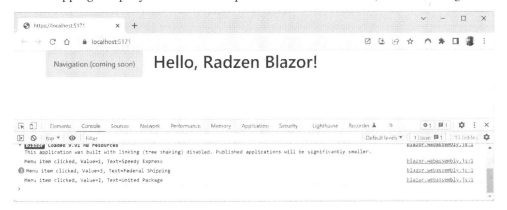

*Figure 17.2: The browser console showing the visitor clicked some items in the context menu*

6.  Close the browser and shut down the web server.

## Using the Radzen notification and dialog components

Let's use the notification and dialog components to show which shipping company the visitor selected:

1.  In the Pages folder, in Index.razor, add statements to inject the notification and dialog services, as shown in the following code:

    ```
    @inject NotificationService notificationService
    @inject DialogService dialogService
    ```

2.  In Index.razor, in the OnMenuItemClick method, make the method asynchronous, comment out the statement that writes the message to the browser console, and then after closing the context menu, add statements to either pop up a dialog or pop up a notification to show what the visitor clicked in the context menu, depending on whether they held down the *Ctrl* key when they clicked, as shown highlighted in the following code:

    ```
    async void OnMenuItemClick(MenuItemEventArgs args)
    {
        //Console.WriteLine(
        // $"Menu item clicked, Value={args.Value}, Text={args.Text}");

        contextMenuService.Close();

        if (args.CtrlKey) // show dialog box
        {
            bool? clickedYes = await dialogService.Confirm(
                message: $"Visitor selected: {args.Text}",
                title: $"Value={args.Value}",
                new ConfirmOptions() { OkButtonText = "Yes", CancelButtonText =
    "No" });

            string title = string.Format("You clicked \"{0}\"",
                (clickedYes.GetValueOrDefault(true) ? "Yes" : "No"));

            DialogOptions options = new()
            {
                CloseDialogOnOverlayClick = true,
                CloseDialogOnEsc = true
            };

            dialogService.Open(title, ds =>
                @<div>
                    <div class="row">
                        <div class="col-md-12">
                            @title
                        </div>
    ```

```
            </div>
          </div>
        , options);
    }
    else // show notification
    {
      NotificationMessage message = new()
        {
          // 1=Info/Speedy Express
          // 2=Success/United Package
          // 3=Warning/Federal Shipping
          Severity = (NotificationSeverity)args.Value,
          Summary = $"Value={args.Value}",
          Detail = $"Visitor selected: {args.Text}",
          Duration = 4000 // milliseconds
        };

      notificationService.Notify(message);
    }
}
```

3. Start the `Northwind.BlazorLibraries.Server` project without debugging.

4. On the home page, right-click the heading, click **United Package**, and note the notification that pops up for four seconds, as shown in *Figure 17.3*:

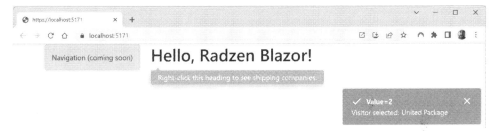

*Figure 17.3: A notification message with the success color scheme and icon*

5. Right-click the heading, hold down the *Ctrl* key and click **United Package**, and note the dialog box that pops up, as shown in *Figure 17.4*:

*Figure 17.4: A confirmation dialog box with Yes and No button choices*

6. Click **Yes**, and note the dialog box appears with custom content, as shown in *Figure 17.5*:

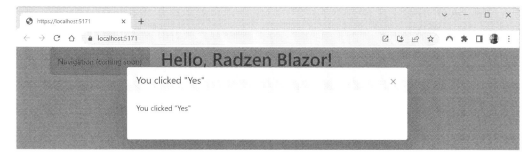

*Figure 17.5: A dialog box with custom content and a close button*

7. Either click the close button or click outside the dialog box to close it.

8. Select the other shipping company menu items and note the difference in color scheme and icons for the notifications.

9. Close the browser and shut down the web server.

# Building a web service for Northwind entities

Now that you have seen the minimum implementation of an entity component, we can add the functionality to fetch entities. In this case, we will use the Northwind database context to fetch employees from the database and expose it as a Minimal API web service:

1. In `Northwind.BlazorLibraries.Server.csproj`, add a reference to the Northwind database context project for SQL Server, as shown in the following markup:

```
<ItemGroup>
  <ProjectReference Include="..\..\..\Chapter02\Northwind.Common.DataContext
.SqlServer\Northwind.Common.DataContext.SqlServer.csproj" />
</ItemGroup>
```

 **Warning!** Unlike previous projects, relative path references for shared projects like the entity models and the database are three levels up, for example, `"..\..\..\"`, because we have additional depths of folders for **Server**, **Client**, and **Shared**.

2. Build the `Northwind.BlazorLibraries.Server` project at the command line or terminal.

3. In the `Northwind.BlazorLibraries.Server` project, in `Program.cs`, import namespaces for working with Minimal API attributes, registering the Northwind database context extension method, and serializing JSON, as shown in the following code:

```
using Microsoft.AspNetCore.Mvc; // [FromServices]
using Packt.Shared; // AddNorthwindContext extension method
using System.Text.Json.Serialization; // ReferenceHandler
using Microsoft.EntityFrameworkCore; // Include extension method
```

```
using HttpJsonOptions = Microsoft.AspNetCore.Http.Json.JsonOptions;
```

4.  In `Program.cs`, after the call to `CreateBuilder`, add a statement to configure the registered dependency service for JSON options and set its reference handler to preserve references, so that the reference between an employee and their manager does not cause a runtime exception due to circular references, as shown in the following code:

```
builder.Services.Configure<HttpJsonOptions>(options =>
{
  options.SerializerOptions.ReferenceHandler = ReferenceHandler.Preserve;
});
```

5.  In `Program.cs`, before the call to `Build`, add a statement to register the Northwind database context in the dependency services collection, as shown in the following code:

```
builder.Services.AddNorthwindContext();
```

6.  In `Program.cs`, before the call to the `MapRazorPages` method, add statements to define some endpoints to `GET` categories and orders, as shown in the following code:

```
app.MapGet("api/categories", (
  [FromServices] NorthwindContext db) =>
    Results.Json(
      db.Categories.Include(c => c.Products))
  .WithName("GetCategories")
  .Produces<Category[]>(StatusCodes.Status200OK);

app.MapGet("api/orders/", (
  [FromServices] NorthwindContext db) =>
    Results.Json(
      db.Orders.Include(o => o.OrderDetails)))
  .WithName("GetOrders")
  .Produces<Order[]>(StatusCodes.Status200OK);
```

## Using the Radzen tabs, image, and icon components

Let's use the tabs component to show the categories and their products from the Northwind database.

There are eight categories in the Northwind database. If we use the category names for the tabs, then they will be too wide. Instead, we will choose an icon for each category that will be shown in the tab.

Radzen has an icon component that uses Google Material Icons, as shown in the following markup:

```
<RadzenIcon Icon="facebook" />
<RadzenIcon Icon="accessibility" />
<RadzenIcon Icon="accessibility" IconStyle="IconStyle.Primary">
```

Some other components, like the `<RadzenTabsItem>` component, have an `Icon` property that can be set to the same keywords.

You can search for appropriate icons at the following link: `https://fonts.google.com/icons?selected=Material+Icons`.

Microsoft has open-sourced its Fluent Emoji, a collection of familiar, friendly, and modern emojis. We will use some of them to add a brighter, more colorful image icon for each category.

You can review and download the collection of Fluent Emoji at the following link: `https://github.com/microsoft/fluentui-emoji`.

Each category has a `Picture` property that is a byte array containing a low-quality JPEG image. We will create a helper extension method for byte arrays to encode the JPEG image as a Base64 string, for use as the `src` attribute for an `<img>` element on a web page.

Let's go!

1. In `Northwind.BlazorLibrary.Shared.csproj`, in the `SharedClass.cs` file, add statements to define an extension method, as shown in the following code:

   ```
   namespace Packt.Shared;

   public static class NorthwindExtensionMethods
   {
     public static string ConvertToBase64Jpeg(this byte[] picture)
     {
       return string.Format("data:image/jpg;base64,{0}",
         Convert.ToBase64String(picture));
     }
   }
   ```

2. In `Northwind.BlazorLibrary.Client.csproj`, add a reference to the Northwind entities project for SQL Server, as shown in the following markup:

   ```
   <ItemGroup>
     <ProjectReference Include="..\..\..\Chapter02\Northwind.Common.
   EntityModels.SqlServer\Northwind.Common.EntityModels.SqlServer.csproj" />
   </ItemGroup>
   ```

3. Build the `Northwind.BlazorLibrary.Client` project at the command line or terminal.

4. In the project folder, in `_Imports.razor`, import the namespaces for serializing JSON, and the Northwind entities so that Blazor components that we build do not need to import the namespaces individually, as shown in the following markup:

```
@using Packt.Shared
@using System.Text.Json
@using System.Text.Json.Serialization
```

5. In `MainLayout.razor`, remove the temporary "coming soon" text and add statements to define navigation links to the home page and a `Categories` page component, as shown in the following markup:

```
<nav class="nav nav-pills flex-column">
  <div class="nav-item px-3">
    <NavLink class="nav-link" href="/" Match="NavLinkMatch.All">
      Home
    </NavLink>
  </div>
  <div class="nav-item px-3">
    <NavLink class="nav-link" href="categories" Match="NavLinkMatch.All">
      Categories
    </NavLink>
  </div>
</nav>
```

6. In the `Northwind.BlazorLibraries.Client` project, in the `Pages` folder, add a new **Razor Component** named `Categories.razor`.

7. In `Categories.razor`, add statements to define a tab for each category and a list of products on each tab, as shown in the following code:

```
@page "/categories"

@inject IHttpClientFactory httpClientFactory

<h3>Categories</h3>

<RadzenTabs>
  <Tabs>
    @if (categories is null)
    {
      <RadzenTabsItem Text="None">
        <h3>No category found.</h3>
        <div class="alert alert-info">
          No products found for this category.
        </div>
      </RadzenTabsItem>
    }
    else
    {
      @foreach (Category category in categories)
      {
```

```
            <RadzenTabsItem Icon="@ConvertToIcon(category.CategoryName)">
              <h3>
                <RadzenImage Path="@ConvertToEmoji(category.CategoryName)"
                             Style="height:48px;width:48px;" />
                @category.CategoryName
                <RadzenBadge BadgeStyle="BadgeStyle.Warning" IsPill="true"
                             Text="@category.Products.Count().ToString()" />
              </h3>
              <div class="alert alert-info">
                @foreach (Product product in category.Products)
                {
                  <RadzenBadge BadgeStyle="BadgeStyle.Info"
                               Text="@product.ProductName" />
                }
              </div>
              @if (category.Picture is not null)
              {
                <div>
                  <img class="rounded float-start"
                       src="@category.Picture.ConvertToBase64Jpeg()" />
                </div>
              }
            </RadzenTabsItem>
          }
        }
      </Tabs>
  </RadzenTabs>

@code {
  private IQueryable<Category>? categories;

  private string ConvertToIcon(string categoryName)
  {
    return categoryName switch
    {
      "Beverages" => "coffee", // Google Material Icons
      "Condiments" => "liquor",
      "Confections" => "cake",
      "Dairy Products" => "water_drop",
      "Grains/Cereals" => "breakfast_dining",
      "Meat/Poultry" => "kebab_dining",
      "Produce" => "restaurant",
      "Seafood" => "set_meal",
      _ => "device_unknown"
    };
  }
```

```
private string ConvertToEmoji(string categoryName)
{
  return categoryName switch
  {
    // These paths are relative to the wwwroot folder.
    "Beverages" => "assets/Hot beverage/3D/hot_beverage_3d.png",
    "Condiments" => "assets/Honey pot/3D/honey_pot_3d.png",
    "Confections" => "assets/Lollipop/3D/lollipop_3d.png",
    "Dairy Products" => "assets/Cheese wedge/3D/cheese_wedge_3d.png",
    "Grains/Cereals" => "assets/Bread/3D/bread_3d.png",
    "Meat/Poultry" => "assets/Cut of meat/3D/cut_of_meat_3d.png",
    "Produce" => "assets/Leafy green/3D/leafy_green_3d.png",
    "Seafood" => "assets/Lobster/3D/lobster_3d.png",
    _ => "assets/Pot of food/3D/pot_of_food_3d.png"
  };
}

protected override async Task OnParametersSetAsync()
{
  Category[]? categoriesArray = null;

  // Web API service uses "Preserve" so
  // we must control how references are handled.
  JsonSerializerOptions jsonOptions = new()
    {
      ReferenceHandler = ReferenceHandler.Preserve,
      PropertyNameCaseInsensitive = true
    };

  HttpClient client = httpClientFactory.CreateClient(
    "Northwind.BlazorLibraries.ServerAPI");

  string path = "api/categories";

  try
  {
    categoriesArray = (await client.GetFromJsonAsync<Category[]?>(
        path, jsonOptions));
  }
  catch (Exception ex)
  {
    Console.WriteLine($"{ex.GetType()}: {ex.Message}");
  }

  if (categoriesArray is not null)
```

```
        {
           categories = categoriesArray.AsQueryable();
        }
     }
  }
```

8.  Start your browser and navigate to the GitHub repository at the following link: `https://github.com/microsoft/fluentui-emoji`.

9.  Click the green **Code** button and then click **Download ZIP**.

10. Extract the ZIP file.

11. In the `Northwind.BlazorLibraries.Client` project, in the `wwwroot` folder, create a folder named `assets`.

12. From the `fluentui-emoji-main\assets` folder, copy the folders for the images used by the categories, as shown in the following list and in *Figure 17.6*:

    -   `assets/Hot beverage/3D/hot_beverage_3d.png`
    -   `assets/Honey pot/3D/honey_pot_3d.png`
    -   `assets/Lollipop/3D/lollipop_3d.png`
    -   `assets/Cheese wedge/3D/cheese_wedge_3d.png`
    -   `assets/Bread/3D/bread_3d.png`
    -   `assets/Cut of meat/3D/cut_of_meat_3d.png`
    -   `assets/Leafy green/3D/leafy_green_3d.png`
    -   `assets/Lobster/3D/lobster_3d.png`
    -   `assets/Pot of food/3D/pot_of_food_3d.png`

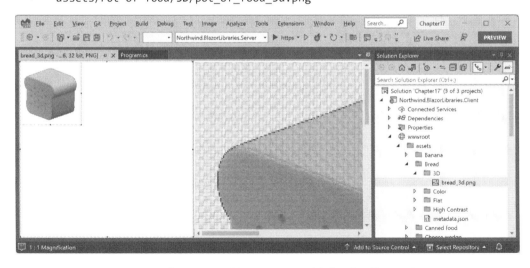

*Figure 17.6: Fluent UI Emoji image assets added to the Client project*

13. Start the `Northwind.BlazorLibraries.Server` project without debugging.

14. On the home page, in the left navigation, click **Categories**, and note the tabs for the eight Northwind categories, as shown in *Figure 17.7*:

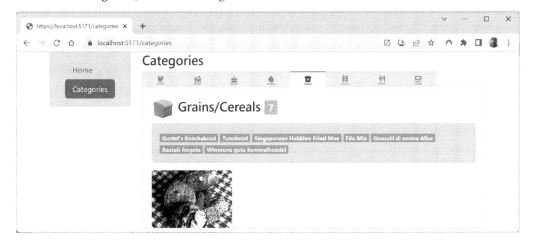

*Figure 17.7: The Grains/Cereals tab selected to show its products and image from the database*

15. Close the browser and shut down the web server.

## Using the Radzen HTML editor component

Now we will use the Radzen HTML editor component to provide an editing experience:

1. In the Pages folder, add a new file named HtmlEditor.razor.

2. In HtmlEditor.razor, add statements to define an instance of the Radzen HTML editor component and bind it to a string property that contains some simple HTML, as shown in the following code:

```
@page "/htmleditor"

<RadzenHtmlEditor @bind-Value=@HtmlValue />

@code {
  [Parameter]
  public string HtmlValue { get; set; } =
    "<h1>Hello, Radzen Blazor!</h1><p></p>";
}
```

3. In MainLayout.razor, add statements to define a navigation link to the HTML Editor page component, as shown in the following markup:

```
<div class="nav-item px-3">
  <NavLink class="nav-link" href="htmleditor">
    HTML Editor
  </NavLink>
</div>
```

4.  Start the `Northwind.BlazorLibraries.Server` project without debugging.

5.  On the home page, in the left navigation, click **HTML Editor**, and note the HTML editor with its toolbar, as shown in *Figure 17.8*:

*Figure 17.8: The HTML editor component in action*

6.  Close the browser and shut down the web server.

 You can learn more about customizing the HTML editor component at the following link: `https://blazor.radzen.com/docs/guides/components/htmleditor.html`.

# Using the Radzen chart component

Now we will use the Radzen chart component to visualize some numeric data about orders in the Northwind database:

1.  In the `Pages` folder, add a new file named `OrdersBarChart.razor`.

2.  In `OrdersBarChart.razor`, add statements to inject the HTTP client factory and then use it to output a bar chart of revenue grouped by country, as shown in the following code:

```
@page "/orders-bar-chart"
@using System.Globalization
@inject IHttpClientFactory httpClientFactory

<RadzenCheckBox @bind-Value="@showDataLabels"
                Name="dataLabels"></RadzenCheckBox>
<RadzenLabel Text="Show Data Labels" For="dataLabels"
             Style="margin-left: 8px; vertical-align: middle;" />

<RadzenChart>
  <RadzenBarSeries Data="@revenue" CategoryProperty="Country"
                   LineType="LineType.Dashed" ValueProperty="Revenue">
    <RadzenSeriesDataLabels Visible="@showDataLabels" />
  </RadzenBarSeries>
```

```
  <RadzenValueAxis Formatter="@FormatAsUSD">
    <RadzenGridLines Visible="true" />
    <RadzenAxisTitle Text="Revenue in USD" />
  </RadzenValueAxis>
  <RadzenBarOptions Radius="5" />
  <RadzenLegend Visible="false" />
</RadzenChart>

@code {
  bool showDataLabels = false;

  class DataItem
  {
    public string? Country { get; set; }
    public decimal Revenue { get; set; }
  }

  private string FormatAsUSD(object value)
  {
    return ((double)value).ToString("C0",
      CultureInfo.GetCultureInfo("en-US"));
  }

  private DataItem[]? revenue;

  protected override async Task OnParametersSetAsync()
  {
    Order[]? ordersArray = null;

    // Web API service uses "Preserve" so
    // we must control how references are handled.
    JsonSerializerOptions jsonOptions = new()
      {
        ReferenceHandler = ReferenceHandler.Preserve,
        PropertyNameCaseInsensitive = true
      };

    HttpClient client = httpClientFactory.CreateClient(
      "Northwind.BlazorLibraries.ServerAPI");

    string path = "api/orders";

    try
    {
      ordersArray = (await client.GetFromJsonAsync<Order[]?>(
        path, jsonOptions));
```

```
        revenue = ordersArray?
          .GroupBy(order => order.ShipCountry)
          .Select(group => new DataItem
           {
              Country = group.Key,
              Revenue = group.Sum(order => order.OrderDetails.Sum(
              detail => detail.UnitPrice * detail.Quantity))
           })
          .OrderByDescending(dataitem => dataitem.Revenue)
          .ToArray();
      }
      catch (Exception ex)
      {
        Console.WriteLine($"{ex.GetType()}: {ex.Message}");
      }
    }
  }
}
```

3.  In the Pages folder, add a new file named CategoriesPieChart.razor.

4.  In CategoriesPieChart.razor, add statements to inject the HTTP client factory and then use it to output a pie chart of the number of products in each category, as shown in the following code:

```
@page "/categories-pie-chart"

@inject IHttpClientFactory httpClientFactory

<RadzenCheckBox @bind-Value="@showDataLabels" Name="dataLabels">
</RadzenCheckBox>
<RadzenLabel Text="Show Data Labels" For="dataLabels"
             Style="margin-left: 8px; vertical-align: middle;" />

<RadzenChart>
  <RadzenPieSeries Data="@categoryProducts" Title="Product Count"
      CategoryProperty="Category" ValueProperty="ProductCount">
    <RadzenSeriesDataLabels Visible="@showDataLabels" />
  </RadzenPieSeries>
</RadzenChart>

@code {
  bool showDataLabels = false;

  class DataItem
  {
    public string? Category { get; set; }
    public decimal ProductCount { get; set; }
```

```
    }

  private DataItem[]? categoryProducts;

  protected override async Task OnParametersSetAsync()
  {
    Category[]? categoriesArray = null;

    // Web API service uses "Preserve" so
    // we must control how references are handled.
    JsonSerializerOptions jsonOptions = new()
      {
        ReferenceHandler = ReferenceHandler.Preserve ,
        PropertyNameCaseInsensitive = true
      };

    HttpClient client = httpClientFactory.CreateClient(
      "Northwind.BlazorLibraries.ServerAPI");

    string path = "api/categories";

    try
    {
      categoriesArray = (await client.GetFromJsonAsync<Category[]?>(
        path, jsonOptions));

      categoryProducts = categoriesArray?
        .Select(category => new DataItem
          {
            Category = category.CategoryName,
            ProductCount = category.Products.Count()
          })
        .OrderByDescending(dataitem => dataitem.ProductCount)
        .ToArray();
    }
    catch (Exception ex)
    {
      Console.WriteLine($"{ex.GetType()}: {ex.Message}");
    }
  }
}
```

5.  In MainLayout.razor, add statements to define navigation links to the Orders Bar Chart and Categories Pie Chart page components, as shown in the following markup:

```
<div class="nav-item px-3">
  <NavLink class="nav-link" href="orders-bar-chart">
```

```
      Orders Bar Chart
    </NavLink>
  </div>
  <div class="nav-item px-3">
    <NavLink class="nav-link" href="categories-pie-chart">
      Categories Pie Chart
    </NavLink>
  </div>
```

6. Start the `Northwind.BlazorLibraries.Server` project without debugging.

7. Start Chrome and navigate to `https://localhost:5171/`.

8. In the left navigation menu, click **Orders Bar Chart**, select the **Show Data Labels** checkbox, hover over one of the bars, and note that the tooltip shows details of the total revenue for that country, as shown for the UK in *Figure 17.9*:

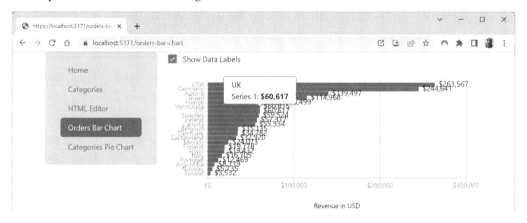

*Figure 17.9: A bar chart of order revenue per country*

9. In the left navigation menu, click **Categories Pie Chart**, and note that categories in the chart are ordered from the highest to the lowest number of products, starting with **Condiments**, which has 13 products, as shown in *Figure 17.10*:

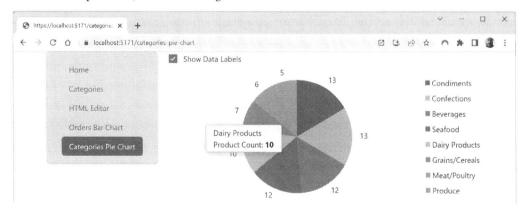

*Figure 17.10: A pie chart of the number of products per category*

10. Select **Show Data Labels** and hover over a pie segment to see a tooltip.

11. Close Chrome and shut down the web server.

## Using the Radzen form components

Now we will use the Radzen form components to enable the viewing and editing of employees in the Northwind database:

1. In the `Northwind.BlazorLibraries.Server` project, in `Program.cs`, before the call to the `MapRazorPages` method, add statements to define some endpoints to `GET` and `PUT` employees and related data like a list of cities and countries, as shown in the following code:

```
app.MapGet("api/employees/", (
  [FromServices] NorthwindContext db) =>
    Results.Json(db.Employees, jsonOptions))
  .WithName("GetEmployees")
  .Produces<Employee[]>(StatusCodes.Status200OK);

app.MapGet("api/countries/", (
  [FromServices] NorthwindContext db) =>
    Results.Json(db.Employees.Select(emp => emp.Country).Distinct()))
  .WithName("GetCountries")
  .Produces<string[]>(StatusCodes.Status200OK);

app.MapGet("api/cities/", (
  [FromServices] NorthwindContext db) =>
    Results.Json(db.Employees.Select(emp => emp.City).Distinct()))
  .WithName("GetCities")
  .Produces<string[]>(StatusCodes.Status200OK);

app.MapPut("api/employees/{id:int}", async (
    [FromRoute] int id,
    [FromBody] Employee employee,
    [FromServices] NorthwindContext db) =>
  {
    Employee? foundEmployee = await db.Employees.FindAsync(id);

    if (foundEmployee is null) return Results.NotFound();

    foundEmployee.FirstName = employee.FirstName;
    foundEmployee.LastName = employee.LastName;
    foundEmployee.BirthDate = employee.BirthDate;
    foundEmployee.HireDate = employee.HireDate;
    foundEmployee.Address = employee.Address;
    foundEmployee.City = employee.City;
    foundEmployee.Country = employee.Country;
    foundEmployee.Region = employee.Region;
```

```
        foundEmployee.PostalCode = employee.PostalCode;
        foundEmployee.ReportsTo = employee.ReportsTo;
        foundEmployee.Title = employee.Title;
        foundEmployee.TitleOfCourtesy = employee.TitleOfCourtesy;
        foundEmployee.Notes = employee.Notes;

        int affected = await db.SaveChangesAsync();

        return Results.Json(affected);
    })
    .Produces(StatusCodes.Status200OK)
    .Produces(StatusCodes.Status404NotFound);
```

2.  In `MainLayout.razor`, add statements to define navigation links to the `Employees` page component, as shown in the following markup:

```
<div class="nav-item px-3">
  <NavLink class="nav-link" href="employees">
    Employees
  </NavLink>
</div>
```

3.  In the `Northwind.BlazorLibraries.Client` project, in the `Pages` folder, add a new file named `Employees.razor`.

4.  In `Employees.razor`, add statements to inject the HTTP client factory and then use it to output a form to select, and then edit employees, as shown in the following code:

 This is a long section of code because employees have more than 20 properties and each must be data bound to a control to edit it. You might prefer to copy it from the GitHub repository and then review it line by line rather than enter it yourself. I have highlighted the most interesting blocks of code, and there are notes about them after the code.

```
@page "/employees"
@using System.Net
@inject IHttpClientFactory httpClientFactory
@inject NotificationService notificationService

<h3>Employees</h3>

<RadzenCard>
  <RadzenListBox AllowFiltering="true" TValue="int"
                 FilterCaseSensitivity="FilterCaseSensitivity.
CaseInsensitive"
                 Data=@employees
                 TextProperty="FirstName"
```

```
                            ValueProperty="EmployeeId"
                            Change=@(args => OnChange(args, "ListBox with filtering"))
                            Style="height:150px" Class="w-100" />
</RadzenCard>
<hr />
@if (employee != null)
{
    <RadzenTemplateForm Data="@employee"
        Submit="@((Employee employee) => { Submit(employee); })">
        <div class="row">
            <div class="col-md-6">
                <RadzenFieldset Text="Employee Details">
                    <div class="row">
                        <div class="col-md-4 align-items-center d-flex">
                            <RadzenLabel Text="Employee ID" />
                        </div>
                        <div class="col-md-8">
                            <RadzenNumeric style="width: 100%;" Name="EmployeeId"
                                @bind-Value="employee.EmployeeId" ReadOnly="true" />
                        </div>
                    </div>
                    <div class="row">
                        <div class="col-md-4 align-items-center d-flex">
                            <RadzenLabel Text="Title" />
                        </div>
                        <div class="col-md-8">
                            <RadzenTextBox style="width: 100%;" Name="Title"
                                @bind-Value="employee.Title" />
                        </div>
                    </div>
                    <div class="row">
                        <div class="col-md-4 align-items-center d-flex">
                            <RadzenLabel Text="Title of Courtesy" />
                        </div>
                        <div class="col-md-8">
                            <RadzenTextBox style="width: 100%;" Name="TitleOfCourtesy"
                                @bind-Value="employee.TitleOfCourtesy" />
                        </div>
                    </div>
                    <div class="row">
                        <div class="col-md-4 align-items-center d-flex">
                            <RadzenLabel Text="First Name" />
                        </div>
                        <div class="col-md-8">
                            <RadzenTextBox style="width: 100%;" Name="FirstName"
```

```
                        @bind-Value="employee.FirstName" />
          </div>
        </div>
        <div class="row">
          <div class="col-md-4 align-items-center d-flex">
            <RadzenLabel Text="Last Name" />
          </div>
          <div class="col-md-8">
            <RadzenTextBox style="width: 100%;" Name="LastName"
              @bind-Value="employee.LastName" />
          </div>
        </div>
        <div class="row">
          <div class="col-md-4 align-items-center d-flex">
            <RadzenLabel Text="Birth Date" />
          </div>
          <div class="col-md-8">
            <RadzenDatePicker style="width: 100%;" Name="BirthDate"
              @bind-Value="employee.BirthDate" />
          </div>
        </div>
        <div class="row">
          <div class="col-md-4 align-items-center d-flex">
            <RadzenLabel Text="Hire Date" />
          </div>
          <div class="col-md-8">
            <RadzenDatePicker style="width: 100%;" Name="HireDate"
              @bind-Value="employee.HireDate" />
          </div>
        </div>
        <div class="row">
          <div class="col-md-12">
            <RadzenTextArea style="width: 100%;" Name="Notes"
              @bind-Value="employee.Notes" Rows="6" />
          </div>
        </div>
      </RadzenFieldset>
    </div>
    <div class="col-md-6">
      <RadzenFieldset Text="Home Address">
        <div class="row">
          <div class="col-md-4 align-items-center d-flex">
            <RadzenLabel Text="Country" />
          </div>
          <div class="col-md-8">
```

```
                    <RadzenDropDown TValue="string" @bind-Value="employee.
Country"
                        Placeholder="USA" Data="@countries" style="width: 100%;"
                        Name="Country">
                    </RadzenDropDown>
                </div>
            </div>
            <div class="row">
                <div class="col-md-4 align-items-center d-flex">
                    <RadzenLabel Text="City" />
                </div>
                <div class="col-md-8">
                    <RadzenDropDown TValue="string" @bind-Value="employee.City"
                        Data="@cities" style="width: 100%;" Name="City">
                    </RadzenDropDown>
                </div>
            </div>
            <div class="row">
                <div class="col-md-4 align-items-center d-flex">
                    <RadzenLabel Text="Region" />
                </div>
                <div class="col-md-8">
                    <RadzenTextBox style="width: 100%;" Name="Region"
                        @bind-Value="employee.Region" />
                </div>
            </div>
            <div class="row">
                <div class="col-md-4 align-items-center d-flex">
                    <RadzenLabel Text="Postal Code" />
                </div>
                <div class="col-md-8">
                    <RadzenTextBox style="width: 100%;" Name="PostalCode"
                        @bind-Value="employee.PostalCode" />
                </div>
            </div>
            <div class="row">
                <div class="col-md-4 align-items-center d-flex">
                    <RadzenLabel Text="Building/Street" />
                </div>
                <div class="col-md-8">
                    <RadzenTextBox style="width: 100%;" Name="Address"
                        @bind-Value="employee.Address" />
                </div>
            </div>
            <div class="row">
                <div class="col-md-4 align-items-center d-flex">
```

```
                    <RadzenLabel Text="Home Phone" />
                </div>
                <div class="col-md-8">
                    <RadzenTextBox style="width: 100%;" Name="HomePhone"
                       @bind-Value="employee.HomePhone" />
                </div>
            </div>
            <div class="row">
                <div class="col-md-4 align-items-center d-flex">
                    <RadzenLabel Text="Picture" />
                </div>
                <div class="col-md-8">
                    @if (employee.Photo is not null)
                    {
                        <div>
                            <img class="rounded float-start"
                               src="@employee.Photo.ConvertToBase64Jpeg()" />
                        </div>
                    }
                </div>
            </div>
        </RadzenFieldset>
      </div>
    </div>
    <div class="row justify-content-center">
        <div class="col-md-12 d-flex align-items-end justify-content-
center"
            style="margin-top: 16px;">
        <RadzenButton ButtonType="ButtonType.Submit" Icon="save"
            Text="Save Changes" />
        </div>
    </div>
  </RadzenTemplateForm>
}

@code {
  private IQueryable<Employee>? employees;
  private string[]? countries;
  private string[]? cities;

  private Employee? employee = null;

  // Web API service uses "Preserve" so
  // we must control how references are handled.
  private JsonSerializerOptions jsonOptions = new()
    {
```

```
      ReferenceHandler = ReferenceHandler.Preserve,
      PropertyNameCaseInsensitive = true
    };

  protected override async Task OnParametersSetAsync()
  {
    Employee[]? employeesArray = null;

    HttpClient client = httpClientFactory.CreateClient(
      "Northwind.BlazorLibraries.ServerAPI");

    string path = "api/employees";

    try
    {
      employeesArray = (await client.GetFromJsonAsync<Employee[]?>(
        path, jsonOptions));

      employees = employeesArray?.AsQueryable();

      countries = (await client.GetFromJsonAsync<string[]?>(
        "api/countries"));

      cities = (await client.GetFromJsonAsync<string[]?>(
        "api/cities"));
    }
    catch (Exception ex)
    {
      Console.WriteLine($"{ex.GetType()}: {ex.Message}");
    }
  }

  void OnChange(object value, string name)
  {
    string? str = value is IEnumerable<object> ?
      string.Join(", ", (IEnumerable<object>)value) :
      value.ToString();

    Console.WriteLine($"{name} value changed to {str}");

    if (str != null)
    {
      employee = employees?.FirstOrDefault(employee =>
        employee.EmployeeId == int.Parse(str));
    }
  }
```

```
  private async void Submit(Employee employee)
  {
    HttpClient client = httpClientFactory.CreateClient(
      "Northwind.BlazorLibraries.ServerAPI");

    string path = $"api/employees/{employee.EmployeeId}";

    try
    {
      HttpResponseMessage response = await client
        .PutAsJsonAsync<Employee>(path, employee);

      NotificationMessage message = new()
        {
          Severity = response.StatusCode == HttpStatusCode.OK ?
            NotificationSeverity.Success : NotificationSeverity.Error,
          Summary = $"{response.StatusCode}",
          Detail = $"Employees affected: {await response.Content.
ReadAsStringAsync()}",
          Duration = 5000 // milliseconds
        };

      notificationService.Notify(message);
    }
    catch (Exception ex)
    {
      Console.WriteLine($"{ex.GetType()}: {ex.Message}");
    }
  }
}
```

Note the following:

- The RadzenListBox component is bound to a list of employees. The text shown in the list is the FirstName. The value selected is the EmployeeId. When the list selection changes, the OnChange method is called.

- If the employee property is not null, then a RadzenTemplateForm is bound to it. Within the template, two RadzenFieldset components (visual groups) are used to separate the left and right halves of the form, titled Employee Details and Home Address.

- RadzenLabel components are used to label each field within the form, like **Employee ID**.

- A read-only RadzenNumeric component is bound to the EmployeeId property. We do not want the user changing the value used as the primary key for an employee.

- A RadzenTextBox component is bound to the Title property. The same is used for the TitleOfCourtesy, FirstName, LastName, Region, PostalCode, Address, and HomePhone properties.

- A RadzenDatePicker component is bound to the BirthDate property. The same is used for the HireDate property.
- A RadzenTextArea component with six rows is bound to the Notes property.
- A RadzenDropDown component is bound to the Country property. It binds to the countries property to supply the list of country text values. A similar one is used for the City property. It binds to the cities property to supply the list of city text values.
- If the Photo property is not null, then an img element has its src set to the bytes of the Photo property converted into a Base64-encoded JPEG image.
- At the bottom of the form is a RadzenButton labeled **Save Changes**.
- In the @code block, note the employees, countries, cities, and employee fields that are bound to by various components.
- When parameters for this component are set, an HttpClient is used to get all the employee entities and lists of cities and countries from the web service, and this data is then stored in the local fields.
- When the list of employees above the form changes, the OnChange method writes the selected employee name to the console output and then uses the selected employee ID to set the local employee field that is bound to the form.
- When the **Save Changes** button is clicked, the form is submitted, and an HttpClient is used to send an HTTP PUT request to the web service, to update the appropriate employee in the database with the current values bound to the employee field. A notification message appears for five seconds.

## Testing the employees page component

Now, we can try out the interactions with the Employees page component:

1. Start the Northwind.BlazorLibraries.Server project without debugging.
2. Start Chrome and navigate to https://localhost:5171/.
3. In the left navigation menu, click **Employees**, enter ne in the search box, and note the list is filtered to only show the two employees with ne in their first name, **Janet** and **Anne**, as shown in *Figure 17.11*:

*Figure 17.11: Filtering employees by first name*

4.  Click **Janet**, and note that all her details are shown in a form below the list box, as shown in *Figure 17.12*:

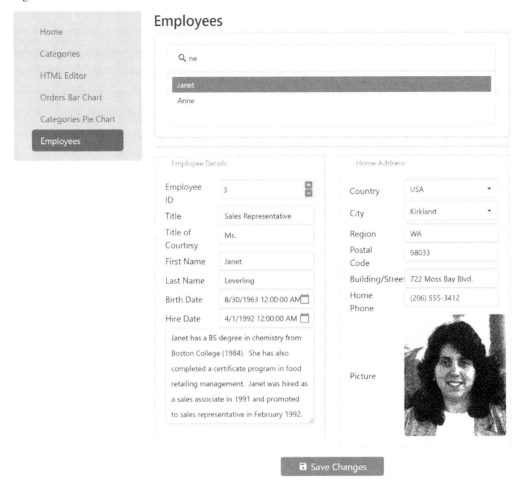

*Figure 17.12: Details for the employee named Janet*

5.  Change some of the details for Janet and note that while the Blazor app is open, those changes remain in memory. However, if you were to close the browser tab or window, those changes would be lost.

6.  Click the **Save Changes** button and note the notification message to inform you that the changes were successfully saved to the database, as shown in *Figure 17.13*:

*Figure 17.13: A successful update to an employee in the database*

7. Close Chrome and shut down the web server.

8. Start the `Northwind.BlazorLibraries.Server` project without debugging.

9. Start Chrome and navigate to `https://localhost:5171/`.

10. In the left navigation menu, click **Employees**, search for Janet, and confirm that her details were saved correctly.

11. Close Chrome and shut down the web server.

# Practicing and exploring

Test your knowledge and understanding by answering some questions, getting some hands-on practice, and exploring this chapter's topics with deeper research.

## Exercise 17.1 – Test your knowledge

Answer the following questions:

1. Why is the Radzen Blazor component library a good choice compared to alternatives like DevExpress or SyncFusion?

2. Does using the Radzen Blazor component library require your project to also use Bootstrap?

3. Which four Radzen Blazor components require you to register dependency services?

4. In a `NotificationMessage`, what does setting the `Severity` property to 1, 2, or 3 do?

5. What is the name of the icon library that can be used by default to set icons for tabs and other components?

6. How can you customize the formatting of data values in a `RadzenChart`?

7. How do you two-way data bind a `RadzenTextBox` component to a property?

8. What three properties should be set on a `RadzenListBox` or `RadzenDropDown` component to display the list of items to select from?

9. How can you trigger a `Submit` event for a form?

10. Which component provides visual grouping in a form?

## Exercise 17.2 – Practice by exploring MudBlazor

Create a new solution and set of projects to explore the MudBlazor component library. You can follow the instructions to get started with it at the following link: `https://mudblazor.com/getting-started/installation#manual-install`.

MudBlazor has similar components to Radzen Blazor, so you should try completing all the tasks in this chapter using MudBlazor instead of Radzen Blazor to see the subtle differences and all the similarities.

## Exercise 17.3 – Explore topics

Use the links on the following GitHub repository to learn more detail about the topics covered in this chapter:

`https://github.com/markjprice/apps-services-net7/blob/main/book-links.md#chapter-17--using-open-source-blazor-component-libraries`

## Summary

In this chapter, you learned:

- How to install Radzen Blazor and enable its services for features like notifications.
- How to use tooltip and context menu components.
- How to use notification and dialog components.
- How to use tabs, images, and icon components.
- How to use HTML editor, chart, and form components.

In the next chapter, you will learn how to build cross-platform apps for mobile and desktop devices using .NET MAUI.

# 18

# Building Mobile and Desktop Apps Using .NET MAUI

This chapter is about learning how to make **graphical user interface** (**GUI**) apps by building a cross-platform mobile and desktop app for iOS and Android, macOS Catalyst, and Windows using **.NET MAUI** (**Multi-platform App UI**).

You will see how **eXtensible Application Markup Language** (**XAML**) makes it easy to define the user interface for a graphical app.

Cross-platform GUI development cannot be learned in a single chapter, but like web development, it is so important that I want to introduce you to some of what is possible. Think of this chapter as an introduction that will give you a taste to inspire you, and then you can learn more from a book dedicated to mobile or desktop development.

The app will allow the listing and management of customers in the Northwind database. The mobile app that you create will call an ASP.NET Core Minimal APIs web service.

Either a Windows computer with Visual Studio 2022 for Windows version 17.4 or later, or a macOS computer with Visual Studio 2022 for Mac version 17.4, can be used to create a .NET MAUI project. But you will need a computer with Windows to compile WinUI 3 apps, and you will need a computer with macOS and Xcode to compile for macOS Catalyst and iOS.

Although you can create a .NET MAUI project at the command line and then edit it using Visual Studio Code, there is no official tooling to help you yet.

In this chapter, we will cover the following topics:

- Understanding XAML
- Understanding .NET MAUI
- Building mobile and desktop apps using .NET MAUI
- Using shared resources
- Using data binding

- Understanding MVVM
- Consuming a web service from a .NET MAUI app

# Understanding XAML

Let's start by looking at the markup language used by .NET MAUI.

In 2006, Microsoft released **Windows Presentation Foundation** (**WPF**), which was the first technology to use **eXtensible Application Markup Language** (**XAML**). Silverlight, for web and mobile apps, quickly followed, but it is no longer supported by Microsoft. WPF is still used today to create Windows desktop applications; for example, Visual Studio for Windows is partially built using WPF.

XAML can be used to build parts of the following apps:

- **.NET MAUI apps** for mobile and desktop devices, including Android, iOS, Windows, and macOS. It is an evolution of a technology named **Xamarin.Forms**.
- **WinUI 3 apps** for Windows 10 and 11.
- **Universal Windows Platform** (**UWP**) **apps** for Windows 10 and 11, Xbox, Mixed Reality, and Meta Quest VR headsets.
- **WPF apps** for Windows desktop, including Windows 7 and later.
- **Avalonia** and **Uno Platform apps** using cross-platform third-party technologies.

## Simplifying code using XAML

XAML simplifies C# code, especially when building a user interface.

Imagine that you need two or more pink buttons, which execute a method for their implementation when clicked, laid out horizontally to create a toolbar.

In C#, you might write the following code:

```
HorizontalStackPanel toolbar = new();

Button newButton = new();
newButton.Content = "New";
newButton.Background = new SolidColorBrush(Colors.Pink);
newButton.Clicked += NewButton_Clicked;
toolbar.Children.Add(newButton);

Button openButton = new();
openButton.Content = "Open";
openButton.Background = new SolidColorBrush(Colors.Pink);
openButton.Clicked += OpenButton_Clicked;
toolbar.Children.Add(openButton);
```

In XAML, this could be simplified to the following lines of code. When this XAML is processed, the equivalent properties are set, and methods are called to achieve the same goal as the preceding C# code:

```
<HorizontalStackPanel x:Name="toolbar">
```

```
  <Button x:Name="newButton" Background="Pink"
          Clicked="NewButton_Clicked">New</Button>
  <Button x:Name="openButton" Background="Pink"
          Clicked="OpenButton_Clicked">Open</Button>
</StackPanel>
```

You can think of XAML as an alternative and easier way of declaring and instantiating .NET types, especially when defining a user interface and the resources that it uses.

XAML allows resources like brushes, styles, and themes to be declared at different levels, like a UI element, a page, or globally for the application to enable resource sharing.

XAML allows data binding between UI elements or between UI elements and objects and collections.

If you choose to use XAML to define your user interface and related resources at compile time, then the code-behind file must call the `InitializeComponent` method in the page constructor, as shown highlighted in the following code:

```
public partial class MainPage : ContentPage
{
  public MainPage()
  {
    InitializeComponent(); // process XAML
  }

  private void NewButton_Clicked(object sender, EventArgs e)
  {
    ...
  }

  private void OpenButton_Clicked(object sender, EventArgs e)
  {
    ...
  }
}
```

Calling the `InitializeComponent` method tells the page to read its XAML, create the controls defined in it, and set their properties and event handlers.

# .NET MAUI namespaces

.NET MAUI has several important namespaces where its types are defined:

| Namespace | Description |
|---|---|
| Microsoft.Maui | Utility types like FlowDirection, IButton, IImage, and Thickness |

| Microsoft.Maui.<br>Controls | Common controls, pages, and related types like Application,<br>Brush, Button, CheckBox, ContentPage, Image, and<br>VerticalStackPanel |
|---|---|
| Microsoft.Maui.<br>Graphics | Types for graphics like Color, Font, ImageFormat, PathBuilder,<br>Point, and Size |

To import a namespace using XAML, you add xmlns attributes in the root element. One namespace is imported as the default, and others must be named using a prefix.

For example, .NET MAUI types are imported by default, so the element names do not need a prefix; general XAML syntax is imported using the x prefix for doing common things like naming a control or the class name that the XAML will be compiled as; and your project types are often imported using the local prefix, as shown in the following markup:

```
<?xml version="1.0" encoding="utf-8" ?>
<ContentPage xmlns="http://schemas.microsoft.com/dotnet/2021/maui"
             xmlns:x="http://schemas.microsoft.com/winfx/2009/xaml"
             xmlns:local="clr-namespace:MyMauiApp.Controls"
             x:Class="MyMauiApp.MainPage"
             ...>

  <Button x:Name="NewFileButton" ...>New File</Button>
  <local:CustomerList x:Name="CustomerList" ... />
  ...
</ContentPage>
```

In the example above, the project is named MyMauiApp and its controls like the CustomerList control are defined in a namespace named MyMauiApp.Controls. This namespace has been registered with the prefix local, so when an instance of the CustomerList control is needed, it is declared using <local:CustomerList>.

You can import as many namespaces with different prefixes as you need.

## Type converters

Type converters convert XAML attribute values that must be set as string values into other types. For example, the following button has its background property set to the string value "Pink":

```
<Button x:Name="newButton" Background="Pink" ...
```

This is converted into a SolidColorBrush instance using a type converter, as shown in the following equivalent code:

```
newButton.Background = new SolidColorBrush(Colors.Pink);
```

There are many type converters provided by .NET MAUI, and you can create and register your own. These are especially useful for custom data visualizations.

# Choosing between .NET MAUI controls

There are lots of predefined controls that you can choose from for common user interface scenarios. .NET MAUI (and most dialects of XAML) support these controls:

| Controls | Description |
|---|---|
| Button, ImageButton, MenuItem, ToolbarItem | Executing actions |
| CheckBox, RadioButton, Switch | Choosing options |
| DatePicker, TimePicker | Choosing dates and times |
| CollectionView, ListView, Picker, TableView | Choosing items from lists and tables |
| CarouselView, IndicatorView | Scrolling animated views that show one item at a time |
| AbsoluteLayout, BindableLayout, FlexLayout, Grid, HorizontalStackLayout, StackLayout, VerticalStackLayout | Layout containers that affect their children in different ways |
| Border, BoxView, Frame, ScrollView | Visual elements |
| Ellipse, Line, Path, Polygon, Polyline, Rectangle, RoundRectangle | Graphical elements |
| ActivityIndicator, Label, ProgressBar, RefreshView | Displaying read-only text and other read-only displays |
| Editor, Entry | Editing text |
| GraphicsView, Image | Embedding images, videos, and audio files |
| Slider, Stepper | Selecting within ranges of numbers |
| SearchBar | Adding a search feature |
| BlazorWebView, WebView | Embedding Blazor and web components |
| ContentView | Building custom controls |

.NET MAUI defines its controls in the Microsoft.Maui.Controls namespace. It has some specialized controls too:

- Application: Represents a cross-platform graphical application. It sets the root page, manages windows, themes, and resources, and provides app-level events like PageAppearing, ModalPushing, and RequestedThemeChanged. It also has methods that you can override to hook into app events like OnStart, OnSleep, OnResume, and CleanUp.
- Shell: A Page control that provides user interface features that most applications require, like flyout or tab bar navigation, navigation tracking and management, and navigation events.

Most .NET MAUI controls derive from View. One of the most important characteristics of View-derived types is that they can be nested. This allows you to build complex custom user interfaces.

## Markup extensions

To support some advanced features, XAML uses markup extensions. Some of the most important enable element and data binding and the reuse of resources, as shown in the following list:

- {Binding} links an element to a value from another element or a data source
- {OnPlatform} sets properties to different values depending on the current platform
- {StaticResource} and {DynamicResource} link an element to a shared resource
- {AppThemeBinding} links an element to a shared resource defined in a theme

.NET MAUI provides the OnPlatform markup extension to allow you to set different markup depending on the platform. For example, iPhone X and later introduced the notch that takes up extra space at the top of the phone display. We could add extra padding to an app that applies to all devices, but it would be better if we could add that extra padding only to iOS, as shown in the following markup:

```
<VerticalStackLayout>
  <VerticalStackLayout.Padding>
    <OnPlatform x:TypeArguments="Thickness">
      <On Platform="iOS" Value="30,60,30,30" />
      <On Platform="Android" Value="30" />
      <On Platform="WinUI" Value="30" />
    </OnPlatform>
  </VerticalStackLayout.Padding>
```

There is a simplified syntax too, as shown in the following markup:

```
<VerticalStackLayout Padding"{OnPlatform iOS='30,60,30,30', Default='30'}">
```

## Understanding .NET MAUI

To create a mobile app that only needs to run on iPhones, you might choose to build it with either the Objective-C or Swift language and the UIKit libraries using the Xcode development tool.

To create a mobile app that only needs to run on Android phones, you might choose to build it with either the Java or Kotlin language and the Android SDK libraries using the Android Studio development tool.

But what if you need to create a mobile app that can run on iPhones *and* Android phones? And what if you only want to create that mobile app once using a programming language and development platform that you are already familiar with? And what if you realized that with a bit more coding effort to adapt the user interface to desktop-size devices, you could target macOS and Windows desktop devices too?

.NET MAUI enables developers to build cross-platform mobile apps for Apple iOS (iPhone), iPadOS, macOS using Catalyst, Windows using WinUI 3, and Google Android using C# and .NET, which are then compiled to native APIs and executed on native phone and desktop platforms.

Business logic layer code can be written once and shared between all platforms. User interface interactions and APIs are different on various mobile and desktop platforms, so the user interface layer is sometimes custom for each platform.

Like WPF and UWP apps, .NET MAUI uses XAML to define the user interface once for all platforms using abstractions of platform-specific user interface components. Applications built with .NET MAUI draw the user interface using native platform widgets, so the app's look and feel fits naturally with the target mobile platform.

A user experience built using .NET MAUI will not perfectly fit a specific platform in the same way as one that's custom-built with native tools for that platform, but for mobile and desktop apps that will not have millions of users, it is good enough. And with some effort, you can build beautiful apps, as illustrated by the Microsoft challenge that you can read about at the following link:

https://devblogs.microsoft.com/dotnet/announcing-dotnet-maui-beautiful-ui-challenge/

## Development tools for mobile first, cloud first

Mobile apps are often supported by services in the cloud.

Satya Nadella, CEO of Microsoft, famously said the following:

> *To me, when we say mobile first, it's not the mobility of the device, it's actually the mobility of the individual experience. [...] The only way you are going to be able to orchestrate the mobility of these applications and data is through the cloud.*

As you have seen earlier in this book, to create an ASP.NET Core Web API service to support a mobile app, we can use Visual Studio Code. To create .NET MAUI apps, developers can use either Visual Studio 2022 for Windows or Visual Studio 2022 for Mac.

When installing Visual Studio 2022, you must select the **.NET Multi-platform App UI development** workload that is in the **Desktop & Mobile** section, as shown in *Figure 18.1*:

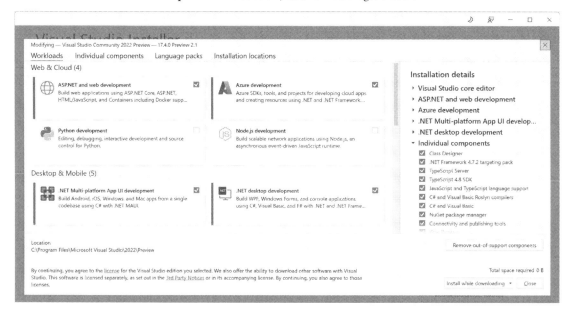

*Figure 18.1: Selecting the .NET MAUI workload for Visual Studio 2022 for Windows*

## Installing .NET MAUI workloads manually

Installing Visual Studio 2022 for Windows or Mac should install the required .NET MAUI workloads. If you get errors later, then you can make sure that the workloads are installed manually.

To see which workloads are currently installed, enter the following command:

```
dotnet workload list
```

The currently installed workloads will appear in a table, as shown in the following output:

```
Installed Workload Ids      Manifest Version       Installation Source
-----------------------------------------------------------------------
maui-maccatalyst            6.0.486/6.0.400        SDK 7.0.100
```

To see which workloads are available to install, enter the following command:

```
dotnet workload search
```

The currently available workloads will appear in a table, as shown in the following output:

```
Workload ID           Description
-----------------------------------------------------------------------
android               .NET SDK Workload for building Android applications.
android-32            Support for Android API-32.
android-33            Support for Android API-33.
ios                   .NET SDK Workload for building iOS applications.
```

```
maccatalyst           .NET SDK Workload for building macOS applications...
macos                 .NET SDK Workload for building macOS applications.
maui                  .NET MAUI SDK for all platforms
maui-android          .NET MAUI SDK for Android
maui-desktop          .NET MAUI SDK for Desktop
maui-ios              .NET MAUI SDK for iOS
maui-maccatalyst      .NET MAUI SDK for Mac Catalyst
maui-mobile           .NET MAUI SDK for Mobile
maui-tizen            .NET MAUI SDK for Tizen
maui-windows          .NET MAUI SDK for Windows
runtimes-windows      workloads/runtimes-windows/description
tvos                  .NET SDK Workload for building tvOS applications.
wasm-experimental     workloads/wasm-experimental/description
wasm-tools            .NET WebAssembly build tools
```

To install the .NET MAUI workloads for all platforms, enter the following command at the command line or terminal:

```
dotnet workload install maui
```

To update all existing workload installations, enter the following command:

```
dotnet workload update
```

To add missing workload installations required for a project, enter the following command:

```
dotnet workload restore <projectname>
```

## Using Windows to create iOS and macOS apps

If you want to use Visual Studio 2022 for Windows to create an iOS mobile app or a macOS Catalyst desktop app, then you can connect over a network to a **Mac build host**. Instructions can be found at the following link:

```
https://docs.microsoft.com/en-us/dotnet/maui/ios/pair-to-mac
```

## .NET MAUI user interface components

.NET MAUI includes some common controls for building user interfaces. They can be divided into four categories:

- **Pages** represent cross-platform application screens, for example, `Shell`, `ContentPage`, `NavigationPage`, `FlyoutPage`, and `TabbedPage`.
- **Layouts** represent the structure of a combination of other user interface components, for example, `Grid`, `StackLayout`, and `FlexLayout`.
- **Views** represent a single user interface component, for example, `CarouselView`, `CollectionView`, `Label`, `Entry`, `Editor`, and `Button`.
- **Cells** represent a single item in a list or table view, for example, `TextCell`, `ImageCell`, `SwitchCell`, and `EntryCell`.

## Shell control

The Shell control is designed to simplify app development by providing standardized navigation and search capabilities. In your project, you would create a class that inherits from the Shell control class. Your derived class defines components like a TabBar, which contains Tab items, FlyoutItem instances, and ShellContent, which contain the ContentPage instances for each page. A TabBar should be used when there are only up to about four or five pages to navigate between. FlyoutItem navigation should be used when there are more items because they can be presented as a vertical scrollable list. You can use both, with the TabBar showing a subset of items. The Shell will keep them synchronized.

Flyout navigation is when a list of items flies out (or slides) from the left side of a mobile device's screen or desktop app's main window. The user invokes it by tapping on a "hamburger" icon with three horizontal lines stacked on top of each other. When the user taps a flyout item, its page is instantiated when needed, as the user navigates around the user interface.

The top bar automatically shows a **Back** button when needed to allow the user to navigate back to a previous page.

## ListView control

The ListView control is used for long lists of data-bound values of the same type. It can have headers and footers and its list items can be grouped.

It has cells to contain each list item. There are two built-in cell types: text and image. Developers can define custom cell types.

Cells can have context actions that appear when the cell is swiped on iPhone, long pressed on Android, or right-clicked on a desktop OS. A context action that is destructive can be shown in red, as shown in the following markup:

```
<TextCell Text="{Binding CompanyName}" Detail="{Binding Location}">
  <TextCell.ContextActions>
    <MenuItem Clicked="Customer_Phoned" Text="Phone" />
    <MenuItem Clicked="Customer_Deleted" Text="Delete" IsDestructive="True" />
  </TextCell.ContextActions>
</TextCell>
```

## Entry and Editor controls

The Entry and Editor controls are used for editing text values and are often data-bound to an entity model property, as shown in the following markup:

```
<Editor Text="{Binding CompanyName, Mode=TwoWay}" />
```

 **Good Practice:** Use Entry for a single line of text. Use Editor for multiple lines of text.

## .NET MAUI handlers

In .NET MAUI, XAML controls are defined in the `Microsoft.Maui.Controls` namespace. Components called **handlers** map these common controls to native controls on each platform. On iOS, a handler will map a .NET MAUI `Button` to an iOS-native `UIButton` defined by UIKit. On macOS, `Button` is mapped to `NSButton` defined by AppKit. On Android, `Button` is mapped to an Android-native `AppCompatButton`.

Handlers have a `NativeView` property that exposes the underlying native control. This allows you to work with platform-specific features like properties, methods, and events, and customize all instances of a native control.

## Writing platform-specific code

If you need to write code statements that only execute for a specific platform like Android, then you can use compiler directives.

For example, by default, `Entry` controls on Android show an underline character. If you want to hide the underline, you could write some Android-specific code to get the handler for the `Entry` control, use its `NativeView` property to access the underlying native control, and then set the property that controls that feature to `false`, as shown in the following code:

```
#if __ANDROID__
  Handlers.EntryHandler.EntryMapper[nameof(IEntry.BackgroundColor)] = (h, v) =>
  {
    (h.NativeView as global::Android.Views.Entry).UnderlineVisible = false;
  };
#endif
```

Predefined compiler constants include the following:

- `__ANDROID__`
- `__IOS__`
- `WINDOWS`

The compiler `#if` statement syntax is slightly different from the C# `if` statement syntax, as shown in the following code:

```
#if __IOS__
  // iOS-specific statements
#elif __ANDROID__
  // Android-specific statements
#elif WINDOWS
  // Windows-specific statements
#endif
```

# Building mobile and desktop apps using .NET MAUI

We will build a mobile and desktop app for managing customers in Northwind.

**Good Practice:** If you have a Mac and you have never run Xcode on it, then run it now until you see the Start window. This will ensure that all its required components are installed and registered. If you do not do this, then you might get errors with your projects later in Visual Studio 2022 for Mac.

# Creating a virtual Android device for local app testing

To target Android, you must install at least one Android SDK. A default installation of Visual Studio 2022 with the mobile development workload already includes one Android SDK, but it is often an older version to support as many Android devices as possible.

To use the latest features of .NET MAUI, you must configure a more recent Android virtual device:

1.  In Windows, start **Visual Studio 2022**. If you see the **Start** window, then click **Continue without code**.

2.  Navigate to **Tools | Android | Android Device Manager**. If you are prompted by **User Account Control** to allow this app to make changes to your device, click **Yes**.

3.  In the **Android Device Manager**, click the **+ New** button the create a new device.

4.  In the dialog box, make the following choices, as shown in *Figure 18.2*:

    *   **Base Device: Pixel 5**
    *   **Processor: x86_64**
    *   **OS: Android 13.0 – API 33**
    *   **Google APIs:** Selected
    *   **Google Play Store:** Cleared

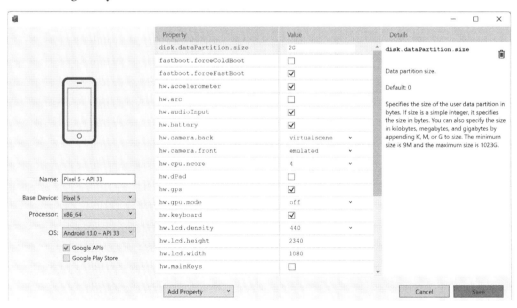

*Figure 18.2: Selecting the hardware and OS for a virtual Android device*

5. Click **Save**.

6. Accept any license agreements.

7. Wait for any required downloads.

8. In the **Android Device Manager**, in the list of devices, in the row for the device that you just created, click **Start**, as shown in *Figure 18.3*:

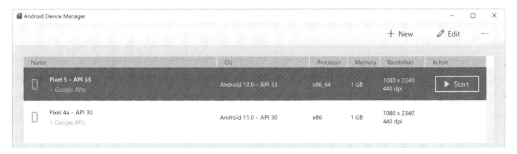

*Figure 18.3: Android Device Manager*

9. When the Android device has finished starting, click the browser and test that it has access to the network by navigating to `https://www.bbc.co.uk/news`.

10. Close the emulator.

11. Close **Android Device Manager**.

12. Restart Visual Studio 2022 to ensure that it is aware of the new emulator.

## Enabling Windows developer mode

To create apps for Windows, you must enable developer mode:

1. Navigate to **Start** | **Settings** | **Privacy & security** | **For developers**, and then switch on **Developer Mode,** as shown in *Figure 18.4*:

*Figure 18.4: Enabling Developer Mode in Windows 11*

2. Accept the warning about how it "could expose your device and personal data to security risk or harm your device," and then close the **Settings** app.

# Creating a .NET MAUI solution

We will now create a project for a cross-platform mobile and desktop app:

1.  In Visual Studio for Windows, add a new project, as defined in the following list:

    -   Project template: **.NET MAUI App**/maui

     You can select **C#** for the language and **MAUI** for the project type to filter and show only the appropriate project templates, as shown in *Figure 18.5*.

    -   Workspace/solution file and folder: Chapter18
    -   Project file and folder: Northwind.Maui.Client

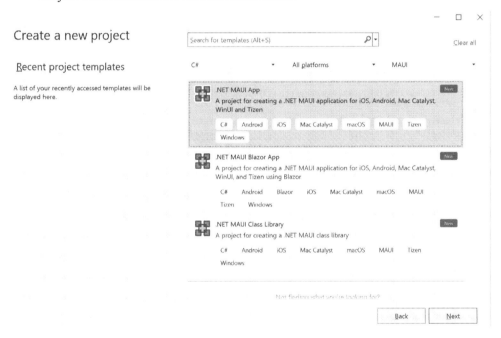

*Figure 18.5: Applying filters to show only the three .NET MAUI project templates*

2.  On Windows, if you see a Windows Security Alert that **Windows Defender Firewall has blocked some features of Broker on all public and private networks**, then select **Private networks** and clear **Public networks**, and then click the **Allow access** button.

3.  In the project file, note the element that targets iOS, Android, and Mac Catalyst, and the element to enable Windows targeting if the OS is Windows, as well as the elements that set the project to be a single project MAUI project, as shown highlighted in the following partial markup:

```
<Project Sdk="Microsoft.NET.Sdk">

  <PropertyGroup>
```

```
    <TargetFrameworks>net7.0-ios;net7.0-android;net7.0-maccatalyst</
TargetFrameworks>
    <TargetFrameworks Condition="$([MSBuild]::IsOSPlatform('windows'))
and '$(MSBuildRuntimeType)' == 'Full'">$(TargetFrameworks);net7.0-
windows10.0.19041.0</TargetFrameworks>
    <!-- Uncomment to also build the tizen app. You will need to install
tizen by following this: https://github.com/Samsung/Tizen.NET -->
    <!-- <TargetFrameworks>$(TargetFrameworks);net7.0-tizen</
TargetFrameworks> -->
    <OutputType>Exe</OutputType>
    <RootNamespace>Northwind.Maui.Client</RootNamespace>
    <UseMaui>true</UseMaui>
    <SingleProject>true</SingleProject>
```

If you see the error Error NU1012 Platform version is not present for one or more target frameworks, even though they have specified a platform: net7.0-ios, net7.0-maccatalyst, then at the command prompt or terminal, in the project folder, restore workloads for the project, as shown in the following command:

```
dotnet workload restore
```

4.  To the right of the **Run** button in the toolbar, set the **Framework** to **net7.0-android**, and select the **Pixel 5 - API 33 (Android 13.0 - API 33)** emulator image that you previously created, as shown in *Figure 18.6*:

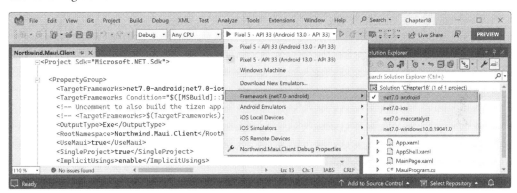

*Figure 18.6: Selecting an Android device as the target for startup*

5.  Click the **Run** button in the toolbar and wait for the device emulator to start the Android operating system and launch your mobile app.

If you're doing this for the first time, there might be another Google license agreement to confirm.

6.  In the .NET MAUI app, click the **Click me** button to increment the counter three times, as shown in *Figure 18.7*:

*Figure 18.7: Incrementing the counter in the .NET MAUI app on Android*

7.  Close the Android device emulator.

8.  To the right of the **Run** button in the toolbar, set the **Framework** to **net7.0-windows**, and then select **Windows Machine**.

As well as the more general **net7.0-windows**, you can also have a version-specific identifier, for example, **net7.0-windows10.0.19041.0**. This is controlled in the project file, as shown in the following markup:

```
<TargetFrameworks Condition="$([MSBuild]::IsOSPlatform('wi
ndows'))">$(TargetFrameworks);net7.0-windows10.0.19041.0</
TargetFrameworks>
```

9.  Make sure that the **Debug** configuration is selected and then click the green triangle start button labeled **Windows Machine**.

10. After a few moments, note that the Windows app displays with the same **Click me** button and counter functionality, as shown in *Figure 18.8*:

*Figure 18.8: Incrementing the counter in the .NET MAUI app on Windows*

.NET MAUI apps will automatically use the operating system's dark mode if it is enabled. The above screenshot shows the .NET MAUI app running on Windows 11 in light mode. During this chapter, I recommend that you switch to light mode because the color schemes work best with that. In future editions of this book, I could cover how to support dark mode if readers want me to prioritize that over other topics.

11. Close the Windows app.

**Good Practice**: You should test run your .NET MAUI app on all the potential devices that it will need to run on. In this chapter, even if I do not explicitly tell you to do so, I recommend that you try the app by running it on your emulated Android device and on Windows after each task to add a new feature. That way, you will have at least seen how it looks on a mobile device with a primarily tall and thin portrait size, and on a desktop device with a larger landscape size. If you are using a Mac, then I recommend that you test it in the iOS simulator, Android emulator, and as a Mac Catalyst desktop app.

## Adding shell navigation and more content pages

Now, let's review the existing structure of the .NET MAUI app and then add some new pages and navigation to the project:

1. In the Northwind.Maui.Client project, in MauiProgram.cs, note that the builder object calls UseMauiApp and specifies App as its generic type, as shown highlighted in the following code:

```
using Microsoft.Extensions.Logging;
```

```
namespace Northwind.Maui.Client;

public static class MauiProgram
{
  public static MauiApp CreateMauiApp()
  {
    var builder = MauiApp.CreateBuilder();
    builder
      .UseMauiApp<App>()
      .ConfigureFonts(fonts =>
      {
        fonts.AddFont("OpenSans-Regular.ttf", "OpenSansRegular");
        fonts.AddFont("OpenSans-Semibold.ttf", "OpenSansSemibold");
      });

#if DEBUG
    builder.Logging.AddDebug();
#endif

    return builder.Build();
  }
}
```

2.  In **Solution Explorer**, expand `App.xaml`, open `App.xaml.cs`, and note the `MainPage` property of the `App` is set to an instance of `AppShell`, as shown highlighted in the following code:

```
namespace Northwind.Maui.Client;

public partial class App : Application
{
  public App()
  {
    InitializeComponent();

    MainPage = new AppShell();
  }
}
```

3.  In `AppShell.xaml`, note that the shell disables flyout mode and only has a single content page named `MainPage`, as shown highlighted in the following code:

```
<?xml version="1.0" encoding="UTF-8" ?>
<Shell
  x:Class="Northwind.Maui.Client.AppShell"
  xmlns="http://schemas.microsoft.com/dotnet/2021/maui"
  xmlns:x="http://schemas.microsoft.com/winfx/2009/xaml"
  xmlns:local="clr-namespace:Northwind.Maui.Client"
  Shell.FlyoutBehavior="Disabled">
```

```
<ShellContent
  Title="Home"
  ContentTemplate="{DataTemplate local:MainPage}"
  Route="MainPage" />

</Shell>
```

 A shell with only one content page does not show any navigation. You must have at least two shell content items to show any navigation.

4. In the `Resources` folder, in the `Images` folder, add images for some icons that we will use for flyout items in the navigation we are about to add.

 You can download the images from the GitHub repository at the following link: `https://github.com/markjprice/apps-services-net7/tree/main/vs4win/Chapter18/Northwind.Maui.Client/Resources/Images`.

5. In `AppShell.xaml`, enable flyout mode, set the background to a pale blue color, add an icon for the `MainPage` content, add a flyout header, and then add some flyout items with more shell content, as shown highlighted in the following markup:

```
<?xml version="1.0" encoding="UTF-8" ?>
<Shell
  x:Class="Northwind.Maui.Client.AppShell"
  xmlns="http://schemas.microsoft.com/dotnet/2021/maui"
  xmlns:x="http://schemas.microsoft.com/winfx/2009/xaml"
  xmlns:local="clr-namespace:Northwind.Maui.Client"
  Shell.FlyoutBehavior="Flyout"
  FlyoutBackgroundColor="AliceBlue">

  <Shell.FlyoutHeader>
    <HorizontalStackLayout Spacing="10" HorizontalOptions="Start">
      <Image Source="wind_face_3d.png"
            WidthRequest="80" HeightRequest="80" />
      <Label Text="Northwind" FontFamily="OpenSansSemibold"
            FontSize="32" VerticalOptions="Center" />
    </HorizontalStackLayout>
  </Shell.FlyoutHeader>

  <ShellContent
    Title="Home"
    Icon="file_cabinet_3d.png"
```

```
            ContentTemplate="{DataTemplate local:MainPage}"
            Route="MainPage" />

    <ShellContent Title="Categories"
                  Icon="delivery_truck_3d.png"
                  ContentTemplate="{DataTemplate local:CategoriesPage}"
                  Route="Categories" />

    <ShellContent Title="Products"
                  Icon="cityscape_3d.png"
                  ContentTemplate="{DataTemplate local:ProductsPage}"
                  Route="Products" />

    <ShellContent Title="Customers"
                  Icon="card_index_3d.png"
                  ContentTemplate="{DataTemplate local:CustomersPage}"
                  Route="Customers" />

    <ShellContent Title="Employees"
                  Icon="identification_card_3d.png"
                  ContentTemplate="{DataTemplate local:EmployeesPage}"
                  Route="Employees" />

    <ShellContent Title="Settings"
                  Icon="gear_3d.png"
                  ContentTemplate="{DataTemplate local:SettingsPage}"
                  Route="Settings" />

</Shell>
```

6.  Right-click the `Northwind.Maui.Client` project folder, choose **Add | New Item...**, select **.NET MAUI** in the template types tree, select **.NET MAUI ContentPage (XAML)**, enter the name `SettingsPage.xaml`, and click **Add**, as shown in *Figure 18.9*:

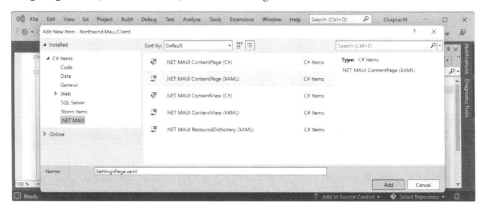

*Figure 18.9: Adding a new XAML Content Page item*

7. Repeat the previous step to add content pages named:

    - `CategoriesPage.xaml`
    - `CustomersPage.xaml`
    - `CustomerDetailPage.xaml`
    - `EmployeesPage.xaml`
    - `ProductsPage.xaml`

8. In **Solution Explorer**, double-click on the `CategoriesPage.xaml` file to open it for editing. Note that Visual Studio 2022 does not yet have a graphical design view for XAML.

9. In the `<ContentPage>` element, change the `Title` to `Categories`, and in the `<Label>` element, change the `Text` to `Categories`.

10. Navigate to **View | Toolbox** or press *Ctrl + W, X*. Note that the toolbox has sections for **Controls, Layouts, Cells**, and **General**, as shown in *Figure 18.10*:

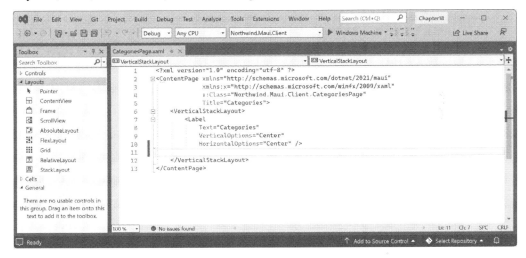

*Figure 18.10: The toolbox showing .NET MAUI layout controls*

11. At the top of the toolbox is a search box. Enter the letter b, and then note that the list of controls is filtered to show controls like **Button, ProgressBar**, and **AbsoluteLayout**.

12. Drag and drop the **Button** control from the toolbox into the XAML markup after the existing `<Label>` control, and change its `Text` property to `Hello!`, as shown in the following markup:

```
<Button Text="Hello!" />
```

13. Set the startup to **Windows Machine** and then start the `Northwind.Maui.Client` project with debugging. Note that the Visual Studio status bar shows us that **XAML Hot Reload** is connected.

14. In the top-left corner of the app, click the flyout menu (the "hamburger" icon) and note the header and the images used for the icons in the flyout items, as shown in *Figure 18.11*:

*Figure 18.11: A flyout with image icons*

15. In the flyout menu, click **Categories**, and note that the text on the button says **Hello!** and that it stretches across the width of the app window.

16. Leave the app running and then, in Visual Studio, change the Text property to Click Me, add an attribute to set the WidthRequest property to 100, and note that the XAML Hot Reload feature automatically reflects the changes in the **XAML Live Preview** window and in the app itself, as shown in *Figure 18.12*:

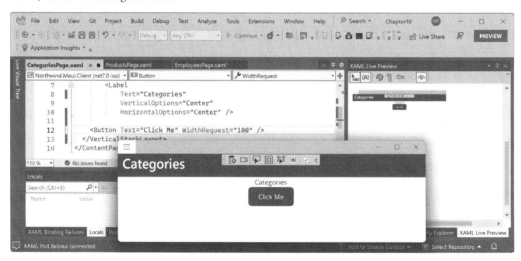

*Figure 18.12: XAML Hot Reload automatically updating changes in the XAML in the live app*

17. Close the app.

18. Modify the Button element to give it a name of ClickMeButton and a new event handler for its Clicked event, as shown in *Figure 18.13*:

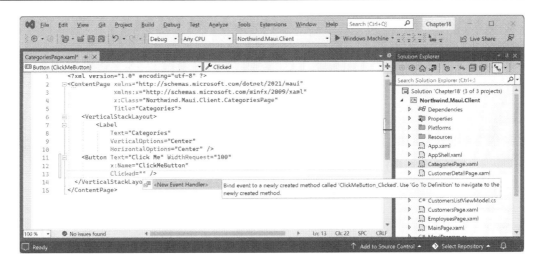

*Figure 18.13: Adding an event handler to a control*

19. Right-click the event handler name and select **Go To Definition** or press *F12*.

20. Add a statement to the event handler method that sets the content of the button to the current time, as shown highlighted in the following code:

```
private void ClickMeButton_Click(object sender, EventArgs e)
{
    ClickMeButton.Text = DateTime.Now.ToString("hh:mm:ss");
}
```

21. Start the `Northwind.Maui.Client` project with debugging with at least one mobile device and one desktop device.

> **Good Practice:** When deploying to an Android emulator or an iOS simulator, the old version of the app could still be running. Make sure to wait for the deployment of the new version of your app before interacting with it. You can keep an eye on the Visual Studio status bar to track deployment progress or just wait until you see the message **XAML Hot Reload connected**.

22. Navigate to **Categories**, click the button, and note that its text label changes to the current time.

23. Close the app.

## Implementing more content pages

Now, let's implement some of the new pages:

1. In `EmployeesPage.xaml`, change the `Title` to `Employees` and add markup to define the user interface for a simple calculator, as shown highlighted in the following markup:

```
<?xml version="1.0" encoding="utf-8" ?>
<ContentPage xmlns="http://schemas.microsoft.com/dotnet/2021/maui"
```

```xml
      xmlns:x="http://schemas.microsoft.com/winfx/2009/xaml"
      x:Class="Northwind.Maui.Client.EmployeesPage"
      Title="Employees">

  <VerticalStackLayout>

    <Grid Background="DarkGray" Margin="10"
          Padding="5" x:Name="gridCalculator"
          ColumnDefinitions="Auto,Auto,Auto,Auto"
          RowDefinitions="Auto,Auto,Auto,Auto">
      <Button Grid.Row="0" Grid.Column="0" Text="X" />
      <Button Grid.Row="0" Grid.Column="1" Text="/" />
      <Button Grid.Row="0" Grid.Column="2" Text="+" />
      <Button Grid.Row="0" Grid.Column="3" Text="-" />
      <Button Grid.Row="1" Grid.Column="0" Text="7" />
      <Button Grid.Row="1" Grid.Column="1" Text="8" />
      <Button Grid.Row="1" Grid.Column="2" Text="9" />
      <Button Grid.Row="1" Grid.Column="3" Text="0" />
      <Button Grid.Row="2" Grid.Column="0" Text="4" />
      <Button Grid.Row="2" Grid.Column="1" Text="5" />
      <Button Grid.Row="2" Grid.Column="2" Text="6" />
      <Button Grid.Row="2" Grid.Column="3" Text="." />
      <Button Grid.Row="3" Grid.Column="0" Text="1" />
      <Button Grid.Row="3" Grid.Column="1" Text="2" />
      <Button Grid.Row="3" Grid.Column="2" Text="3" />
      <Button Grid.Row="3" Grid.Column="3" Text="=" />
    </Grid>
    <Label x:Name="Output" FontSize="24"
           VerticalOptions="Center"
           HorizontalOptions="Start" />

  </VerticalStackLayout>
</ContentPage>
```

2.  Add an event handler for the page's Loaded event, as shown highlighted in the following markup:

```xml
Title="Employees"
Loaded="ContentPage_Loaded">
```

3.  In EmployeesPage.xaml.cs, add statements to resize each button in the grid and hook up an event handler for the Clicked event, as shown in the following code:

```csharp
private void ContentPage_Loaded(object sender, EventArgs e)
{
  foreach (Button button in gridCalculator.Children.OfType<Button>())
  {
    button.FontSize = 24;
    button.WidthRequest = 54;
```

```
    button.HeightRequest = 54;
    button.Clicked += Button_Clicked;
  }
}
```

4. Add a `Button_Clicked` method, with statements to handle the clicked button by concatenating the text of the button to the output label, as shown in the following code:

```
private void Button_Clicked(object sender, EventArgs e)
{
  string operationChars = "+-/X=";

  Button button = (Button)sender;

  if (operationChars.Contains(button.Text))
  {
    Output.Text = string.Empty;
  }
  else
  {
    Output.Text += button.Text;
  }
}
```

 This is not a proper implementation for a calculator because the operations have not been implemented. It just simulates one for now because we are focusing on how to build UIs with .NET MAUI. You can google how to implement a simple calculator as an optional exercise.

5. Start the `Northwind.Maui.Client` project with debugging. Try it with at least one desktop and one mobile device.

6. Navigate to **Employees**, click some of the buttons, and note that the label updates to show what is clicked, as shown on a Windows machine in *Figure 18.14*:

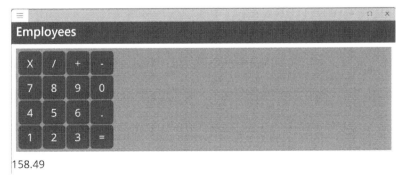

*Figure 18.14: A simulated calculator on Windows*

7.  Close the app.

# Using shared resources

When building graphical user interfaces, you will often want to use a resource such as a brush to paint the background of controls or an instance of a class to perform custom conversions. Resources can be defined at the following levels and shared with everything at that level or lower:

- Application
- Page
- Control

## Defining resources to share across an app

A good place to define shared resources is at the app level, so let's see how to do that:

1.  In the `Resources` folder, in the `Styles` folder, add a new **.NET MAUI Resource Dictionary (XAML)** project item named `Northwind.xaml`.

2.  Add markup inside the existing `ResourceDictionary` element to define a linear gradient brush with a key of `rainbow`, as shown highlighted in the following markup:

```xml
<?xml version="1.0" encoding="utf-8" ?>
<ResourceDictionary xmlns="http://schemas.microsoft.com/dotnet/2021/maui"
            xmlns:x="http://schemas.microsoft.com/winfx/2009/xaml"
            x:Class="Northwind.Maui.Client.Resources.Styles.Northwind">

  <LinearGradientBrush x:Key="rainbow">
    <GradientStop Color="Red" Offset="0" />
    <GradientStop Color="Orange" Offset="0.1" />
    <GradientStop Color="Yellow" Offset="0.3" />
    <GradientStop Color="Green" Offset="0.5" />
    <GradientStop Color="Blue" Offset="0.7" />
    <GradientStop Color="Indigo" Offset="0.9" />
    <GradientStop Color="Violet" Offset="1" />
  </LinearGradientBrush>

</ResourceDictionary>
```

3.  In `App.xaml`, add an entry to the merged resource dictionaries to reference the resource file in the `Styles` folder named `Northwind.xaml`, as shown highlighted in the following markup:

```xml
<?xml version = "1.0" encoding = "UTF-8" ?>
<Application xmlns="http://schemas.microsoft.com/dotnet/2021/maui"
            xmlns:x="http://schemas.microsoft.com/winfx/2009/xaml"
            xmlns:local="clr-namespace:Northwind.Maui.Client"
            x:Class="Northwind.Maui.Client.App">
  <Application.Resources>
    <ResourceDictionary>
```

```
        <ResourceDictionary.MergedDictionaries>
          <ResourceDictionary Source="Resources/Styles/Colors.xaml" />
          <ResourceDictionary Source="Resources/Styles/Styles.xaml" />
          <ResourceDictionary Source="Resources/Styles/Northwind.xaml" />
        </ResourceDictionary.MergedDictionaries>
      </ResourceDictionary>
    </Application.Resources>
</Application>
```

# Referencing shared resources

Now we can reference the shared resource:

1.  In `CategoriesPage.xaml`, modify the `ContentPage` to set its background to the brush resource
    with the key of `rainbow`, as shown highlighted in the following markup:

    ```
    <ContentPage xmlns="http://schemas.microsoft.com/dotnet/2021/maui"
                 xmlns:x="http://schemas.microsoft.com/winfx/2009/xaml"
                 x:Class="Northwind.Maui.Client.CategoriesPage"
                 Background="{StaticResource rainbow}"
                 Title="Categories">
    ```

     `StaticResource` means the resource is read once when the app first starts. If the
    resource changes after that, any elements that reference it will not be updated.

2.  Start the `Northwind.Maui.Client` project with debugging.

3.  Navigate to **Categories** and note that the background of the page is a rainbow.

4.  Close the app.

# Changing shared resources dynamically

Now we can implement a settings page to allow the user to change some colors used in the user interface at runtime:

1.  In `Northwind.xaml`, add markup inside the `ResourceDictionary` element to control the width
    and other properties of the `Entry` control so they are usable on Android, and to define a pair
    of color resources that will be used for the text and background colors of labels and buttons,
    as shown in the following markup:

    ```
    <Style TargetType="Entry">
      <Setter Property="TextColor" Value="{DynamicResource PrimaryTextColor}"
    />
      <Setter Property="FontFamily" Value="OpenSansRegular" />
      <Setter Property="HorizontalOptions" Value="Start" />
      <Setter Property="WidthRequest" Value="300" />
    </Style>
    ```

```xml
<Color x:Key="TextColor">Black</Color>
<Color x:Key="BackgroundColor">Silver</Color>
```

2. In `MainPage.xaml`, set the `TextColor` property of the labels, and both the `TextColor` and `BackgroundColor` properties of the button to use the appropriate resource dynamically, as shown highlighted in the following markup:

```xml
<?xml version="1.0" encoding="utf-8" ?>
<ContentPage xmlns="http://schemas.microsoft.com/dotnet/2021/maui"
             xmlns:x="http://schemas.microsoft.com/winfx/2009/xaml"
             xmlns:local="clr-namespace:Northwind.Maui.Client"
             x:Class="Northwind.Maui.Client.MainPage">

  <ScrollView>
    <VerticalStackLayout Spacing="25" Padding="30,0"
                         VerticalOptions="Center">

      <Image Source="dotnet_bot.png" SemanticProperties.Description=
             "Cute dot net bot waving hi to you!"
             HeightRequest="200" HorizontalOptions="Center" />

      <Label TextColor="{DynamicResource TextColor}"
             Text="Hello, World!"
             SemanticProperties.HeadingLevel="Level1"
             FontSize="32" HorizontalOptions="Center" />

      <Label TextColor="{DynamicResource TextColor}"
             Text="Welcome to .NET Multi-platform App UI"
             SemanticProperties.HeadingLevel="Level2"
             SemanticProperties.Description="Welcome to dot net Multi
platform App U I"
             FontSize="18"
             HorizontalOptions="Center" />

      <Button TextColor="{DynamicResource TextColor}"
              BackgroundColor="{DynamicResource BackgroundColor}"
              x:Name="CounterBtn" Text="Click me"
              SemanticProperties.Hint="Counts the number of times you
click"
              Clicked="OnCounterClicked" HorizontalOptions="Center" />

    </VerticalStackLayout>
  </ScrollView>

</ContentPage>
```

3. In `SettingsPage.xaml`, add a handler for the content page's `Loaded` event, change the `Title` to `Settings`, set the `Padding` of the vertical stack layout to `10`, add content to define a form for changing the two colors, and note that the button is also dynamically bound to the color resources so the user will see the effect immediately, as shown highlighted in the following markup:

```xml
<?xml version="1.0" encoding="utf-8" ?>
<ContentPage xmlns="http://schemas.microsoft.com/dotnet/2021/maui"
             xmlns:x="http://schemas.microsoft.com/winfx/2009/xaml"
             x:Class="Northwind.Maui.Client.SettingsPage"
             xmlns:local="clr-namespace:Northwind.Maui.Client"
             Loaded="ContentPage_Loaded"
             Title="Settings">

  <VerticalStackLayout Padding="10">

    <Label Text="Text Color" />
    <Entry x:Name="TextColorEntry"
           TextChanged="TextColorEntry_TextChanged" />

    <Label Text="Background Color" />
    <Entry x:Name="BackgroundColorEntry"
           TextChanged="BackgroundColorEntry_TextChanged" />

    <Button x:Name="ApplyButton" Text="Apply"
            TextColor="{DynamicResource TextColor}"
            BackgroundColor="{DynamicResource BackgroundColor}"
            Clicked="ApplyButton_Clicked" IsEnabled="false" />

  </VerticalStackLayout>

</ContentPage>
```

4. In `SettingsPage.xaml.cs`, add statements to handle the events for changing the two colors, as shown highlighted in the following code:

```csharp
using System.Reflection; // FieldInfo

namespace Northwind.Maui.Client;

public partial class SettingsPage : ContentPage
{
  public SettingsPage()
  {
    InitializeComponent();
  }
```

```csharp
private const string textColorKey = "TextColor";
private const string backgroundColorKey = "BackgroundColor";

private async void ApplyButton_Clicked(object sender, EventArgs e)
{
  try
  {
    App.Current.Resources[textColorKey] =
      Color.Parse(TextColorEntry.Text);

    App.Current.Resources[backgroundColorKey] =
      Color.Parse(BackgroundColorEntry.Text);
  }
  catch (Exception ex)
  {
    await DisplayAlert(title: "Exception",
      message: ex.Message, cancel: "OK");
  }
}

private async void ContentPage_Loaded(object sender, EventArgs e)
{
  try
  {
    object color;

    if (App.Current.Resources.TryGetValue(textColorKey, out color))
    {
      TextColorEntry.Text = GetNameFromColor(color as Color);
    }

    if (App.Current.Resources.TryGetValue(backgroundColorKey, out
color))
    {
      BackgroundColorEntry.Text = GetNameFromColor(color as Color);
    }
  }
  catch (Exception ex)
  {
    await DisplayAlert(title: "Exception",
      message: ex.Message, cancel: "OK");
  }
}

private string GetNameFromColor(Color color)
{
```

```
        Type colorsType = typeof(Colors);

        FieldInfo info = colorsType.GetFields().Where(
          field => field.GetValue(field) == color).SingleOrDefault();

        return info?.Name;
    }

    private void TextColorEntry_TextChanged(
      object sender, TextChangedEventArgs e)
    {
      if (!ApplyButton.IsEnabled) ApplyButton.IsEnabled = true;
    }

    private void BackgroundColorEntry_TextChanged(
      object sender, TextChangedEventArgs e)
    {
      if (!ApplyButton.IsEnabled) ApplyButton.IsEnabled = true;
    }
}
```

5.   Start the `Northwind.Maui.Client` project with debugging. Try it with at least one desktop and mobile device.

6.   Note that the color of the text in the labels on the home page is black and the button background is silver.

7.   Navigate to **Settings** and note that the color resource names are loaded into the two `Entry` controls so the user can change them, and the **Apply** button is currently disabled, as shown on a Windows machine in *Figure 18.15*:

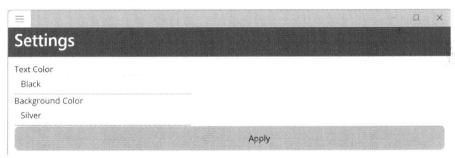

*Figure 18.15: A Settings page for changing text and background colors on Windows*

8.   Change the text color from **Black** to **Navy**, change the background color from **Silver** to **Pink**, click the **Apply** button, and note that the button changes its colors.

9.   Navigate to the **Home** page and note that the labels and button colors have changed here too.

10.  Return to the **Settings** page, change the text color to `Green` and the background color to `LightYellow`, and then click the **Apply** button.

11. Navigate to the **Home** page and note that the labels and button colors have changed again, as shown in *Figure 18.16*:

Figure 18.16: Text and background colors of the Home page button have changed on Windows

12. Close the app.

**Good Practice:** A resource can be an instance of any object. To share it within an application, define it in the `App.xaml` file and give it a unique key. To set an element's property with a resource once when the app first starts, use `{StaticResource key}`. To set an element's property with a resource whenever the resource value changes during the lifetime of the app, use `{DynamicResource key}`. To load a resource using code, use the `TryGetValue` method of the `Resources` property. If you treat the `Resources` property as a dictionary and use array-style syntax, like `Resources[key]`, it will only find resources defined directly in the dictionary, not in any merged dictionaries

Resources can be defined and stored inside any element of XAML, not just at the app level. For example, if a resource is only needed on `MainPage`, then it can be defined there. You can also dynamically load XAML files at runtime.

**More Information:** You can read more about .NET MAUI resource dictionaries at the following link: `https://docs.microsoft.com/en-us/dotnet/maui/fundamentals/resource-dictionaries`. In particular, note the section about resource lookup behavior.

# Using data binding

When building graphical user interfaces, you will often want to bind a property of one control to another, or to some data.

## Binding to elements

The simplest type of binding is between two elements. One element acts as a source for a value and the other element acts as the target:

1.  In `CategoriesPage.xaml`, under the existing button in the vertical stack layout, add a label for instructions, another label to show the current degree of rotation, a slider for selecting a rotation, and a rainbow square to rotate, as shown highlighted in the following markup:

```xml
<?xml version="1.0" encoding="utf-8" ?>
<ContentPage xmlns="http://schemas.microsoft.com/dotnet/2021/maui"
             xmlns:x="http://schemas.microsoft.com/winfx/2009/xaml"
             x:Class="Northwind.Maui.Client.CategoriesPage"
             Background="{StaticResource rainbow}"
             Title="Categories">

  <VerticalStackLayout>

    <Button Text="Click Me" WidthRequest="100"
            x:Name="ClickMeButton"
            Clicked="ClickMeButton_Clicked" />

    <Label Margin="10">
      Use the slider to rotate the square:
    </Label>

    <Label BindingContext="{x:Reference Name=sliderRotation}"
           Text="{Binding Path=Value, StringFormat='{0:N0} degrees'}"
           FontSize="30" HorizontalTextAlignment="Center" />

    <Slider Value="0" Minimum="0" Maximum="180"
            x:Name="sliderRotation" Margin="10,0" />

    <Rectangle HeightRequest="200" WidthRequest="200"
               Fill="{StaticResource rainbow}"
               BindingContext="{x:Reference Name=sliderRotation}"
               Rotation="{Binding Path=Value}" />

  </VerticalStackLayout>

</ContentPage>
```

2.  Note that the text of the label and the angle of the rotation of the rectangle are both bound to the slider's value using a binding context and the `{Binding}` markup extension.
3.  Start the `Northwind.Maui.Client` project with debugging.
4.  Navigate to the **Categories** page.

5. Click and pull the slider to change the rotation of the rainbow square, as shown in *Figure 18.17*:

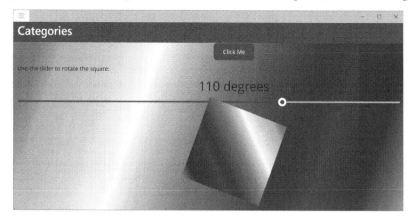

*Figure 18.17: A slider data-bound to a label and the rotation of a rectangle on Windows*

6. Close the app.

# Understanding MVVM

Model-View-ViewModel (**MVVM**) is a design pattern like MVC. The letters in the acronym stand for:

- **Model:** An entity class that represents a data object in a store like a relational database.
- **View:** A way to represent data in a graphical user interface including fields to show and edit data fields and buttons and other elements to interact with the data.
- **ViewModel:** A class that represents the data fields, actions, and events that can then be bound to elements like text boxes and buttons in a view.

In MVC, models passed to a view are read-only because they are only passed one-way into the view. That is why immutable records are good for MVC models. But view models are different. They need to support two-way interactions and if the original data changes during the lifetime of the object, the view needs to dynamically update.

## INotifyPropertyChanged interface

The INotifyPropertyChanged interface enables a model class to support two-way data binding. It works by forcing the class to have an event named PropertyChanged, with a parameter of type PropertyChangedEventArgs, as shown in the following code:

```
namespace System.ComponentModel
{
  public class PropertyChangedEventArgs : EventArgs
  {
    public PropertyChangedEventArgs(string? propertyName);
    public virtual string? PropertyName { get; }
  }
```

```
  public delegate void PropertyChangedEventHandler(
    object? sender, PropertyChangedEventArgs e);

  public interface INotifyPropertyChanged
  {
    event PropertyChangedEventHandler PropertyChanged;
  }
}
```

Inside each property in the class, when setting a new value, you must raise the event (if it is not null) with an instance of PropertyChangedEventArgs containing the name of the property as a string value, as shown in the following code:

```
private string companyName;

public string CompanyName
{
  get => companyName;
  set
  {
    companyName = value; // store the new value being set
    PropertyChanged?.Invoke(this,
      new PropertyChangedEventArgs(nameof(CompanyName)));
  }
}
```

When a user interface control is data-bound to the property, it will automatically update to show the new value when it changes.

To simplify the implementation, we can use a compiler feature to get the name of the property by decorating a string parameter with the [CallerMemberName] attribute, as shown in the following code:

```
private void NotifyPropertyChanged(
  [CallerMemberName] string propertyName = "")
{
  // if an event handler has been set then invoke
  // the delegate and pass the name of the property
  PropertyChanged?.Invoke(this,
    new PropertyChangedEventArgs(propertyName));
}

public string CompanyName
{
  get => companyName;
  set
  {
    companyName = value; // store the new value being set
    NotifyPropertyChanged(); // caller member name is "CompanyName"
  }
}
```

> You can reference the .NET Community Toolkit NuGet package to make implementing
> MVVM easier. You can read more about it at the following link: `https://devblogs.`
> `microsoft.com/dotnet/announcing-the-dotnet-community-toolkit-800/`.

## ObservableCollection class

Related to `INotifyPropertyChanged` is the `INotifyCollectionChanged` interface, which is implemented by the `ObservableCollection<T>` class. This gives notifications when items get added or removed
or when the collection is refreshed. When bound to controls like `ListView` or `TreeView`, the user
interface will update dynamically to reflect changes.

## Creating a view model with two-way data binding

We need to create a view model that will allow us to show and modify a customer entity, so the class
should implement two-way data binding:

1.  In the `Northwind.Maui.Client` project folder, create two classes, one named
    `CustomerDetailViewModel.cs` to show the details of a single customer and one named
    `CustomersListViewModel.cs` to show a list of customers.

2.  In `CustomerDetailViewModel.cs`, modify the statements to define a class that implements the
    `INotifyPropertyChanged` interface and has six read-write properties that will support two-way
    data binding and one read-only property, as shown in the following code:

```csharp
using System.ComponentModel; // INotifyPropertyChanged
using System.Runtime.CompilerServices; // [CallerMemberName]

namespace Northwind.Maui.Client;

public class CustomerDetailViewModel : INotifyPropertyChanged
{
  public event PropertyChangedEventHandler PropertyChanged;

  private string customerId;
  private string companyName;
  private string contactName;
  private string city;
  private string country;
  private string phone;

  // this attribute sets the propertyName parameter
  // using the context in which this method is called
  private void NotifyPropertyChanged(
    [CallerMemberName] string propertyName = "")
  {
    // if an event handler has been set then invoke
```

```csharp
    // the delegate and pass the name of the property
    PropertyChanged?.Invoke(this,
      new PropertyChangedEventArgs(propertyName));
}

public string CustomerId
{
  get => customerId;
  set
  {
    customerId = value;
    NotifyPropertyChanged();
  }
}

public string CompanyName
{
  get => companyName;
  set
  {
    companyName = value;
    NotifyPropertyChanged();
  }
}

public string ContactName
{
  get => contactName;
  set
  {
    contactName = value;
    NotifyPropertyChanged();
  }
}

public string City
{
  get => city;
  set
  {
    city = value;
    NotifyPropertyChanged();
    NotifyPropertyChanged(nameof(Location));
  }
}
```

```
public string Country
{
  get => country;
  set
  {
    country = value;
    NotifyPropertyChanged();
    NotifyPropertyChanged(nameof(Location));
  }
}

public string Phone
{
  get => phone;
  set
  {
    phone = value;
    NotifyPropertyChanged();
  }
}

public string Location
{
  get => $"{City}, {Country}";
}
}
```

Note the following:

- The class implements INotifyPropertyChanged, so a two-way bound control like Editor will update the property and vice versa. There is a PropertyChanged event that is raised whenever one of the properties is modified, using a NotifyPropertyChanged private method to simplify the implementation.
- In addition to properties for storing values retrieved from the HTTP service, the class defines a read-only Location property. This will be bound to a summary list of customers to show the location of each one. Whenever the City or Country property changes, we also need to notify any data bindings that the Location has changed, or any views bound to Location would not update correctly.

3. In CustomersListViewModel.cs, modify the statements to define a class that inherits from ObservableCollection<T> and has a method to populate sample data, as shown in the following code:

```
using System.Collections.ObjectModel; // ObservableCollection<T>

namespace Northwind.Maui.Client;
```

```
public class CustomersListViewModel :
  ObservableCollection<CustomerDetailViewModel>
{
  // for testing before calling web service
  public void AddSampleData(bool clearList = true)
  {
    if (clearList) Clear();

    Add(new CustomerDetailViewModel
    {
      CustomerId = "ALFKI",
      CompanyName = "Alfreds Futterkiste",
      ContactName = "Maria Anders",
      City = "Berlin",
      Country = "Germany",
      Phone = "030-0074321"
    });

    Add(new CustomerDetailViewModel
    {
      CustomerId = "FRANK",
      CompanyName = "Frankenversand",
      ContactName = "Peter Franken",
      City = "München",
      Country = "Germany",
      Phone = "089-0877310"
    });

    Add(new CustomerDetailViewModel
    {
      CustomerId = "SEVES",
      CompanyName = "Seven Seas Imports",
      ContactName = "Hari Kumar",
      City = "London",
      Country = "UK",
      Phone = "(171) 555-1717"
    });
  }
}
```

Note the following:

- After loading from the service, which will be implemented later in this chapter, the customers are cached locally using ObservableCollection<T>. This supports notifications to any bound user interface components, such as ListView, so that the user interface can redraw itself when the underlying data adds or removes items from the collection.

- For testing purposes, when the HTTP service is not available, there is a static method to populate three sample customers.

## Creating views for the customers list and customer details

You will now add a view to show a list of customers and a view to show the details for a customer:

1. In `CustomersPage.xaml`, change the `Title` to `Customers`, add padding and spacing to the vertical stack layout, and then modify its contents to define a list view of customers, each one showing their company name and location, as shown highlighted in the following markup:

```xml
<?xml version="1.0" encoding="utf-8" ?>
<ContentPage xmlns="http://schemas.microsoft.com/dotnet/2021/maui"
             xmlns:x="http://schemas.microsoft.com/winfx/2009/xaml"
             x:Class="Northwind.Maui.Client.CustomersPage"
             Title="Customers">

  <VerticalStackLayout Spacing="15" Padding="20">

    <HorizontalStackLayout Spacing="10">
      <Label Text="Customers" FontSize="Title" />
      <Button Text="Add" Clicked="Add_Clicked" HorizontalOptions="End" />
    </HorizontalStackLayout>
    <ListView ItemsSource="{Binding .}"
              VerticalOptions="Start"
              HorizontalOptions="Start"
              IsPullToRefreshEnabled="True"
              ItemTapped="Customer_Tapped"
              Refreshing="Customers_Refreshing">
      <ListView.ItemTemplate>
        <DataTemplate>
          <TextCell Text="{Binding CompanyName}"
                    Detail="{Binding Location}"
                    TextColor="{DynamicResource PrimaryTextColor}"
                    DetailColor="{DynamicResource PrimaryTextColor}" >
            <TextCell.ContextActions>
              <MenuItem Clicked="Customer_Phoned" Text="Phone" />
              <MenuItem Clicked="Customer_Deleted" Text="Delete"
                        IsDestructive="True" />
            </TextCell.ContextActions>
          </TextCell>
        </DataTemplate>
      </ListView.ItemTemplate>
    </ListView>

  </VerticalStackLayout>

</ContentPage>
```

Note the following:

- ListView has its IsPullToRefreshEnabled set to true.
- An **Add** button is in the list view header so that users can navigate to a detail view to add a new customer.
- A data template defines how to display each customer: larger text for the company name and smaller text for the location underneath.
- Event handlers have been written for the following events:

  - Customer_Tapped: A customer being tapped or clicked to show their details.
  - Customers_Refreshing: The list being pulled down to refresh its items.
  - Customer_Phoned: A cell being swiped left on iPhone, long pressed on Android, or right-clicked on Windows, and then tapping or clicking **Phone**.
  - Customer_Deleted: A cell being swiped left on iPhone, long pressed on Android, or right-clicked on Windows, and then tapping or clicking **Delete**.
  - Add_Clicked: The **Add** button being clicked or tapped.

2. In CustomersPage.xaml.cs, modify the contents to create the view model, populate it with sample data, and set it as the binding context, as well as implement event handlers for all the control events, as shown highlighted in the following code:

```
namespace Northwind.Maui.Client;

public partial class CustomersPage : ContentPage
{
  public CustomersPage()
  {
    InitializeComponent();

    CustomersListViewModel viewModel = new();
    viewModel.AddSampleData();
    BindingContext = viewModel;
  }

  async void Customer_Tapped(object sender, ItemTappedEventArgs e)
  {
    if (e.Item is not CustomerDetailViewModel c) return;

    // navigate to the detail view and show the tapped customer
    await Navigation.PushAsync(new CustomerDetailPage(
      BindingContext as CustomersListViewModel, c));
  }

  async void Customers_Refreshing(object sender, EventArgs e)
  {
    if (sender is not ListView listView) return;
```

```csharp
  listView.IsRefreshing = true;

  // simulate a refresh
  await Task.Delay(1500);

  listView.IsRefreshing = false;
}

void Customer_Deleted(object sender, EventArgs e)
{
  MenuItem menuItem = sender as MenuItem;
  if (menuItem.BindingContext is not CustomerDetailViewModel c) return;
  (BindingContext as CustomersListViewModel).Remove(c);
}

async void Customer_Phoned(object sender, EventArgs e)
{
  MenuItem menuItem = sender as MenuItem;
  if (menuItem.BindingContext is not CustomerDetailViewModel c) return;

  if (await DisplayAlert("Dial a Number",
    "Would you like to call " + c.Phone + "?",
    "Yes", "No"))
  {
    try
    {
      if (PhoneDialer.IsSupported)
      {
        PhoneDialer.Open(c.Phone);
      }
    }
    catch (Exception ex)
    {
      await DisplayAlert(title: "Failed",
        message: string.Format(
          "Failed to dial {0} due to: {1}", c.Phone, ex.Message),
        cancel: "OK");
    }
  }
}

async void Add_Clicked(object sender, EventArgs e)
{
  await Navigation.PushAsync(new CustomerDetailPage(
```

```
        BindingContext as CustomersListViewModel));
    }
}
```

Note the following:

- BindingContext is set to an instance of CustomersViewModel that is populated with sample data in the constructor of the page.
- When a customer in the list view is tapped, the user is taken to a details view (which you will implement in the next step).
- When the list view is pulled down, it triggers a simulated refresh that takes 1.5 seconds.
- When a customer is deleted in the list view, they are removed from the bound customers view model.
- When a customer in the list view is swiped, and the **Phone** button is tapped, a dialog prompts the user as to whether they want to dial the number, and if so, the platform-native implementation will be retrieved using the dependency resolver and then used to dial the number.
- When the **Add** button is tapped, the user is taken to the customer detail page to enter details for a new customer.

3. In CustomerDetailPage.xaml, modify its contents to define a user interface to review and edit the details of a customer, as shown highlighted in the following markup, and note the following:

- The Title of the content page has been set to Customer Detail.
- A Grid with two columns and six rows is used for the layout.
- Entry views are two-way data bound to properties of the CustomerViewModel class.
- InsertButton has an event handler to execute code to add a new customer:

```xml
<?xml version="1.0" encoding="utf-8" ?>
<ContentPage
    xmlns="http://schemas.microsoft.com/dotnet/2021/maui"
    xmlns:x="http://schemas.microsoft.com/winfx/2009/xaml"
    x:Class="Northwind.Maui.Client.CustomerDetailPage"
    Title="Customer Detail">

    <VerticalStackLayout>

        <Grid ColumnDefinitions="Auto,Auto"
              RowDefinitions="Auto,Auto,Auto,Auto,Auto,Auto">
            <Label Text="Customer Id" VerticalOptions="Center" Margin="6" />
            <Entry Text="{Binding CustomerId, Mode=TwoWay}" Grid.Column="1"
                   MaxLength="5" TextTransform="Uppercase" />
            <Label Text="Company Name" Grid.Row="1"
                   VerticalOptions="Center" Margin="6" />
            <Entry Text="{Binding CompanyName, Mode=TwoWay}"
```

```
                    Grid.Column="1" Grid.Row="1" />
        <Label Text="Contact Name" Grid.Row="2"
                    VerticalOptions="Center" Margin="6" />
        <Entry Text="{Binding ContactName, Mode=TwoWay}"
                    Grid.Column="1" Grid.Row="2" />
        <Label Text="City" Grid.Row="3"
                    VerticalOptions="Center" Margin="6" />
        <Entry Text="{Binding City, Mode=TwoWay}"
                    Grid.Column="1" Grid.Row="3" />
        <Label Text="Country" Grid.Row="4"
                    VerticalOptions="Center" Margin="6" />
        <Entry Text="{Binding Country, Mode=TwoWay}"
                    Grid.Column="1" Grid.Row="4" />
        <Label Text="Phone" Grid.Row="5"
                    VerticalOptions="Center" Margin="6" />
        <Entry Text="{Binding Phone, Mode=TwoWay}"
                    Grid.Column="1" Grid.Row="5" />
    </Grid>
    <Button x:Name="InsertButton" Text="Insert Customer"
                Clicked="InsertButton_Clicked" />

  </VerticalStackLayout>

</ContentPage>
```

> A control that is a child of a `Grid` automatically has its `Grid.Row` and `Grid.Column` set to 0. Therefore, controls like the `Customer Id` label do not need those properties to be explicitly set, and controls like the `CustomerId` entry only need the column set.

4.  In `CustomerDetailPage.xaml.cs`, modify its contents to create a view model and set it as the binding context, and implement the **Insert** button, as shown highlighted in the following code:

```
namespace Northwind.Maui.Client;

public partial class CustomerDetailPage : ContentPage
{
  private CustomersListViewModel customers;

  public CustomerDetailPage(CustomersListViewModel customers)
  {
    InitializeComponent();

    this.customers = customers;
    BindingContext = new CustomerDetailViewModel();
    Title = "Add Customer";
```

```
        }

    public CustomerDetailPage(CustomersListViewModel customers,
        CustomerDetailViewModel customer)
    {
        InitializeComponent();

        this.customers = customers;
        BindingContext = customer;
        InsertButton.IsVisible = false;
    }

    async void InsertButton_Clicked(object sender, EventArgs e)
    {
        customers.Add((CustomerDetailViewModel)BindingContext);
        await Navigation.PopAsync(animated: true);
    }
}
```

Note the following:

- The default constructor has been deleted.

- The constructor with a `customers` parameter sets the binding context to a new customer instance and the view title is changed to **Add Customer**.

- The constructor with a `customers` parameter and a `customer` parameter sets the binding context to that instance and hides the **Insert** button because it is not needed when editing an existing customer due to two-way data binding.

- When the **Insert** button is tapped, the new customer is added to the customers view model and the navigation is moved back to the previous view asynchronously.

5. In the `Platforms` folder, in the `Android` folder, open the `AndroidManifest.xml` file and add entries to enable phone dialing, as shown highlighted in the following markup:

```
<?xml version="1.0" encoding="utf-8"?>
<manifest xmlns:android="http://schemas.android.com/apk/res/android">
  <application android:allowBackup="true"
               android:icon="@mipmap/appicon"
               android:roundIcon="@mipmap/appicon_round"
               android:supportsRtl="true"></application>
  <uses-permission android:name="android.permission.ACCESS_NETWORK_STATE"
/>
  <uses-permission android:name="android.permission.INTERNET" />
  <queries>
    <intent>
      <action android:name="android.intent.action.DIAL" />
      <data android:scheme="tel"/>
    </intent>
```

```
    </queries>
  </manifest>
```

# Testing the .NET MAUI app

We will now test the app using the Android device emulator so that we can see the phone caller functionality:

1.  In Visual Studio 2022, to the right of the **Run** button in the toolbar, set the target **Framework** to **net7.0-android** and select the Android emulator.

2.  Start the project with debugging. The project will build, and then after a few moments, the Android device emulator will appear with your running .NET MAUI app.

3.  Navigate to **Customers**, as shown in *Figure 18.18*:

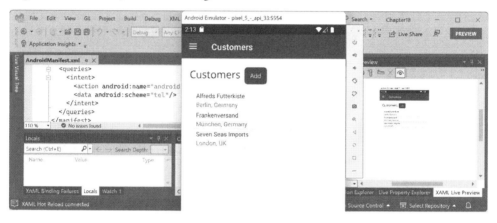

*Figure 18.18: The Android device emulator running the Northwind .NET MAUI app and showing Customers*

4.  Click **Seven Seas Imports** and modify **Company Name** to `Seven Oceans Imports`, as shown in the following screenshot of the **customer detail** page in *Figure 18.19*:

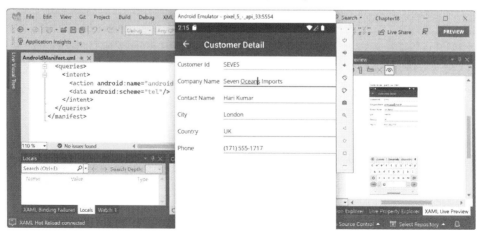

*Figure 18.19: Editing a company name on the Customer Detail page*

5. Click the back button to return to the list of customers and note that the company name has been updated due to the two-way data binding.

6. Click **Add**, and then fill in the fields for a new customer, as shown in *Figure 18.20*.

 By default, in the Android device emulator, the virtual keyboard is shown when typing on a physical keyboard. To hide the virtual keyboard, click the keyboard icon to the right of the square Android soft button, and then toggle **Show virtual keyboard**.

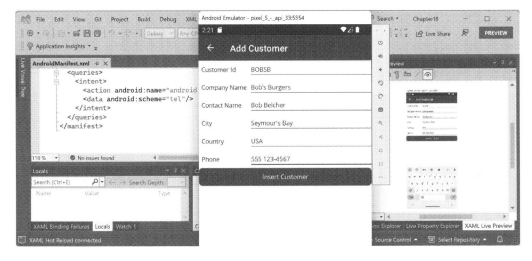

*Figure 18.20: Completing the details to add a new customer*

7. On the **Customer Detail** page, click the **Insert Customer** button and, after being returned to the list of customers, note that the new customer has been added to the bottom of the list.

8. Click and hold on one of the customers to reveal two action buttons, **Phone** and **Delete**, as shown in *Figure 18.21*:

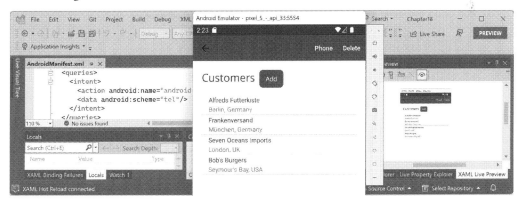

*Figure 18.21: Extra commands for a selected customer*

9.  Click **Phone** and note the pop-up prompt to the user to dial the number of that customer with
    **Yes** and **No** buttons, as shown in *Figure 18.22*:

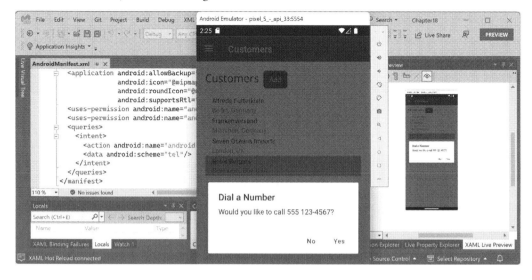

*Figure 18.22: Prompting to dial a phone number*

10. Click **Yes**.

11. Note the app switches to the device's native phone dialer, as shown in *Figure 18.23*:

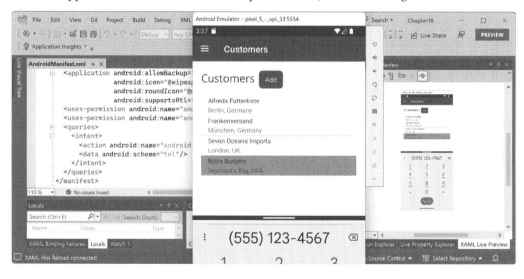

*Figure 18.23: The native device phone dialer*

12. In the emulator, click the back button (the back-pointing triangle) three times to return to
    the app.

13. Click and hold on one of the customers to reveal two action buttons, **Phone** and **Delete**, and
    then click on **Delete**, and note that the customer is removed.

14. Click, hold, and drag the list down and then release, and note the animation effect for refreshing the list, but remember that this feature is simulated, so the list does not change.

15. Close the Android device emulator.

We will now make the app call a web service to get the list of customers.

# Consuming a web service from a mobile app

Apple's **App Transport Security** (**ATS**) forces developers to use good practice, including secure connections between an app and a web service. ATS is enabled by default and your mobile apps will throw an exception if they do not connect securely. Since Android 9, Google has had a similar policy.

If you need to call a web service that is secured with a self-signed certificate like our `Northwind.Maui.WebApi.Service` project is, it is possible but complicated. For simplicity, we will allow unsecure connections to the web service and disable the security checks in the mobile app.

## Creating a Minimal API web service for customers

We will create a web service for working with customers in the Northwind database:

1.  In the `Chapter18` solution, add a web service project, as defined in the following list:

    *   Project template: **ASP.NET Core Web API**/`webapi --use-minimal-apis`
    *   Workspace/solution file and folder: `Chapter18`
    *   Project file and folder: `Northwind.Maui.WebApi.Service`
    *   **Authentication type:** None
    *   **Configure for HTTPS:** Selected
    *   **Enable Docker:** Cleared
    *   **Use controllers (uncheck to use minimal APIs):** Cleared
    *   **Enable OpenAPI support:** Selected
    *   **Do not use top-level statements:** Cleared

2.  Add a project reference to the Northwind database context project for SQL Server that you created in *Chapter 2, Managing Relational Data Using SQL Server*, as shown in the following markup:

    ```
    <ItemGroup>
      <ProjectReference Include="..\..\Chapter02\Northwind.Common.DataContext
    .SqlServer\Northwind.Common.DataContext.SqlServer.csproj" />
    </ItemGroup>
    ```

The path cannot have a line break. If you did not complete the task to create the class libraries in *Chapter 2, Managing Relational Data Using SQL Server*, then download the solution projects from the GitHub repository.

3. At the command line or terminal, build the `Northwind.Maui.WebApi.Service` project to make sure the entity model class library projects outside the current solution are properly compiled, as shown in the following command:

```
dotnet build
```

4. In the `Properties` folder, in `launchSettings.json`, modify the `applicationUrl` to use port 5181 for `https` and port 5182 for `http`, as shown highlighted in the following configuration:

```
"profiles": {
  "http": {
    "commandName": "Project",
    "dotnetRunMessages": true,
    "launchBrowser": true,
    "launchUrl": "swagger",
    "applicationUrl": "http://localhost:5182",
    "environmentVariables": {
      "ASPNETCORE_ENVIRONMENT": "Development"
    }
  },
  "https": {
    "commandName": "Project",
    "dotnetRunMessages": true,
    "launchBrowser": true,
    "launchUrl": "swagger",
    "applicationUrl": "https://localhost:5181;http://localhost:5182",
    "environmentVariables": {
      "ASPNETCORE_ENVIRONMENT": "Development"
    }
  },
```

5. In `Program.cs`, delete the statements about the weather service and replace them with statements to configure endpoints for CRUD operations on customers, as shown highlighted in the following code:

```
using Microsoft.AspNetCore.Mvc; // [FromServices]
using Packt.Shared; // AddNorthwindContext extension method

var builder = WebApplication.CreateBuilder(args);

// Add services to the container.
// Learn more about configuring Swagger/OpenAPI at https://aka.ms/
aspnetcore/swashbuckle
builder.Services.AddEndpointsApiExplorer();
builder.Services.AddSwaggerGen();

builder.Services.AddNorthwindContext();
```

```csharp
var app = builder.Build();

// Configure the HTTP request pipeline.
if (app.Environment.IsDevelopment())
{
  app.UseSwagger();
  app.UseSwaggerUI();
}

app.UseHttpsRedirection();

app.MapGet("api/customers", (
  [FromServices] NorthwindContext db) => db.Customers)
  .WithName("GetCustomers")
  .Produces<Customer[]>(StatusCodes.Status200OK);

app.MapGet("api/customers/{id}", (
  [FromRoute] string id,
  [FromServices] NorthwindContext db) => db.Customers
    .FirstOrDefault(c => c.CustomerId == id))
  .WithName("GetCustomer")
  .Produces<Customer>(StatusCodes.Status200OK);

app.MapPost("api/customers", async (
  [FromBody] Customer customer,
  [FromServices] NorthwindContext db) =>
{
  db.Customers.Add(customer);
  await db.SaveChangesAsync();
  return Results.Created($"api/customers/{customer.CustomerId}",
customer);
}).WithOpenApi()
  .Produces<Customer>(StatusCodes.Status201Created);

app.MapPut("api/customers/{id}", async (
  [FromRoute] string id,
  [FromBody] Customer customer,
  [FromServices] NorthwindContext db) =>
{
  Customer? foundCustomer = await db.Customers.FindAsync(id);

  if (foundCustomer is null) return Results.NotFound();

  foundCustomer.CompanyName = customer.CompanyName;
  foundCustomer.ContactName = customer.ContactName;
  foundCustomer.ContactTitle = customer.ContactTitle;
```

```
  foundCustomer.Address = customer.Address;
  foundCustomer.City = customer.City;
  foundCustomer.Region = customer.Region;
  foundCustomer.PostalCode = customer.PostalCode;
  foundCustomer.Country = customer.Country;
  foundCustomer.Phone = customer.Phone;
  foundCustomer.Fax = customer.Fax;

  await db.SaveChangesAsync();

  return Results.NoContent();
}).WithOpenApi()
  .Produces(StatusCodes.Status404NotFound)
  .Produces(StatusCodes.Status204NoContent);

app.MapDelete("api/customers/{id}", async (
  [FromRoute] string id,
  [FromServices] NorthwindContext db) =>
{
  if (await db.Customers.FindAsync(id) is Customer customer)
  {
    db.Customers.Remove(customer);
    await db.SaveChangesAsync();
    return Results.NoContent();
  }
  return Results.NotFound();
}).WithOpenApi()
  .Produces(StatusCodes.Status404NotFound)
  .Produces(StatusCodes.Status204NoContent);

app.Run();
```

6. Start the web service project with the `https` profile and note the Swagger documentation, as shown in *Figure 18.24*:

*Figure 18.24: Swagger documentation for the Northwind Web API service*

7.  Click **GET /api/customers** to expand that section.

8.  Click the **Try it out** button, click the **Execute** button, and note that customer records are returned.

9.  Close the browser and shut down the web server.

## Configuring the web service to allow unsecure requests

Next, we will enable the web service to handle unsecure connections:

1.  In the `Northwind.Maui.WebApi.Service` project, in `Program.cs`, in the section that configures the HTTP pipeline, comment out the HTTPS redirection, as shown in the following code:

    ```
    // app.UseHttpsRedirection();
    ```

2.  Start the `Northwind.Maui.WebApi.Service` project without debugging.

3.  Start Chrome and test that the web service is returning customers as JSON by navigating to `http://localhost:5182/api/customers/` and note the returned JSON document, as shown in *Figure 18.25*:

*Figure 18.25: Customers returned as a JSON document*

4.  Close Chrome but leave the web service running.

## Connecting to local web services while testing

When testing a .NET MAUI app on the Windows machine, it has normal access to the local network including any web services you are hosting on localhost. The iOS emulator also has normal access to the local network. So, both Windows- and iOS-targeted .NET MAUI apps can connect directly to a web service hosted at an endpoint like `http://localhost:5182/api/customer`.

But when testing a .NET MAUI app on an emulated Android device, it is separated from your local network by a virtual router. To connect to a web service hosted on localhost, you must use a special IP address `10.0.2.2` that the virtual router maps to `127.0.0.1`, aka localhost. So, Android-targeted .NET MAUI apps can connect to a web service hosted at an endpoint like `http://localhost:5182/api/customer` by using `http://10.0.2.2:5182/api/customer`.

## Configuring the iOS app to allow unsecure connections

To allow unsecure connections to web services in an iOS app, we have a couple of choices:

- Set `NSAppTransportSecurity` to `NSAllowsArbitraryLoads`. This allows cleartext in all scenarios.
- Set `NSAppTransportSecurity` to `NSAllowsLocalNetworking`. This allows cleartext only in local scenarios.

Now you will configure the `Northwind.Maui.Customers` project to disable ATS to allow unsecure HTTP requests to the web service:

1. In the `Northwind.Maui.Client` project, in the `Platforms/iOS` folder, right-click the `Info.plist` file and open it with the **XML (Text) Editor**.

2. At the bottom of the dictionary, add a new key named `NSAppTransportSecurity` that is a dictionary, and in it, add a key named `NSAllowsArbitraryLoads` that has a value of `true`, as shown highlighted in the following partial markup:

```xml
<?xml version="1.0" encoding="UTF-8"?>
<!DOCTYPE plist PUBLIC "-//Apple//DTD PLIST 1.0//EN"
          "http://www.apple.com/DTDs/PropertyList-1.0.dtd">
<plist version="1.0">
<dict>
  <key>LSRequiresIPhoneOS</key>
  <true/>
  ...
  <key>XSAppIconAssets</key>
  <string>Assets.xcassets/appicon.appiconset</string>
  <key>NSAppTransportSecurity</key>
  <dict>
    <key>NSAllowsArbitraryLoads</key>
    <true/>
  </dict>
</dict>
</plist>
```

3. Save and close `Info.plist`.

**Warning!** If you run a .NET MAUI app using the iOS simulator on Windows, the app is actually running on the connected Mac even though it visually appears on Windows. It therefore cannot connect to local web services. It would have to connect remotely to the web service, or you could run the web service on the Mac.

## Configuring the Android app to allow unsecure connections

In a similar way to Apple and ATS, with Android 9 (API level 28) cleartext (that is, non-HTTPS) support is disabled by default.

Now you will configure the project to enable cleartext to allow unsecure HTTP requests to the web service:

1. In the `Platforms/Android` folder, in the `Resources` folder, add a new folder named `xml`.

2. In the `xml` folder, add a new XML file named `network_security_config.xml`, and add entries to enable cleartext when connecting over the virtual router's special IP address that maps out to localhost, as shown in the following markup:

```xml
<?xml version="1.0" encoding="utf-8" ?>
<network-security-config>
  <domain-config cleartextTrafficPermitted="true">
    <domain includeSubdomains="true">10.0.2.2</domain>
  </domain-config>
</network-security-config>
```

3. In the `Android` folder, in `AndroidManifest.xml`, add an attribute to the `<application>` element to reference the new XML file, as shown highlighted in the following markup:

```xml
<?xml version="1.0" encoding="utf-8"?>
<manifest xmlns:android="http://schemas.android.com/apk/res/android">
  <application android:allowBackup="true"
               android:icon="@mipmap/appicon"
               android:networkSecurityConfig="@xml/network_security_config"
               android:roundIcon="@mipmap/appicon_round"
               android:supportsRtl="true">
  </application>
  <uses-permission android:name="android.permission.ACCESS_NETWORK_STATE" />
  <uses-permission android:name="android.permission.INTERNET" />
  <queries>
    <intent>
      <action android:name="android.intent.action.DIAL" />
      <data android:scheme="tel"/>
    </intent>
  </queries>
</manifest>
```

4. Save all the changes.

## Getting customers from the web service

Now, we can modify the customers list page to get its list of customers from the web service instead of using sample data:

1.  In the `Northwind.Maui.Client` project, in `CustomersPage.xaml`, add a label to show information about the web service endpoint and a label to show any error message, as shown in the following markup:

```
<VerticalStackLayout Spacing="15" Padding="20">
  <HorizontalStackLayout Spacing="10">
    <Label Text="Customers" FontSize="Title" />
    <Button Text="Add" Clicked="Add_Clicked" HorizontalOptions="End" />
  </HorizontalStackLayout>
  <Label x:Name="InfoLabel" />
  <Label x:Name="ErrorLabel" IsVisible="false" />
  <ListView ItemsSource="{Binding .}"
```

2.  In `CustomersPage.xaml.cs`, import the following additional namespaces:

```
using System.Net.Http.Headers; // MediaTypeWithQualityHeaderValue
using System.Net.Http.Json; // ReadFromJsonAsync<T>
```

3.  Modify the `CustomersPage` constructor to load the list of customers using the service proxy and only call the `AddSampleData` method if an exception occurs, as shown in the following code:

```
public CustomersPage()
{
  InitializeComponent();

  CustomersListViewModel viewModel = new();

  try
  {
    HttpClient client = new()
    {
      BaseAddress = new Uri(DeviceInfo.Platform == DevicePlatform.Android ?
        "http://10.0.2.2:5182" : "http://localhost:5182")
    };

    InfoLabel.Text = $"BaseAddress: {client.BaseAddress}";

    client.DefaultRequestHeaders.Accept.Add(
      new MediaTypeWithQualityHeaderValue("application/json"));

    HttpResponseMessage response = client
      .GetAsync("api/customers").Result;
```

```
    response.EnsureSuccessStatusCode();

    IEnumerable<CustomerDetailViewModel> customersFromService =
      response.Content.ReadFromJsonAsync
      <IEnumerable<CustomerDetailViewModel>>().Result;

    foreach (CustomerDetailViewModel c in customersFromService
      .OrderBy(customer => customer.CompanyName))
    {
      viewModel.Add(c);
    }

    InfoLabel.Text += $"\n{viewModel.Count} customers loaded.";
  }
  catch (Exception ex)
  {
    ErrorLabel.Text = ex.Message + "\nUsing sample data instead.";
    ErrorLabel.IsVisible = true;

    viewModel.AddSampleData();
  }

  BindingContext = viewModel;
}
```

4. Navigate to **Build | Clean Northwind.Maui.Client** because changes to `Info.plist` and `AndroidManifest.xml`, like allowing unsecure connections, sometimes require a clean build.

5. Navigate to **Build | Build Northwind.Maui.Client**.

6. If you did not previously leave the web service running, then start the `Northwind.Maui.WebApi.Service` project and note the endpoints it is listening on, as shown highlighted in the following output:

```
info: Microsoft.Hosting.Lifetime[14]
      Now listening on: https://localhost:5181
info: Microsoft.Hosting.Lifetime[14]
      Now listening on: http://localhost:5182
info: Microsoft.Hosting.Lifetime[0]
      Application started. Press Ctrl+C to shut down.
info: Microsoft.Hosting.Lifetime[0]
      Hosting environment: Development
info: Microsoft.Hosting.Lifetime[0]
      Content root path: C:\apps-services-net7\Chapter18\Northwind.Maui.
WebApi.Service
```

7. Run the `Northwind.Maui.Client` project, navigate to the **Customers** page, and note that 91 customers are loaded from the web service, as shown in *Figure 18.26*:

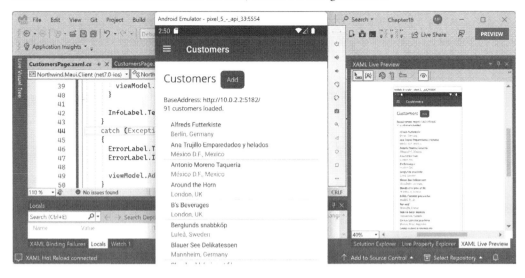

*Figure 18.26: Loading customers from a web service into the Northwind .NET MAUI app*

8. Close the app.

# Practicing and exploring

Test your knowledge and understanding by answering some questions, getting some hands-on practice, and exploring this chapter's topics with more in-depth research.

## Exercise 18.1 – Test your knowledge

Answer the following questions:

1. What are the four categories of .NET MAUI user interface components, and what do they represent?
2. What is the benefit of the `Shell` component and what kinds of UI does it implement?
3. How can you enable a user to perform an action on a cell in a list view?
4. When would you use an `Entry` instead of an `Editor`?
5. What is the effect of setting `IsDestructive` to `true` for a menu item in a cell's context actions?
6. You have defined a `Shell` with a content page, but no navigation is shown. Why might this be?
7. What is the difference between `Margin` and `Padding` for an element like a `Button`?
8. How are event handlers attached to an object using XAML?
9. What do XAML styles do?
10. Where can you define resources?

## Exercise 18.2 — Explore topics

Use the links on the following GitHub repository to learn more detail about the topics covered in this chapter:

```
https://github.com/markjprice/apps-services-net7/blob/main/book-links.md#chapter-18--
-building-mobile-and-desktop-apps-using-net-maui
```

# Summary

In this chapter, you learned:

- How to build a cross-platform mobile and desktop app using .NET MAUI.
- How to define shared resources and reference them.
- How to use data binding with common controls.
- How to consume data from a web service.

In the next chapter, you will learn how to integrate a .NET MAUI app with native mobile features.

# 19

# Integrating .NET MAUI Apps with Blazor and Native Platforms

This chapter is about integrating .NET MAUI apps with Blazor components and native platform features to build hybrid apps that make the most of the operating system they run on.

In *Chapter 16, Building Web Components Using Blazor WebAssembly*, you saw how easy it is to create components using web user interface technologies including HTML and CSS and common user interface style libraries like Bootstrap.

In *Chapter 17, Leveraging Open-Source Blazor Component Libraries*, you saw that there are many free open-source libraries for Blazor with great components like charts and data grids.

In *Chapter 18, Building Mobile and Desktop Apps Using .NET MAUI*, you saw that .NET MAUI enables you to build cross-platform apps that work using native controls on each device and its operating system.

In this chapter, you will see how to get the best of all those worlds by building .NET MAUI apps that host Blazor components and retain the ability to closely integrate with native features, including the look and feel.

By the end of this chapter, you will be able to make sensible decisions about what technology to use for an app, from purely native using .NET MAUI with the user interface defined using XAML to purely web using Blazor with the user interface defined using HTML and CSS, as shown in *Figure 19.1*:

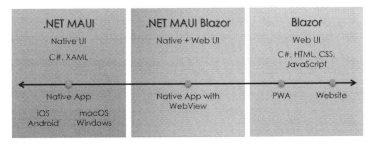

*Figure 19.1: A spectrum of choices for app development*

This chapter will cover the following topics:

- Building .NET MAUI Blazor Hybrid apps
- Integrating with native platforms
- Using third-party control libraries

# Building .NET MAUI Blazor Hybrid apps

In *Chapter 18*, *Building Mobile and Desktop Apps Using .NET MAUI*, you learned how to build .NET MAUI apps with native controls. By **native**, I mean the controls provided by the operating system. So, when Apple updates the look and feel of iOS, your apps will update too because .NET MAUI uses those native controls. Supported operating systems and their native control libraries are shown in the following list:

- **Windows**: Windows App SDK, and WinUI 3
- **macOS**: Catalyst, UIKit, and AppKit
- **iOS**: UIKit, ARKit, AVKit, CarPlay, and so on
- **Android**: android.widget and AndroidX libraries

In this section, you will learn how to build a hybrid app that combines the best of .NET MAUI app capabilities with the best of Blazor web components. This means you are not limited to building a user interface using .NET MAUI controls that use native OS capabilities. You can also leverage all the great component libraries for Blazor and simpler web user interfaces. But you still get all the benefits of close native integrations with platform features like geolocation, sensors, access to the local filesystem, notifications, and so on.

 .NET MAUI does have support for detecting and adjusting to system themes like dark mode if the operating system supports it but this book does not cover that feature. If you use dark mode, please switch it off while working on this chapter. You can read about system theme change support at the following link: `https://learn.microsoft.com/en-us/dotnet/maui/user-interface/system-theme-changes`.

## Creating a .NET MAUI Blazor project

We will now create a project for a cross-platform mobile and desktop app that can have Blazor components embedded in it. We will use the project template that enables mixing .NET MAUI controls and Blazor components in the same project.

Let's go!

1. In Visual Studio 2022 for Windows, add a new project, as defined in the following list:
    - Project template: **.NET MAUI Blazor App**/`maui-blazor`. In Visual Studio 2022 for Windows, you can select **C#** for the language and **MAUI** for the project type to show only the appropriate project templates.
    - Workspace/solution file and folder: `Chapter19`
    - Project file and folder: `Northwind.Maui.Blazor.Client`

2. If you see a Windows Security Alert that **Windows Defender Firewall has blocked some features of Broker on all public and private networks**, then select **Private networks** and clear **Public networks**, and then click the **Allow access** button.

3. In the Resources folder, in the Images folder, add images for some icons that we will use for tab items in the navigation we are about to add.

 You can download the images from the GitHub repository at the following link: https://github.com/markjprice/apps-services-net7/tree/main/vs4win/Chapter19/Northwind.Maui.Blazor.Client/Resources/Images.

4. In the Northwind.Maui.Blazor.Client project, in MauiProgram.cs, note the extra statements compared to the equivalent project template for just .NET MAUI. The statements enable embedding Blazor components by adding support for web view and registering a local weather service, as shown highlighted in the following code:

```
using Microsoft.Extensions.Logging;
using Northwind.Maui.Blazor.Client.Data;

namespace Northwind.Maui.Blazor.Client;

public static class MauiProgram
{
  public static MauiApp CreateMauiApp()
  {
    var builder = MauiApp.CreateBuilder();
    builder
      .UseMauiApp<App>()
      .ConfigureFonts(fonts =>
      {
        fonts.AddFont("OpenSans-Regular.ttf", "OpenSansRegular");
      });

    builder.Services.AddMauiBlazorWebView();

#if DEBUG
    builder.Services.AddBlazorWebViewDeveloperTools();
    builder.Logging.AddDebug();
#endif

    builder.Services.AddSingleton<WeatherForecastService>();

    return builder.Build();
  }
}
```

# Adding a shell and .NET MAUI pages

By default, the .NET MAUI Blazor project template assumes Blazor will be used for the user interface, so immediately after creating the project, we will add a shell and four page views and configure a tab bar for navigation between those pages.

We will add a `Views` folder to keep the .NET MAUI pages separate from the Razor files used by Blazor that are stored in the `Pages` folder by default. We will also create subfolders for each .NET MAUI page with all the files needed for that page, including models and view models. The .NET MAUI page views will be assigned to the project `Views` namespace to make them easier to reference in the shell.

Let's go:

1.  In the `Northwind.Maui.Blazor.Client` project, add a new folder named `Views`.
2.  In the `Views` folder, create new subfolders named `Categories`, `Employees`, `Home`, and `Orders`.

     Although we have created subfolders for each view for organizational purposes, we want all views to be in the same namespace for namespace import purposes, so we will do that manually for each view we define.

3.  In the `Views/Categories` folder, add a new **.NET MAUI ContentPage (XAML)** project item named `CategoriesPage.xaml`.
4.  In `CategoriesPage.xaml`, modify the `x:Class` attribute so that the class that is automatically generated from the XAML will be in the `Views` namespace rather than the subfolder `Views`. `Categories` namespace, as shown highlighted in the following markup:

    ```
    <ContentPage xmlns="http://schemas.microsoft.com/dotnet/2021/maui"
                 xmlns:x="http://schemas.microsoft.com/winfx/2009/xaml"
                 x:Class="Northwind.Maui.Blazor.Client.Views.CategoriesPage"
                 ...
    ```

5.  In `CategoriesPage.xaml.cs`, modify the namespace, as shown in the following code:

    ```
    namespace Northwind.Maui.Blazor.Client.Views;
    ```

6.  In the `Views/Categories` folder, add a new **.NET MAUI ContentPage (XAML)** project item named `CategoryPage.xaml`, and repeat the namespace changes on the markup and code-behind files. This page view will be used to show a single category for editing purposes.
7.  In the `Views/Employees` folder, add a new **.NET MAUI ContentPage (XAML)** project item named `EmployeesPage.xaml`, and repeat the namespace changes on the markup and code-behind files.
8.  In the `Views/Orders` folder, add a new **.NET MAUI ContentPage (XAML)** project item named `OrdersPage.xaml`, and repeat the namespace changes on the markup and code-behind files.
9.  Move the `MainPage.xaml` file from the project folder to the `Views/Home` folder, and make the appropriate namespace changes to the markup and code-behind files.
10. In `MainPage.xaml`, set the `Title` to `Home`, as shown highlighted in the following markup:

```xml
<?xml version="1.0" encoding="utf-8" ?>
<ContentPage xmlns="http://schemas.microsoft.com/dotnet/2021/maui"
             xmlns:x="http://schemas.microsoft.com/winfx/2009/xaml"
             xmlns:local="clr-namespace:Northwind.Maui.Blazor.Client"
             x:Class="Northwind.Maui.Blazor.Client.Views.MainPage"
             Title="Home"
             BackgroundColor="{DynamicResource PageBackgroundColor}">

  <BlazorWebView x:Name="blazorWebView" HostPage="wwwroot/index.html">
    <BlazorWebView.RootComponents>
      <RootComponent Selector="#app" ComponentType="{x:Type local:Main}" />
    </BlazorWebView.RootComponents>
  </BlazorWebView>

</ContentPage>
```

11. In the project folder, add a new **.NET MAUI ContentPage (XAML)** project item named AppShell.xaml.

12. In AppShell.xaml:

   • Delete the existing `<VerticalStackLayout>` element.

   • Change the root element to `<Shell>` and change the title.

   • Import the project Views namespace using the views prefix.

   • Add a `<TabBar>` element with some `<Tab>` items and shell content for the main, categories, employees, and orders pages, as shown highlighted in the following markup:

```xml
<?xml version="1.0" encoding="UTF-8" ?>
<Shell xmlns="http://schemas.microsoft.com/dotnet/2021/maui"
       xmlns:x="http://schemas.microsoft.com/winfx/2009/xaml"
       x:Class="Northwind.Maui.Blazor.Client.AppShell"
       xmlns:views="clr-namespace:Northwind.Maui.Blazor.Client.Views"
       Title="Northwind .NET MAUI + Blazor App">

  <TabBar>
    <Tab Title="Home" Icon="wind_face_high_contrast.svg" >
      <ShellContent Route="home"
        ContentTemplate="{DataTemplate views:MainPage}" />
    </Tab>
    <Tab Title="Categories" Icon="file_cabinet_high_contrast.svg">
      <ShellContent Route="categories"
        ContentTemplate="{DataTemplate views:CategoriesPage}" />
    </Tab>
    <Tab Title="Employees" Icon="identification_card_high_contrast.svg">
      <ShellContent Route="employees"
```

```
                ContentTemplate="{DataTemplate views:EmployeesPage}" />
        </Tab>
        <Tab Title="Orders" Icon="euro_banknote_high_contrast.svg">
          <ShellContent Route="orders"
                ContentTemplate="{DataTemplate views:OrdersPage}" />
        </Tab>
      </TabBar>

    </Shell>
```

 Route names are case-sensitive.

13. In `AppShell.xaml.cs`, change the class to inherit from `ContentPage` to `Shell`, as shown high-lighted in the following code:

```
public partial class AppShell : Shell
```

14. In **Solution Explorer**, expand `App.xaml`, open `App.xaml.cs`, and note that the `MainPage` property of the `App` class is set to an instance of `MainPage`, as shown highlighted in the following code:

```
namespace Northwind.Maui.Blazor.Client;

public partial class App : Application
{
  public App()
  {
    InitializeComponent();

    MainPage = new MainPage();
  }
}
```

15. In `App.xaml.cs`, change the main page property to an instance of the `AppShell` class, as shown in the following code:

```
MainPage = new AppShell();
```

16. To the right of the **Run** button in the toolbar, set the **Framework** to **net7.0-android**, and select the **Pixel 5 - API 33 (Android 13.0 - API 33)** emulator image.

17. Click the **Run** button in the toolbar and wait for the device emulator to start the Android operating system and launch your mobile app.

18. In the .NET MAUI + Blazor app, note the title bar labeled **Home** at the top and the tab bar at the bottom that has four labeled icons provided by the .NET MAUI native controls. The **Home** page titled **Northwind.Maui.Blazor.Client** with its hamburger menu has a web user interface provided by Blazor, as shown in *Figure 19.2*:

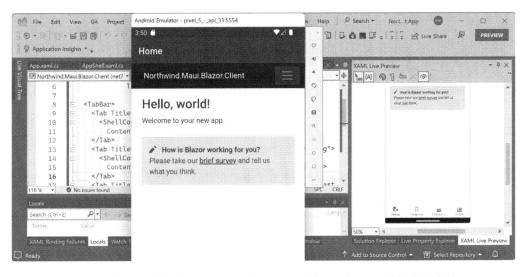

*Figure 19.2: The Northwind .NET MAUI + Blazor app with a main page UI built with Blazor on Android*

19. In the Blazor hamburger menu, click **Counter**.

20. On the **Counter** page, click the **Click me** button to increment the counter three times.

21. Close the Android device emulator.

22. In Visual Studio 2022, to the right of the **Run** button in the toolbar, set the **Framework** to **net7.0-windows**, and then select **Windows Machine**.

23. Make sure that the **Debug** configuration is selected and then click the green triangle start button labeled **Windows Machine**.

24. After a few moments, note that the Windows app appears, with the tab bar at the top of the window, as shown in *Figure 19.3*:

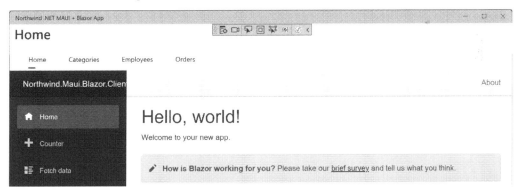

*Figure 19.3: The Northwind .NET MAUI + Blazor app with a main page UI built with Blazor on Windows*

25. Navigate to the **Counter** page.

26. On the **Counter** page, click the **Click me** button to increment the counter three times.

27. Close the Windows app.

 You could now replace the **Counter** or **Fetch data** Razor components with any of your own Blazor components that you learned how to build in *Chapter 16, Building Web Components Using Blazor WebAssembly,* or any open-source components that you learned how to use in *Chapter 17, Leveraging Open-Source Blazor Component Libraries.*

# Creating a minimal API web service for categories

We will create a web service for working with categories and products in the Northwind database:

1. In the Chapter19 solution, add a web service project, as defined in the following list:

   - Project template: **ASP.NET Core Web API**/webapi --use-minimal-apis
   - Workspace/solution file and folder: Chapter19
   - Project file and folder: Northwind.Maui.WebApi.Service
   - **Authentication type:** None
   - **Configure for HTTPS:** Selected
   - **Enable Docker:** Cleared
   - **Use controllers (uncheck to use minimal APIs):** Cleared
   - **Enable OpenAPI support:** Selected
   - **Do not use top-level statements:** Cleared

2. Add a project reference to the Northwind database context project for SQL Server that you created in *Chapter 2, Managing Relational Data Using SQL Server,* as shown in the following markup:

```
<ItemGroup>
  <ProjectReference Include="..\..\Chapter02\Northwind.Common.DataContext
.SqlServer\Northwind.Common.DataContext.SqlServer.csproj" />
</ItemGroup>
```

 The path cannot have a line break. If you did not complete the task to create the class libraries in *Chapter 2, Managing Relational Data Using SQL Server,* then download the solution projects from the GitHub repository.

3. At the command line or terminal, build the Northwind.Maui.WebApi.Service project to make sure the entity model class library projects outside the current solution are properly compiled, as shown in the following command:

```
dotnet build
```

4. In the Properties folder, in launchSettings.json, modify the applicationUrl to use port 5191 for https and port 5192 for http, as shown highlighted in the following configuration:

```
"profiles": {
```

```
"http": {
    "commandName": "Project",
    "dotnetRunMessages": true,
    "launchBrowser": true,
    "launchUrl": "swagger",
    "applicationUrl": "http://localhost:5192",
    "environmentVariables": {
      "ASPNETCORE_ENVIRONMENT": "Development"
    }
},
"https": {
    "commandName": "Project",
    "dotnetRunMessages": true,
    "launchBrowser": true,
    "launchUrl": "swagger",
    "applicationUrl": "https://localhost:5191;http://localhost:5192",
    "environmentVariables": {
      "ASPNETCORE_ENVIRONMENT": "Development"
    }
},
```

5. In `Program.cs`, delete the statements about the weather service and replace them with statements to disable HTTPS redirection while developing and to configure minimal API endpoints for data operations on categories, as shown highlighted in the following code:

```csharp
using Microsoft.AspNetCore.Mvc; // [FromServices]
using Packt.Shared; // AddNorthwindContext extension method

var builder = WebApplication.CreateBuilder(args);

// Add services to the container.
// Learn more about configuring Swagger/OpenAPI at https://aka.ms/
aspnetcore/swashbuckle
builder.Services.AddEndpointsApiExplorer();
builder.Services.AddSwaggerGen();

builder.Services.AddNorthwindContext();

var app = builder.Build();

// Configure the HTTP request pipeline.
if (app.Environment.IsDevelopment())
{
  app.UseSwagger();
  app.UseSwaggerUI();
}
else
```

```csharp
{
  app.UseHttpsRedirection();
}

app.MapGet("api/categories", (
  [FromServices] NorthwindContext db) => db.Categories)
  .WithName("GetCategories")
  .Produces<Category[]>(StatusCodes.Status200OK);

app.MapGet("api/categories/{id:int}", (
  [FromRoute] int id,
  [FromServices] NorthwindContext db) =>
    db.Categories.Where(category => category.CategoryId == id))
  .WithName("GetCategory")
  .Produces<Category[]>(StatusCodes.Status200OK);

app.MapPost("api/categories", async (
  [FromBody] Category category,
  [FromServices] NorthwindContext db) =>
{
  db.Categories.Add(category);
  await db.SaveChangesAsync();
  return Results.Created($"api/categories/{category.CategoryId}",
category);
}).WithOpenApi()
  .Produces<Category>(StatusCodes.Status201Created);

app.MapPut("api/categories/{id:int}", async (
  [FromRoute] int id,
  [FromBody] Category category,
  [FromServices] NorthwindContext db) =>
{
  Category? foundCategory = await db.Categories.FindAsync(id);

  if (foundCategory is null) return Results.NotFound();

  foundCategory.CategoryName = category.CategoryName;
  foundCategory.Description = category.Description;
  foundCategory.Picture = category.Picture;

  await db.SaveChangesAsync();

  return Results.NoContent();
}).WithOpenApi()
  .Produces(StatusCodes.Status404NotFound)
  .Produces(StatusCodes.Status204NoContent);
```

```
app.MapDelete("api/categories/{id:int}", async (
  [FromRoute] int id,
  [FromServices] NorthwindContext db) =>
{
  if (await db.Categories.FindAsync(id) is Category category)
  {
    db.Categories.Remove(category);
    await db.SaveChangesAsync();
    return Results.NoContent();
  }
  return Results.NotFound();
}).WithOpenApi()
  .Produces(StatusCodes.Status404NotFound)
  .Produces(StatusCodes.Status204NoContent);

app.Run();
```

6. Start the web service project and note the Swagger documentation.

7. Click **GET /api/categories** to expand that section.

8. Click the **Try it out** button, click the **Execute** button, and note that category entities are returned.

9. Close the browser and shut down the web server.

## Configuring the .NET MAUI app to allow unsecure connections

Now you will configure the `Northwind.Maui.Blazor.Client` project to allow unsecure HTTP requests to the web service:

1. In the `Northwind.Maui.Blazor.Client` project, in the `Platforms/iOS` folder, open the `Info.plist` file by right-clicking and opening it with the **XML (Text) Editor**.

2. At the bottom of the dictionary, add a new key named `NSAppTransportSecurity` that is a dictionary, and in it, add a key named `NSAllowsArbitraryLoads` that has a value of `true`, as shown highlighted in the following partial markup:

```xml
<?xml version="1.0" encoding="UTF-8"?>
<!DOCTYPE plist PUBLIC "-//Apple//DTD PLIST 1.0//EN"
        "http://www.apple.com/DTDs/PropertyList-1.0.dtd">
<plist version="1.0">
<dict>
  <key>LSRequiresIPhoneOS</key>
  <true/>
  ...
  <key>NSAppTransportSecurity</key>
  <dict>
    <key>NSAllowsArbitraryLoads</key>
    <true/>
  </dict>
```

```
    </dict>
  </plist>
```

3. Save and close `Info.plist`.

4. In the `Platforms/Android` folder, in the `Resources` folder, add a new folder named `xml`.

5. In the `xml` folder, add a new XML file named `network_security_config.xml`, and add entries to enable cleartext when connecting over the virtual router's special IP address that maps out to `localhost`, as shown in the following markup:

```xml
<?xml version="1.0" encoding="utf-8" ?>
<network-security-config>
  <domain-config cleartextTrafficPermitted="true">
    <domain includeSubdomains="true">10.0.2.2</domain>
  </domain-config>
</network-security-config>
```

6. In the `Android` folder, in `AndroidManifest.xml`, add an attribute to the `<application>` element to reference the new XML file, as shown highlighted in the following markup:

```xml
<?xml version="1.0" encoding="utf-8"?>
<manifest xmlns:android="http://schemas.android.com/apk/res/android">
  <application android:allowBackup="true"
               android:icon="@mipmap/appicon"
               android:networkSecurityConfig="@xml/network_security_config"
               android:roundIcon="@mipmap/appicon_round"
               android:supportsRtl="true">
  </application>
  <uses-permission android:name="android.permission.ACCESS_NETWORK_STATE"
/>
  <uses-permission android:name="android.permission.INTERNET" />
</manifest>
```

7. Save all the changes.

## Implementing the Model-View-ViewModel pattern

The **Model-View-ViewModel** (**MVVM**) pattern separates an application's business and presentation logic from its user interface markup. This makes the app easier to test, maintain, and add or modify features over time. You were briefly introduced to MVVM in *Chapter 18*, *Building Mobile and Desktop Apps Using .NET MAUI*, so you could go back and review it there if you need a refresher.

There are three parts of MVVM:

- **Model:** An entity model class like `Category` or `Product`.
- **View Model:** A class that represents the business logic, like validation rules, and presentation logic, like properties for all data values that might need to appear in a view. Examples of data values include a category name or a unit price of a product.

> Examples of business logic include commands for actions that need to be taken, like creating a new product or saving a change to a category, and events like "the data has changed," without any specific user interface.

- **View**: A markup file that represents a user interface that can be bound to a view model. You could have different views for different scenarios, like desktop or mobile. In the desktop view, the data might be bound to a horizontally oriented carousel view and show a picture of each category that the user swipes left and right through. In the mobile view, the data might be bound to a simple vertical list view with just text that the user scrolls up and down through.

MVVM can be a pain to implement because it requires a lot of boilerplate code. For example, the properties in the view model must implement the `INotifyPropertyChanged` interface and raise the `PropertyChanged` event so that the view gets notified when it needs to update.

 You can learn about the MVVM design pattern and how to implement it for .NET MAUI apps at the following link: `https://docs.microsoft.com/en-us/dotnet/architecture/maui/mvvm`.

The MVVM Toolkit has source generators to do that work for you. For example, just inherit from the `ObservableObject` class, define a `private` field named using camel casing, and decorate with the `[ObservableProperty]` attribute, as shown in the following code, and then the source generators will do the rest:

```
// ObservableObject, [ObservableProperty]
using CommunityToolkit.Mvvm.ComponentModel;

partial class Category : ObservableObject
{
  [ObservableProperty]
  private string? categoryName;

  // Other members.
}
```

If a class already needs to inherit from another class and so it cannot inherit from `ObservableObject`, then you can decorate the class with a special attribute, as shown in the following code:

```
// [INotifyPropertyChanged], [ObservableProperty]
using CommunityToolkit.Mvvm.ComponentModel;

[INotifyPropertyChanged]
partial class Category : SomeOtherClass
{
  [ObservableProperty]
  private string? categoryName;

  // Other members.
}
```

**Good Practice:** To create an observable class, it is best to inherit from `ObservableObject`. If you cannot, then decorate with `[INotifyPropertyChanged]`, but this will be less efficient because code must be duplicated.

You can learn about the MVVM Toolkit at the following link: `https://docs.microsoft.com/en-us/dotnet/communitytoolkit/mvvm/`.

Now, let's define a model and a view model for working with categories:

1.  In the `Northwind.Maui.Blazor.Client` project file, add package references for the .NET MAUI Community Toolkit and for the MVVM Community Toolkit, as shown in the following markup:

```
<ItemGroup>
  <PackageReference Include="CommunityToolkit.Maui" Version="1.3.0" />
  <PackageReference Include="CommunityToolkit.Mvvm" Version="8.0.0" />
</ItemGroup>
```

2.  Build the project to restore packages.

Note that you will see a warning because the .NET MAUI Community Toolkit runs a code analyzer that checks to see if you have called the extension method to use the toolkit. You will do that in the next step.

3.  In `MauiProgram.cs`, add a call to an extension method to enable the .NET MAUI Community Toolkit, as shown highlighted in the following code:

```
var builder = MauiApp.CreateBuilder();
builder
  .UseMauiApp<App>()
  .UseMauiCommunityToolkit()
  .ConfigureFonts(fonts =>
```

4.  In the `Views/Categories` folder, add a new class named `Category.cs`. Modify it to use the MVVM Community Toolkit to implement an observable category model that matches the `Category` entity models defined in the SQL Server EF Core models, but with an extra property to generate a path to a picture of each category as an alternative to the bytes stored in the database, as shown in the following code:

```
// ObservableObject, [ObservableProperty]
using CommunityToolkit.Mvvm.ComponentModel;

namespace Northwind.Maui.Blazor.Client.Views.Categories;
```

```
internal partial class Category : ObservableObject
{
  // The field names must be camelCase because the source-generated
  // public property names will be TitleCase.

  [ObservableProperty]
  [NotifyPropertyChangedFor(nameof(PicturePath))]
  private int categoryId;

  [ObservableProperty]
  private string categoryName;

  [ObservableProperty]
  private string description;

  [ObservableProperty]
  private byte[] picture;

  [ObservableProperty]
  private string picturePath;
}
```

The PicturePath property will use the pattern categoryX_small.jpeg, where X is the category ID. Therefore, if the category ID changes, we must notify any data bindings that anything bound to the PicturePath will also need to be updated.

5. In the Views/Categories folder, add a new class named CategoriesViewModel.cs, and modify it to inherit from ObservableCollection<T>, have some commands, and get the categories from the web service, as shown in the following code:

```
using CommunityToolkit.Mvvm.Input; // [RelayCommand]
using System.Collections.ObjectModel; // ObservableCollection<T>
using System.Net.Http.Headers; // MediaTypeWithQualityHeaderValue
using System.Net.Http.Json; // ReadFromJsonAsync<T>

namespace Northwind.Maui.Blazor.Client.Views.Categories;

internal partial class CategoriesViewModel : ObservableCollection<Category>
{
  // These property do not need to support two-way binding
  // because they are set programmatically to display to user.

  public string InfoMessage { get; set; } = string.Empty;
```

```csharp
public string ErrorMessage { get; set; } = string.Empty;

public bool ErrorMessageVisible { get; set; }

public CategoriesViewModel()
{
  try
  {
    HttpClient client = new()
    {
      BaseAddress = new Uri(
        DeviceInfo.Platform == DevicePlatform.Android ?
        "http://10.0.2.2:5192" : "http://localhost:5192")
    };

    InfoMessage = $"BaseAddress: {client.BaseAddress}. ";

    client.DefaultRequestHeaders.Accept.Add(
      new MediaTypeWithQualityHeaderValue("application/json"));

    HttpResponseMessage response = client
      .GetAsync("api/categories").Result;

    response.EnsureSuccessStatusCode();

    IEnumerable<Category> categories =
      response.Content.ReadFromJsonAsync
      <IEnumerable<Category>>().Result;

    foreach (Category category in categories)
    {
      int offset = 78; // to remove the OLE header

      category.Picture = category.Picture.AsSpan(
        offset, category.Picture.Length - offset).ToArray();

      category.PicturePath = $"category{category.CategoryId}_small.jpeg";

      Add(category);
    }

    InfoMessage += $"{Count} categories loaded.";
  }
  catch (Exception ex)
```

```
        {
          ErrorMessage = ex.Message;
          ErrorMessageVisible = true;
        }
      }

      [RelayCommand]
      private void AddCategoryToFavorites()
      {
        Console.WriteLine("Add category to favorites");
      }

      [RelayCommand]
      private void DeleteCategory()
      {
        Console.WriteLine("Delete category");
      }
    }
```

# Getting categories from the web service

Now, we can modify the categories page to show the categories in a carousel:

1.  In App.xaml, modify the resources for the PageBackgroundColor and PrimaryTextColor, and
    the BackgroundColor for buttons, as shown highlighted in the following markup:

```xml
<?xml version="1.0" encoding="UTF-8" ?>
<Application xmlns="http://schemas.microsoft.com/dotnet/2021/maui"
             xmlns:x="http://schemas.microsoft.com/winfx/2009/xaml"
             xmlns:local="clr-namespace:Northwind.Maui.Blazor.Client"
             x:Class="Northwind.Maui.Blazor.Client.App">
  <Application.Resources>
    <ResourceDictionary>

      <Color x:Key="PageBackgroundColor">LightGray</Color>
      <Color x:Key="PrimaryTextColor">SlateGray</Color>

      <Style TargetType="Label">
        <Setter Property="TextColor"
                Value="{DynamicResource PrimaryTextColor}" />
        <Setter Property="FontFamily" Value="OpenSansRegular" />
      </Style>

      <Style TargetType="Button">
        <Setter Property="TextColor"
                Value="{DynamicResource PrimaryTextColor}" />
        <Setter Property="FontFamily" Value="OpenSansRegular" />
        <Setter Property="BackgroundColor"
```

```
                    Value="{DynamicResource PageBackgroundColor}" />
          <Setter Property="Padding" Value="14,10" />
      </Style>

    </ResourceDictionary>
  </Application.Resources>
</Application>
```

2. In `CategoriesPage.xaml`, import namespaces for working with types defined at the project level using the prefix `local` and types in the `Categories` folder using the prefix `categories`, then create an instance of the categories view model for the binding context of the content page. Then, in the vertical stack layout, add a label to show information about the web service endpoint, a label to show any error message, and a carousel with indicator lights, as shown highlighted in the following markup:

```
<?xml version="1.0" encoding="utf-8" ?>
<ContentPage xmlns="http://schemas.microsoft.com/dotnet/2021/maui"
             xmlns:x="http://schemas.microsoft.com/winfx/2009/xaml"
             x:Class="Northwind.Maui.Blazor.Client.Views.CategoriesPage"
             xmlns:local="clr-namespace:Northwind.Maui.Blazor.Client"
             xmlns:categories=
               "clr-namespace:Northwind.Maui.Blazor.Client.Views.
Categories"
             xmlns:toolkit=
               "http://schemas.microsoft.com/dotnet/2022/maui/toolkit"
             Title="Categories"
             BackgroundColor="{StaticResource PageBackgroundColor}">

  <ContentPage.BindingContext>
    <categories:CategoriesViewModel />
  </ContentPage.BindingContext>

  <VerticalStackLayout>

    <HorizontalStackLayout Spacing="20" Padding="20">
      <Label Text="{Binding InfoMessage}" />
      <Label Text="{Binding ErrorMessage}" TextColor="Red"
             IsVisible="{Binding ErrorMessageVisible}" />
    </HorizontalStackLayout>

    <CarouselView x:Name="carouselView"
                  ItemsSource="{Binding .}"
                  IndicatorView="indicatorView"
                  PeekAreaInsets="10"
                  Loop="False">

      <CarouselView.EmptyView>
```

```xml
        <ContentView>
          <VerticalStackLayout HorizontalOptions="Center"
                               VerticalOptions="Center">
            <Label Text="No results matched your filter."
                   Margin="10,25,10,10"
                   FontAttributes="Bold"
                   FontSize="18"
                   HorizontalOptions="Fill"
                   HorizontalTextAlignment="Center" />
          </VerticalStackLayout>
        </ContentView>
      </CarouselView.EmptyView>

      <CarouselView.ItemTemplate>
        <DataTemplate>
          <VerticalStackLayout>
            <Frame HasShadow="True"
                   BorderColor="{StaticResource PrimaryTextColor}"
                   CornerRadius="10"
                   Margin="20"
                   HeightRequest="450"
                   HorizontalOptions="Center"
                   VerticalOptions="Center">

              <VerticalStackLayout>
                <Label Text="{Binding CategoryName}"
                       FontAttributes="Bold"
                       FontSize="18"
                       HorizontalOptions="Center"
                       VerticalOptions="Center" />
                <Image Source="{Binding PicturePath}"
                       Aspect="AspectFill"
                       HeightRequest="250"
                       WidthRequest="375"
                       HorizontalOptions="Center" />
                <Label Text="{Binding Description}"
                       FontAttributes="Italic"
                       HorizontalOptions="Center"
                       MaxLines="5"
                       LineBreakMode="TailTruncation" />
              </VerticalStackLayout>

            </Frame>
          </VerticalStackLayout>
        </DataTemplate>
      </CarouselView.ItemTemplate>
```

```
            </CarouselView>

            <Frame BackgroundColor="{StaticResource PrimaryTextColor}"
                    CornerRadius="5" HorizontalOptions="Center">
                <IndicatorView x:Name="indicatorView"
                                IndicatorColor="{StaticResource PageBackgroundColor}"
                                SelectedIndicatorColor="DeepSkyBlue"
                                HorizontalOptions="Center" />
            </Frame>

        </VerticalStackLayout>

    </ContentPage>
```

3. Start the `Northwind.Maui.WebApi.Service` project using the `https` profile, and note the endpoints it is listening on, as shown highlighted in the following output:

```
info: Microsoft.Hosting.Lifetime[14]
      Now listening on: https://localhost:5191
info: Microsoft.Hosting.Lifetime[14]
      Now listening on: http://localhost:5192
info: Microsoft.Hosting.Lifetime[0]
      Application started. Press Ctrl+C to shut down.
info: Microsoft.Hosting.Lifetime[0]
      Hosting environment: Development
info: Microsoft.Hosting.Lifetime[0]
      Content root path: C:\apps-services-net7\Chapter19\Northwind.Maui.
WebApi.Service
```

4. Run the `Northwind.Maui.Blazor.Client` project using the Android emulator, navigate to the **Categories** page, and note that eight categories are loaded from the web service and displayed in the carousel, with indicator lights at the bottom of the page view, as shown in *Figure 19.4*:

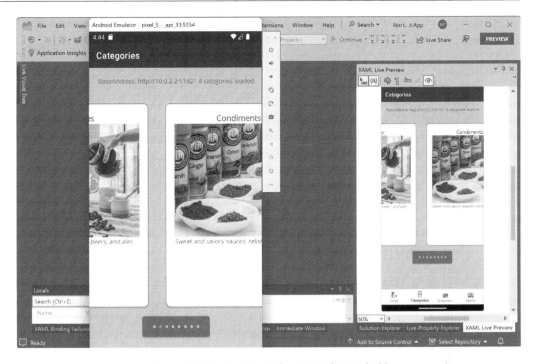

*Figure 19.4: Categories in the carousel on Android*

5. Note that the user can swipe left and right to flip between categories or click the dots in the indicator view to quickly jump to the matching category.

6. Close the Android emulator.

7. Run the `Northwind.Maui.Blazor.Client` project using the Windows machine, navigate to the **Categories** page, and note that eight categories are loaded from the web service and displayed in the carousel, with indicator lights at the bottom of the page view, as shown in *Figure 19.5*:

*Figure 19.5: Categories in the carousel on Windows*

8. Note that the user can use the horizontal scrollbar at the bottom to scroll between categories or click the dots in the indicator view to quickly jump to the matching category.

9. Close the Windows app.

# Integrating with native platforms

.NET MAUI provides cross-platform APIs for native device features. Examples include:

- Working with the system clipboard
- Picking files and media from the local filesystem
- Storing data securely in a local dictionary for key-value storage
- Getting information about the device like the operating system version
- Reading sensors like an accelerometer or compass
- Checking network connectivity
- Using native user interface interactions like menu systems and toast notifications

Let's look at example code for some of these native platform integrations.

## Working with the system clipboard

You often need to integrate your app with the clipboard on the local device. For example, a user might have a description of a category in another app like a word processor or notes app. While editing a category, they might want to copy and paste the description from that other app. The clipboard integration only works with text.

Let's enable integration with the clipboard:

1. In the `Views/Employees` folder, in `EmployeesPage.xaml`, change the title, set the vertical spacing in the stack to `10`, and replace the existing label element with a frame, an entry, and a pair of buttons to copy and paste to and from the box whatever text is currently in the clipboard, as shown highlighted in the following markup:

```xml
<?xml version="1.0" encoding="utf-8" ?>
<ContentPage xmlns="http://schemas.microsoft.com/dotnet/2021/maui"
             xmlns:x="http://schemas.microsoft.com/winfx/2009/xaml"
             x:Class="Northwind.Maui.Blazor.Client.Views.EmployeesPage"
             Title="Employees">

    <VerticalStackLayout Spacing="10">

        <Frame BorderColor="{StaticResource PrimaryTextColor}"
               Margin="5" Padding="5">
            <VerticalStackLayout Spacing="10">
                <Label Text="Clipboard Examples"
                       VerticalOptions="Center"
                       HorizontalOptions="Center" />
                <Entry x:Name="NotesTextBox"
```

```
                    HorizontalOptions="Fill" />
        <HorizontalStackLayout Spacing="10">
          <Button Text="Copy to Clipboard"
                  x:Name="CopyToClipboardButton"
                  Clicked="CopyToClipboardButton_Clicked"
                  HorizontalOptions="Center" />
          <Button Text="Paste from Clipboard"
                  x:Name="PasteFromClipboardButton"
                  Clicked="PasteFromClipboardButton_Clicked"
                  HorizontalOptions="Center" />
        </HorizontalStackLayout>
      </VerticalStackLayout>
    </Frame>

  </VerticalStackLayout>

</ContentPage>
```

2.  In `EmployeesPage.xaml.cs`, add statements to the event handlers to call the default clipboard methods for setting and getting text, as shown highlighted in the following code:

```csharp
namespace Northwind.Maui.Blazor.Client.Views;

public partial class EmployeesPage : ContentPage
{
  public EmployeesPage()
  {
    InitializeComponent();
  }

  private async void CopyToClipboardButton_Clicked(
    object sender, EventArgs e)
  {
    await Clipboard.Default.SetTextAsync(NotesTextBox.Text);
  }

  private async void PasteFromClipboardButton_Clicked(
    object sender, EventArgs e)
  {
    if (Clipboard.HasText)
    {
      NotesTextBox.Text = await Clipboard.Default.GetTextAsync();
    }
  }
}
```

3.  Start the project in the Android emulator.

4. Navigate to the **Employees** page.

5. Enter some text into the entry box, for example, `Hello, Clipboard!`.

6. Click the **Copy to Clipboard** button.

7. Start Notepad on Windows. (The Android emulator integrates automatically with the Windows clipboard.)

8. Paste, and note the text is whatever you typed into the entry box.

9. Type some new text into Notepad, for example, `Hello, .NET MAUI app!`, and then select it and copy it to the clipboard.

10. In the app, click the **Paste from Clipboard** button and note that the correct text appears in the entry box, as shown in *Figure 19.6*:

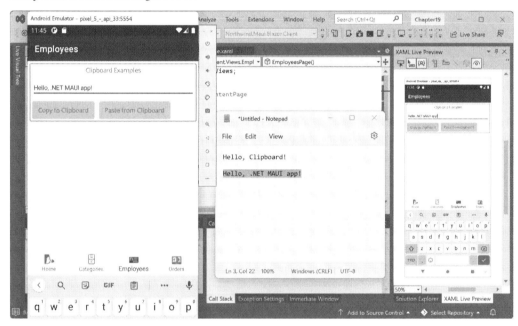

*Figure 19.6: Pasting from the system clipboard on Android*

11. Close the Android emulator.

12. Repeat this test of the app on a Windows machine and note that it has the same functionality.

# Picking files from the local filesystem

You often need to allow the app user to access the local filesystem on their device to select a file, for example, a photo that they have taken.

To access the media and file picker functionality in a .NET MAUI app, platform-specific configuration is required.

## Enabling media and file picking on Windows

In the `Platforms/Windows` folder, in `Package.appxmanifest`, add entries to the `<Capabilities>` section, as shown highlighted in the following markup:

```
<Capabilities>
  <rescap:Capability Name="runFullTrust" />
  <DeviceCapability Name="microphone"/>
  <DeviceCapability Name="webcam"/>
</Capabilities>
```

 By default, Visual Studio 2022 opens a graphical editor for the `Package.appxmanifest` file. To modify the XML directly, you must choose to open the file with the **XML (Text) Editor**.

## Enabling media and file picking on Android

In the `Platforms/Android` folder, in `AndroidManifest.xml`, add entries in the manifest node, as shown in the following markup:

```
<uses-permission android:name="android.permission.MANAGE_EXTERNAL_STORAGE" />
<uses-permission android:name="android.permission.READ_EXTERNAL_STORAGE" />
<uses-permission android:name="android.permission.WRITE_EXTERNAL_STORAGE" />
<uses-permission android:name="android.permission.MANAGE_MEDIA" />
<uses-permission android:name="android.permission.CAMERA" />
```

For Android 11 with API 30 or later, you must also add entries in `AndroidManifest.xml`, as shown in the following markup:

```
<queries>
  <intent>
    <action android:name="android.media.action.IMAGE_CAPTURE" />
  </intent>
</queries>
```

## Enabling media and file picking on iOS

In the `Platforms/iOS` folder, in the `Info.plist` file, add keys and values to the root `<dict>` element, as shown in the following markup:

```
<key>NSCameraUsageDescription</key>
<string>This app needs access to the camera to take photos.</string>
<key>NSMicrophoneUsageDescription</key>
<string>This app needs access to the microphone for taking videos.</string>
<key>NSPhotoLibraryAddUsageDescription</key>
<string>This app needs access to the photo gallery for adding photos and
videos.</string>
<key>NSPhotoLibraryUsageDescription</key>
```

```
<string>This app needs access to the photos gallery for picking photos and
videos.</string>
```

 By default, Visual Studio 2022 opens a graphical editor for the `Info.plist` file. To modify the XML directly, you must choose to open the file with the **XML (Text) Editor**.

## Integrating with the media and file picker

Let's enable the user to select a new image for a category:

1.  In the `Views/Employees` folder, in `EmployeesPage.xaml`, add another frame, a label, an image, and a pair of buttons to pick a text file or an image file and show them in the label or image control, as shown highlighted in the following markup:

```xml
<?xml version="1.0" encoding="utf-8" ?>
<ContentPage ...
             Title="Employees">

  <VerticalStackLayout Spacing="10">
    ...

    <Frame BorderColor="{StaticResource PrimaryTextColor}"
           Margin="5" Padding="5">
      <VerticalStackLayout Spacing="10">
        <Label Text="Picker Examples"
               VerticalOptions="Center"
               HorizontalOptions="Center" />
        <HorizontalStackLayout Spacing="10">
          <Button Text="Pick Text File"
                  x:Name="PickTextFileButton"
                  Clicked="PickTextFileButton_Clicked"
                  HorizontalOptions="Center" />
          <Button Text="Pick Image"
                  x:Name="PickImageButton"
                  Clicked="PickImageButton_Clicked"
                  HorizontalOptions="Center" />
          <Button Text="Take a Photo"
                  x:Name="TakePhotoButton"
                  Clicked="TakePhotoButton_Clicked"
                  HorizontalOptions="Center" />
        </HorizontalStackLayout>
        <Label x:Name="FilePathLabel"
               HorizontalOptions="Fill" />
        <Label x:Name="FileContentsLabel"
               HorizontalOptions="Fill" />
```

```xml
            <Image x:Name="FileImage"
                   HeightRequest="375"
                   WidthRequest="250"/>
        </VerticalStackLayout>
      </Frame>

  </VerticalStackLayout>

</ContentPage>
```

2. In `EmployeesPage.xaml.cs`, add statements to the event handlers. When the user clicks the **Pick Text File** button, use the default file picker with a list of file types to define plain text for each platform, and then read the file into the label. When the user clicks the **Pick Image** button, use the default media picker to read an image file and then load it into the image control. When the user clicks the **Take a Photo** button, use the default media picker to capture a photo and then load it into the image control, as shown in the following partial code:

```csharp
namespace Northwind.Maui.Blazor.Client.Views;

public partial class EmployeesPage : ContentPage
{
  ...

  private async void PickTextFileButton_Clicked(object sender, EventArgs e)
  {
    try
    {
      FilePickerFileType textFileTypes = new(
        new Dictionary<DevicePlatform, IEnumerable<string>>
        {
          { DevicePlatform.iOS, new[] { "public.plain-text" } },
          { DevicePlatform.Android, new[] { "text/plain" } },
          { DevicePlatform.WinUI, new[] { ".txt" } },
          { DevicePlatform.Tizen, new[] { "*/*" } },
          { DevicePlatform.macOS, new[] { "txt" } }
        });

      PickOptions options = new()
      {
        PickerTitle = "Pick a text file",
        FileTypes = textFileTypes
      };

      FileResult result = await FilePicker.Default.PickAsync(options);

      if (result != null)
```

```
      {
        using var stream = await result.OpenReadAsync();
        FileContentsLabel.Text = new StreamReader(stream).ReadToEnd();
      }

      FilePathLabel.Text = result.FullPath;
    }
    catch (Exception ex)
    {
      await DisplayAlert(title: "Exception",
        message: ex.Message, cancel: "OK");
    }
  }

  private async void PickImageButton_Clicked(object sender, EventArgs e)
  {
    FileResult photo = await MediaPicker.Default.PickPhotoAsync();

    if (photo != null)
    {
      FileImage.Source = ImageSource.FromFile(photo.FullPath);

      FilePathLabel.Text = photo.FullPath;
    }
    else
    {
      await DisplayAlert(title: "Exception",
        message: "Photo was null.", cancel: "OK");
    }
  }

  private async void TakePhotoButton_Clicked(object sender, EventArgs e)
  {
    if (MediaPicker.Default.IsCaptureSupported)
    {
      FileResult photo = await MediaPicker.Default.CapturePhotoAsync();

      if (photo != null)
      {
        FileImage.Source = ImageSource.FromFile(photo.FullPath);

        FilePathLabel.Text = photo.FullPath;
      }
      else
      {
        await DisplayAlert(title: "Exception",
```

```
            message: "Photo was null.", cancel: "OK");
        }
      }
      else
      {
        await DisplayAlert(title: "Sorry",
          message: "Image capture is not supported on this device.",
          cancel: "OK");
      }
    }
  }
}
```

3.  Start the project in the Android emulator.

4.  In the .NET MAUI app, navigate to the **Employees** page.

5.  In the emulator, start the Chrome browser.

6.  Navigate to `https://raw.githubusercontent.com/markjprice/apps-services-net7/main/sample.txt`.

7.  Download the `sample.txt` file. In Chrome for Android, you can click the dots menu and then click the down-pointing arrow in the mini toolbar.

8.  Switch back to the .NET MAUI app.

9.  Tap **Pick Text File**.

10. Select the `sample.txt` file, and note that the local path to the file and its contents are displayed in the two labels, as shown in *Figure 19.7*:

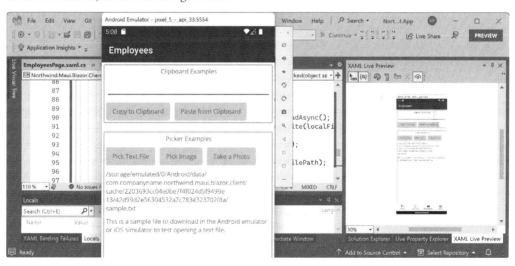

*Figure 19.7: Showing the file path and contents for a picked text file*

11. Switch to the Chrome browser.

12. Navigate to `https://github.com/markjprice/apps-services-net7/blob/main/images/Categories-small/categories-small.jpeg`.

13. Download the small image of categories, as shown in *Figure 19.8*:

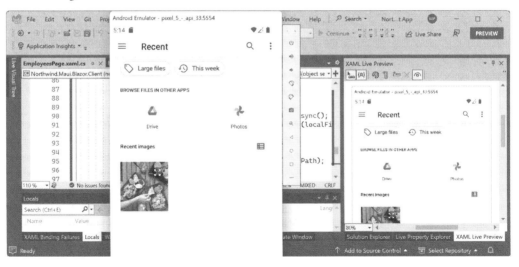

*Figure 19.8: Downloading an image of categories in the Android emulator*

14. When the notification appears indicating the image has downloaded, tap it to view it. This will add the image to the most recent list of images.

15. Tap **Pick Image** and select the small picture of categories from the list of recent images, as shown in *Figure 19.9*:

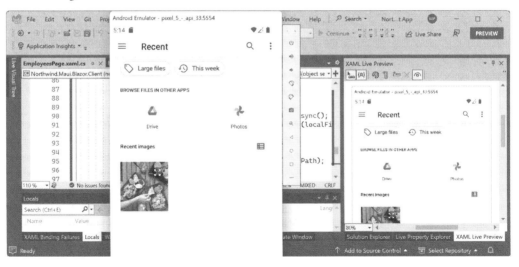

*Figure 19.9: The native image picker on Android*

16. The image is shown at the bottom of the app, as shown in *Figure 19.10*:

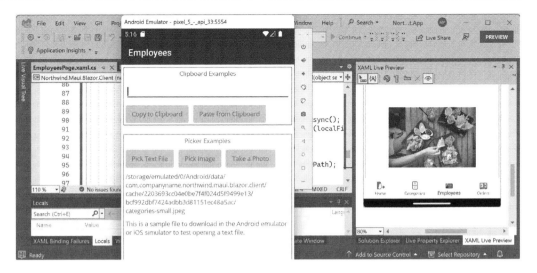

*Figure 19.10: The selected image visible in the .NET MAUI app*

17. Tap **Take a Photo** and note the permission request, as shown in *Figure 19.11*:

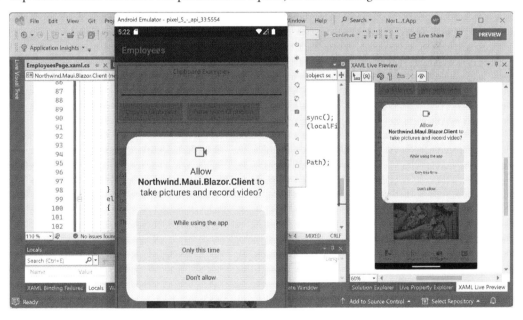

*Figure 19.11: A .NET MAUI app requesting permission to use the camera*

18. Close the app.

# Creating new windows

The defining characteristic of the Windows operating system is… windows! The old Xamarin.Forms technology did not support creating windows because mobile device operating systems do not support windows. But .NET MAUI can target desktop operating systems, so .NET MAUI adds the capability of creating a new window.

Let's go!

1. In the `Views\Orders` folder, in `OrdersPage.xaml`, change the title, set the spacing in the vertical stack to `10`, and then replace the existing label with a frame containing a label and button, as shown highlighted in the following markup:

```xml
<?xml version="1.0" encoding="utf-8" ?>
<ContentPage xmlns="http://schemas.microsoft.com/dotnet/2021/maui"
             xmlns:x="http://schemas.microsoft.com/winfx/2009/xaml"
             x:Class="Northwind.Maui.Blazor.Client.Views.OrdersPage"
             Title="Orders">

  <VerticalStackLayout Spacing="10">

    <Frame BorderColor="{StaticResource PrimaryTextColor}"
           Margin="5" Padding="5">
      <VerticalStackLayout Spacing="10">
        <Label Text="Windowing"
               VerticalOptions="Center"
               HorizontalOptions="Center" />
        <Button Text="New Window" x:Name="NewWindowButton"
                Clicked="NewWindowButton_Clicked"
                HorizontalOptions="Center" />
      </VerticalStackLayout>
    </Frame>

  </VerticalStackLayout>

</ContentPage>
```

2. In `OrdersPage.xaml.cs`, add a handler for the button event that creates a new window with a starting page that is a new instance of `AppShell` and opens it, as shown highlighted in the following code:

```csharp
namespace Northwind.Maui.Blazor.Client.Views;

public partial class OrdersPage : ContentPage
{
  public OrdersPage()
  {
    InitializeComponent();
  }

  private void NewWindowButton_Clicked(object sender, EventArgs e)
  {
    Window window = new() { Page = new AppShell() };
    Application.Current.OpenWindow(window);
  }
}
```

```
    }
```

3. Start the app on **Windows Machine**.

4. Navigate to the **Orders** page, click the **New Window** button, and note that a new window appears, as shown in *Figure 19.12*:

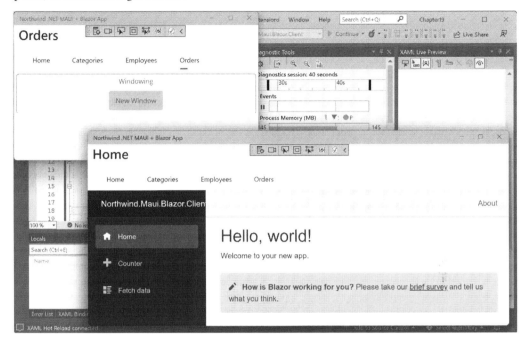

*Figure 19.12: Multiple windows in a Windows app*

5. Close the new window and then close the Windows app.

 Mobile devices do not support windows. For example, if you click the **New Window** button on an Android device, it will close and restart the app. It would be better to disable this button on mobile devices using the following markup: `IsEnabled="{OnPlatform False, WinUI=True}"`. Or you could make the button invisible.

# Getting device information

You often need to get information about the device that the app is running on, including about network connectivity and sensor readings.

## Enabling device information on Android

To get information about the battery on Windows or iOS, you do not need to ask for permission. But on Android you must request permission by adding an entry to `AndroidManifest.xml`, as shown in the following markup:

```
<uses-permission android:name="android.permission.BATTERY_STATS" />
```

# Adding device information to the app

Let's show some useful information about the device:

1.  In the `Views/Orders` folder, add a new class named `DeviceInfoViewModel.cs`, and define some properties to bind to, as shown in the following code:

```
namespace Northwind.Maui.Blazor.Client.Views.Orders;

internal class DeviceInfoViewModel
{
  public string DisplayPixelWidth =>
    $"{DeviceDisplay.Current.MainDisplayInfo.Width} pixel width";

  public string DisplayDensity =>
    $"{DeviceDisplay.Current.MainDisplayInfo.Density} pixel density";

  public string DisplayOrientation =>
    $"Orientation is {DeviceDisplay.Current.MainDisplayInfo.
Orientation}";

  public string DisplayRotation =>
    $"Rotation is {DeviceDisplay.Current.MainDisplayInfo.Rotation}";

  public string DisplayRefreshRate =>
    $"{DeviceDisplay.Current.MainDisplayInfo.RefreshRate} Hz refresh
rate";

  public string DeviceModel => DeviceInfo.Current.Model;

  public string DeviceType =>
    $"{DeviceInfo.Current.DeviceType} {DeviceInfo.Current.Idiom} device";

  public string DeviceVersion => DeviceInfo.Current.VersionString;

  public string DevicePlatform =>
    $"Platform is {DeviceInfo.Current.Platform}";
}
```

2.  In `OrdersPage.xaml`, instantiate the class to bind to, as shown highlighted in the following markup:

```
<?xml version="1.0" encoding="utf-8" ?>
<ContentPage xmlns="http://schemas.microsoft.com/dotnet/2021/maui"
             xmlns:x="http://schemas.microsoft.com/winfx/2009/xaml"
             xmlns:orders=
                 "clr-namespace:Northwind.Maui.Blazor.Client.Views.Orders"
             x:Class="Northwind.Maui.Blazor.Client.Views.OrdersPage"
```

```
                    Title="Orders">

<ContentPage.BindingContext>
    <orders:DeviceInfoViewModel />
</ContentPage.BindingContext>
```

3. In `OrdersPage.xaml`, add markup in the `ContentPage` element below the existing frame to define a frame for showing device information, as shown in the following markup:

```
<Frame BorderColor="{StaticResource PrimaryTextColor}"
        Margin="5" Padding="5">
  <VerticalStackLayout Spacing="10">
    <Label Text="Device Information"
            VerticalOptions="Center"
            HorizontalOptions="Center" />
    <HorizontalStackLayout Spacing="20">
      <Label Text="Listen to battery events"
              VerticalOptions="Center" />
      <Switch Toggled="BatterySwitch_Toggled"
              x:Name="BatterySwitch"
              VerticalOptions="Center"/>
    </HorizontalStackLayout>
    <Label x:Name="BatteryStateLabel" />
    <Label x:Name="BatteryLevelLabel" />
    <Label Text="{Binding DeviceModel}" />
    <Label Text="{Binding DeviceType}" />
    <Label Text="{Binding DevicePlatform}" />
    <Label Text="{Binding DeviceVersion}" />
    <Label Text="{Binding DisplayOrientation}" />
    <Label Text="{Binding DisplayRotation}" />
    <Label Text="{Binding DisplayDensity}" />
    <Label Text="{Binding DisplayPixelWidth}" />
    <Label Text="{Binding DisplayRefreshRate}" />
  </VerticalStackLayout>
</Frame>
```

4. In `OrdersPage.xaml.cs`, add an event handler for when the battery information has changed and call it in the constructor so that the page immediately shows the information when it first loads, as shown highlighted in the following code:

```
namespace Northwind.Maui.Blazor.Client.Views;

public partial class OrdersPage : ContentPage
{
  public OrdersPage()
  {
    InitializeComponent();
```

```csharp
    UpdateBatteryInfo(Battery.Default);
}

private void NewWindowButton_Clicked(object sender, EventArgs e)
{
  Window window = new() { Page = new AppShell() };
  Application.Current.OpenWindow(window);
}

private void Battery_BatteryInfoChanged(object sender,
  BatteryInfoChangedEventArgs e)
{
  UpdateBatteryInfo(Battery.Default);
}

private void UpdateBatteryInfo(IBattery battery)
{
  BatteryStateLabel.Text = battery.State switch
  {
    BatteryState.Charging => "Battery is currently charging",
    BatteryState.Discharging =>
      "Charger is not connected and the battery is discharging",
    BatteryState.Full => "Battery is full",
    BatteryState.NotCharging => "The battery isn't charging.",
    BatteryState.NotPresent => "Battery is not available.",
    BatteryState.Unknown => "Battery is unknown",
    _ => "Battery is unknown"
  };

  BatteryLevelLabel.Text =
    $"Battery is {battery.ChargeLevel * 100}% charged.";
}

private void BatterySwitch_Toggled(object sender, ToggledEventArgs e) =>
  WatchBattery(Battery.Default);

private bool _isBatteryWatched;

private void WatchBattery(IBattery battery)
{
  if (!_isBatteryWatched)
  {
    battery.BatteryInfoChanged += Battery_BatteryInfoChanged;
  }
  else
```

```
    {
        battery.BatteryInfoChanged -= Battery_BatteryInfoChanged;
    }

    _isBatteryWatched = !_isBatteryWatched;
    }
}
```

5. Start the app on **Windows Machine**.

6. Navigate to the **Orders** page, switch on listening for battery events, unplug your laptop charger cable (if you have a laptop; do not unplug a desktop computer!), and note the battery information and other device information, as shown in *Figure 19.13*:

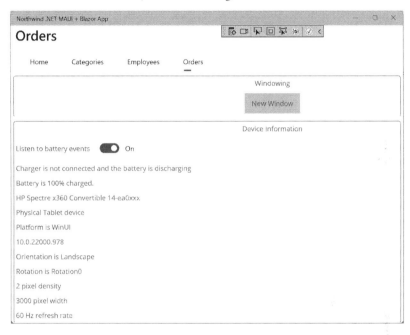

*Figure 19.13: Showing battery and device information on a Windows 11 laptop*

 On a desktop computer, the battery information will show **Battery is not available.**

7. Close the Windows app.

8. Start the app on the Android emulator.

9. Navigate to the **Orders** page, switch on listening for battery events, click the more (three dots) menu in the emulator toolbar, in the **Extended Controls** dialog box, select **Battery**, and then change the settings, including **Battery status**.

Note the battery information updates in the .NET MAUI app, as shown in *Figure 19.14*:

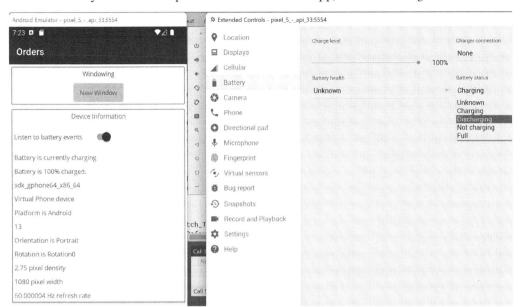

*Figure 19.14: Showing battery and device information on an emulated Android device*

10. Close the app.

# Integrating with desktop menu bars

For desktop operating systems, users will expect menu bars to access functionality. We will implement this functionality using both traditional events and relay commands to see the difference.

Let's add a small menu bar to the app for use on Windows:

1.  In the Views\Orders folder, in DeviceInfoViewModel.cs, import the namespaces for working with MVVM observable objects and defining relay commands, as shown in the following code:

    ```
    using CommunityToolkit.Mvvm.ComponentModel; // ObservableObject
    using CommunityToolkit.Mvvm.Input; // [RelayCommand]
    ```

2.  In DeviceInfoViewModel.cs, make the class a partial observable object, as shown highlighted in the following code:

    ```
    internal partial class DeviceInfoViewModel : ObservableObject
    ```

3.  In DeviceInfoViewModel.cs, add statements to define a command to navigate between pages, as shown in the following code:

    ```
    [RelayCommand]
    private async Task NavigateTo(string pageName)
    {
      await Shell.Current.GoToAsync($"//{pageName}");
    }
    ```

4. In `OrdersPage.xaml.cs`, add statements to define an event handler to navigate between pages, as shown in the following code:

```
private async void Menu_Clicked(object sender, EventArgs e)
{
  MenuFlyoutItem menu = sender as MenuFlyoutItem;

  if (menu != null)
  {
    await Shell.Current.GoToAsync($"//{menu.CommandParameter}");
  }
}
```

5. In `OrdersPage.xaml`, after the binding context, add markup in the `ContentPage` element to define a menu bar, as shown highlighted in the following markup:

```
<ContentPage.BindingContext>
  <orders:DeviceInfoViewModel />
</ContentPage.BindingContext>

<ContentPage.MenuBarItems>
  <MenuBarItem Text="File">
    <MenuFlyoutItem Text="Exit" />
  </MenuBarItem>
  <MenuBarItem Text="View">
    <MenuFlyoutItem Text="Home" Clicked="Menu_Clicked"
                    Command="{Binding NavigateToCommand}"
                    CommandParameter="home" />
    <MenuFlyoutItem Text="Categories" Clicked="Menu_Clicked"
                    Command="{Binding NavigateToCommand}"
                    CommandParameter="categories" />
    <MenuFlyoutItem Text="Employees" Clicked="Menu_Clicked"
                    Command="{Binding NavigateToCommand}"
                    CommandParameter="employees" />
    <MenuFlyoutItem Text="Orders" Clicked="Menu_Clicked"
                    Command="{Binding NavigateToCommand}"
                    CommandParameter="orders" />
    <MenuFlyoutItem Text="Refresh" />
  </MenuBarItem>
</ContentPage.MenuBarItems>
```

6. Start the app on **Windows Machine**.

7. Navigate to the **Orders** page, and note the menu bar, as shown in *Figure 19.15*:

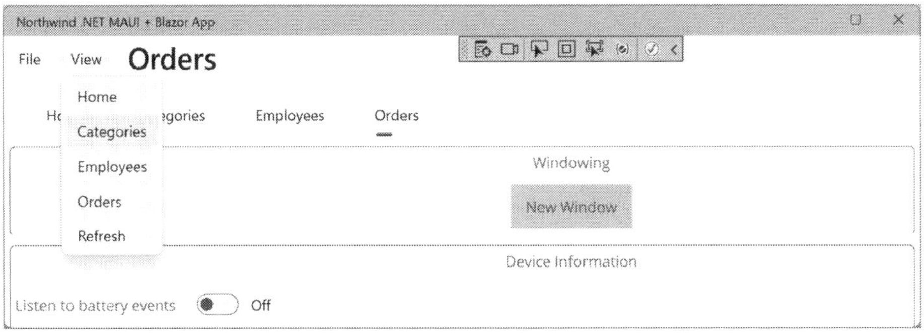

*Figure 19.15: On a desktop OS, the app has a menu bar*

8. Navigate to **View | Categories** and note that you are taken to the **Categories** page.

9. Navigate back to the **Orders** page to see the menu.

10. Navigate to **View | Home** and note that you are taken to the **Home** page.

11. Close the Windows app.

## Popping up a toast notification

The .NET MAUI Community Toolkit makes some tasks for integrating with the native platform easier, for example, if you want to show a pop-up toast notification.

Let's get the app to show a toast notification on the native platform:

1. In `DeviceInfoViewModel.cs`, import the namespaces for working with toast, as shown in the following code:

```
using CommunityToolkit.Maui.Alerts; // Toast
using CommunityToolkit.Maui.Core; // IToast, ToastDuration
```

2. In `DeviceInfoViewModel.cs`, add a relay command to show some toast, as shown in the following code:

```
[RelayCommand]
private async Task PopupToast()
{
  IToast toast = Toast.Make(message: "This toast pops up.",
    duration: ToastDuration.Short, textSize: 18);

  await toast.Show();
}
```

3. In `OrdersPage.xaml.cs`, import the namespaces for working with toast, as shown in the following code:

```
using CommunityToolkit.Maui.Alerts; // Toast
```

```
using CommunityToolkit.Maui.Core; // IToast, ToastDuration
```

4.  In `OrdersPage.xaml.cs`, add statements to define an event handler to show some toast, as shown in the following code:

```
private async void ToastMenu_Clicked(object sender, EventArgs e)
{
  MenuFlyoutItem menu = sender as MenuFlyoutItem;

  if (menu != null)
  {
    IToast toast = Toast.Make(message: "This toast pops up.",
      duration: ToastDuration.Short, textSize: 18);

    await toast.Show();
  }
}
```

5.  In `OrdersPage.xaml`, at the bottom of the menu bar, add a new menu, as shown in the following markup:

```
<MenuBarItem Text="Notify">
  <MenuFlyoutItem Text="Popup Toast" Clicked="ToastMenu_Clicked"
                  Command="{Binding PopupToastCommand}" />
</MenuBarItem>
```

6.  Start the app on **Windows Machine**.

7.  Navigate to the **Orders** page, in the **Notify** menu, click **Popup Toast**, and note that the toast notification appears, as shown in *Figure 19.16*:

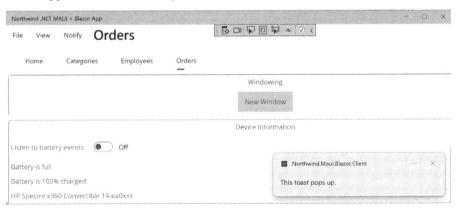

*Figure 19.16: Toast notification pops up on Windows*

8.  Close the Windows app.

# Using third-party control libraries

There are not as many free or open-source third-party libraries for .NET MAUI as there are for Blazor. This is probably because creating Blazor components is easier. You only need to concern yourself with supporting one user interface target, the web. When building a .NET MAUI control library, you would want to implement each control for native iOS, Android, Windows, macOS, and hopefully Linux in the future. That is a lot of tricky work.

The only major component library software manufacturer that gives away a control library for .NET MAUI for free is DevExpress, and its library only supports the two mobile platforms, iOS and Android. It is also not open-source.

 You can learn more about the DevExpress library at the following link: `https://www.devexpress.com/maui/`.

Other .NET MAUI component library software manufacturers charge license fees for their libraries, for example, Progress Telerik ($999 for a single developer license with priority support) and Syncfusion ($2,495 for a single developer license for the first year, $900 for the second year). Both have free trials.

# Practicing and exploring

Test your knowledge and understanding by answering some questions, getting some hands-on practice, and exploring this chapter's topics with deeper research.

## Exercise 19.1 – Test your knowledge

Answer the following questions:

1.  Modern .NET is cross-platform. Windows Forms and WPF apps can run on modern .NET. Can those apps therefore run on macOS and Linux?

2.  Is .NET MAUI a .NET developer's only choice for creating cross-platform graphical user interfaces?

3.  How do you enable a .NET MAUI app that targets iOS and Android to allow unsecure HTTP connections, i.e., use `http` as well as `https`?

4.  What does the .NET MAUI Community Toolkit do to make sure you have configured it?

5.  What domain must a .NET MAUI app use to connect to a locally hosted web service when testing in (a) the Android emulator and (b) the iOS simulator?

6.  In a .NET MAUI app, how would you store the text "Hello, World!" in the system clipboard?

7.  To use file and media pickers, as well as writing code, what must you do?

8.  When picking a file in a .NET MAUI app, how do you set a filter to limit which types of files can be selected?

9.  What information about a device can you access in a .NET MAUI app?

10. What are some benefits of using the .NET MAUI Community Toolkit?

## Exercise 19.2 – Explore the code samples

Review the official .NET MAUI code samples at the following link:

```
https://docs.microsoft.com/en-us/samples/browse/?expanded=dotnet&products=dotnet-maui
```

## Exercise 19.3 – Explore topics

Use the links in the following GitHub repository to learn more about the topics covered in this chapter:

```
https://github.com/markjprice/apps-services-net7/blob/main/book-links.md#chapter-19--
-integrating-net-maui-apps-with-blazor-and-native-platforms
```

# Summary

In this chapter, you learned:

- How to create a hybrid .NET MAUI and Blazor app.
- How to use the MVVM Community Toolkit to implement the Model-View-ViewModel pattern with bindable properties and commands.
- How to use the carousel view with current position indicators.
- How to integrate apps with platform features like the clipboard, picking files, and getting device information.
- How to use desktop features like menu bars and new windows.
- How to use the .NET MAUI Community Toolkit to add notifications.

In the next chapter, you will learn about a survey project challenge that I designed for this book, which you can optionally build to practice all the technologies that you have learned about in this book.

# 20

# Introducing the Survey Project Challenge

This chapter is about the Survey Project Challenge, an optional complete solution to a common set of problems that will give you a real-world set of projects to build.

This chapter will cover the following topics:

- What have you learned in this book?
- Why a survey project?
- What are the product requirements?
- Promote your abilities

## What have you learned in this book?

A lot!

## Technologies covered in this book

In this book, you have learned about many of the most important and popular technologies for building apps and services with .NET, as shown in *Figure 20.1*:

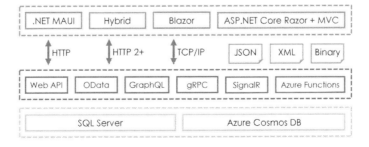

*Figure 20.1: Technologies for building apps and services with .NET*

The technologies can be divided into layers:

- **Presentation** (green; at the top): This layer presents information and handles interactions with the user like editing and showing notifications.
- **Transport** and **data exchange format** (gray; second from the top): This layer transports data between other layers. There are two main factors that affect efficiency: the transport protocol, and the data exchange format. Text-based formats like JSON and XML are easier to debug since they are human-readable. Binary formats are more efficient for larger amounts of data. Older protocols like HTTP/1.1 are more interoperable but less efficient. Newer protocols like HTTP/2 are faster but less well supported.
- **Services** (blue; third from the top): This layer implements core functionality like business logic, acts as an interaction layer to expose data that clients might not be able to directly talk to themselves, and enables users to switch between devices while working on a task. For example, from mobile to desktop to websites while checking their email.
- **Data** (yellow; at the bottom): This layer stores and manages data. Data stores often have their own special protocols for communicating with them, like **Tabular Data Stream** (**TDS**) for SQL Server. More modern data stores tend to use more open protocols like HTTP.

There are also features that can be implemented at multiple layers, like caching and queuing, to improve scalability, reliability, and overall performance.

Important decisions about which technology would best solve a specific development problem are tricky because they do not just involve the technology itself, like .NET MAUI, but also the technologies relating to it, like the transport protocol used to communicate with other layers of the solution and the format of data documents that are exchanged between layers.

# Why a survey project?

Before I explain the survey project challenge, let's talk about the best way to learn any new skill or technology.

## What is the best way to learn?

The best way to learn how to build apps and services with .NET is to work on real projects that you would use yourself or that at least spark an interest in you.

If you are a student, or a professional developer who has no choice over the projects or technologies that you implement, how can you work on a real project that needs the technologies you are interested in learning about?

In this chapter, I will introduce my idea for how to achieve that goal.

## Attributes of a good learning project

To help us learn all the different technologies that .NET developers need to know these days, we need a project that:

- Genuinely needs a mix of technologies and skills.

- Is cool, fun, and practical, so it will stretch our skills both from an engineering perspective as well as creatively.

- Is as real as possible and that we would use ourselves.

- Has already been implemented by others with public products that we can be inspired by, preferably with some open-source examples so we can even review code implementations, but even if not, a product with screenshots of all their features so we can scope out a **product requirements document (PRD)**.

 A PRD contains a listing of the features for a product to allow someone to understand *what* it should do. It does not say *how* it should do it. That would be defined in a functional specification that is more detailed.

- Has a small enough **minimal viable product (MVP)** that we have an achievable short-term goal to aim for.

- Has a large enough potential that it stretches to something much more complex long-term.

When you're struggling with a bug, you need to stay motivated. The best way to stay motivated is to work on a project that you will use yourself. Eat your own dog food, as they say.

## Alternative project ideas

A common suggestion for this type of project is to build your own **content management system (CMS)**. This is a thriving market with everything from the "big boys" like Optimizely and Adobe, to SaaS solutions like SquareSpace, via open-source solutions like Piranha and Umbraco.

 You can learn more about CMS solutions at the following link: `https://github.com/markjprice/apps-services-net7/blob/main/docs/cms/README.md`.

## Features of survey and polling tools

Personally, I have used survey and polling software to gain insight into my students and readers. For example, the most popular survey product is probably SurveyMonkey, although there are dozens of alternatives, as shown in the following list:

- SurveyMonkey: `https://www.surveymonkey.com/`
- Google Forms: `https://www.google.com/forms/about/`
- Microsoft Forms: `https://www.microsoft.com/en-us/microsoft-365/online-surveys-polls-quizzes`
- Poll Everywhere: `https://www.polleverywhere.com/`
- TechRadar's best list: `https://www.techradar.com/best/best-survey-tools`

Most survey tools have a free tier so you can try them out. For example, SurveyMonkey has a Basic plan that is free. Their best value paid plan, Advantage Annual, is £384/US$453 per year for an individual, or £99 per month if you want to stop paying at any time. That gets expensive fast!

Their free Basic plan has the following limitations:

- 10 questions per survey
- 40 responses per survey
- No response exports
- Limited question types (no star ratings, no freeform rich text)

So, I am motivated to create my own survey solution and I have the skills to do it! ☺

## Question types

There are dozens of question types, from multiple choice to scale selection via matrix and freeform text, as shown in *Figure 20.2*:

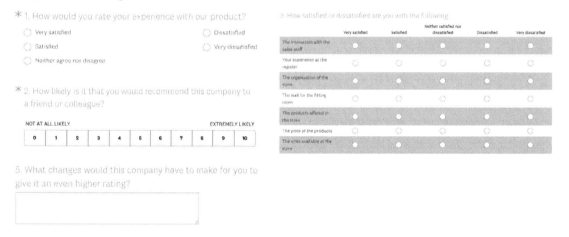

*Figure 20.2: Types of survey questions in SurveyMonkey*

Some of these question types should be easy enough to implement, like the plain text response or selecting one option from many. Others are likely to be harder to implement once you think about all the potential possibilities.

## Polling and quizzes

Survey tools have similar features to other tools like live polling and quiz builders. They all need some way to build the survey, poll, and quiz, and some way to take it, and finally ways to analyze the results.

I often deliver live training sessions and webinars. It is useful to ask the audience a bit about themselves, like where in the world they are, what their current experience is, and what they expect to get out of the session. The main difference between a survey and a live poll is the duration that question items are available to answer. The main difference with a quiz is the concept of a correct answer and scoring at the end.

Quizzes also share a lot of similarities. The main difference is the breadth of question item types. You can imagine that a quiz builder for learning mathematics or physics could have some quite elaborate components with complex implementations.

## Analyzing the responses

Another major feature of survey tools is the ability to analyze the results using everything from basic charts to complex machine learning artificial intelligence algorithms to spot unusual patterns.

# What are the product requirements?

A product requirements document is the result of analyzing a business problem. It defines a set of suggested features that solve the problems that the software is supposed to address.

## Minimal requirements overview

A minimal viable product for a survey tool would include:

- A website to take a survey anonymously
- An app to view the survey results
- Data storage for the survey question items
- Data storage for the responses
- Services to integrate the above functionality

## Minimal website requirements

To take a survey, the solution should provide a website. This is to make the surveys as accessible to as many people as possible. Every device has a web browser so a website will have the broadest reach. We can also easily share surveys using hyperlinks.

The website should respond to a request to take a survey identified by a unique value, as shown in the following link:

```
https://www.survey.com/123456
```

The website should allow anonymous visitors, present the question items to them, and record their responses. To keep it simple, there could be no restrictions on taking the survey multiple times. There would be no registering or authentication checks.

## Minimal question item types

The website should support the following question types:

- Single line plain text.
- Multi-line plain text.
- Rating (1-10).
- Multiple choice (one selection). Shows radio buttons.

Each item type should allow a plain text question.

## Minimal survey design requirements

An interactive survey design tool would be a lot of work. For the MVP, we will limit it to a basic JSON editor. The structure of the JSON document will be defined for the minimal question item types, but a plain text editor with templates for each item type is the only option for creating and editing them.

## Minimal data storage requirements

How should a survey and their responses be stored? It needs to be simple yet flexible. A document-based data storage solution would be best. A relational database would require normalization and therefore unnecessary complexity and potential performance issues.

- Each survey could be stored as a single document, with nested items.
- Each visitor who completes a survey could also be stored as a document.

Analyzing the results would benefit from duplicating some information from the individual responses, for example, so we could show a chart of how many respondents selected each radio button in a multiple choice item.

## Minimal analysis app requirements

The analysis app should show a list of all surveys and their status, for example, if they are active, if they are complete, how many have taken them, the details of their answers, and summaries of the results. Numeric results should appear as tabular data as well as charts, as shown in *Figure 20.3*:

*Figure 20.3: A chart of survey responses*

# Ideas for extended requirements

One of my favorite aspects of a survey tool is that there are many areas where you can choose to extend the minimal product:

- A website that a visitor can register with and track the surveys they have completed
- Dozens of different question types
- Dozens of ways to analyze the results
- Multiple ways to store the questions and results, from a fully normalized database to document-based cloud storages
- Multiple ways to process the results and provide a service layer above the data stores

## Extended website requirements

A visitor should be able to register with the website and store basic profile information, like a contact email address, demographic details, and a list of the surveys that they have taken. This information should follow good practice in allowing the visitor to update and delete their data at any time.

## Extended question item types

The website could support the following additional question types:

- Multi-line rich text. (Either provide a toolbar or allow markdown syntax.)
- Multiple choice (one selection). Shows radio buttons or a dropdown list.
- Multiple choice (multiple selection). Shows check boxes or a dropdown list of checkboxes.
- Rating (five stars with half values).
- Rating (customizable shape and maximum number of values). Choice to show as graphics or slider.
- Matrix of radio buttons.
- Clicking a position on an image.
- Ranking a list of items.

Each item type should allow a rich text question for each item and allow arbitrary rich text and images throughout a survey.

SurveyMonkey keeps the cool item types for the paid tiers, as shown in *Figure 20.4*:

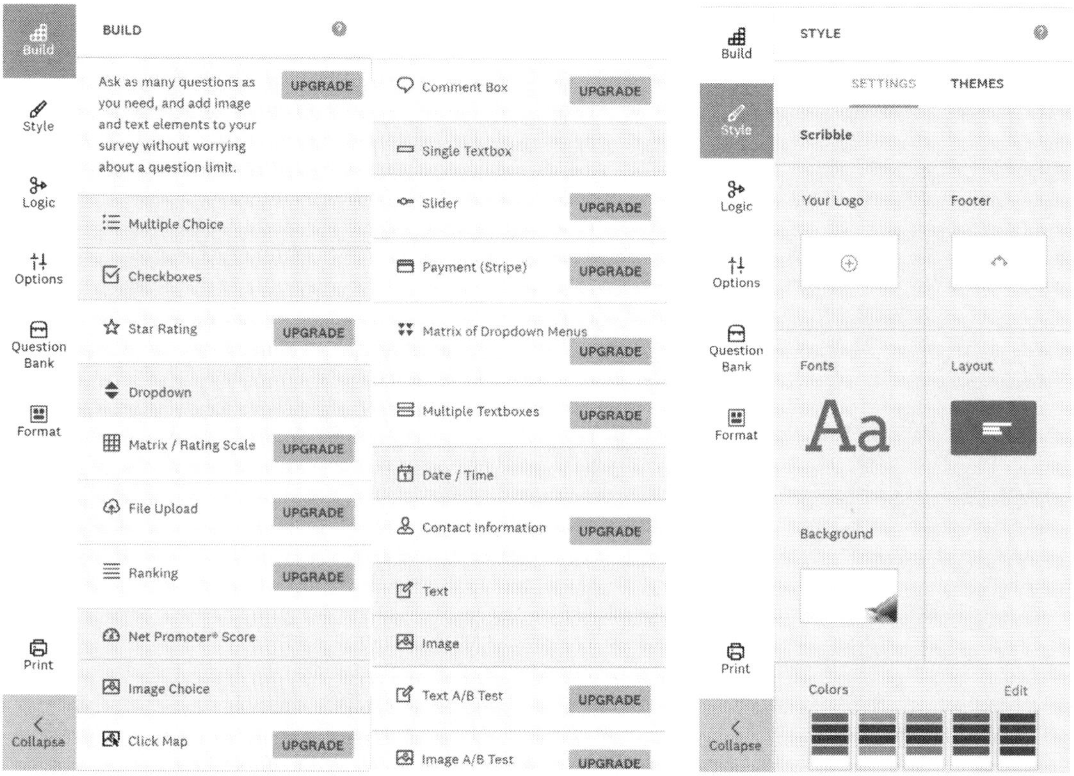

Figure 20.4: Upgrade SurveyMonkey to unlock most item types

# Extended survey design requirements

The minimal product stores the surveys and their question items but does not provide an easy way to create or edit them. We could provide a website or an app to enable someone to register an account and manage their own surveys and question items.

This will require authentication and authorization checks. The create and edit functionality could get quite complex because showing a question item is easier than providing an editing experience for one.

Either a website or app should provide a friendly survey creation and editing experience that closely matches what the survey taker would experience. In other words, a what-you-see-is-what-you-get editing experience.

For a survey tool that will be sold commercially, the organizations will want to brand their surveys with logos, images, colors, and so on.

# Extended data storage requirements

Even with a minimal product, the data storage requirements need to be flexible enough to store multiple different item types, a flexible number of items per survey, and the responses when someone takes a survey.

The main extended addition might be storing pre-created analysis data to improve performance, especially in a NoSQL cloud data storage example where each survey response is stored as a separate document.

### Extended analysis app requirements

If you have data science skills, then you could integrate the ML.NET libraries to add machine learning algorithms to process survey results to reveal interesting insights that humans might overlook.

 You can learn more about ML.NET at the following link: `https://dotnet.microsoft.com/en-us/apps/machinelearning-ai/ml-dotnet`.

# Promote your abilities

Pick one of the parts of the survey project to implement.

If you are more visually creative, then design and build a question item or a graphical analytics component. Even if you cannot build it yourself, you could sketch out your idea, and someone else might be inspired to implement it.

If you are more engineering-oriented, then perhaps optimizing the plumbing appeals to you more. You could define service requirements and then implement them using multiple technologies. Then create tests to compare the performance of each.

You can share ideas, discuss potential solutions, and get help from fellow readers and even me on the Discord channel for this book, found at the following link:

`https://packt.link/apps_and_services_dotnet7`

Publish your work in a public GitHub repository to share your achievement with the world. The best work will be promoted in the second edition of this book planned to be published in November 2023. I will link to your GitHub repository or your website so readers can learn more about your work. I am excited to see what my readers produce!

I plan to have a go myself during the first half of 2023 and I will share my projects in separate GitHub repositories. I will link to them from the GitHub repository for this book, so if you're interested, then keep an eye out for links to them here:

`https://github.com/markjprice/apps-services-net7`

# Summary

In this chapter, you learned about the survey project challenge. Hopefully you were inspired to have a go at implementing one or more of its components, if not a full solution, and to share your hard work with the world.

In the *Epilogue*, you will learn how to continue your learning journey with apps and services for .NET.

# Join our book's Discord space

Join the book's Discord workspace for *Ask me Anything* sessions with the author.

https://packt.link/apps_and_services_dotnet7

# 21

# Epilogue

I wanted this book to be different from the others on the market. I hope that you found it to be a brisk, fun read, packed with practical hands-on walkthroughs of each subject.

This epilogue contains the following short sections:

- Second edition coming November 2023
- Next steps on your C# and .NET learning journey
- Good luck!

## Second edition coming November 2023

I have already started work identifying areas for improvement for the next edition, which we plan to publish with the release of .NET 8 in November 2023. While I do not expect major new features at the level of .NET MAUI, I do expect .NET 8 to make worthwhile improvements to all aspects of .NET.

If you have suggestions for topics that you would like to see covered or expanded upon, or you spot mistakes that need fixing in the text or code, then please let me know the details via the GitHub repository for this book, found at the following link:

```
https://github.com/markjprice/apps-services-net7
```

## Next steps on your C# and .NET learning journey

For subjects that you wanted to learn more about than I had space to include in this book, I hope that the notes, good practice tips, and links in the GitHub repository pointed you in the right direction:

```
https://github.com/markjprice/apps-services-net7/blob/main/book-links.md
```

If you are looking for other books from my publisher that cover related subjects, there are many to choose from, as shown in *Figure 21.1*:

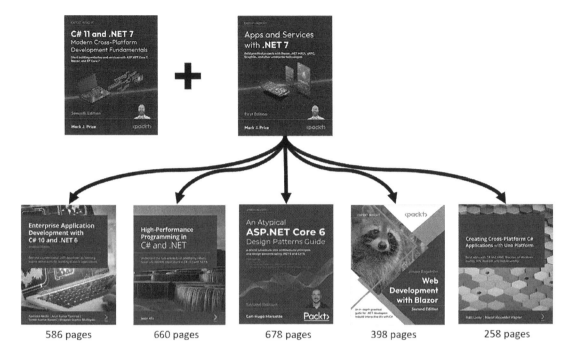

*Figure 21.1: Packt books to take your apps and services with .NET learning further*

# Good luck!

I wish you the best of luck with all your .NET projects!

# Index

# Download a free PDF copy of this book

Thanks for purchasing this book!

Do you like to read on the go but are unable to carry your print books everywhere?

Is your eBook purchase not compatible with the device of your choice?

Don't worry, now with every Packt book you get a DRM-free PDF version of that book at no cost.

Read anywhere, any place, on any device. Search, copy, and paste code from your favorite technical books directly into your application.

The perks don't stop there. You can get exclusive access to discounts, newsletters, and great free content in your inbox daily.

Follow these simple steps to get the benefits:

1. Scan the QR code or visit the link below:

https://packt.link/free-ebook/9781801813433

2. Submit your proof of purchase.
3. That's it! We'll send your free PDF and other benefits to your email directly.

Made in United States
Troutdale, OR
07/19/2023

11391430R10452